ECONOMIC THEORY AND MODELS: DERIVATIONS, COMPUTATIONS AND APPLICATIONS FOR POLICY ANALYSES

ECONOMIC THEORY AND MODELS: DERIVATIONS, COMPUTATIONS AND APPLICATIONS FOR POLICY ANALYSES

Keshab Bhattarai
Lecturer in Economics
The University of Hull Business School, England, UK

SERIALS PUBLICATIONS
NEW DELHI (INDIA)

First Published - 2008

ISBN: 978-81-8387-141-9

Published by

SERIALS PUBLICATIONS
4830/24, Prahlad Street, Ansari Road
Darya Ganj, New Delhi-110002 (India)
Phone : 23245225. Fax : 91-11-23272135
E-mail: serials@satyam.net.in

Contents

FOREWORD

Economists use static, dynamic, gametheoretic and econometric models to analyse various important policy issues. Techniques of analysis vary to some extent by the nature of questions asked for or the depth and comprehensiveness of answers required. I have tried to put together articles that I have written myself or jointly with my coauthors in the past few years for reader, interested in applying economic model for policy analysis. Eighteen out of twendy two papers were published either in refereed journals or as working papers and seven of them are couthored ones. Readings of these should be complemented by derivations, proofs, programming, computation and estimation in the class room. Where applicable the author acknowledges following sources for permission to publish these articles in this book format. I dedicate this work to people who inspired me for this and to students and researchers who may benefit from reading this book and for peace and prosperity in the whole world.

1. Consumption, Investment and Financial Intermediation in Ramsey Models, Applied Financial Economics Letters, *Applied Financial Economics Letters* 1(6).
2. Macroeconomic Impacts of Consumption and Income Taxes: A General equilibrium Analysis, *Research Memorandum no, 41 Business School*, University of Hull.
3. Multi-Sectoral Multi-Household General Equilibrium Tax Model: an Application, *Problems and Perspectives in Management*, 3/2004.
4. Efficiency and Factor Reallocation Effects and Marginal Excess Burden of Taxes in the UK Economy, *European Research Studies*, 2003, V. 6, iss. 3-4, pp. 177-205.
5. Welfare Impacts of Equal-Yield Tax Experiment in the UK Economy, forthcoming in *Applied Economics*.
6. Multi-household dynamic general equilibrium analysis of poverty and income redistribution.
7. Political Economy of Conflict and Growth: Nepalese Dilemma.

8. Keynesian Models of macroeconomic policy (Casino conference, 2005).
9. Interest Determination Rule four UK and Other Four Major Industrial Economies, *Research Memorandum No. 42* Business School, University of Hull.
10. Economic Growth: Models and Global Evidence, *Research Memorandum* No. 48 Business School, University of Hull.
11. Unemployment and inflation in OECD Economies.
12. Determinants of wage and labour supply in the UK, *Hull Economics Research Paper No. 277.*
13. Wage dynamics in the UK.
14. Discreteness and the Welfare Cost of Labour Supply Tax Distortions, *International Economic Review* 44:3:1117-1133, August 2003 joint work of Bhattarai and Whalley.
15. Division and Size of Gains from Liberalization of Trade in Services, *Review of International Economics,* 14:3:348-361. Bhattarai K and J Whalley (2006).
16. Welfare Gains to UK from a Global Free Trade, the *European Research Studies,* Vol. IV, Issue 3-4, 2001.
17. Redistribution Effects of Transfers, *National Bureau of Economic Research,* Working Paper No. 6281. joint work of Bhattarai K and J Whalley.
18. Welfare and distributional Impacts of financial liberalisation in a developing economy: Lessons from a forward looking CGE model of Nepal, *Working Paper No. 7*, Hull Advances in Policy Economics Research Papers.
19. General Equilibrium Modelling of UK Tax Policy in S. Holly and M Weale (eds.) *Econometric Modelling: Techniques and Applications,* pp. 69-93, the Cambridge University Press, 2000, (with J Whalley).
20. Role of Heterogeneity of Labour Demand in Tax Incidence Analysis in Baldev Raj and R. Boadway (Eds.) *Advances on Public Economics, pp.47-69, Physica-Verlag, 2000.* and Empirical Economics, 24:4, 1999, pp.599-620 (with J Whalley).
21. On some properties of a trade closure widely used in numerical modelling, *Economic Letters*, 62 no. 1 1999, pp. 13-21, (with M Ghosh and J Whalley).
22. More on Trade Closure in L Raut and G Ranis (eds.) Trade, Growth and Development: Essays in Honour of Professor T N Srinivasan, *Contribution to Economic Analysis 242,* Elsevier, NorthHolland 1999. (With M Ghosh and J Whalley).

1

Consumption, Investment and Financial International in a Ramsey Model

Keshab Bhattarai[1]

INTRODUCTION

The Ramsey (1928) model of optimal consumption and saving in a growing economy, extended by Goodwin (1961) and Cass (1965) and others, has been applied frequently to analyse consumption, saving, investment and capital accumulation over time. It focuses on the optimal rate of saving and the long run growth in contrast to a model with a constant and exogenously fixed rate of saving that preoccupies itself with the fluctuations in the short run as in Keynes (1936) and Hicks (1937) and their followers. The Ramsey model has become prominent more recently and remained a benchmark model for sophisticated analyses of consumption and saving in Caballero (1991), Deaton (1992) Pemberton (1997) and Blundell and Preston (1999), Gul and Pesendorfer (2004) and Meghir (2004). Despite this it is hard to find a study that links the productivity of capital stock and the cost of financial intermediation and impacts of these on consumption, saving, investment and capital accumulation and economic growth under a simple version of Ramsey model. Using analytical solutions and numerical examples this paper shows how output, capital stocks, consumption and saving can be sensitive to the parameters of preferences, production and financial intermediation in a growing economy. Analyses contained here complement various other studies found in applied economics literature in recent years that use either a VAR model for impulse response analyses or macroeconometric model for simulations or panel or multiple regression models to test economic hypotheses as in Dawson (2003), Kim (2003), Ataullah, Cockerill and Le (2004), Liu and Shu (2004), Mallick (2004), Park and Lim (2004).

1. Corresponding Address K. R. Bhattarai@hull.ac.uk.

INFINITE HORIZON RAMSEY MODEL OF CONSUMPTION AND SAVING

In Ramsey (1928), a benevolent social planner or a representative household optimises the lifetime utility from consumption in each period and his saving equals investment in equilibrium. Investment generates additional capital stock and enhances the productive capacity of the economy. The basic Ramsey model can be expressed in five functions expressing the utility of a representative household, production of a firm, the process of capital accumulation, conditions for market clearing and the initial state of the economy:

$$\text{Preference: Max}\, U = \sum_{t=0}^{\infty} \beta^t \ln(C_t) \quad 0 < \beta < 1 \tag{1}$$

Subject to:

$$\text{Output and the technology constraint: } Y_t = AK_t^{\alpha} \quad 0 < \alpha < 1 \tag{2}$$

$$\text{Market clearing condition: } C_t + I_t = Y_t \tag{3}$$

$$\text{Capital formation: } K_{t+1} = K_t(1-\delta) + I_t \quad 0 < \delta < 1 \tag{4}$$

$$\text{Boundary (initial) condition } K_0 = K_0 \tag{5}$$

The solutions for optimal consumption from this infinite horizon problem can be obtained by substituting the consumption term from the market clearing condition in the utility function and using the standard first order conditions for utility maximisation and by analysing optimal conditions for any two periods in terms of control and state variables that apply to all other periods in the model as illustrated below.

$$C_t = Y_t - I_t \rightarrow C_t = AK_t^{\alpha} - K_{t+1} - K_t(1-\delta) \tag{6}$$

$$U_t = \sum_{t=0}^{\infty} \beta^t \ln\left(AK_t^{\alpha} - K_{t+1} + K_t(1-\delta)\right) \tag{7}$$

Two periods of this infinite sum actually can be sliced as:

$$\begin{aligned} U_t &= +\beta^t \ln\left(AK_t^{\alpha} - K_{t+1} + K_t(1-\delta)\right) \\ &+\beta^{t+1} \ln\left(AK_{t+1}^{\alpha} - K_{t+2} + K_{t+1}(1-\delta)\right) + .. + \end{aligned} \tag{8}$$

For optimal consumption and savings, the loss in utility by not consuming at period *t* should equal gain from production (consumption) next period, *t*+1. This can be ascertained by comparing the first order conditions or the Euler equations taking consumption and investment as control and capital stock as the state variables.

$$\frac{\partial U_t}{\partial C_t}\frac{\partial C_t}{\partial C_{t+1}}\frac{\partial C_{t+1}}{\partial K_{t+1}} = ..-\frac{\beta^t}{C_t}+\frac{\beta^{t+1}}{C_{t+1}}\left(\alpha A K_{t+1}^{\alpha-1}+(1-\delta)\right)+..=0 \tag{9}$$

$$\rightarrow \frac{C_{t+1}}{C_t}=\beta\left(\alpha A K_{t+1}^{\alpha-1}+(1-\delta)\right) \tag{10}$$

This equation implies that the ratio of consumption between two periods should equal discounted value of the marginal product of capital in the next period, and in a competitive equilibrium this should equal the gross interest rate.

The level of consumption and capital stock are constant in the steady state; $..=K_{t-1}=K_t=K_{t+1}=..=\bar{K}$ and $..=C_{t-1}=C_t=C_{t+1}=..=\bar{C}$. When this steady state value of capital stock is substituted in the parenthesis of (7) the life time utility becomes a constant number and the $\bar{K}$ term can be taken out of the summation sign as $U_t=\ln\left(A\bar{K}^{\alpha}-\bar{K}+\bar{K}(1-\delta)\right)\sum_{t=0}^{\infty}\beta^t$. The steady state capital stock $\bar{K}$ can be found using steady state values of consumption in equation (10).

$$\frac{C_{t+1}}{C_t}=\frac{\bar{C}}{\bar{C}}=\beta\left(\alpha A\bar{K}^{\alpha-1}+(1-\delta)\right)\rightarrow\left(\alpha A\bar{K}^{\alpha-1}+(1-\delta)\right)=\left(\frac{1}{\beta}\right)$$

$$\rightarrow\left(\bar{K}^{\alpha-1}\right)=\frac{1}{\alpha A}\left(\frac{1}{\beta}-(1-\delta)\right)$$

$$\left(\bar{K}^{\alpha-1}\right)=\frac{1}{\alpha A}\left(\frac{1-\beta(1-\delta)}{\beta}\right)\rightarrow\bar{K}=\left(\frac{1-\beta(1-\delta)}{\alpha A\beta}\right)^{\frac{1}{\alpha-1}}$$

$$\rightarrow\bar{K}=\left(\frac{\alpha A\beta}{1-\beta(1-\delta)}\right)^{\frac{1}{1-\alpha}} \tag{11}$$

Output in the steady state is obtained by substituting the steady state capital stock in the production function: $\bar{Y}=A\bar{K}^{\alpha}\rightarrow\bar{Y}=A^{\frac{2-\alpha}{1-\alpha}}\left(\frac{\alpha\beta}{1-\beta(1-\delta)}\right)^{\frac{\alpha}{1-\alpha}}$ (12)

Investment and consumptions in the steady state are:

$$\bar{I}=\bar{K}-(1-\delta)\bar{K}\rightarrow\bar{I}=\delta\bar{K}\rightarrow\bar{I}=\delta\bar{K}=\delta\left(\frac{\alpha A\beta}{1-\beta(1-\delta)}\right)^{\frac{1}{1-\alpha}} \tag{13}$$

$$\bar{C} = \bar{Y} - \bar{I} \rightarrow \bar{C} = \left(\frac{\alpha A\beta}{1-\beta(1-\delta)}\right)^{\frac{\alpha}{1-\alpha}} - \delta\left(\frac{\alpha A\beta}{1-\beta(1-\delta)}\right)^{\frac{1}{1-\alpha}} \quad (14)$$

Thus the output, capital stock and consumption in the steady state of this economy are ultimately functions of preference of the social planner or the representative consumer(β) , technological factor (A), the elasticity of output to the capital stock(α) and the rate of depreciation (δ). The implications to higher or lower depreciation rate on long run growth of the economy is clear from above derivations as the steady state values for consumptions, investment and capital stock significantly differ when $0<\delta<1$ than when $\delta=1$.

IMPACTS OF COST OF FINANCIAL INTERMEDIATION

The above two scenarios assume an ideal benevolent social planner and a smooth and efficient financial market. The financial markets are incomplete in the real world and the investments are not equal to saving because of intermediation cost. When θ represents a charge imposed by financial institutions in the intermediation process with a higher value of θ representing more inefficiency in the financial system then $\phi=(1+\theta)$ of saving is required for one unit of investment. Higher intermediation cost, (higher values of ϕ) reduces capital, output, consumption and investment and modifies the macroeconomic balance to:

$$C_t = Y_t - I_t \rightarrow C_t = AK_t^{\alpha} - \phi\left\{K_{t+1} - K_t(1-\delta)\right\} \quad (15)$$

Now the financial system deviates from the standard Arrow-Debreau competitive equilibrium; only $1/(1+\theta)$ fraction of saving is channelled to investment; thus the investment equals savings net of intermediation cost $S_t = \phi I_t = (1+\theta) I_t$ as in Pagano (1993); $\theta.I_t$ amount of savings is wasted in process of financial intermediation. As such a higher value ϕ represents more inefficiency in the financial system. Solutions of models with $0<\delta<1$ and $\phi \geq 1$ are further modified as:

$$C_t = Y_t - I_t \rightarrow C_t = AK_t^{\alpha} - \phi\left\{K_{t+1} - K_t(1-\delta)\right\} \quad (16)$$

$$U_t = \sum_{t=0}^{\infty} \beta^t \ln\left[AK_t^{\alpha} - \phi\left\{K_{t+1} - K_t(1-\delta)\right\}\right] \quad (17)$$

As before part of this infinite sum actually can be written as:

$$U_t = +\beta^t \ln\left[AK_t^\alpha - \phi\left\{K_{t+1} - K_t\left(1-\delta\right)\right\}\right] + \beta^{t+1}$$
$$\ln\left[AK_{t+1}^\alpha - \phi\left\{K_{t+2} - K_{t+1}\left(1-\delta\right)\right\}\right] + .. +$$

First order conditions or the Euler equation in terms of consumption as a control and capital stock as a state variable changes to

$$\frac{\partial U_t}{\partial C_t} = .. - \frac{\phi\beta^t}{C_t} + \frac{\beta^{t+1}}{C_{t+1}}\left(\alpha AK_{t+1}^{\alpha-1} + \phi\left(1-\delta\right)\right) + .. = 0$$

$$\rightarrow \frac{C_{t+1}}{C_t} = \frac{\beta}{\phi}\left(\alpha AK_{t+1}^{\alpha-1} + \phi\left(1-\delta\right)\right) \qquad (18)$$

As above this equation implies that the ratio of consumption between two periods should equal the discounted value of the marginal product of capital in the next period, in a competitive equilibrium this should equal the gross interest rate. Again for an optimal allocation between consumption and savings, loss in utility by not consuming now should equal gain from production (consumption) next period.

As above in a steady state both capital and consumption remain constant; $.. = K_{t-1} = K_t = K_{t+1} = .. = \overline{K}$ and also $.. = C_{t-1} = C_t = C_{t+1} = .. = \overline{C}$. Like in (7) above the term in the parenthesis of (17) becomes a constant number and can be taken out of the summation sign $U_t = \ln\left(A\overline{K}^\alpha - \phi\overline{K} + \overline{K}\phi\left(1-\delta\right)\right)\sum_{t=0}^{\infty}\beta^t$.

This again gives a constant utility in the steady state. The steady state capital stock $\overline{K}$ can be found using steady state values of consumption in equation (18).

$$\frac{C_{t+1}}{C_t} = \frac{\overline{C}}{\overline{C}} = \frac{\beta}{\phi}\left(\alpha A\overline{K}^{\alpha-1} + \phi\left(1-\delta\right)\right) \rightarrow \left(\alpha A\overline{K}^{\alpha-1} + \phi(1-\delta)\right) = \left(\frac{\phi}{\beta}\right)$$

$$\rightarrow \left(\overline{K}^{\alpha-1}\right) = \frac{1}{\alpha A}\left(\frac{\phi}{\beta} - \phi(1-\delta)\right) \quad \left(\overline{K}^{\alpha-1}\right) = \frac{1}{\alpha A}\left(\frac{\phi - \beta\phi(1-\delta)}{\beta}\right)$$

$$\rightarrow \overline{K} = \left(\frac{\phi - \beta\phi(1-\delta)}{\alpha A\beta}\right)^{\frac{1}{\alpha-1}} \rightarrow \overline{K} = \left(\frac{\alpha A\beta}{\phi - \beta\phi(1-\delta)}\right)^{\frac{1}{1-\alpha}} \qquad (19)$$

Thus in case of financial intermediation the output, investment and consumption in the steady state are:

$$\overline{Y} = A\overline{K}^{\alpha} \rightarrow \overline{Y} = \left(\frac{\alpha A\beta}{\phi - \beta\phi(1-\delta)}\right)^{\frac{\alpha}{1-\alpha}} \tag{20}$$

$$\overline{I} = \overline{K} - (1-\delta)\overline{K} \rightarrow \overline{I} = \delta\overline{K} \rightarrow \overline{I} = \delta\overline{K} = \delta\left(\frac{\alpha A\beta}{\phi - \beta\phi(1-\delta)}\right)^{\frac{1}{1-\alpha}} \tag{21}$$

$$\overline{C} = \overline{Y} - \overline{I} \rightarrow \overline{C} = \left(\frac{\alpha A\beta}{\phi - \beta\phi(1-\delta)}\right)^{\frac{\alpha}{1-\alpha}} - \delta\left(\frac{\alpha A\beta}{\phi - \beta\phi(1-\delta)}\right)^{\frac{1}{1-\alpha}} \tag{22}$$

In addition to β, A, α and δ the steady state consumption, investment and capital stock also depend on the cost of intermediation $\phi = (1+\theta)$.

NUMERICAL EXAMPLE

The numerical solutions of three versions of the infinite horizon model are summarised in table below. The upper part of table lists the set of parameters used in each scenario and the corresponding model solutions for the steady state are given at the lower part of the table.

Capital Stock, Output, Consumption and Investment in the Steady State

Parameters of the Infinite Horizon Model									
I	*II*	*III*	*IV*	*V*	*VI*	*VII*	*VIII*	*IX*	
Technology (A)	44	44	44	44	44	44	100	100	100
Productivity of capital (α)	0.4	0.4	0.2	0.6	0.6	0.6	0.4	0.4	0.6
Discount rate (β)	0.9	0.9	0.9	0.9	0.9	0.9	0.9	0.9	0.9
Initial capital (K_0)	100	100	100	100	100	100	100	100	100
Depreciation rate (δ)	1	0.05	0.05	0.05	0.05	0.05	1	0.05	0.05
Intermediation cost (ϕ)	1	1	1	1	1.2	1.05	1	1	1. 05
Infinite Horizon Economy in the Steady State									
Capital Stock (K)	100	2,499	149	344,202	218,202	304,677	392	9,807	2,369,142
Output (Y)	278	1,006	120	92,424	70,310	85,902	1,090	3,950	667,967
Consumption (C)	178	882	112	75,214	59,400	70,668	698	3,460	549,509
Investment (I)	100	125	7	17,210	10,910	15,234	392	490	118,457

Scenarios I to IV are solutions without intermediation cost as given above in equations (11) to (14); scenarios I and II compare role of depreciation, scenarios I-IV demonstrate the role of productivity of capital. The scenarios IV-VI illustrate distortions due to intermediation costs as presented in equations (19) to (22) and scenarios VII to IX show impact of technical progress for varying rate of depreciation and intermediation costs.

The major points emerging from analyses of results in this table are following:

1. Greater the productivity of capital larger is the level of capital stock, output, consumption and investment in the steady state (I-IV). This implies that countries with higher capital share or productivity of capital (α) have higher level of output and consumption.
2. Higher financial intermediation cost (A) reduces the level of output in the steady state but it is less important than the productivity of capital (V-VI). Higher productivity of capital can compensate for higher cost of financial intermediation. Economies that can employ capital more efficiently can grow faster despite higher transaction costs of financial intermediation.
3. Higher rate of technological progress leads to higher level of income in the steady state (VII-IX). Countries that are able to complement technical progress with larger amount of capital have better prospect of economic growth.
4. Countries with the higher rate of depreciation of the capital (δ) experience lower rate of growth of output (I and II).
5. When the subjective discount factor (β) was changed to 0.8 from 0.9 in scenario IX the levels of capital stock, output, consumption and investments were 500,728, 262,882, 237,846 and 25,036 respectively. Countries that discount the future consumption heavily have lower level of output in the steady state.

Analytical and numerical results from a simple Ramsey model presented above shows the role of productivity and depreciation rates of capital, level of technology, the cost of financial intermediation and discount factors for future relative to current consumption and how the real factors of financial sector determine the rate and space of economic growth in an economy. These results should be studied together with the results from the other models as mentioned in section I considering the fact that a greater space of financial deepening brings a larger proportion of the real physical assets into financial assets making expectations of investors and consumers more important and complicated than simply productivity based arbitrage conditions used here in allocation of resources between consumption and investment. More complex issues like this are beyond the scope of this paper.

CONCLUSION

The optimal allocations of income between consumption and investment over time in a growing economy is shown with analytical solutions as well as numerical examples from a simple version of the Ramsey model with production and cost of financial intermediation in an infinite horizon setting. On the consumption side, economies with strong preferences for future consumption (that have a lower discount rate and higher saving rate) grow faster and have higher level of capital stock, output and consumption in the steady state than economies that discount future consumption at a higher rate. On the production side, economies with higher rate of productivity of capital will have higher level of standard of living. Similarly lower rate of depreciation and lower cost of financial intermediation raises the level of output and capital stock in the steady state. Model results show that productivity of capital and discount rate for future consumption are found to be more important than the cost of financial intermediation.

REFERENCES

Ataullah A. T. Cockerill and H Le (2004), Financial Liberalisation and Bank Efficiency: a Comparative Analysis of India and Pakistan, *Applied Economics*, 36:1915-1924.

Blundell R and I. Preston (1999), Consumption Inequality and Income Uncertainty, *Quarterly Journal of Economics*, 113, 603-640.

Caballero R. J. (1991), Earning Uncertainty and Aggregate Wealth Accumulation, *American Economic Review*. Vol. 81, No. 4, 859-871.

Cass, D. (1965), Optimum Growth in Aggregative Model of Capital Accumulation, *Review of Economic Studies*, 32:233-240.

Dawson P. J. (2003), Financial Development and Growth in Economies in Transition, *Applied Economics* Letters, 10:833-836.

Deaton A. (1992), *Understanding Consumption*, Oxford University Press.

Goodwin R. M. (1961), The Optimal Growth Path for an Underdeveloped Economy, *Economic Journal*, 71: 284: 756-774.

Gul F. and W Pesendorfer (2004), Self-Control and the Theory of Consumption, *Econometrica*, 72:1:119-158.

Hicks, J. R.(1937), Mr. Keynes and the "Classics"; A Suggested Interpretation, *Econometrica* 5: 2:, 147-159.

Keynes (1936), *The General Theory of Employment, Income and Interest Rate*, Cambridge University Press.

Kim J. U. (2003), Economic growth and returns to scale for reproducible factors, *Applied Economics Letters*, 10:925-928.

Liu X. and C Shu (2004), Consumption and Stock Markets in Greater China, *Applied Economics Letters*, 11:365-368.

Mallick S. K. (2004), A Dynamic Macroeconometric Model for short-run Stabilisation, *Applied Economics*, 36:261-276.

Meghir C. (2004), A Retrospective on Friedman's Theory of Permanent Income, *Economic Journal*, 114, June, F293-F306.

Pagano M. (1993), Financial Markets and Growth: An Overview, *European Economic Review*, 37(2-3, April) 613-622.

Park C and P. F. Lim (2004), Excess Sensitivity of Consumption, Liquidity Constraints, and Mandatory Saving, Applied Economics Letters, 11:771-774.

Pemberton J. (1997), The Empirical Failure of the Life Cycle Model with Perfect Capital Markets, *Oxford Economic Papers*. vol. 49, pp 129-151.

Ramsey, F. P. (1928), A Mathematical Theory of Saving, *Economic Journal* 38:543-559.

2

Macroeconomic Impacts of Consumption and Income Taxes: A General Equilibrium Analysis

Keshab Bhattarai[2]

INTRODUCTION

The multiplier analysis of changes in government expenditure, investment or exports in the presence of lump sum or proportional income taxes under the fixed price ISLM model, as commonly found in the usual macro-textbooks, is not sufficient for analysis of impacts of taxes in an economy. Taxes have wide ranging impacts both in supply and demand sides of the markets for goods and services and factors of production and they distort commodity prices, wage rates which significantly affect the allocation of resources in the economy. Reduction of taxes on commodities not only shifts the aggregate demand towards right by increasing the disposable income of the households but also causes an increase in spending along the aggregate demand line as lower prices induce more demand by households with accompanying income and substitution effects. A reduction in the labour income tax rate lowers the cost of production of the firms and raises the demand for labour. It also raises labour supply in response to higher net of tax wage rate. More production reduces prices of commodities from the supply side and raises the real income of households who supply labour to a firm. Higher real income may induce further increase in the demand for leisure and reduce the supply of labour. An increase in both direct and indirect tax rates have similar effect on the opposite direction.

Overall macroeconomic effects of taxes involve very complicated substitution and income effects at micro level, which should not be missed in a formal analysis of the fiscal policy. The incidence of tax may fall either on consumer or producer though ultimately consumers pay the gross of tax prices prevailing in the market including the wedge above the net of tax prices that is actually received by the

2. The Correspondence Address: *K.R.Bhattarai@hull.ac.uk*

firms. Similarly firms pay gross of tax wage rates to its workers but can recover the amount of taxes they paid by charging higher prices on commodities to the households. It is the net of tax wage rate that really matters when a household makes labour-leisure and consumption-saving decisions. Absence of evaluation of these direct and indirect impacts of taxes in discussion of expansionary or contractionary fiscal or monetary policy is a serious shortcoming of the traditional ISLM models built in tradition of Keynes (1936) and Hicks (1937).

There is a long standing debate on relative merits and demerits of the direct and indirect taxes in terms of their incidence and impact to the tax payers. Microeconomic analysis based on Marshallian or Hicksian analysis of demand and supply takes a partial equilibrium view which may be true from the point of a single firm or the consumer but not sufficient from the perspective of the economy as a whole. A partial equilibrium approach to analyse economy wide problem often generates misleading results. The public finance literature as in Ramsey (1927), Pigou(1947), Atkinson and Stiglitz (1976), Mirlees (1971), Whalley (1975), Boadway and Bruce (1992), Peroni (1995), Hutton and Ruocco (1999) Iwamoto and Shibata (1999) Seidman and Lewis (1999) make this point to some extent but very few of these studies investigate the macroeconomic impacts and miss explicit general equilibrium solution of the tax induced macroeconomic impacts on output and employment as clearly as desirable (Rebelo(1991)). Most of these analyses focus on impact on welfare of individuals or redistribution impacts of transfers (Pechman (1987), Atkinson and Stiglitz (1976)).

The simplest possible general equilibrium model is often presented for a Crusoe type economy taking interaction between consumption and production by a representative household. Such a model can be used to evaluate the impact of both direct and indirect taxes on consumption, leisure, labour supply, output and employment. The welfare cost is measured in terms of reduction in the utility of a representative household, who supplies labour to the firm, by examining the optimality of income or consumption taxes separately or jointly under the general equilibrium framework in which the decisions of households to maximize utility subject to its budget constraint are linked to the decision of producers to maximize profit choosing the optimal units of employment through the real wage rate. The analytical solution of the model with no taxes is presented in section II, with taxes in section III, a numerical illustration for a hypothetical economy in section IV before applying the model to the actual data set for the UK economy in section V. Paper ends with conclusions followed by references.

MICRO-FOUNDED GENERAL EQUILIBRIUM MODEL WITH A REPRESENTATIVE HOUSEHOLD AND A REPRESENTATIVE FIRM

A simple general equilibrium model represents an economy in which a representative household maximises utility by consuming goods and services supplied by producers and paying for them by income that it receives in return of supply of labour and capital inputs to the producers. Firms optimise profit combining inputs with the existing technology in production and rewarding inputs according to its marginal productivity. Tax policies of government influence both production and consumption sides of the economy by affecting prices of inputs and outputs. By distorting the marginal conditions of optimisation, these taxes influence choices of goods and services by households and use of inputs by producers. The incidence and impact of taxes on consumption may differ from taxes on labour income depending on the key parameters for share or elasticities of substitution in consumption or in the production sides of the economy.

A general equilibrium implies a set of prices that eliminate excess supply or excess demand and where these prices and wage rates are consistent with the preferences and endowments of households and technology of firms. The perfect match between demand and supply for both goods and services and inputs of production follow from the properties of utility and production functions as given by explicit analytical solutions in the next section.

Household's Problem

Consider an economy with a representative household and a representative firm. The household tries to maximise utility by consuming goods and services and enjoying leisure subject to its budget constraint. The producer wants to maximise profit by selling goods produced using the labour supplied by the household. The household maximisation problem can be stated in terms of preferences, budget and time constraints as the following:

$$Max \quad U = c^{\phi} l^{1-\phi}$$

Subject to:

i. $l + h^s = 1$ time constraint

ii. $wh^s + \pi = pc$ budget constraint

iii. $c \geq 0; l \geq 0; h^s \geq 0$ non-negativity constraint (1)

where c is consumption, l is leisure and h^s is labour supply, p is the price of the commodity, w is the wage rate; π is the profit from owning the firm, ϕ is weight of consumption and $(1-\phi)$ weight of leisure in utility.

For simplicity, normalise labour endowment to 1, define leisure as $l = 1 - h^s$ and substitute it into the utility function to get, $U = c^{\phi}\left(1 - h^s\right)^{1-\phi}$

The Lagrangian function for the constrained optimisation is given by

$$L(c,l,\lambda) = c^{\phi}\left(1 - h^s\right)^{1-\phi} + \lambda\left[wh^s + \pi - pc\right] \tag{2}$$

It has three choice variables (c,l,λ), λ is shadow price of income. The first order conditions (FOC) for utility maximisation are:

$$\frac{\partial L(c,l,\lambda)}{\partial c} = \phi c^{\phi-1}\left(1-h^s\right)^{1-\phi} - \lambda p = 0 \tag{3}$$

$$\frac{\partial L(c,l,\lambda)}{\partial h^s} = (1-\phi)c^{\phi}\left(1-h^s\right)^{-\phi}(-1) + \lambda w = 0 \tag{4}$$

$$\frac{\partial L(c,l,\lambda)}{\partial \lambda} = wh^s + \pi - pc = 0 \tag{5}$$

Equation (3) and (4) give the marginal utility from consumption and leisure respectively. These three equations can be used to solve for three choice variables.

Demand for consumption goods can be derived by dividing FOC (3) by FOC (4) and solving for c.

$$\frac{\dfrac{\partial L(c,l,\lambda)}{\partial h^s}}{\dfrac{\partial L(c,l,\lambda)}{\partial c}} = \frac{(1-\phi)c^{\phi}\left(1-h^s\right)^{-\phi}(-1)}{\phi c^{\phi-1}\left(1-h^s\right)^{1-\phi}} = \frac{w}{p} \tag{6}$$

This optimising condition implies that the marginal rate of substitution between leisure and consumption should equal the real wage rate in equilibrium. It is clear that the consumption demand depends on real wage rate and the work efforts.

$$c = \left(\frac{\phi}{1-\phi}\right)\left(1-h^s\right)\frac{w}{p}$$

(7)

In the absence of taxes, the market clearing condition in this single good economy implies that the income of the household equals spending on consumption: $wh^s + \pi = pc$. Using (7) this budget constraint can be rewritten as:

$$h^s\frac{w}{p} + \frac{\pi}{p} = c = \left(\frac{\phi}{1-\phi}\right)\left(1-h^s\right)\frac{w}{p} \tag{8}$$

Now (8) can be solved for the household's labour supply

$$h^s\frac{w}{p} + \frac{\pi}{p} = \left(\frac{\phi}{1-\phi}\right)\left(1-h^s\right)\frac{w}{p} \Rightarrow h^s\left(1+\frac{\phi}{1-\phi}\right)\frac{w}{p} = \left(\frac{\phi}{1-\phi}\right)\frac{w}{p} - \frac{\pi}{p}$$

$$h^s\left(\frac{1}{1-\phi}\right)\frac{w}{p} = \left(\frac{\phi}{1-\phi}\right)\frac{w}{p} - \frac{\pi}{p}\frac{1-\phi}{1-\phi}$$

$$h^s \frac{w}{p} = \phi \frac{w}{p} - \frac{\pi}{p}(1-\phi) \tag{9}$$

From the optimising behaviour of a representative household the supply of labour, demand for leisure and consumption become functions of the real wage rate and profit.

$$h^s = \frac{\phi \frac{w}{p} - \frac{\pi}{p}(1-\phi)}{\frac{w}{p}} \text{; leisure } l = 1 - h^s = 1 - \frac{\phi \frac{w}{p} - \frac{\pi}{p}(1-\phi)}{\frac{w}{p}} \tag{10}$$

$$c = \left(\frac{\phi}{1-\phi}\right)\left(1-h^s\right)\frac{w}{p} = c = \left(\frac{\phi}{1-\phi}\right)\left(1 - \frac{\phi \frac{w}{p} - \frac{\pi}{p}(1-\phi)}{\frac{w}{p}}\right)\frac{w}{p} \tag{11}$$

The real wage rate that is consistent with optimal demand for labour and profit from the firm's side of optimisation is found in the next section.

Firm's Problem

The representative firm receives the net of tax price of goods by selling them to the households and pays the gross of tax wage rate for labour. Its maximisation problem, given the technology, input and output prices can be stated as:

$$Max \ \pi = py - wh^d$$

Subject to :

i. $y \le \left(h^d\right)^{\alpha}$ technology constraint

ii. $y \ge 0; h^d \ge 0$ non negativity constraint (12)

where y is the output supplied by the firm and h^d is its demand for labour.

All above conditions can be collapsed into one objective function for the firm.

$$\text{Max } \pi = py - wh^d = p\left(h^d\right)^{\alpha} - wh^d \tag{13}$$

From the first order condition, firm's demand for labour input can be derived using the profit maximisation condition, which implies

$$\frac{\partial \pi}{\partial h^d} = p\alpha \left(h^d\right)^{\alpha-1} - w = 0 \Rightarrow h^d = \left(\frac{1}{\alpha}\frac{w}{p}\right)^{\frac{1}{\alpha-1}} \tag{14}$$

This optimal demand for labour by the firm in terms of the real wage rate can be substituted in the objective function of the firm (12) to express profit in terms of the real wage rate.

$$\frac{\pi}{p} = y - w\frac{h^d}{p} = \left(h^d\right)^{\alpha} - \frac{w}{p}h^d = \left(\frac{1}{\alpha}\frac{w}{p}\right)^{\frac{\alpha}{\alpha-1}} - \frac{w}{p}\left(\frac{1}{\alpha}\frac{w}{p}\right)^{\frac{1}{\alpha-1}}$$

$$= \left(\frac{w}{p}\right)^{\frac{\alpha}{\alpha-1}}\left[\left(\frac{1}{\alpha}\right)^{\frac{\alpha}{\alpha-1}} - \left(\frac{1}{\alpha}\right)^{\frac{1}{\alpha-1}}\right] \tag{15}$$

Definition of a Competitive Equilibrium

In this model a competitive equilibrium is obtained by a real wage rate that guarantees the demand for labour by firms to be exactly equal to the supply of labour by households, the time endowments of households to be exactly equal to the sum of supply of labour and demand for leisure, and the production (supply) of output to be exactly equal to the demand for consumption by the household. Given the convexity of preferences and technology such equilibrium exists, is unique and stable.

The real wage rate can be determined by using the labour market clearing condition where the demand for labour by the firm equals the supply of labour by the household, $h^d = h^s$. That implies in equilibrium the demand for labour, $h^d = \left(\frac{1}{\alpha}\frac{w}{p}\right)^{\frac{1}{\alpha-1}}$, should equal the supply of labour, $h^s = \frac{\phi\frac{w}{p} - \frac{\pi}{p}(1-\phi)}{\frac{w}{p}}$. Then using the expression for the real profit from (15) this equality should fulfil the following identity.

$$h^d = \left(\frac{1}{\alpha}\frac{w}{p}\right)^{\frac{1}{\alpha-1}} = h^s = \frac{\phi\frac{w}{p} - \frac{\pi}{p}(1-\phi)}{\frac{w}{p}}$$

$$\frac{\phi\frac{w}{p}-\left(\frac{w}{p}\right)^{\frac{\alpha}{\alpha-1}}\left[\left(\frac{1}{\alpha}\right)^{\frac{\alpha}{\alpha-1}}-\left(\frac{1}{\alpha}\right)^{\frac{1}{\alpha-1}}\right](1-\phi)}{\frac{w}{p}} \tag{16}$$

Two sides of the labour market in (16) can be solved for equilibrium real wage rate as a function of preference and technology parameters of the model.

$$\frac{w}{p}=\frac{\phi^{\alpha-1}}{\left[(1-\phi)\left(\frac{1}{\alpha}\right)^{\frac{\alpha}{\alpha-1}}+\phi\left(\frac{1}{\alpha}\right)^{\frac{1}{\alpha-1}}\right]^{\alpha-1}} \tag{17}$$

The equilibrium quantities of l and h^d are determined by this equilibrium wage rate:

$$\hat{h}^d=\hat{h}^s=\left(\frac{1}{\alpha}\frac{\phi^{\alpha-1}}{\left[(1-\phi)\left(\frac{1}{\alpha}\right)^{\frac{\alpha}{\alpha-1}}+\phi\left(\frac{1}{\alpha}\right)^{\frac{1}{\alpha-1}}\right]^{\alpha-1}}\right)^{\frac{1}{\alpha-1}} \tag{18}$$

the demand for leisure:

$$\hat{l}=1-\hat{h}^s=1-\left(\frac{1}{\alpha}\frac{\phi^{\alpha-1}}{\left[(1-\phi)\left(\frac{1}{\alpha}\right)^{\frac{\alpha}{\alpha-1}}+\phi\left(\frac{1}{\alpha}\right)^{\frac{1}{\alpha-1}}\right]^{\alpha-1}}\right)^{\frac{1}{\alpha-1}} \tag{19}$$

Given the real wage rate and labour supply and leisure, the amount of consumption (c) and the level of output supplied (y) in the no tax case can be obtained by substituting real wage rate from (17) into the demand for consumption function in (7) and labour demand function in (14)

$$,\quad \hat{c} = \left(\frac{\phi}{1-\phi}\right)\left(1 - \left(\frac{1}{\alpha}\frac{\phi^{\alpha-1}}{\left[(1-\phi)\left(\frac{1}{\alpha}\right)^{\frac{\alpha}{\alpha-1}} + \phi\left(\frac{1}{\alpha}\right)^{\frac{1}{\alpha-1}}\right]^{\alpha-1}}\right)^{\frac{1}{\alpha-1}}\right)$$

$$\frac{\phi^{\alpha-1}}{\left[(1-\phi)\left(\frac{1}{\alpha}\right)^{\frac{\alpha}{\alpha-1}} + \phi\left(\frac{1}{\alpha}\right)^{\frac{1}{\alpha-1}}\right]^{\alpha-1}} \tag{20}$$

Equilibrium output is then given by substituting the equilibrium labour input in the production function in (12)

$$\hat{y} = \left(\frac{1}{\alpha}\frac{\phi^{\alpha-1}}{\left[(1-\phi)\left(\frac{1}{\alpha}\right)^{\frac{\alpha}{\alpha-1}} + \phi\left(\frac{1}{\alpha}\right)^{\frac{1}{\alpha-1}}\right]^{\alpha-1}}\right)^{\frac{\alpha}{\alpha-1}} \tag{21}$$

The representative household maximises utility using these optimal values of consumption and leisure in the utility function, $\hat{U} = \hat{c}^{\phi}\hat{l}^{1-\phi}$. This example explicitly shows how the price system allocates resources in an economy.

MICRO-FOUNDED GENERAL EQUILIBRIUM MODEL WITH CONSUMPTION AND LABOUR INCOME TAXES

When both consumption and incomes taxes are applied to raise the revenue the budget constraint changes to $w(1-t_l)h^s + \pi + R = p(1+t_c)c$, where t_c is tax rate on consumption and t_l is the tax rate on labour income and R is the tax revenue which is given back to households as transfers. The household problem modifies but the firms problem remains the same as before as we have not considered taxes at the firm's profit.

$$Max \quad U = c^{\phi} l^{1-\phi}$$

Subject to:

i. $l + h^s = 1$ time constraint

ii $p(1+t_c)c = w(1-t_l)h^s + \pi + R$ budget constraint with taxes

iii. $pt_c c + wt_l h^s = R$ tax revenue and transfer

iv. $c \geq 0; l \geq 0; h^s \geq 0$ non-negativity constraint (1')

The optimisation problem in the tax case is similar but need to be take account of the tax distorted conditions. When the tax revenue function, R is substituted into the budget constraint, the tax budget constraint returns the no tax budget constraint.

$$p(1+t_c)c = w(1-t_l)h^s + \pi + R \rightarrow \quad wh^s + \pi = pc \tag{2'}$$

The term R can be treated as constant when the equal yield revenue constraint is imposed in the model otherwise it varies depending on the tax instruments and tax rates.

The optimal closed form solution of this model in the presence of tax requires tax-distorted first order conditions in the model which can be obtained using the Lagrangian function for constrained optimisation as:

$$L(c,l,\lambda) = c^{\phi}\left(1-h^s\right)^{1-\phi} + \lambda\left[w(1-t_l)h^s + \pi + R - p(1+t_c)c\right] \tag{3'}$$

The household has three choice variables (c,l,λ), where λ is the shadow price of income and tax rates are among the choice variables in the optimal tax model. The first order necessary conditions (FOC) give the marginal utility of consumption, and leisure or the disutility of work and the budget constraint as given below.

$$\frac{\partial L(c,l,\lambda)}{\partial c} = \phi c^{\phi-1}\left(1-h^s\right)^{1-\phi} - \lambda p(1+t_c) = 0 \tag{4'}$$

$$\frac{\partial L(c,l,\lambda)}{\partial h^s} = (1-\phi)c^{\phi}\left(1-h^s\right)^{-\phi}(-1) + \lambda w(1-t_l) = 0 \tag{5'}$$

$$\frac{\partial L(c,l,\lambda)}{\partial \lambda} = w(1-t_l)h^s + \pi + R - p(1+t_c)c = 0 \text{ or } wh^s + \pi = pc \qquad (6')$$

In equilibrium the marginal rate of substitution between consumption and leisure (ratio of FOC (4') to FOC (5')) equals the after tax real wage rate:

$$\frac{\dfrac{\partial L(c,l,\lambda)}{\partial h^s}}{\dfrac{\partial L(c,l,\lambda)}{\partial c}} = \frac{(1-\phi)c^{\phi}(1-h^s)^{-\phi}(-1)}{\phi c^{\phi-1}(1-h^s)^{1-\phi}} = \frac{w(1-t_l)}{p(1+t_c)} \qquad (7')$$

Using results (4') to (7') the demand for consumption goods is obtained as a function of labour supply (h^s) and the real wage rate $\left(\frac{w}{p}\right)$ and the consumption tax rate (t_c) and labour income tax rate t_l.

$$c = \left(\frac{\phi}{1-\phi}\right)(1-h^s)\frac{w(1-t_l)}{p(1+t_c)} \qquad (8')$$

The household's labour supply h^s need to be solved as a function of $\frac{w}{p}$ and which can be done using equation (2') $\frac{w}{.p}h^s + \frac{\pi}{p} = c$.The counterpart of the equation (8) in the tax case is:

$$h^s\frac{w}{p} + \frac{\pi}{p} = c = \left(\frac{\phi}{1-\phi}\right)(1-h^s)\frac{w}{p}\left(\frac{1-t_l}{1+t_c}\right) \qquad (9')$$

The equation (9') is derived after cancelling the tax revenue and transfer components of the tax distorted budget constraint as given in equation (2'). Collecting the terms of the household labour supply:

$$h^s\frac{w}{p} + \left(\frac{\phi}{1-\phi}\right)\frac{w}{p}\left(\frac{1-t_l}{1+t_c}\right)h^s = c = \left(\frac{\phi}{1-\phi}\right)\frac{w}{p}\left(\frac{1-t_l}{1+t_c}\right) - \left(\frac{\pi}{p}\right) \qquad (10')$$

$$h^s\frac{w}{p}\left(\frac{\phi}{1-\phi}\left(\frac{1-t_l}{1+t_c}\right)+1\right) = c = \left(\frac{\phi}{1-\phi}\right)\frac{w}{p}\left(\frac{1-t_l}{1+t_c}\right) - \left(\frac{\pi}{p}\right) \qquad (11')$$

$$h^s = \frac{\left(\frac{\phi}{1-\phi}\right)\frac{w}{p}\left(\frac{1-t_l}{1+t_c}\right)-\left(\frac{\pi}{p}\right)}{\frac{w}{p}\left(\frac{\phi}{1-\phi}\left(\frac{1-t_l}{1+t_c}\right)+1\right)} \tag{12'}$$

Using the value of optimal profit

$$h^s = \frac{\left(\frac{\phi}{1-\phi}\right)\frac{w}{p}\left(\frac{1-t_l}{1+t_c}\right)-\left(\left(\frac{w}{p}\right)^{\frac{\alpha}{\alpha-1}}\left[\left(\frac{1}{\alpha}\right)^{\frac{\alpha}{\alpha-1}}-\left(\frac{1}{\alpha}\right)^{\frac{1}{\alpha-1}}\right]\right)}{\frac{w}{p}\left(\frac{\phi}{1-\phi}\left(\frac{1-t_l}{1+t_c}\right)+1\right)} \tag{13'}$$

The definition of a competitive equilibrium does not change much in the tax distorted economy compared to no tax economy except that the real wage rate now reflects the tax distorted choices and equilibrium. The demand for labour by firms are reduced, the supply of labour by households may rise or fall though the labour market clearing conditions still holds implying the sum of the labour supply and leisure demand to be equal to the total time endowment of the households. The labour market equilibrium should be consistent to the goods market clearing condition whereby the output of the firm equals consumption demand by the household. In addition the government spending should equal tax revenue, which is met in this model by transferring all collected revenue to the household. Using these definitions of a competitive economy, the tax equilibrium can be determined by the real wage rate that equates the demand for and supply of labour in the tax distorted economy.

$$h^d = \left(\frac{1}{\alpha}\frac{w}{p}\right)^{\frac{1}{\alpha-1}} = h^s = \frac{\left(\frac{\phi}{1-\phi}\right)\frac{w}{p}\left(\frac{1-t_l}{1+t_c}\right)-\left(\left(\frac{w}{p}\right)^{\frac{\alpha}{\alpha-1}}\left[\left(\frac{1}{\alpha}\right)^{\frac{\alpha}{\alpha-1}}-\left(\frac{1}{\alpha}\right)^{\frac{1}{\alpha-1}}\right]\right)}{\frac{w}{p}\left(\frac{\phi}{1-\phi}\left(\frac{1-t_l}{1+t_c}\right)+1\right)} \tag{14'}$$

$$\left(\frac{1}{\alpha}\frac{w}{p}\right)^{\frac{1}{\alpha-1}}\left(\frac{\phi}{1-\phi}\left(\frac{1-t_l}{1+t_c}\right)+1\right)$$

$$=\left(\frac{\phi}{1-\phi}\right)\left(\frac{1-t_l}{1+t_c}\right)-\left(\left(\frac{w}{p}\right)^{\frac{1}{\alpha-1}}\left[\left(\frac{1}{\alpha}\right)^{\frac{\alpha}{\alpha-1}}-\left(\frac{1}{\alpha}\right)^{\frac{1}{\alpha-1}}\right]\right) \tag{15'}$$

$$\left(\frac{1}{\alpha}\frac{w}{p}\right)^{\frac{1}{\alpha-1}}\left(\frac{\phi}{1-\phi}\left(\frac{1-t_l}{1+t_c}\right)+1\right)+\left(\left(\frac{w}{p}\right)^{\frac{1}{\alpha-1}}\left[\left(\frac{1}{\alpha}\right)^{\frac{\alpha}{\alpha-1}}-\left(\frac{1}{\alpha}\right)^{\frac{1}{\alpha-1}}\right]\right)$$

$$=\left(\frac{\phi}{1-\phi}\right)\left(\frac{1-t_l}{1+t_c}\right) \quad (16')$$

$$\left(\frac{w}{p}\right)^{\frac{1}{\alpha-1}}\left[\left(\frac{1}{\alpha}\right)^{\frac{1}{\alpha-1}}\left(\frac{\phi}{1-\phi}\left(\frac{1-t_l}{1+t_c}\right)+1\right)+\left\{\left(\frac{1}{\alpha}\right)^{\frac{\alpha}{\alpha-1}}-\left(\frac{1}{\alpha}\right)^{\frac{1}{\alpha-1}}\right\}\right]$$

$$=\left(\frac{\phi}{1-\phi}\right)\left(\frac{1-t_l}{1+t_c}\right) \quad (17')$$

$$\left(\frac{w}{p}\right)^{\frac{1}{\alpha-1}}=\frac{\left(\frac{\phi}{1-\phi}\right)\left(\frac{1-t_l}{1+t_c}\right)}{\left[\left(\frac{1}{\alpha}\right)^{\frac{1}{\alpha-1}}\left(\frac{\phi}{1-\phi}\left(\frac{1-t_l}{1+t_c}\right)+1\right)+\left\{\left(\frac{1}{\alpha}\right)^{\frac{\alpha}{\alpha-1}}-\left(\frac{1}{\alpha}\right)^{\frac{1}{\alpha-1}}\right\}\right]} \quad (18')$$

Thus the real wage rate in equilibrium is given by

$$\frac{w}{p}=\left[\frac{\left(\frac{\phi}{1-\phi}\right)\left(\frac{1-t_l}{1+t_c}\right)}{\left[\left(\frac{1}{\alpha}\right)^{\frac{1}{\alpha-1}}\left(\frac{\phi}{1-\phi}\left(\frac{1-t_l}{1+t_c}\right)+1\right)+\left\{\left(\frac{1}{\alpha}\right)^{\frac{\alpha}{\alpha-1}}-\left(\frac{1}{\alpha}\right)^{\frac{1}{\alpha-1}}\right\}\right]}\right]^{\alpha-1} \quad (19')$$

Once we have this real wage rate, the amount of labour supplied and demanded in the tax distorted economy can be evaluated using the labour demand equation in (14). Firms pay the gross of tax wage rate but households receive the net of tax wage. Households pay gross of tax prices for goods and services and firm's receive net of tax prices. The differences between these prices accrue to the government as the tax revenue. It cause distortions though the government ploughs back all of the revenues to households directly as transfers or as public goods or services.

From the above analysis it is obvious that the commodity and labour income taxes create a wedge between the producer prices received by firms and market prices paid by households in the goods market. The labour income tax puts a wedge between the gross of tax wage rate paid by firms and net of tax wage rate received by the households. These wedges may differ between these two tax instruments and may have different impacts on consumption, labour supply, output and demand for leisure.

$$h^d = \left(\frac{1}{\alpha}\frac{w}{p}\right)^{\frac{1}{\alpha-1}} \rightarrow$$

$$h^s = h^d = \left(\frac{1}{\alpha}\right)^{\frac{1}{\alpha-1}} \left[\frac{\left(\frac{\phi}{1-\phi}\right)\left(\frac{1-t_l}{1+t_c}\right)}{\left[\left(\frac{1}{\alpha}\right)^{\frac{1}{\alpha-1}}\left(\frac{\phi}{1-\phi}\left(\frac{1-t_l}{1+t_c}\right)+1\right)+\left\{\left(\frac{1}{\alpha}\right)^{\frac{\alpha}{\alpha-1}}-\left(\frac{1}{\alpha}\right)^{\frac{1}{\alpha-1}}\right\}\right]}\right] \quad (20')$$

The labour supply in equations (20') is expressed also in terms of the real wage rate by using the equilibrium condition in the labour market, where demand for labour by the firms is consistent with the supply of the labour by the household. The labour supply then determines the level of output as:

$$\hat{y} = \left(\frac{1}{\alpha}\right)^{\frac{\alpha}{\alpha-1}} \left[\frac{\left(\frac{\phi}{1-\phi}\right)\left(\frac{1-t_l}{1+t_c}\right)}{\left[\left(\frac{1}{\alpha}\right)^{\frac{1}{\alpha-1}}\left(\frac{\phi}{1-\phi}\left(\frac{1-t_l}{1+t_c}\right)+1\right)+\left\{\left(\frac{1}{\alpha}\right)^{\frac{\alpha}{\alpha-1}}-\left(\frac{1}{\alpha}\right)^{\frac{1}{\alpha-1}}\right\}\right]}\right]^{\alpha} \quad (21')$$

Leisure demand is then given by the difference between the endowment and labour supply.

$$\hat{l} = 1-\left(\frac{1}{\alpha}\right)^{\frac{1}{\alpha-1}} \left[\frac{\left(\frac{\phi}{1-\phi}\right)\left(\frac{1-t_l}{1+t_c}\right)}{\left[\left(\frac{1}{\alpha}\right)^{\frac{1}{\alpha-1}}\left(\frac{\phi}{1-\phi}\left(\frac{1-t_l}{1+t_c}\right)+1\right)+\left\{\left(\frac{1}{\alpha}\right)^{\frac{\alpha}{\alpha-1}}-\left(\frac{1}{\alpha}\right)^{\frac{1}{\alpha-1}}\right\}\right]}\right] \quad (22')$$

Consumption demand is obtained using the leisure in (22') above in (8').

$$\hat{c} = \left(\frac{\phi}{1-\phi}\right)\left[1-\left(\frac{1}{\alpha}\right)^{\frac{1}{\alpha-1}}\left[\frac{\left(\frac{\phi}{1-\phi}\right)\left(\frac{1-t_l}{1+t_c}\right)}{\left[\left(\frac{1}{\alpha}\right)^{\frac{1}{\alpha-1}}\left(\frac{\phi}{1-\phi}\left(\frac{1-t_l}{1+t_c}\right)+1\right)+\left\{\left(\frac{1}{\alpha}\right)^{\frac{\alpha}{\alpha-1}}-\left(\frac{1}{\alpha}\right)^{\frac{1}{\alpha-1}}\right\}\right]}\right]\right]$$

$$\frac{w(1-t_l)}{p(1+t_c)} \qquad (23')$$

The level of utility to the representative household in the tax distorted economy is given by $\hat{U} = \hat{c}^{\phi}\hat{l}^{1-\phi}$.

As can be seen from the above derivation the price and real wage rates are the basis of all consumption and production decisions. Production occurs because there is demand for products by the households. Firms demand factors to produce output. They pay labour according to its marginal product. The remuneration for labour services provides income to the households, which they use to purchase consumption goods. Once the equilibrium price is determined that determines all other quantities, such as the demand for goods and leisure and the supply of labour by households and the demand for labour and supply of commodities by firms. Both labour and capital income taxes distort the equilibrium quantities and prices and have discernible impacts in allocation of resources in the economy.

A NUMERICAL EXAMPLE FOR THE GENERAL EQUILIBRIUM TAX MODEL

A simple numerical example is provided here for the above general equilibrium tax model and used it to measure the relative impacts of consumption and income taxes in the economy. These impacts vary according to the preferences of households in relation to technology of production available to firms. If households strongly prefer leisure rather than consumption, the costs of income taxes are likely to be higher than those of the consumption taxes. On the other hand if the households have stronger preferences for consumption than for leisure then consumption taxes might be costlier. As stated above these preference and technology factors jointly determine the prices and prices influence allocation of resources in the economy. Numerical values of model parameters are given in Table 1.

Table 1
Parameters of the model in the base scenario

Parameter of the model	*Numerical value in the base model*
Utility weight on consumption (ϕ)	0.6
Utility weight on leisure (1- ϕ)	0.4
Elasticity of output to labour input (α)	0.6
Value of Endowment	68 hours
Consumption tax rate in the base model	0.17
Income tax rate in the base case	0.35

Normalisation of price $w + p = 1$. Time endowments of 68 ours per week is used here as is customary in the literature.

Two types of simulations are conducted using this model. The first one is the base case scenario constructed using a reasonable set of preference and technology parameters as given in Table 1. Then there is a no tax scenario where all taxes are eliminated, followed by scenarios with taxes either only on consumption or only on labour income. The impacts of tax policy experiments are determined by comparing the utility and changes in output and employment before and after the change in taxes.

Experiments for the tax reform
Use of both consumption and income taxes and lump sum transfers (base case)
Elimination of all taxes and no transfer
Only labour income tax and lump sum transfers
Only consumption tax and lump sum transfers

In addition sensitivity analyses are conducted to see how the welfare and macroeconomic impacts change in response to a distribution of households by preference and that of firms by the production technology. The grids of parameters for sensitivity analyses are in Table 2. Again impacts of taxes are measured in terms of levels and changes in utility, output, leisure, labour supply and consumption.

Table 2

Parameter of the model	*Numerical value in the base model*
Share of spending on consumption (ϕ)	0.25 to 0.6 with steps size of 0.05
Share of spending on leisure (1- ϕ)	0.75 to 0.4 with steps size of 0.05
Elasticity of output to labour input (α)	0.3 to .65 with steps size of 0.05
Value of Endowment	68 to 108 hours with steps size of 5
Consumption tax rate in the base model	0.17 to 0.67 with steps size of 0.05
Income tax rate in the base case	0.40 to 0.85 with steps size of 0.05

ANALYSIS OF MODEL RESULTS

The benchmark economy includes consumption tax rate of 17 per cent and income tax rate of 35 per cent, similar to the one that actually exists in many of the OECD countries including the UK. In all experiments the government returns tax revenue to the household in the form of a lump sum transfer. The model is then used to evaluate the impacts of four different tax reform experiments: (1) the distortionary cost of both income and consumption taxes; (2) impact of a complete switch to the labour income tax holding the revenue fixed; (3) impact of a complete switch towards the consumption tax; and (4) the test of reliability and robustness of the model by examining the sensitivity to the key parameters of the model.

Table 3
Overall Welfare Impacts of Tax Changes in the General Equilibrium Model of Taxes

	Equivalent Variation	*Compensating Variation*
Elimination of all taxes	3.2%	-3.1%
Labour tax only	-6.2%	6.7%
Consumption tax only	-0.05%	0.05%

The Hicksian equivalent variations (EV) are presented in terms of the money metric utility in the counter factual scenario in comparison to the benchmark scenario by asking how much the household benefits from the tax changes equivalent in terms of the original equilibrium. The corresponding compensating variation is also in terms of the money metric utility measuring the amount of compensation a consumer needs to bring back her to the original level of utility after the changes in tax rates.

Table 4
Macroeconomic Impacts of Alternative Taxes

Variables	*Both Taxes*	*Not Tax*	*Labour Income Tax*	*Consumption Tax*
Utility	14.142	14.601	13.689	14.526
Output	6.505	8.032	5.849	7.431
Leisure	45.333	35.789	49.012	39.703
Labour Supply	22.667	32.211	18.988	28.297
Consumption	6.505	8.032	5.849	7.431
Revenue	2.109	—	1.687	1.687
Wage	0.147	0.13	0.156	0.136
Price	0.853	0.87	0.844	0.864
Profit	14.142	14.601	13.689	14.526
Consumption tax	0.17	—	—	0.263
Labour income tax	0.35	—	0.57	

The overall welfare costs of taxes, as presented in Table 3 above, show that the costs of using both consumption and income taxes are higher than of using only either the consumption or only the labour income tax. The overall distortionary impacts of both consumption and labour income taxes are up to 3.2 per cent of the benchmark utility. This compares to results as contained in Bhattarai and Whalley (1999, 2003). If the revenue is returned as a lump sum form to the households, the model results confirm that the labour income tax has highly distortionary impact in the economy. It may cost up to 6.2 per cent of the benchmark utility. Higher rate of labour income tax first reduces labour supply and output and consumption consequently. In comparison, sole reliance on only consumption taxes significantly lowers distortions than labour income taxes. Model calculations suggest that the cost of moving towards only consumption taxes is 0.05 per cent of the benchmark utility. Thus the overall costs are lower when tax is only on consumption than when taxes are both on consumption and labour income simultaneously.

For this hypothetical economy taxes affect the aggregate output, employment, leisure, labour supply as well as consumption of the household as shown in Table 4 to Table 7. It is obvious that the adverse macroeconomic impacts of only labour income taxes are a lot higher than those of only consumption taxes.

Table 5
Impact of Alternative Taxes: Per centage changes compared to the base case

	Base two tax case	*Labour only tax*	*Consumption tax*
Output	23.471	-27.174	-7.478
Leisure	-21.053	36.946	10.936
Labour supply	42.105	-41.051	-12.151
Consumption	23.471	-27.174	-7.478
Revenue	-100	—	—
Wage rate	-11.406	19.868	4.595
Price	1.964	-2.972	-0.687
Profit	25.896	-29.339	-8.114
Utility	3.246	-6.246	-0.511

When both labour income and consumption taxes are removed, households lose the amount of transfer income from the government but still it has a very good positive impact on output, consumption and utility level of the representative household. In contrast the labour income tax discourages labour supply relative to both the no tax and consumption tax only cases leading to highly distortionary effects on the economy.

This model generates predictable results when subject to sensitivity tests along the various rates of consumption and labour income tax rates. It confirms that the welfare costs of taxes rise proportionately to the squares of tax rates as suggested by the famous Harberger triangle, a measure of the dead weight loss of taxes.

The model also behaves well when subject to changes in the endowments. Households receive higher utility as their endowments rise but at a decreasing rate given the law of diminishing marginal utility. Since the consumer values both consumption and leisure, the increase in utility of increasing only consumption show a diminishing utility as does the increase in the share of labour in production which raises the marginal productivity of labour and reduces the amount of leisure in the utility function.

Table 6
Sensitivity of Welfare cost to Tax Changes

Scenarios	*EV*	*Consumption tax rate*	*Labour Income tax rate*
1	4.727	0.22	0.4
2	6.567	0.27	0.45
3	8.83	0.32	0.5
4	11.607	0.37	0.55
5	15.03	0.42	0.6
6	19.289	0.47	0.65
7	24.685	0.52	0.7
8	31.71	0.57	0.75
9	41.246	0.62	0.8
10	55.092	0.67	0.85

The welfare cost of taxes rises when tax rates increase as shown in Table 6. Changes in the base case utility are sensitive to time endowment of household (for instance in the case of a two member household compared to a single member household). The welfare levels are sensitive to the preferences and labour supply elasticity as shown in Table 7. The costs of a consumption tax are higher in an economy which prefers more leisure than consumption but are lower in an economy which prefers more consumption than leisure. This confirms to the diminishing marginal utility theory of consumption. Similarly labour bears the most burden of taxes when elasticity of labour demand is lower rather than when it is higher as shown in the last two columns in Table 7.

Table 7
Sensitivity of Model Results in Comparison to the Base Case

Endowment	*Change in utility*	*Alpha*	*Change in utility*	*Phi*	*Change in utility*
73	5.54	0.3	-44.054	0.25	106.269
78	10.99	0.35	-38.744	0.3	81.531
83	16.357	0.4	-32.729	0.35	61.117
88	21.647	0.45	-25.937	0.4	44.153
93	26.865	0.5	-18.286	0.45	29.991
98	32.016	0.55	-9.677	0.5	18.144
103	37.104	0.6	-9.40E-12	0.55	8.241

All above results show how the relative prices of commodities and labour determine the allocation of resources in an artificial economy. This model, however, can be applied to a real economy to assess the impacts of alternative tax measures on output, consumption, labour supply, leisure, price of a commodity and wage rate in an economy. Though very simple, this model can answer a number of key policy questions that may confront the policy makers while considering the fiscal policy for an economy.

The model was applied taking actual data on endowments, consumption share and production share of the UK Economy for 2002. The consumption tax rate is set to 17 per cent which is close enough to the standard VAT rate and the labour income tax rate is set to 35 per cent. This is fairly representative tax rate in the UK when one considers the average of the base and higher income tax rates along with the national insurance payments that are applied to labour income in the UK. The labour endowment measured in terms of efficiency units, is set at 1000 billion which is close to the size of the economy of 2002. From the income distribution tables of the Office of National Statistics (2002) the share parameter (phi) in the consumption function is set to 0.6 and the elasticity of output to the labour input (alpha) set to 0.75. These values were confirmed by an econometric estimation.

The first scenario considers the efficiency impacts of removing all the taxes and transfers in the UK. When a representative household does not pay tax it also does not receive any transfer from the government. This is an extreme scenario in which all public services are provided by the private sector. The second scenario considers switching completely to the labour income tax and eliminating all indirect taxes. The third scenario, on the other hand is switching completely to consumption taxes and removing all taxes on the labour income. The results of the model are very intuitive.

Efficiency Gains in the UK from elimination of all taxes and transfers

(Measured as a per cent of benchmark utility level of a representative household)

Equivalent Variation = 3.715
Compensating Variation = -3.582

Efficiency Gains from Switching to Labour income Taxes
Equivalent Variation = -6.9
Compensating Variation = 7.0

Efficiency Gains from Switching to Consumption Taxes
Equivalent Variation = 2.967
Compensating Variation = -2.882

Table 8
Macroeconomic Impacts of Consumption and Labour Income Taxes in the UK

Variable	*BenchmarkBoth taxes*	*Labour Income tax only*	*Consumption tax only*
Utility	190.073	188.757	195.713
Output	86.85	84.687	100.008
Leisure	615.385	628.104	535.791
Labour supply	384.615	371.896	464.209
Consumption	86.85	84.687	100.008
Revenue	32.122	25.698	25.698
wage rate	0.145	0.146	0.139
Price	0.855	0.854	0.861
Profit	190.073	188.757	195.713
Optimal Consumption tax rate	0.17	—	0.298
Optimal labour income tax rate	0.35	0.474	—

The key results of this exercise in the general equilibrium impacts of tax reforms are the following:

(1) The efficiency gains from switching to only consumption taxes are about 80 per cent of the gains of eliminating all the taxes. Optimal consumption tax rate given the revenue constraint set equal to 80 per cent of the benchmark revenue level is 2.9 per cent. This seems a very sensible result considering the fact that consumers ultimately bear the burden of all taxes. Similarly consumers make a choice whether to consume a certain product or not depending upon its price. If the prices are high because of taxes they can increase utility by not consuming the heavily taxed good and by taking more leisure instead of work.

(2) Labour income tax is highly distortionary in this model for various reasons. As before 47 per cent tax rate of labour income is optimal to meet the required revenue target. It reduces the labour supply. Both output and consumption becomes smaller after such a tax is imposed. The efficiency losses from switching to this sort of taxes can be up to 6.9 per cent of the original utility.

(3) The first result shows that the net deadweight loss of the current tax and transfer system is about 4 per cent of GDP.

CONCLUSION

An analytical solution is provided to a simplest possible general equilibrium model, with households, firms and the government, to analyse how the price and real wage rate are determined in equilibrium and to assess the macroeconomic impacts on consumption and labour income taxes in an economy. In a numerical example, where a given revenue need to be raised for transfers, the welfare cost and macroeconomic impacts are higher when both consumption and income taxes are applied together than when only one of these two taxes are in use because of the compounding effects of taxes. When revenues are returned to households in the form of lump sum transfers the labour income taxes are found more distortionary than the consumption taxes.

The model is applied to assess three policy reform scenarios in the UK and found that switching to only consumption taxes would improve the efficiency in the economy which are about 80 per cent of the welfare gains from the elimination of all tax and transfers and far better than switching completely to the labour income taxes. Since the ultimate burden of taxes lies on consumers, consumption taxes remove the inefficiency caused by the tax system more than any other taxes.

Acknowledgement: I appreciate a lecture from Professor Stephen Parente then at Northeastern and some comments from Professor Richard Green in the earlier draft of this paper and the Centre of Economic Policy of the Hull University Business School for publishing an earlier version of this paper as a Research Memorandum. All errors and omissions are my own.

REFERENCES

Atkinson A.B. and J. E. Stiglitz (1976), "The design of the tax structure: direct versus indirect taxation", *Journal of Public Economics*, 6:1-2:55-75.

Bhattarai, K. and J. Whalley (1999), "The Role of Labour Demand Elasticities in Tax Incidence Analysis with Heterogeneous Labour," *Empirical Economics* 24:4:599-619, November.

Bhattarai K. and J. Whalley (2003), "Discreteness and the Welfare Cost of Labour Supply Tax Distortions" *International Economic Review* 44:3:1117-1133, August.

Boadway, R. N. Bruce (1992), Problems with Integrating Corporate and Personal Income Taxes in an Open Economy, J*ournal of Public Economics*, June, 48:1:39-66.

GAMS Development Corporation, GAMS: A User's Guide, Washington DC 20007, USA.

Hicks J. R. (1948), Value and Capital, Oxford.

Hutton, J. P. A. Ruocco (1999), Tax Reform and Employment in Europe *International Tax and Public Finance*, August, 6:3:263-87.

Iwamoto, Y. A. Shibata (1999), Foreign Tax Credit and the Current Account *International Tax and Public Finance*, 6:2:131-48, May.

Keynes JM (1936), The General Theory of Employment, Interest and Money, Macmillan.

Pechman J. A. (1987), Tax Reform: Theory and Practice *The Journal of Economic Perspectives*, 1:1:11-28, Summer.

Mirlees, J. A. (1971), "An exploration in the theory of optimum income taxation", *Review of Economic Studies*, 38:175-208.

Office of National Statistics (2002), Economic Trends London.

Perroni, C. (1995), "Assessing the Dynamic Efficiency Gains of Tax Reform When Human Capital is Endogenous," *International Economic Review* 36:907-925.

Pigou A.C. (1947), A Study in Public Finance (3rd edition) McMillan, London.

Ramsey, F. P. (1927), "A contribution to the theory of taxation", *Economic Journal*, 37:47-61.

Rebelo, S. (1991), "Long-run Policy Analysis and Long-run Growth," *Journal of Political Economy* 99:500-521.

Seidman, L. S., K. A. Lewis (1999), The Consumption Tax and the Saving Elasticity *National Tax Journal*, March, 52:1: 67-78.

Whalley J. (1975), "A General Equilibrium Assessment of the 1973 United Kingdom tax reform", *Economica*, 42:166:139-161.

A Brief GAMS Code for the numerical part of the model parameters

```
phi
alph
endow
endow0
lmd
*tc
*tl
;
phi = 0.6;
alph =0.6;
endow =68;
endow0 =endow;
*tc=0.17;
*tl=0.35;
lmd =100;

variables
u
c
l
ls
w
y
p
prf
rv
tc
tl
;

equations
util
time
budg
dmc
dls
prd
mkt
eprf
gov
rlprice
;

util..

u =e= (c**phi)*(l**(1-phi));

time..
  (l+ls)-endow =e= 0;
budg..
  p*(1+tc)*c =e=w*(1-tl)*ls+prf+rv;
dmc..
      c=e=  (phi/(1-phi))*(endow-
ls)*(w*(1-tl)/(p*(1+tc)));

dls..
   ls=e=
{(1/alph)*(w/p)}**(1/(alph-1));
gov..
   rv =e= tc*c*P+tl*w*ls;
prd..
  y =e= ls**alph;
mkt..
  y=e=c;
eprf..
  prf =e= p*y-w*ls;
rlprice..
  p+w =e=1;
model tax /util, time, budg,dmc,prd,
dls,mkt,eprf,gov, rlprice/;

p.lo=0.01;
c.lo=0.0001;
l.lo=0.0001;
ls.lo=0.0001;
w.lo=0.0001;
p.lo=0.0001;
y.lo=0.0001;
prf.lo=0.00;
rv.lo=-inf;
tc.fx=0.17;
tl.fx=0.35;
tax.iterlim =10000;
Solve tax maximising u using nlp;
```

3

Multi-Sectoral Multi-Household General Equilibrium Tax Model: An Application

Keshab R. Bhattarai*

A PROTOTYPE OF A GENERAL EQUILIBRIUM TAX MODEL

Applied general equilibrium models have been used increasingly to evaluate the resource reallocation and redistribution impacts of tax reforms in an economy[1]. We here present two versions and simple numerical examples of a GE tax model for expository purposes. We begin with a four sector three household model with three tax instruments (sales, income and VAT taxes), similar to that considered earlier by Piggott and Whalley (1985). We then report on a version with a labour-leisure choice component added to the basic model. For these two platform models we briefly discuss the specification of preferences and technology, and then describe the construction of the micro-consistent data sets required for model implementation.

We also discuss the methods used for model calibration and choice of the elasticity parameters in preferences and production functions. Once the model replicates the base year economy, we can then solve for a counterfactual equilibrium without taxes in order to evaluate the welfare costs of tax distortions. The tax experiments executed with the platform model and reported here are illustrative.

---

* Research reported in this paper was undertaken under an ESRC project on General Equilibrium and Dynamic Modelling for the Analysis of UK Policy Issues in the University of Warwick. I am grateful to Professor John Whalley for guidance in this research. Model developed here were also discussed in a workshop on applied general equilibrium analysis at the economics department of the University of Hull during July 2-6, 2001. I appreciate comments and suggestions from Carlo Perroni, T.F. Rutherford and Mike Ryan in the earlier version of the paper. Correspondence address *K.R.Bhattarai@hull.ac.uk*. Phone (44) 1482-466483 Fax: (44) 1482-466216. Earlier version of this paper has appeared as Working Paper 9 in the series of Hull Advances in Policy Economics. Author is solely responsible for any errors and omissions in the paper.

Specification for a Standard Static General Equilibrium Tax Model

In this section we present a platform version of a standard general equilibrium tax model, to illustrate the basic structure and use of GE model for tax policy analyses. Basic ingredients of these models are as found in the standard Arrow-Debreu economy (Arrow and Debreu (1954)). Households maximise utility subject to their budget constraints, and producers maximise profits subject to technology constraints. Both the utility of households and production by firms are given by standard CES (concave, monotonic, homothetic and continuous) functions. The equilibrium conditions imply that markets for goods, labour and

capital clear, firms receive zero profits in equilibrium, and income is equal to expenditure for all households. The role of the government in these platform models is to affect the distribution of income through tax revenue financed transfer programs, by taxing households and corporations on their income and collecting value added taxes from final purchases. Labour supply decisions of the households are in the platform model 2, in which a labour-leisure choice is explicitly included in household utility functions, and labour market clearing takes account of leisure consumed by households. The current model incorporates all standard equilibrium conditions that are characteristics of the computable general equilibrium literature. This class of models is used in both static and dynamic studies of tax reform policies (Ballard, Fullerton, Shoven and Whalley (1985)).

Demands

The household maximises utility which is described by a CES function defined over commodities (i=1 ..N) and leisure, subject to a budget constraint. This utility function can be written as

$$U_h = \left(\sum_i \alpha_{i,h} C_{i,h}^{\rho_h} + \beta_h L_h^{\rho_h} \right)^{\frac{1}{\rho_h}} \tag{1}$$

where U_h is the utility of household h, $C_{i,h}$ is the consumption of good i by household h, L_h is the leisure taken by household h, $\alpha_{i,h}$ is the share of the full income of household h spent on consumption of good i, β_h is the share of full income spent on leisure, and ρ_h is the elasticity parameter in the utility function, the elasticity of substitution between goods (and leisure) being equal to $\sigma_h = \dfrac{1}{1-\rho_h}$ (Varian (1992)). In versions of the model in which leisure does not appear $\beta_h = 0$ and $\sum_{i=1}^{N} \alpha_{i,h} = 1$.

Households receive income from capital and labour endowments, and transfers from the government. They pay taxes on household and capital income. The disposable income of a household is given by

$$I_h = r(1-t_k)\bar{K}_h + (1-t_l^h)w\bar{L}_h + TR_h \tag{2}$$

where I_h is the full income of the household, $\bar{K}_h$ is its endowment of capital, $\bar{L}_h$ is its endowment of labour, TR_h are the transfers received by household *h*, *r* is the rental rate of capital, *w* is the wage rate, t_l^h is the tax rate on household h's labour income[2], and t_k is the tax rate on capital income.

The demand functions for goods and leisure are obtained by maximising (1) with respect to (2), and take the following form

$$C_{i,h} = \left(\frac{\alpha_{i,h} I_h}{\left(P_i(1+t_i^v)\right)^{\sigma h} \left(\sum_i \alpha_{i,h} \left(P_i\left(1+t_i^v\right)\right)^{\sigma h} + \beta_h \left(w\left(1-t_l^h\right)\right)^{\sigma h} \right)} \right) \tag{3}$$

where t_i^v is value added tax rate and t_l^h tax rate on labour income, and P_i is the price of commodity *i*.

Consumption of leisure is given by

$$L_h = \left(\frac{\beta_h . I_h}{\left(w\left(1-t_l^h\right)\right)^{\sigma h} \left(\sum_i \alpha_{i,h} \left(P_i\left(1+t_i^v\right)\right)^{\sigma h} + \beta_h \left(w\left(1-t_l^h\right)\right)^{\sigma h} \right)} \right) \tag{4}$$

In versions of the model where there is no demand for leisure households have demand functions only for goods. In that case equation (4) does not exist, and equation (3) is modified by setting $\beta_h = 0$.

In the one household case, the labour supply of the household LS_h is given by the difference between the household labour endowment, and the demand for leisure, L_h.

$$LS_h = \bar{L}_h - L_h \tag{5}$$

In equilibrium, this labour supply by the household must be consistent with the total demand for labour derived from the profit maximisation behaviour of firms as set out in the following section.

Production

Producers use labour and capital in each of N sectors to yield value added. This also is given by CES functions.

$$Y_i = \Omega_i((1-\delta_i)(K_i)^{\gamma_i} + \delta_i(L_i)^{\gamma_i})^{\frac{1}{\gamma_i}} \quad (i = 1..N) \tag{6}$$

where Y_i is the value added of sector i, Ω_i is a shift parameter in the production function, K_i and L_i are the amounts of capital and labour used in sector i, δ_i is the share parameter on labour in the CES function, and γ_i is the CES factor substitution parameter.

The gross output of each sector reflects the use of value added, Y_i, and intermediate inputs. We assume fixed coefficients both among intermediate inputs, and between value added and intermediate inputs; $M_{i,j}$ is the intermediate use of good *i* in the production of good *j* and X_i is the gross output of sector *i*. At any set of prices, producers in each sector maximise profits subject to their technology constraint

$$\max \Pi_i = P_i X_i - wL_i - rK_i - \sum_j P_j M_{j,i} \tag{7}$$

where Π_i is the profit of sector *i*. In equilibrium, factor demands by sectors are determined where the value marginal product of factors equal factor prices, and there are no positive profits for producers.

Government Budget

The government collects revenue from taxes on capital and labour income and value-added taxes. All the tax revenues collected are transferred to households in lump sum form; ie.

$$\sum_h TR_h = \sum_i t_k rK_i + \sum_h t_i^v P_i C_{i,h} + \sum_h t_l^h wLS_h \tag{8}$$

where t_k is the tax rate on capital income, t_i^v is the *ad valorem* tax rate on final sales, t_l^h is the tax rate on labour income of the household.

These taxes, particularly when they are levied at different rates on different sectors and households, have distortionary impacts on the allocation of resources in the economy. These are captured by the model. Government budget balance is a property of an equilibrium

Model Equilibrium Conditions

In this model a competitive equilibrium is given by prices of consumption goods, P_i ; the rental rate of capital r ; a wage rate for labour, w; and levels of gross output, Y_i; capital use, K_i ; and sectoral use of labour, L_i ; such that,

(i) markets for goods and services, labour and capital clear; and

(ii) the government budget constraint is satisfied.

More specifically, the market clearing condition for the goods market is given by

$$X_i = C_i + \sum_{j=1}^{N} a_{ij} X_j \tag{9}$$

where $C_i = \sum_h C_{i,h}$ is household final consumption, and $\sum_j a_{ij} X_j$ the intermediate demand.

The capital market clearing condition implies

$$\sum_h \bar{K}_h = \sum_i K_i \tag{10}$$

and labour market clearing implies:

$$\sum_h LS_h = \sum_i LS_i \tag{11}$$

Government budget balance is given by (8). When there are n different markets in the economy, relative prices that clear n-1 markets clears the nth market as well.

A SIMPLE MICRO-CONSISTENT DATA SET FOR A PLATFORM GE TAX MODEL

We can illustrate the operation of this platform model using a simple example of a micro-consistent data set taken from Piggott and Whalley (1985). This data set meets the equilibrium conditions for a competitive economy: demand equals supply for all goods and factors, non-positive profits are made in all industries and the government budget constraint in the presence of taxes is satisfied (Mansur and Whalley (1984) and St- Hilaire and Whalley (1983)). The input-output data of firms in Tables 1, 2 and 3 are illustrative, but they are separately available for the UK economy in National Accounts and related sources as the starting point for base year model calibration. If the required balance conditions do not hold in the raw data, various adjustments become necessary. The construction of such a data set, based on UK national accounts and other data sources, is discussed in section four and appendix 1.

Table 1
Illustrative Input-output Value Transactions Matrix For The Platform Model

Sectors	*Sector 1*	*Sector 2*	*Sector 3*	*Sector 4*
Sector 1	2	1	2	3
Sector 2	4	3	1	2
Sector 3	2	1	1	1
Sector 4	2	1	1	0

Our simple example of a data set for use in the platform model includes four sectors, three households, a government sector, and three types of tax instruments: taxes on capital income, household income and value added. These are displayed in tables 1-3, where data reported are in transactions (or value) terms.[3] This platform model is a closed economy model with an implicit assumption that foreign trade balances in general.

Table 2
Illustrative Data On Consumption, Income, Output And Taxes For The Platform Model

Sectors	*Sector 1*	*Sector 2*	*Sector 3*	*Sector 4*
Consumption 1	4	2	4	1
Consumption 2	2	3	1	3
Consumption 3	1	1	3	4
Capital Income	1	2	3	1
Labour Income	2	4	3	1
Indirect Taxes	1	2	1	1
Vat	1	2	1	3
Base Year Price	1	1	1	1
Total Output	15	16	13	12

Table 3
Illustrative Data On Sources Of Income to The Households For The Platform Model

	Household 1	*Household 2*	*Household 3*
Interest Income	5	1	1
Wage Income	3	3	4
Transfer Income	6	7	6
Household Taxes	3	2	2

Tables 1-3 provide the basic data required for the implementation of the first platform model. The input-output transactions for this illustrative economy are given in Table 1, in which rows represent purchases of intermediate goods by other sectors and columns represent purchases of intermediate goods by a particular sector. For instance, the first column represents the purchase of intermediate inputs by sector 1, and the first row represents the sale of intermediate goods by sector 1 to other sectors. Input-output coefficients, which give the input requirements from sector i per unit of output in sector j, provide forward and backward linkages in the production sectors of the economy.

Information on consumption of each of three households and value added payments to capital and labour, indirect business taxes, VAT on final consumption and base-year prices are given in Table 2. The economy wide balance requires that total output be equal to the total of intermediate demand and final consumption.

Sectoral payments of wages and salaries and interest accrue to households, which provide these labour and capital services to producers. The allocation of wage and interest income among various households is as described in Table 3. From this table, it is evident that household 1 owns more capital and receives a larger amount of capital income compared to other households. It also pays more taxes in comparison to other households, and receives less in transfers than household 2.

CALIBRATION OF PARAMETERS AND ELASTICITIES USED IN THE PLATFORM MODEL

The computer code used in implementing these platform models, MPSGE/GAMS programmes[4], proto.gms and leisure.gms are presented in appendices[5].

We use the data presented in tables 1 to 3 to calibrate the share parameters in the CES functions used in the platform version of the model, as specified in the previous section. The calibrated share parameters in consumption and production presented below are consistent with the replication of the benchmark data by the model equilibrium solutions.

Table 4
Calibrated Share Parameters In Consumption In Illustrative Example Of A Platform Economy

Sectors	*Sector 1*	*Sector 2*	*Sector 3*	*Sector 4*
Household 1	0.429	0.167	0.338	0.078
Household 2	0.245	0.286	0.125	0.268
Household 3	0.122	0.100	0.375	0.357

The figures in Table 4 show that households differ in preferences over consumption goods. For instance, household 1 spends more on commodities 1 and 3 than on commodities 2 and 4. Household 3 spends more on commodities 3 and 4 than on commodities 1 and 2. Consumption preferences of household 2 lies between those of households 1 and 3.

Capital and labour are the only two primary factors of production for each sector considered in the platform model 1 (equation 6). With constant returns to scale in production, the value of output at factor cost will equal the remuneration of capital and labour. The production side calibrated share parameters are given in Table 5, which shows sector 1 and 2 are labour intensive while sectors 3 and 4 use equal shares of labour and capital.

Table 5
Calibrated Shares Of Capital And Labour In Production In Illustrative Example Of A Platform Economy

Sectors	*Share of Capital Income*	*Share of Labour Income*
Sector 1	0.333	0.667
Sector 2	0.333	0.667
Sector 3	0.500	0.500
Sector 4	0.500	0.500

To calibrate share parameters to base year data, we also need numerical values of elasticities of substitution in utility and production. Numerical values of these estimates can be crucial in deriving model results. Following a standard practice common to applied general equilibrium modellers, we select elasticity parameters close to literature based estimates as presented in Table 6 (see appendix for various estimates of elasticity of substitution).

Table 6
Elasticity of Substitution in Consumption and Production

	Elasticity of Substitution
Among Consumption Goods	1.5
Capital and Labour	0.75

Table 7
Capital and Value Added Tax Rates in the Base Year in Illustrative Example of a Platform Economy

Sectors	*Tax Rate on Capital Income*	*Value-added Tax Rates*
S1	1.00	0.17
S2	1.00	0.50
S3	0.33	0.14
S4	1.00	0.60

The above discussion implies that we are now able to use the platform version of this model for general equilibrium analysis of tax policy. The basic platform model has three different tax instruments: taxes on capital income, value-added taxes on sales of final goods, and taxes on household income. Tax rates on capital and household income are given in Tables 7 and 8. Tax rates on household income are given in Table 8, which also shows net transfer as fraction of household income.

Table 8
Household Tax Rates in Illustrative Example of a Platform Economy

Households	*Household Income Tax Rates*	*Net Transfers as Fraction of Household Income*
H1	0.27	0.27
H2	0.22	0.55
H3	0.22	0.44

A standard test of the code of an applied general equilibrium model lies in the replication of the benchmark equilibrium with the use of calibrated parameters and selected values of elasticities. Unless the model reproduces the base year data as a solution to the specified model, the calibration process is not complete. This puts limitations on the admissible set of parameters in a calibrated model. Only parameters that are consistent with the replication of the base year equilibrium are meaningful for policy analysis.

After checking the replication of the benchmark economy, we solve the base case of platform model 1 with existing taxes on production and consumption as given by the tax rates in Tables 7-8. Basic economic theory suggests that these taxes distort the allocation of resources in the economy, causing inefficiency in consumption and production, and affecting the distribution of income among households (Varian (1992)). We now turn to defining measures of the welfare cost from tax distortions in the platform economy.

WELFARE AND DISTRIBUTIONAL IMPACTS OF TAX CHANGES IN THE PLATFORM MODEL

We use comparative static analysis to measure the welfare costs of tax distortions, by comparing an equilibrium with taxes to an equilibrium without taxes. Traditionally equivalent and compensating variation measures are used to compute the welfare costs of tax distortions. Hicksian equivalent variation measures changes in money metric utility between tax and no-tax equilibria. Compensating variation measures the amount of money required to bring a household back to the same level of utility as in the benchmark equilibrium following changes in prices in counterfactual equilibrium. In the linear homogenous utility case, implied by the CES functions, the equivalent and compensating variation can be defined as[6]:

$$EV^h = \left(\frac{U_C^h - U_B^h}{U_B^h} \right) I_C^h \tag{12}$$

$$CV^h = \left(\frac{U_B^h - U_C^h}{U_C^h} \right) I_B^h \tag{13}$$

where subscripts C and B stand for counterfactual and benchmark equilibria, EV^h and CV^h are the equivalent and compensating variation due to tax changes, U_C^h and U_B^h are utility levels in counterfactual and benchmark scenarios, and I_C^h and I_B^h are levels of income in counterfactual and benchmark equilibria. Equations (12) and (13) provide the basis for an economy wide calculation of the distorting welfare cost of any given set of sales and/or labour income taxes. The total welfare cost is computed by taking the arithmetic sums of *EV*s and *CV*s across households, *h*. We then express these sums as a fraction (or percentage) of the relevant sum of economy wide income measures:

$$TEV = \frac{\sum_h EV^h}{\sum_h I_o^h} \tag{14}$$

$$TCV = \frac{\sum_h CV^h}{\sum_h I_n^h} \tag{15}$$

where TEV and TCV are the economy-wide total equivalent and compensating variation from the tax changes.

The welfare costs (gains from removal) of tax distortions in the platform model are reported in Table 9.

Table 9
Welfare Gains from Removing Tax Distortions in the Platform Model
(Ev, Cv As A Fraction of Income)

Households	*Equivalent Variation*	*Compensating Variation*
H1	0.299	-0.230
H2	-0.226	0.291
H3	-0.119	0.135

The welfare costs presented here show significant effects on the distribution of income among households. Household one gains by 29 per cent of its benchmark income. Before tax reform, this household was paying the highest rate of income tax, and received a lower share of transfers compared to other households. Tax reform reduces their tax burden and they lose their transfer component of income, but this is less than that of other households. Meanwhile households 2 and 3 are worse off because of the tax change. This is mainly due to the loss of the transfer component of their income.

It should be noted that money metric gains occurring for household 1 are sufficient to compensate the money metric losses to households 2 and 3. The overall economy wide impact of tax distortions, measured through Equivalent Variation is 0.00703 (and the corresponding compensating variation is -0.00716). Though this economy-wide tax reform has only a small gain in comparison to the magnitudes of tax rates existing in the platform economy, model results show the redistribution of income among households which take place due to the change. However, we would expect a larger net overall gain to the economy after the removal of distortions caused by the taxes to the allocation of resources under a further refinement to the platform model, to include the labour-leisure choices made by households. This is discussed in the next section.

LABOUR-LEISURE CHOICE IN THE PLATFORM MODEL

The implicit assumption in implementing the platform version of the model so far has been that households only value commodities, and they supply all of their labour endowment as labour services to producers. However, households care for leisure as well as their labour income when maximizing utility, given their time endowments. There is a trade off between labour and leisure, and a labour-leisure choice can be incorporated in the model by including leisure in the utility function. The choice of leisure, given the time and budget constraints of the households, implies a labour supply decision consistent with maximization of utility by households. An explicit consideration of a labour leisure choice is central to any consideration of the labour supply impacts of tax reforms.

The data presented earlier in Tbles 1-3 have been modified in order to incorporate a labour-leisure choice in the platform general equilibrium tax model. These modified data are presented in Tables 10-12.

Table 10
Input-output Table for Platform Model 2

Sectors	*Sector 1*	*Sector 2*	*Sector 3*
Sector 1	2	1	5
Sector 2	4	3	3
Sector 3	4	2	3

Table 11
Data on Consumption, Income, Output And Taxes For Platform Model 2

Sectors	*Sector 1*	*Sector 2*	*Sector 3*
Consumption 1	4	2	4
Consumption 2	2	3	2
Consumption 3	1	1	5
Capital Income	1	2	3
Labour Income	1	3	1
Indirect Taxes	1	3	1
Vat	1	2	4
Base Year Price	1	1	1
Total Output	14	14	16

Table 12
Income Source Data for Platform Model 2

	Household 1	*Household 2*	*Household 3*
Interest Income	5	1	1
Transfer Income	6	6	7
Household Taxes	3	2	2
Leisure	1	1	3
Labour Supply	2	2	1
Labour Supply To S1	1	0	0
Labour Supply To S2	1	2	0
Labour Supply To S3	0	0	1
Price of Leisure	1	1	1

Calibrated parameters used in the GE tax model with a labour-leisure choice are presented in Tables 13-15. The utility function contains two nests. First a composite good is constructed using the elasticity of substitution among commodities, as shown in Table 16. Then households choose between leisure and the composite good. The budget shares spent on composite good and consumption of leisure by household are given in Table 13.

Table 13
Shares of Consumption and Leisure in the With Leisure Utility Function in Platform Model 2

Households	*Share of Full Income Spent on Consumption*	*Share of Full Income Spent on Leisure*
H1	0.913	0.087
H2	0.831	0.169
H3	0.588	0.412

Poor households (*i.e.* type H2 and H3) take more leisure compared to rich households of type H1 whereas the share of consumption in full income is higher for the high income households. This indicates that the richer households supply more labour than the poor households as the opportunity cost of labour is higher for them.

Table 14
Calibrated Shares in Consumption in Platform Model 2

Households	*Sector 1*	*Sector 2*	*Sector 3*
H1	0.429	0.167	0.318
H2	0.286	0.333	0.212
H3	0.107	0.083	0.398

Figures in Table 14 shows the pattern of preference for consumption by the three households. Household 1 spends more on sector 1 good, while household 3 likes more sector 3 goods.

Table 15
Calibrated Shares of Capital and Labour in Production

Sectors	*Share of Capital Income*	*Share Of Labour Income*
S1	0.333	0.667
S2	0.600	0.400
S3	0.250	0.750

The factor intensity differs among sectors in a multisectoral model. Some sectors are capital intensive and some others are labour intensive in the production process. Figures in Table 15 show that sector 1 and sector 3 are labour intensive sectors while sector 2 is a capital intensive sector.

Table 16
Elasticities of Substitution in Consumption and Production in Platform Model 2

	Elasticity of Substitution
Leisure and Consumption	0.75
Among Consumption Goods	2.0
Capital and Labour	2.0

As with platform model 1, we use platform model 2 to evaluate the distortionary cost of taxes for this illustrative economy. This is done by comparative static analysis of tax and no tax equilibria.

The tax rates on capital and labour income and value added taxes similar to Table 7 are presented in Table 17.

Table 17
Tax Rates Used In The Base Case In The Platform 2 Model

Sectors	*Tax Rate on Capital Income*	*Value-added Tax Rates*
S1	0.5	0.17
S2	1.5	0.50
S3	0.33	0.571

This prototype model includes household tax rates, which are reported in Table 18.

Table 18
Household Tax Rates in the Platform 2 Model

Households	*Household Income Tax Rates*	*Net Transfers as Fraction of Household Income*
H1	0.27	0.27
H2	0.22	0.56
H3	0.22	0.44

To measure the distortionary cost of taxes in this case we compute equivalent and compensating variations for each household, comparing money-metric utility measures of households before and after the tax changes, as given by equations 12-15.

Table 19
Welfare Gains From Removal of Tax Distortions in Platform Model 2

Households	*Equivalent Variation*	*Compensating Variation*
H1	-0.31	0.31
H2	0.44	-0.44
H3	0.57	-0.57

The redistributive impacts of these tax changes are again significant. Contrary to platform model 1, household 1 is worse off after the change, while households

2 and 3 gain. This result is due to differences in the valuation of leisure by these households. Because household 1 values leisure less than households 2 and 3, a reduction in the cost of leisure after the tax change is more favourable to households 2 and 3 than household 1. Thus we show that taking account of leisure significantly changes the model outcome.

The economy-wide impacts of these tax changes are positive. The overall EV is equal to 2.4 per cent of the total income of the economy (the corresponding CV was equal to -2.5 percent). This result is strikingly different from the small but positive effect of tax reforms reported in the case of version 1 of the platform model.

Another useful way of measuring the cost of tax distortions is to find the welfare cost of each additional pound of tax revenue raised by extra taxation. Economists have used the marginal excess burden of taxes (MEB) concept to measure these additional welfare costs. This measure gives the loss of welfare (money metric utility) in an incremental tax equilibrium compared to the before (base case tax) tax equilibrium. In version 2 of the platform model, an extra pound raised by means of incremental taxes (i.e. scaling all existing tax rates proportionately) has an excess burden equal to 21 pence. This MEB figure is comparable to those found in earlier general equilibrium analysis of tax policies (e.g. Ballard, Fullerton, Shoven and Whalley (1985), and Piggott and Whalley (1985), Goulder and Summers (1989); see the appendix for an elaborated list).

CONCLUSION

We use two prototypes of closed economy multi-sector multi-household static general equilibrium tax model with the government collecting taxes on capital income, value-added taxes on commodities and taxes on household income and redistributing income by means of transfers to households. Labour supply is exogenous in the first, while labour-leisure choice is endogenous in the second model.

The value-added tax influences the composition of final demand, income tax and accompanying transfers influence the labour supply decisions of the households. Differential rates of capital income across sectors distort the allocation of capital resources across sectors. Production subsidies reduce the selling price of commodities below the cost of production.

When taxes are eliminated household 1, which was paying the highest rate of income tax and received a lower share of transfers compared to household 2 and 3 gains, by 29 percent of its benchmark income. Tax reform reduces its tax burden. Meanwhile households 2 and 3 are worse off by 22 and 11 percent of their base income because of the tax change. This is mainly due to the loss of the transfer component of their income. Money metric gains occurring for household 1 are sufficient to compensate the money metric losses to households 2 and 3. The overall economy wide impact of tax distortions, measured through Equivalent Variation is 0.00703 (and the corresponding compensating variation is -0.00716). Though this economy-wide tax reform has only a small gain in comparison to the magnitudes of tax rates existing in the platform economy, model results show the redistribution of income among households which take place due to the change.

The redistributive impacts of these tax changes are significant even in the second model, where we consider labour leisure choice endogenously. Contrary to platform model 1, household 1 is worse off after the change, while households 2 and 3 gain. This result is due to differences in the valuation of leisure by these households. Because household 1 values leisure less than households 2 and 3, a reduction in the cost of leisure after the tax change is more favourable to households 2 and 3 than household 1. Thus we show that taking account of leisure significantly changes the model outcome.

The economy-wide impacts of these tax changes are positive. The overall EV is equal to 2.4 percent of the total income of the economy (the corresponding CV was equal to -2.5 percent). This result is strikingly different from the small but positive effect of tax reforms reported in the case of version 1 of the platform model. In version 2 of the platform model, an extra pound raised by means of incremental taxes (i.e. scaling all existing tax rates proportionately) has an excess burden equal to 21 pence.

REFERENCES

Arrow, K. J. and F. H. Hahn (1971), *General Competitive Analysis*, San Franscisco; Holden-Day.

Arrow, K. J. and G. Debreu (1954), "Existence of an Equilibrium for a Competitive Economy" *Econometrica* 22, 265-90.

Adelman, I. and S. Robinson (1978), *Income Distribution Policy in Developing Countries: A Case of South Korea*, Standford University Press, Stanford, California.

Auerbach, A. J. and L. J. Kotlikoff (1987), *Dynamic Fiscal Policy*. Cambridge University Press.

Ballard, C. L., D. Fullerton, J. B. Shoven and J.Whalley (1985), *A General Equilibrium Model for Tax Policy Evaluation*, University of Chicago Press, Chicago.

Bhattarai, K. and J. Whalley (2003), "Discreteness and the Welfare Cost of Labour Supply Tax Distortions" *International Economic Review* 44:3:1117-1133, August.

Bhattarai, K. and J. Whalley (2000), "General Equilibrium Modelling of UK Tax Policy" *in* Sean Holly and Martin Weale (eds.) *Econometric Modelling: Technique and Applications*, Cambridge University Press.

Bhattarai, K. and J. Whalley (1999), "The Role of Labour Demand Elasticities in Tax Incidence Analysis with Heterogeneous Labour," *Empirical Economics* 24(4) November.

Bhattarai, K., M. Ghosh and J.Whalley (1999), "On some properties of a trade closure widely used in numerical modelling", *Economics Letters* 62 13-21.

Bhattarai, K. and J. Whalley (1997), "Redistributive Effects of Transfers", *NBER Working Paper* No. 6281, November.

Brook, A K., D. Kendtrick, A. Meeraus (1992), *GAMS: Users's Guide*, release 2.25, The Scientific Press, San Francisco, CA.

Browning, E. K. (1987), "On the Marginal Cost of Taxation", *American Economic Review*, 77(1), March, pp. 11-23.

Browning, E. K. and Johnson, W. R. (1984), "The Trade-off between Equality and Efficiency", *Journal of Political Economy*, 1984 vol. 92. no. 21 pp. 175-203.

Central Statistical Office (CSO (1995)), *Family Spending*: A report on the 1994-95 Expenditure Survey.

Debreu, G. (1954), *The Theory of Value*, Yale University Press, New Haven.

Dervis, K., J.De Melo, and S.Robinson (1985), *General Equilibrium Models for Development Policy*, CUP, New York.

Devarajan, S., J. D. Lewis, S. Robinson (1996), *A Bibliography of Computable General Equilibrium Models Applied to Developing Countries*, Harvard Institute of International Development, DDP No. 224.

Dirkse, S. P. and M. C. Ferris (1995), "CCPLIB: A collection of nonlinear mixed complementarity problems" *Optimization Methods and Software*. 5:319-345.

Dirkse, S. P. and M.C. Ferris (1996), "A pathsearch damped Newton method for computing general equilibria" *Annals of Operations Research*, 1996.

Dixon P. B., Parmenter B. R., Powell A. A. and Wilcoxen P.J. (1992), Notes and Problems in Applied General Equilibrium Economics, North-Holland.

Ferris, M. C. and J. S. Pang (1997), "Engineering and economic applications of complementarity problems" *SIAM Review*, 39:669–713.

Financial Markets Group, LSE "How to Use P-Tax" and Manual for Turbo P-tax.

Fleming, M. J. (1962), "Domestic Financial Policies Under Fixed and Under Floating Exchange Rates", IMF Staff Papers 9, 3, 369-379.

Fullerton, D. and D. L. Rogers (1993), *Who Bears the Lifetime Tax Burden?* Brookings Institution, Washington D.C.

Giles, C. and P. Johnson (1994), "Tax Reform in the UK and Changes in the Progressivity of the Tax System, 1985-95", *Fiscal Studies*, vol. 15, no. 3, pp. 64-86.

Ginsburgh and Keyzer (1997), The Structure of Applied General Equilibrium Models, MIT Press.

Goulder, L. H., J. Shoven and J. Whalley (1983), "Domestic Tax Policy and Foreign Sector: The Importance of Alternative Foreign Sector Formulations to Results from a General Equilibrium Tax Analysis Model" in M. Feldstein ed. *Behavioral Simulation Methods in Tax Policy Analysis*, Chicago University Press.

Goulder, L. H., and L. H. Summers (1989), "Tax Policy, Asset Prices, and Growth: A General Equilibrium Analysis", *Journal of Public Economics*, 38:265-296, North Holland.

Hamermesh, D. S. (1993), *Labour Demand*, Princeton University Press, New Jersey.

Harberger, A. C. (1962), "The incidence of the corporation income tax" *Journal of Political Economy* 70 (June):215-40.

Harrison G. W., Rutherford, T. F. et al. ed. (2000), Using Dynamic General Equilibrium Models for Policy Analysis, North-Holland.

HMSO (1995), *New Earnings Survey*, London.

Inland Revenue (1991), "How to Use P-Tax", *memio*, Economics Unit, London.

Kehoe, T. J. (1991), "Computation and Multiplicity of Equilibria" in *Handbook of Mathematical Economics*, Volume IV, Elsevier Science Publishers B.V.

Killingsworth, M. (1983), *Labour Supply*, Cambridge University Press.

King, M.A. and D. Fullerton (1984), *The taxation of income from capital : a comparative study of the United States, the United Kingdom, Sweden and West Germany* Chicago University Press.

King, M. A. and M. H. Robson (1988), "Manual for Turbo P-tax", *LSE*, London.

Kotlikoff, L. (1998), "Two Decades of A-K Model", *NBER working Paper*, August Lau M. L. A. Pahlke and T. F. Rutherford (2002), Approximating infinite-horizon models in a complementarity format: A primer in dynamic general equilibrium analysis, Journal of Economic Dynamics and Control 26 577-609.

Mansur, A. and J. Whalley (1984), "Numerical Specification of Applied General Equilibrium Models: Estimation, Calibration and Data", in Scarf Herbert E and Shoven John B. (1984) *Applied General Equilibrium Analysis*, CUP.

Mercenier, J. and Srinivasan, T. N. ed. (1994), *Applied General Equilibrium and Economic Development: Present Achievement and Future Trends*, University of Michigan Press, Ann Arbor.

Mundell, R. A. (1968), *International Economics*, Macmillan, New York. Office of National Statistics (ONS (1995)) *Input Output : Tables for the United Kingdom*, HMSO, London.

———(1992), *United Kingdom National Accounts: Sources and Methods*.

———(1996), *United Kingdom National Accounts:* the Blue Book.

———(1997), *Financial Statistics*, February.

Piggott, J. and J.Whalley (1985), *UK Tax Policy and Applied General Equilibrium Analysis*, Cambridge University Press.

Robinson, S. (1991), "Macroeconomics, Financial Variables, and Computable General Equilibrium Models" *World Development*, Vol.19, No.11, pp.1509-1523, Pergamon Press plc.

Rutherford, T. F. (1995), "Extension of GAMS for Complementary Problems Arising in applied Economic Analysis" *Journal of Economic Dynamics and Control* 19 1299-1324.

Rutherford, T. F. (1997), *The GAMS/ MPSGE and GAMS/MILES user notes*, GAMS Development Corporation, Washington D.C.

Scarf, H. E. (1986), The Computation of Equilibrium Prices, in Scarf H. E. and Shoven John B. ed. *Applied General Equilibrium Analysis*, Cambridge University Press.

Siddorn, G. (1999), Derivation of 1995 Symmetric Use Matrices, *mimeo*, *Economics Unit*, Inland Revenue, F4 West Wing, Somerset House, Strand, London WC2R 1LB.

St-Hilaire F. and J. Whalley (1983), "A micro consistent equilibrium data set for Canada for use in tax policy analysis", *Review Income and Wealth*, 29, 175-204.

Shoven, J. B. and J. Whalley (1992), *Applying General Equilibrium*, Cambridge University Press, 1992.

Shoven, J. B. and J. Whalley (1973) "General Equilibrium with Taxes: A Computation Procedure and an Existence Proof" *Review of Economic Studies* 40, 475-90.

Shoven, J. B. and J. Whalley (1977), "Equal Yield Tax Alternatives: General Equilibrium Computational Techniques." *Journal of Public Economics* 8, 211-24.

Shoven, J. B. and J. Whalley (1984), "Applied General-Equilibrium Models of Taxation and International Trade: An Introduction and Survey", *Journal of Economic Literature*, vol. XXII, Sept,pp.1007-1051.

Taylor, L. ed. (1990), *Socially Relevant Policy Analysis: Structuralist Computable General Equilibrium Models for the Developing World,* MIT Press, Cambridge 1990.

Varian, H. R. (1992), *Microeconomic Analysis*, 3rd edition, W.W. Norton and Company, New York.

Walras, L. *Elements of Pure Economics*, Allen and Unwin, London, 1954.

Whalley, J. (1985), *Trade Liberalization Among Major World Trading Areas*, MIT Press, Cambridge.

Whalley, J. and B. Yeung (1983), "External Sector `Closing' Rules in Applied General Equilibrium Models" *Journal of International Economics*,15, pp.1-16.

APPENDIX

GAMS/MPSGE code for the Prototype General Equilibrium Tax Model

A1.***Prototype Multisectoral General Equilibrium Model

```
$OFFLISTING
Option decimals=5;

SET
        I       Sectors  /
        S1      Sector   1
        S2      Sector   2
        S3      Sector   3
        S4      sector   4
        /
        HH      Households and labour categories    /
                H1       Household 1
                H2       Household 2
                H3       Household 3
        /;

ALIAS (I,J), (LC,HH), (H,HH);

TABLE IOF (I,J) Input-output flows
        S1      S2      S3      s4
S1      2       1       2       3
S2      4       3       1       2
S3      2       1       1       1
s4      2       1       1       0
```

```
TABLE ZZ (*,I) MISCELLANEOUS PARAMETERS AND INITIAL DATA
           S1      S2      s3      S4
Cons1      4       2       4       1
cons2      2       3       1       3
cons3      1       1       3       4
Tax        1       2       1       1
Ka         1       2       3       1
Lb         2       4       3       1
vat        1       2       1       3
XD         14      14      12      9
p0         1       1       1       1

Table income (*,hh) Sources of Income to the households
           h1      h2      h3
intr       5       1       1
wage       3       3       4
trns       6       7       6
hhtx       3       2       2
;

PARAMETER
              C0(hh,I)       gross of VAT consumption
              D0(HH,I)       net of VAT consumption
              GREV           government revenue
              HIT(HH)        taxes on household income
               HIT0(HH)      taxes on household income
               HTX(HH)       revenue of taxes on household income
              IN0(I,J)       input of sector i good to sector j output
              I0(HH)         gross income of househods
              INTR(HH)       interest income
              K0(I)          capital services used per sector
              L0(I)          labour used in each sector
              p0(I)          benchmark prices of commodities
              rk0(i)
              tk(i)          tax rates on capital services
              TL(I)          tax rates on labour
              TR(HH)         transfer to households
              NTR(HH)        net transfer to households
              ntrr(hh)       net transfer rate to households
              VA0(I)         value added in benchmark
              vAt(I)         value added tax revenue in the benchmark
              WAG(HH)        labour endowment of households
              Y0(I)          output per-sector
              tk0(i)         base year capital tax rate
              vt(i)          value-added tax rate
              vt0(i)         base year value-added tax rate
              ;
```

```
* Extract some data:
y0(I) = ZZ("XD",I);
C0("H1",I) = ZZ("CONS1",I);
C0("H2",I) = ZZ("CONS2",I);
C0("H3",I) = ZZ("CONS3",I);
D0(HH,I) =C0(HH,I);
IN0(I,J) = IOF(I,J);
K0(I) = ZZ("KA",I);
L0(I) = ZZ("LB",I);
P0(I) = ZZ("P0",I);
VAT(I) = ZZ("VAT",I);
WAG(hh) =INCOME("WAGE",HH);

INTR(HH) =INCOME("INTR",HH);
TR(HH) = INCOME("TRNS",HH);
HTX(HH) =INCOME("HHTX",HH);
NTR(HH) =TR(HH)-HTX(HH);

I0(HH) =WAG(HH)+INTR(HH)+NTR(HH);

* Impose a marginal income
HIT(HH) =HTX(HH)/I0(HH);
ntrr(hh) =ntr(hh)/i0(hh);

* Calibrate capital tax rates to the data:
tk(i) =ZZ("Tax",I)/k0(i);
rk0(i) = 1 + tk(i);
display tk;

* Calibrate the value-added tax from the data:
VT(I) =VAT(I)/(SUM(HH,C0(HH,i))-VAT(i));
p0(i) = 1 + vt(i);
D0(HH,I) =C0(HH,I)/(1+VT(I));
GREV = SUM(I,VAT(I)+ZZ("Tax",I))+SUM(HH,HTX(HH));
DISPLAY Y0,VT,I0, TK,D0,IN0,K0,L0,TR,HTX,GREV;

*Check the zero profit condition in the base year

PARAMETER prf(i), MKT(*), IB(HH), PL0, RK0;
PL0=1;

* Zero profit:
prf(i) = y0(i) - sum(j, iof(j,i)) - l0(i) - k0(i)*rk0(i);
display prf;

* Market clearance:
mkt(i) = y0(i) - sum(j,iof(i,j)) - sum(hh,d0(hh,i));
mkt("l") = sum(hh, wag(hh)) - sum(i, l0(i));
```

```
mkt("k") = sum(i, k0(i)) - sum(hh,intr(hh));
display mkt;
```

*** Check income balance condition for households**

```
IB(HH) =SUM(I,(D0(HH,I)*P0(I))) -WAG(HH)*PL0 -INTR(HH) -NTR(HH);
DISPLAY IB,hit,ntrr;
$ONTEXT
$MODEL:pjw
$COMMODITIES:
        P(I) ! SUPPLY PRICE
        RK ! CAPITAL RENTAL RATE
        PL ! WAGE RATE
        PT ! value of transfers
        PU(HH) ! unit expenditure cost index

$SECTORS:
        Y(I) ! PRODUCTION
        U(HH) ! consumpion

$CONSUMERS:
        RA(HH) ! PRIVATE HOUSEHOLDS
        govt ! tax income account

$PROD:Y(I) s:0 VA:1.5
        O:P(I) Q:Y0(I)
        I:P(J) Q:IOF(J,I)
        I:PL Q:L0(I) VA:
        I:RK Q:K0(I) VA: A:GOVT T:TK(I) P:rk0(i)

$PROD:U(HH) S:0.75
        O:PU(HH) Q:I0(HH)
        I:P(I) Q:D0(HH,I) A:GOVT T:VT(I) P:P0(I)

$DEMAND:GOVT
        D:PT Q:grev

$DEMAND:RA(HH)
        E:PL Q:WAG(HH)
        E:RK Q:INTR(HH)
        E:PT Q:NTR(HH)
        D:PU(HH)

$REPORT:
        V:Y1(I) O:P(I) PROD:Y(I)
        V:U1(HH) O:PU(HH) PROD:U(HH)
        V:L1(I) I:PL PROD:Y(I)
        V:K1(I) I:RK PROD:Y(I)
        V:W(HH) W:RA(HH)
```

```
$OFFTEXT

*OPTION SYSOUT =ON;
$SYSINCLUDE mpsgeset PJW
PJW.ITERLIM = 0;
$INCLUDE PJW.GEN
SOLVE PJW USING MCP;

***Retrieving parameters consistent with the equilibrium *****
parameter va(i), betak(i),betal(i),netinc(h),alpha(h,i);
va(i) =PL.L*L1.L(I) +RK.L*K1.L(I);
netinc(h) =ra.L(H)-HTX(H);
betal(i) =(PL.L*L1.L(I))/va(i) ;
betak(i) = (rk.L*K1.L(I))/va(i);
*alpha(h,i) =p.l(I)*d0(H,I)/NETINC(H);
alpha(h,i) =p.l(i)*d0(H,I)/netinc(H);
display va,betak,betal,netinc,alpha;

* Assign base year taxes:
vt0(i) = vt(i);
hit0(hh) = hit(hh);
tk0(i) = tk(i);

DISPLAY "FIRST", P.L,PL.L,RK.L,PU.L;

PARAMETER WA(HH),EV0(HH),CV0(HH),EV,CV;
WA(HH) =W.L(HH);

*Tax reform: elimination of all taxes

VT(I) =0.01;
TK(I) =0.01;
hIt(hh) =0.0;

PJW.ITERLIM = 1000;
$INCLUDE PJW.GEN
SOLVE PJW USING MCP;
DISPLAY P.L,PL.L,RK.L,PU.L;
CV0(HH) =(W.L(HH)-WA(HH))/WA(HH);
EV0(HH) =(WA(HH)-W.L(HH))/W.L(HH);
EV =SUM(HH,EV0(HH))/SUM(HH,WA(HH));
CV =SUM(HH,CV0(HH))/SUM(HH,W.L(HH));
DISPLAY WA,W.L,EV0,CV0,EV,CV;
```

A2. * Labour Leisure choice Model**

```
$OFFLISTING
$offsymlist offsymxref
SET
```

```
        I       Sectors /
        S1      Sector 1
        S2      Sector 2
        S3      Sector 3
        /

        HH      Households and labour categories /
        H1      Household 1
        H2      Household 2
        H3      Household 3
        /;

ALIAS (I,J), (LC,HH), (H,HH);

TABLE IOF(I,J) Input-output flows
        S1      S2      S3
S1      2       1       5
S2      4       3       3
S3      4       2       3

TABLE ZZ(*,I) MISCELLANEOUS PARAMETERS AND INITIAL DATA
        S1      S2      s3
Cons1   4       2       4
cons2   2       3       2
cons3   1       1       5
Tax     1       3       1
Ka      2       2       3
Lb      1       3       1
vat     1       2       4
XD      14      14      16
p0      1       1       1

TABLE ZZ1(HH,*) Leisure accounts of the households
        Le      la      ls1     ls2     ls3     intr    trns    hhtx    PLE0
h1      1       2       1       1       0       5       6       3       1
h2      1       2       0       2       0       1       6       2       1
h3      3       1       0       0       1       1       7       2       1
;

PARAMETER
                C0(hh,I)
                D0(HH,I)
                LE0(HH,I)
                LA0(HH,I)
                GREV
                HTX(HH)
                HIT(HH)
                hit1(hh)
```

```
                    IN0(I,J)
                    I0(HH)
                    INTR(HH)
                    K0(I)
                    L0(I)
                    p0(I)
                    PLE0(HH)

                    tk(i)
                    tk1(i)
                    TR(HH)
                    NTR(HH)
                    Tx(I)
                    VA0(I)
                    vAt(I)
                    VT(I)
                    vt1(i)
                    WAG(HH)
                    WLE(HH)
                    Y0(I)
                    ;

y0(I) = ZZ("XD",I);
C0("H1",I) = ZZ("CONS1",I);
C0("H2",I) = ZZ("CONS2",I);
C0("H3",I) = ZZ("CONS3",I);
D0(HH,I) =C0(HH,I);
IN0(I,J) = IOF(I,J);
K0(I) = ZZ("KA",I);
L0(I) = ZZ("LB",I);
P0(I) = ZZ("P0",I);
VAT(I) = ZZ("VAT",I);

PLE0(HH) = ZZ1(HH,"PLE0");
WAG(HH) = ZZ1(HH,"LA");
WLE(HH) = ZZ1(HH,"LE");

INTR(HH) =ZZ1(HH,"INTR");
TR(HH) = ZZ1(HH,"TRNS");
HTX(HH) =ZZ1(HH,"HHTX");

NTR(HH) =TR(HH)-HTX(HH);

I0(HH) =WAG(HH)+INTR(HH)+NTR(HH);

HIT(HH) = HTX(HH)/I0(HH);

I0(HH) =WAG(HH)+INTR(HH)+NTR(HH);
```

```
HIT(HH) =HTX(HH)/I0(HH);
tk(i) =ZZ("Tax",I)/k0(i);

VT(I) =VAT(I)/(SUM(HH,C0(HH,i))-VAT(i));

D0(HH,I) =C0(HH,I)/(1+VT(I));

GREV = SUM(I,VAT(I)+ZZ("Tax",I))+SUM(HH,HTX(HH));

DISPLAY Y0,D0,HTX,I0,IN0,K0,L0,VAT,INTR,TR,GREV,TK,VT,HIT;

PARAMETER MKT(I), IB(HH), PL0, RK0;

PL0=1; RK0=1;
MKT(I) =Y0(I)-SUM(J,IN0(I,J))-SUM(HH,D0(HH,I));
IB(HH) =SUM(I,(1+VT(i))*(D0(HH,I)*P0(I))) -WAG(HH)*PL0 -INTR(HH)*RK0 -
TR(HH)+HTX(HH);

DISPLAY MKT, IB;
tk1(i) =tk(i);
vt1(i) =vt(i);
hit1(hh)=hit(hh);

$ONTEXT

$MODEL:pjw

*$PEPS: 1.0E-6
*$echOP:.TRUE
*$FUNLOG:.TRUE

$COMMODITIES:
        P(I) ! SUPPLY PRICE
        RK ! CAPITAL RENTAL RATE
        PL ! WAGE RATE
        PT
        PLE(HH)
        PU(HH)

$SECTORS:
        Y(I) ! PRODUCTION
        LS(HH)
        U(HH)

$CONSUMERS:
        RA(HH) ! PRIVATE HOUSEHOLDS
        govt
```

```
$PROD:Y(I) s:0 VA:2
        O:P(I)          Q:Y0(I)
        I:P(J)          Q:IOF(J,I)
        I:PL            Q:L0(I) VA:
        I:RK            Q:K0(I) VA: A:GOVT T:TK(I) P:(rk0*(1+TK1(I)))

$PROD:LS(HH)
        O:PL            Q:WAG(HH)
        I:PLE(HH)               Q:WAG(HH)

$PROD:U(HH) s:0.75 a:2.0
        O:PU(HH)        Q:(I0(HH)+WLE(HH))
        I:P(I)          Q:D0(HH,I) A:GOVT T:VT(I) P:(P0(I)*(1+VT1(I))) a:
        I:PLE(HH)       Q:WLE(HH)

$DEMAND:GOVT
        D:PT Q:(SUM(I,(VT(I) *p0(i) *SUM(HH,D0(HH,I)))+(TK(I) *rk0
*K0(I)))+(SUM(HH,HIT(HH) *I0(HH))))

$DEMAND:RA(HH) s:1.5
        E:PLE(HH)       Q:(WAG(HH)+WLE(HH))
        E:RK            Q:INTR(HH)
        E:PT            Q:(TR(HH)-HIT1(hh)*I0(HH))
        D:PU(HH)        Q:(I0(HH)+WLE(HH))

$REPORT:
        V:Y1(I)         O:P(I)   PROD: Y(I)
        V:IO(I,J)       I:P(J)   PROD: Y(I)
        V:L1(I)         I:PL     PROD:Y(I)
        V:K1(I)         I:RK     PROD:Y(I)
        V:LS1(HH)       I:PLE(HH) PROD:LS(HH)
        V:U1(HH)        O:PU(HH) PROD:U(HH)
        V:C1(HH,I)      I:P(I)   PROD:U(HH)
        V:LE(HH)        I:PLE(HH)        PROD:U(HH)
        V:W1(hh)        D:PU(HH)         DEMAND:RA(HH)
        V:PT1           D:PT     DEMAND:GOVT
        V:W(HH)         W:RA(HH)

$OFFTEXT

*OPTION SYSOUT =ON;
$SYSINCLUDE mpsgeset PJW

pl.fx =1;

PJW.ITERLIM = 0;
$INCLUDE PJW.GEN
SOLVE PJW USING MCP;
```

```
DISPLAY HTX;

***Retrieving parameters consistent with the equilibrium *****
parameter va(i), betak(i),betal(i),netinc(h),alpha(h),alphal(H),alphac(h,i);
va(i) =PL.L*L1.L(I) +RK.L*K1.L(I);
netinc(h) =ra.L(H)-HTX(H);
betak(i) =(PL.L*L1.L(I))/va(i) ;
betal(i) = (rk.L*K1.L(I))/va(i);
alpha(h) =SUM(I,p.l(I)*C1.l(H,I))/NETINC(H);
alphaL(H) = 1-alpha(h);
alphac(h,i) = p.l(I)*C1.l(H,I)/NETINC(H);
display va,betak,betal,netinc,alpha,alphal, alphac;

*$ontext
PARAMETER WA(HH),UA(HH),REVA, REPORT,REPHH, REPORT1,REPHH1,
REPORT2,REPHH2;
UA(HH) =U.L(HH);
WA(HH) =W1.L(HH);
REPORT("OUTPUT", I) =Y1.L(I);
REPORT("PRICES", I) =P.L(I);
REPORT("CAPITAL", I) =K1.L(I);
REPORT("LUSE", I) =L1.L(I);
REPORT("SALES TAX",I) =VT(I);
REPORT("KI-TAX",I) =TK(I);

REPHH("LSUPPLY", HH) =LS1.L(HH);
REPHH("UTILITY", HH) =U1.L(HH);
REPHH("INCOME", HH) =W1.L(HH);
REPHH("INCTAX",HH) =HIT(HH);
REVA =govt.L;

PARAMETER LMD,MEB,EV0(HH), CV0(HH),EV1,CV1,EV2,CV2;

PJW.ITERLIM =5000;

VT(I) =0.01;
TK(I) =0;
HIT(HH) =0;

$INCLUDE PJW.GEN
SOLVE PJW USING MCP;

VT(I) =0.7;
TK(I) =0.5;
HIT(HH) =0.6;

$INCLUDE PJW.GEN
SOLVE PJW USING MCP;
```

```
EV0(HH) =((U.L(HH)-UA(HH))/U.L(HH))*W1.L(HH);
CV0(HH) =((UA(HH)-U.L(HH))/UA(HH))*WA(hh);
EV1 =SUM(HH,EV0(HH))/SUM(HH,W1.L(HH));
CV1 =SUM(HH,CV0(HH))/SUM(HH,WA(HH));

REPORT1("OUTPUT", I) =Y1.L(I);
REPORT1("PRICES", I) =P.L(I);
REPORT1("CAPITAL", I) =K1.L(I);
REPORT1("LUSE", I) =L1.L(I);
REPHH1("LSUPPLY", HH) =LS1.L(HH);
REPHH1("UTILITY", HH) =U1.L(HH);
REPHH1("INCOME", HH) =W1.L(HH);
REPORT1("SALES TAX",I) =VT(I);
REPORT1("KI-TAX",I) =TK(I);
REPHH1("INCTAX",HH) =HIT(HH);

REPHH1("EV-HH", HH) =EV0(HH);
REPHH1("CV-HH", HH) =CV0(HH);

DISPLAY EV1;

LMD =1.001;

VT(I) =VT(I)*LMD;
TK(I) =TK(I)*LMD;
HIT(HH) =HIT(HH)*LMD;

$INCLUDE PJW.GEN
SOLVE PJW USING MCP;

EV0(HH) =((U.L(HH)-UA(HH))/U.L(HH))*W1.L(HH);

MEB =SUM(HH,EV0(HH))/(REVA-govt.L);

DISPLAY MEB;

*$ONTEXT
VT(I) =0.3;
TK(I) =0.4;
HIT(HH) =0.3;

$INCLUDE PJW.GEN
SOLVE PJW USING MCP;

REPORT2("OUTPUT", I) =Y1.L(I);
REPORT2("PRICES", I) =P.L(I);
REPORT2("CAPITAL", I) =K1.L(I);
REPORT2("LUSE", I) =L1.L(I);
```

```
REPHH2("LSUPPLY", HH) =LS1.L(HH);
REPHH2("UTILITY", HH) =U1.L(HH);
REPHH2("INCOME", HH) =W.L(HH);
REPORT2("SALES TAX",I) =VT(I);
REPORT2("KI-TAX",I) =TK(I);
REPHH2("INCTAX",HH) =HIT(HH);
REPHH2("EV-HH", HH) =EV0(HH);
REPHH2("CV-HH", HH) =CV0(HH);

EV0(HH) =(PU.L(HH)-UA(HH))/UA(HH);
CV0(HH) =(UA(HH)-PU.L(HH))/PU.L(HH);
EV2 =SUM(HH,EV0(HH))/SUM(HH,W.L(HH));
CV2 =SUM(HH,CV0(HH))/SUM(HH,WA(HH));
```

***DISPLAY**

```
REPORT,REPHH,REPORT1,REPHH1,REPORT2,REPHH2,EV1,CV1,EV2,CV2;
DISPLAY REPORT,REPHH,REPORT1,REPHH1,EV1;
```

***$offtext**

4

Efficiency and Factor Reallocation Effects and Marginal Excess Burden of Taxes in the UK Economy[9]

Keshab R. Bhattarai*

INTRODUCTION

The public sector total receipts were about 39 per cent of GDP in the UK in 2002. More than 50 per cent of it was collected from direct tax instruments such as the labour income tax, the national insurance contribution, the corporate income tax and the council tax. The indirect tax instruments such as value added tax (VAT) and excise and tariffs contributed to the rest of it. While increased demand for public services has required collection of more tax revenue, there is a widespread concern among public about the economic burden of these taxes. In theory, all taxes are distortionary; but some of them are less distortionary than others. Both public and policy makers like to know which one of these taxes hurt the least and is a more efficient way of raising the target revenue. Model presented in this paper, which fairly mimics the structure of the UK economy in 1995, provides a method to evaluate the welfare gains from tax reform in terms money metric equivalent or compensating variations for a representative household of the economy. This study aims to complement a number of tax impact studies of the UK found in the literature which more often focus on labour supply and income distribution (King (1983), Giles and McCrae (TAXBEN (1983)), King and Fullerton (1984), Institute of Fiscal Studies (2002), Blundell-Duncan and Meghir

* Major part of work for this paper was undertaken under an ESRC project on General Equilibrium and Dynamic Modelling for the Analysis of UK Policy Issues. I am grateful to Professor John Whalley at the universities of Warwick and Western Ontario for guidance and support for this research. I appreciate Graham Siddorn and Bill McNie who were at the Economics Unit of the Inland Revenue at the time of this study and to Tobi Kendall for various information and suggestions. I acknowledge comments made by colleagues and participants of a seminar organised by the Centre for Economic Policy in Hull in May 2000. All errors and shortcomings are my own. Correspondence address: Economic Group, Business School, University of Hull, Cottingham Road HU6 7RX, Hull. K.R.Bhattarai@hull.ac.uk, phone: 44-1482-466483; fax: 44-1482-466216.

(1995)). Most of these studies are based on Marshallian partial equilibrium analysis. We use a general equilibrium model, as in Piggot and Whalley (1985) and Bhattarai and Whalley (2000), Bhattarai (2000) to capture the widespread reallocation and readjustment in both demand and supply of goods and factors by consumers and producers in process of shifting the burden of taxes until it settles down to the ultimate payer of these taxes.

Applied general equilibrium models have been in use for fiscal policy analysis for almost four decades[1]. Here we specify and calibrate the model that has a representative household, 16 production firms, a government and the Rest of the World using the benchmark data set for 1995. The model is then applied to evaluate the efficiency and factor reallocation impacts and to measure the marginal excess burden of each of the above tax instruments in the UK economy.

Model outlined here has many features of a standard Arrow-Debreu general equilibrium model for an open economy (Debreu (1954), Arrow and Hahn (1971)). Both households and firms maximise utility and profit subject to their budget and technology constraints taking goods and factor prices as given. In equilibrium, prices adjust until the demand for goods, labour and capital equal their supplies; profit of firms become zero at the margin; income and expenditure of households, investors and the government become equal; and the value of exports equals the value of imports. A general equilibrium model thus provides a consistent structure of the economy as parameters describing the behaviour of households and firms and the government and the Rest of the World sector are calibrated using the benchmark data set. The calibrated model that replicates the benchmark economy[2] is then used for analysis of tax policy reform using the money metric measure of welfare obtained by summing up those values for households, investors and the government in the counterfactual cases relative to the benchmark economy.

SPECIFICATION OF THE GENERAL EQUILIBRIUM TAX MODEL OF THE UK ECONOMY

Household Preferences, Demand Structure and Technology

Utility of a representative household is assumed to be given by a CES function of leisure and composite consumption. A representative household maximises utility, which is described by a nest of CES functions defined over composite consumption and leisure, subject to a budget constraint including a composite price for the commodity and leisure. The composite commodity demand is derived from i number of these sub-composite goods ($i = 1,..., N$). Each of these sub composites is obtained from domestic and imported sources. At the top of the nest the utility function is written as

$$U = \left(\alpha C^{\rho} + \beta \ L^{\rho}\right)^{\frac{1}{\rho}} \tag{1}$$

where U is the utility of household, C is the consumption of the composite good, L is the leisure taken by the household, aa is the share of full income of household spent on consumption of the composite good, β is the share of full income spent on leisure, and rr is the elasticity parameter in the utility function; the elasticity of substitution between goods (and leisure) being equal to $\sigma = \frac{1}{1-\rho}$.

The household receives income from capital and labour endowments, and transfers from the government, pays taxes on household and capital income. The disposable income of a household is given by

$$H = \sum_j \sum_i r_j (1 - t_{j,i}) \theta_{j,i} \overline{K}_j + (1 - t_l) w\overline{L} + TR \tag{2}$$

where H is the income, $\theta_{j,i}$ is the share of type j asset used in sector i, $\overline{K}_j$ is the endowment of capital type j for the household, $\overline{L}$ is the endowment of labour, TR are the transfers received, r is the rental rate of capital by type j, w is the wage rate, t_l is the tax rate on labour income[3], and $t_{j,i}$ is the tax rate in sector i on rental income from capital of type j.

$$P(1 + t_v)C + w(1 - t_l)L = H \tag{3}$$

where P and C are prices and quantities of composite goods respectively, and t_v is the effective tax rate on consumption; consisting of tariffs, duties and levies, value added taxes and subsidies.

The demand functions for goods and leisure are obtained by maximising (1) with respect to (2) and (3), and take the following form

$$C = \left(\frac{\alpha \; H}{(P(1+t_v))^{1-\sigma} \left(\alpha \left(P(1+t_v) \right) \right)^{1-\sigma} + \beta \left(w\left(1-t_l\right) \right)^{1-\sigma}} \right) \tag{4}$$

Consumption of leisure is given by

$$L = \left(\frac{\beta \; H}{(w(1-t_l))^{1-\sigma} \left(\alpha \left(P(1+t_v) \right) \right)^{1-\sigma} + \beta \left(w\left(1-t_l\right) \right)^{1-\sigma}} \right) \tag{5}$$

In the one household case, the labour supply of each household LS is given by the difference between the household labour endowment, and the demand for leisure, L.

$$LS = \overline{L} - L \tag{6}$$

In equilibrium, the labour supplied by the household must be consistent with the total demand for labour derived from the profit maximising behaviour of firms (as set out in the following section).

Composite consumption covers N sub-composite goods in the model,

$$C = \psi\left(\sum_i \delta_i^c CC_i^{\frac{\sigma-1}{\sigma}}\right)^{\frac{\sigma}{\sigma-1}} \tag{7}$$

where CC_i is the ith good composite of domestic and imported consumption goods, ψ is the unit parameter of the CES composite function and δ_i^c is the share of the consumption good. The overall value of composite consumption should satisfy:

$$P \cdot C = \sum_i P_i \cdot CC_i \quad \text{for} \quad i = 1..N \tag{8}$$

The term p is the price of composite consumption net of indirect taxes, and CC_i is composite consumption good of both domestic and import of the ith good.

International Trade

The total supply, A_i, for each sector is produced using domestic and imported goods, and is given by a CES (Armington (1969)) function as following:

$$A_i = \Phi\left((1-\delta_i^m)D_i^{\frac{\sigma_m-1}{\sigma_m}} + \delta_i^m M_i^{\frac{\sigma_m-1}{\sigma_m}}\right)^{\frac{\sigma_m}{\sigma_m-1}} \tag{9}$$

where A_i is the CES aggregate of domestic supplies D_i and import supplies M_i. δ_i^d is the share of domestic supplies for good i, and δ_i^m is the share of imports in good i, σ_m is the elasticity of substitution in the aggregate supply function, and Φ is the shift parameter of the aggregate supply function. Overall market clearing in the product market implies that

$$A_i = CC_i + G_i + I_i \tag{10}$$

where G_i and I_i represent composite consumption by the government and investment respectively (discussed below). In value terms,

$$PA_i \ A_i = PD_i \ D_i + PM_i \ M_i \tag{11}$$

where D_i and M_i are domestic and import supplies at prices PD_i and PM_i respectively, and PA_i is the price of total supply in sector i.

In the above equation, domestic supply, D_i, is the part of the output sold in the domestic market. The rest of domestic output is sold abroad, and given by the product transformation function.

$$Y_i = \Theta\left((1-\delta_i^e) D_i^{\frac{\sigma_y - 1}{\sigma_y}} + \delta_i^e E_i^{\frac{\sigma_y - 1}{\sigma_y}} \right)^{\frac{\sigma_y}{\sigma_y - 1}} \tag{12}$$

where E_i is exports, D_i is domestic supplies, σ_y is the elasticity of substitution in total supplies, δ_i^e is the share of exports, and QQ is the shift parameter in the production function. The total value of gross domestic product is composed of value of domestic sales and exports.

$$PY_i \ Y_i = PD_i \ Y_i + PE_i \ E_i \tag{13}$$

The value of exports is equal to the value of imports in equilibrium.

$$\sum_i PE_i E_i = \sum_i PM_i M_i \tag{14}$$

where PE_i and PM_i are the world prices of exported and imported commodities in terms of the numeraire. These import and export prices could be different than the domestic prices because of differentiation between domestic and foreign products in this model. Gross of export tax or tariff prices of domestic commodities tends to be close to the world prices as the elasticity of transformation between domestic sales and exports and elasticity of substitution between domestic supplies and imports reach to the infinity.

Production

Producers use labour and capital in each of N sectors to yield value added. This also is given by CES functions.

$$VA_i = \Omega_i \left((1-\delta_i)(K_i)^{\gamma_i} + \delta_i (LS_i)^{\gamma_i} \right)^{\frac{1}{\gamma_i}} \tag{15}$$

where VA_i is the gross value added of sector i, Ω_i is a shift parameter in the production function, K_i and LS_i are the amounts of capital and labour used in sector i, δ_i is the share parameter of labour in the CES function, and γ_i is the CES factor substitution parameter.

The gross output of each sector Y_i contains value added, VA_i and intermediate inputs. We allow substitution between domestic and imported intermediate inputs, and between value added and intermediate inputs.

$$PY_iY_i = PV_i.VA_i + \sum_j PA_i\,(1+t^d_{i,j})DI_{i,j} + \sum_j PM_i(1+t^m_{i,j})MI_{i,j} \qquad (16)$$

where $DI_{i,j}$ is the demand for domestic intermediate input and $MI_{i,j}$ is demand for imported intermediate inputs, PV_i is the composite price of value added, and VA_i is the value added component of gross output, $t^d_{i,j}$ and $t^m_{i,j}$ are taxes on intermediate demands.

At any set of prices, producers in each sector maximise profits subject to their technology constraint

$$\Pi_i = PY_i\;Y_i - wL_i - \sum_{j,i} r_jK_{j,i} - \sum_j PA_j(1+t^m_{i,j})MI_{j,i}$$

$$-\sum_j PA_j(1+t^d_{i,j})DI_{j,i} \qquad (17)$$

where Π_i is the profit of sector i. In equilibrium, factor demands by sectors are determined where the value of the marginal product of factors equal factor prices, and there are no positive profits for producers.

Treatment of the public sector

Government Budget

The government collects direct and indirect taxes from households on their income and consumption, production and capital income taxes from corporations, and import duties from traders. All tax revenues collected are either used to purchase public goods or transferred to households in lump sum form; *i.e.*

$$G + TR = \sum_J \sum_i t^k_{j,i} r_j K_{j,i} + \sum_i t^{vc}_i P_i CC_i + \sum_i t^{vg}_i P_i G_i + \sum_i t^{vk}_i P_i I_i + \sum_i t_l wLS$$

$$+\sum_i t^m_i M_i + \sum_j \sum_i PA_j t^m_{i,j} MI_{j,i} + \sum_j \sum_i PA_j t^d_{i,j} DI_{j,i} \qquad (18)$$

where G is public consumption, and $t^k_{j,i}$ is the tax rate on capital income from asset j used in sector i. These rates are taken from P-Tax formulae. There are four different indirect taxes in the model: tariffs, duties and levies, VAT and subsidies. Here, t^{vc}_l is the effective *ad valorem* tax rate on final consumption of households, t^{vg}_i is effective indirect tax rate on public consumption and t^{vk}_i is effective tax rate on investment, t_l is the tax rate on labour income, and t_i^m is the tariff on imports, $t_{i,j}^d$ and $t_{i,j}^m$ are taxes on intermediate demands.

These taxes, particularly when they are levied at different rates on different sectors and households, have distortionary impacts on the allocation of resources in the economy. These are captured by the model. The value of government consumption is given by:

$$G = \sum_i PA_i GD_i + \sum_i PA_i GM_i \tag{19}$$

where GD_i is government consumption of domestic goods and GM_i is government consumption of imported goods.

Model closures and savings and investment

Total investment demand I equals the use of investment goods from domestic and imported sources.

$$I = \sum_i PA_i ID_i + \sum_i PA_i IM_i \tag{20}$$

where ID_i is investment demand for domestic good i, and IM_i is investment demand for imported good i. The savings-investment identity closes this model where I is the gross of indirect taxes.

We have taken a closed capital market view until so far. This essentially means the allocation of assets across sectors sums up to the domestic endowments of assets which implies:

$$\bar{K}_j = \sum_i K_{i,j} \quad j=1,..5 \tag{21}$$

where $\bar{K}_j$ is the endowment of jth type of asset and $K_{i,j}$ allocation of type j asset in sector i. Reallocation occurs until the rental rate of capital is same across all sectors.

Capital moves freely according to domestic and foreign rate of returns in an open economy resulting in inflows or outflows depending on relative returns (Whalley (1985)).

$$\bar{K}_j + FK_j = \sum_i K_{i,j} \tag{22}$$

Here FK_j represents net inflow or outflow of asset type j. The inflow and outflow of capital asset depends upon the gap between the rental rate in the UK and the Rest of the World.

$$r_j^{UK} \geq r_j^{w} \Rightarrow FK_j \geq 0 \tag{23}$$

$$r_j^{UK} \leq r_j^{w} \Rightarrow FK_j \leq 0 \tag{24}$$

where r_j^{UK} is the net of tax return in asset j in the UK and r_j^{w} is the net return in the world market. Thus the amount of inflow or outflow depends upon the gap between the domestic and world rental rate of capital. We implicitly have assumed that the rate of return from capital in the UK is equal to the rate of return in the global capital market.

Model Equilibrium Conditions and Closure

In this model a competitive equilibrium is given by prices of consumption goods, P_i; the rental rate of capital assets r_j; a wage rate for labour, w; levels of gross output, Y_i (gross of intermediate use); capital use, K_i; and sectoral use of labour, L_i; imports M_i, exports X_i, intermediate inputs $DI_{i,j}$, $MI_{i,j}$ investment I_i, government consumption G_i, private consumption C_i, such that,

(i) The markets for goods and services, labour and capital clear; and

(ii) Budget constraints of households, the government and investors are satisfied.

More specifically, the market clearing condition for the goods market is given by

$$Y_i = F_i^d + \sum_{j=1}^{N} a_{i,j}^d Y_j \tag{25}$$

where $F_i^d = C_i^d + I_i^d + G_i^d + E_i^d$ is a decomposition of final demand into household consumption, investment, and government consumption, $\sum_j a_{ij}^d Y_j$ is total domestic intermediate demand, and $a_{i,j}^d$ is sector i input per unit of sector j output.

$$M_i = F_i^m + \sum_{j=1}^{N} a_{i,j}^m Y_j \tag{26}$$

where $F_i^m = C_i^m + I_i^m + G_i^m + E_i^m$ represents a decomposition of final demand for imports and $\sum_j a_{i,j}^m Y_j$ is total imports for intermediate inputs.

The capital market clearing condition, in the closed capital market case, implies

$$\bar{K}_{\bar{j}} = \sum_i K_{i,j} \quad j=1,..5 \tag{27}$$

The capital market clearing condition in the open capital market scenario implies

$$\bar{K}_j + FK_j = \sum_i K_{i,j} \tag{28}$$

and labour market clearing implies:

$$LS = \sum_i LS_i \tag{29}$$

where LS_i represents labour demand in the ith sector. This model assumes mobility of goods across economies rather than that of labour considering the labour market facts of the UK economy.

The prices and quantities in each of above market clear simultaneously in a general equilibrium solution. By Walras' (1954) law only n-1 relative prices can be determined endogenously in such a model because the price of nth good is determined in terms of those n-1 prices. In practice one of them, such as money, can act as a numeraire. This model is very complex. A numerical technique is used to solve it as it is almost impossible to find a closed form analytical algebraic solutions of it.

We use prices and quantities in the benchmark and counterfactual scenarios to compute the Hicksian equivalent (*EV*) and compensating variations (CV) to compare welfare gains or losses across different tax reform scenarios. A positive EV represents a gain compared to the old equilibrium and a negative EV represents a loss. For each value of a positive Hicksian EV there is a corresponding but negative value of Hicksian CV, which represents the amount of money that needs to be taken away from the consumer to keep her at the old utility level. EV measure uses benchmark prices (*i.e.* prices before the reduction in taxes) to compute the money metric measure of utility while the *CV* measure uses new prices (*i.e.* price after the tax change). As in Shoven and Whalley (1992), for homothetic preferences the values of EV and CV between a benchmark and counterfactual scenarios can be computed as:

$$EV = E(U^N, P^0) - E(U^0, P^0) \tag{30}$$

$$CV = E(U^N, P^N) - E(U^0, P^N) \tag{31}$$

where superscripts *N* and *O* represent new and old values of the variable on which they appear, and *E* the money metric utility, *U* the utility and *P* the price level. If utility functions are linear homogeneous then the original and the new equilibria

Table A1

Aggregation of 123 sectors into 16 sectors from 1990 Input-Output Sectoral Classification

Industry/Asset	*1990 I-O Sectors*	*1990 sectoral code*	*1995 sectoral code*
Agriculture	Agriculture, Forestry, Fishing	1,2,3	1-3
Extraction	Extraction – oil and gas	5	5
Other mining & quarrying	Coal extraction, stone, clay, sand, gravel, metal ores and minerals	4,14, 10	4,6,7
Chemicals	Coke ovens, oil proc, nuclear fuel, inorganic chemicals, organic chemicals, fertilisers, synthetic resins, paints, dyes, printing ink, special chemical for industry, pharmaceutical products, soap and toilet preparations, chemical products, man-made fibres	6, 20-29	35-46
Metals and mineral products	Iron and Steel, Aluminium, other non-ferrous metals, structural clay products, Cement, lime and plaster, concrete, asbestos, abrasive prods, glass, refractory and ceramic goods, metal casting, metal doors, windows, packaging products of metals, industrial plant and steel work, engineers small tools	11-13, 15-19, 30-34, 37	49-61
Engineering	Agricultural machinery and tractors, metal working machine tools, textile etc machinery, process machinery and contractors, mining equipment, mech power transmission equipment, other machinery, ordnance samll arms and ammunition, insulated wires and cables, basic electrical equipment, industrial electrical equipment, telecommunications etc. equipment, electronic components, electronic consumer goods, demestic electric appliances, electric lighting equipment, instrument engineering	35,36, 38-52, 57	62-76
Food, drinks and tobacco	Oils and fats, slaughtering and meat processing, milk and products, fruit vegetable and fish processing, grain milling and starch, bread, biscuits, sugar, confectionary, animal feeding stuffs, miscellaneous foods, alcoholic drink soft drinks, tobacco	58-70	8-20
Other manufacturing	Motor vehicles and parts, shipbuilding and repairing, aerospace etc, other vehicles, woollen and worsted, cotton spinning and weaving, hosiery and other knitted goods, textile finishing, carpets, jute, leather and leather goods, footwear, clothing furs, household and other textiles, timber and wood products, wooden furniture, pulp, paper and board,	53-56, 71-90	21-34, 47-48,77-84

Contd....

Industry/Asset	*1990 I-O Sectors*	*1990 sectoral code*	*1995 sectoral code*
	paper and board products, printing and publishing, rubber products, processing of plastics, jewellery and coins, sports goods and toys, other goods		
Electricity, gas and water	Electricity production, gas, water supply	7,8,9	85-87
Construction	Construction	91	88
Distribution, hotels, etc.	Wholesale distribution, retail distribution, distribution and vehicles repairs, hotels catering, pubs etc.	92,93,94,95	89-92
Transport, storage, and communication	Railways, road and other inland transport, sea transport, air transport, transport services, postal services, telecoomunication	96-102	93-99
Financial sector	Banking and finance, insurance, auxiliary financial services, estate agents, legal services, accountancy services, other professional services, advertising, computing services, other business services, renting of movables, owning and dealing in real estate, research and development	103-114, 118	100-103, 105-114
Public administration	Public administration	115	115
Education, health and social work	Sanitary services, education, health services, recreation and welfare services, personal services, domestic services	116, 117, 119-122	116-123
Housing services	Ownership of dwelling	123	104

differ by a radial expansion in the utility surface. Therefore the change in the welfare between benchmark and counterfactual solutions of a model is proportional to the change in income or the percentage change in the area of radial projection between two consumption points. The values of both EV and CV are sensitive to elasticities of substitution in production and consumption. It is necessary to evaluate the sensitivity of the EV/GDP ratios to a set of relevant substitution elasticities for robustness of the tax reform analysis.

EFFICIENCY AND REALLOCATION IMPACTS OF CAPITAL INCOME AND INDIRECT TAX REFORM

The model outlined above is calibrated using the benchmark data set for 1995 which includes taxes on five types of capital assets and labour income and four types of indirect taxes in commodities and services as given in Table A4 and A5 in the appendix. The five types of capital assets are buildings, short and long lived plant and machinery, vehicles and dwellings; the four types of indirect taxes are import duties, subsidies, duties and levies and value added taxes on intermediate and final demands.

First, we consider four different policy reform scenarios. First scenario is moving to a yield preserving uniform 26.5 per cent tax rate from the existing taxes for central and unit elasticity cases. The next scenario considers a uniform 30 per cent tax rate from the existing taxes without any equal yield requirements

Table A2

A 16 Sector Industry by Industry Input-Output Table of the United Kingdom 1995

I x I Domestic Use Matrix	Agricul-ture	Extrac-tion	Other-Mining	Chemi-cals	Metals	Engine-ering	Food, drink	Other Manuf.	Utili-ties	Constru-ction	Distri-bution	Trans-port	Finan-cial	Pub-lic Ad-min	Educ. Health,	Hous-ing	Total interme diate	Consu-mers' expen-diture	GG FC	GDF CF	Stocks	Exports	Total final demand	Total
Agriculture	2,096	0	14	27	7	5	12,132	435	0	4	564	48	15	0	148	0	15,495	6,730	42	0	0	1,942	8,713	24,208
Extraction	0	2,439	0	4,697	3	0	0	0	3,622	0	0	0	0	0	0	0	10,762	0	0	0	0	6,942	6,942	17,704
Other Mining	20	0	353	218	846	26	45	130	1 897	401	105	17	8	0	57	0	4,124	339	47	0	0	983	1,369	5,493
Chemicals	1,433	10	37	3,899	433	546	571	1,484	466	737	1,299	1,254	913	0	3,204	19	16,304	3,764	3,116	0	261	28,663	35,804	52,108
Metals	110	162	192	1,225	7,249	6,320	1,831	5,197	50	7,074	503	389	5	0	84	0	30,392	346	588	7,158	779	10,230	19,101	49,493
Engineering	0	576	317	682	1,254	5,705	528	2,432	534	788	848	1,808	1,018	0	1,567	36	18,192	0	1,589	2,613	332	50,923	55,457	73,649
Food, drink	2,797	52	25	356	82	120	6,382	350	64	51	6,589	650	1,058	0	1,796	4	20,377	25,904	411	0	153	10,270	36,737	57,114
Other Manuf.	583	80	134	1,781	1,839	3,005	2,816	16,404	474	4,242	6,702	4,139	8,242	0	3,340	283	54,064	18,082	3,872	8,933	1,185	39,858	71,928	125,992
Utilities	279	0	160	1,330	1,596	1,189	931	1,980	12,273	272	1,201	857	1,184	0	705	23	23,981	16,353	1,323	0	0	62	17,738	41,719
Construction	172	0	122	109	32	56	0	31	0	21,085	603	151	1,985	0	146	3,929	28,420	3,521	4,414	47,764	285	0	55,983	84,404
Distribution	1,005	200	206	1,479	2,489	4,115	1,647	3,724	355	1,371	4,164	2,470	2,276	0	790	0	26,289	111,181	1,229	2,586	0	13,701	128,698	154,987
Transport	245	704	335	1,232	2,047	1,415	1,583	3,614	183	887	14,871	15,642	17,082	0	3,175	198	63,216	19,715	2,637	779	0	12,194	35,324	98,540
Financial	1,949	671	471	4,070	2,781	6,194	4,205	9,177	1,834	10,483	22,425	12,387	50,836	0	13,435	15,221	156,189	25,373	8,458	8,483	0	12,545	54,859	211,047
Public Admin	0	0	0	0	0	0	0	0	0	0	0	0	0	0	0	0	0	0	63,843	0	0	0	63,843	63,843
Educ. Health,	378	1	41	520	253	581	496	2,618	179	242	1,001	1,369	4,031	0	7,756	67	19,535	43,653	46,265	0	0	4,504	94,422	113,957
Housing	0	0	0	0	0	0	0	0	0	0	0	0	0	0	0	0	0	53,269	0	0	0	0	53,269	53,269
Total intermediate	11,067	4,895	2,410	21,626	20,912	29,276	33,168	47,576	22,081	47,638	60,876	41,182	88,652	0	36,201	19,781	487,339	328,229	137,832	78,316	2,995	192,816	740,188	1,227,527
Imports	1,630	989	425	10,639	7,613	15,965	8,827	30,336	3,612	5,151	3,532	4,895	3,949	0	2,960	19	100,541	52,021	9,995	28,174	1,563	2,494	94,248	194,789
Duty on imports	34	6	5	136	101	214	171	405	48	66	51	26	2	0	9	0	1,273	547	91	382	20	32	1,073	2,346
VAT	0	0	0	0	0	0	0	0	0	0	0	218	3,259	0	1,181	0	4,658	33,257	3,915	3,731	0	0	40,902	45,561
Duties and levies	211	2	103	1,175	344	176	460	331	1,378	130	1,275	2,026	896	0	344	36	8,887	22,713	434	0	0	0	23,147	32,034
Other taxes and sub sidies	-265	-25	-10	-50	-53	-46	-1,454	-212	-10	-34	-443	-404	-409	0	-186	-6	-3,607	4,559	-577	-45	4	-556	3,384	-223
Value added – Labour	7,143	1,409	1,822	10,151	15,790	18,529	9,691	36,483	5,492	29,947	61,877	35,191	70,149	60,316	69,067	0	433,059	0	0	0	0	0	0	433,059
Value added – Gross profits etc	4,388	10,428	738	8,432	4,786	9,536	6,250	11,074	9,118	1,505	27,820	15,406	44,549	3,527	4,381	33,440	195,376	0	0	0	0	0	0	195,376
Total inputs	24,208	17,704	5,493	52,108	49,493	73,649	57,114	125,992	41,719	84,404	154,987	98,540	211,047	63,843	113,957	53,269	1,227,526	441,325	151,691	110,558	4,582	194,786	902,942	2,130,468

Source: ONS, Input-Output Tables of the United Kingdom, 1995

Table A3

Industry by Industry Import Use Matrix for the UK economy 1995

I x I Domestic Use Matrix	*Agricul-ture*	*Extrac-tion*	*Other-Min ing*	*Chemi-cals*	*Metals*	*Engine-ering*	*Food, drink*	*Other Manuf.*	*Utili-ties*	*Constru-ction*	*Distri-bution*	*Trans-port*	*Finan-cial*	*Pub-lic Ad-min*	*Educ. Health,*	*Hous-ing*	*Total interme diate*	*Consu-mers' expen-diture*	*GG FC*	*GDF CF*	*Stocks*	*Exports*	*Total final demand*	*Total*
Agriculture	462	0	0	2	0	0	2,342	394	0	0	546	9	0	0	0	0	3,755	1,471	0	0	0	46	1,517	5,272
Extraction	0	133	0	1,532	0	0	0	0	1,613	0	0	0	0	0	0	0	3,278	0	0	0	0	0	0	3,278
Other Mining	0	0	68	359	540	31	4	50	312	540	0	0	0	0	0	0	1,905	29	3	0	0	2,003	2,035	3,941
Chemicals	802	11	142	7,931	1,028	1,274	844	7,476	382	196	165	609	22	0	299	0	21,182	2,259	873	0	199	165	3,495	24,677
Metals	26	180	57	222	5,249	2,251	378	1,745	0	1,690	64	0	0	0	0	0	11,863	0	0	3	220	0	222	12,085
Engineering	45	161	61	13	286	11,980	22	2,177	855	770	46	791	78	0	119	0	17,403	6,220	3,123	22,859	148	164	32,513	49,916
Food, drink	291	0	0	275	0	0	4,641	36	0	0	936	53	0	0	0	0	6,232	8,812	348	0	18	19	9,198	15,430
Other Manuf.	0	0	79	300	478	369	565	18,399	12	1,900	1,206	641	60	0	357	0	24,365	24,075	2,893	5,312	979	98	33,357	57,722
Utilities	0	0	0	3	4	1	2	3	432	0	0	0	0	0	0	0	446	0	0	0	0	0	0	446
Construction	0	0	0	0	0	0	0	0	0	44	0	0	0	0	0	0	44	0	0	0	0	0	0	44
Distribution	0	0	0	0	0	0	0	0	0	0	0	0	0	0	0	0	0	3,518	0	0	0	0	3,518	3,518
Transport	0	504	11	0	5	0	4	0	0	2	530	2,720	375	0	60	0	4,211	4,036	342	0	0	0	4,378	8,590
Financial	4	1	8	0	20	50	22	0	4	10	35	33	3,369	0	886	19	4,463	0	1,328	0	0	0	1,328	5,791
Public Admin	0	0	0	0	0	0	0	0	0	0	0	0	0	0	0	0	0	0	416	0	0	0	416	416
Educ. Health,	0	0	0	1	3	8	2	55	2	0	3	38	45	0	1,238	0	1,395	1,035	669	0	0	0	1,704	3,099
Housing	0	0	0	0	0	0	0	0	0	0	0	0	0	0	0	0	0	566	0	0	0	0	566	566
Total Imports	1,630	989	425	10,639	7,613	15,965	8,827	30,336	3,612	5,151	3,532	4,895	3,949	0	2,960	19	100,541	52,021	9,995	28,174	1,563	2,494	94,248	194,789

Source: ONS, Input-Output Tables of the United Kingdom, 1995.

for low and high labour elasticity cases. For each of these scenarios, we compute changes in aggregate welfare for the economy by summing up money metric equivalent variations for households, investors and the government and study reallocation of capital assets and employment across sectors and corresponding changes in output. To be comprehensive, we take percentage changes in total money metric equivalent variations as a percentage of UK GDP for various alternative capital tax arrangements. Then robustness of each of above experiments is checked by using model solutions for low (0.15) and high (0.3) values of labour supply elasticities by computing the sensitivity of the EV/GDP ratios and a set of substitution elasticities between capital and labour as well as among capital assets. Then we report on the marginal excess burdens of each pound of additional revenue raised by different tax instruments and welfare implications of replacing the current taxes by a system of lump sum taxes on household income.

Efficiency effects of tax reform

A summary of results of capital income tax reform under four different scenarios is given in Table 1. The two scenarios in case A show welfare gains when capital income tax rates existing in 1995 (see Table A4) are replaced by a uniform 26.5 per cent rate across sectors and assets for a low labour supply elasticity for two cases of elasticities of substitution as reported in Table A6. In the central case, there is an improvement in efficiency of 0.035 per cent of UK GDP (£219 million in terms of 1995 prices). Note that the gross value added was 628 billion as given in the input-output table in A2. The improvement is 0.022 per cent of UK GDP (£139 million) in the case of unit elasticity specification.

Table A4

Effective Tax rates on capital income by assets for year 1995 used in the UK tax mode

Industry/Asset	*Buildings*	*P&M Long*	*P&M Short*	*Vehicles*	*Dwellings*	*P & M long life (new life 95)*
Agriculture	46.2	14.6	25.3	16.9	0.0	25.3
Extraction	51.1	15.9	27.8	21.3	0.0	27.8
Other mining & quarrying	44.3	14.6	23.3	21.3	0.0	23.3
Chemicals	39.9	13.0	17.9	21.3	0.0	17.9
Metals and mineral products	39.7	12.0	17.1	21.3	0.0	17.1
Engineering	39.7	12.0	18.3	21.3	0.0	18.3
Food, drinks and tobacco	39.7	12.4	17.8	21.3	0.0	17.8
Other manufacturing	39.7	12.9	19.1	22.7	0.0	19.1
Electricity, gas and water	40.8	13.6	30.0	21.3	0.0	30.0
Construction	39.7	14.6	23.5	21.3	0.0	23.5
Distribution, hotels, etc.	39.7	13.3	23.9	21.3	0.0	23.9
Transport, storage, and communication	39.7	16.4	26.5	18.5	0.0	26.5
Financial sector	50.7	13.3	24.7	21.3	0.0	24.7
Public administration	50.7	13.3	23.8	21.3	0.0	23.8
Education, health and social work	51.3	13.3	22.2	21.3	0.0	22.2
Housing services	0.0	0.0	0.0	0.0	0.0	0.0

Source: P-Tax calculator, Inland Revenue 1998.

Table A5
Composite indirect tax Rates on Final Demand Expressed as per cent of net Prices for year 1995

	Tax on Household Consumption		*Tax on Investment*		*Tax in Government Consumption*	
	Domestic sales	*Imports*	*Domestic sales*	*Imports*	*Domestic sales*	*imports*
Agric	-10.9	4.9			-7.1	2.6
Minin	5.4	5.4			16.0	16.0
Chemi	163.1	167.2		1.5	14.7	16.3
Metal	17.3	17.3	3.3	4.7	17.5	17.5
Engin	15.4	16.9	5.0	6.6	16.6	18.2
Foodd	47.5	49.0			2.0	3.1
Othma	14.6	16.0	5.4	6.8	10.8	12.3
Power	9.0	9.0			16.9	16.9
Const	13.9	14.0	2.4	2.5	17.0	17.1
Distr	12.8	12.8			7.9	7.9
Trans	5.9	8.7	-2.2	0.3	6.7	9.3
Finan	1.1	1.1	0.3	0.3	6.1	6.1
Educa	6.3	7.5			-0.8	0.3
House	-2.0					

Source: GE data set, Inland Revenue 1998.

When we relax the equal yield constraint in Cases B of Table 1 the size of government can, and usually does, change after the tax reform without any adjustment to other taxes. The efficiency gain from replacing existing taxes by uniform capital income tax rates in the no equal yield capital tax reform was about 0.281 per cent of UK GDP (1.8 billion pounds) for the low labour supply elasticity case and 0.283 per cent for the high labour supply elasticity. It can be up to 0.3 per cent of the UK GDP (about £20 billion) when the capital income tax is replaced by yield preserving lump-sum taxes.

Table 1
Aggregate Welfare Results of Replacing Capital Income Taxes By Uniform Rates in Equal and No-equal-yield Cases (with labour supply elasticity of 0.15)

A. Equal Yield Case

Tax Experiments	*Hicksian equivalent variation as % of GDP*	*Hicksian compensating variation as % of GDP*
Replacing the Existing Capital Income Taxes By Yield Preserving Uniform Rates (Central case)	0.035	-0.036
Replacing the Existing Capital Income Taxes By Yield Preserving Uniform Rates (Unit elasticity Case)	0.022	-0.022

B. No equal yield central elasticity case with low and high labour supply elasticities

Tax Experiments	*Hicksian equivalent variation as % of GDP*	*Hicksian compensating variation as % of GDP*
Replacing the Existing Capital Income Taxes By Uniform Rates (Low case)	0. 281	-0.279
Replacing the Existing Capital Income Taxes By Uniform Rates (High case)	0.283	-0.281

Note: See section 4 for numerical values of substitution elasticities in central and unit cases.

Welfare gains reported here are lower than those reported in Piggot and Whalley (1985) and Shoven and Whalley (1992) mainly because the benchmark year 1995 had already witnessed a significant amount of tax reform compared to the benchmark taxes in their studies. These gains are in similar magnitude to those in Bhattarai and Whalley (2000, 1999) and in Bhattarai (2000).

Sensitivity analysis of model results

The robustness of the welfare impact results outlined above is tested by means of sensitivity analysis of the results to four different sets of substitution elasticities among assets (ss_k), keeping elasticities of substitution between labour and capital (ss_v) fixed; and four different sets of elasticities of substitution between labour and capital, keeping substitution elasticities among assets fixed. Table 2 includes the results of sensitivity analysis for replacing the existing level of capital income taxes by yield preserving uniform capital income tax rates, for both low and high labour supply elasticities.

Table 2
Sensitivity of aggregate welfare as a percentage of UK GDP to substitution elasticities between capital and labour, and to substitution elasticities across capital assets

A. Labour supply elasticity 0.15

$ss_k ss_v$	*0.75*	*1.0*	*3.0*	*5.0*
0.75	0.01513	0.01705	0.0316	0.04594
1.0	0.01951	0.0223	0.03607	0.05046
3.0	0.04999	0.05252	0.06898	0.08426
5.0	0.07694	0.08039	0.09992	0.11647

B. Labour supply elasticity 0.3

$ss_k ss_v$	*0.75*	*1.0*	*3.0*	*5.0*
0.75	0.01496	0.01688	0.03143	0.04576
1.0	0.0193	0.02124	0.03587	0.05026
3.0	0.04947	0.05206	0.06866	0.08399
5.0	0.07616	0.07971	0.09953	0.11618

Note: ss_v is the elasticity of substitution between capital and labour
ss_k is the elasticity of substitution among capital assets.

For all pairs of elasticities, the welfare impacts of moving to a yield preserving capital income tax from a set of existing taxes is positive and almost linear in the value of substitution elasticities among assets, for a particular set of elasticities of substitution between labour and capital assets. Similarly, it is also almost linear in the values of substitution elasticities between capital and labour for any particular value of substitution elasticities among capital assets. When both ss_v and ss_k are very high, each assuming a value of 5.0, the welfare impact of switching to a uniform tax rate was about 0.11 per cent of UK GDP, which amounts to nearly £691 million.

Reallocation of capital assets and labour in production

Firms use capital and labour services in production. Following convention in general equilibrium analysis, before tax prices of these factors are set to unity in the benchmark. Producers, or users of these inputs, however, pay the gross of tax prices but the owners of these factors receive net of tax payments. Government collects the tax revenue. In this model capital income taxes are collected at the sectoral level. The labour tax does not differ by sector and is collected from households[1].

In 15 out of 16 sectors, capital services are split between four different assets: buildings, short lived plant and machinery, long lived plant and machinery, and vehicles. Labour is homogeneous across all these sectors. The housing services sector is peculiar in terms of input use, as it uses dwellings as its only input. Housing sector is isolated from other sectors. It uses none of the other assets nor any labour.

Table 3

Capital Asset Reallocation from Equal Yield Replacement of Capital Income Taxes by Uniform Tax Rates By Industry (% Change in Capital Use (By Asset By Sector)

(a) *Central Case Elasticity Specification*					(b) *Unit Elasticity Specification*				
Asset Class	*Buildings*	*PM Long*	*PM Short*	*Vehicles*	*Asset Class*	*Buildings*	*PM Long*	*PM Short*	*Vehicles*
Agric	2.05		2.76	-5.3	Agric	2.1		2.17	-4.63
Extr	21.17	-0.45	10.26	2.11	Extr	16.21	2.46	9.15	4.06
Min	-1.47		0.3	2.49	Min	-0.6		0.09	1.46
Chem	-8.98	-0.52	-5.79	7.88	Chem	-5.15	-0.46	-3.63	4.58
Metal	-11.62	-4.93	-9.55	4.81	Metal	-7.29	-3.53	-6.41	2.54
Eng	-12.06	-5.88	-8.12	3.06	Eng	-8.76	-5.05	-6.51	0.92
Food	-5.87	-1.08	-3.72	4.64	Food	-5.51	-1.24	-3.82	4.52
OTHMA	-6.74	-1.97	-3.45	4.24	OTHMA	-7.04	-2.28	-3.85	4.69
Power	-6.26	0.38	20.12	6.89	Power	-3.96	-0.02	12.92	4.29
Constr	-8.31	-1.15	0.85	1.92	Constr	-7.91	-1.23	0.86	1.86
Distr	-10.82	-1.66	4.68	5.63	Distr	-6.6	-1.24	2.82	3.31
Trans	-11.56	3.34	9.65	-1.03	Trans	-7	1.99	5.97	-0.76
Fin	14.18	-8.78	-1.34	-2.01	Fin	9.42	-5.6	-0.73	-1.25
PubAD	18.89	-5.02	0.91	2.03	PubAD	12.12	-3.27	0.58	1.19
EducA	20.89		-2.55	1.96	EducA	13.39		-1.54	1.22

Note: The capital income tax rates used here may be different from the capital income tax rates in use in the Inland Revenue.

Equal yield uniform capital tax rate 26.5%
Aggregate Welfare Effect: £218.1 mill (95)
Aggregate Welfare Effect: +£140 mill (95)
= 0.0347% of UK 1995 GDP
= 0.0223% of UK 1995 GDP

The relative prices of capital assets differ across sectors in the benchmark, mainly for the reason that capital income tax rates differ by assets and sectors. The equal yield uniform tax reform reduces these inter-sectoral and inter-asset differences in the relative user cost of capital in the counterfactual scenarios. Consequently we see a significant reallocation of capital and labour resources across sectors occurring in comparison to the base year.

The capital reallocation results in Table 3 show intra-asset reallocation of capital assets with the central case elasticity specification for both low and high labour supply elasticity cases. The model results confirm our assertion about the reallocation effects of changes in the relative prices. Based on changes in relative prices of capital between sectors, we expect more use of building type assets in the agriculture, extraction, financial services, public administration and education sectors. The relative prices of building type assets decrease in these sectors when capital income taxes become uniform across sectors and assets, compared to the benchmark relative prices. The sector-by-sector results in the first row in Table 3 show that in the case of low labour supply elasticity, reallocation is actually happening in our model solutions. The use of building type assets increases by 21 per cent in education, 19 per cent in public administration, 21 per cent in extraction, 14 per cent in financial services, and around 2 per cent in the agriculture sector. The use of buildings decreases in the other sectors because of a rise in the relative price of building assets in those sectors compared to the base year.

Table 4
% Changes in Employment and Output
Equal Yield Replacement of Capital Income Taxes by Uniform Tax Rates

(Central Case Specification of Elasticities)

	Labour Supply Elasticity 0.15	
Industry	*% change in employment(labour use)*	*% change in output*
Agric	-0.989	-0.065
Extra	-0.843	1.606
Minin	-0.207	-0.367
Chemi	4.758	-0.251
Metal	1.850	-0.731
Engin	0.352	-0.970
Food	2.797	-0.044
Othma	0.951	-0.241
Power	4.084	-0.262
Constr	0.130	-0.040
Distr	2.673	-0.121
Trans	1.818	-0.015
Finan	-4.757	0.124
PubAD	-0.827	0.035
EducA	-0.897	0.107
House		

0.01

The reallocation results for other assets, long and short lived plant and machinery and vehicles could also be interpreted in this manner. We see positive changes in the use of a particular asset in which the user cost of the asset has reduced relative to the base year.

Besides inter-sectoral reallocation, we also see inter-asset substitution and capital labour reallocation after the uniform tax reform. Given that we have a fixed endowment of each type of capital asset in both the benchmark and the counterfactual scenarios, total reallocation is subject to this capital stock constraint.

Reallocation between asset types also occurs when the relative prices of these assets change in counterfactual scenarios. Inter-asset reallocation in response to capital tax reform is reflected in terms of positive changes for some assets, followed by negative changes in the use of other assets within a sector. For every sector, some assets change positively and some other assets change negatively in response to the uniform tax reform. For instance, in the agriculture sector, use of the buildings type asset increases by 2 per cent, use of plant and machinery with short life also increases by 2.8 per cent, while there is a reduction of 5.3 per cent in the use of vehicle type assets.

The capital reallocation effect explained in this section is sensitive to elasticity configurations. We consider a unit elasticity case in Table 3.b. Generally the direction of changes in the allocation of assets is the same as in the central elasticity specification outlined in Table 3, while the magnitude of such changes is smaller for the unit elasticity specification than in the central elasticity specification.

Besides inter-sectoral and inter-asset redistribution, changes in the relative user cost of capital have a significant effect on the use of labour across sectors. When capital inputs become relatively cheaper than the labour input, producers tend to substitute capital for labour. As outlined above, capital becomes relatively cheaper in certain sectors such as agriculture, finance, public administration, and education, and relatively expensive in some other sectors, particularly manufacturing, after a uniform tax reform. For this reason we see substitution between capital and labour in the model solutions.

The figures in Table 4 show that replacing low capital income tax rates in the base year by a 26.5 per cent uniform tax rate increases the user cost of capital in manufacturing sectors and some service sectors (chemicals, metals, engineering, food, other manufacturing, power, construction, distribution and transport). We see substitution of capital by labour in these sectors. Thus the effect of the reduction in capital assets is not completely compensated for by increased use of labour. Therefore output decreases in most of the manufacturing sectors, though not by as much as would have been warranted by the reduction in the use of capital in these sectors. Figures in Table 4 also show that labour is substituted by capital assets, because capital becomes less expensive, in the financial services and education sectors. Benefiting from cheaper capital services, these sectors substitute capital for labour and experience positive changes in output. For instance, two extreme cases of factor substitution are seen in the financial and chemical sectors: capital substitutes for labour substantially in the financial sector while labour substitutes for capital in the chemical sector.

Aggregate Welfare for Indirect Tax Reform

The basic UK model included here has four types of indirect taxes on intermediate inputs and final demand: tariffs, subsidies, duties and levies, and value added tax. Rates of indirect taxes vary across sectors (Table A5 in the appendix) and final demand categories as reported in the previous section.

The aggregate welfare impacts of replacing a non-uniform indirect tax by a uniform tax rate and lump sum taxes are reported in Table 5.

For the central case specification, the welfare gain from replacing equal yield non-uniform VAT by uniform VAT was about 0.019 per cent of UK GDP. Such a welfare gain occurs because of the removal of distortions caused by differentiated VAT rates in the base year.

Equal yield replacement of all differentiated indirect tax rates by uniform tax rates across sectors leads to a gain of 0.017 per cent of UK GDP. This figure is also very close to the gains from the uniform VAT case.

Finally, when we replace indirect tax rates by an equal yield lump sum tax, the welfare gain rises to 1.72 per cent of UK GDP (10.8 billion), which is bigger than in all the other tax experiments reported earlier.

Table 5
Aggregate Welfare for other cases
(as % of GDP)

Equal Yield Replacement of non-uniform VAT By Uniform Rates - Central Case Specification of Elasticities	0.0186% of UKGDP
Equal Yield Replacement of all indirect Taxes By Uniform Indirect Tax Rates	0.01704% of UKGDP
Equal Yield Replacement of all indirect Taxes By equal yield lump-sum Tax	1.723% of UKGDP
Equal Yield Replacement of household income taxes By equal yield lump-sum tax	3.67% of UKGDP

As the last equal yield scenario shows, moving completely away from the household income tax to the lump sum income taxes generates even more efficiency gain equal to 3.67 per cent of the GDP (21.98 billion).

MARGINAL EXCESS BURDEN OF TAXES IN THE UK MODEL

The marginal excess burden (MEB) of taxes measures the extra cost to society, in terms of money metric welfare, of each pound of revenue raised by means of a certain tax instrument. We have computed the MEB for each tax instrument included in the UK model by dividing the change in welfare (ΔW_t) by the net change in the government revenue (ΔR_t). The net change in government revenue reflects the share (g) of revenue retained by the public sector.

$$MEB_t = \frac{\Delta W_t}{g.\Delta R_t} \tag{32}$$

The popular measure of the marginal excess burden of taxes, given by the area of the Harberger triangle, is related with the elasticity of demand for goods. Let P be the before tax price of a commodity and $P(1+t)$ be its value after tax rate t is imposed in it. Change in price, DDP, equals tax rate. It causes a change in demand by DDq. In a partial equilibrium analysis the area of triangle under the demand curve before and after taxes represents the dead weight loss of tax changes, which is $dwl = \frac{1}{2}\Delta q \Delta p$. This area is proportional to the square of the tax rate and the elasticity of demand. The price elasticity of demand is $e = \frac{\Delta q}{\Delta p}\frac{p}{q}$. Then the relation between the change in quantity and the elasticity is $\Delta q = \frac{\Delta pq}{p}e$. Inserting this value of Δq in the equation for the dead weight loss formula we get $dwl = \frac{1}{2}\left(\frac{\Delta pq}{p}\right)e\Delta p$. The tax rate and change in prices are equal, implying $\Delta p = t$ and $dwl = \frac{1}{2}t^2\frac{eq}{p}$; normalising $p=1$, $dwl = \frac{1}{2}t^2 eq$. In case of general equilibrium such formula need to take account of cross price elasticities as well as changes in quantity demands various sectors that are triggered by an imposition of tax in a certain sector. After all these calculations values of marginal excess burden are given by (32).

The results show that MEB figures differ according to the type of tax instrument used to raise additional revenue. Results of the UK model in terms of changes in revenue, Hicksian EVs and MEB are given in Table 6.

Table 6

Marginal Excess Burden of Taxes (pence/per £ of additional revenue: low elasticity case)

Tax instrument	*Low Elasticity Case*			*High Elasticity Case*		
	MEB	*Change in revenue*	*Hicksian money metric EV*	*MEB*	*Change in revenue*	*Hicksian money metric EV*
Capital income tax	-0.350	11305	-3962	-0.660	4449	-2936
Production tax	-0.544	6585	-3582	-0.673	876	-590
Labour income tax	-0.435	7984	-3473	-0.580	8182	-4750
Household consumption tax	-0.517	6911	-3574	-0.669	4519	-3025
Indirect tax on government consumption	-0.540	6629	-3578	-0.540	6629	-3578
Indirect tax on Investment goods	-0.542	6609	-3581	-0.614	344	-211

For the low labour supply elasticity case, the MEB ranges from 35 pence in the case of capital income taxes to 54 pence per pound of additional revenue from production taxes. The MEB figures reflect the degree of distortion for the tax instrument used to raise the additional revenue. Production taxes in intermediate goods and indirect taxes on investment goods seem to be the most distortionary tax instrument in the UK economy. The marginal excess burden (MEB) of all other taxes are between these two figures.

A6
Elasticity Parameters used in the UK tax model (central case)

Industry	*(a) Elasticity of substitution between labour and capital*	*(b) Elasticity substitution among capital assets*	*(c) Elasticity substitution among domestic supplies and imports*	*(d) Elasticity transformation between domestic supplies and exports*	*(e) Central tendency values of own prices elasticities household demand functions*
Agriculture	0.90	0.90	2.12	1.46	-0.475
Extraction	1.19	1.19	2.82	1.93	-0.305
Other mining & quarrying	1.11	1.11	2.63	1.80	-0.362
Chemicals	1.18	1.18	2.80	1.92	-0.542
Metals and mineral products	1.22	1.22	2.89	1.98	-0.503
Engineering	1.11	1.11	2.63	1.80	-0.275
Food, drinks and tobacco	0.74	0.74	1.75	1.20	-0.795
Other manufacturing	1.18	1.18	2.80	1.92	-0.530
Electricity, gas and water	1.11	1.11	2.63	1.80	-0.000
Construction	0.74	0.74	1.75	1.20	-0.000
Distribution, hotels, etc.	1.18	1.18	2.80	1.92	-0.489
Transport, storage, and communication	1.18	1.18	2.80	1.92	0.321
Financial sector	1.22	1.22	2.89	1.98	-0.000
Public administration	0.67	0.67	1.58	1.08	-0.481
Education, health and social work	1.18	1.18	2.80	1.92	-0.253
Housing services	0.74	0.74	1.75	1.20	-0.000

Source: These values are comparable to those used by Piggott and Whalley (1985).

These MEB figures are comparable to theoretical and empirical results on MEB available in the literature. Theoretical studies about the marginal excess burden of taxes as reported in Harberger (1962) King (1983), Browning and Johnson (198e),Browning (1987), Mayshar (1990), Atkinson (1995) state how the excess burden of taxes can rise with extra amount of distortionary taxes in an economy. On empirical side Piggott and Whalley (1985) stated that "about one quarter of the revenue raised by the UK government each year are foregone through dead weight loss". Shoven and Whalley (1984) summarising some earlier studies of tax reform studies state that "welfare loss per extra dollar of revenues raised from existing United States distortionary taxes may approach a dollar". BFSW(1985), Goulder and Shoven and Whalley (1983) and Fullerton and Rogers

(1993) had slightly lower estimates of MEB. Our MEB estimate between 35 to 54 pence per pound of additional revenue is consistent with these findings in the MEB literature.

We find MEB measures to be sensitive to the elasticities of substitution in both the consumption and production sides of the economy. As figures in Tables 6 show, MEB figures are higher for higher values of elasticities compared to corresponding numbers with lower elasticities.

CONCLUSION

We present a multisectoral multiple capital asset general equilibrium tax model that can be used for analysing the fiscal policy taking account of more detailed structure of the UK economy. Model is calibrated to the micro-consistent benchmark data set for 1995 and used to evaluate the welfare gains that can be achieved by replacing existing differentiated capital income tax rates by a uniform rate of 26.5 per cent across all sectors and assets. Then the model was used to evaluate the welfare gains from replacing the existing taxes by yield preserving uniform taxes and also to evaluate the marginal excess burden of various taxes. The major findings from our study using the model are the following:

1. We compute the welfare gains by replacing the capital income tax rates existing in 1995 by a uniform yield preserving 26.5 per cent rate across sectors and assets for low labour supply elasticity to be equal to 0.035 per cent of UK GDP (£219 million).
2. The efficiency gain from replacing existing capital income taxes by uniform capital income tax rates without equal yield constraint is about 0.281 per cent of UK GDP (£1.8 billion) for the low labour supply elasticity case and 0.283 for high elasticity case.
3. The computed efficiency gain from replacing capital income tax by yield preserving lump-sum taxes can be about 0.3 per cent of UK GDP (£20 billion).
4. We check the robustness of the welfare results by means of sensitivity analysis. The welfare impacts of moving to a yield preserving capital income tax from a set of existing taxes is positive and almost linear in the values of substitution elasticities among assets

(σ_k) for a particular set of elasticities of substitution between labour and capital assets (σ_v). Similarly, it is also linear in the values of substitution elasticities between capital and labour for any particular value of substitution elasticities among capital assets. When both σ_v and σ_k are very high, each assuming a value of 5.0, the welfare impact of switching to a uniform tax rate was about 0.11 per cent of UK GDP, which amounts to nearly £691 million.

5. Changes in the relative prices of capital assets across sectors compared to the benchmark following the yield preserving capital income tax reform leads to a reallocation of capital assets across sectors. The equal yield uniform tax reform reduces the inter-sectoral and inter-asset differences

in the relative user cost of capital in the counterfactual scenarios. Consequently we see a significant reallocation, up to a 20 per cent increase or up to a 10 per cent reduction in the use of capital assets in a low labour supply elasticity case. The use of labour input also varies of between –5 and 5 per cent across sectors, occurring in comparison to the base year. Both capital and labour reallocation effects are robust with respect to labour supply elasticity.

6. When capital inputs become relatively cheaper than labour input, producers tend to substitute capital for labour; this happens in the agriculture, finance, public administration, and education sectors. Capital becomes relatively expensive in manufacturing sectors, after a uniform tax reform. We see substitution of capital by labour in these sectors. The effect of the reduction in capital assets is however not completely compensated for by increased use of labour. Therefore output levels decrease in most of the manufacturing sectors, though not by as much as would have been warranted by the reduction in the use of capital in these sectors.

8. The marginal excess burden (MEB) of taxes is computed as a ratio of loss in welfare to a net change in government revenue. It varies according to the tax instruments in use for raising the additional pound of revenue. For the low labour supply elasticity case, the MEB ranges from 35 pence in case of capital income taxes to 54 pence per pound of additional revenue from production taxes. The effects of other taxes lie between these two numbers. If MEB figures reflect the degree of distortion for the tax instrument used to raise the additional revenue, production taxes in intermediate goods and indirect taxes on investment goods seem to be the most distortionary tax instruments in the UK economy. MEB figures are higher for higher values of labour supply elasticities compared to corresponding numbers for lower labour supply elasticities. These MEB figures are comparable to rates available in the literature (Shoven and Whalley (1984), Piggott and Whalley (1985) and BFSW(1985)).

REFERENCES

Atkinson A.B. (1995), *Public Economics in Action: the Basic Income/Flat Tax Proposal*, Oxford University Press.

Armington, P.S. (1969), "A Theory of Demand for Products Distinguished by Place of Production", International Monetary Fund *Staff Papers* 16, 159-76.

Arrow, K.J. and F.H. Hahn (1971), *General Competitive Analysis*, San Franscisco: Holden-Day.

Arrow, K.J. and G. Debreu (1954), "Existence of an Equilibrium for a Competitive Economy" *Econometrica* 22, 265-90.

Ballard, C.L., D. Fullerton, J.B. Shoven and J.Whalley (1985), *A General Equilibrium Model for Tax Policy Evaluation*, University of Chicago Press, Chicago.

Bhattarai, K. and J. Whalley (1999), "Role of Labour Demand Elasticities in Tax Incidence Analysis with Heterogeneous Labour Model" *Empirical Economics*, 24(4) 599-619.

Bhattarai, K. and J. Whalley (2000), "General Equilibrium Modelling of UK Tax Policy" *in* Sean Holly and Martin Weale (eds.) *Econometric Modelling: Technique and Applications*, Cambridge University Press.

Blundell, Duncan and Meghir (1995), Estimating Labour Supply Responses Using Tax Reforms, *Working paper 95/7*, Institute of Fiscal Studies, London.

Browning, E.K. (1987), "On the Marginal Cost of Taxation", *American Economic Review*, 77(1), March, pp.11-23.

Browning, E.K. and Johnson, W.R. (1984), "The Trade-off between Equality and Efficiency", *Journal of Political Economy*, 1984 Vol.92. No.21 pp.175-203.

Central Statistical Office (CSO (1995)), *Family Spending*: A report on the 1994-95 Expenditure Survey.

Debreu, G. (1954) *The Theory of Value*, Yale University Press, New Haven.

Dervis, K., J.De Melo, and S.Robinson (1985), *General Equilibrium Models forDevelopment Policy*, CUP, New York.

Dirkse, S. P. and M. C. Ferris (1995) "CCPLIB: A Collection of Nonlinear Mixed Complementarity Problems" *Optimization Methods and Software*. 5:319-345.

Fullerton, D. and D.L. Rogers (1993), *Who Bears the Lifetime Tax Burden?* Brookings Institution, Washington D.C.

Giles C. and J McCrae (1983), TAXBEN: The IFS Microsimulation Tax and Benefit Model, *Working paper 95/19*, Institute of Fiscal Studies, London, UK9 (http//www.ifs.org.uk).

Giles, C. and P. Johnson (1994) "Tax Reform in the UK and Changes in the Progressivity of the Tax System, 1985-95", *Fiscal Studies*, Vol. 15, No. 3, pp. 64-86.

Goulder, L.H., J. Shoven and J. Whalley (1983), "Domestic Tax Policy and Foreign Sector:

The Importance of Alternative Foreign Sector Formulations to Results from a General Equilibrium Tax Analysis Model" in M. Feldstein ed. *Behavioral Simulation Methods in Tax Policy Analysis*, Chicago University Press.

Goulder, L.H., and L.H. Summers (1989), "Tax Policy, Asset Prices and Growth: A General Equilibrium Analysis", *Journal of Public Economics*, 38:265-296, North Holland.

Harberger, A.C. (1962), The Incidence of the Corporation Income Tax *Journal of Political Economy* 70 (June):215-40.

Institute of Fiscal Studies (2002), *Green Budget*, Institute of Fiscal Studies, London.

Inland Revenue (1991), "How to Use P-Tax", *Memio*, Economics Unit, London.

King M.A. (1983), Welfare Analysis of Tax Reform Using Household Data, Journal of Public Economics, 21 183.214.

King, M.A. and D. Fullerton (1984), *The Taxation of Income from Capital: a Comparative Study of the United States, the United Kingdom, Sweden and West Germany* Chicago University Press.

King, M.A. and M.H. Robson (1988), "Manual for Turbo P-tax", *LSE*, London.

Mayshar J. (1990), On Measures of Excess Burden and Their Application, Journal of Public Economics, 43, pp.263-289.

Mercenier, J. and Srinivasan, T.N. ed. (1994), *Applied General Equilibrium and Economic Development: Present Achievement and Future Trends*, University of Michigan Press, Ann Arbor.

Office of National Statistics (ONS (1995)), *Input Output : Tables for the United Kingdom*, HMSO, London.

Piggott, J. and J.Whalley (1985), *UK Tax Policy and Applied General Equilibrium Analysis*, Cambridge University Press.

Robinson, S. (1991), "Macroeconomics, Financial Variables, and Computable General Equilibrium Models," *World Development* 19, 1509-1523.

Rutherford, T. F. (1995), "Extension of GAMS for Complementary Problems Arising in applied Economic Analysis" *Journal of Economic Dynamics and Control* 19 1299-1324.

Rutherford, T. F. (1997), *The GAMS/ MPSGE and GAMS/MILES user notes*, GAMS Development Corporation, Washington D.C.

Scarf, H. E. (1986), The Computation of Equilibrium Prices, in Scarf H. E and Shoven John B. ed. *Applied General Equilibrium Analysis*, Cambridge University Press.

Siddorn, G. (1999), Derivation of 1995 Symmetric Use Matrices, *mimeo*, *Economics Unit*, Inland Revenue, F4 West Wing, Somerset House, Strand, London WC2R 1LB.

Shoven, J. B. and J.Whalley (1992), *Applying General Equilibrium*, Cambridge University Press, 1992.

Shoven, J. B. and J. Whalley (1973), "General Equilibrium with Taxes: A Computation Procedure and an Existence Proof" *Review of Economic Studies* 40, 475-90.

Shoven, J. B. and J. Whalley (1977), "Equal Yield Tax Alternatives: General Equilibrium Computational Techniques." *Journal of Public Economics* 8, 211-24.

Shoven, J. B. and J. Whalley (1984), "Applied General-Equilibrium Models of Taxation and International Trade: An Introduction and Survey", *Journal of Economic Literature*, vol. XXII, Sept,pp.1007-1051.

Taylor, L. ed. (1990), *Socially Relevant Policy Analysis: Structuralist Computable GeneralEquilibrium Models for the Developing World*, MIT Press, Cambridge 1990.

Walras, L. (1954), *Elements of Pure Economics*, Allen and Unwin, London.

Whalley, J. (1985), *Trade Liberalization Among Major World Trading Areas*, MIT Press, Cambridge.

NOTES

1. Some key references in applied general equilibrium models are Harberger (1959), Shoven and Whalley (1972, 1977, 1984,1992) Ballard-Fullerton-Shoven-Whalley (BFSW(1985)), Atkinson (1985), Scarf (1986), Piggott and Whalley (1985), Goulder and Summers (1989), Taylor (1990), Robinson (1991), Fullerton and Rogers (1993), Mercenier and Srinivasan (1994), Rutherford (1997). The development of the mixed complementarity solution technique in 1990s, particularly with the GAMS/MPSGE software in recent years has made it easier to solve large scale models (Brook, Kendrick and Meeraus (1992), Rutherford (1997), Dirkse and Ferris (1995)).
2. Numerical im plementation of a general equilibrium model involves five steps, namely, preparing a micro-consistent benchmark data set, declaration of the model, calibration

or replication, counterfactual solution and evaluation of welfare gains or losses. Model dimensions (sets) are declared and all base year data are read in tabular, parameter or scalar form while preparing the micro-consistent data set for the base year. Then the modeller specifies equations for preferences of households, production technology of firms, revenues and income constraints for each economic agents and the markets for the economy as a whole. A model is calibrated when the base year economy is reproduced by the model as its solution. This step is known as benchmark replication. The fourth step involves determining various taxes or exogenous variables and changes in them according the policy preference and assessing the efficiency and reallocation effects of proposed changes in composition and structure of tax transfer system. Finally, the summary of all interaction are reported in the form of money metric equivalent and compensating variations to judge whether proposed tax reform is likely to generate gains or losses in the economy. We find the GAMS/MPSGE to be a very handy software for solving a large scale Arrow-Debreu model as specified in this paper.

3. The effect of tax distortions on the labour-leisure choice can be captured through a subsidy to the consumption of leisure at rate t_l .
4. Though social security, national insurance contributions could be thought of as taxes on labour use.

5

Welfare Impacts of Equal-Yield Tax Reforms in the UK Economy[14]

Keshab R. Bhattarai

INTRODUCTION

Applied general equilibrium models have been in use for many years for the evaluation of short and long run impacts of fiscal policy. Depending on the specification of households, sectors of production and other economic institutions, these models provide numerical illustration of economy wide impacts of tax-transfer programmes. Plenty of studies exist in which these tools are used for analysis of policy alternatives available to a government (Harberger (1962), Ballard, Fullerton, Shoven and Whalley (1984), Piggott and Whalley (1985) Auerbach and Kotlikoff (1987) Goulder and Summers (1989), Robinson (1991), Hutton and Kenc (1994) and Perroni (1995)). Benchmarked to a dynamic reference path, these models provide the basis for numerical analyses of economic policies designed to increase growth rates, improve income distribution and assure efficiency in inter sectoral reallocation of resources over time going beyond the single sector model as in Ramsey (1928), Solow (1956), Uzawa (1962), Cass (1965), Lucas (1988), Romer (1989) and Rebelo (1991).

Here we focus on empirical results obtained from a dynamic multisectoral tax policy model, which contains a representative household, an investor, sixteen different firms, a government as well as the international sector. Advancement in computing technology has made it possible to compute more decentralised markets

14. This paper builds on research undertaken as part of the ESRC project on General Equilibrium and Dynamic Modelling for the Analysis of UK Policy Issues. I am grateful to Professors John Whalley, Carlo Perroni and Thomas F. Rutherford for guidance, to Graham Siddorn and Bill McNie who were at the Economics Unit of the Inland Revenue at the time of study for data support. I acknowledge suggestions made by Professor Richard Green, Tobi Kendall and a seminar group in the University of Hull and by two anonymous referees in the earlier working paper version of this paper. Correspondence address: *K.R.Bhattarai@hull.ac.uk*, phone: 44-1482-466483; fax: 44-1482-466216. All errors and omissions are my own.

in recent years (Rutherford (1995), Ferris and Munson (2004)). Micro-founded models of decentralised economies have become increasingly popular tools for evaluating macroeconomic policy issues in recent years (Rankin (1992)). The model here provides a numerical example of a decentralised market that takes a 65 years' horizon and is implemented with the micro-consistent data set for the UK economy received from the Inland Revenue and the ONS (see Tables A1, A2 and A3 in the appendix).

Table A1
Aggregation of 123 sectors into 16 sectors from 1990 Input-Output Sectoral Classification

Industry/Asset	*1990 I-O Sectors*	*1990 sectoral code*	*1995 sectoral code*
Agriculture	Agriculture, Forestry, Fishing	1,2,3	1-3
Extraction	Extraction – oil and gas	5	5
Other mining & quarrying	Coal extraction, stone, clay, sand, gravel, metal ores and minerals	4,14, 10	4,6,7
Chemicals	Coke ovens, oil proc, nuclear fuel, inorganic chemicals, organic chemicals, fertilisers, synthetic resins, paints, dyes, printing ink, special chemical for industry, pharmaceutical products, soap and toilet preparations, chemical products, man-made fibres	6, 20-29	35-46
Metals and mineral products	Iron and Steel, Aluminium, other non-ferrous metals, structural clay products, Cement, lime and plaster, concrete, asbestos, abrasive prods, glass, refractory and ceramic goods, metal casting, metal doors, windows, packaging products of metals, industrial plant and steel work, engineers small tools	11-13, 15-19, 30-34, 37	49-61
Engineering	Agricultural machinery and tractors, metal working machine tools, textile etc machinery, process machinery and contractors, mining equipment, mech power transmission equipment, other machinery, ordnance samll arms and ammunition, insulated wires and cables, basic electrical equipment, industrial electrical equipment, telecommunications etc. equipment, electronic components, electronic consumer goods, demestic electric appliances, electric lighting equipment, instrument engineering	35,36, 38-52, 57	62-76
Food, drinks and tobacco	Oils and fats, slaughtering and meat processing, milk and products, fruit vegetable and fish processing, grain milling and starch, bread, biscuits, sugar, confectionary, animal feeding stuffs, miscellaneous foods, alcoholic drink soft drinks, tobacco	58-70	8-20

Industry/Asset 1995 code	*1990 I-O Sectors*	*sectoral*	*1990 sectoral code*
Other manufacturing	Motor vehicles and parts, shipbuilding and repairing, aerospace etc, other vehicles, woollen and worsted, cotton spinning and weaving, hosiery and other knitted goods, textile finishing, carpets, jute, leather and leather goods, footwear, clothing furs, household and other textiles, timber and wood products, wooden furniture, pulp, paper and board, paper and board products, printing and publishing, rubber products, processing of plastics, jewellery and coins, sports goods and toys, other goods	53-56, 71-90	21-34, 47-48,77-84
Electricity, gas and water	Electricity production, gas, water supply	7,8,9	85-87
Construction	Construction	91	88
Distribution, hotels, etc.	Wholesale distribution, retail distribution, distribution and vehicles repairs, hotels catering, pubs etc.	92,93,94,95	89-92
Transport, storage, and communication	Railways, road and other inland transport, sea transport, air transport, transport services, postal services, telecoomunication	96-102	93-99
Financial sector	Banking and finance, insurance, auxiliary financial services, estate agents, legal services, accountancy services, other professional services, advertising, computing services, other business services, renting of movables, owning and dealing in real estate, research and development	103-114, 118	100-103, 105-114
Public administration	Public administration	115	115
Education, health and social work	Sanitary services, education, health services, recreation and welfare services, personal services, domestic services	116, 117, 119-122	116-123
Housing services	Ownership of dwelling	123	104

Essential features of the model are presented in section I followed by model specification in section II. A brief discussion of the calibration technique is provided in section III. Numerical specification of parameters and benchmark tax rates are given in section IV. Results of the model are discussed in section V followed by conclusions and references.

FEATURES OF A DYNAMIC MULTISECTORAL GENERAL EQUILIBRIUM TAX MODEL

Every applied general equilibrium model begins with specifications for consumption, production, price and quantity adjustment process in goods and factor markets. The model behind this paper contains a single representative consumer, producers representing the sixteen different sectors, a government sector and the rest of the world. With its focus on analysis of fiscal policy it has a more

Figure A1
Impact of Tax Reform in the Capital Accumulation Access Sectors

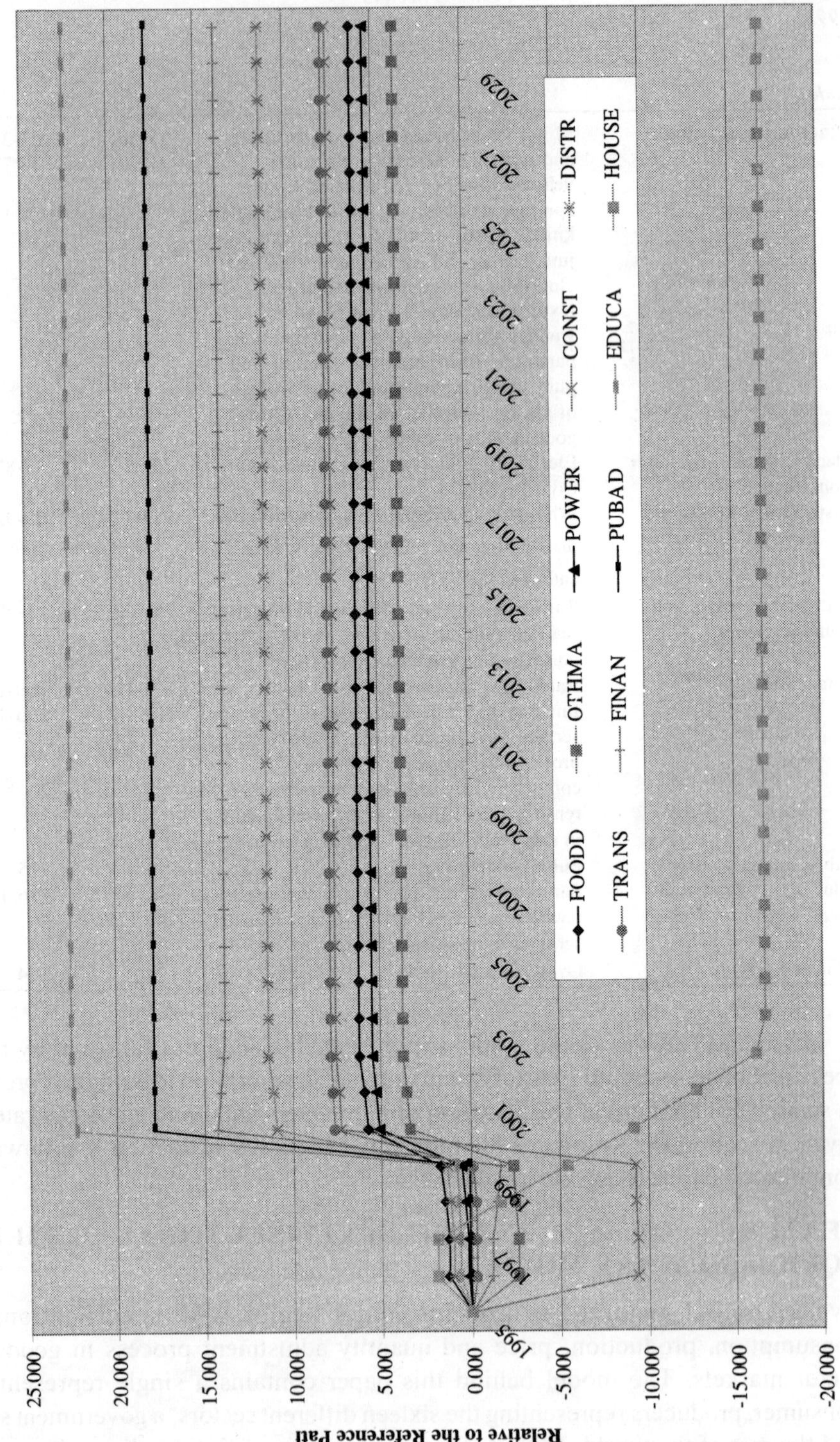

Table A2

A 16 Sector Industry by Industry Input-Output Table of the United Kingdom 1995

I x I Domestic Use Matrix	*Agricul-ture*	*Extrac-tion*	*Other-Min ing*	*Chemi-cals*	*Metals*	*Engine-ering*	*Food, drink*	*Other Manuf.*	*Utili-ties*	*Constru-ction*	*Distri-bution*	*Trans-port*	*Finan-cial*	*Pub-lic Ad-min*	*Educ. Health,*	*Hous-ing*	*Total interme diate*	*Consu-mers' expen-diture*	*GG FC*	*GDF CF*	*Stocks*	*Exports*	*Total final demand*	*Total*
Agriculture	2,096	0	14	27	7	5	12,132	435	0	4	564	48	15	0	148	0	15,495	6,730	42	0	0	1,942	8,713	24,208
Extraction	0	2,439	0	4,697	3	0	0	0	3,622	0	0	0	0	0	0	0	10,762	0	0	0	0	6,942	6,942	17,704
Other Mining	20	0	353	218	846	26	45	130	1,897	401	105	17	8	0	57	0	4,124	339	47	0	0	983	1,369	5,493
Chemicals	1,433	10	37	3,899	433	546	571	1,484	466	737	1,299	1,254	913	0	3,204	19	16,304	3,764	3,116	0	261	28,663	35,804	52,108
Metals	110	162	192	1,225	7,249	6,320	1,831	5,197	50	7,074	503	389	5	0	84	0	30,392	346	588	7,158	779	10,230	19,101	49,493
Engineering	0	576	317	682	1,254	5,705	528	2,432	634	788	848	1,808	1,018	0	1,567	36	18,192	0	1,589	2,613	332	50,923	55,457	73,649
Food, drink	2,797	52	25	356	82	120	6,382	350	64	51	6,589	650	1,058	0	1,796	4	20,377	25,904	411	0	153	10,270	36,737	57,114
Other Manuf.	583	80	134	1,781	1,839	3,005	2,816	16,404	474	4,242	6,702	4,139	8,242	0	3,340	283	54,064	18,082	3,872	8,933	1,185	39,858	71,928	125,992
Utilities	279	0	160	1,330	1,596	1,189	931	1,980	12,273	272	1,201	857	1,184	0	705	23	23,981	16,353	1,323	0	0	62	17,738	41,719
Construction	172	0	122	109	32	56	0	31	0	21,085	603	151	1,985	0	146	3,929	28,420	3,521	4,414	47,764	285	0	55,983	84,404
Distribution	1,005	200	206	1,479	2,489	4,115	1,647	3,724	355	1,371	4,164	2,470	2,276	0	790	0	26,289	111,181	1,229	2,586	0	13,701	128,698	154,987
Transport	245	704	335	1,232	2,047	1,415	1,583	3,614	183	887	14,871	15,642	17,082	0	3,175	198	63,216	19,715	2,637	779	0	12,194	35,324	98,540
Financial	1,949	671	471	4,070	2,781	6,194	4,205	9,177	1,884	10,483	22,425	12,387	50,836	0	13,435	15,221	156,189	25,373	8,458	8,483	0	12,545	54,859	211,047
Public Admin	0	0	0	0	0	0	0	0	0	0	0	0	0	0	0	0	0	0	63,843	0	0	0	63,843	63,843
Educ. Health,	378	1	41	520	253	581	496	2,618	179	242	1,001	1,369	4,031	0	7,756	67	19,535	43,653	46,265	0	0	4,504	94,422	113,957
Housing	0	0	0	0	0	0	0	0	0	0	0	0	0	0	0	0	0	53,269	0	0	0	0	53,269	53,269
Total intermediate	11,067	4,895	2,410	21,626	20,912	29,276	33,168	47,576	22,081	47,638	60,876	41,182	88,652	0	36,201	19,781	487,339	328,229	137,832	78,316	2,995	192,816	740,188	1,227,527
Imports	1,630	989	425	10,639	7,613	15,965	8,827	30,336	3,612	5,[illegible]51	3,532	4,895	3,949	0	2,960	19	100,541	52,021	9,995	28,174	1,563	2,494	94,248	194,789
Duty on imports	34	6	5	136	101	214	171	405	48	66	51	26	2	0	9	0	1,273	547	91	382	20	32	1,073	2,346
VAT	0	0	0	0	0	0	0	0	0	0	0	218	3,259	0	1,181	0	4,658	33,257	3,915	3,731	0	0	40,902	45,561
Duties and levies	211	2	103	1,175	344	176	460	331	1,378	130	1,275	2,026	896	0	344	36	8,887	22,713	434	0	0	0	23,147	32,034
Other taxes and sub sidies	-265	-25	-10	-50	-53	-46	-1,454	-212	-10	-34	-443	-404	-409	0	-186	-6	-3,607	4,559	-577	-45	4	-556	3,384	-223
Value added – Labour	7,143	1,409	1,822	10,151	15,790	18,529	9,691	36,483	5,492	29,947	61,877	35,191	70,149	60,316	69,067	0	433,059	0	0	0	0	0	0	433,059
Value added – Gross profits etc	4,388	10,428	738	8,432	4,786	9,536	6,250	11,074	9,118	1,505	27,820	15,406	44,549	3,527	4,381	33,440	195,376	0	0	0	0	0	0	195,376
Total inputs	24, 208	17, 704	5, 493	52, 108	49, 493	73, 649	57, 114	125, 992	41, 719	84, 404	154, 987	98, 540	211, 047	63, 843	113, 957	53, 269	1,227, 526	441, 325	151, 691	110, 558	4, 582	194, 786	902, 942	2,130, 468

Source: ONS, Input-Output Tables of the United Kingdom, 1995.

Figure A2
Impact of Tax Reform in Accumulation of Capital Stock Across Sectors

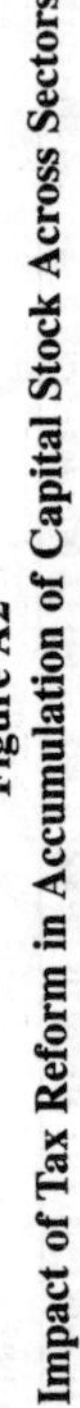

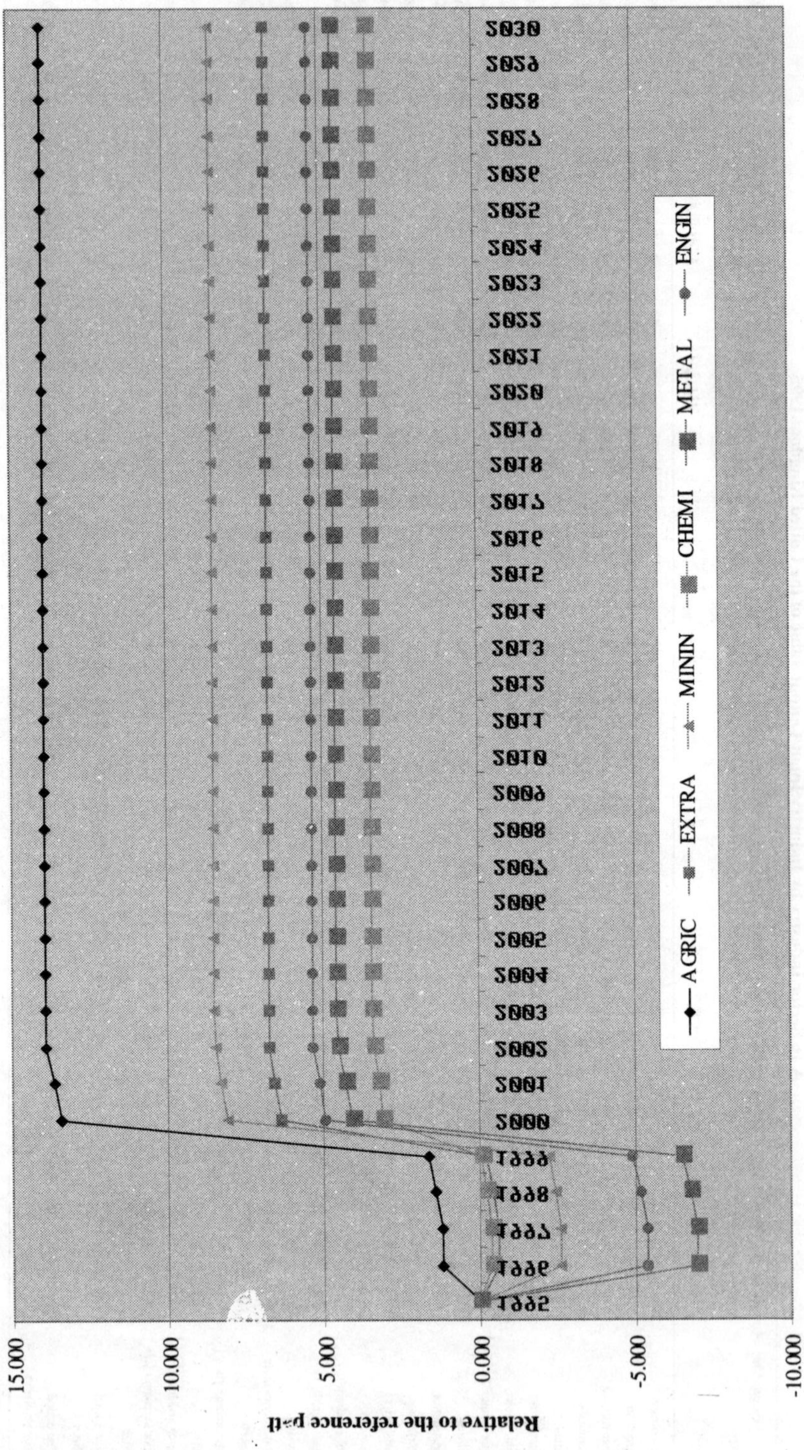

Table A3
Industry by Industry Import Use Matrix for the UK economy 1995

I x I Domestic Use Matrix	*Agricul-ture*	*Extrac-tion*	*Other-Mining*	*Chemi-cals*	*Metals*	*Engine-ering*	*Food, drink*	*Other Manuf.*	*Utili-ties*	*Constru-ction*	*Distri-bution*	*Trans-port*	*Finan-cial*	*Pub-lic Ad-min*	*Educ. Health,*	*Hous-ing*	*Total interme diate*	*Consu-mers' expen-diture*	*GG FC*	*GDF CF*	*Stocks*	*Exports*	*Total final demand*	*Total*
Agriculture	462	0	0	2	0	0	2,342	394	0	0	546	9	0	0	0	0	3,755	1,471	0	0	0	46	1,517	5,272
Extraction	0	133	0	1,532	0	0	0	0	1,613	0	0	0	0	0	0	0	3,278	0	0	0	0	0	0	3,278
Other Mining	0	0	68	359	540	31	4	50	312	540	0	0	0	0	0	0	1,905	29	3	0	0	2,003	2,035	3,941
Chemicals	802	11	142	7,931	1,028	1,274	844	7,476	382	196	165	609	22	0	299	0	21,182	2,259	873	0	199	165	3,495	24,677
Metals	26	180	57	222	5,249	2,251	378	1,745	0	1,690	64	0	0	0	0	0	11,863	0	0	3	220	0	222	12,085
Engineering	45	161	61	13	286	11,980	22	2,177	855	770	46	791	78	0	119	0	17,403	6,220	3,123	22,859	148	164	32,513	49,916
Food, drink	291	0	0	275	0	0	4,641	36	0	0	936	53	0	0	0	0	6,232	8,812	348	0	18	19	9,198	15,430
Other Manuf.	0	0	79	300	478	369	565	18,399	12	1,900	1,206	641	60	0	357	0	24,365	24,075	2,893	5,312	979	98	33,357	57,722
Utilities	0	0	0	3	4	1	2	3	432	0	0	0	0	0	0	0	446	0	0	0	0	0	0	446
Construction	0	0	0	0	0	0	0	0	0	44	0	0	0	0	0	0	44	0	0	0	0	0	0	44
Distribution	0	0	0	0	0	0	0	0	0	0	0	0	0	0	0	0	0	3,518	0	0	0	0	3,518	3,518
Transport	0	504	11	0	5	0	4	0	0	2	530	2,720	375	0	60	0	4,211	4,036	342	0	0	0	4,378	8,590
Financial	4	1	8	0	20	50	22	0	4	10	35	33	3,369	0	886	19	4,463	0	1,328	0	0	0	1,328	5,791
Public Admin	0	0	0	0	0	0	0	0	0	0	0	0	0	0	0	0	0	0	416	0	0	0	416	416
Educ. Health,	0	0	0	1	3	8	2	55	2	0	3	38	45	0	1,238	0	1,395	1,035	669	0	0	0	1,704	3,099
Housing	0	0	0	0	0	0	0	0	0	0	0	0	0	0	0	0	0	566	0	0	0	0	566	566
Total Imports	1,630	989	425	10,639	7,613	15,965	8,827	30,336	3,612	5,151	3,532	4,895	3,949	0	2,960	19	100,541	52,021	9,995	28,174	1,563	2,494	94,248	194,789

Source: ONS, Input-Output Tables of the United Kingdom, 1995.

elaborate specification of production sectors and the tax structure as close as possible to the UK economy. The essential features of it can be summarised in terms of the following five points.

1. We use the constant elasticity of substitution (CES) for the utility of an infinitely lived representative household, which allocates its lifetime income between consumption and savings and total time endowment between leisure and labour supply in order to maximise utility subject to its intertemporal budget constraint. The consumption, leisure and labour supply activities of households are related to each other. The representative household uses its time endowment either to supply labour to productive firms or to enjoy leisure. Its consumption level in turn depends upon labour and capital income and transfers. Besides its time endowment, the household is also endowed with the initial capital stock, which accumulates over time as savings provide for investment in each period. This household also owns production firms and acts as an investor to allocate the accumulated capital stock among various firms to maximise the rate of return from its investment activities. Intertemporal equilibrium is consistent with intra-temporal equilibrium among economic agents in each period. The government influences household decisions by means of taxes on labour and capital income and on consumption and transfers.
2. Firms use labour and capital as well as intermediate inputs to produce goods for the market while maximising their own profit over time. In this model the marginal productivity is the only investment criteria for investment across sectors. More productive sectors get more input as the investor is interested in gaining higher net of tax returns from each unit of investment. Tax distorted rates of return vary across sectors as taxes distort allocations affecting input or output prices, even shutting down investment in certain sectors that cannot promise reasonable net of tax returns.
3. Government plays a key role in the resource allocation process by means of its tax and transfer scheme. Its revenue comprises direct and indirect taxes and tariffs which is either spent on government consumption, or on provision of production subsidies to firms or to transfer income to the household. The government budget is balanced over time like that of the representative consumer or those of firms.
4. This model assumes a competitive global economy exporting and importing commodities to and from the rest of the world. We use the Armington specification of differentiated products in which imports are aggregated with domestic supply using CES function and domestic output is divided between domestic supplies and exports by a constant elasticity of transformation (CET) function. Export subsidies and import tariffs cause domestic prices to differ from those in the rest of the world (ROW).

The international payments are balanced as export earnings pay for imports over time.

5. The price mechanism plays a key role in allocating resources in this economy. Quantities and prices adjust until demands equal to supplies in goods, labour and financial markets. Tax wedges between basic and market prices distort the allocation of resources by firms and the consumer, which gives a less efficient outcome than that in a non-distorted economy.

SPECIFICATION OF THE MODEL

Intertemporal preferences and household demand

We assume forward-looking behaviour by consumers and producers, in the sense that they have perfect foresight with regard to their income, resources and prices of commodities in the economy. In the model, infinitely-lived households allocate lifetime income to maximise lifetime utility, which is defined as

$$\sum_{t=0}^{\infty} \beta^t \frac{U_t^{1-\sigma} - 1}{1-\sigma} \tag{1}$$

where *b* is the discount factor, which depends on the rate of time preference; U_t is composite commodity in the instantaneous utility function as given in (2). This composite commodity is made of consumption and leisure. We choose a constant relative risk aversion (CRRA) CES functional form for this utility function in (1)[1] in which *1/s* measures the elasticity of substitution between the present and future composite commodity. The smaller is *s*, the more slowly marginal utility falls as the quantity of the composite commodity rises, so households are more willing to allow changes in the composite commodity over time. Thus a smaller *s* implies a higher elasticity of substitution between current and future consumption or a higher degree of consumption smoothing and substitution over time.

Instantaneous utility *U* is a function of composite consumption and leisure:

$$U(C_t, L_t) = \left(\alpha_c C_t^{\frac{\gamma-1}{\gamma}} + (1-\alpha_c) L_t^{\frac{\gamma-1}{\gamma}} \right)^{\frac{\gamma}{\gamma-1}} \tag{2}$$

where C_t is composite consumption in period *t*, and L_t is leisure in period *t*. Here g represents the elasticity of substitution between consumption and leisure; the larger the value of g, the more responsive are consumption and labour supply to changes in commodity prices and wage rates.

The representative household faces an intertemporal budget constraint whereby the present value of its consumption and leisure in all periods cannot exceed the present value of infinite lifetime full income (wealth constraint). Life-time income in this model includes the value the household's labour endowment and other income:

$$\sum_{t=0}^{\infty} R_t^{-1}(P_t(1+t^{vc})C_t + w_t(1-t_l)L_t) = W \tag{3}$$

where, $R_t^{-1} = \prod_{s=0}^{t-1} 1/(1+r_s)$ is a discount factor; r_s represents the real interest rate on assets at time s; P_t is the price of composite consumption (which is based on goods' prices), t^{vc} is value added tax on consumption, t^l is labour income taxes, and C_t is composite consumption, which is composed of sectoral consumption goods, *i.e.* $P_t = \vartheta \prod_{i=1}^{n} \alpha_i p_{i,t}^{\alpha_i}$, and $C_t = \prod_{i=1}^{n} C_{i,t}^{\alpha_i}$ where α_i gives the share of spending on good i by the representative household, $C_{i,t}$ is a composite of domestic and foreign sector j products and $p_{i,t}$ its gross-of-tax price, and ϑ is a constant price index in the base year. W is the life time wealth of the household, defined as

$$W_{0,h} = \frac{J_{0,h}}{1+r_0^c} + \frac{J_{1,h}}{(1+r_0^c)(1+r_1^c)} + ... + \frac{J_{t,h}}{\Pi_s^t(1+r_s^c)} + ... = \sum_{t=0}^{\infty} \mu(t) J_{t,h} \tag{4}$$

where J_t is disposable household full income in period t, which includes the value of labour endowments and capital income plus transfers:

$$J_t = (1-t_l)w_t\bar{L}_t + (1-t_k)r_tK_t + TR_t \tag{4'}$$

where w_t is the wage rate, $\bar{L}_t$ is labour endowment, r_t is the rental rate of capital, K_t is the capital stock, TR_t is the transfer from the government to the household, t_l is the tax rate in labour and t_k is the tax rate in capital.

We combine equations (1) to (4) to form the Lagrangian for the consumer's inter-temporal allocation problem in (5).

$$\Im = \sum_{t=0}^{\infty}\left(\frac{1}{1+\rho}\right)^t \frac{\left(\left(\alpha_c C_t^{\frac{\gamma-1}{\gamma}} + (1-\alpha_c)L_t^{\frac{\gamma-1}{\gamma}}\right)^{\frac{\gamma}{\gamma-1}}\right)^{1-\sigma} - 1}{1-\sigma} + \lambda\left[\sum_{t=0}^{\infty} R_t^{-1}(P_t(1+t^{vd})C_t + w_t(1-t_l)L_t) - W_t\right] \tag{5}$$

Here, γ is the intratemporal elasticity of substitution between consumption and leisure, λ is the shadow price of income in terms of the present value of utility, and b in (1) is replaced by $\frac{1}{1+\rho}$, where $\rho > 0$ is the rate of time preference, which indicates the degree to which the household prefers leisure and consumption in earlier rather than in later years. The larger the value of, the more the household is willing to spend resources under its disposal earlier in life. This parameter is thus crucial in determining the amount of saving that the household wants to carry out in each period. Non-satiation in preferences implies that the inter-temporal budget constraint will hold with equality at an optimum.

The instantaneous utility function used to model intratemporal substitution possibilities by consumers contains three levels of nesting. At the top level, utility is a function of leisure and composite consumption, as in (1). How a single composite consumption good is made from sixteen sub-composite goods is shown in the second level of the nest. Finally each sub-composite good again represents a combination of domestic and imported goods. Elasticities of substitution used in actual calculations are given in Table 1.

Table 1
Basic Parameters of the UK Model

Steady state growth rate for sectors (g)	0.02
Net interest rate in non-distorted economy (r)	0.02
Reference quantity index of output, capital and labour for each sector, Q_{rf}	$(1+g)^{t-1}$
Reference index of price of output, capital and labour for each sector, P_{rf}	$1/(1+r)^{t-1}$
Elasticity of transformation between UK's domestic supplies and exports to the Rest of the World (ROW), σ_y	1.5
Elasticity of substitution between UK's domestic products and imports from Rest of the World (ROW), σ_m	1.5
Intertemporal elasticity of substitution, σ	0.5
Intra temporal elasticity of substitution between leisure and composite goods, γ	0.5
Elasticity of substitution in consumption goods across sectors, σ_c	0.5

Like consumption, investment and government consumption demand also comprise domestic and imported sources, but their composition depends on relative price of commodities.

Saving, investment, and labour supply

Economy wide savings, S_t, is the total of household savings (we assume that the government pursues a balanced budget policy over the model horizon). Household savings are the part of income that is not consumed:

$$S_t = J_t - P_t(1+t^{vc})C_t \tag{6}$$

For a given rate of time preference and inter-temporal rate of substitution (and if some other conditions are satisfied), individuals will save more when the rate of interest is higher than when it is lower. The lower the inter-temporal elasticity of substitution and the smaller the time preference parameter, the larger are the savings in the economy. A higher rate of interest on savings raises the cost of current consumption in terms of future consumption. At the same time, it lowers lifetime wealth as future income is discounted at a higher rate. The first effect tends to induce more savings, while the second tends to raise consumption. If the former effect dominates the latter, which is the case given our model parameterisation, savings will rise.

Note that, in reality, it is possible that the rate of return on saving received by households may be less than the cost of capital to the investors if financial intermediaries charge interest on the mobilisation of resources, the transaction cost of intermediation thus taking the form of a wedge between the prices faced by savers and investors. Here, we simply assume that the gross-of-intermediation cost of capital is equal to the return on savings.

Economy wide balance requires that income be equal to total expenditure. Government revenue is constrained to be equal to its expenditure. In the closed-capital market version of the model, we also assume trade balance (equality between the value of imports and the value of exports) in each period; whereas the trade balance must be satisfied in present value terms over the model horizon (see the next section) when we allow for international capital flows.

Investors employ savings to purchase investment goods. The market rental rate of capital is determined by the equality of the demand for and the supply of capital. Total investment demand equals the use of investment goods from domestic and imported sources:

$$I_t = \sum_i PD_{i,t} ID_{i,t} + \sum_i PM_{i,t} IM_{i,t} \tag{7}$$

where $ID_{i,t}$ is domestic supply of investment goods, and is imported investment goods. Ideally one would need to include a capital composition matrix to specify how a unit of investment good in a particular sector is made from the capital inputs from various sectors. In the absence of information on the sectoral composition of investment by sector of origin, we simply specify a composite investment good using information on total investment demand from the input-output table. This composite good is then allocated to sector-specific investment so as to equalize the marginal productivity of capital across sectors.Investment opportunities are arbitraged when the net rate of return from each investment activity does not exceed the rate of interest, and is equal to it when investment is undertaken at a positive level in that sector, *i.e.*

$$R_{i,t} - \delta_i \le r_t \quad I_{i,t} \ge 0 \quad I_{i,t}(R_{i,t} - \delta_i - r_t) = 0 \tag{8}$$

where $R_{i,t}$ is the gross-of-depreciation rate of return in sector i at time t, is the sector-specific depreciation rate, and r_t is the rate of interest at t. This arbitraging condition implies that sectors with higher gross return and lower depreciation rate generate more gross investment demand. On a balanced-growth path, investment will grow at the same rate in all sectors, and the return to capital will be equalized everywhere. However, during the transition to a balanced-growth path, it is possible for the net return in a sector to fall below the return elsewhere in the economy, and, as a result, for investment to "shut down" in that sector.

Sectoral assets are subject to economic depreciation. Thus, in every period, gross sectoral investment replenishes depleted capital, and increases the capital stock (*net* investment). Capital accumulation in sector i in period $t+1$ then is given by the capital stock of period t net of depreciation and investment:

$$K_{i,t+1} = K_{i,t}(1 - \delta_i) + I_{i,t} \tag{9}$$

Growth in sectoral output depends both upon the growth of employment and the growth of the capital stock in that sector. On a balanced-growth path, where all prices are constant and all real economic variables grow at a constant rate, capital stocks must grow at a fast enough rate to sustain growth. This condition can be expressed as

$$I_{i,T} = K_{i,T}(g + \delta_i) \tag{10}$$

where the subscript T denotes the terminal period of the model.

For simplicity, in the open capital markets version of the dynamic model we simply assume the UK to be a price taker in capital markets, and allow capital inflows and outflows to take place so as to ensure that the UK rate of interest remains constant and equal to the world rate of return. A more realistic analysis of capital asset flows would require a model structure where the UK economy is explicitly modelled as part of the global economy.

Labour supply, LS_t, for each household is given by the difference between the household labour endowment, and the demand for leisure, .

$$LS_t = \bar{L}_t - L_t \tag{11}$$

In equilibrium, the wage rate must be such that the labour supplied by the household equals the total demand for labour derived from the profit maximising behaviour of firms (as set out in the following section).

Technology and trade

The structure of production in the model is shown in Figure A2 in the appendix. At the bottom of the figure one type of composite capital stock[2] combines with labour to form value added for the sixteen sectors in the model. Then this value added aggregate combines with domestic and imported intermediate inputs from sixteen sectors to produce gross output for each sector. Gross output is either sold in domestic markets or exported to the rest of the world.

Following a well-established convention in open-economy applied general equilibrium models, we adopt an "Armington (1969)" specification whereby products are differentiated according to the location of production. Thus domestic and imported goods, even in the same sector, are qualitatively different and are not perfect substitutes, and intra-industry trade can occur (Shoven and Whalley (1984), Devarajan and Lewis (1990), Harrison, Rutherford and Tarr (1997)). The Armington aggregation function, with given shares and substitution elasticity, describes how the domestic and imported goods are combined:

$$A_{i,t} = \Phi\left(\left(\delta_i^d\right)^{\frac{1}{\sigma_m}} D_{i,t}^{\frac{\sigma_m - 1}{\sigma_m}} + \left(\delta_i^m\right)^{\frac{1}{\sigma_m}} M_{i,t}^{\frac{\sigma_m - 1}{\sigma_m}} \right)^{\frac{\sigma_m}{\sigma_m - 1}} \tag{12}$$

where $A_{i,t}$ is the Armington CES aggregate of domestic supplies $D_{i,t}$ and import supplies $M_{i,t}$ for each sector, δ_i^d is the share of domestically produced goods, δ_i^m is the share of good i imports, σ_m is the elasticity of substitution in the aggregate supply function, and Φ is the shift parameter of the aggregate supply function.

The aggregate value of supply in the economy must be equal to the sum of the values of domestic supplies and imports:

$$PA_{i,t} A_{i,t} = PD_{i,t} D_{i,t} + PM_{i,t} M_{i,t} \tag{13}$$

where $D_{i,t}$ and $M_{i,t}$ are domestic and import supplies respectively, $PD_{i,t}$ is gross price of domestic supplies, $PM_{i,t}$ is price of imported goods gross of tariffs, and $PA_{i,t}$ is the gross price of composite commodity i.

Overall market clearing in the product market implies

$$A_{i,t} = CC_{i,t} + G_{i,t} + I_{i,t} + \sum_j DI_{i,j,t} + \sum_j MI_{i,j,t} \tag{14}$$

where $CC_{i,t}$ is composite consumption, $G_{i,t}$ and $I_{i,t}$ represent composite consumption by the government and investment respectively (discussed below), $DI_{i,j}$ is the demand for domestic intermediate input and $MI_{i,j}$ is demand for imported intermediate inputs,.

Domestic supply, $D_{i,t}$, in equations (15,16), is the part of gross output sold in the domestic market. The rest of domestic output is exported. The split between domestic sales and exports is given by a constant elasticity transformation function:

$$GY_{i,t} = \Theta\left((1-\delta_i^e) D_{i,t}^{\frac{\sigma_y - 1}{\sigma_y}} + \delta_i^e E_{i,t}^{\frac{\sigma_y - 1}{\sigma_y}} \right)^{\frac{\sigma_y}{\sigma_y - 1}} \tag{15}$$

where $GY_{i,t}$ is output (gross of intermediate inputs), $E_{i,t}$ is exports, $D_{i,t}$ is domestic supplies, σ_y is the elasticity of transformation in total supply, δ_i^e is the share of exports, and Θ is the shift or scale parameter in the transformation function. The value of gross supplies in the economy must be equal to the sum of the gross values of domestic supplies and exports:

$$P_{i,t} GY_{i,t} = PD_{i,t} D_{i,t} + PE_{i,t} E_{i,t} \tag{16}$$

where $D_{i,t}$ and $E_{i,t}$ are domestic and export supplies respectively, $PD_{i,t}$ is gross prices of domestic supplies, $PE_{i,t}$ is price of exported goods gross of export taxes, and $P_{i,t}$ is the price of domestic supplies of commodity *i*.

The import and export prices in equations (16) and (20) will generally differ from domestic prices because of tariffs and export taxes applied considering product differentiation between domestic and foreign products. The gross-of-export-tax prices of exportable goods and the gross-of-tariff prices of importable commodities tend to get closer to world prices as the elasticity of transformation between domestic sales and exports in production and the elasticity of substitution between domestically produced goods and imports in consumption approach infinity.

On the production front, producers use labour and capital in each of *N* sectors to produce value added. The amount of each type of these inputs employed by a producer in a particular sector is based upon the sector specific production technology and input prices. We use a CES function to express this relationship:

$$Y_{i,t} = \Omega_i \left((1-\delta_i)(K_{i,t})^{\gamma_i} + \delta_i (LS_{i,t})^{\gamma_i} \right)^{\frac{1}{\gamma_i}} \tag{17}$$

where $Y_{i,t}$ is the gross value added of sector i, Ω_i is a shift or scale parameter in the production function, $K_{i,t}$ and $LS_{i,t}$ are the amounts of capital and labour used in sector *i*, δ_i is the share parameter of labour in production, and γ_i is the CES substitution elasticity parameter. This is a constant return to scale production function. Euler's product exhaustion theorem implies that total output (value added) equals payments to labour and capital and each factor receives remuneration at the rate of its marginal productivity:

$$PY_{i,t}Y_{i,t} = w_t LS_{i,t} + r_t K_{i,t} \tag{18}$$

where w_t is the gross-of-tax wage rate and r_t is the gross rental rate of capital.

The relationship between the intermediate inputs and gross output is expressed by input-output coefficients, which form a fixed physical non-price based constraint in the production system. The general form of production function is

$$GY_{i,t} = \min\left(Y_{i,t}, \left(\frac{DI_{i,j,t}}{a^d_{i,j}}\right)_{i=j}, \left(\frac{MI_{i,j,t}}{a^m_{i,j}}\right)_{i=j}\right) \tag{19}$$

where $a^d_{i,j}$ are input-output coefficients for domestic supply of intermediate goods; $a^m_{i,j}$ are input-output coefficients for imported supply of intermediate goods, $DI_{i,j}$ is the supply of domestic intermediate input and $MI_{i,j}$ is the supply of imported intermediate inputs. The presence of input-output linkages in the model enables us to assess various kinds of backward and forward impacts of policy changes. For instance a tax on agricultural output has a direct effect on demands for agricultural goods, and a backward impact that spreads to many other sectors which provide inputs to that sector. Similarly, through forward linkages, the tax affects the cost of agricultural inputs to other sectors.

The objective of a firm in the *j*th sector of the economy is to maximise the present value of profits subject to production technology constraints. Sectoral profits are given by the differences between the revenue from sales and the cost of supply. The unit revenue function is a constant elasticity transformation (CET) composite of the unit price of domestic sales and the unit price of exports. The unit costs are divided between value-added, i.e. payments to labour and capital, and domestic and imported intermediate inputs:

$$\Pi^y_{j,t} = [((1-\delta^e_i)PD_{i,t}^{\frac{\sigma_y - 1}{\sigma_y}} + \delta^e_i PE_{i,t}^{\frac{\sigma_y - 1}{\sigma_y}})]^{\frac{1}{\sigma_y - 1}}$$

$$-\theta^v_j PY^v_{j,t} - \theta^d_j \sum_i a^d_{i,j} P_{i,t} - \theta^m_j \sum_i a^m_{i,j} PM_{j,t} \tag{20}$$

where: $\Pi^y_{j,t}$ is the unit profit of activity in sector *j*; $PE_{j,t}$ is the export price of good *j* $PD_{j,t}$ is the domestic price of good *j*; $PY^v_{j,t}$ is the price of value added per unit of output in activity *j*; s_y is a transformation elasticity parameter ; $P_{i,t}$ is the price of final goods used as intermediate goods; δ_j^e is the share parameter for exports in total production; θ_j^v is the share of costs paid to labour and capital; θ_j^d is the cost share of domestic intermediate inputs; θ_j^m is the cost share of imported intermediate inputs; $a_{i,j}^d$ are input-output coefficients for domestic supply of intermediate goods; $a_{i,j}^m$ are input-output coefficients for imported supply of intermediate goods.

In equilibrium, with free entry and perfect competition, profits will be zero in each period. The zero-profit condition for sector j in period t can be written in dual form in terms of composite prices of commodities and inputs (see appendix for details):

$$\Pi_{j,t}^y \leq 0 \tag{21}$$

With respect to international trade, zero trade balance is a property of any general equilibrium model. In the version with no international capital flows, we have, therefore, assumed that the value of exports (gross of UK taxes and subsidies) equals the value of imports (net of UK taxes and subsidies) in equilibrium in each period:

$$\sum_i PE_{i,t} E_{i,t} = \sum_i PM_{i,t} M_{i,t} \tag{22}$$

No inter-temporal borrowing occurs in this case. In the version with international capital flows, this condition must be satisfied in the present value terms, *i.e.*

$$\sum_t (1+r^W)^{-t} \sum_i PE_{i,t} E_{i,t} = \sum_t (1+r^W)^{-t} \sum_i PM_{i,t} M_{i,t} \tag{23}$$

where r^W is the world rate of interest.

Public consumption

The government collects revenue from various taxes and spends that revenue to purchase goods and services for public consumption and to make transfers to households.

The value of government consumption is given by

$$G = \sum_i PA_i GD_i + \sum_i PA_i GM_i \tag{24}$$

where GD_i is government consumption of domestic goods, and GM_i is government consumption of imported goods. Like households, the government chooses between domestic and imported goods for its consumption on the basis of their relative prices.

Tax revenue is collected through taxes on capital and labour income and value added taxes on final demand, production taxes on intermediate inputs, and tariffs on imports:

$$REV_t = \sum_i t_i^k r_t K_{i,t} + \sum_i t_i^{vc} P_{i,t} CC_{i,t} + \sum_i t_i^{vg} P_{i,t} G_{i,t} + \sum_i t_i^{vk} P_{i,t} I_{i,t}$$

$$+ \sum_i t_l w LS_t + \sum_i t_i^m PM_{i,t} M_{i,t} + \sum_i t_i^p P_{i,t} GY_{i,t} \qquad (25)$$

where REV_t is total government revenue and t_i^k is a composite tax rate on capital income from sector *i*. These rates are derived from the P-Tax model of capital income tax rates, originally written by King and Robson (1988) using methodology devised by King and Fullerton (1984); and used in the Inland Revenue for a number of years. t_l^{vc} is the *ad valorem* tax rate on final consumption by households, t_i^{vg} is that on public consumption and t_i^{vk} is the ad valorem tax rate on investment, t_l is the tax rate on labour income of the household, t_i^p is the tax on production, and t_i^m is the tariff on imports. All of these taxes, particularly when they are levied at different rates on different sectors and households, have distortionary impacts on the allocation of resources in the economy.

Tax revenues are either used to finance public consumption, or to make transfers to households in lump sum form:

$$REV_t = G_t + TR_t \qquad (26)$$

Definition of a dynamic competitive equilibrium

A dynamic competitive equilibrium is a combination of sequences of prices of gross output $P_{i,t}$, price of domestic supplies, $PD_{i,t}$; import prices, $PM_{i,t}$; export prices, $PE_{i,t}$; prices of value added, $PY_{i,t}$; prices of capital goods, $P_{j,t}^k$; prices of terminal capital, $PTK_{j,t}$; wage rates of labour, w_t; prices of government services, PG_t; values of transfers to households, PR_t; prices of composite of consumption and leisure, PU_t; rental rate of capital for each sector, r_1^k : R+ ®R, and sequences of gross output, $GY_{i,t}$; total supply of domestic intermediate inputs, $DI_{i,j,t}$ and imported intermediate inputs, $MI_{i,j,t}$; sectoral capital stock, $K_{i,t}$; labour demands, $LS_{i,t}$; value added, $Y_{i,t}$; sectoral investment, $I_{i,t}$; exports, $E_{i,t}$;

imports, $M_{i,t}$ government revenue, REV_t; services, G_t; consumption of households, CC_t; labour supply, LS_t and leisure demand, L_t; and level of household utility from consumption, U_t, such that given these prices and quantities, the following conditions are satisfied:

1. households maximise inter-temporal utility subject to their wealth constraint;
2. investors maximise inter-temporal profits subject to arbitrage conditions in capital markets;
3. producers minimise costs subject to technology constraints;
4. unit profits are zero in all production sectors;
5. markets for goods and services clear;
6. the government account constraint is satisfied;
7. the balance of payments condition is fulfilled
8. the economy grows at a constant rate beyond a certain terminal period *T*.

In such an equilibrium, consumers have perfect foresight, capital accumulation is consistent with household's and producers' optimisation and income and expenditures balance over the life period. An agent is doing the best he or she can in light of actions taken by others, and actions taken together are feasible given technologies and resources.

DYNAMIC CALIBRATION[1]

The dynamics in this model arise from an endogenous process of capital accumulation and exogenous growth rate of the labour force. We rule out uncertainty and rely on the perfect foresight of households and firms, which means that actual and expected values of variables are the same. Leisure is assumed to be 75 percent of net of tax wage income in this model. We have a single vintage of capital. Embodiment of technical progress through multiple vintages of capital, though important from practical point of view, has not been modelled here because of complexity in computation. Consistency of this dynamic model is assured by replication of the benchmark economy (Rutherford (1995,1998), Bhattarai (1997, 1999), Lau et. al (2002)).

There are essentially five steps involved in calibration of this dynamic model. The first step relates to forming a relation between the price of investment good at period *t*, P_t and the price of capital in period *t+1*, P^k_{t+1}. It also needs specifying a link between prices of capital stock at periods *t* and *t+1*, P^k_t and, with due account of the rental on capital and the depreciation rate. For instance, one unit of investment made using one unit of output in period *t* produces one unit of capital stock in period *t+1*. This implies,, where is the price of one output in period *t* and is the *t* period price of one unit of capital in period *t+1*.

Capital depreciates at the rate of δ . One unit of capital at the beginning of period *t* earns a rental R_t^l and delivers (*1-d*) units of capital at the end of period *t* (or at the start of the *t+1* period), $(1-\delta)P_{t+1}^k$. Here R_t^l is also measured in term of P_{t+1}^K or P_t .We therefore must have:

$$P_t^k = R_t^l + (1-\delta)P_{t+1}^k \tag{27}$$

In a perfect foresight world price of capital in period *t* really reflects the sum of discounted rental over time. A sum of geometric series of declining values of investment income can be used to expand terms for P_t^K and P_{t+1}^K as following:

$$P_t^K = R_t^l + \frac{R_t^l(1-\delta)}{1+r} + .. = R_t^l\left(\frac{1+r}{r+\delta}\right) \tag{28}$$

$$P_{t+1}^K = R_t^l(1-\delta) + \frac{R_t^l(1-\delta)^2}{1+r} + .. = R_t^l\left(\frac{1+r}{r+\delta}\right)(1-\delta) \tag{29}$$

A unit of capital generates less revenue next period because of depreciation, $R_{t+1}^l = R_t^l(1-\delta)$. The second step of calibration involves setting up a link of the rental rate with the benchmark interest rate and the depreciation. The rental covers depreciation and interest payment for each unit of investment. When rental is paid at the end of the period

$$R_t^l = (r+\delta)P_t^k \tag{30}$$

where *r* is the benchmark real rate of interest. If the rental rates are paid in the beginning of the period *t* then from intertemporal arbitrage the equation (28) changes to $\frac{R_t^l}{P_{t+1}^k} = \frac{r+\delta}{1+r}$.

Third step of calibration involves forming relation between the future and the current price of capital. Use equation (28) and (29) together to get

$$\frac{P_{t+1}^k}{P_t^k} = \frac{1}{1+r} \approx (1-\delta) \tag{31}$$

This means that the ratio of prices of the capital at period *t* and *t+1* equals to the market discount factor in the model, which is $(1-\delta)$. This discount factor can also be approximated by $\frac{1}{1+r}$. In addition, the spot price of capital stock in period *t+1* equals ${}_{t+1}P_{t+1}^{K} = \frac{R_t'(1-\delta)(1+r)}{(r+\delta)}$. When an expectation is made in period *t* about the period *t+1* it needs to be discounted by factor $\frac{1}{1+r}$. That means expected price of a unit of *t+1* capital at *t* is given by ${}_{t}P_{t+1}^{K} = \frac{R_t'(1-\delta)}{(r+\delta)}$. In equation (28) above we have spot price of unit of capital defined as ${}_{t}P_{t}^{K} = \frac{R_t'(1+r)}{(r+\delta)}$. Thus the ratio of price of capital in period *t* and *t+1* is $\frac{{}_{t}P_{t+1}^{k}}{{}_{t}P_{t}^{k}} = \frac{1-\delta}{1+r}$. In this case both the discount rate and δ the benchmark interest rate *r* are involved in linking price of capital at periods *t* and *t+1*.

The fourth step of calibration involves setting up equilibrium relation between capital earning (value added from capital) and the cost of capital. We compute values for sectoral capital stocks from sectoral capital earnings in the base year. If capital income in sector *i* in the base year is $\bar{V}_i$, we can write $\bar{V}_i = R_i K_i$. Since the return to capital must be sufficient to cover interest and depreciation, we can also write

$$\bar{V}_i = (r+\delta_i)P_{t+1}^{k} K_i, \quad \text{or} \quad K_i = \frac{\bar{V}_i}{(r+\delta_i)}. \qquad \text{Since } P_t = P_{t+1}^{k} = 1 \tag{32}$$

The fifth step of calibration involves setting up relation between the investment and capital earning on the balanced growth path[1]. Investment should be enough to provide for growth and depreciation, $I_i = (g_i + \delta_i)K_i$, which together with (32) implies

$$I_i = \frac{(g_i+\delta_i)}{(r+\delta_i)} \bar{V}_i \tag{33}$$

The balance between investment and earnings from capital is restored here by adjustment in the growth rate g_i that responds to changes in the marginal productivity of capital associated to changes in investment. Readjustment of capital stock and investment continues until this growth rate and the benchmark interest rates become equal.

If the growth rate in sector i is larger than the benchmark interest rate then more investment will be drawn to that sector. The capital stock in that sector rises as more investment takes place setting the diminishing return on capital. Eventually the declining marginal productivity of capital retards growth in that sector. We also have built scenarios for closed and open capital markets and anticipated and unanticipated tax reforms. The lending and borrowing is permitted in response to trade imbalances in the open capital market case. The households and producers use announced tax rates in the base year instead of current ones in anticipated scenario while they use existing taxes until the reform occurs in the unanticipated scenario.

Thus investment per sector is tied to earnings per sector. In the benchmark equilibrium, all reference quantities grow at the rate of labour force growth, g, and reference prices are discounted on the basis of the benchmark rate of return as given by equation (31) above.

To solve the model, we allow for a time horizon sufficient for a balanced-growth path to be attained. In our simulations we use a sixty-five year horizon. In practice, the model's variables typically converge to an approximate balanced-growth path after about twenty to thirty years. We formulate and solve the model using the GAMS/MPSGE software (Rutherford (1995), Brook et. al. (1992)).

PARAMETERS, ELASTICITIES AND TAX RATES

The model is calibrated following the steps outlined above using a micro consistent data set for the UK economy for the year 1995 (Siddorn (1999)). Implicitly, following a general practice in the applied equilibrium analysis, we assume that the UK economy was on a balanced-growth path in that year. Once the model is calibrated in this way, the baseline growth path shows how the economy would move forward, *ceteris paribus*, if the current economic policies were to continue.

Besides capital stocks for each production sector, a careful selection of other model parameters is crucial to the general equilibrium analysis of model results. The intertemporal rate of substitution in the household's utility function, the elasticity of substitution between composite consumption and leisure, the elasticity of substitution between domestic and imported commodities and the elasticity of substitution between the capital and labour inputs in production are the crucial parameters which determine the behaviour of the current model. It also needs the elasticity of transformation between domestic and foreign trade, popularly known as the Armington (1969) elasticity, the growth rate of the labour force, the benchmark rate of interest, and rates of depreciation by sector. Table 1 and Table 2 list the values assumed for these parameters in the current model.

The capital income tax rate for each sector, as given in Table 2, is derived from the asset specific tax rates obtained from the calculations of the P-TAX model received from the Inland Revenue. The P-tax calculates tax wedge using sector specific financial structure and depreciation allowances for each type of asset. The wide variation in these rates across sectors thus not only reflects statutory rates but also underlying differences in depreciation allowances and debt-equity or self-financing structure. Taxes on building type assets were higher than for plant and machinery or for the vehicles type assets for each sector in the benchmark. Further more, effective tax rates were higher if the investment project were financed by debt rather than equities. Sectors that had a larger proportion of building asset and relied on debt financing such as the financial services, education and public administration sector and agricultural sector had higher effective rates of capital income taxes.

Table 2
Depreciation, Capital Income and Indirect Tax Rates (%)

Industry	*Elasticity substitution between labour and capital (y)*	*Deprecia-tion rate (annual %)*	*Capital income tax rate*	*Indirect tax on private consump-tion*	*Indirect tax on public consump-tion*	*Indirect tax on invest-ment*	*Produc-tion tax rates*	*Tariff rates*
Agric	1.2	8.3	41.4	1.6	7.7		-10.9	2.5
Extra	1.7	16.6	26.2					2.5
Minin	1.5	10.4	31.0	12.5			-0.6	2.5
Chemi	1.7	5.6	24.0	15.4	8.3		14.3	2.5
Metal	1.6	5.4	25.3			3.8	0.0	2.5
Engin	1.5	6.0	27.6		31.1	4.9	0.0	2.5
Food	1.0	5.4	28.0	17.0	3.5		12.2	2.5
Othma	0.9	6.4	26.2	26.3	19.	6.1	0.0	2.5
Power	1.5	4.1	28.9	5.7	22.1		3.4	2.5
Constr	1.0	9.4	30.3	13.3	27.8	2.5	-0.1	
Distr	1.6	5.9	33.9	4.4			5.4	
Trans	1.6	7.5	29.7	8.3	15.3	0.1	-2.2	2.5
Finan	1.6	6.9	41.9	1.0	11.0	0.3	2.0	2.5
PubAD	1.6	4.	45.8					2.5
EducA	1.6	3.8	48.1	7.5	0.6		1.9	2.5
House	1.0	2.0					-0.3	2.5

Source and Notes: We have done some sensitivity analysis while choosing the values of the elasticity of substitution between labour and capital. These values are close to those used by Piggott and Whalley (1985). The aggregate depreciation rate per sector is derived from the P-tax sector-asset specific discount rates (King and Robson (1988); tax and tariff rates rely on Bhattarai (1999) and Siddorn (1998).

TAX POLICY EXPERIMENTS: EQUAL-YIELD TAX REFORMS

By removing distortions equal yield tax reforms aim for an efficient, fair and simple tax system holding revenue constant. However, there are several practical question relating to the tax base, information about the tax reform and the level of distortions due to one tax versus another. Should revenue be raised by direct or indirect taxes? Should it be from capital or labour income? Are the effects of tax reforms different when people have some anticipation of future taxes or when such reforms come all of a sudden? Are the impacts of reform different in closed capital markets or open capital markets? These are key issues that we would like to answer by assessing the dynamic efficiency and reallocation effects of taxes using the dynamic tax model described in the previous section. In each equal yield tax reform we ask what happens if we replace the differentiated tax rates existing in the UK in 1995 by uniform rates across all sectors. The actual benchmark tax rates as reported in Table 2 and their counterfactual rates for our analysis are as given in Table 3 below. Removing distortions with lower uniform rates of one particular tax instead of its benchmark rates may reduce or increase the overall distortions in the economy. Efficiency gains are expected to be positive if that tax has more distortionary impact on production and consumption than other taxes in the system, while efficiency losses may occur if less distortionary taxes are replaced by more distortionary taxes in order to maintain the equal yield constraint. Therefore whether aggregate welfare improves by changing one particular tax depends on its degree of relative distortions rather than in absolute tax rates.

Table 3
Counterfactual tax rates in the dynamic UK model

Tax	*Capital income tax rate*	*Indirect tax on private consumption*	*Indirect tax on public consumption*	*Indirect tax on invest ment*	*Production tax rates*	*Tariff rates*	*Household income tax rate*
Counterfactual tax rates	25.0	10.0	5.0	5.0	5.0	1.0	15.0

We use overall efficiency gains to measure the impact of a tax reform. These gains are measures in terms of changes in money metric utility to the consumer relative to that in the base year, which is computed as the change in the present value of lifetime utility relative to base expressed as a percentage of base year UK GDP as:

$$UW = 100 \quad (LU - 1)\frac{C_0}{GDP_0} \tag{34}$$

here UW is a measure of the present value of welfare to the representative household for the period of the model horizon, LU is the unit of composite lifetime utility which is equal to one in the base case solution, C_0 is the composite of consumption and leisure in the base year, and GDP_0 is the base year GDP (the adjustment factor $\frac{C_0}{GDP_0}$ corrects for the fact that the value of household composite consumption in the model includes the value of leisure and excludes government consumption).

Table 4
Efficiency effects of tax reform in the dynamic UK model
Change in life time utility as a percentage of base GDP (%)

	Closed capital market with no anticipation	*Closed capital market with anticipation*	*Open capital market with no anticipation*
Capital income tax	0.699	0.633	0.768
Labour income tax	-2.054	-2.054	-2.195
Production tax	1.421	1.284	1.442
Investment tax	-0.085	-0.048	-0.106
Household consumption tax	0.112	0.557	0.693
Government consumption tax	0.297	0.256	0.317
Tariffs	0.070	0.053	0.081

The dynamic welfare gains of equal yield tax reform associated with seven different taxes for three different scenarios are as shown in Table 4. The efficiency gain from reform of five different taxes, as set out in Table 2 and 3 above, with the equal-yield constraint is positive. This indicates removal of sector specific distortions in the economy. Model results show loss in welfare with reform in investment and labour income taxes. The welfare loss in case of investment tax reflects an increase in the tax rate in the counterfactual scenarios because tax rates were lower in the benchmark case. The negative welfare gains from the labour income tax reform, when its rate is reduced from 25 to 15 percent indicates that the labour income tax is less distortionary than other taxes. As its rate declines it causes more distortions in the system as there is an equi-proportional increase in other more distortionary taxes. A reduction in revenue due to lower labour income taxes has to be compensated by higher rates of more distortionary taxes to meet the equal yield constraint.

In the "anticipated" scenario, we assume that private agents can foresee the tax change occurring five years before it is implemented, and can therefore immediately adjust their choices in anticipation of the change. People do not know about tax changes in advance in unanticipated scenario. Welfare gains, which are generally lower with anticipation than without anticipation, reflect the fact that producers, traders, government and owners of capital are more capable of adjusting their economic behaviour when they know how taxes are going to change in the future. The presence of announcement effects, however, has an ambiguous effect on the welfare impacts of tax reform. On the one hand, announcing tax changes in advance enables the private sector to better adjust to the change, immediately undoing some of the distortions associated with the taxes to be reduced. On the other hand, when new distortionary policies are introduced, announcing policy changes in advance actually raises the efficiency costs of the policy, as individuals' choices are immediately affected by the change. The model solutions show that dynamic welfare effects are generally larger when there are international capital flows.

The efficiency gains or losses signal underlying quantity and price adjustments across sectors because of the above taxes. Capital income tax reform impacts growth path of the economy. Model-based numerical simulations for the various experiments provide results that show impacts on sectoral investment, capital stocks, output and employment relative to the baseline "business as usual" reference path case. We report series of capital stock across the sectors in the appendix.

When capital income tax rates, which range from 24 percent in the chemical sector to 48 percent in the education sector in the base year, are set to a uniform twenty-five percent rate in the counterfactual scenario, it has positive impact on the growth path of investment, capital stock, employment and output across all sectors relative to their benchmark. In an unanticipated case it raises investment by more than fifteen percent in production sectors and other sectors, before it settles down between five and fifteen percent above the reference path of the economy. The agriculture, finance, distribution, mining and construction sectors, which are relatively more distorted in the benchmark, experience more expansion than other sectors. In contrast, housing investment shuts down for more than five years and remains depressed afterwards.

Capital stocks in each sector follow the growth in investment. In the long run, the capital stock in agriculture remains above fifteen percent higher than in the baseline; other sectors experience a ten percent increase compared to the reference path (see Figures A1 and A2 in the appendix for instance). This again depends on the degree of distortion in that particular sector in the benchmark. For instance, the growth path of the capital stock in the chemical sector does not deviate much from the reference path, due to the capital tax rate in that sector remaining relatively unaffected by the reform.

The general pattern of investment and capital stock effects described above is not very different in closed and open capital market except that the convergence is faster and smoother in the open capital market case than with closed capital markets.

Besides inter-sectoral asset reallocation, changes in the relative user cost of capital have a significant effect on employment across sectors. When capital inputs become relatively cheaper than the labour input, producers tend to substitute capital for labour. As outlined above, capital becomes relatively cheaper in certain sectors such as agriculture, finance, public administration, and education, and relatively expensive in some other sectors, particularly manufacturing, after a uniform tax reform.

The levels of employment and output under a uniform capital income tax reform remain within –5 and 5 percent of the reference path in this model. Growth of the agriculture sector is above the reference path across all market scenarios, while that of the engineering sector remains below the reference path in all scenarios. This reflects the fact that the capital income tax in the agriculture sector has reduced from 41 percent to 25 percent and it has a relatively lower depreciation rate compared to other sectors. The construction sector experiences a big shock after the tax change, but bounces back to above the benchmark reference path over time.

The presence of announcement effects causes investment to begin adjusting earlier, in anticipation of the new taxes. When tax changes are known in advance, there are incentives, immediately after the announcement, to postpone investment to periods where it enjoys relatively better tax treatment. As the time of the reform approaches, however, investment changes go in the same directions as the post-reform changes (with the exception of the initial spike immediately following the reform).

Looking at these numbers on investment and capital stock we may conclude that the impact of capital income tax reform varies across sectors and the size of this impact depends upon the benchmark rates of capital income tax and depreciation. Sectors subject to higher tax rates and lower depreciation rates in the benchmark realise growth paths significantly above the reference path of the economy and sectors with lower tax and depreciation rates stay on or below the reference path.

The general equilibrium impacts of capital income tax changes affect the reference paths of employment and output but the size of the employment and output effects are smaller than those on investment and capital stock by sector. Changes in the capital stock have some knock on effects on employment and then on output. Output effects are more extreme in the extraction and distribution sectors, which are more capital-intensive than service sectors such as public administration and education. Our above empirical findings on aggregate and sector specific impacts of capital income taxes for the UK economy are also close to the conclusions of some other studies on the US economy as analysed in Boskin (1978), Fullerton, Shoven, and Whalley (1983) and Auerbach and Kotlikoff (1987).

In contrast to positive impacts of capital income tax reform, a reduction in the labour income tax rate from 24 percent in the benchmark economy to 15 percent in the counterfactual depresses investment, capital stock, output and employment in all but the housing sector. Given the equal-yield constraint, the reduction in revenue due to lower labour income taxes causes equi-proportional increases in other taxes. This is the main reason for such depressing impacts of reducing labour income tax which contributes to 55 percent of the total tax revenue in the economy, with the dynamic efficiency loss of 2.05% of the base year GDP as reported earlier. Though labour taxes may influence the labour leisure choice of individuals, given the structure of this model it is more "neutral" than any other taxes. More elaborate explanation of redistribution impacts of taxes is outside the scope of the current model, which has only a representative agent.

Besides capital and labour income taxes this model contains five other taxes: production tax, tax on investment goods, taxes on private consumption, taxes on public consumption and a tariff.

When we replace all sector-specific production tax rates in the benchmark, which vary from –11 to 14 percent in the base year, by a uniform rate of 5 percent, it has a positive impact both on growth and efficiency. Investment, capital stock, employment and output expand. The overall efficiency effect of the replacement is a sizeable 1.4 percent of the base year GDP. There is little variation between the open and closed capital markets cases.

Reform of indirect tax rates on investment goods exhibits a very different pattern of impacts on the model economy in comparison with other experiments, and we see a significant difference between the open and closed capital market scenarios, with and without announcement effects. Since investment taxes are small in the benchmark, however, all the associated impacts are relatively modest. In the long run, the growth paths of most sectors are 2 percent above or below the reference path. The efficiency loss from moving to a uniform 5 percent investment tax from the existing differentiated but lower tax rates ranges from 0.08 percent to -0.1 percent of base year GDP, suggesting that this tax is relatively more distortionary than other taxes.

In the current model tax rates on household consumption[5] vary from 1.6 percent in the agriculture sector to 26 percent in 'other manufactures' in the base year. In our experiment, these differentiated rates are replaced by a flat ten percent rate. The pattern of growth effects relative to the reference path varies significantly across sectors. Production sectors generally experience higher growth rates relative to the reference path while other sectors experience a negative impact. This pattern is very different from what we observe for other tax experiments, because consumers are less able to shift the burden of taxes in comparison to producers. Tax relieves on consumption increases demand by reducing distortions in relative prices faced by consumers and raises the effective wage rate for the household.

Taxes on public consumption vary from 0.6 percent to 32 percent in the data. Such differentiated tax rates on public consumption create distortions in public demand choices. In our counterfactual experiment, we reduce these rates to a uniform rate of 5 percent. Simulation results show that most of the sectors experience increased growth. Again, sectors with higher tax rates in the base year are above the reference path, and sectors with low taxes on public consumption do not show much variation.

Table 5
Sensitivity of Lifetime Utility to Key Elasticities in the Model

Ten different configurations for key elasticities in the model (Scenarios)	*Intertemporal substitution between consumption and leisure*	*Sensitivity of lifetime utility to elasticities of substitution in consumption and production (as percentage change of utility relative to it value in the benchmark)*
S1	0.6	0.080001
S2	0.72	0.080000
S3	0.86	0.080000
S4	1.02	0.080001
S5	1.2	0.080002
S6	1.4	0.080001
S7	1.62	0.079999
S8	1.86	0.079999
S9	2.12	0.080001
S10	2.4	0.079997

Following a long process of intra-regional and international trade liberalisation over more than five decades, very little room is left for further gains from liberalisation of commodity trade alone. Still we find some mild efficiency effects and more or less uniformly positively distributed effects of tariff reform across sectors. These results show that as the UK economy is quite liberalised already, gains from such moves may be very small, even when dynamic linkages are taken into account.

The results discussed above are robust to the various specifications to the values of elasticities of substitution as shown in Table 5 below. The lifetime utilities do not vary much just by changes in these elasticities. For ten different values of these elasticities, that range form 0.6 to 2.4, we notice changes in the lifetime utility by only 0.08 percent of thc benchmark scenario. This sensitivity result indicates that the model results that were discussed above, are robust enough to elasticity configurations. The welfare impacts of tax reform, reported in table 3 and 4 above, indeed reflect the cost of distortions from the tax system.

CONCLUSION

The major advantage of the dynamic model presented here, in comparison to the static version of the models, lies in its ability to track both short- and long-run impacts of tax and trade policy measures on the growth path of the economy via their effects on capital formation. In the dynamic model, the process of capital accumulation, both in the short and in the long run, is determined endogenously through consumption-saving decisions of households and investment allocation decisions of producers. The structure of the model allows us to look at the differential impacts of tax reform on investment by sector and to capture the possibility of transitory shutdowns in sectoral investment.

The model is calibrated using 1995 micro consistent data for the UK economy. It is then used to perform a number of equal-yield tax replacement experiments, whereby a certain tax is reduced and the remaining taxes increased in order to guarantee a constant period-by-period level of government spending without any change in public borrowing. For each experiment, we assess overall dynamic efficiency impacts as well as transitional and long-run effects on sectoral output, employment, and capital formation. In each case, we investigate whether impacts differ when people can anticipate tax changes occurring in the future or when they encounter tax changes all of a sudden without any anticipation. We also investigate how results in a closed capital market specification differ from those in an open capital market setting.

The dynamic efficiency effects and the growth path impacts of tax reform vary significantly across experiments. When distortionary capital income tax rates ranging from 24 to 48 percent in the base year are replaced by a uniform capital income tax rate of 25 percent, the dynamic efficiency gains are about 0.77 percent of the base year GDP. Some sectors, such as agriculture, where the relative capital input cost has been reduced in the counterfactual scenario by lower capital income tax rates, experience an expansion. Other sectors, such as engineering, where the capital income tax has not been reduced that much in the counterfactual scenario relative to the benchmark, experience slower growth.

Reducing labour income tax from 24 percent in the benchmark year to 15 percent results in a welfare loss of up to 2.05 percent of the base year GDP, mainly because more distortionary taxes have to be increased to make up for lost revenues. Replacing differential tax rates on production by a uniform 5 percent rate across sectors results in a welfare gain of 1.4 percent of the base year GDP. Similarly replacing differentiated household consumption taxes by a uniform 5 percent rate causes a gain of 0.6 percent of GDP. We find similar gains in welfare from a reform in the taxes on government consumption and tariffs.

The private sector's ability to anticipate reform affects transitional effects as well as the dynamic efficiency effects of reform, raising them in some cases and lowering them in others. Simulation results appear to be robust with respect to changes in the degree of international openness of capital markets and a range of values for the intertemporal and entra-temporal substitution elasticities. In all cases, convergence to a new balanced-growth path occurs more quickly when private agents anticipate future tax changes and when capital markets are internationally open.

REFERENCES

Armington, P.S. (1969), "A Theory of Demand for Products Distinguished by Place of Production", International Monetary Fund *Staff Papers* 16, 159-76.

Arrow, K.J., H.B. Chenery, B.C. Minhas and R.M. Solow (1961), "Capital-Labour Substitution and Economic Efficiency," *Review of Economics and Statistics* 43, 225- 250.

Auerbach, A.J. and L.J. Kotlikoff (1987), *Dynamic Fiscal Policy*. Cambridge University Press.

Ballard, C.L., D. Fullerton , J.B. Shoven and J. Whalley (1985), *A General Equilibrium Model for Tax Policy Evaluation*. University of Chicago Press, Chicago.

Bhattarai K. R (1997) Financial Deepening and Economic Development in Nepal :A Forward Looking CGE Model with Financial Intermediation, Ph.D. dissertation Northeastern University, Boston, Massachussetts.

Bhattarai, K. (1999), A Forward-Looking Dynamic Multisectoral General Equilibrium Tax Model of the UK Economy, Hull Economics Research Papers no. 269, University of Hull, HU6 7RX, UK.

Bhattarai, K. and J. Whalley (2000), "General Equilibrium Modelling of UK Tax Policy" *in* Sean Holly and Martin Weale (eds.) *Econometric Modelling: Technique and Applications*, Cambridge University Press.

Bhattarai, K. and J. Whalley (1999), "The Role of Labour Demand Elasticities in Tax Incidence Analysis with Heterogeneous Labour," *Empirical Economics* 24(4) November; also in Boadway and Baldev Raj (eds.) Advances in Public Economics, pp. 47-67 Physica-Verlag, 2000.

Boskin, M.J. (1978), "Taxation Saving and the Rate of Interest," *Journal of Political Economy* 86:s3-s28.

Brook, A K., D. Kendtrick, A. Meeraus (1992), *GAMS: User's Guide,* Release 2.25, The Scientific Press, San Francisco, CA.

Cass, D. (1965), "Optimal Growth in an Aggregative Model of Capital Accumulation," *Review of Economic Studies* 32:233-240.

Cooley T. F., J Greenwood, M. Yorukoglu (1997), The Replacement Problem, Journal of Monetary Economics, 40 457-499.

Debreu, G. (1954), *The Theory of Value*. Yale University Press, New Haven.

Devarajan, Shantayanan, and J.D. Lewis (1990), "Policy Lessons from Trade Focused Two-Sector Models", *Journal of Policy Modeling* 12(4):625-657.

Fullerton, D., J. Shoven and J. Whalley (1983), "Dynamic General Equilibrium Impacts of Replacing the US Income tax with a Progressive Consumption Tax," *Journal of Public Economics* 38, 265-96.

Ferris M.C. and T.S. Munson (2004), Path 4.6 in GAMS: The Solver Manuals, GAMS Development Corporation, Washington DC.

Goulder, L.H., and L.H. Summers (1989), "Tax Policy, Asset Prices, and Growth: A General Equilibrium Analysis," *Journal of Public Economics*, 38, 265-296.

Harberger A.C. (1962), "The Incidence of the Corporation Income Tax," *Journal of Political Economy* 70, 215-40.

Harrison, G.W., T.F. Rutherford and D.G. Tarr (1997) "Quantifying the Uruguay Round", *Economic Journal* vol. 107 no. 444, September, pp.1405-1430,

Harrison, W.J. and K.R. Pearson (1996), "Computing Solutions for Large General Equilibrium Models Using GEMPACK," *Computational Economics* 9, 83-127.

Hutton, J. and T. Kenc (1994), "Representative UK Income Tax with a Progressive Consumption Tax," University of Cambridge Department of Applied Economics *Working Paper* 9413, June.

King M.A. and D. Fullerton (1984), "The taxation of Income from Capital", *The University of Chicago Press Ltd.*

King M. A. and Robson (1988), "Manual for TURBO PTAX", *London School of Economics Financial Markets Group.*

Kotlikoff, L.J. (1988), " Intergenerational Transfers and Savings," *Journal of Economic Perspectives* 2, 41-58.

King, R.G. and R. Levine (1993), "Finance and Growth: Schumpeter Might Be Right," *Quarterly Journal of Economics*, Aug., pp.717-737.

Lau M.L. A. Pahlke and T.F. Rutherford (2002), Approximating infinite-horizon models in a complementarity format: A primer in dynamic general equilibrium analysis, Journal of Economic Dynamics and Control 26 577-609.

Lucas R.E. (1988), "On the Mechanics of Economic Development", Journal of Monetary Economics, 22:3-42.

Perroni, C. (1995), "Assessing the Dynamic Efficiency Gains of Tax Reform When Human Capital is Endogenous," *International Economic Review* 36, 907-925.

Piggott, J. and J. Whalley (1985), *UK Tax Policy and Applied General Equilibrium Analysis.* Cambridge University Press.

Ramsey, F.P. (1928), "A Mathematical Theory of Saving," *Economic Journal* 38, 543-559.

Rebelo, S. (1991), "Long-run Policy Analysis and Long-run Growth," *Journal of Political Economy* 99, 500-521.

Robinson, S. (1991), "Macroeconomics, Financial Variables, and Computable General Equilibrium Models," *World Development* 19, 1509-1523.

Romer, P. (1989), "Endogenous Technological Change", *Journal of Political Economy,* 98: 5: 2: S71-S102.

Rankin Neil (1992), Imperfect Competition, Expectations and the Multiple Effects of Monetary growth, the Economic Journal 102: 743-753.

Rutherford, T.F. (1995), "Extension of GAMS for Complementary Problems Arising in Applied Economic Analysis," *Journal of Economic Dynamics and Control* 19, 1299-1324.

Rutherford, T.F. (1998), GAMS:MPSGE Guide, GAMS Development Corporation, Whashington DC.

Siddorn, G. (1999), Derivation of 1995 Industry-by-Industry Use Matrices, *Mimeo, Economics Unit*, Inland Revenue, F4 West Wing, Somerset House, Strand, London WC2R 1LB.

Solow, R.M. (1956), "A Contribution to the Theory of Economic Growth." *Quarterly Journal of Economics* 70, 65-94.

Shoven, J.B. and J. Whalley (1984), "Applied General-Equilibrium Models of Taxation and International Trade: An Introduction and Survey," *Journal of Economic Literature* 22, 1007-1051.

Summers, L.H. (1980), "Capital Taxation and Accumulation in a Life Cycle Growth Model," *American Economic Review* 71, 533-44.

Uzawa, H. (1962), "On a Two-Sector Model of Economic Growth," *Review of Economic Studies* 29, 40-47.

NOTES

1. When $\sigma = 1$, we have $U(C_t) = \ln U_t$.
2. Disaggregation of assets into five different capital assets ¾ long-lived plant and machinery, short lived plant and machinery, vehicles, buildings and dwellings, as in our static model, is left for a future version of the model.
3. I appreciate very useful and extensive comments made by the editor of the Economic Issues for this section.
4. This model assumes a uniform growth path across the sectors in the steady state. There may be a set of dynamic paths in which some sectors might be expanding and some others remain contracting or even eliminated over time. Analysis of this sort of

economy requires a more complicated model left as an open question for further research.

5. The main excise duties on tobacco, alcohol and fuel were included in
6. Production Taxes' here in line with ONS Input-Output definitions; although in a later tax aggregation provided by the Inland Revenue and used in our Static Model (Bhattarai (1999)) such excise taxes were incorporated within consumption taxes (see also Siddorn (1999)).

6

Analyses of Poverty and Income Redistribution: Some Lessions from Games and Multi-Household Multi-Sectoral Dynamic Equilibrium Models

Keshab Bhattarai[20]

INTRODUCTION

Poverty is a relative concept irrespective to the level of development of an economy. For Adam Smith (1776) poverty meant:

"... not only the commodities which are indispensably necessary of the support of life but whatever the custom of the country renders it indecent for creditable people ... to be without. A linen shirt is strictly speaking not a necessity of life. The Greeks and Romans lived very comfortably though they had no linen. But in the present time ... a creditable day-laborer would be ashamed to appear in public without a linen shirt..."[1].

Marx also noted 'necessary wants of the workers as the product of historical development that depended to a great extent on the degree of civilization of the country'[2]. The absolute concept to poverty was first formally used by Rowntree (1899) in a study of minimum living standard for a respectable life in York in Britain more than a hundred years ago[3]. In his study a family was considered to be living in poverty if its total earnings were insufficient to obtain the minimum necessaries for the maintenance of merely physical needs. In 1899, taking American nutritionist Atwater's estimate on the minimum requirements of protein and calories, Rowntree calculated a daily food expenditure on porridge and skim milk for breakfast, bread and cheese for lunch, vegetable broth, bread, cheese, dumpling for dinner, and bread and porridge for supper. All these would cost 5s 6d for a single person, 9s 2d for a couple, and 10s 6d for a couple with four children, with the addition in each of rent paid. Orshansky (1965) did similar study for the United

20. Corresponding address: *K.R.Bhattarai@hull.ac.uk;* Phone 44-1482-463207 Fax: 44-1482-463484.
Author acknowledges the EPSRC grant GR/S28082/01.

States. Critically assessing both of these studies on measurement of poverty Atkinson (1970) concluded that ".. poverty line cannot be defined in a vacuum, but only in relation to a particular society at a particular date". An accurate measurement of poverty has been an issue of theoretical investigation since then (Sen (1976), Foster and Shorrocks (1985), Basu (1985), Vaughan (1987), Preston (1995), Shorrocks (1995) and Chakravarty (1997), Davidson and Duclos (2000)). As research progressed the head-count and the income-gap ratios, two widely used measures of poverty by Rowntree (1901) and Townsend (1954, 1979) were thought inadequate to reflect the effect of intra-group transfers. Sen (1976)[4] suggested an ordinal approach for measurement of poverty that would fulfill the axioms of monotonicity, transfer, relative equity, ordinal rank and monotonic welfare. Many more empirical studies have appeared recently that aim to justify and monitor programmes aimed at reducing poverty, such as the poverty reduction strategy framework under the Millennium Development Goals (OECD (1976), UNDP (1991), Slesnick (1996), World Bank (1991), Ravallion (1996), Stifel and Thorbekcek (2003)).

A NUMERICAL EXAMPLE ON THE MEASUREMENT AND ALLEVIATION OF POVERTY

Consider an economy inhabited by N number of individuals where income of each is denoted by y_i for each $i = 1,2, \ldots, N$. Income vary among individuals for economic, social, political, cultural or many other less obvious reasons; $y_i \neq y_j$ for all $\forall_i$. A strict ordering implies $y_1 < y_2 < .. < y_N$, with corresponding ordering of welfare with lower income individuals having lower level of welfare. Infinite numbers of income configurations (distributions) are possible which often are summarised by their mean and variances. Some distributions, with lower variances, are more equal than others. Poverty line relates to average income of individuals; particularly with questions such as how many people fall below the average income, $\bar{y} = \sum_{i}^{N} \frac{y_i}{N}$ or how many of them are above this level of income. Many countries adopt one half of the average income as a cut-off point for absolute poverty line; $z = \frac{1}{2}\bar{y}$, which is then used to come up with either the head count ratio, which is the ratio of number of people below the poverty line divided by the total number of individuals in the population. The head count ratio is however not an adequate indicator. It cannot show the depth of poverty. Income gap ratio, which is given by the deficiency of income of individuals to reach the poverty gap $I = \frac{\sum_{i}^{n}(y_i - z)}{z.n}$ measures the depth of poverty. Sen (1976) argues that even this indicator violates the monotonicity assumption as it is insensitive to transfer from poorest poor to less poor person and proposes further refinement of this in a measure of poverty that takes account of this distribution as:

$$P = H.I + (1 - I)G \tag{1}$$

Here P is a composite poverty index of poverty, H the headcount ratio, I the income gap ratio, G the Gini coefficient; higher values of H, I, and G means greater degree of poverty. Consider the following table for a numerical example that can illustrate these concepts more accurately.

Table 1
Measuring Poverty in a Hypothetical Economy

y	N	cy	cp	yshre	cyshre	pshare	cpshare	triangle	Rectangle	Area	ygap
10	1	10	1	0.01	0.01	0.1	0.1	0.0005	0	0.0005	-90
20	1	30	2	0.02	0.03	0.1	0.2	0.001	0.001	0.002	-80
30	1	60	3	0.03	0.06	0.1	0.3	0.0015	0.003	0.0045	-70
40	1	100	4	0.04	0.1	0.1	0.4	0.002	0.006	0.008	-60
50	1	150	5	0.05	0.15	0.1	0.5	0.0025	0.01	0.0125	-50
60	1	210	6	0.06	0.21	0.1	0.6	0.003	0.015	0.018	-40
90	1	300	7	0.09	0.3	0.1	0.7	0.0045	0.021	0.0255	-10
100	1	400	8	0.1	0.4	0.1	0.8	0.005	0.03	0.035	0
200	1	600	9	0.2	0.6	0.1	0.9	0.01	0.04	0.05	100
400	1	1000	10	0.4	1	0.1	1	0.02	0.06	0.08	300

Column y gives the income by households, N the number of households in each income category, *cy* and *cp* are cumulative income and population; *yshre* and *cyshre* columns present income share of each decile and cumulative shares; *pshre* and *cpshre* columns present income share of each decile and cumulative shares; area under the Lorenz curve is approximated using triangle and rectangles.

The total income is 1000, with 10 households, average income is 100. Area under the Lorenz curve is 0.236, that between the Lorenz curve and equality line is 0.264; this implies a Gini coefficient of 0.528; higher G reflecting more unequal distribution.

By the headcount ratio seventy percent of population is poor if the accepted poverty line is the average income $\bar{y} = 100$ but only 40 percent is poor when absolute poverty line is established as the half of this average income $z = \frac{1}{2}\bar{y} = 50$ as only four individuals are below the poverty line. As stated above this head count ratio does not indicate the depth of poverty. The income gap ratio, $I = \frac{\sum_{i}^{n}(y_i - z)}{z.n} = \frac{40 + 30 + 20 + 10}{50 \cdot 4} = \frac{100}{200} = 0.5$. In terms of Sen's poverty index, poverty in this economy is

$$P = H.I + (1 - I)G = 0.4 \times 0.5 + (1 - 0.5)0.528 = 0.2 + 0.264 = 0.464$$

This index would have larger value if the income distribution was more unequal. The elimination of the absolute poverty in this example requires transfers of 100 to poor individuals with $T_1 = 40$ for the poorest household and $T_2 = 30$, $T_3 = 20$ and $T_4 = 10$ accordingly to other other three households below the poverty line. This transfer can be funded by a 10 percent and 20 percent tax on the income of 9th and 10th deciles raising 20 and 80 respectively. This brings *H* to zero and *I* to 1 making *P* to zero (see Appendix 1 for cross country comparisons, Appenix 2 for UK income distribution and Appendix 3 for the Social Accounting Matrix of the US, Appendices 5 and 6 for input-output tables of Nepal and UK economies respectively).

It is obvious that the value of poverty index is influenced by the choice of the poverty line. When income is perfectly equally distributed no one is below poverty line with *H* zero and *G* also equals zero with no poverty, $P = 0$; but these are extreme cases only of theoretical possibility. In the real world, values of *P* range between zero and one, $0 < P < 1$, with higher *P* indicating to the higher level of poverty. This means when looked from this point of view, the poverty is everywhere, in relative sense there are poor in every society. Variation in the level of poverty emanates from the basic structure of the socio-economic model adopted by the country.

Poverty measure us sensitive the choice of the poverty line. There is more poverty in the economy when the mean of the income is taken as a poverty line than when the half of the income is taken for it. A more unequal society has greater poverty than the more equal society. More fundamentally the degree and depth of poverty can be changed by influencing the choices of individuals and households and by adopting economic programmes that are more efficient and generate best outcome.

It is often argued that poverty can be eliminated by means of tax and transfer as illustrated in the numerical example in Table 1. Broader questions arise regarding the impact of such transfer programme. First relates to its impact on labour supply of rich and poor. Higher taxes may discourage rich individuals to work and transfer receipts may reduce the need to work to earn for living for poor. Secondly, higher taxes may discourage incentives of saving and investment. Third, modality of transfer payment may be crucial for long term growth. Providing in kind transfer in the form of education and health spending may be better than cash transfers to empower productive capacity of poor. Fourth, in addition to transfer payment government needs to provide public goods for the entire population. As everyone consumes the public goods these should be provided by taxing on income of both rich and poor.

GAME OF POVERTY

Limitations of one time transfers to end poverty have made alleviation of poverty one of the major global agenda in recent years (Millennium Development Goals (MDG), G8 meeting and Live 8 concerts 2005; poverty alleviations strategies of many developing economies including the OECD, China and India). As mentioned above poverty is not only the problem of developing economies but also of advanced economies. Effective implementation of these require strategic thinking among three major players in the poverty game; poor themselves who are often considered beneficiaries of aids, grants and transfers, rich individuals who bear the burden of taxes to pay for those transfers and the government that is involved not only in determining the depth of poverty and setting objectives, targets and programmes that aim to eliminate poverty but also is subject to corruption and misuse of public money. This effectively involves designing an effective incentive structure in the economy and the balance of economic and political power among these three players.

Ideally high income individuals would like to see the end of poverty as has been campaigned by public and private sectors in advanced countries in recent year. In the mean time they also expect that poor who receive benefit should make good efforts to get out of the poverty trap by investing their time and resources in education, skill and training and health care taking a longer time view rather than taking transfers to pay only for current spending. Government, made of representatives of both poor and rich people, might bring very sound and ideal programmes and propose rules and regulations but they become ineffective in removing poverty if there is not enough cooperation from tax payers and the recipients of the aid. A small game theoretic model is presented here to explain the dynamic situation of poverty. The solutions differ when all players use cooperative strategy and when they play a non-cooperative strategy. In a utility or welfare maximising world, model results will be based on comparison of expected welfare in each strategy.

Model of the Poverty Game

Each player in the model (poor, rich and government) has a set of strategies available to it (s, l, and k respectively). The outcome of the game is the strategy contingent income for poor and rich, $y_t^P(s,l,k)$ and $y_t^R(s,l,k)$. The probability of being in particular state like this is given by $\pi_t^P(s,l,k)$ and $\pi_t^R(s,l,k)$ respectively. The state-space of the game rises exponentially with the length of time period t. The objective of these two players is to maximize the expected utility and government can influence this outcome by means of taxes and transfers. More specifically, following conditions should hold in this poverty alleviation game.

Condition 1: The state contingent money metric expected utility of poor is less than that of rich, which can be expressed as:

$$\sum_{s=1}^{s}\sum_{l=1}^{l}\sum_{k=1}^{k}\sum_{t}^{T}\pi_t^P(s,l,k)\cdot\delta_t^P u\left(y_t^P(s,l,k)\right)$$

$$<\sum_{s=1}^{s}\sum_{l=1}^{l}\sum_{k=1}^{k}\sum_{t}^{T}\pi_t^R(s,l,k)\cdot\delta_t^R u\left(y_t^R(s,l,k)\right)$$

where $\pi_t^P(s,l,k)$ gives the probability of choosing one of strategies by poor given that the rich and the government has chosen l and k strategies. Utility is derived from income as given by $u\left(y_t^P(s,l,k)\right)$ and $\delta_t^P = \frac{1}{\left(1+r_t^P\right)}$ is the discount factors for poor and the discount factor for rich.

Condition 2: Transfer raises money metric expected utility of poor and reduces the utility of rich.

$$\sum_{s=1}^{s}\sum_{l=1}^{l}\sum_{k=1}^{k}\sum_{t}^{T}\pi_t^P(s,l,k)\cdot\delta_t^P u\left(y_t^P(s,l,k)+T_t^P(s,l,k)\right)$$

$$<\sum_{s=1}^{s}\sum_{l=1}^{l}\sum_{k=1}^{k}\sum_{t}^{T}\pi_t^R(s,l,k)\cdot\delta_t^R u\left(y_t^R(s,l,k)-T_t^P(s,l,k)\right)$$

Condition 3: Incentive compatibility requires that

$$\sum_{s=1}^{s}\sum_{l=1}^{l}\sum_{k=1}^{k}\sum_{t}^{T}\pi_t^P(s,l,k)\cdot\delta_t^P u\left(y_t^P(s,l,k)+T_t^P(s,l,k)\right)>$$

$$\sum_{s=1}^{s}\sum_{l=1}^{l}\sum_{k=1}^{k}\sum_{t}^{T}\pi_t^P(s,l,k)\cdot\delta_t^P u\left(y_t^P(s,l,k)\right)$$

and

$$\sum_{s=1}^{s}\sum_{l=1}^{l}\sum_{k=1}^{k}\sum_{t}^{T}\pi_t^R(s,l,k)\cdot\delta_t^R u\left(y_t^R(s,l,k)-T_t^P(s,l,k)\right)$$

$$<\sum_{s=1}^{s}\sum_{l=1}^{l}\sum_{k=1}^{k}\sum_{t}^{T}\pi_t^R(s,l,k)\cdot\delta_t^R u\left(y_t^R(s,l,k)\right)$$

Condition 4: Growth requires that income of both poor and rich are rising over time:

$$T_t^P(s,l,k)<T_{t+1}^P(s,l,k)<T_{t+2}^P(s,l,k)<..<T_{t+T}^P(s,l,k)$$

$$Y_t^P(s,l,k) < Y_{t+1}^P(s,l,k) < Y_{t+2}^P(s,l,k) < .. < Y_{t+T}^P(s,l,k)$$

$$Y_t^R(s,l,k) < Y_{t+1}^R(s,l,k) < Y_{t+2}^R(s,l,k) < .. < Y_{t+T}^R(s,l,k)$$

Condition 5: Termination of poverty requires that every poor individual has at least the level of income equal to the poverty line determined by the society. When the poverty line is defined one half of the average income this can be stated as:

$$Y_{t+T}^P(s,l,k) \geq \frac{1}{2}\sum_{p=1}^{P} Y_{t+T}^P(s,l,k)$$

Above five conditions comprehensively incorporate all possible scenarios in the Poverty Game mentioned above. Conditions 2-5 present optimistic scenarios for a chosen horizon *T*.

Testing above propositions in a real world situation is very challenging exercise. It requires modelling of the entire state space of the economy. Moreover in real situation economy is more complicated than depicted in the model above. Many households with different endowment of labour and capital supply factors to many producers across agricultural, manufacturing, production or service sectors of the economy with government in possession of vaious instruments to guide the choices of those consumers and producers in the economy. In essence it requires a general equilibrium set up of an economy where poor and rich households participate freely in economic activities taking their share of income received from supplying labour and capital inputs that are affected by tax and transfer system. This aspect modelling is briefly specified in the next section and examined in details using the general equilibrium models of three different economies: Nepal, UK and USA in section V. These dynamic multi-household-multi-sectoral computable general equilibrium models are solved using the GAMS/MPSGE software (Rutherford (1998)).

POVERTY IN MULTI-SECTORAL MULTI-HOUSEHOLD DYNAMIC GENERAL EQUILIBRIUM MODEL

Poverty reduction strategy requires a thorough appreciation of the production as well as the consumption sides of the economy and the structure of the markets, government and the foreign sectors. This section aims to present a simple multi-household multi-sectoral computable dynamic general equilibrium model in which the government uses taxes and spending strategy to alleviate the depth of poverty. It is possible to evaluate the life time welfare of households and evaluate the impacts of public policy in redistribution of income using this framework.

The models of Nepal and the economies consist of ten different households, $h_1 \ldots h_{10}$ ranked according to their income status, 10 different firms $i_1 \ldots i_{10}$, a government that collects taxes from labour and capital income taxes on use of inputs and household income taxes and tariffs and the rest of the world sector. The US model consist seven categories of households. The growth of the economy and distribution of income among households depends on the capital accumulation process and growth rate of productivity of labour force.

It is impossible to have an explicit analytical solution for a big model like this therefore numerical technique is used to solve the model. Household preferences and technology of firms are similar to those in Bhattarai (2005).

$$\text{Max } U_0^h = \sum_{t=0}^{\infty} \beta^t U_t^h \left(C_t^h, l_t^h\right)$$

Subject to

$$\sum_{t=0}^{\infty} R_t^{-1} \left[P_t (1 + t^{vc}) C_t^h + w_t (1 - t_l) l_t^h \right]$$

$$= \sum_{t=0}^{\infty} \left[(1 - t_l) w_t L_t^h + (1 - t_k) r_t K_t^h + TR_t^h \right]$$

where C_t^h, l_t^h and L_t^h are respectively composite consumption, leisure and labour supplies of household *h* in period *t*, $R_t^{-1} = \prod_{s=0}^{t-1} 1/(1 + r_s)$ is a discount factor; r_s represents the real interest rate on assets at time *s*; t^{vc} is value added tax on consumption, t^l is labour income taxes, and K_t^h is the composite consumption, which is composed of sectoral consumption goods, P_t is the price of composite consumption (which is based on goods' prices), *i.e.* $P_t = \vartheta \prod_{i=1}^{n} \alpha_i p_{i,t}^{\alpha_i}$, and $C_t^h = \prod_{i=1}^{n} C_{i,t}^{\alpha_i^h}$.

Industries of the economy are represented by firms that combine both capital and labour input in production and supply goods and services to the market.

$$\Pi_{j,t}^y = [((1 - \delta_i^e) PD_{i,t}^{\frac{\sigma_y - 1}{\sigma_y}} + \delta_i^e PE_{i,t}^{\frac{\sigma_y - 1}{\sigma_y}})]^{\frac{1}{\sigma_y - 1}} - \theta_j^v PY_{j,t}^v - \theta_j^d \sum_i a_{i,j}^d P_{i,t}$$

where: $\Pi_{j,t}^y$ is the unit profit of activity in sector *j*; $PE_{j,t}$ is the export price of good *j* $PD_{j,t}$ is the domestic price of good *j*; $PY_{j,t}^v$ is the price of value added per unit of output in activity j; s_y is a transformation elasticity parameter ; $P_{i,t}$ is the price of final goods used as intermediate goods; δ_j^e is the share parameter for exports in total production; θ_j^v is the share of costs paid to labour and capital; θ_j^d is the cost share of domestic intermediate inputs; $a_{i,j}^d$ are input-output coefficients for domestic supply of intermediate goods.

These are open economy models in which goods produced at home and foreign countries are considered closed substitutes, Armington assumption, popular in the applied general equilibrium literature and the production process is given by a nested production and trade functions.

Figure 1
Structure of Production and Trade in the Dynamic Multi-household Models

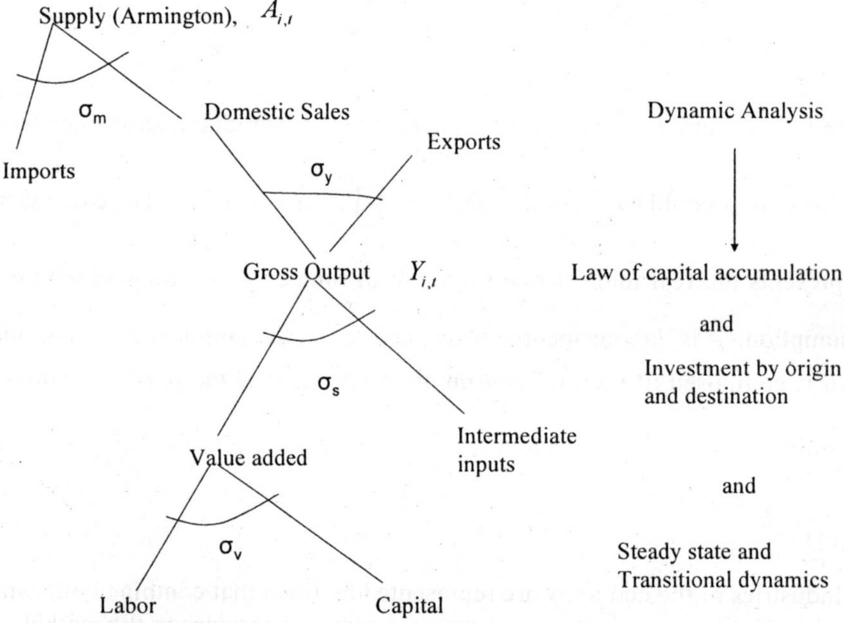

The households pay taxes to the government and government returns part of this income to the poor households and spends rest of it to provide public services.

$$REV_t = \sum_{i,h} t_i^k r_t K_{i,t} + \sum_i t_i^{vc} P_{i,t} C_{i,t}^h + \sum_i t_i^{vg} P_{i,t} G_{i,t}$$

$$+\sum_i t_i^{vk} P_{i,t} I_{i,t} + \sum_{i,h} t_l w LS_t^h + \sum_i t_i^m PM_{i,t} M_{i,t} + \sum_i t_i^p P_{i,t} GY_{i,t} \qquad (25)$$

where REV_t is total government revenue and t_i^k is a composite tax rate on capital income from sector *I*, t_i^{vc} is the *ad valorem* tax rate on final consumption by households, t_i^{vg} is that on public consumption and t_i^{vk} is the ad valorem tax rate on investment, t_l is the tax rate on labour income of the household, t_i^p is the tax on production, and t_i^m is the tariff on imports.

The steady equilibrium growth path of the economy is determined in terms of the interest rate, discount factor and relative prices of goods and factors in which the excess demand for goods and factors are eliminated and resource balance condition holds for the economy and each household and the government and rest of the world sectors in each period and over the model horizon. It also shows how the income of each type of household evolves over time as a function of the relative prices of goods and share of households in income. Government transfers can alter this equilibrium.

CALIBRATION

Above model is applied to the Nepal and UK and US economies to study the income distribution impact of public policy among the households of the various groups with dynamics as in Bhattarai (2005). The issue of labour-leisure choice analysed in the static context in Bhattarai and Whalley (1999) takes inter-temporal dimension in this model. The micro-consistency in the model is obtained by construction, the demand and supply sides balance for each sector in an input-output model, the income of households equals consumption plus saving, and investment equals total of savings by the households.

Table 2

Sectoral share of Consumption by Households α_i^h

	Agric	*Min*	*Manu*	*Utils*	*Const*	*Distb*	*Trans*	*Busi*	*OthSect*
H1	0.018	0.018	0.018	0.018	0.018	0.018	0.018	0.018	0.018
H2	0.026	0.026	0.026	0.026	0.026	0.026	0.026	0.026	0.026
h3	0.041	0.041	0.041	0.041	0.041	0.041	0.041	0.041	0.041
h4	0.057	0.057	0.057	0.057	0.057	0.057	0.057	0.057	0.057
h5	0.074	0.074	0.074	0.074	0.074	0.074	0.074	0.074	0.074
h6	0.094	0.094	0.094	0.094	0.094	0.094	0.094	0.094	0.094
h7	0.111	0.111	0.111	0.111	0.111	0.111	0.111	0.111	0.111
h8	0.118	0.118	0.118	0.118	0.118	0.118	0.118	0.118	0.118
h9	0.141	0.141	0.141	0.141	0.141	0.141	0.141	0.141	0.141
h10	0.322	0.322	0.322	0.322	0.322	0.322	0.322	0.322	0.322

The sectoral composition of consumption by households are approximated by the net of tax and transfer income of households and assumed to remain same across all goods as presented in Table 2. In addition based on economic survey data is used for getting the estimates of the distribution of wage, interest rate and transfer income for households.

Table 3
Distribution of Wage and Interest Income, Leisure and Household Tax Rate

	H1	*h2*	*H3*	*h4*	*H5*	*h6*	*h7*	*H8*	*h9*	*h10*
Wage	3436	9935	18974	29170	37692	47379	54874	61726	72055	97817
Intr	2682	1370	4257	6006	9155	12975	17115	15599	21022	105197
Leisure	2577	7451	14230	21877	28269	35535	41156	46294	54041	73363
Hit	0	0.05	0.1	0.15	0.2	0.25	0.3	0.35	0.4	0.45

Table 4
Key Parameters of the Model

Elasticity of Substitution	1.5
Growth rate of Output	0.02
Benchmark Interest Rate	0.05
Rate of Depreciation	0.1
Elasticity of Intertemporal Substitution	1.1

In my knowledge this is the first applied dynamic general equilibrium model of the UK and Nepal economies with the dynamic and multisectoral structure and could be applied to other economies with information on consumption income and labour leisure choice and labour supply as contained in the social accounting matrix of the economy as shown in the SAM for the US economy and Input Output Tables for Nepal and the UK at the appendix.

POLICY SCENARIOS

The income redistribution effect in the model occurs through the differentiated tax rates of household income, value added taxes on consumption of goods and services, labour income tax and capital income tax rates. All these tax experiments should constrain the amount of revenue and find the best optimal rates of taxes given that revenue requirement.

Table 5
Labour and capital input taxes in the UK model

	Capial input tax	*Labour input tax*
Agriculture	-0.0011	-0.0021
Mining and forests	0.0018	0.0188
Manufacturing	0.0106	0.014
Utilities	0.0388	0.1934
Construction	0.0269	0.0041
Distribution	0.0079	0.0107
transports	0.0303	0.0398
Business	0.0121	0.0404
Other Sectors	0.0426	0.0078

Table 6
Labour and Capital Input Taxes in the Nepal Model

Benchmark Data for Nepal	*Tax on labour input*	*Tax on capital input*
Agriculture	0.037	0.003
Manufacturing	0.242	0.299
Chemicals	0.482	0.989
Metal	0.088	0.306
Gas electricity and water	0.896	0.014
Hotel	0.279	0.018
Transport and communication	0.642	0.045
Finance	0.075	2.78E-04
Social Services	0.002	0.046

The above benchmark labour and capital input taxes are replaced by uniform rates of 0.3 and 0.2 in the counterfactual scenario. Model solutions show how these reforms affect the distribution income and welfare among households. Results are presented briefly in the following diagrams. The model solutions show that no household gains from such a reform. Implementing a flat tax like this would make poor households even poorer. These results are shown in a series of graphs generated from the benchmark and counterfactual results of these models. These results are preliminary and reflect the income and substitution impacts of policy measures that affect both product and factor markets in these economies. Various other scenarios are under consideration and are being investigated further.

All the model scenarios arise from growing economies. These systems are distorted in the benchmark and are that are removed under the counterfactual scenarios. Tax reform though important seems to have not very significant impact in developing country like Nepal which requires more investment in physical infrastructure and human capital. Properly designed tax reforms can remove the risk of income uncertainty in the UK as they lead to steady flow of household wellbeing under the counter-factual scenario against the cyclical patterns of income and wellbeing in the benchmark economy. On the other hand the Fair Tax reforms proposals in the US seem to reward households in the low and high income categories where the most the burden of switching to commodity taxes falls up the middle income households.

The US model is larger than above two models in terms of sectoral specification and included both federal and local governments. The tax experiment involved replacing all federal indirect taxes by consumption tax and gave the following pattern on the redistribution effects of tax reforms (Tuerck, Haughton, Bhattarai, Ngo and S-Penalvar (2006) for details).

The dynamic models contain a lot more result on the economy than what could be discussed above. They show the evolutionary path for these economies and generate patterns of investment, capital accumulation, employment and output by sectors, relative prices of commodities and factors of production, importable and exportable, government spending and expenditure, composition leisure, consumption and labour supply by households for each model scenario. It is not

Figure 2
Redistribution Impacts of Policy Reforms in the Nepal Model

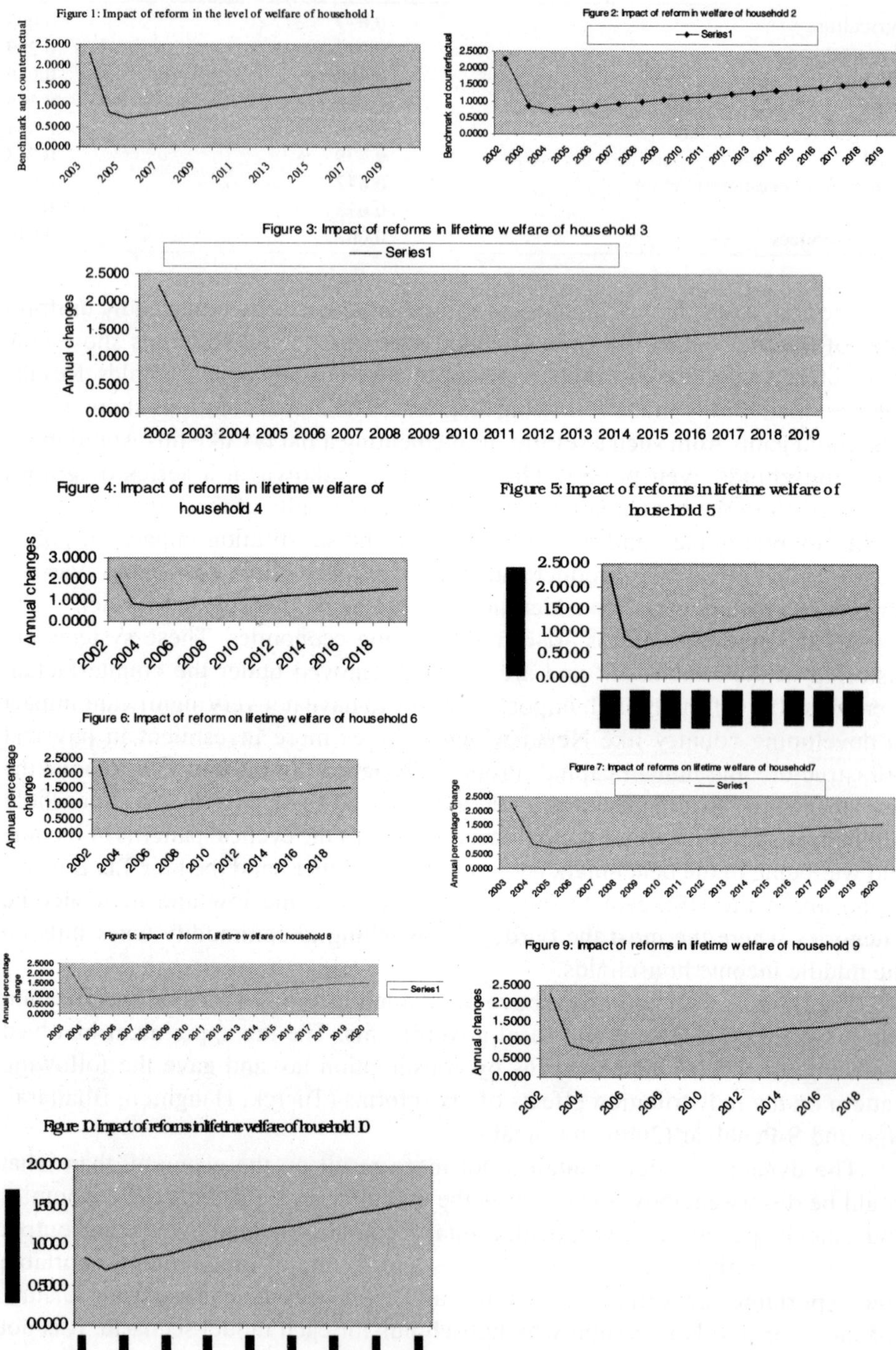

Figure 3
Redistribution Impacts of Tax Reforms in the UK Model

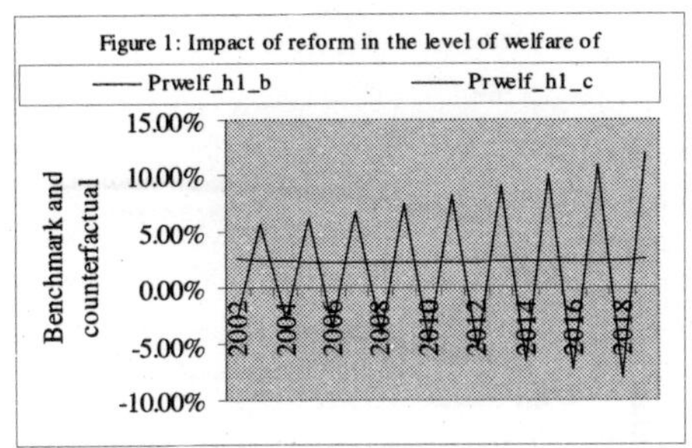

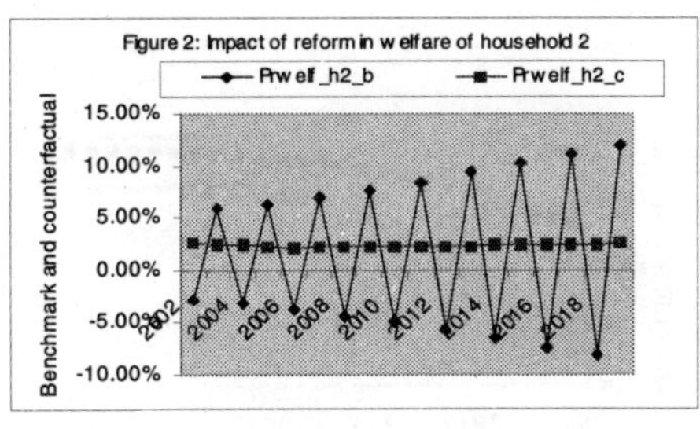

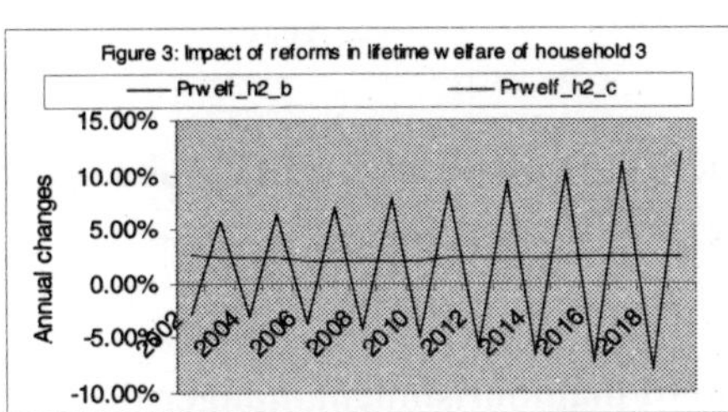

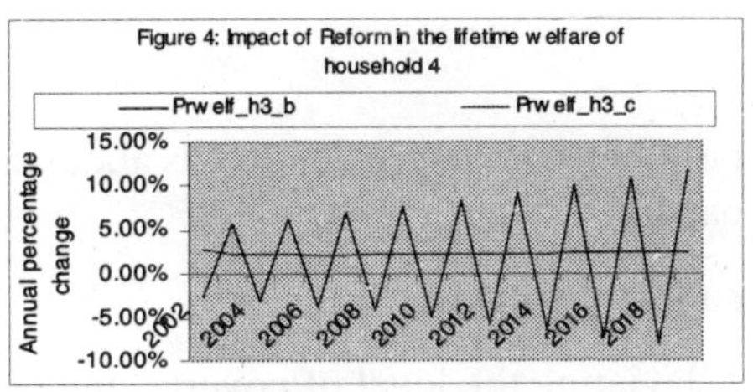

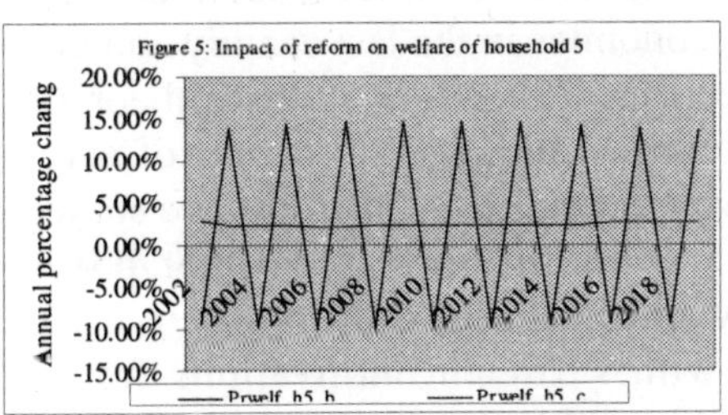

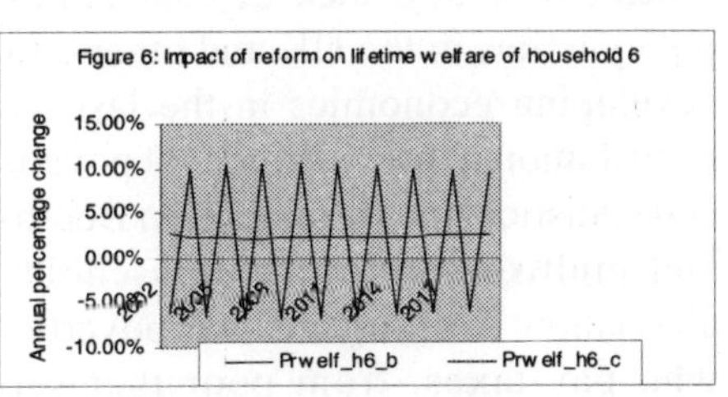

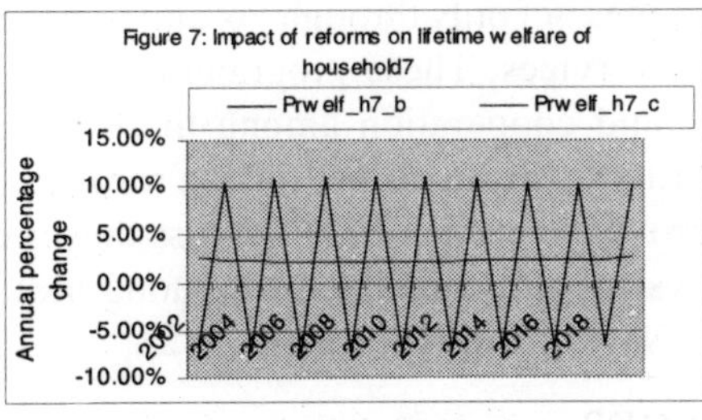

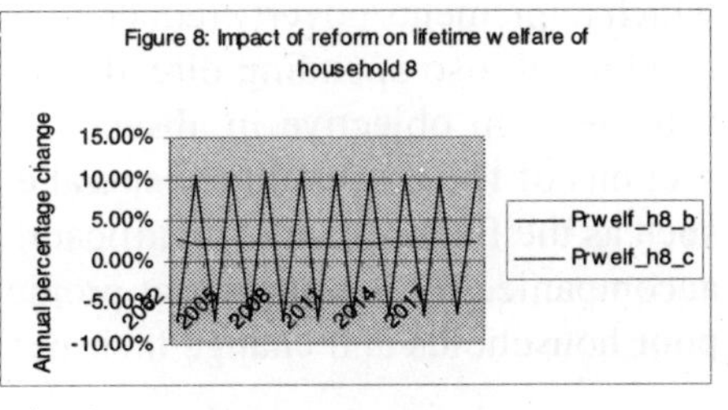

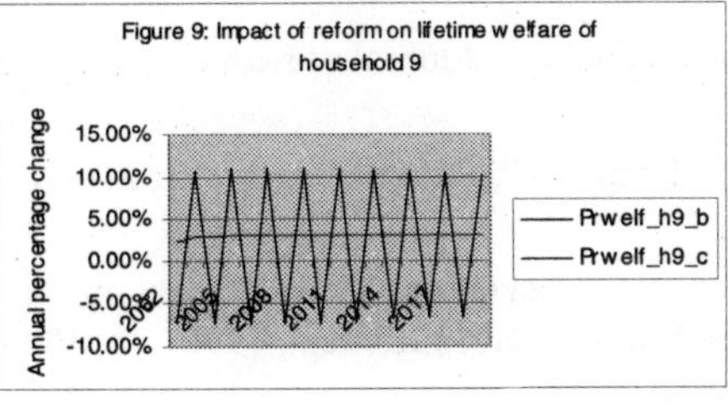

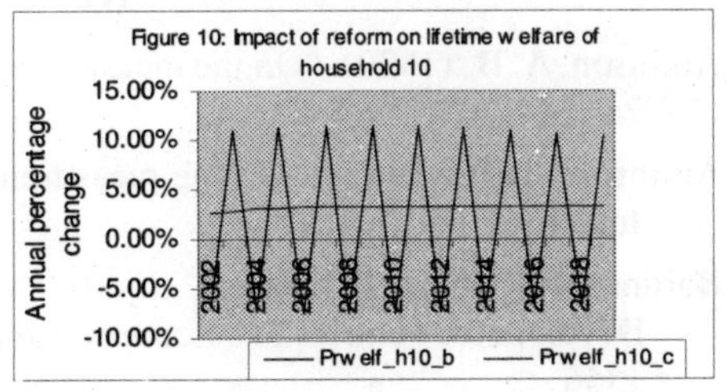

Figure 4
Redistribution Impacts of Tax Reforms in the US Model

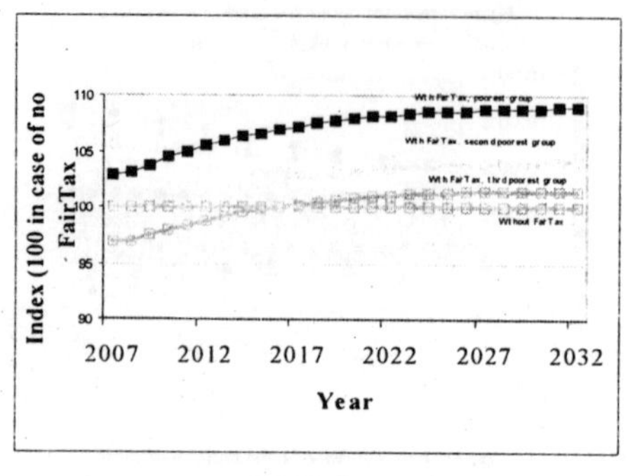

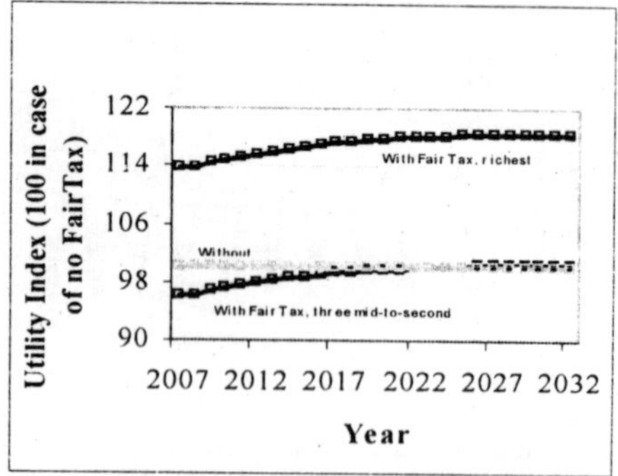

possible to go in greater details about them here but will be reviewed in subsequent papers.

CONCLUSION

Alleviating the level of poverty -the problem of malnourishment, hunger-disease-illness, illiteracy, lack of education and skills- has remained one of the major policy issues in the UK and other OECD economies in the last century and many developing economies in the last five decades. This paper assesses theoretical contribution in measurement of poverty in terms of Atkinson-Sen indices of poverty and statistical measurements in Booth-Rowntree tradition and proposes a strategic and multisectoral multi-household general equilibrium models for poverty alleviation. It is argued that poverty alleviation requires cooperation from rich, who pay taxes, from poor themselves with sufficient motivations for skill enhancement and precautions against unforeseeable future and the government which implements poverty reduction programmes not only through tax and transfer system but also spending directly on public services. These programmes fail to achieve such objective in absence of trust and cooperation among these three sections of the community. General equilibrium analysis of tax reform measures such as the flat tax cannot significantly improve the status of poor unless they are accompanied by measures that promote physical and capital assets among these poor households and change their patters of saving and investment.

REFERENCES

Atkinson, A. B.:(1970), "On the measurement of inequality", Journal of Economic Theory, 2:3:244-263.

Atkinson, A. B.:(1987), "On the measurement of poverty", Econometrica, 55: 4:749 64 July

Bardhan P. (1996), Efficiency, Equity and Poverty Alleviation: Policy Issues in Less Developed Countries *The Economic Journal* Vol. 106, No. 438 (Sep., 1996), pp. 1344-1356

Bhattarai K and J Whalley (1999), Role of Heterogeneity of Labour Demand in Tax Incidence Analysis *Empirical Economics*, 24:4, pp.599-620.

Bhattarai K (2005), Welfare impacts of equal-yield tax reforms in the UK economy, Applied Economics, forthcoming.

Department of Social Security (1999), Opportunity for all: Tackling Poverty and Social Exclusion - The Changing Welfare State, First Annual Report, cm 4445, London, Stationary Office.

Desai, M. and A. Shah (1988), "An econometric approach to the measurement of poverty", Oxford Economic Papers, v40 p505 22 September.

Davidson, R and J.Y. Duclos (2000), Statistical inference for stochastic dominance and for the measurement of poverty and inequality, Econometrica, 68:6:1435-1464, November.

Foster J. E. and A. F. Shorrocks (1988), Poverty orderings: notes and comments, Econometrica, 56:1:173-177.

Glennester H. J.Huills, D. Piachaud and J. Webb (2004), One hundred years of poverty and policy, Joseph Rawntree Foundation, York, (www.jrf.org.uk).

Jenkins, S.P. (1991), "Poverty measurement and the within household distribution: agenda for action", Journal of Social Policy v20 p457 83 October.

Myles G.D. (2001), Economic mismeasurement and the bias in policy choice, the Public Economic Theory, 3:2:139-166.

Orshansky M.(1965) Counting the poor: another look at poverty profile, Social Security Bulletin, 28:1:3-29, Jan.

Pyatt G (1987), Measuring welfare, poverty and inequality, Economic Journal, 97:386:459-467.

Preston I. (1995), Sampling distributions of relative poverty statistics, Applied Statistics, 44:1:91-99.

Ravallion M. (1996), Issues in measuring and modeling poverty, *Economic Journal*, 106:438:1328-1343.

Rutherford T.F (1998), Economic Modelling with GAMS: An Introduction to GAMS/MCP and GAMS/MOSGE, GAMS Corporation, GAMS/MPSGE guide.

Sen A. (1976), Poverty: An Ordinal Approach to Measurement, *Econometrica*, 44:2:219-231.

Shorrocks A. F. (1995), Revisiting the Sen Poverty Index, Econometrica, 63:5:1225-1230.

Slesnick D.T. (1996), Consumption and poverty: how effective are in-kind transfers, *The Economic Journal* Vol. 106, No. 438 Sep., pp. 1527-1545

Stifel, D.C. Thorbecke, E.(2003), A dual-dual CGE model of an archetype African economy: trade reform, migration and poverty. Journal of Policy Modeling, Apr, Vol. 25 Issue 3, p207, 29p;

Tuerck, Haughton, Bhattarai, Ngo and S-Penalvar (2006), The Economic Effects of the Fair Tax: Results from The Beacon Hill Institute CGE Model, Beacon Hill Institute at Suffolk University, Boston, USA.

Townsend, P (1979), Poverty in the United Kingdom, Allen Lane and Penguin, London.

UNDP (1991), Human Development Report.

Vaughan, R. N (1987), "Welfare approaches to the measurement of poverty", The Economic Journal v97 supp p160 70.

World Bank (1990), "Poverty: The World development Report 1990", OUP, Washington D.C.

The World Bank, Nepal: Poverty and Incomes, Washington D. C., 1991.

NOTES

1. Quoted in A. K. Sen's (1983), 'Poor, Relatively Speaking' Oxford Economic Papers 35, p.161.
2. Quoted by Atkinson (1988), The Economics of Inequality, OUP, London, p189.
3. See Glennester, Huills, Piachaud and Webb (2004) for a historical account on the measurement of poverty in Great Britain.
4. Sen (1988), 'Poverty: An Ordinal Approach to Measurement', Oxford University Paper, pp.219-231.

Appendix 1
Reality of Poverty and Income Redistribution

Information about the depth of poverty is obtained from the living standard surveys conducted by statistical offices. Though these surveys constitute a wide range of questions regarding the quality of human life measured by level of education and health access to modern means of communication and transportation and many other environmental factors the distribution of consumption and income are often considered the most important factors to study the issue of poverty and income distribution often expressed by deciles of households as contained in Table A1 for a number of economies.

Table A1
Income of households in local currency units

	Bolivia	*Chile*	*Ghana*	*Nepal*	*South Korea*	*Switzer land*	*Taiwan*	*Tunisia*	*UK*	*USA*
h1	23	3,183	55,701	3,190	783,280	5,619	30,171	134	710	1,478
h2	38	5,352	83,186	4,820	1,276,662	10,070	41,341	181	1,590	3,235
h3	49	7,015	105,938	6,061	1,574,922	11,992	48,632	226	2,019	4,586
h4	61	8,685	128,276	7,394	1,850,881	14,043	55,736	277	2,361	5,782
h5	75	10,609	149,574	8,846	2,118,479	16,338	63,157	331	2,744	6,976
h6	91	13,037	172,952	10,545	2,416,738	18,883	71,287	399	3,168	8,333
h7	110	16,221	201,659	13,098	2,790,259	22,386	81,423	482	3,637	10,014
h8	144	21,199	242,501	16,734	3,289,217	27,059	94,182	624	4,277	12,046
h9	203	32,201	303,300	23,845	4,047,409	33,638	115,828	891	5,204	15,299
h10	474	112,568	539,155	57,145	7,698,998	64,669	194,204	1,165	8,455	24,266

Source: http://www.worldbank.org/research/inequality/data.htm; CBS for Nepal.

Absolute distribution like above can be used to derive absolute poverty measures based on certain criteria, such as the mean of income, half of the mean of income or a dollar a day as shown in Table A2.

Table A2
Mean income and poverty line and population below it across economies

	Bolivia	*Chile*	*Ghana*	*Nepal*	*South Korea*	*Switzer land*	*Taiwan*	*Tunisia*	*UK*	*USA*
Mean income	127	23007	198224	15168	2784685	22470	79596	471	3417	9202
Income in US dollars	27	57	305	312	3469	15182	3016	471	5099	9202
Poverty line-hmi	63	11504	99112	7584	1392342	11235	39798	236	1708	4601
Income gap-hmi	-83	-22674	-59337	-8871	-724743	-6781	-9627	-166	-1117	-4503
Income gap ratio-hmi	0.163	0.197	0.150	0.146	0.130	0.151	0.121	0.117	0.163	0.163
Percent below PL	40	50	20	40	20	20	10	30	20	30
Income gap-mi	-441	-96947	-493718	-52221	-6687145	-57957	-167253	-1278	-7907	-24819
Income gap ratio_mi	0.496	0.527	0.415	0.492	0.400	0.368	0.350	0.452	0.386	0.450
Percent below PL	70	80	60	70	60	70	60	60	60	60
Total income	1268	230070	1982242	151678	27846845	224697	795961	4710	34165	92015
Population (million)	8.06	13.77	16.45	19.27	44.06	6.94	20.9	8.57	58.19	258.14
Exchange rate (for $)	4.7	404.35	649.06	48.61	802.67	1.48	26.39	1	0.67	1

Authors own calculations. Symbol * indicates monthly series.

Absolute poverty measures do not violate the monotonicity axiom of distribution. As Sen (1976) and Foster and Shorrocks (1988) argued it is important to incorporate the degree of inequality in the measurement of poverty. This requires computing the Gini coefficient as contained in Table A4 and Table A5 along with head count and income gap ratios contained Table A2 and Table A3. Comparing the pattern of shares of income going to different households across countries gives a rough idea about the relative position of a particular household in the income distribution. EU economies such as the UK and Switzerland as well as the African economies such as the Ghana and Tunisia have more equal distribution of income than the US. East Asian economies such as South Korea and Taiwan seem to be with more equal income distribution than the South Asian economies such as Nepal. Latin American economies, Chile and Bolivia have highly unequal distribution of income.

Table A3
Structure of income distribution across countries

	Bolivia	*Chile*	*Ghana*	*Nepal*	*South Korea*	*Switzer land*	*Taiwan*	*Tunisia*	*UK*	*USA*
H1	0.018	0.014	0.028	0.021	0.028	0.025	0.038	0.028	0.021	0.016
H2	0.030	0.023	0.042	0.032	0.046	0.045	0.052	0.038	0.047	0.035
H3	0.039	0.030	0.053	0.040	0.057	0.053	0.061	0.048	0.059	0.050
H4	0.048	0.038	0.065	0.049	0.066	0.062	0.070	0.059	0.069	0.063
H5	0.059	0.046	0.075	0.058	0.076	0.073	0.079	0.070	0.080	0.076
H6	0.072	0.057	0.087	0.070	0.087	0.084	0.090	0.085	0.093	0.091
H7	0.087	0.071	0.102	0.086	0.100	0.100	0.102	0.102	0.106	0.109
H8	0.114	0.092	0.122	0.110	0.118	0.120	0.118	0.132	0.125	0.131
H9	0.160	0.140	0.153	0.157	0.145	0.150	0.146	0.189	0.152	0.166
H10	0.374	0.489	0.272	0.377	0.276	0.288	0.244	0.247	0.247	0.264
	1.000	1.000	1.000	1.000	1.000	1.000	1.000	1.000	1.000	1.000

It is possible to measure a comprehensive poverty index as in equation (1) using the data on income distribution contained in Tables A1-A3. These comprehensive poverty indices are given in Table A4. Theoretically value of such index varies between zero and one but it is between these two extremes in reality. Economies that score low in terms of absolute income can score high in terms relative distribution.

Table A4
Cumulative share of income distribution across countries

	Bolivia	*Chile*	*Ghana*	*Nepal*	*South Korea*	*Switzer land*	*Taiwan*	*Tunisia*	*UK*	*USA*
H1	0.018	0.014	0.028	0.021	0.028	0.025	0.038	0.028	0.021	0.016
H2	0.048	0.037	0.070	0.053	0.074	0.070	0.090	0.067	0.067	0.051
H3	0.087	0.068	0.124	0.093	0.131	0.123	0.151	0.115	0.126	0.101
H4	0.135	0.105	0.188	0.142	0.197	0.186	0.221	0.174	0.196	0.164
H5	0.194	0.151	0.264	0.200	0.273	0.258	0.300	0.244	0.276	0.240
H6	0.266	0.208	0.351	0.269	0.360	0.342	0.390	0.329	0.369	0.330
H7	0.353	0.279	0.453	0.356	0.460	0.442	0.492	0.431	0.475	0.439
H8	0.466	0.371	0.575	0.466	0.578	0.562	0.610	0.563	0.600	0.570
H9	0.626	0.511	0.728	0.623	0.724	0.712	0.756	0.753	0.753	0.736
H10	1.000	1.000	1.000	1.000	1.000	1.000	1.000	1.000	1.000	1.000

Table A5
Sen's Poverty indices in cross section of countries

	Income Gap Ratio_mi	*Income Gap Ratio_hmi*	*Gini coefficient*	*Poverty index -mi*	*Poverty index-hmi*
Bolivia	0.102326	0.079653	0.624132	0.631896	0.60628
Chile	0.123093	0.090413	0.702367	0.702076	0.675029
Ghana	0.119833	0.10950	0.516766	0.538724	0.50398
Nepal	0.098711	0.072422	0.61786	0.625968	0.602082
South Korea	0.119786	0.109359	0.507487	0.530548	0.495733
Switzerland	0.124988	0.124965	0.526959	0.548587	0.511093
Taiwan	0.103491	0.120949	0.465898	0.490125	0.457928
Tunisia	0.11925	0.071833	0.534544	0.554274	0.524879
UK	0.132031	0.146092	0.498815	0.525377	0.484379
USA	0.139896	0.113125	0.544104	0.565913	0.527802

Source: Department of Work and Pension

Appendix 2

TABLE 14 (Appendix 1): Average incomes, taxes and benefits by decile groups of ALL households, 2003-04

	Decile groups of all households ranked by equivalised disposable income										*All house-holds*
	Bottom	*2nd*	*3rd*	*4th*	*5th*	*6th*	*7th*	*8th*	*9th*	*Top*	
Average per household (£ per year)											
Decile points (equivalised £)			9348	11667	13712	15956	18444	21206	24486	29555	38420
Number of households in the population ('000s)	2464	2469	2465	2468	2465	2469	2468	2466	2467	2468	24670
Original income											
Wages and salaries	1340	3110	5382	9368	13884	18617	22556	29741	36014	58843	19885
Imputed income from benefits in kind	8	-	26	30	97	144	278	432	716	1573	330
Self-employment income	439	578	695	1268	1018	1346	2232	2522	4326	12745	2717
Occupational pensions, annuities	401	890	1250	1871	2216	2623	2520	3021	2962	3515	2127
Investment income	256	233	240	381	480	563	612	917	1452	3572	871
Other income	141	99	113	187	219	221	269	161	226	360	200
Total	2586	4910	7706	13105	17915	23514	28467	36794	45695	80608	26130
Direct Benefits in Cash											
Retirement pension	1807	2754	2838	2422	2322	1758	1537	1174	925	553	1809
Job seeker's allowance (Contribution based)	58	40	11	14	15	6	4	3	5	4	16
Incapacity benefit	337	554	375	284	179	209	163	162	36	25	232
Widows' benefits	32	28	36	56	52	54	22	28	19	3	33
Statutory Maternity Pay/Allowance	1	3	1	1	2	7	17	15	13	44	10
Non-contributory											
Income support1	914	1075	728	471	345	190	174	25	39	6	397
Child benefit	404	397	363	452	425	402	367	354	276	229	367
Housing benefit	714	875	920	592	474	246	223	64	74	13	420
Job seeker's allowance (Income based)	173	86	46	8	31	2	15	0	-	-	36
Invalid care allowance	34	43	116	74	36	51	18	22	13	3	41
Attendance allowance	8	46	90	71	73	85	63	11	21	-	47
Disability living allowance	149	253	422	437	398	331	295	157	85	42	257
War pensions/War widows' pensions	2	18	6	23	28	34	34	41	43	-	23
Severe disablement allowance	50	34	43	60	37	63	13	1	14	4	32
Industrial injury disablement benefit	5	28	23	33	34	38	15	26	15	3	22
Student support	14	30	15	58	36	40	18	16	35	103	37
Government training schemes	15	8	10	9	12	5	3	3	12	-	8
Tax credits 2	170	319	366	390	278	185	90	68	60	15	194

Contd....

	Decile groups of all households ranked by equivalised disposable income										*All house-holds*
	Bottom	*2nd*	*3rd*	*4th*	*5th*	*6th*	*7th*	*8th*	*9th*	*Top*	
Other non-contributory *benefits*	181	173	189	137	139	101	75	72	55	44	117
Total cash benefits	5067	6763	6598	5591	4915	3805	3147	2242	1740	1091	4096
Gross income	7654	11673	14304	18697	22829	27319	31614	39037	47436	81700	30226
Direct taxes and Employees' NIC											
Income tax	287	455	854	1548	2258	3170	4190	5675	7478	16287	4220
less: Tax credits3	16	96	170	271	232	211	186	167	65	21	144
Employees' NI contributions	92	183	330	610	925	1301	1622	2161	2616	3326	1317
Council tax and Northern Ireland rates 4	730	766	746	814	828	862	899	952	1027	1142	876
less: Council tax benefit/Rates rebates	278	265	214	139	93	55	48	13	10	7	112
Total	815	1043	1545	2563	3686	5066	6477	8609	11046	20726	6158
Disposable income	6839	10630	12759	16134	19144	22253	25137	30428	36390	60973	24069
Equivalised disposable income	6706	10527	12698	14818	17243	19874	22824	26827	33303	60042	22486
Indirect taxes											
Taxes on final goods and services											
VAT	968	1098	1133	1538	1685	1989	2110	2381	2758	3563	1922
Duty on tobacco	287	339	347	263	325	316	366	266	300	210	302
Duty on beer and cider	54	83	79	100	118	127	142	175	172	143	119
Duty on wines & spirits	76	79	104	121	141	184	140	186	252	250	153
Duty on hydrocarbon oils	212	225	255	366	417	495	525	617	655	730	450
Vehicle excise duty	65	67	76	107	125	140	148	179	186	195	129
Television licences	86	79	85	90	93	98	104	110	109	110	96
Stamp duty on house purchase	44	30	38	68	66	86	107	131	188	395	115
Customs duties	16	17	18	22	23	27	28	31	36	44	26
Betting taxes	20	23	27	32	52	40	61	35	36	25	35
Insurance premium tax	23	23	26	33	38	46	52	60	65	85	45
Air passenger duty	11	21	6	10	15	15	25	29	37	53	22
Camelot National Lottery Fund	33	45	48	48	64	56	59	65	62	35	52
Other	8	13	7	21	29	12	31	25	23	19	19
Intermediate taxes											
Commercial and industrial rates	153	161	166	205	222	254	265	296	339	419	248
Employers' NI contributions	255	268	277	341	371	424	442	493	566	699	414
Duty on hydrocarbon oils	103	108	112	138	150	171	179	199	229	283	167

Contd....

	Decile groups of all households ranked by equivalised disposable income										*All house-holds*
	Bottom	*2nd*	*3rd*	*4th*	*5th*	*6th*	*7th*	*8th*	*9th*	*Top*	
Vehicle excise duty	21	22	23	29	31	35	37	41	47	58	35
Other	137	144	149	184	200	229	238	266	305	377	223
Total indirect taxes	2572	2847	2976	3716	4166	4746	5058	5587	6367	7692	4573
Post-tax income	4267	7783	9783	1241	14978	17506	20079	24841	30023	53281	19496
Benefits in kind											
Education	2612	1908	1566	2113	1995	1775	1605	1477	1254	822	1713
National health service	3037	3430	3351	3160	3120	2874	2697	2520	2234	2074	2850
Housing subsidy	80	89	83	67	49	38	27	15	5	0	45
Rail travel subsidy	25	13	15	24	23	39	43	56	78	106	42
Bus travel subsidy	57	61	55	62	53	58	46	50	53	41	54
School meals and welfare milk	80	60	39	28	14	9	9	4	4	1	25
Total	5890	5559	5109	5455	5254	4794	4428	4122	3628	3044	4728
Final income	10157	13342	14892	17873	20232	22300	24507	28963	33651	56326	24224

1. Including pension credit
2. Child tax credit and working tax credit payments which are treated as benefits (see Appendix 2, paragraph 22).
3. Child tax credit and working tax credit payments which are treated as negative income tax. Also includes tax relief at source on life assurance premiums.
4. Council tax and Northern Ireland rates after deducting discounts.©s

7

Political Economy of Conflict, Cooperation and Economic Growth: Nepalese Dilemma

Keshab Bhattarai[25]

INTRODUCTION

Capital, labour and technology have been central factors in determining the rate of economic growth in the classical, neo-classical and endogenous models of economic growth. Both theoretical and empirical studies abound on how these variables impact on economic growth and why these growth rates vary from one country to another even if they have similar rates of saving, endowment and growth rates of labour, and the level of technology[1]. These models rely on competitive markets where factors are paid according to their marginal productivities. Very little discussion is found in the literature, however, on how conflicts among various economic agents in the economy reduce the rates of economic growth as seen in growth disaster countries and how the cooperation among them can generate spectacular rates of growth in growth miracle countries over time. Persistence of conflicts and violence paralyses markets and stops investment and production activities and creates economic crises. It destroys existing infrastructure and prevents creation of new ones. Why big economies are able to control such violence but small ones not? This paper aims to analyse the role of conflict and cooperation in economic growth with the help of a simple game-theoretic model and illustrates its application using the Nepalese dilemma on impacts of conflict on economic retardation and prospect of cooperation on growth. Section two introduces a political economy model[2] to analyse the effects of conflicts and cooperation in economic growth. The political economy structure of Nepal is presented in

25. I very much appreciate my brothers Kedar Bhattarai in Kathmanud for painfully gathering survey information for the empirical part of this paper and for Bishnu Bhattarai in Boston for some discussions on the formulation of questionnaire and my mother Hari Maya Bhattarai, Sisters Manu Maya Bhattarai and Basundhara Khanal and millions of Nepalese people for invaluable inspiration for this study. All errors and omissions are my own.

section three with further analysis of solution on the conflict in section four. The conclusion of the study and recommendations along with references are given in the last section. Appendix contains graphical representation of the model of conflict and growth, sample structure and summary for empirical support of the model, salient features of the Nepalese economy in comparison to her South Asian neighbours.

POLITICAL ECONOMY MODEL OF CONFLICT AND COOPERATION

Take a developing economy that produces Y amount of total output in each year using labour, capital and technology inputs. This Y includes both private (C) and public (G) commodities and services. The government fails to provide private goods as it does not know preferences of households and technology of firms and market fails to provide public goods because of positive and negative externalities in consumption and productions. Public goods including education and health, neither market nor the government can provide sufficiently and efficiently. Public sector goods (G) are provided by tax revenue (T) and the consumption C equals the output net of taxes (Y-T). This economy is inhibited by N number of people in total and $n1$, $n2$ or $n3$ numbers in three different groups each with distinct positions and roles in the economy with consumption $c1$, $c2$ or $c3$ and public goods $g1$, $g2$ or $g3$ and corresponding utility levels U1(c1,g1), U2(c2,g2) and U3(c3,g3) respectively. Questions such as who should decide the level of tax, $T = \{T1, T2, T3\}$, and how it should be collected and how should G be allocated among the sections of communities, $G = \{g1, g2, g3\}$, are the major sources of political disagreement and conflict among power contenders. Some arrangements and allocations are growth enhancing and others are growth retarding. In fact inequality in the distribution of public goods according to the need of people and insecurity of personal freedom and protection of property rights to tax payers is the major issue of conflict.

At the higher level of echelon there are $n1$ number the elites, feudal landlords or hereditary rulers. Their wealth and power more owes to their hereditary status, assets or claims than to their competence, creativity and productive contribution to the economy. Members of this group, through well knit connections and favour, often take the whole of the state machinery as their own private property despite themselves being an insignificant minority of population. Workers and rebel, who do not really have an access to this machinery perceive that this group is parasite that sucks their blood and takes a large share of the Y because of administrative or property rights they have established on resources of the economy and protected by laws and regulations they promulgated over generations using their dominance on state machinery. In many instances these rulers protect their position in the society through loyal armies or military and clever strategic networks spread throughout the economy. Kings at the centre and feudal landlords or tribal lords at the local level represent these groups. This group uses this political power and connections to oppress opponents and to secure economic gains. They enjoy more both of private luxury goods as well as public goods. Power is proportional to the size of army and amount of defence goods which are funded by the tax revenue mainly raised from the income of workers.

Then there are *n2* numbers of middle class working people that make the majority of population. They are self-employed as farmers, entrepreneurs or traders; a small fraction of them work in service sectors; others work for organised political parties. Politically members of this group are influenced by ideas of democracy, freedom and individual liberties; economically they are keen to achieve more by using their talents and capabilities on the basis of a fair playing field in their trades; socially they communicate to each other through media, newspapers, journals, conferences, mass-meetings and rallies. A significant diversity and heterogeneity among them appears due to economic, ethnic, religious and cultural backgrounds. They are divided on the basis of their origin or profession and are individually very vulnerable to whims of rulers though collectively they belong to the most powerful economic group in the economy. Since they are divided on the basis of their origins, believes, professions or personal interests, coordination among them is very difficult. Rulers take advantage of this fact and keep a policy that divides them and makes them even weaker by making them play against each other using subtle tactics of pecuniary or political favours. It is in their interest to make this group economically and morally corrupt and weaker to challenge rulers' hereditary claims to the power.

Then there are *n3* numbers of people who have been economically marginalised, lack decent jobs or occupation and have been struggling to meet their basic needs. They have little education or professional skills or property to be economically self-dependent. They face serious income uncertainty and are struggling to meet their basic needs problems. Because of these weak economic reasons, people in this group can easily be mobilised by radicals for a little payment of money for their livelihood. Such marginalisation occurs for several reasons. First one relates to declining inheritance of family property. In a traditional economy and family system each successive generation climbs down the property ladder more often than climbing up. Upon the death of a property holder parent, his/her property is divided equally among children. Thus hereditary property diminishes in each generation according to the number of children in the family. Secondly, they have growing burden of debts incurred for purchasing food, clothes, medicine for activities for survival or for social activities such as weddings or funerals. It is possible that a child in such family is born in debt, grows in debt and dies leaving more debt to its children. They never recover from it and cannot invest in any human capital enhancing activities. Thirdly, children of little educated parents have harder time to get a decent opportunity of education; they drop out in early stage of education cycle and do not have necessary qualifications to compete for jobs and professions in a modern sector. There is very little learning in family setting as none of the parents of such children are likely to happen to be educated. Fourth, they spend more on feasts and festivals whenever they have some savings and have very little collateral to borrow from formal financial sectors. Fifth they hardly have anything to sale except their labour. A significant number of them are found squatting to public lands for a long time without any entitlement or property right to their house or gardens. This puts down their morale, bargaining power and collateral position in the market. Sixth, the state is often not able to provide public goods including education, health and job insurance to poor who remain very insecure and vulnerable through out their lives.

The global economy impacts this economy through trade and flows of capital, ideas and technology. The benefits of these links flow according to the economic powers of these groups, elites benefit the most from international contacts than people in the working group. Part of their activities involves maintaining good external contacts for economic or personal reasons. The marginal group hardly have any access to these international factors.

Division of Income and Power

The level of growth and development of this economy depends on interactions among these groups. In an ideal and egalitarian society share of income for each group depends on the relative proportion in their population such as

$s_i = \frac{n_i}{n_1 + n_2 + n_3} Y$ where i = 1..3, s_i denotes the share of income Y for group i

which is in proportion to their size in population $\frac{n_i}{n_1 + n_2 + n_3}$, where

$Y = Y_1 + Y_2 + Y_3$ and $C_1 = C_2 = C_3$ and $g_1 = g_2 = g_3$. The real economy, that has evolved over hundred of years, since this primordial society, is far from this ideal scenario. The rulers have used opportunity of tax and spend on public goods to alter their own shares as manifested in their palaces and buildings, lands and business and entitlements from state provisions. The dynamic factors originating from economic relations have distorted the distribution as there has been a tendency among the ruling group to accumulate more economic resources and take ownership of new sources of economic growth as the utility of each group depends on income that they get, which further depends on the degree of concentration of the political power.

How does economic power relate to the political power? In democracy each citizen of a country, even with unequal endowments, should have equal political power, $p_i = \frac{1}{N}$ for a population size of N, which they can use to make collective choices[3]. However, an individual vote would not take its meaning unless it is expressed collectively $P = \sum_i^N p_i$ where P is the total power and N is the total size of population. There is no society in the world where all individuals have the same opinion on any one issue. Therefore this power is often clustered around the groups of individuals with same or similar opinions. In the context of above analysis with three groups in a developing economy each specific group has its utility function that it tries to maximise, $U_i = P_i$ where P_i represents the political power it commands from individuals subscribing to views and ideas that this of group represent. When the power is normalised to one, $\sum_{i=1}^{3} P_i = 1$, then it becomes important to know how this power is distributed among various contesting groups in the economy. Economic growth is enhanced when this power is used efficiently through a social contract that has consent of each section of the society. Misuse of power causes conflict and retardation.

There is a constant struggle in the division of power between elites, workers and paupers. As an increase in the power of one group reduces power of another group, each of them continuously tries to increase its own power. People become more rational with more education and are ready to challenge any source of power that are not directly linked to votes of common people. Real support for the aims and objectives of a group is the real source of powers, which can be increased or reduced by force or coercion for sometime until the fundamentals are realised. At any point of time there is an efficient power sharing bargaining solution that maximises the social objective function subject to the unit power constraint. Maximising a social welfare function with arguments of power for each group of the economy $W = P_1 P_2 P_3$ subject to the power constraint $U = P_1 + P_2 + P_3$ can generate optimal distribution of power among sections. In a real situation each group has a reservation or threshold level of power, represented by the numbers of votes of committed followers, which it is available to that group in any circumstances. The amount of additional part of support fluctuates depending on circumstances of the economy and is closely monitored. Each of them to tries to increase power if an opportunity exists. If this reservation power or the disagreement point in power-sharing agreement is added to the above problem, the efficient solution is obtained by maximum Nash product $W = (P_1 - d_1)(P_2 - d_2)(P_3 - d_3)$ subject to power constraint $U = P_1 + P_2 + P_3$ where represent the disagreement point as illustrated in diagram 1 below.

Further, in a three party situation with Elites (E), Workers (W) and Rebels (R) there are six possible coalitions: three absolute power singletons $\{E\}$, $\{W\}$ and $\{R\}$; two intermediate coalitions $\{E, W\}$ and $\{E, R\}$; and one grand coalition $\{E, W, R\}$. In a winner takes all arrangement the singleton prevails whenever one of the above group manages to win others. When any one particular party cannot clearly win majority votes, two or all of them can form a coalition on the basis of power-sharing agreement. Such agreements tend to be very unstable as each of the coalition partners has an incentive to deviate from the agreement realistically or unrealistically in aspiration of control over all power. The grand coalition is more a theoretical possibility rather than a practical solution. If this can assure political stability, that can be very vital for achieving the higher rate of economic growth.

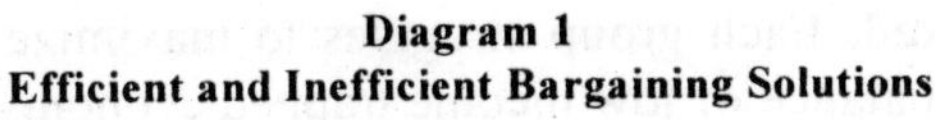

Diagram 1
Efficient and Inefficient Bargaining Solutions

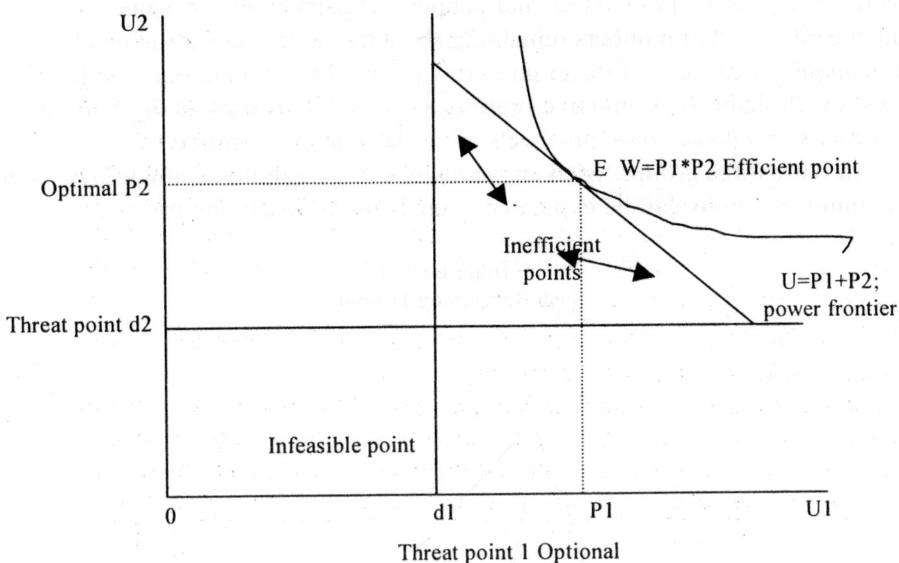

ROLE OF CONFLICTS AND COOPERATION IN THE GROWTH PROCESS

There were very little differences between rulers and common people in the agricultural society. Such differences tend to grow with the development of industry and commerce which not only opens new opportunities but also creates new base of taxes. The gap in the living standards of people between the rulers and the common people rises continuously. This further intensifies the desire of the ruling group to remain in power and increase its economic strengths by investing in securities, insurances and new businesses that would further expand their power. Reforms in such system are unavoidable for a stable and growing economy. Democracies have produced better solution for dynamic economies than communism (Schumpeter (1942) Downs (1957), Myrdal (1982), Sen (1983), Perkins (1994), Przeworski and Limongi (1993), Huber et. al (1993), Shleifer and Treisman (2005), Gunning (1986), Wintrobe (1998), Morris (2001), Paldam (2002), Verwimp (2003), McMillan and Zoido (2005)). Working people are the real producers of goods and services in the economy. They are often free to carry out their ideas in actions independently but have to solicit for permits, licences to carry business and pay taxes to rules to be able to conduct their business. Decisions of rulers can either promote their business or harm their business depending on incentive structure that it generates.

One can think of two different scenarios for conflict and cooperation in this economy as presented in Figures 1 in the appendix. The conflict scenario in part A at the end takes a static and dull view of the economy in which size of economy is considered to be fixed. Each group struggles to maximize its share from this constant share. The balance of low income trapped economy means the share of income going to rulers, workers and paupers remains about the same over time with the ratio of their numbers remaining about the same. Such a static outlook of an economy is cause of disaster and growing number of marginal people in the economy. Probability of massive protests and revolution rises as the intensity of poverty rises and economic prospects of workers do not improve.

All these three groups listed above involve in bargaining continuously. Their bargaining positions can be explained using a Nash Bargaining triangle.

Diagram 2
Nash Bargaining Triangle

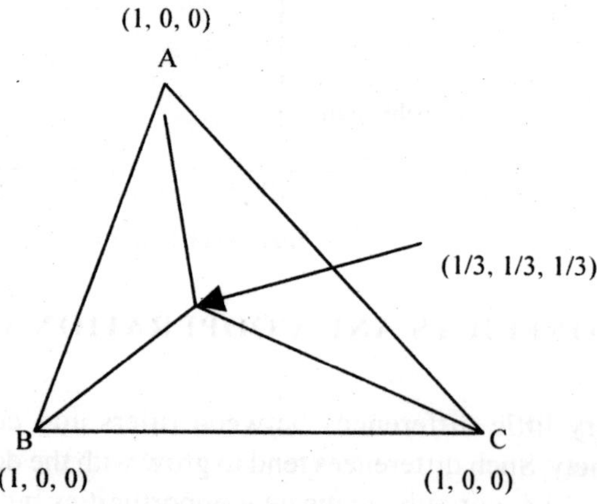

In this bargaining triangle the position A represents a dictatorial position of the ruler, which assumes all powers and represses all people to stabilise and increase his power. At point B the working group retain all power, eliminate the traditional power of Kings. Point C represents rule of extreme rebels. Given the nature of economy non of these three extremes are possible solutions in itself and the bargaining solution is dividing the national income among these three groups as shown by point D. Once such bargain is struck it would be optimal to establish a set of rules that binds each party and let economy move from scenarios A to scenario B in Figure 1 in the appendix. Whether this solution is stable one depends on the gap between the expected outcome and the bargaining result achieved by each party. It is more likely that bargained contracts are broken by one or another party demanding a revision on the contract made earlier according to the new situation. Emergence of new sectors of economy, beginning of new organisations and opportunities, several other reasons may cause such contract to be violated. One group may become stronger than another group to warrant more share in the bargain. Possibility of continuous conflict deters stability of the economy and productive activities.

Figure 1
Short and Far-sighted view of Growth and Development Dynamics in an Economy

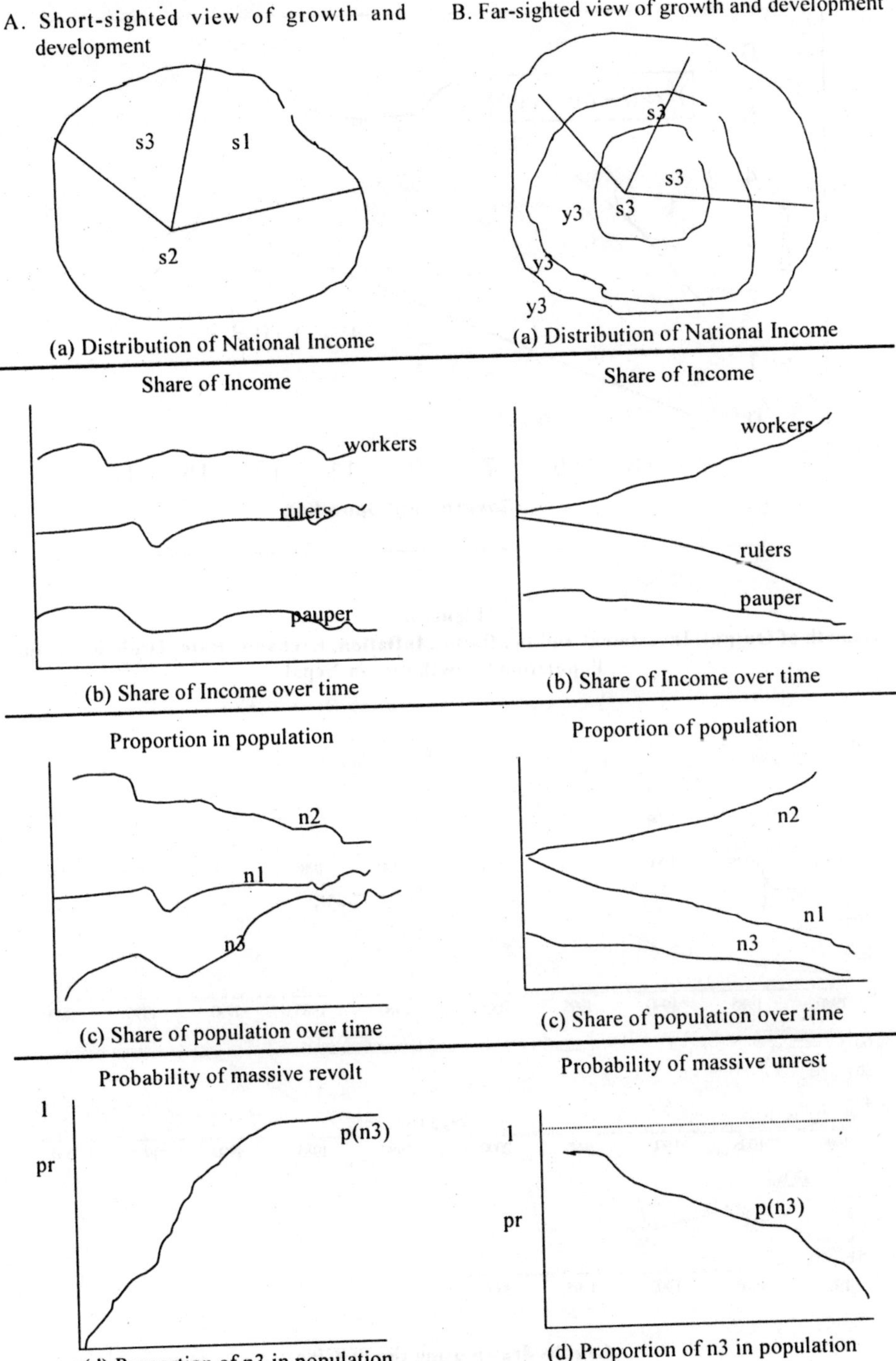

Figure 2
Levels of Income and Size of Government under Kingship, Democracy and Rebels

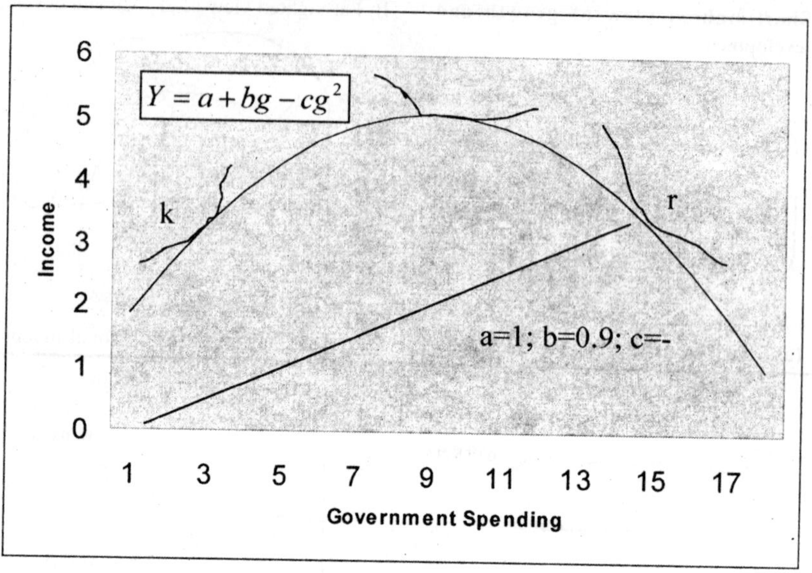

Figure 3
Growth of Output, Investment and tax Ratios, Inflation, Exchange Rate, Trade Ratio and Population Growth rate in Nepal

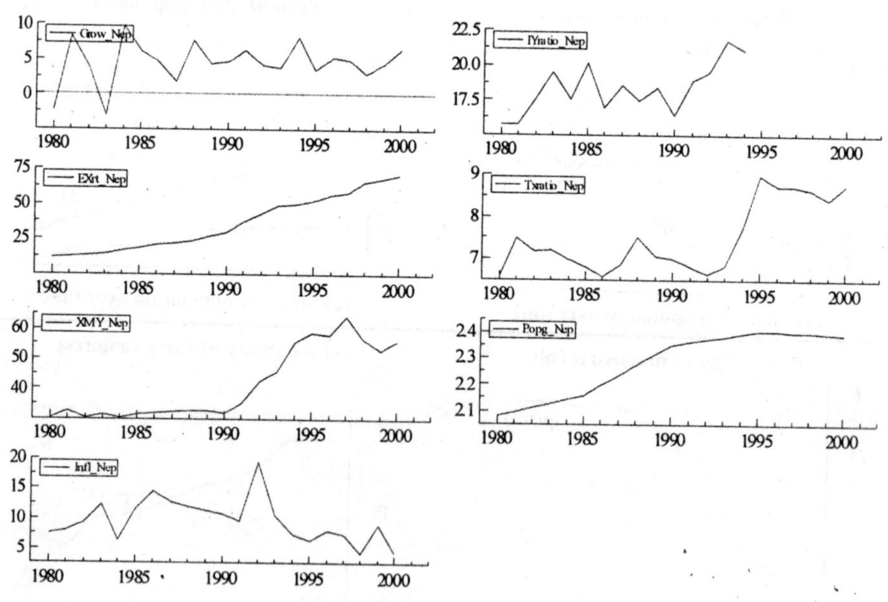

Graphs drawn using the PCGive

Figure 4
Growth, Investment, Tax and inflation in South Asia

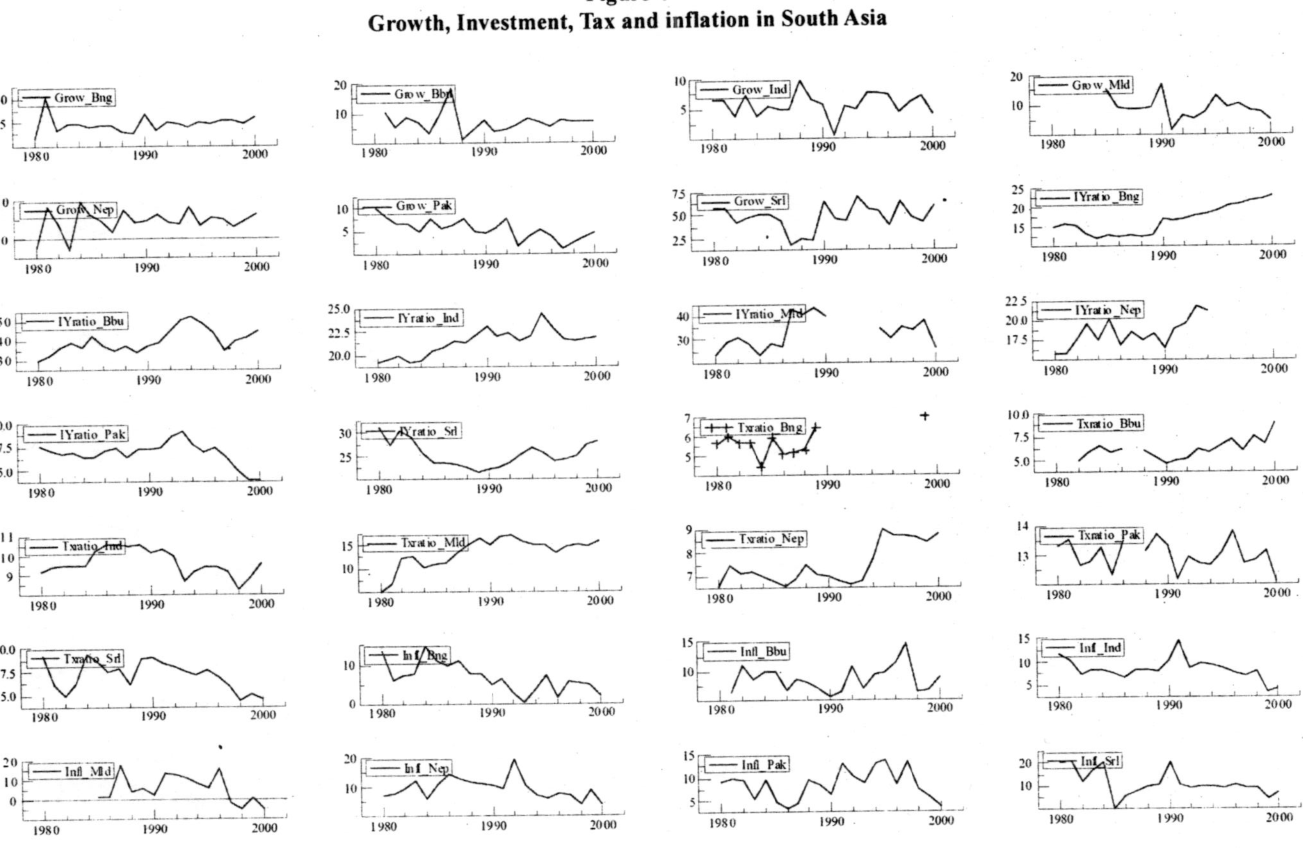

Graphs drawn using the PCGive

Figure 5
Exchange Rate, Trade Ratio and Population Growth Rate in South Asia

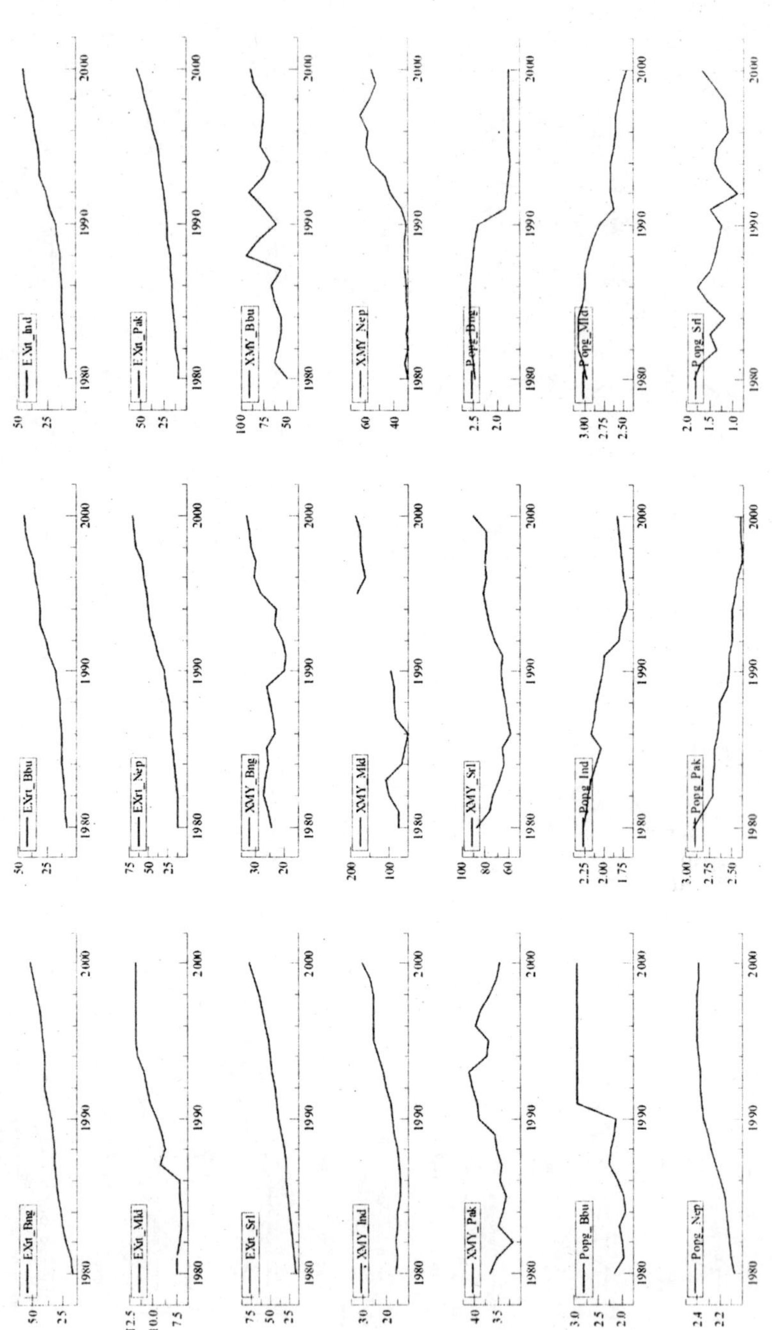

Graphs Drawn Using the PCGive

Table 1
Structure of Random Strategic Sampling on Conflict, Cooperation and Growth in Nepal

Geographic Area	*Sample*	*Age Group*	*Sample*	*Gender*	*Sample*
Tanahun	73	Below 20	34	Male	146
Chitwan	46	20-29	72	Female	84
Kathmandu	22	30-39	44	Total	230
Nawalparasi	36	40-49	45		
Morang	3	50-59	20		
Sunsari	7	60-69	11		
Kaski	6	70-79	4		
Gorkha	4	80-89	0		
Others	33				
Total	230		230		

Ethnicity of Respondents	*Sample*	*Educational Background*	*Sample*	*Profession*	*Sample*
Brahmin	113	Masters	41	Teaching	44
Chhetri	26	Diploma	62	Student	81
Newar	17	Intermediate	40	Business	20
Magar	17	S.L.C.	38	Farmer	26
Guring	13	High School	8	Housewife	17
Rai	5	Primary	15	Government Employee	21
Others	39	Illiterate	14	University Teacher	5
		PhD	8	Other	16
		Other	4		
Total	230		230		230

Table 2
Summary of Answers from the Strategic Sampling on Conflict, Cooperation and Growth in Nepal

How do you think this problem should be solved?	
a. by dialogue among parties and democracy	146
b. abolition of monarch	39
c. People's republic as proposed by Maoists	27
d. absolute monarchy	
Why is not Nepal growing? (1 least)	
a. Corruption	104
b. Low investment	2
c. Political conflict	62
d. Lack of ideas and technology adoption	17
e. Poverty	27
f. Low education	17
g. fewer health facilities	
h. communication and transportation	
i. inefficient market	
What is the problem with political parties?	
a. lack of internal democracy	54
b. personal ambition	129
c. lack of coordination	46

What is Problem with the King?	
a. lacks understanding	63
b. does not know what he is doing	77
c. ambition to retain absolute monarchy	
What is the Problem with Maoists?	
a. violent means	117
b. unreasonable vision	
Do you own any Property?	
House	115
Land	36
Stocks	7
Bank deposits	24
None	24

The far sighted scenario (Figure 1 part B) offers a better solution. Here fundamentals of markets hold, there is some link between the marginal productivity of workers and their remunerations. Entrepreneurs are encouraged to start new businesses and take advantage of latest available technology. Such economy opens opportunities for paupers to upgrade themselves to belong to the working group through means of education and training. It also appeals to elites who join hands with the working group rather than being idle rent-seekers as in the static world. Both these factors raise the proportion of the middle group people relative to those of rulers and paupers.

Diagram 3
Growth of Income and Transition to a Steady economy with Coordination

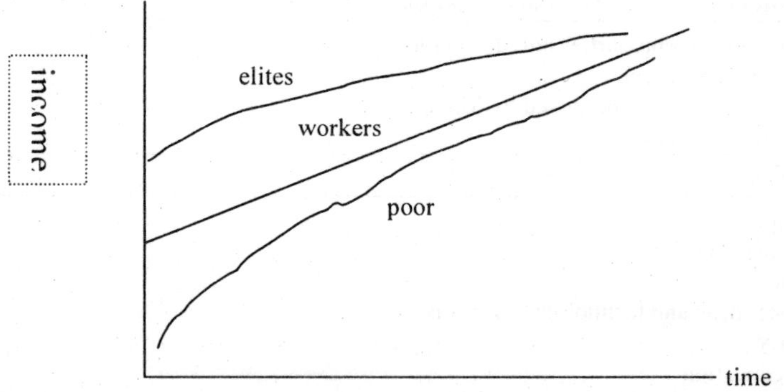

The nature of the solution should look like something as presented in Diagram 3. This solution is not automatic. It may take one generation or two to transform the structure of economy and relative position of these three groups as shown in this diagram. It is possible to achieve this by putting reasonable rates of taxes on the income of rulers and property owners to raise revenue that can be used to finance on education and skill of children from the poor income group along with reforms regarding their fair access to employment and other economic opportunities.

There is more pessimistic dynamic version of the solution to the above game which shows a continuous deterioration of the economy. Permanent conflicts, chaos, and lack of law and order situation due to continued terror and violence in which infrastructure and properties are destroyed, morality and creativeness of investors is harassed. There is massive capital flight and emigration. Such economy is trapped into a vicious circle of poverty.

STRUCTURE OF POLITICAL ECONOMY OF NEPAL

Nepal is one of the poorest countries in the world; 60 percent of its people live in absolute poverty, below the subsistence level. Power contenders are King, political parties and Maoist rebels representing elites, workers and marginal groups as presented in the model outlined in section two. The political conflict has affected prospects of growth in Nepal as in many other developing economies of Asia, Africa, Caribbean and Latin American economies (see figures 2-5 in the appendix). King is interested in maintaining the status quo along with his hereditary power, various political parties have plans and programmes for growth but squabble each other in forming and operating the government and the Maoists are committed to establish a dictatorship of proletariats by eliminating class enemies that include both King and workers running the political parties and have coerced the marginal poor people to join their army for violence and terror in the process of peoples War. An account of each of these elements is given below in order to apply the bargaining model stated in the above section.

The King

King has remained a dominant political power ever since the creation of modern state of Nepal but many people hate the traditional and hereditary nature of King and think that to be a major reason for backwardness of the economy. It is true that about 200 years ago then King P. N. Shah unified this country from 22 and 24 kingdoms scattered in the Western and Eastern parts of current Nepal. He was a popular King because he directed and fought wars with soldiers in the battle fields. Despite being popular in his brevity in war he was less farsighted in setting the hereditary rules by which the eldest son of a King would automatically access on the throne upon his demise. Hereditary King does not have do be aware of real aspirations, problems , objectives and constraints of common people as he neither has experience of tough competition in business or entrepreneurship nor has enough knowledge of recent technologies or ideas that can promote economic growth. Such rules have made the Kingship very unpopular among people. Because of his vested interests in maintaining traditional values and culture that has divided the Nepalese society by casts, ethnicity, economic classes and made them uncritical and subjugated secondary citizens, his ability to be a role model for coming generation is limited. He misused more of this power than used it for productive purposes. This was part of the reason why Ranas were able to relegate them to status of dummy Kings during 104 years of tyrant and autocratic rules during a period of Industrial revolution in the West. Kings came in forefront of Nepalese politics after Ranas relinquished power under the pressure of democratic movements in 1951. Despite that King has not learnt enough lessons and continues betraying people whenever any opportunity arises in which he could have made a difference in the lives of the common people. King has never shown any real initiative for a free, fair and liberalised democratic system and prosperous economy. He is happier in concentrating all powers in him and maintaining a status quo regarding freedom and democracy. He enjoys more a dictatorial regime and absolute power rather than a democratic regime. The history of Nepal is full of stories on conspiracy and assassinations in the Royal family as the Royal massacre of 2002 is very recent in the memory of many people around the world. The glories of Kings in ancient India and Nepal are just myths as far as their relevance in concerned in solving economic problem of current time. The King is simply a dictator who assumes power because of the royal military. Various political events since 1950s such as seizure of elected multi-party government in 1960 and imposition of authoritarian Panchayat regime from 1960 to 1990, re-instalment of dictatorial regime with dissolution of elected parliament and government in 2002 and 2005 are clear evidences for this assertion. Kingship is a regressive not progressive force for the economy and has always betrayed common people. Even though people secured Kings Position as constitutional monarch in 1990, the current King has acted against this good faith while dismantling the elected government and strengthening and elongating the dictatorial regime further in recent years. For a check and balance, it might have been appropriate to warn the government that was inefficient in fulfilling its promises and forgotten the aspirations of people but no one would support the tendency towards dictatorship as justifiable move. It is generating widespread protests from political parties and rebels against the King. People are also concerned because the resources of economy are being spent on managing these conflicts rather than investing in economic growth.

The political parties

Winds of movements for democracy, socialism and desire for modern economic prosperity blew to Nepal from the UK, the Western Europe and the United States through the Indian subcontinent during the time of the movement of freedom and independence in South Asia in 1940s. Ideas of a constitution that guarantees individual freedom and defines state machinery with a clear division of power among legislature, executive and judiciary; has provision of regular free and fair election of representatives in all levels of the government; makes the bureaucracy responsible to elected officials came along with greater emphasis on individual freedom and property rights for a free, open and liberal society and a growing economy. The appeal to Marxist-Leninist ideas of class-struggle, classless society and dictatorship of proletariats in line of the Bolshevik revolution in the Soviet Union and communist revolution in China had less impact in Nepal till early 1960s was evident from the overwhelming majority of the Nepali Congress party in the first parliamentary election held in 1960. Communist ideas spread more after King imposed dictatorial regime dissolving the democratically elected multi-party parliament in 1961. It took thirty years for people to fight back their rights and to curb on the absolute dictatorial power of the King. A successful movement of restoration of democracy in 1990 was seen a very positive political development. It was consistent with a move towards more liberalism in India and China. Nepal was up to date in terms of political system with the rest of the world. This was made possible through a united front made by the social democrats (Nepali Congress) and leftist parties (Communist party of Nepal) representing the major political forces in the country.

The Nepali Congress Party had remained at the forefront in the movement of democracy and socialism in Nepal as practiced in many European countries. Its ideology is also influenced by the socialist groups of India. It was started by BP Koirala in late 1940s and has remained one of the strongest party through-out the democratic movement in Nepal, has support of liberal minded people and professionals and has remained continuously in direct conflict with Kings regarding the supremacy of elected parliament over monarchy. The influence of the Communist Party (Marxist-Leninist) increased during the Kings' dictatorial regime between 1960 and 1990. Initially the King had used them strategically to counterbalance the growing power of the Congress party. Communists did not hesitate to compromise to remain themselves under the King though he was their topmost class enemy under the communist ideology. In terms of ideology the Congress party was committed more towards the liberalism and democracy than the Communist Party. For an outsider there seems to be a little difference between them as both of them have accepted constitutional monarchy and were aspiring for a socialist economy. This apparent contradiction in the main group of Nepalese communists who participated in the process of multi-party democracy with a constitutional monarch has given a rise to the more extreme leftist parties such as Nepal Peasants and Workers' Party (NMKP) and the deadliest Nepalese Maoist party of rebels after 1990. There are other minor parties representing the interests of ethnic groups such as Sadbhavana and rightist royal elements such as Nepal Rastriya Prajatantra Party. Though each of above parties claim to represent farmers, traders, entrepreneurs, employees of public and private sectors and other people in the working group at national, district and village levels, the Nepali Congress Party and the Communist Party of Nepal (CPN-UML) were the prominent ones in terms of influence and the two main contenders of political power in the parliamentary democracy that started in 1990.

The government of the Nepali Congress had taken good initiatives to reform economic policies after it came to power in the beginning of 1990s winning the general election under the multi-party system. For internal stability, prices were stabilised adopting careful balance in the budget deficit by introducing VAT to broaden the tax base, exchange rates were left to the market, trades and financial sector were liberalised and made more competitive; system of licences and quota was dismantled and Nepal became a member of WTO, more expenditure was allocated to the education and health sectors, many public enterprises were sold to the private sector to enhance efficiency. The basic needs including provision of drinking water and electricity were among the top priority and there were policies for balanced development of communication and transportation networks. Despite these measures these parties promised a lot for reducing poverty but achieved very little. Problem further increased because of increase in corruption and lack of discipline in many politicians and distorted economic decisions and raised concerns from the opposition and rebels. No party could hang on to power continuously. The Communist Party and the party of royalists have also formed their own or the coalition government in the parliament when the Congress lost its majority in 1996.

It is clear that none of the parties have been able to retain their clean and clear image in front of the people. Each of them has suffered from the lack of discipline within their organisation and in government and has used power for corruption and malpractices. They have forgotten the promises they made to the people in the election once they were in office and busy in the power struggle. Though there had been some progress in liberalisation of the economy, in education, health and transportation sectors, the poor growth record shows that these parties did not make enough efforts for growth and investment in the economy; their focus was more on distribution rather than in economic growth. They were weaker in implementation and were more corrupt than people in the Congress government. Despite these weaknesses, the freedom of expression and liberty that the system provided to common people had given an open environment in which people could think about their future. These economic and individual freedoms were taken away when the King snatched people's power in 2002.

Maoists

The Maoist ideology entered in Nepal during King's dictatorial regime between 1960 and 1990; the policy of playing against India with China and vice-versa might have attracted some development aids manifested in roads or transportation networks from China but they came along with the Maoist ideology. Despite theoretical contradiction communists strategically accepted King as their leader and strengthened their organisation while following rules set by the absolute monarch. This was the genesis the Maoist movement and radical rebels in Nepal though it is true that Mao himself was not clear what the Maoism stood for. The Chinese Communist Party has already abandoned this ideology as early as mid 1970s. It is an irony that while the Maoism has been discarded as an ideology in the mainland China with its swift transition to the more efficient market system with property rights and individual freedom on economic activities resulting in unprecedented rates of economic growth, the Moaist rebels are becoming stronger and more effective in creating violence and terror in the name of so called Peoples War in Nepal. In principle Maoism was revision on the Soviet model of Marxist-Leninist and Stalinist ideas and was a cult that preached "equality, opposition of bureaucratism and corruption, an idealisation of frugal lifestyles, a denial of individual selfishness and devotion to the public good, a demand for mass participation in political administration, championing of mass criticism and the rights to rebel, and a theory how a new ruling class emerges within the Party" (Walder (1987)). It is said that this cult creates "a paranoid view of political world among its followers by branding as traitor for someone who has insufficient enthusiasm in the worship of Mao, a mentality that encourage the treatment of enemies as non-humans subjectable to any form of humiliation or torture, a notion of democracy that enforces slavish conformity to a single dictator." In Nepal such extreme Maoist party was formed under the freedom of expression and organisation provided by the Constitution of Nepal of 1990. It had six (out of 235) parliamentarians in the first parliament and all of them committed to protest the parliamentary system from inside the parliament. They boycotted the second general election in 1996 and started Peoples War using any means of terrorism. They have formed a parallel government, looted arms and ammunitions from military barracks, killed people and created fears and tensions in the minds of people. They destabilised the whole system and created confusion and uncertainty among common people including entrepreneurs, traders and business people. They have strongholds in remote poverty belts of Nepal and mobilised the marginal groups massively for terror activities. More than 12000 people have been killed in last 10 years because of the violence and terror created by Maoists and brought the country to a bloody civil war. Peaceful country of Buddha has become very frightening war zone, full of explosions, riots and attacks. This conflict has reduced the rates of investment and saving and economic growth in Nepal. It seems that it is not possible to solve current impasse without bringing Maoists into the main-stream of the political economy of Nepal. More failure in bargaining means more violence and more terror.

NEPALESE DILEMMA: CONFLICT RESOLUTION AND COOPERATION FOR GROWTH

Nepal is in conflict and crises because of inherent contradiction among three political economic forces mentioned in the previous section. King wants to increase his power, political parties want to form their own governments but have proved incompetent while they had an opportunity to do so, and Maoists want to eliminate both of them and create their own state. Conflicts and growing internal tensions have reduced investment and other economic activities, deterred donors to continue developmental activities in Nepal and frightened tourists from visiting Nepal. It has created hatred among people and demoralised investors and created sense of fear among consumers and producers. Cumulative effect of all these political disagreement is leading to a civil war and permanent crises. It is urgent to sort out his problem before any initiative for long run growth. How can a bargaining model be applied successfully to solve this problem? If there is no agreement among these three, this economy will further face a situation of dynamic deterioration. Nepal will be left permanently in poverty and crises. Entrepreneurs and skilled workers will abandon the country, science and technology will not reach out there, it will not benefit from the rapid space of globalisation, it will remain isolated and a basket case of poverty. Any solution that does not satisfy each of these parties is bound to fail. Application of force and coercion may suppress the situation for a while but the problem will rise again.

It is clear from above analysis that King (*K*), parties (*P*) and rebels (*R*) do not have ability to run the government own their own. The singletons $\{K\}$, $\{P\}$ and $\{R\}$ are not feasible solutions, politically, economically or socially; two intermediate coalitions $\{K, P\}$ and $\{K, R\}$ have been tried out and failed; and one grand coalition $\{K, P, R\}$ seems the only solution that has not been put in practice efficiently. As stated in section two at any time there is an efficient bargaining solution for such strategic economic problem where parties maximise their social objective function subject to the unit power constraint (Max $W = P_1P_2P_3$ subject to $U = P_1 + P_2 + P_3$ as given in section 2). If this reservation power or the disagreement point in power-sharing agreement is added to the above problem the efficient solution is obtained by maximum Nash product 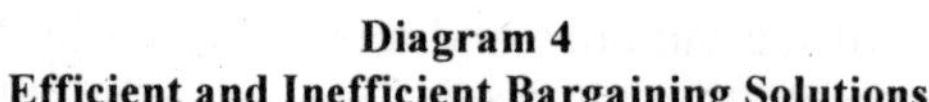 $W = (P_1 - d_1)(P_2 - d_2)(P_3 - d_3)$ subject to power constraint where represent the disagreement point. In a two party case solution looks like in diagram 4.

Diagram 4
Efficient and Inefficient Bargaining Solutions

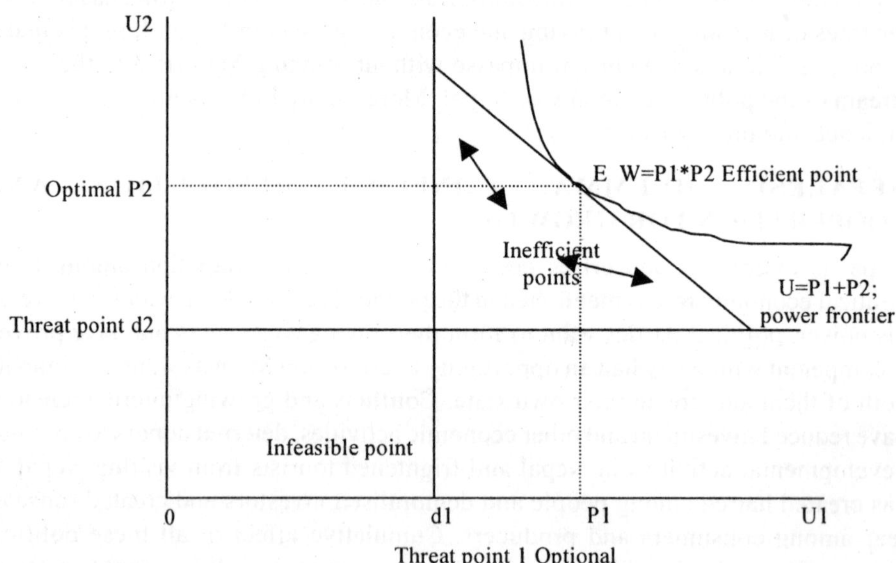

Returning to three-pronged Nepalese dilemma each party is pivotal for the bargaining solution. King should understand that returning to absolute monarchy is inconsistent with democracy and for the growth of the economy and be satisfied with the titular position as practiced in the many of the western democracies including Britain, Denmark and Spain. Political parties should put economic growth in top priority and adopt efficient and prudent policies taking a view of long horizon. Maoists should reconsider not to introduce failed ideology in Nepal if they are really concerned about uplifting the lives of marginal and poor people taking lessons from the failure of communism and move towards market based allocations and greater democracy and socialism both in Russia and China (Walder (1987), Perkins (1994), Shleifer and Treisman (2005)). The grand coalition that all agree will be one which can come with a solution, at least in the long run in which, $W = (P_1 - d_1)(P_2 - c_1 + g_1 = c_2 + g_2 = c_3 + g_3 d_2)(P_3 - d_3)$ where each have prospects of having equal sum of private and public consumption. This can occur only when the tax revenues from the high income group pays for the public goods of low income groups. The solutions of this bargaining problem may be summarised in terms of following points.

(a) Make "a grow Nepal contract" and put growth as the first objective of the political economic system. Put a system that promotes economic growth and remove features that are harmful for economic growth. Make sure that fruits of growth are distributed more evenly among people.

(b) The parliament should decide a tax rate on income of the King and he should pay these taxes without any hesitation. The King should not be treated more than an ordinary citizen for tax purposes and he should be elected but not hereditary. If King does not heed to people's demand he should be overthrown and his land and palaces should be used for starting schools and universities to educate children from the poor background.

(c) Political parties should run their organisations in true spirit of democracy and have a system of punishing corrupt party officials according to amount of such corruption. Any citizen should be able to make a case against such corruption.

(d) Extra resources should be channelled for education, health care, job security of the marginal groups. Maoists should abandon their arms as well as the violence and terror as a means of achieving their political objectives. They should not threaten common people.

(e) The nation should give each citizen an equal starting point by means of education and training and let their creativity and productivity prosper according to their abilities through competitive system and elimination of corruption.

(f) Each party should respect the fundamental human rights and individual freedom. It should commit itself to establish the rule of law, strengthen laws for property rights, establish liberal system of tax and transfer, ensure transparency in use of public funds and system of eliminating corruptions.

Cooperative solution can improve the situation significantly and let economy to move on the path of prosperity. The Ninth and Tenth Plans of Nepal in NPC

(1997, 2002) contain details on the Nepalese economy but they lack sufficient analytical structure required by the challenge of the time. To my knowledge Bhattarai (2000) goes one step towards detailed economic modelling of the Nepalese economy taking account of the structure details of demand, supply and production and trade sides of economy. Acharya (2000) suggests measures necessary to institutional set up for a parliamentary democracy suitable to Nepal. Panday (1999) points regarding implementations of plans and Hutt (2005) on recent problems are noteworthy.

The international community can contribute significantly in solving this conflict on the basis of collective experiences that has been accumulated over years in solving these types of problems around the globe. Many lessons can be learnt from the experience of democratic struggles and transformation in many of the Western countries in the past and Eastern countries in recent years, and particularly on how the adult franchise and the market economy can offers better solutions for growth, technical progress and redistribution than by authoritative regimes.

EMPIRICAL SUPPORT FOR THE ABOVE MODEL

A strategic random sampling survey on opinions of Nepalese male and female belonging various age groups, living in different parts of country and working in cross sections of occupations was conducted during the period between January to March 2006. They were asked to express their opinions about how the existing conflict among the political parties, King, and Maoists had affected their lives, how these problems should be solved and express their believes on which one of them would be able to solve these problems. They also were asked to express their ranking of various factors hindering growth of Nepal, what were the major problems of each of above political forces. The structure of sample and the responses are as reported in Tables 1 and 2.

Sample represented opinions of people from 26 out of 75 districts in Nepal, though the sample was more clustered in Tanahun (32%), Chitwan (20%), Nawalparasi (15.7%) and Kathmandu (9.6%). Out of 230 people surveyed 63 percent were males. These people represented 26 ethnic groups though mainly dominated by Brahmin and Chhetri (61%). Respondents were quite educated by Nepalese standards.

Majority of people reported their daily activities to be seriously affected by the conflict and the major way out of this crisis was a political dialogue (64%) rather than absolute monarchy (17%) or people's republic (11.3%). Corruption (45%). Political conflict (27%) and poverty (12%) were pointed to be major obstacles to economic growth. Personal ambition of political leaders (56%), lack of the internal democracy (24%) and coordination were major weaknesses of political parties, while the ambition to retain the absolute power (39%), lack of understanding of the problem (27 %). Another 31 percent thought that he did not know what he was doing. Most respondents were critical of violent means of Maoists and they accused them for unreasonable vision.

CONCLUSION

Conflict among feudal factors led by the King, working people in trade and industry led by political parties, marginal, poverty trapped people threatened and mobilised by Maoist rebels has created a very unproductive environment where investors and entrepreneurs do not get any productive opportunity. Non-cooperation among competing political and economic forces has brought Nepal into crisis and a growth disaster. The major reason for conflict is short-sighted horizon of these players with constant sum view who try to maximise their own current share on GDP taking its size as a constant. It has discouraged productive economic activities and transfer of better technology and knowledge and resources from abroad with dangerous consequences to the economy. A solution is offered here in terms of a contract in more objectives and specific growth oriented rules that bounds each of them to the policy rules in which each of these groups has incentive to stick for peace and prosperity, adoption and use of knowledge and technology for growth. This is possible if they take a more optimistic grow-Nepal strategy to maximise the growth rate of the economy.

REFERENCES

Acharya N.H. (2000), *Naya Nepalko Prastavana* (Proposal for New Nepal), Kathmandu Nepal.

Bardhan P. (1997), Methods and Madness: A political economy analysis of ethnic conflicts in less developed countries, World Development, 25:1381-1398.

Besley T. and S. Coate (2003), Sources of inefficiency in a representative democracy: A Dynamic Analysis, *American Economic Review*, 88:1:139-156.

Bhattarai KR (2004), Economic Growth: Models and Global Evidence, Research Memorandum , University of Hull.

Bhattarai KR (2000), Welfare and distributional Impacts of financial liberalisation in a developing economy: Lessons from a forward looking CGE model of Nepal, Working Paper no. 7, Hull Advances in Policy Economics Research Papers.

Downs A. (1957), *Economic Theory of Democracy*, Harper and Row, New York.

Easterly W. (2001), The elusive quest for growth: economists' adventure and misadventures in the tropics, MIT press, MA.

Gunning P. J. (1986), An economic Approach to Riot Analysis, *Public Choice*, 13:31-47.

Huber E . D. Rueschemeyer and J. D. Stephens (1993), The Impact of Economic Development on Democracy, *Journal of Economic Perspective*, 7:3:71-85.

Hutt M. (2005), Nepal and Bhutan: Two Kings, Two Features, Asian Survey, XLV:1:83-87, Jan/Feb.

Maskin E. and J. Tirole (2004), The Politician and the Judge: Accountability in Government, *American Economic Review*, 94:4:1034-1054.

McMillan J. and P. Zoido (2005), How to Subvert Democracy: Montesinos in Peru, *Journal of Economic Perspective*, 18:4:69-92.

Mehrling P. G. (1986), A classical model of the class struggle: A game-Theoretic Approach, Journal of Political Economy, 94:6:1280-1303.

Morris S. (2001), Political Correctness, *Journal of Political Economy*, 109:2:231-65.

Myrdal G. (1982), Asian Drama: An Inquiry Into the Poverty of Nations, Kalyani Publishers, New Dehli.

National Planning Commission (1997 and 2002), The Ninth and Tenth Plans of Nepal, Kathmandu, Nepal.

Paldam M. (2002), The cross country pattern of corruption: economics, culture and the seasaw dynamics, *European Journal of Political Economy*, 18:215-240.

Panday D. R. (1999), Nepal's Failed Development: Reflection on the Mission and the Maladies, Kathmandu, Nepal.

Perkins D. (1994), Completing China's Move to the Market, *Journal of Economic Perspective*, 8:2:23-46.

Przeworski A. and F. Limongi (1993), Political Regimes and Economic Growth, *Journal of Economic Perspective*, 7:3:51-69.

Schumpeter J. (1942), Capitalism, Socialism and Democracy, Harper.

Sen A. K. (1983), Development: which way now? *Economic Journal*, 93:372-745-62.

Shleifer A. and D. Treisman (2005), A Normal Country: Russia After Communism, *Journal of Economic Perspective*, 19:1:151-174.

Verwimp P. (2003), The political economy of coffee, dictatorship and genocide, *European Journal of Political Economy*, 19:161-181.

Walder A. G. (1987). Actually Existing Maoism, *Australian Journal of Chinese Affairs*, 18:155-166 July.

Wintrobe A. (1988), *The political economy of dictatorship*, Cambridge University Press.

Wittman D. (1989), Why democracies produce efficient results? *Journal of Political Eocnomy*, December 97:6:1395-426.

NOTES

1. See Ramsey (1928), Harrod (1939), Domar (1947), Solow (1956), Cass (1965), Koopmans (1965), Lucas (1988), Romer (1989) for theories and Madison (1991) Mankiw, Romer and Weale (1992), Barro and Sala-i-Martin (1995), Temple (1999), Bhattarai (2004) for empirical studies.
2. See Gunning (1986), Bardhan (1997), Easterly (2001) for studies on riots and ethnic conflicts and Schumpeter (1942), Myrdal(1982), Sen (1983), Przeworski and Limongi (1993), Wittman (1989), Easterly (2001), Virwimp (2003) on models of development and democracy and Mehrling (1986), Besley and Coate (2003), Maskin and Tirole (2004) for models of political economy
3. Such political power can mitigate the inequality caused by the market. In evolution of the election system with one person one vote were behind the adoption of the social democratic system by majority of Western economies, as their economies industrialised in the last century and adoption of general welfare system in the second half of the 20th century.

8

Keynesian Models for Analysis of Macroeconomic Policy[29]

Keshab R. Bhattarai

INTRODUCTION

Macroeconomic models have been in use for formulation of economic policy almost in every country in the world. These models not only provide an analytical framework to link the demand and supply sides and the resource allocation process in an economy but also may help in reducing fluctuations and enhancing the economic growth, which are two major aspects of any economy. Classical, Keynesian, new classical and new Keynesian approaches have evolved over time to analyse fluctuations of output, employment and price level over years (Keynes (1936), Hicks (1937), Samuelson (1939), Phillips (1958), Friedman (1968), Phelps (1968), Tobin (1969), Barro and Gordon (1983), Sargent (1986) Goodhart (1989), Nickell (1990), Lockwood Miller and Zhang (1998), IMF (1992)). Empirical validity of these models are tested using either macro-econometric simulations models, applied multisectoral general equilibrium models or by using stochastic dynamic general equilibrium models (Wallis (1989), MPC (1999), Pagan and Wickens (1989), Kydland and Prescott (1977)). There is a considerable controversy about the causes, consequences and remedies for the macroeconomic fluctuations in the short run in the literature. New classical and new Keynesian models use rational expectation and market imperfections and frictions in the labour market or technological shocks in explaining these fluctuations. There is less controversy in the literature about the economic events in the long run despite plenty of work that has been done in area of endogenous and exogenous growth models (Solow

29. Correspondence Address: Business School, University of Hull, HU6 7RX, UK. E-mail: *K.R.Bhattarai@hull.ac.uk* Phone: 01482-463207 and Fax: 01482-643484. This paper was presented at the Keynesian Legacy to the Macroeconomic Modelling Conference in Cassino, Italy in September 2005.

(1956), Lucas (1988), Romer (1990), Mankiw, Romer and Weil (1992), Parente and Prescott (1993)).

Price system played a crucial role in the classical macroeconomic models. Real wages that equate demand for labour to its supply, determined the level of employment and that determined the level of output. Income is either spent on the current consumption or saved for the future consumption. The real sector equilibrium is guaranteed by equality between the saving and investment. The price level is proportional to supply of money and the monetary neutrality is maintained by perfectly flexible real prices. Unemployment or glut cannot happen in the classical system because of the flexibility of prices. Aggregate demand always equals the aggregate supply. The major objective of government is to ensure law and order so that business enterprises could thrive. As such less intervention is considered better. Capital accumulation and saving drives the dynamics of economy in the classical system. More saving means more investment and larger amount of capital stock and higher output. Rapid rate of economic growth through out the 19th century, except few interruptions, provided a strong support for the classical system that influenced thoughts of policy makers from the time of Adam Smith (1776) up to Marshall or Pigou in 1920s. This was the period of industrial revolution and structural transformation and unprecedented improvement in production technology as well as in the living standards of the majority of people in the Western economies.

The assumption of equality between aggregate demand and aggregate supply did not hold true in late 1920s. Factories were producing a lot more than they could sell. Firms laid off employees, people became pessimistic about their future prospects and started spending less. This further reduced the aggregate demand and production capacity became under utilised. More than a quarter of working population became unemployed causing both social and economic problems. Inefficiency of aggregate demand had far reaching consequences on employment and output. This is the starting point of the Keynesian macroeconomic analysis.

Keynes showed how deficiency in aggregate demand may continue for a long period if the government does not step in to solve the problem. In the national income identity, sum of consumption, investment, government spending and net exports, the aggregate demand, should equal aggregate supply. The aggregate demand may remain less than aggregate supply and the productive capacity may be under utilised. Keynes spent a significant amount of time in explaining consumption and investment behaviour of the economy. Values of multiplier and accelerator coefficients were determined based on the key structural parameters such as the marginal propensity to consume, productivity of capital and the sensitivity of imports to the national income. While the ratios of consumption, investment, government expenditure and trade balances to the GDP provide broad indicators of resource constraints, the behavioural assumption behind each of these demand components give a good framework for analysing how fiscal, monetary and exchange rate policies that determine the level of aggregate output, employment and savings and investment activities in the economy. Though the supply shocks, such as the rise in the oil prices in 1970s, gave rise to new classical and new Keynesian approaches with more focus in the supply side of the economy, the basic structure of Keynesian model are still very useful in policy analysis. These models are popular because they are simple and easy to understand. They can be used to compute the impacts of various policy scenarios such as tax cuts, increase in spending, increase in money supply or increase in external demand or change in the behaviour of consumers and producers in an economy.

Macro-econometric models aim to test a macroeconomic model with time series or cross section data on major economic variables (Wallis (1989), MPC (1999), Pagan and Wickens (1989), Hendry (1995), Holly Weale (2000)). Once these models can mimic an actual economy then they are used for policy analysis. Structural parameters such as the marginal propensity of consume and imports, elasticities of investment to the interest rate or change in aggregate demand, elasticity of production to capital and labour inputs. When real parameters are known then a model can be used for policy simulation. Policy makers have control over policy instruments such as the tax rate, or government spending or exchange rate or the interest rate. They like to know how the real output, employment and trade balances change when certain policy measures are implemented. Macro models provide a systematic framework to analyse these questions. These exogenous variables include judgement and decisions of policy makers regarding taxes, money supply, exchange rate, division of resources across various sectors or between consumption and saving. They may include perception of people regarding inflation and expected wages rates and their labour supply behaviour. Traditional econometric models were based on Keynesian structural models as found in the Macro Modelling Bureaus. After the Lucas Critique (Sargent and Wallace (1975), Lucas (1976), King and Plosser (1984)) there has been more effort in modelling the supply side, dynamic optimisation, and incorporating fiscal or monetary or exchange rate policy rules based on fundamentals of an economy.

The applied general equilibrium models of an economy have more elaborate specification about the price mechanism, consumption, production, trade in the economy. These models use input-output tables that provide micro consistent data set on income, expenditure and demand side of the more decentralised economy (Shoven and Whalley (1984), Aurbach and Kotlikoff (1987), Bhattarai (1999), Rutherford (1995), Perroni (1995), Bhattarai and Whalley (1999 and 2003), Kehoe, Srinivasan and Whalley (2005)). A calibrated applied general equilibrium model can reproduce the sufficiently decentralised benchmark economy as its solution and can act as a laboratory of economic policy analyses in which one can estimate the impact of various policy alternatives available to the policy makers. These models can be single country, multiple country or the global economy models which can be used to analyse the impacts of not only domestic policies but also the impacts of external events in the domestic economy. The general equilibrium impacts of tax, trade, labour market, financial sector policies, monetary and fiscal policy measures can be quite deep and penetrating when the all sorts of chain reactions of policy actions are taken into account. These general equilibrium models aim to capture these impacts.

Stochastic dynamic general equilibrium models are outcome of the research programme of new classical economists who oppose the interventionist idea of Keynes to contain economic fluctuations. These models claim that economies are always in equilibrium and fluctuations are outcome of optimising behaviour of economic agents. Economic policies are ineffective in generating real impacts in an economy. The shocks to the production technology or government spending are outcome of a random process. Workers supply more hours when wage rates are high due to technological breakthrough and less hours when wage rates are low. The degree of response depends upon the inter-temporal substitution of labour supply. The model generated solutions are often used to analyse the underlying factors behind macroeconomic series by comparing their variance or covariance to actual time series. Infinite period economy is approximated by steady state characterisation of the first order conditions linking two consecutive periods.

An attempt is made here to provide a general review about the aspects of these macroeconomic models, particularly in its three aspects a simple Keynesian model for analysis of economic policy and its empirical counterpart simultaneous equation model, comparative static analysis in the Keynesian model with a production function and a neoclassical growth model which takes many features of the Keynesian model for the long run prospects of the economy.

A SIMPLE MACROECONOMIC MODEL

Macro economic models aim to explain the level of aggregate demand, employment, interest rates, price level, trade balances, consumption, investment and saving activities of the households and firms and government expenditure and net exports. Keynesian models assume the aggregate supply to be perfectly flexible in the short run with a constant level of prices. Behavioural parameters such as the marginal propensities to consume and import and tax rates determine the impact of policy in the real sectors of the economy. A simple version of Keynesian model can briefly be explained in terms of 12 equations as presented in this section.

Consumption, the major component of the aggregate demand, is determined by disposable income as following

$$C_t = \beta_0 + \beta_1 (Y_t - T_t) \tag{1}$$

where C_t is consumption, Y_t is the national income, T_t is the tax rate. Parameters β_0 and β_1 represent the consumption behaviour in this model; β_0 can be considered as the level of consumption for subsistence and representing the marginal propensity to consume out of disposable income has value between 0 and 1; $0 < \beta_1 = \dfrac{\partial C}{\partial Y} < 1$

Investment is another major component of aggregate demand. In simplest form the investment demand is determined by the rate of interest, the cost of capital and the change in the demand in the previous period as:

$$I_t = \mu_0 + \mu_1 R_t + \phi \Delta Y_{t-1} \tag{2}$$

where I_t is investment demand, R_t is the rate of interest, ΔY_t is the change in demand, *i.e.* $\Delta Y_{t-1} = Y_t - Y_{t-1}$. Interest rate denotes the cost of capital and determines the level of investment, as shown by $\mu_1 = \frac{\partial I}{\partial R} < 0$. Producers invest more if there is more aggregate demand, $\phi = \frac{\partial I}{\partial Y} > 0$.

The government demand (G_t) and exports (X_t) are other two components of aggregate demand. The G_t component is fixed because the government has commitment to a set of public services which cannot be easily altered. The X_t may be determined by the real exchange rate and the foreign income. We assume that both G_t and X_t as exogenous variables in the model.

Imports provide for part of these demand as all goods and services consumed or invested in the economy cannot be produced at home. Most of Keynesian models relate imports to level of domestic income and the real exchange rate:

$$M_t = m_0 + m_1 Y_t + m_2 \lambda_t \tag{3}$$

M_t is the imports and λ_t is the real exchange rate may be defined as $\lambda_t = \frac{eP}{P^*}$ where e is the nominal exchange rate, P is the domestic price level and P^* is foreign price level. Parameters m_0 m_1 and m_2 represent import behaviour of the economy. Import rises with a rise in the level of national income, $\frac{\partial M}{\partial Y} = m_1 > 0$, and the real exchange rate $\frac{\partial M}{\partial \lambda} = m_2 > 0$. Higher real exchange rate makes the domestic economy less competitive in the world. Nominal exchange rate may not always be aligned with the real exchange rate. The purchasing power parity theory implies that currency should appreciate (depreciate) if the domestic inflation rate is lower (higher) than the foreign inflation rate. Evidence suggests that PPP holds in the long run but the risk adjusted uncovered interest parity theory is more appropriate for the short run.

Macroeconomic balance requires the aggregate demand to be equal to aggregate income. Households use part of their income in consumption, other parts to pay taxes or to save as:

$$Y_t = C_t + T_t + S_t \tag{4}$$

This equation defines income constraint of an economy. An economy with more consumption has less amount for saving or taxes or both.

Most often the collection of taxes by the government is mainly determined by the level of income as:

$$T_t = t_0 + t_1 Y_t \tag{5}$$

here t_0 is the collection of lump sum taxes and t_1 is the tax rate proportional to the national income, $\frac{\partial T}{\partial Y} = t_1 > 0$.

The national income identity emerges by putting all above features together from income and demand sides as:

$$C_t + T_t + S_t = Y_t = C_t + I_t + G_t + X_t - M_t \tag{6}$$

where the left hand side represents components of national income and the right hand side represents components of aggregate demand. This also implies that the net national saving, public plus private net savings, should equal the current account balance of the economy, which is often called the fundamental identity of an economy.

$$(T_t - G_t) + (S_t - I_t) = (X_t - M_t) \tag{7}$$

If the net public spending is bigger than the net private saving, it is met by net capital inflow. A country which is less credit worthy or has accumulated heavy debt will not be able to finance its deficit by borrowing from abroad. Imbalances between revenue and government spending represents a change in the national debt $\Delta B_t = (T_t - G_t)$ and debt accumulates over time $B_t = \Delta B_t + rB_{t-1}$. Trade imbalances result in external debt $\Delta D_t = (X_t - M_t)$ and debt accumulates over time $D_t = \Delta D_t + rD_{t-1}$. Persistence in budget or trade imbalances results in massive accumulation of debt.

Equations (1) to (7) represent the real sector in the Keynesian model, where Y_t, C_t, M_t, I_t, R_t and T_t are endogenous variables and $\Delta Y_{t-1}, G_t, X_t$ and λ_t are predetermined or exogenous variables. It assumes that the aggregate supply is fixed in the short run and output is completely determined by the demand side of the economy. Fluctuations in consumption, investment, government consumption or exports are the sources of fluctuation in income and employment in the short run. Hicks(1937) formalised the Keynesian analysis in terms of investment saving and money market equilibrium, IS-LM model in which the IS curve represents the equilibrium in the goods market (IS) given the aggregate supply by a production function, $Y_t = F\left(\bar{K}_t L_t\right)$ in which variation in output is due to variation in employment as the capital stock is fixed in the short run.

National income consistent with equilibrium in the saving and investment (the IS curve) is derived by using (1), (2) and (5) in (6) $\bar{Y}_t = C_t + I_t + G_t + X_t - M_t$ and substituting all demand components (1) to (4) in (5).

$$Y_t = \frac{\beta_0 - \beta_1 c_0 + \mu_0 - m_0 + G_t + X_t}{1 - \beta_1 + \beta_1 t_1 + m_1}$$

$$+ \frac{\mu_1 R_t}{1 - \beta_1 + \beta_1 t_1 + m_1} + \frac{\phi \Delta Y_{t-1}}{1 - \beta_1 + \beta_1 t_1 + m_1} \qquad (8)$$

The first part on the right hand side shows impacts on output due to changes in exogenous or policy variables, the second component shows how the aggregate demand increases (decrease) with low (high) real interest rate, since $\mu_1 < 0$. The third component gives the dynamics of income, the acceleration effect of increase in income in the previous period (we $\Delta Y_{t-1} = 0$ in our first two tables).

We take the above investment saving equilibrium (IS) model of Keynes and solve it for various policy issues specifying eight different policy specifications as presented in Tables 1-4. First is tax cut scenario where tax reduces from 30 percent to 20 percent. It is expected that the tax cut will have expansionary impact on output, consumption and imports. One may expect that government budget surplus to decrease after the tax cut as the government revenue falls due to the lower rate of tax though it rises due to expansion in income which may lead to more collection of taxes after an increase in income. Tax cut results in trade deficit as imports rise while exports are fixed at exogenous level.

Table 1
Parametric Specification of the Keynesian Model

	Parameters	*Base case*	*Tax cut*	*Spending*	*MPC*	*T&G*	*High X*	*High I*	*MMM*
G	200	200	200	400	200	400	200	200	200
X	100	100	100	100	100	100	300	100	100
r	0.1	0.1	0.1	0.1	0.1	0.1	0.1	0.1	0.1
C0	300	300	300	300	300	300	300	300	300
b	0.8	0.8	0.8	0.8	0.9	0.8	0.8	0.8	0.8
I0	50	50	50	50	50	50	50	200	50
d	10	10	10	10	10	10	10	10	10
t0	30	30	30	30	30	30	30	30	30
t	0.3	0.3	0.2	0.2	0.3	0.2	0.3	0.3	0.3
m0	20	20	20	20	20	20	20	20	20
m1	0.25	0.25	0.25	0.25	0.25	0.25	0.25	0.25	0.4

Raising government spending from 200 to 400 has significant impact on output and hence in tax revenue, consumption and imports. It also worsens the trade balance. The national saving fall because of deficit in government budget and balance of payment situation becomes worse as imports rise due to increase in income. When both tax and government spending rise it has more pronounced expansionary impact in the economy.

Table 2
Solutions of the Basic Keynesian Model

	Y	*T*	*C*	*I*	*G*	*X*	*M*	*S*	*T-G*	*X-M*	*S-I*	*Bal*
Base case	876.8	293.0	767.0	49.0	200.0	100.0	239.2	-183.2	93.0	-139.2	-232.2	-139.2
Tax cut	991.8	228.4	910.8	49.0	200.0	100.0	268.0	-147.3	28.4	-168.0	-196.3	-168.0
Spending	1166.7	380.0	929.3	49.0	400.0	100.0	311.7	-142.7	-20.0	-211.7	-191.7	-211.7
MPC	971.0	321.3	884.7	49.0	200.0	100.0	262.7	-235.0	121.3	-162.7	-284.0	-162.7
T&G	1319.7	293.9	1120.6	49.0	400.0	100.0	349.9	-94.9	-106.1	-249.9	-143.9	-249.9
High X	1166.7	380.0	929.3	49.0	200.0	300.0	311.7	-142.7	180.0	-11.7	-191.7	-11.7
High I	1094.2	358.3	888.8	199.0	200.0	100.0	293.6	-152.8	158.3	-193.6	-351.8	-193.6
MMM	720.2	246.1	679.3	49.0	200.0	100.0	308.1	-205.2	46.1	-208.1	-254.2	-208.1

The marginal propensities to consume (MPC) and import (MMM) are very important. While the higher MPC implies more expansion of demand in response to any policy induced or autonomous changes in the system, higher propensity to import implies more leakages of resources from the economy, which sets a contractionary impact to the domestic economy. Higher export like expansion in the government spending has an expansionary impact in the economy.

So far we have taken only the real sector of the economy. More realistic model should take account of both real and monetary sectors. This is done by integrating the monetary and sectors with the goods market presented above under the IS-LM model. The monetary sector has to complement the real side of the economy. Keynes considers that total liquid wealth is divided either in money or bonds. The demand for money arises for transaction, precautionary or speculative purposes. Higher level of income raises the precautionary and transaction demand for money and higher rate of interest reduces demand for money by raising the opportunity cost of holding money. Putting these things together the money demand function takes the following form:

$$\text{Money demand function: } \left(\frac{MM}{P}\right)_t = b_0 + b_1 Y_t - b_2 R_t \tag{9}$$

Money supply $\overline{MM}_t$ is considered a policy variable to be determined by a monetary authority. In every period the rate of interest is set so that the demand for money equals the supply of money. Since the price level is assumed to be fixed both the real and nominal interest rates are equal. The money market equilibrium implies

$$R_t = \frac{b_0}{b_2} - \frac{1}{b_2}\left(\frac{\overline{MM}}{P}\right)_t + \frac{b_1}{b_2}Y_t \tag{10}$$

The intersection points of the IS curve and the LM curves give the overall equilibrium that satisfy both goods and money market equilibrium, this is also the aggregate demand. Substitute (10) in (8) to find out the level of output and the interest rate consistent with simultaneous equilibrium in goods as well as money markets.

$$= \frac{b_2\left(\beta_0 - \beta_1 t_0 + \mu_0 - m_0 + G_t + X_t\right)}{\left(1-\beta_1+\beta_1 t_1+m_1\right)b_2 - \mu_1 b_1} + \frac{b_2 \phi \Delta Y_{t-1}}{\left(1-\beta_1+\beta_1 t_1+m_1\right)b_2 - \mu_1 b_1}$$

$$Y + \frac{b_2 \mu_1}{\left(1-\beta_1+\beta_1 t_1+m_1\right)b_2 - \mu_1 b_1}\left[\frac{b_0}{b_2} - \frac{1}{b_2}\left(\frac{\overline{MM}}{P}\right)_t\right] \tag{11}$$

This is also an aggregate demand function in the Keynesian model which is downward sloping in prices. The equilibrium interest rate is found using the aggregate demand (11) equation in the money market equilibrium condition (10). The interest rate and the level of income are consistent with the equilibrium in both the goods and money markets. No gap remains to be covered between the demand and supply. It becomes a static model if ΔY_{t-1} term is left out.

$$R_t = \frac{b_0}{b_2} - \frac{1}{b_2}\left(\frac{\overline{MM}}{P}\right),$$

$$+ \frac{b_1}{b_2}\left[\frac{b_2\left(\beta_0 - \beta_1 t_0 + \mu_0 - m_0 + G_t + X_t\right)}{\left(1-\beta_1+\beta_1 t_1+m_1\right)b_2 - \mu_1 b_1} + \frac{b_2 \phi \Delta Y_{t-1}}{\left(1-\beta_1+\beta_1 t_1+m_1\right)b_2 - \mu_1 b_1} + \frac{b_2 \mu_1}{\left(1-\beta_1+\beta_1 t_1+m_1\right)b_2 - \mu_1 b_1}\left[\frac{b_0}{b_2} - \frac{1}{b_2}\left(\frac{\overline{MM}}{P}\right)_t\right]\right] \tag{12}$$

Finally, model with a change in income term, $\Delta Y_{t-1} = Y_{t-2} - Y_{t-1}$, would be a multiplier accelerator dynamic IS-LM model. Stating from an initial condition such as $Y_{t-1} = Y_0$, not only the current demand but also the past demand will determine the current equilibrium. This happens because of the adjustment process in investment. If ΔY_t was positive for a given time *t*, depending on the parameter ϕ, in the current formulation, investment component will change.

In a simultaneous system any change in one variable will have repercussion in all other variables. The dynamic path for income over years can be simulated using this equation. More appropriately, as above, one should use both goods and money market equilibrium conditions to do this simulation by modifying the exogenous or policy variables such as the government spending or the level of exports .

Table 3
Parameters of the IS-LM Model

beta0	*10000*	*10000*	*10000*	*10000*	*10000*	*10000*	*10000*	*10000*	*10000*	*10000*	*22114.16*
beta1	0.9	0.9	0.9	0.9	0.9	0.9	0.9	0.9	0.6	0.9	0.459078
mu0	500	500	500	500	500	500	1000	500	500	500	105457
m0	100	100	100	100	100	100	100	100	100	100	-65167
t0	200	500	200	500	200	200	200	200	200	200	-201384
t1	0.3	0.3	0.3	0.3	0.3	0.3	0.3	0.3	0.3	0.3	0.476403
m1	0.2	0.2	0.2	0.2	0.2	0.2	0.2	0.2	0.2	0.3	1.387408
mu1	1000	1000	1000	1000	1000	1000	1000	1000	1000	1000	1720.051
phi	0.6	0.6	0.6	0.6	0.6	0.6	0.6	0.6	0.6	0.6	0.6
G	20000	20000	25000	25000	20000	20000	20000	20000	20000	20000	155880
X	8000	8000	8000	8000	8000	8000	8000	10000	10000	8000	289225
y0	500	500	500	500	500	500	500	500	500	500	500
b0	800	800	800	800	800	800	800	800	800	800	-78809
b1	0.25	0.25	0.25	0.25	0.25	0.25	0.25	0.25	0.25	0.25	0.333992
b2	300000	300000	300000	300000	300000	600000	300000	300000	300000	300000	-1829.75
M4	10000	10000	10000	10000	15000	10000	10000	10000	10000	10000	10000
P	1	1	1	1	1	1	1	1	1	1	1

Table 4
Solution of the IS-LM Model

	R	*Y*	*C*	*I*	*G*	*T*	*M*	*X*	*S*	*X-M*	*S-I*	*T-G*
Base case	0.0251	66901	51968	525	20000	20270	13480	8000	-5337	-5480	-5862	270
More Tax	0.024	65640	50453	524	20000	20692	13228	8000	-5505	-5228	-6029	692
More Spending	0.0324	75660	57486	532	25000	22898	15232	8000	-4724	-7232	-5256	-2102
Tax and Spend	0.032	75187	56918	532	25000	23056	15137	8000	-4787	-7137	-5319	-1944
More money supply	0.0084	66872	51949	508	20000	20262	13474	8000	-5339	-5474	-5847	262
More Sensitive Asset demand	0.0126	66977	52015	513	20000	20293	13495	8000	-5332	-5495	-5844	293
More investment	0.026	67777	52519	1026	20000	20533	13655	8000	-5276	-5655	-6301	533
More Exports	0.028	70405	54175	528	20000	21321	14181	10000	-5092	-4181	-5620	1321
Low MPC	0.01	48985	30454	510	20000	14896	9897	8000	3636	-1897	3126	-5104
High MPM	0.017	56928	45685	517	20000	17278	17178	8000	-6035	-9178	-6552	-2722

The model solutions in response to various policy changes as presented in the above table show that the both fiscal and monetary policy can have significant impact in the economy. These results are subject to the set of parameters presented above. Behaviour of households and importers can have most dramatic macroeconomic effects are shown by the scenarios for lower MPC and higher MPM, both of which are contractionary.

The above tables show comparative static effect of a policy change. This model also can be made recursively dynamic setting a dynamic path for income and the interest rate, consumption, investment, tax revenue and imports by introducing monetary, fiscal and exchange rate policy rule for the economy. However, more information is needed on policy (exogenous) variables on exports and government expenditure, two major exogenous variables in the current model. This model could also be used to study a structural shift in the components of GDP by changing the slopes and intercept parameters, which ideally should come from an econometric estimation.

The aggregate demand (AD) can be derived from the IS-LM model by tracing out the economy in response change in the prices. A downward sloping AD implied that the aggregate spending decreases in higher prices. This happens because of reduced real balances, appreciation of domestic currency and reduction in external demand for goods, or by lowering the expectations of income among people.

Above model can be applied to real economy using the macroeconomic time series data and applied fore economic forecasting and simulation.

Figure 1
Macroeconomic Time Series of the UK,1960-2000

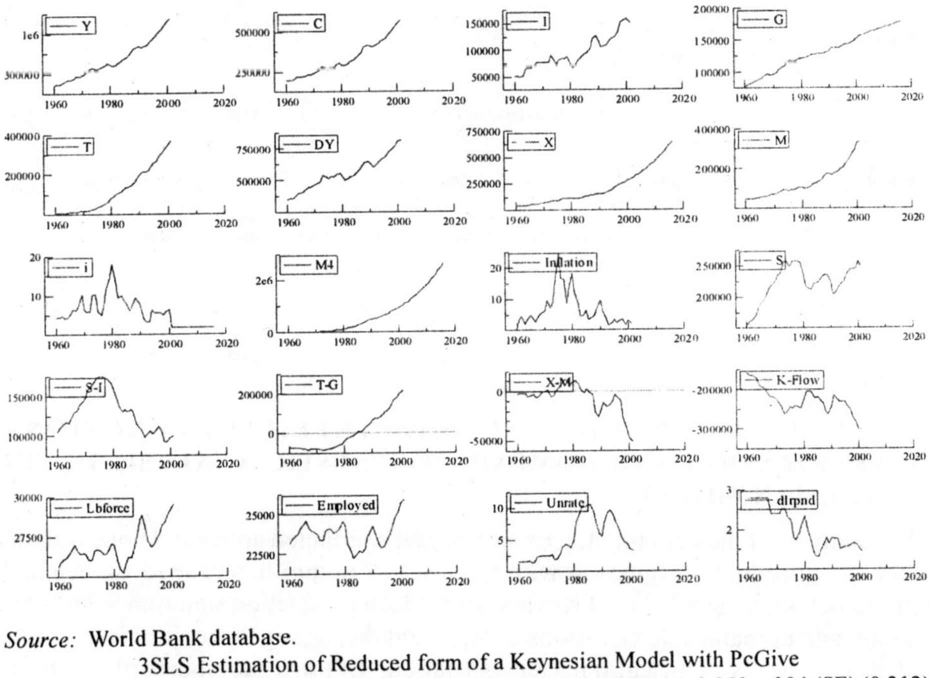

Source: World Bank database.

3SLS Estimation of Reduced form of a Keynesian Model with PcGive

Consumption function C = 1.407*G + 0.1767*X + 0.2128*M4 + 8.059e+004 (SE) (0.212) (0.154) (0.0266) (1.63e+004)

Investment function: I = 0.0684*G + 0.2681*X + 0.02907*M4 + 4.292e+004 (SE) (0.182) (0.132) (0.0229) (1.4e+004)

Tax Reveneu: T = + 0.9521*G - 0.08909*X + 0.3204*M4 - 7.533e+004 (SE) (0.159) (0.116) (0.02) (1.23e+004)

Import function: M = - 0.4738*G + 1.003*X + 0.06508*M4 + 4.34e+004 (SE) (0.157) (0.114) (0.0198) (1.21e+004)

Interest rate: i = 0.0001148*G + 6.273e-005*X - 2.384e-005*M4 - 7.408 (SE)
(4.93e-005) (3.58e-005) (6.2e-006) (3.79)
log-likelihood -1798.42246 -T/2log|Omega| -1500.44537 No. of observations 42 no. of parameters 20

The above model can be applied to simulate and forecast the model economy as illustrated in the following sets of diagrams.

Figure 2
Actual and Simulated values, Cross Plots of actual and simulated values, Fitted and Simulated values and Simulation residuals

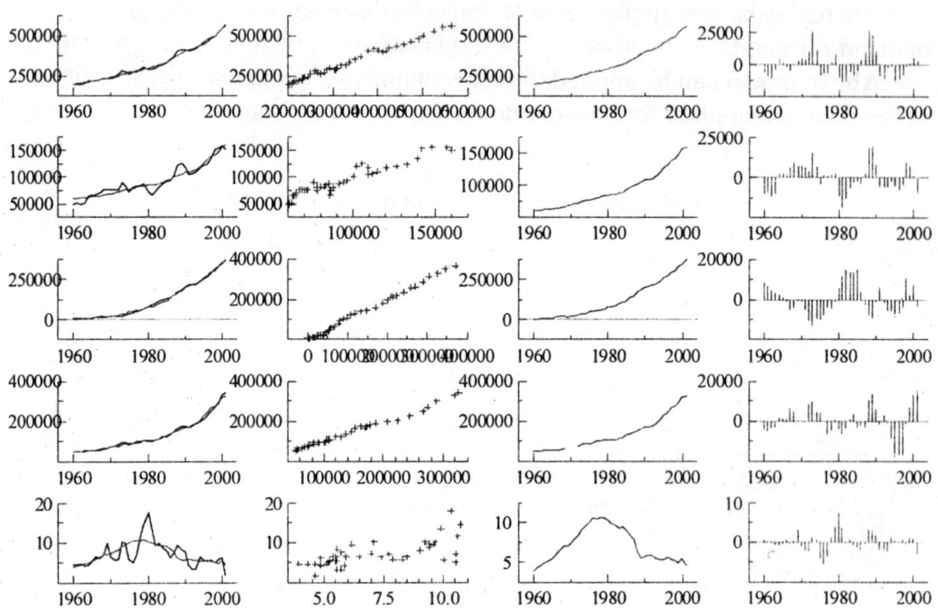

MULTIPLIER ANALYSIS USING IMPLICIT FUNCTIONS: LINEARIZATION AND COMPARATIVE STATIC ANALYSIS IN THE KEYNESIAN MODEL

The analysis of the demand determined model conducted above did not explicitly include a production function with the level of output determined by demand. In a neoclassical synthesis of Keynesian model a production function is included along with demand side equations to represent the aggregate economic activities of the economy. The capital (*K*) and labour (*N*) are the standard inputs in production and each subject to diminishing marginal rate of productivity as following.

$$Y = F(K,N);\ F_N > 0;\ F_K > 0; F_{NN} < 0\ F_{KK} < 0 \qquad (13)$$

The stock of capital is fixed in the short run implying variability of output directly associated with the amount of labour input in use.

Figure 3
Ex-Ante Forecast of the Model Economy

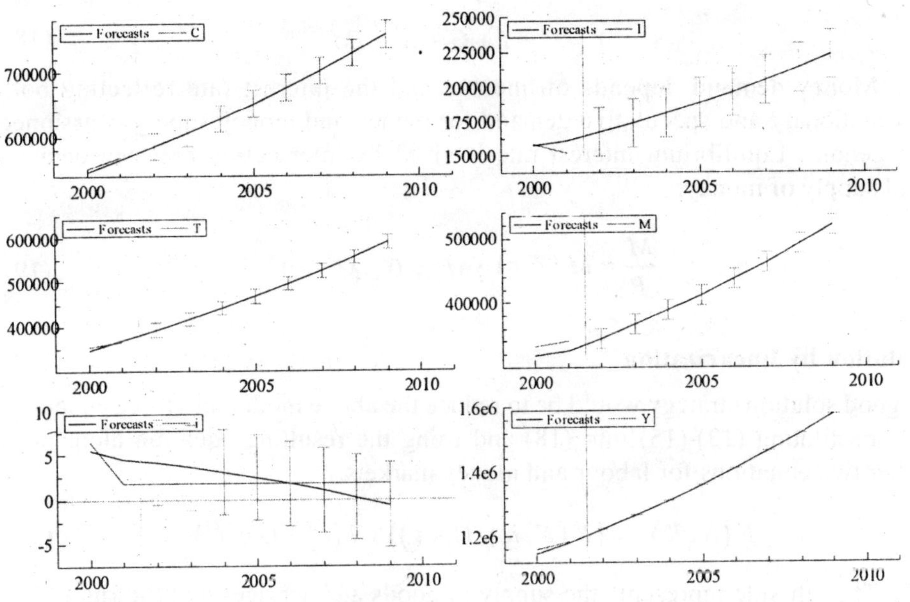

Consumption depends on disposable income

$$C = C\left(Y^d\right) \tag{14}$$

where the disposable income is defined as

$$Y^d = \left(1-\tau\right)Y \tag{15}$$

The demand for labour is given by the marginal productivity of labour

$$\frac{W}{P} = F_N\left(N, K\right) \tag{16}$$

In spirit of the Keynesian model it is assumed that involuntary unemployment exists; not all individuals in the labour force are employed in present of excess supply of labour. It is possible to increase output by increasing demand for labour by fixing the market wage rate to a specific rate such as W_0 until the employment rate reaches a certain point such as $\overline{N}$. The labour market condition in such situation can be represented as $W = W_0 + W\left(N\right)$

$$\text{where, } W\left(N\right) = \begin{cases} 0 \; for & N \le \overline{N} \\ + \; for & N > \overline{N} \end{cases} \tag{17}$$

Finally the aggregate supply equals aggregate demand (aggregate income) as:

$$Y = C + I + G + X - IM \tag{18}$$

Money demand depends on income and the interest rate reflecting both precautionary and speculative demand for money and money supply is assumed exogenous. Equilibrium interest rate is given by intersection between demand and supply of money:

$$\frac{M}{P} = M(Y, r) \; ; M_y > 0 \, , \; M_r < 0 \tag{19}$$

Solution by linearization

A good solution strategy would be to reduce the above model into three equations by substituting (13)-(15) into (18) and using the resulting equation along with other two equations for labour and money markets.

$$F(N, K) = c\left(F(N, K) \cdot (1 - \tau)\right) + I(r) + G + NX \tag{20}$$

The left side represents the supply of goods and services and the right hand side gives the aggregate demand. For simplicity assume exports equals imports and the net export equals to zero.

The demand for labour equals the supply of labour in equilibrium in the classical model and is obtained by combining (4) and (5) which equate real wage rate with the marginal productivity of labour as:

$$\frac{W}{P} = F_N(N, K) \tag{21}$$

The equilibrium interest rate is determined by intersection of demand for and supply of money:

$$\frac{M}{P} = M(Y, r) \tag{22}$$

With the reduced form model consisting of (20) to (22) it is possible to determine the solutions and conduct comparative static analysis taking total differentiation of these three functions resulting in equations for employment, price and the interest rate.

$$F_N dN + F_K dK = c(1 - \tau) d\left(F(N, K)\right) + d\left(c(1 - \tau)\right) F(N, K) + I_r dr + dG$$

or

$$F_N dN + F_K dK = c(1 - \tau) F_N dN + c(1 - \tau) F_K dK - c d\tau F(N, K) + I_r dr + dG \tag{23}$$

$$\frac{dW}{P} - \frac{W}{P^2} dP = F_{NN} dN + F_{NK} dK \tag{24}$$

$$\frac{dM}{P} - \frac{M}{P^2} dP = M_y F_N dN + M_y F_K dK + M_r dr \tag{25}$$

By further expansion and rearrangement for endogenous variable labour (*dN*), price (*dP*) and interest rate (*dr*) this model is succinctly written as:

$$F_N dN - c(1-\tau) F_N dN - I_r dr$$

$$= c(1-\tau) F_K dK - F_K dK - cd\tau F(N,K) + dG \tag{26}$$

$$M_y F_N dN + \frac{M}{P^2} dP + M_r dr = \frac{dM}{P} - M_y F_K dK \tag{27}$$

$$F_{NN} dN + \frac{W}{P^2} dP = \frac{dW}{P} - F_{NK} dK \tag{28}$$

Or this can be written in a matrix notation

$$\begin{bmatrix} (1-c(1-\tau))F_N & 0 & -I_r \\ M_y F_N & \dfrac{M}{P^2} & M_r \\ F_{NN} & \dfrac{W}{P^2} & 0 \end{bmatrix} \begin{bmatrix} dN \\ dP \\ dr \end{bmatrix}$$

$$= \begin{bmatrix} c(1-\tau) F_K dK - F_K dK - cd\tau F(N,K) + dG \\ \dfrac{dM}{P} - M_y F_K dK \\ \dfrac{dW}{P} - F_{NK} dK \end{bmatrix} \tag{29}$$

This matrix can be solved for the changes in the employment, price level and the interest rate if the determinant of the coefficients of endogenous variable in the left side (Jacobian matrix) is non-singular; the determinant of this matrix should be non-zero:

$$\Delta = \begin{vmatrix} (1-c(1-\tau))F_N & 0 & -I_r \\ M_y F_N & \dfrac{M}{P^2} & M_r \\ F_{NN} & \dfrac{W}{P^2} & 0 \end{vmatrix}$$

$$= -M_r \frac{W}{P^2}\left[(1-c(1-\tau))F_N\right] - I_r\left(M_y F_N \frac{W}{P^2} - F_{NN}\frac{M}{P^2}\right) \tag{30}$$

The first term of the determinant is positive since slope of money demand function M_r is negative F_N is positive. The second term also is positive since the slope of the investment function I_r is negative, the production function is subject to the diminishing returns, $F_{NN} < 0$. This means that determinant is non-vanishing and it is possible to find a solution for this model. The Cramer's rule can be applied to find out the solution for each endogenous variable.

$$dN = \frac{1}{\Delta}\begin{bmatrix} c(1-\tau)F_K dK - F_K dK - cd\tau F(N,K) + dG & 0 & -I_r \\ \dfrac{dM}{P} - M_y F_K dK & \dfrac{M}{P^2} & M_r \\ \dfrac{dW}{P} - F_{NK} dK & \dfrac{W}{P^2} & 0 \end{bmatrix} \tag{31}$$

$$dN = \frac{1}{\Delta}\begin{bmatrix} -I_r \dfrac{W}{P^2}\left(\dfrac{dM}{P} - M_y F_K dK\right) + I_r\left(\dfrac{dW}{P} - F_{NK} dK\right)\dfrac{M}{P^2} - \\ M_r \dfrac{W}{P^2}\left(c(1-\tau)F_K dK - F_K dK - cd\tau F(N,K) + dG\right) \end{bmatrix} \tag{32}$$

As can be seen the change in the employment depends upon the monetary and fiscal policy variables as well as the structural parameters of the model. Impact on output can be found using the total derivative of the production function. $dy = F_N dN + F_K dK$ But the capital stock is constant in the short run, $dK = 0$. The above value of dN can be used to solve for dy.

$$dy = \frac{F_N}{\Delta}\begin{bmatrix} -I_r \dfrac{W}{P^2}\left(\dfrac{dM}{P} - M_y F_K dK\right) + I_r\left(\dfrac{dW}{P} - F_{NK} dK\right)\dfrac{M}{P^2} - \\ M_r \dfrac{W}{P^2}\left(c(1-\tau)F_K dK - F_K dK - cd\tau F(N,K) + dG\right) \end{bmatrix} \tag{34}$$

This equation can be used to find the output multiplier of change in tax, or money supply or the government expenditure, or the because of the changes in the structural features of the economy. For instance a multiplier effect of the change in the marginal income tax is given by

$$\frac{dy}{d\tau} = -cF(N,K)\left(-M_r \frac{W}{P^2}\right) \tag{35}$$

Thus increase in the tax rate will reduce the level of income. The size of such reduction depends upon the value of c, M_r and $\frac{W}{P^2}$.

$$dp = \frac{1}{\Delta}\begin{bmatrix} (1-c(1-\tau))F_N & c(1-\tau)F_K dK - F_K dK - cd\tau F(N,K) + dG & -I_r \\ M_y F_N & \dfrac{dM}{P} - M_y F_K dK & M_r \\ F_{NN} & \dfrac{dW}{P} - F_{NK} dK & 0 \end{bmatrix}$$

(36)

$$dr = \frac{1}{\Delta}\begin{bmatrix} (1-c(1-\tau))F_N & 0 & c(1-\tau)F_K dK - F_K dK - cd\tau F(N,K) + dG \\ M_y F_N & \dfrac{M}{P^2} & \dfrac{dM}{P} - M_y F_K dK \\ F_{NN} & \dfrac{W}{P^2} & -\dfrac{dW}{P} - F_{NK} dK \end{bmatrix}$$

(37)

It is even simpler to find the solution of the system for the short run.

For empirical analysis a standard modelling approach is to estimate the structural parameters using time series data, and make these parameters as reliable as possible and compute the values of multiplier and accelerator coefficients under interest and find out the impacts of changes in government spending or tax rates or money supply in output, employment and prices. The major issue, however, remains about the stability of these parameters. A policy change is not only likely to change the levels of variables but also the behaviour of people which further might change the value of those parameters itself. The policy analyses based on a given set of parameters, therefore, are less likely to be accurate though their value in providing a benchmark scenario is unquestionable.

AGGREGATE SUPPLY AND THE PHILLIP'S CURVE

Assumption of the infinite elasticity of aggregate supply (horizontal AS) in a standard Keynesian IS-LM model presented has met with serious criticism in macroeconomics. The first starting point in this direction was the Phillips' curve (1957), which recognised the trade-off between inflation and unemployment and thus an upward sloping AS in the short run. Policy makers can reduce unemployment by increasing demand through expansionary monetary policy but more demand for output exerts extra pressure in both labour and capital markets. This causes increase in factor prices. Higher factor prices lead to an increase in the price level. This fact is presented in the form of short run aggregate supply curve as:

$$Y = \overline{Y} + 50\left(P - P^{e}\right) \text{ and } Y = F\left(\overline{K},\ L\right) = \overline{K}^{\alpha}\,\overline{L}^{\beta} = 1000^{0.3}1000^{0.7} \qquad (38)$$

Lucas critique (1976) introduces rational expectation among economic agents, which states that only unanticipated demand management policies can have real impacts in the economy. Given the structure of a macroeconomic model like above, workers, employers, consumers or producers change their behaviour in order to mitigate the consequences of anticipated changes.

The new Keynesian analysis introduces market imperfection to suggest why the aggregate supply is upward-sloping but not as horizontal as suggested by Keynes (Blanchard and Kiyotaki (1987), Manning (1995), Rankin (1992)). Imperfections ultimately results in mark-up behaviour of firms and workers. The most of these market imperfection models treat labour as the only variable input as the plants and machineries cannot be varied in the short run. The simplest form of the market imperfection model contains monopolistic mark up of product prices by firms and similar mark on wage rates by the union. This process of wage price mark up as follows.

Firm make sure the prices (P) of commodities cover the cost of labour (W). In addition they charge a mark up (θ) over the price. The extra amount is called the mark-up as given by in the equation below.

$$P_t = (1+\theta)W_t \qquad (39)$$

Unions (or workers) care for real wages. They also charge a mark-up over the expected price while negotiating the wage rate from the employer.

$$W_t = (1+\gamma)P_t^e \tag{40}$$

Using (16) in (17) we have

$$P_t = (1+\theta)(1+\gamma)P_t^e \tag{41}$$

Dividing both sides of (41) by P_{t-1} and defining $(1+\pi_t) = \frac{P_t}{P_{t-1}}$, the equation (41) can be written as $(1+\pi_t) = (1+\theta)(1+\gamma)(1+\pi_t^e)$. Using the law of small numbers this can be approximated by $\pi_t = \pi_t^e + \theta + \gamma$.

Both type of mark-ups, θ and γ, are normally higher in boom periods and lower during the recession (Burda and Wyplosz (2002 p. 287) as given by the equation below:

$$\theta + \gamma = a(y_t - \bar{y}) = -b(u_t - \bar{u}) \tag{42}$$

where the term $\theta + \gamma$ are the sum of the mark ups charged by the unions and firms, y is the actual output and $\bar{y}$ is the trend output, thus the term $(y_t - \bar{y})$ reflects the deviation of output from the trend, $(u_t - \bar{u})$ reflects how the actual unemployment rate differs from the natural rate of unemployment. The parameters α and b are positive. The firms can charge higher mark up if the actual aggregate demand is higher than the trend and lower if the actual unemployment is higher than the natural rate of unemployment.

The equation (41) includes only the labour cost. All sorts of non-labour costs in the economy such as an increase in oil prices, increase in the prices of raw materials, increase in the interest rate or the cost of capital are taken by the aggregate supply shock. Then the aggregate supply function or the Phillips curve become:

$$\pi_t = \bar{\pi} + \begin{Bmatrix} a(y - \bar{y}) \\ or \\ -b(u - \bar{u}) \end{Bmatrix} + s \tag{43}$$

The short run dynamics of trade-off between inflation and unemployment are given by the expectation augmented Phillips' curve. In case of an adaptive expectation

$$\pi_t - \pi_{t-1} = -b(u_t - u_n) \tag{44}$$

where π_t is inflation rate; u_t is actual unemployment rate; u_n natural rate of unemployment. The impact of output gap on unemployment is given by Okun curves is presented as:

$$u_t - u_{t-1} = -a\left(g_{y,t} - g_{y,n}\right) \tag{45}$$

$g_{y,t}$ is actual growth rate of output; $g_{y,n}$ is natural growth rate of output .

Finally link between money supply and price level can be derived using a simple version of quantity theory of money PY=M, or by log differentiation

$$g_{y,t} = g_{m,t} - \pi_t \tag{46}$$

$g_{m,t}$ is growth rate of money supply.

Given the actual growth rate of output, increase in money supply raises the price level and which can increase output in the short run but over time workers adjust their expectation about the price level. Wage rates rise in proportion to change in the price level, leaving output and employment levels at their natural rates.

To sum up macroeconomic general equilibrium is characterised by prices, wage rates, interest rates, exchange rates which equate demand and supply in goods, labour, money and foreign exchange markets. Disequilibrium may result when these prices are not free to change because of institutional or policy reasons in the short run but disequilibrium may not continue over a long period as wage rates adjust in proportion to a rise in the price level. The impact of demand management is even smaller under the rational expectation model as there is instantaneous price adjustment in response to an expansionary fiscal policy with no impact of output and employment implying a vertical AS even in the short run.

Policy makers may reduce unemployment below its natural rate in the short run at the cost of higher inflation rate but the economy moves back to the natural rate of unemployment once workers take account of rise in price level in their wage contract. For instance suppose the economy is at point a in the beginning and government wants to reduce unemployment rate below the natural rate,, by using expansionary policy which creates extra demand for labour and reduces the unemployment rate. Overtime, however, workers learn that prices have increased. Their expectation of inflation rises. Phillips curve shifts out and becomes vertical without any real impacts in the output and employment. Living standard of people ultimately depends on the long run economic growth, more even so in case of developing economies.

CRITIQUE ON MULTIPLIERS OF A KEYNESIAN MODEL

As research in macroeconomic models has progressed over years these Keynesian models have been criticised, revised and refined continuously. These criticism and refinements can normally be classified into four categories.

First, Keynesian multipliers as presented above assume constancy of structural parameters such as $\beta_0 \beta_1 \mu_1 \phi\ m_0\ m_1, m_2$, t_0 and t_1. As mentioned above standard Keynesian practice is to use the times series data to estimate these parameters and conduct economic forecasting assuming that these parameters will remain stable. Such econometric forecasting lacks rational expectation (Lucas (1976)). Expectations influence decisions of consumers and producers and economic agents update information set as time goes by. Given a policy action from the public sector there can be even more reaction from the private sector and such interaction significantly changes the values of model parameters. Model results based on constancy of parameters are likely to be flawed. Many suggestions have been made on how the rational expectation could be incorporated in a macroeconomic model (see Sargent and Wallace (1975), Fisher (1977), Wallis (1980), Mankiw (1989), Prescott (1986), Taylor (1987), Taylor (1993), Sargent and Ljungqvists (2000), Minford and Peel (2002), Blake and Weal (2003), Garratt, Lee, Pesaran and Shin (2003)) contain techniques how rational expectation could improve predictions from a macroeconomic model.

Secondly Keynesian models lack sufficient micro foundation to explain the optimising behaviour of consumers and producers in a market economy. Though all endogenous variables are determined simultaneously the equations for consumption, investment, exports and imports or taxes, or interest rates or demand for money are not derived from the optimising framework. Therefore the results of a standard Keynesian model cannot determine whether a solution obtained from the model is optimal one from the perspective of millions of households and firms in the economy. The new classical and new Keynesian models that have appeared in the last two decades have attempted to remedy this problem by explicitly incorporating the optimising framework in the model (Mankiw and Romer (1993)).

Thirdly early Keynesian models lacked a good dynamic structure though some attempts were made in this direction by Samuelson (1939), Phillips (1958), Phelps (1968) and Friedman (1968). Model forecasts depended more on backward looking adaptive expectation framework or on simple autoregressive structure despite the fact that Ramsey (1928) already had developed an explicit dynamic structure for a growing economy with single representative household.

Unhappy with Keynesian pre-occupation with short run fluctuations Harrod (1939), Domar (1947) and Solow (1956) analysed growth taking the Keynesian set up. These growth models involve maximising the utility of the infinitely lived household $\int_0^\infty e^{-\rho t} \frac{C_t^{1-\sigma}}{1-\sigma} dt$ subject to the technology constraint $Y_t = A_t K_t^\alpha N_t^{1-\alpha}$ and capital accumulation process $\dot{K}_t = Y_t - N_t C_t - \delta K_t$. When simplified, assuming $A_t = 1\ \ N_t = 1$, the optimisation problem is often formulated in the form of a current value Hamiltonian as

$$H(c, K, \theta) = \frac{C_t^{1-\sigma}}{1-\sigma} + \theta\left[K_t^{\alpha} - C_t - \delta K_{t-1}\right]$$

where C is consumption, a control variable; K is the capital stock, a state variable, θ is the shadow price of the capital stock in terms of the utility, a co-state variable. Market clearing, implicit in the budget constraint, implies that output is either consumed or invested. The optimal path of capital accumulation is found using four first order conditions:

$$\frac{\partial H}{\partial C_t} = 0 \rightarrow C_t^{-\sigma} = \theta_t \qquad (47)$$

$$\dot{\theta}_t = \rho\theta_t - \frac{\partial H_t}{\partial K_t} \rightarrow \dot{\theta}_t = \rho\theta_t - \theta_t\left[\alpha K_t^{\alpha-1} - \delta\right] \qquad (48)$$

$$\dot{K}_t = K_t^{\alpha} - C_t - \delta K_t \qquad (49)$$

and the transversality condition $\lim_{t \to \infty} e^{-\rho t}\theta_t K_t = 0$ (50)

The first equation denotes the shadow price of capital in terms of the marginal utility of consumption. The second shows how the shadow price is sensitive to subjective discount factor and accumulation constraint. The final terminal condition implies no need for capital accumulation at the end of the planning horizon. Capital stock, consumption and the shadow price of capital remain constant in the balanced growth path; $\frac{\dot{C}}{C} = g_c$; $\frac{\dot{K}}{K} = g_K$ and $\frac{\theta_t}{\theta_t} = g_\theta$. Proof of this follows from (48)

$$\frac{\dot{\theta}_t}{\theta_t} = \rho - \left[\alpha K^{\alpha-1} - \delta\right] \rightarrow \alpha K^{\alpha-1} = \rho - \frac{\dot{\theta}_t}{\theta_t} + \delta \qquad (51)$$

This is the most important equation for deriving the equilibrium in this model. It simply states that the marginal productivity of capital should equal the cost of capital, where the shadow price measures the opportunity cost of capital. By assumption the RHS in (51) is constant. This implies that the LHS also should be a constant, therefore, $\frac{\dot{K}}{K} = 0$. Then from the production function, if the capital stock is not growing then the output is also not growing; and so $\frac{\dot{Y}}{Y} = 0$. From the budget constraint when output and capital stocks are not growing the consumption is also not growing; thus $\frac{\dot{C}}{C}=0$. The shadow price also is not changing in the steady state as is obvious by the log differentiation of (47) $\frac{\dot{\theta}_t}{\theta_t}=-\sigma\frac{\dot{C}_t}{C_t}\rightarrow\frac{\dot{\theta}_t}{\theta_t}=0$.

The values of capital stock and output in the steady state can be solved from (51): $K_t^{\alpha-1}=\frac{\rho+\delta}{\alpha}\rightarrow K^*=\left(\frac{\rho+\delta}{\alpha}\right)^{\frac{1}{\alpha-1}}$ and $Y^*=\left(\frac{\alpha}{\rho+\delta}\right)^{\frac{\alpha}{1-\alpha}}$.

Though the capital stock does not grow the economy needs positive saving to maintain the capital stock intact: $C^*=K^{*\alpha}-\delta K^*$

$$\text{The saving rate}\frac{\delta\ K^*}{Y^*}=\delta\left(K^*\right)^{1-\alpha}=\delta\left[\left(\frac{\alpha}{\rho+\delta}\right)^{\frac{1}{1-\alpha}}\right]^{1-\alpha}=\delta\left[\left(\frac{\alpha}{\rho+\delta}\right)\right] \quad (52)$$

The major difference of this optimal growth model from the standard Keynesian growth model is that the saving rate is determined in terms of parameters of preferences and technology rather than being assumed as a constant fraction of the national income. The higher discount rate for future consumption implies lower saving rate and more productive capital implies higher saving rate. Higher discount rate of capital reduces the steady state capital but raises the level of saving in the steady state.

The transitional dynamics show a process where by the economy converges towards the steady state once it is disturbed from that path. From the second first order condition derived above, $\dot{\theta}_t=\theta_t\left(\rho-\alpha K_t^{\alpha-1}+\delta\right)\rightarrow$ for $\dot{\theta}_t=0$, since $\theta_t>0$

$K^*=\left(\frac{\alpha}{\rho+\delta}\right)^{\frac{1}{1-\alpha}}$ can be used in the (θ_t, K_t) space for the transition dynamics of the shadow price θ_t relative to the steady state capital stock as shown in Figure 1.

Capital stock can be increased above the steady state only by raising the shadow price of capital above its steady state value or if the shadow price is lowered it will reduce the capital stock. Similarly the transition dynamics of the K_t in the (θ_t, K_t) space relative to the steady state of the shadow price θ_t can be found using FOC (1);

$$C_t^{-\sigma}=\theta_t\rightarrow C_t=\theta_t^{-\frac{1}{\sigma}};\ \dot{K}_t=K_t^{\alpha}-N_tC_t-\delta K_t\rightarrow\dot{K}_t=K_t^{\alpha}-\delta K_t-\theta_t^{-\frac{1}{\sigma}}\rightarrow$$
$$K_t^{\alpha}-\delta K_t=\theta_t^{-\frac{1}{\sigma}} \quad (53)$$

Figure 4
Transition Dynamics for Shadow Price of Capital Stock

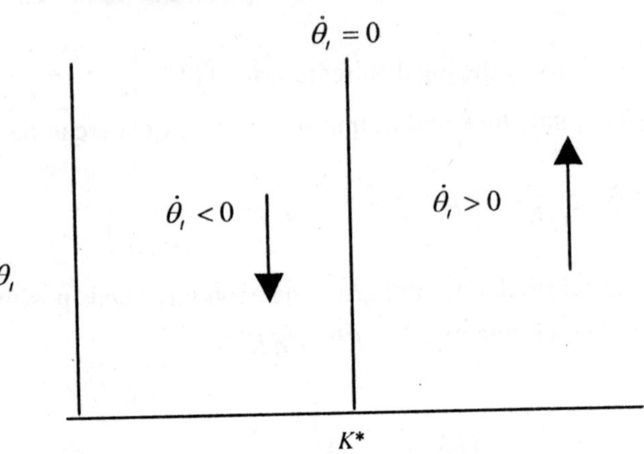

Figure 5
Transition dynamics for capital stock

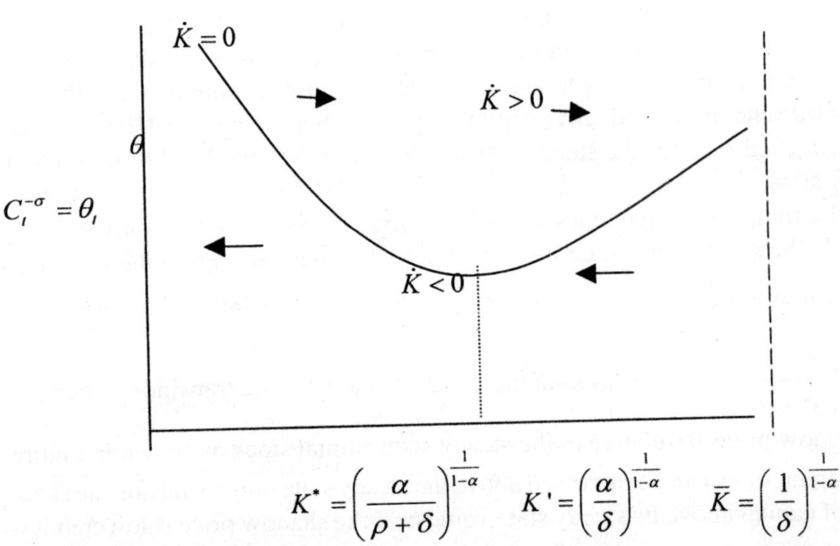

$$K^* = \left(\frac{\alpha}{\rho+\delta}\right)^{\frac{1}{1-\alpha}} \quad K' = \left(\frac{\alpha}{\delta}\right)^{\frac{1}{1-\alpha}} \quad \bar{K} = \left(\frac{1}{\delta}\right)^{\frac{1}{1-\alpha}}$$

For sufficiently large value of K there is no for which (53) will be satisfied. The largest such value of K can be found by setting the right hand side of (53) to zero.

$$K_t^{\alpha} = \delta K_t \rightarrow \bar{K} = \delta^{\frac{1}{\alpha-1}} = \left(\frac{1}{\delta}\right)^{\frac{1}{1-\alpha}} \tag{54}$$

$\bar{K} > K^*$ since $\alpha < 1$ and the $\rho > 1$.

Figure 6
Saddle path for Steady State Solutions

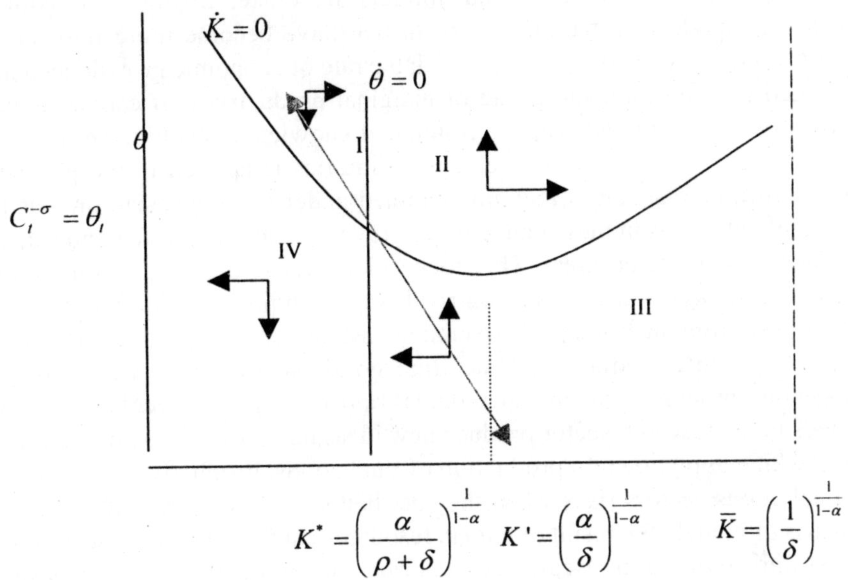

The saddle points for this model consists of points in (θ_t, K_t) space where the economy will converge to its steady state as shown by lines with arrows in region I and II in Figure 6. The $\dot{K} = 0$ path shows set of values of θ, for which there will be no change in the stock of capital. Capital stock is rising above this line and falling below this line. Similarly $\dot{\theta} = 0$ shows capital stock where there is no change in value of. The shadow price is rising to the right of this and falling to the left of this line. Right balance between the shadow price and accumulation is obtained only by the parameter sets in region I and III which guarantee the convergence of the system to the steady state.

As seen from above derivations the long run growth path of the economy is determined by a set of parameters in preferences and technology. Values of these parameters are determined by cultures and institutions. Economies with a hard drive for growth have lower discount rates for future consumption and higher rates of saving than economies that value current consumption more. More efficient economies produce more from the given sets of inputs.

Once the model parameters are specified it is possible to trace the growth paths of consumption, output and capital stock in this model. There can be too much capital if solutions lie in the region II and too little capital if the solution remains in region IV. Analysis of data on economic growth suggests that OECD and many middle income economies fall in convergence regions I and III. Fast growing economies of East Asia belong to region II and they are accumulating too much capital. Growth disaster economies such as those of Sub-Saharan Africa have not saved enough and caught in poverty trap in region IV of the above figure.

Implications of the Keynesian models are closer to the conclusions of endogenous models of economic growth that have become more popular after Lucas (1988) and Romer (1989) in which the rate of economic growth need not to be limited by the diminishing rate of marginal productivity of capital as in the above neoclassical model when accumulated knowledge resulting from work of researchers in universities or research laboratories is applied in the production process. Infinite elasticity of supply assumed under the Keynesian models have same implications as in these endogenous growth models as the demand can drive the rate of economic progress. The stock of knowledge that exists in the form of designs, formulas or models is a non-rival good with positive externality as it can be borrowed from the library. These models assume separate production functions for research, intermediate and the final goods sector while illustrating the endogenous process of technical progress and its impact in economic growth. Workers in the research sector produce new ideas that they sell to an intermediate sector, which apply them in production of final goods. Productivity of workers in the final goods sectors rises when they get better tools to work with. Economic growth is ultimately the result of human resources employed in the research sector such as universities and research laboratories. The production function is similar to the labour augmenting technology in the Solow model with a standard neoclassical production function, $Y = K^{\alpha}\left(AL_{Y}\right)^{\beta}$. Now technology A is the result of efforts of researchers working in the knowledge sector. Total labour resource (L) can either be used in the knowledge sector L_A or in the production of final goods sector L_y: $L = L_y + L_A$. As presented in Jones (1995) any change in the stock of knowledge depends upon the number of people employed in the knowledge sector, , average productivity in the research sector and the stock of existing knowledge A as and . By log differentiating this equation one finds that the growth rate of technology is determined by the rate of population growth in the steady state, . Higher rate of growth of population is beneficial rather than harmful for economic growth because the economy can afford to put more people in research. This type of endogenous growth model shows increasing return to scale relative to all inputs used in production. Since there is imperfect competition in the intermediate goods sector it is possible that inventors can extract profits by selling patent rights to producers of intermediate goods. Protecting research in terms of patent rights or subsidies to researchers becomes optimal as research drives up productivity by increasing the stock of knowledge in the whole economy. More demand drives higher growth rate both in Keynesian and endogenous growth models.

The real economic growth process is much more complicated than explained by the above models. Growth involves structural transformation in production, trade and consumption. Conclusions received from simple single sector models are elegant but can provide little intuition for actual policy analysis that involves assessments of the underlying factors that determine demand and supply in the various sectors of the economy and evaluation of redistribution impacts of policies implemented by public authorities. Analysis of structural change requires more details on technologies production across sectors and system of trade, preferences of households and about the process of capital accumulation and finance. There has been some progress in constructing more disaggregated dynamic general equilibrium models in recent years. Sargent and Ljungqvists (2000) have shown how dynamic programming techniques can be used to provide a consistent dynamic structure of an economy.

Fourth, the majority of Keynesian macro models only have a single good and a representative firm and a household and lack structural details of an economy required for evaluation of a policy that can affect various sectors and sections of the economy in many different ways. Multi-sectoral multi-period dynamic general equilibrium models developed in recent years provide both micro foundation and inter-temporal optimising frameworks required for a policy model (Fullerton, Shoven and Whalley (1983), Auerbach and Kotlikoff (1987), Perroni (1995), Rutherford (1995), Bank of England, NIESR) Bhattarai (1997, 1999), Kehoe, Srinivasan and Whalley (2005)).

CONCLUSION

This paper briefly reviews the Keynesian IS-LM model and the neoclassical and endogenous economic growth models that are widely used in analysing fluctuations of output in the short run and economic growth in the long run. Numerical examples are provided to evaluate impacts to fiscal and monetary policy reforms and to assess the importance of model parameters that describe the behavioural aspect of the economy. Discussion here provides an overview of the macroeconomic models often applied for policy analysis in the literature.

REFERENCES

Abramovitz, Moses (1986), Catching up, forging ahead and falling behind. *Journal of Economic History*, 46(2), June, 386-406.

Aurbach A.J. and L.J. Kotlik off (1987), *Dynamic Fiscal Policy*. Cambridge University Press.

Bank of England *(www.bankofengland.co.uk)*, The Transmission Mechanism of Monetary Policy.

Bhattarai K. (2005), Economic Growth: Models and Global Evidence, Research Memorandum, CEP, Business School, University of Hull; forthcoming in Applied Economics.

Bhattarai and J. Whalley (2000), "General Equilibrium Modelling of UK Tax Policy" in S. Holly and M Weale (Eds.) Econometric Modelling: Techniques and Applications, pp.69-93, the Cambridge University Press, 2000.

Bhattarai (1999), A Forward-Looking Dynamic Multisectoral General Equilibrium Model of the UK Economy, Hull Economics Research Paper no. 269.

Bhattarai K. and J. Whalley (2003), Discreteness and the Welfare Cost of Labour Supply Tax Distortions, *International Economic Review*, vo. 44. No. 3, August.

Bhattarai K. and J. Whalley (1999), "Role of labour demand elasticities in tax incidence analysis with hetorogeneous labour" *Empirical Economics*, 24:4, pp.599-620.

Blake A. P. and M.R. Weal (2003), Policy Rule and Economic Uncertainty, National Institute of Economic and Social Research.

Blanchard, O.J. and L. Summers (1986), "Hysteresis and the European Unemployment Problem," NBER Macroeconomics Annual, the MIT Press.

Blanchard O.J. and Kiyotaki (1987), Monopolistic competition and the effects of aggregate demand, *American Economic Review*, 77: September, pp 647-66.

Barro, Robert J. (2001), Human capital and growth. *American Economic Review*, May, 91(2), 12-17.

Barro, R. J. (1974), "Are Government Bonds Net Wealth?," Journal of Political Economy pp. 1095-1117.

Barro and Gordon (1983), A Positive Theory of Monetary Policy in a Natural Rate Model, *Journal of Political Economy*, 91:4: 589-610.

Burda and Wyplosz (2002), Macroeconomics: a European text, Oxford University, Press.

Cameron G. (2003), Why Did UK Manufacturing Productivity Growth Slow Down in the 1970s and Speed Up in the 1980s? *Economica*, 70:121-141.

Canzoneri M. B. and J. A. Gray (1985), Monetary Policy Games and the Consequences of Non-Cooperatinve Behaviour, *International Economic Review*, 26:3:547-564.

Domar E. (1947), Capital Expansion, Rate of Growth and Employment" *Econometrica*, 14:2:137-147.

Domar E. (1947), Expansion and Employment, *American Economic Review*, 37:1:35-55.

Dornbusch R. (1976), Expectations and Exchange Rate Dynamics, *Journal of Political Economy*, 84:6: 1161-1176.

Doornik J.A. and Hendry D.F. (2001), *Econometric Modelling Using PcGive* vol. I-III. Timberlake Consultants, London.

Edwards, S. (1998), Openness, productivity and growth: what do we really know? *Economic Journal*, 108, March, 383-398.

Goodhart C.E.A. (1994), What should central banks do? What should be their macroeconomic objective and operations?, *Economic Journal*, 104, November, 1424-1436.

Fisher, S.(1977), Long-Term Contracts, Rational Expectations, and the Optimal Money Supply Rule, *Journal of Political Economy*, Vol.85, No.1.

Friedman, M. (1968), The Role of Monetary Policy, *American Economic Review*, No.1 vol. LVIII March.

Freeman R. (19), What Does Modern Growth Analysis Say About Government Policy Towards Growth?

Fleming J. Marcus (1962), Domestic financial policies under fixed and under floating exchange rates, *IMF staff paper* 9, November, 369-379.

Fullerton, D., J.B. Shoven and J. Whalley (1983), "Replacing the U.S. Income Tax with a Progressive Consumption Tax. A Sequenced General Equilibrium Approach", *Journal of Public Economics*, 20, 3-23.

Garratt A., K. Lee, M.H. Pesaran and Y. Shin (2003), A Structural Cointegration VAR Approach to Macroeconometric Modelling, Economic Journal, 113:487:412-455

Hicks, J.R. (1937), Mr. Keynes and the "Classics"; A Suggested Interpretation, *Econometrica* 5.

International Monetary Fund (1992), Macroeconomic Adjustment: Policy Instruments and Issues, IMF.

Institute, Washington D.C.

Jones C.I. (1995), R & D-Based Models of Economic Growth, *Journal of Political Economy*, 103:4:759-784.

Keynes J.M. (1936), The General Theory of Employment, Interest and Money, MacMillan and Cambridge University Press.

Kehoe T, T.N. Srinivasan and J. Whalley (2005), Frontiers in Applied General Equilibrium Modelling, Cambridge University Press.

King R.G.and Plosser C.I. (1984), Money Credit and Prices in a Real Business Cycle, *American Economic Review*, 64 (June) 263-380.

Kydland F.E. and E.C. Prescott (1977), Rules rather than discrection: the Inconsistency of Optimal Plans, *Journal of Political Economy*, 85:3: 473-491.

Lockwood B., M. Miller and L Zhang (1998) Designing Monetary Policy when Unemployment Persists, *Economica* (1998) 65 327-45.

Lucas R.E. (1988), On the Mechanics of Economic Development, *Journal of Monetary Economics*, 22, 3-42.

Lucas R.E. (1976), Econometric Policy Evaluation: A Critique, Carnegie Rochester Conference Series on Public Policy 1: 19-46.

Lucas, Robert Jr. and Sargent, After Keynesian Macroeconomics, Spring 1979, Federal Reserve Bank of Minneapolis Quarterly Review.

Manning, (1995), Development in Labour Market Theory and their implications for macroeconomic Policy, *Scottish Journal of Political Economy*, vol.42, no. 3, August 1995.

Mankiw and Romer (1993), New Keynesian Economics, vol. 1, 2, the MIT Press.

Mankiw N.G. (1989), Real Business cycle: A New Keynesian Perspective, *Journal of Economic Perspectives*, vol. 3, no. 3 pp. 79-90.

Minford P. and D. Peel (2002), Advanced Macroeconomics: A Primer, Edward Elgar Publishing.

Modigliani F. (1986), Life Cycle, Individual Thrift and the Wealth of Nations, American Economic Review 76, 279-313.

MPC Bank of England (www.bankofengland.co.uk), *The Transmission Mechanism of Monetary Policy.*

Mundell R. A. (1962), Capital mobility and stabilisation policy under fixed and flexible exchange rates, *Canadian Journal of Economic and Political Science*, 29, 475-85.

Nelson C.R. and C.I. Plosser (1982), Trends and andom Walks in Macroeconomic Time Series: Some Evidence and Implications, Journal of Monetary Economics.

Nickell, S. (1990), "Inflation and the UK Labor Market," Oxford Review of Economic Policy; 6(4) Winter.

Nordhaus W.D. (1994), Policy Games: Cooperation and Independence in Monetary and Fiscal Policy, *Brookings Papers on Economic Activity*, 2: pp. 139-216.

Pagan A. and M. Wickens (1989), A Survey of Some *Recent Econometric Methods, Economic Journal*, 99 pp. 962-1025.

Perroni, C. (1995), "Assessing the Dynamic Efficiency Gains of Tax Reform When Human Capital is Endogenous," *International Economic Review* 36:907-925.

Phillips A W. (1958), The relation between unemployment and the rate of change of money wage rates in the United Kingdom, Economic Journal, 1861-1957 *Economica*, pp.283-299.

Phelps E.S. (1968), Money wage dynamics and labour market equilibrium, *Journal of Political Economy*, 76, 678-711.

Prescott, E.C. (1986), "Theory Ahead of Business Cycle Measurement," Federal Reserve Bank of Minneapolis, *Quarterly Review*; Fall.

Ramsey, F.P. (1928), "A Mathematical Theory of Saving," *Economic Journal* 38, 543-559.

Plosser Charles I (1989), Understanding Real Business Cycle, *Journal of Economic Perspectives*, vol. 3, no. 3 pp. 51-77.

Rankin Neil (1992), Imperfect Competition, Expectations and the Multiple Effects of Monetary Growth, *the Economic Journal* 102: 743-753.

Rebelo S. (1990), Long Run Policy Analysis and long run growth, *Journal of Political Economy* Vol. 99 No. 3 pp. 500-521.

Rogoff, K. (1999), "International Institutions for Reducing Global Financial Instability", *Journal of Economic Perspectives*, 1999 or NBER WP 7265.

Romer P. (1990), Endogenous Technological Change, Journal of Political Economy, 98:5:2, pp.s71-s102.

Romer, P. Capital Accumulation in the Theory of Long Run Growth" in Barro R. J. (1989) ed. Modern Business Cycle Theory, Harvard University Press.

Samuelson P. A. (1939), Interaction Between the Multiplier Analysis and the Principle of Acceleration, *Review of Economics and Statistics*, 75-78.

Sargent and Ljungqvists (2000), Recursive Macroeconomic Theory, MIT Press.

Sargent, T.J. and N. Wallace (1975), "Rational" Expectations, the Optimal Monetary Instrument, and the Optimal Money Supply Rule, Journal of Political Economy, pp. 241-254.

Shoven, J.B. and J. Whalley (1984), Applied General-Equilibrium Models of Taxation and International Trade: An Introduction and Survey, *Journal of Economic Literature* 22, 1007-1051.

Solow R.M. (1956), "A Contribution to the Theory of Economic Growth", *Quarterly Journal of Economics*, pp. 65-94.

Solow R.M. (2000), Towards a Macroeconomics of Medium Run, *Journal of Economic Perspective* 14:1:Winter 151-158.

Taylor M.P. (1987), *On the Long Run Solution to Dynamic Econometric Equations Under Rational Expectation*, Economic Journal, 97:385:215-218.

Temple, Jonathan R.W. (2001), Growth effects of Education and Social Capital in the OECD Countries. *OECD Economic Studies*, 33, 57-101.

Tobin J. (1969), A general Equilibrium Approach to Monetary Theory, *Journal of Money Credit and Banking* 1 (Feb) 15-29.

Taylor J. (1993), Discretion Versus Policy Rules in Practice, Carnegie Rochester Conference Series on Public Policy 29 Amsterdam.

Wallis K.F. (1989), Macroeconomic Forecasting: A Survey, *The Economic Journal*, Vol. 99, No. 394., pp. 28-61.

Wallis Kenneth (1980), Econometric Implications of the Rational Expectations Hypothesis, Econometrica 48:1, pp, 48-71.

Williamson J. and M. Miller (1987), Targets and Indicators: a Blue print for International co-ordination of Economic Policies, *Institute of International Economics*, Washington.

Yellen J.L. (1984), Efficiency Wage Models of Unemployment, *American Economic Review* Papers and Proceedings.

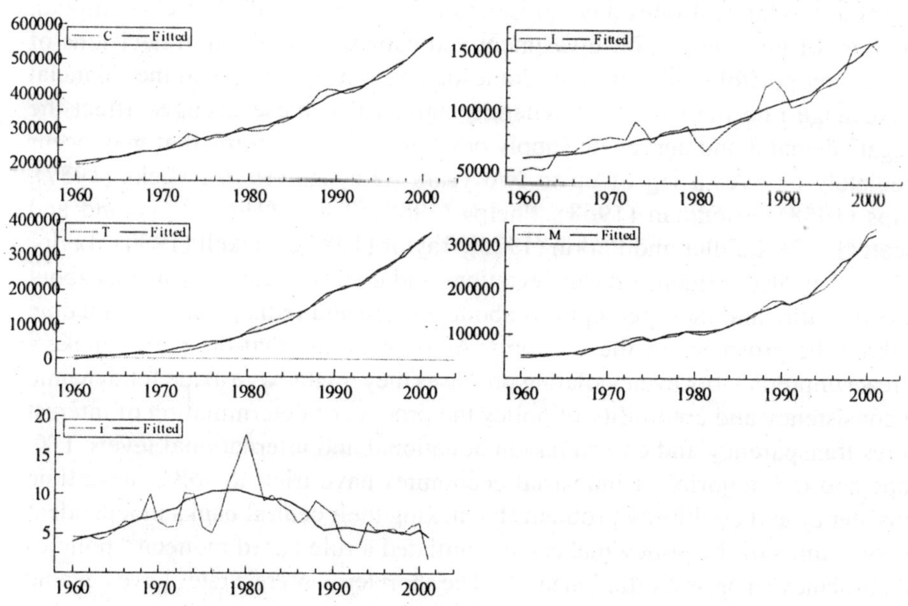

9

An Empirical Study of Interest Rate Determination Rules

Keshab Bhattarai

INTRODUCTION

Changes in the interest rates have profound impacts on saving and consumption behaviours of households, on investment and capital accumulation decisions of firms, and on portfolio allocation of domestic and foreign traders in the financial and exchange rate markets. It is generally agreed that these changes affect the aggregate demand and aggregate supply positions in an economy that may occur immediately or over a lag of up to two years ((Keynes (1936), Hicks (1937), Phillips (1958), Friedman (1968), Phelps (1968), Tobin (1969), Kydland and Prescott (1977), Laidler and Parkin (1975), Taylor (1987), Nickell (1990), Taylor (1993)). They also influence the expectations and plans of economic agents about their own future and their perceptions about welfare and redistribution of income and about the prospects of the economy. As public fears that the policy makers may react unpredictably even violating promises they might have made for dynamic time consistency and credibility of policy the process of determination of interest requires transparency and co-ordination at national and international levels. UK, Europe and the majority of industrial economies have tried to solve these time inconsistency and credibility problems by making their central banks independent from the whims of the policy makers and initiated a rule based monetary policies aimed to achieve a pre-set inflation target. The short term interest rates have become key instruments to be determined by economic realities rather than by the discretion of the policy makers. When the interest rate policy is based on rules like this it is possible to trace out the potential effects of interest rates on market rates on various types of financial transactions and subsequent impacts on asset prices, expectations of households and firms and the exchange rates and ultimately through these prices into the aggregate demand, inflation and the rate of unemployment systematically with minimum errors. How could macroeconomic stability and higher growth rate of output be achieved under such policy rules is explained sufficiently in non-technical terms in MPC (1999) and Bernanke and Mishkin (1997). Taylor (1993) uses a small scale model which shows how the interest rate can be systematically determined looking at the output gaps and inflation gaps to insure internal and external stability and to reduce the degree of fluctuations in aggregate economic activities. Woodford (2001) has shown how even a small Taylor type model can be consistent to detailed optimisation in more elaborate general equilibrium models though more detailed analyses of consequences of the interest rates by a central bank is often analysed using more comprehensive econometric and general equilibrium models, as discussed in Altig, Carlstrom and Lansing (1995), Gali and Gertler (1999) or in Holly and Weale (2000) or in HM Treasury (2002).

Given the strengths of a small scale model in explaining changes in the interest rate and its contribution in reducing the fluctuations in an economy, this paper aims to investigate how Taylor (1993) model fits to the interest rate series of the UK and five major industrial economies over last three decades. It complements to applied economic studies on this topics that have appeared in recent years; particularly those relating to the interdependency of real interest rates among *G7 economies* (Cheung and Westerman (2002), Ghazali and Ramlee (2003)) *or to G3 economies (Yamada (2002)) or to Fisher hypothesis (*Berument and Jelashi (2002), Silvapulle and Hewarathna (2002)*)*. Model discussed in this paper neither directly derives the interest rate rules using optimising models with *non-negativity constraints on the interest rate as found in* Sugo and Teranishi (2005) nor uses predominance of the m*ajority vote rule over the consensus in setting policy a*s discussed in Gerlack-Kristen (2005). *The* empirical results emerging from single equation or simultaneous equations or panel data or VAR-cointegration models generate results that are comparable to findings seen in studies by Asimakopoulos, Goddard and Siriopoulos (2000), Brooks and Skinner(2000), Castelnouvo (2003), Camarero, Ordonez and Tamarit (2002), Bacchetta and Ballabriga (2000) Lee (2002), Den Butter and Jenson (2004), Ferris and Galbraith(2003), Valente (2003), Ghazali and Ramlee (2003),Wetherilt (2003), Buch (2004),Staikouras(2004), Mills and Wood (2002.. Some details on issues, methods and major findings of these various studies are given in the appendix. Study reported here also focuses on the long run relationship of the determinants of interest rate and its impacts on output and prices based on cointegration analyses for long run relationship between the interest rate and time series of output gap and inflation gaps in the UK and G7 economies. A simultaneous equation model is used to investigate the interdependency among these variables and a VAR impulse response model is used for analysing the impacts of unit shocks in output, inflation and the interest rate and for forecasting future values of these variables using information contained in their time series. Determinants of the interest rate in this paper are based analytically on the solutions of a second order difference equation for interest determination rule similar to that of Taylor (1993) in section II. A brief discussion of data set used for study is in section III. Empirical relevance of this model is tested with quarterly macro economic time series data for the UK and annual data for five major industrial economies during last three decades in section IV and conclusions and references are in section V.

A SIMPLE INTEREST RATE DETERMINATION MODEL

A simple interest rate determination model, originally proposed by Taylor (1993) for the Federal Reserves in the US, can be constructed using three equations. First equation states the current output gap $\left(y_t - y^*\right)$, the actual output relative to the trend output, as a function of the deviation of the interest rate one period earlier from the target interest rate of the monetary authority $\left(i_{t-1} - i^*\right)$. This relationship is expected to be negative one as the higher interest rate is expected to slow down expenses by consumers and firms and generate contractionary impacts in the economy such as:

$$y_t - y_t{}^* = -d\left(i_{t-1} - i_{t-1}^*\right) \quad d > 0 \tag{1}$$

where y_t and y_t^* are actual and natural level of output, i_t is the actual rate of interest in period *t*, i_t^* is the target or the natural rate of interest for the monetary authority. This is similar to the equation for the investment-saving equilibrium relation (*IS* curve) in Woodford (2001), particularly when trends and targets are treated as expectations. More than one period lag can be assumed between the periods of the decisions of the interest rate and the changes in the output, though it was found not necessary for the current study.

The next equation shows how the price level in this economy responds to the level of economic activities, the aggregate supply. The expectation augmented Phillips curve in terms of output is given by:

$$\pi_t = \pi_t^* + c\left(y_{t-1} - y_{t-1}^*\right) \quad c > 0 \tag{2}$$

where π_t and π_t^* are actual and target rates of inflation. When the output is above the trend in the last period, it creates an upward pressure in the labour market which raises the wage rate. Increase in the wage rate translates into higher prices and higher rates of inflation. Again this is similar to equation (3) in Woodford (2001) when target inflation rate is treated as expected rate of inflation. A simple interest rate rule is derived by combining (1) and (2) to show how the policy makers like to reduce interest rate when both output and inflation rates are higher relative to their natural rates as:

$$i_t = i_t^* + a\left(y_t - y_t^*\right) + b\left(\pi_t - \pi_t^*\right) \quad a > 0;\ b > 0 \tag{3}$$

If the output gap from (1) and inflation rate gap from (2) are substituted in the interest rate rule in (3) it generates autoregressive reduced form single equation of interest that can explain the cycles of interest rate in terms of reduced form parameters as :.

$$i_t = i_t^* - ad\left(i_{t-1} - i_{t-1}^*\right) - bcd\left(i_{t-2} - i_{t-2}^*\right)$$

$$i_t + adi_{t-1} + bcdi_{t-2} = i_t^* + adi_{t-1}^* + bcdi_{t-2}^* \tag{4}$$

The stability or convergence properties of the second order difference equation (4) essentially depends upon values of the parameters a b, c and d and two initial conditions for i_0 and i_1. For simplicity define $\beta_0 = \left(i_t^* + adi_{t-1}^* + bcdi_{t-2}^*\right)$, and $\beta_1 = ad$ and $\beta_2 = bcd$. Then equation (4) can be written as:

$$i_t + \beta_1 i_{t-1} + \beta_2 i_{t-2} = \beta_0 \tag{5}$$

The general solution to the reduced form difference equation (5) has complementary and particular parts. The particular solution refers to the steady state and the complementary solution shows a dynamic adjustment towards that steady state when the interest rate is above or below its natural rate. It explains the dynamics of the interest rate series. The convergence or divergence from the steady state or the natural rate of interest rate depend on this part of the equation.

The particular or steady state solution is easy, as interest rate in each period equals the steady state interest rate which can be also considered a natural rate of interest, *i.e.* $i_t + \beta_1 i_{t-1} + \beta_2 i_{t-2} = \beta_0 i_t = i_{t+1} = i_{t+2} = \ldots = i_{t+n}$. Thus with some manipulation the steady state or the natural rate of interest rate for the above model can be expressed as:

$$\bar{i} = \frac{i_t^* + adi_{t-1}^* + bcdi_{t-2}^*}{1 + \beta_1 + \beta_2} \text{ or } \bar{i} = \frac{i_t^* + adi_{t-1}^* + bcdi_{t-2}^*}{1 + ad + bcd}$$ in terms of the original model parameters with flexible targets i_{t-2}^* i_{t-1}^* and i_t^* and as

$$\bar{i} = \frac{i_t^*\left(1 + ad + bcd\right)}{1 + ad + bcd} \text{ with fixed targets.} \tag{6}$$

Any short run disturbances from this natural rate should ultimately return to it due to forces of demand and supply in the financial markets and is represented by a homogeneous part of the solution.

$$i_t + \beta_1 i_{t-1} + \beta_2 i_{t-2} = 0 \tag{7}$$

Theoretically the complementary solutions of (7) can have three different cases depending on the values of parameters β_0, and β_1 and β_2:

(a) real and distinct root, when $\beta_1^2 - 4\beta_2 > 0$, guarantees convergence to the steady state.

(b) real and equal roots case, $\beta_1^2 - 4\beta_2 = 0$, generates repeated cycles and

(c) complex roots case with $\beta_1^2 - 4\beta_2 < 0$ gives a cyclical pattern which may converge or diverge from the steady state rate depending the absolute values of parameters.

The general solutions of the model in these three different cases are:

$$i_t = A_1\lambda_1^t + A_2\lambda_2^t + \bar{i} \tag{8}$$

where A_1 and A_2 are arbitrary constants and λ_1^t and λ_2^t are the characteristic roots.

In case (a) the value of $\lambda_1^t = \dfrac{-\beta_1 + \sqrt{\beta_1^2 - 4\beta_2}}{2}$ and $\lambda_2^t = \dfrac{-\beta_1 - \sqrt{\beta_1^2 - 4\beta_2}}{2}$.

Therefore the general solution (8) can be written as:

$$i_t = A_1\left(\frac{-\beta_1 + \sqrt{\beta_1^2 - 4\beta_2}}{2}\right)^t + A_2\left(\frac{-\beta_1 - \sqrt{\beta_1^2 - 4\beta_2}}{2}\right)^t + \bar{i} \tag{9}$$

More specifically using all the parameters of the model this turns to be

$$i_t = A_1\left(\frac{-ad + \sqrt{(ad)^2 - 4bcd}}{2}\right)^t + A_2\left(\frac{ad - \sqrt{(ad)^2 - 4bcd}}{2}\right)^t + \bar{i} \tag{10}$$

The definite solution requires values of constant terms and, which can be obtained using the two initial conditions, and . Values of *a*, *b*, *c* and *d* parameters can be obtained from an econometric estimation. Literature suggests that interest rate, determined objectively in this manner, can be used to achieve price stability and real growth in the economy (Fisher (1977), Hanson (1980), Barro and Gordon (1983a, 1983b), Sargent (1986), Mankiw (1987), Driffil (1988), Goodhart (1989) Ball and Romer (1990), Alesina and Summers (1993), Nordhaus (1995), Dornbush and Fisher (1993), Lockwood, Miller and Zhang (1998), Vickers (1999), Nelson (2000), Corsetti and Pesenti (2001), Benigno(2002), Ellis and Price (2003)).

DATA SET

Interest rates have changed significantly over the years as shown in Figures 1a-1c. In general they were low and helped to generate unprecedented rate of economic growth in major industrial economies till late 1960s; increased and varied significantly and unpredictably in 1970s and 1980s characterising economic problems and have started changing systematically in a predictable manner as many western economies adopted rule based policy of determining these rates after mid 1990. Interest rates have become major tool for stabilising prices and the markets activities more in recent years.

Figure 1a
Monthly Basic Interest Rate Series in UK, USA and Japan

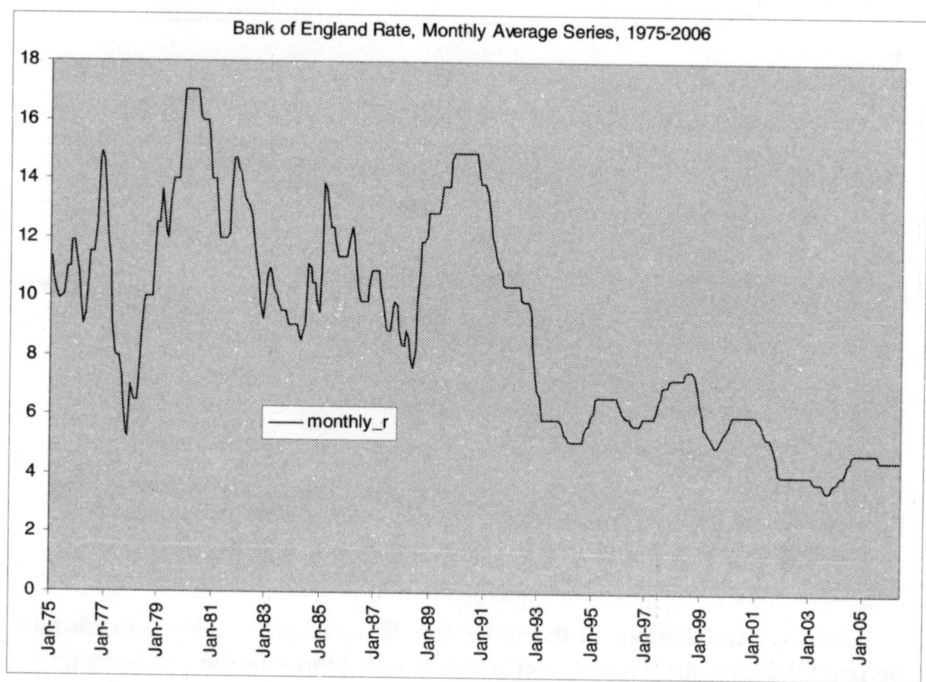

Figure 1b
Federal Fund Rate, 1954-2006

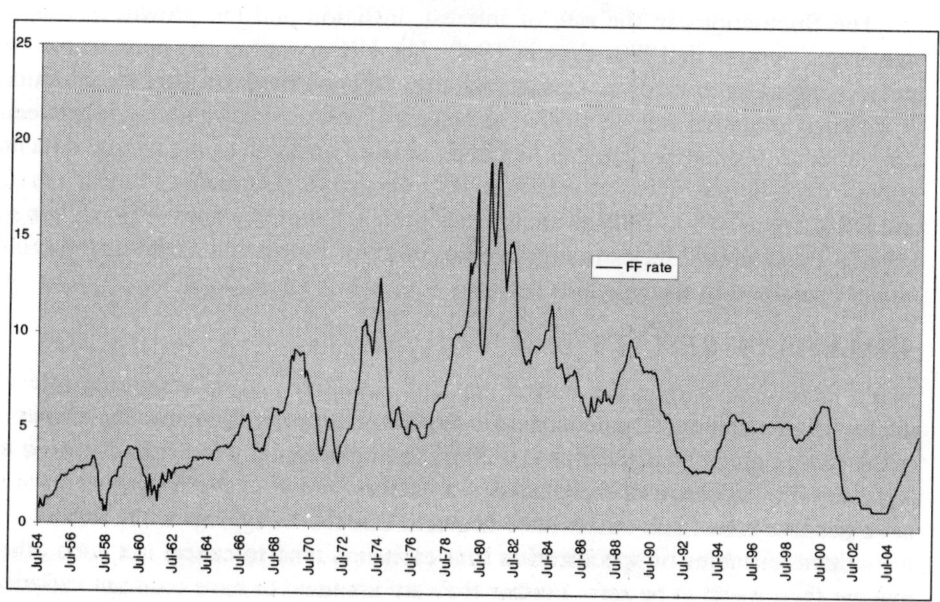

Figure 1c
Monthly Interest Rate Series in Japan

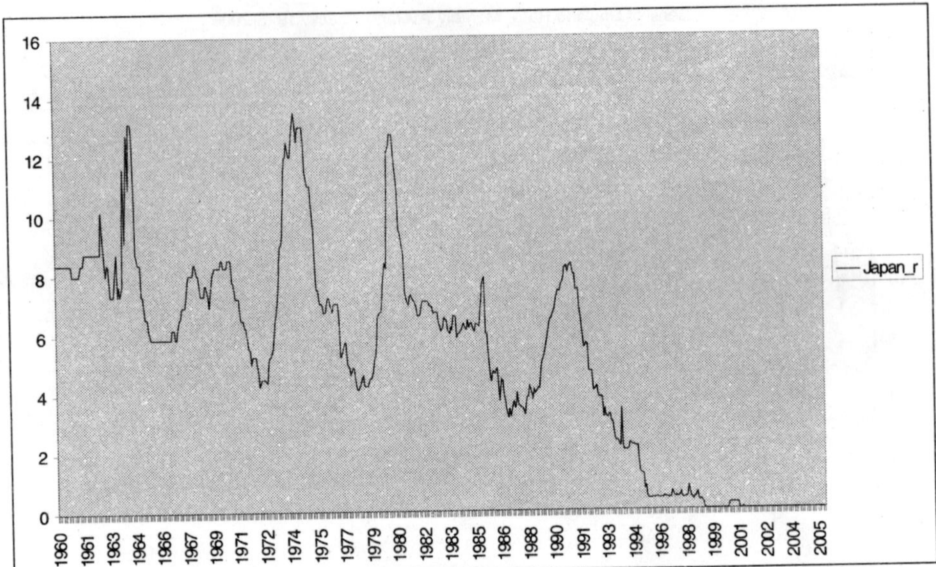

Quarterly fluctuations in the series for the retail price index, growth rate of the real GDP and the Treasury bill rates, which represent the whole varieties of interest rate, from 1970:q2 to 1999:q4 are as presented in Figure 2. These series were obtained from the macro time series data archive in Essex *(http://www.data-archive.ac.uk).*

The fluctuations in the rate of interest, inflation and the growth of output were more serious in 1980s than in 1990. The UK economy has been stabilised and moving more towards its natural rate after 1995 particularly after the adoption of inflation targeting rule in 1997 (see Nelson (2000) for more division between sub periods). Similar pattern can be obtained from analysis of the annual data on growth rates output, rates of inflation and interest for Germany, France, Japan, and USA from 1978 to 2000 as shown in Figure 3. Quarterly time series shown in Figures 2 and annual series in Figure 3 are used for estimation of the interest rule model explained in the previous sections.

ANALYSIS OF RESULTS

Many factors other than the output gap and inflation gap influence the rate of interest in an economy. The econometric models incorporate these missing elements in the model given by equations (1)-(3) including error terms to each equation to represent the influence of these unknown factors. Some of these omitted factors have positive effect and others have negative effects. In aggregate the influences of omitted variables or specification bias elements tend to cancel out each other making their mean to be zero. Further they are assumed to have constant variance to express no systematic relation among the errors. Technically speaking these

Figure 2
Growth rates of output, interest rate and inflation in the UK

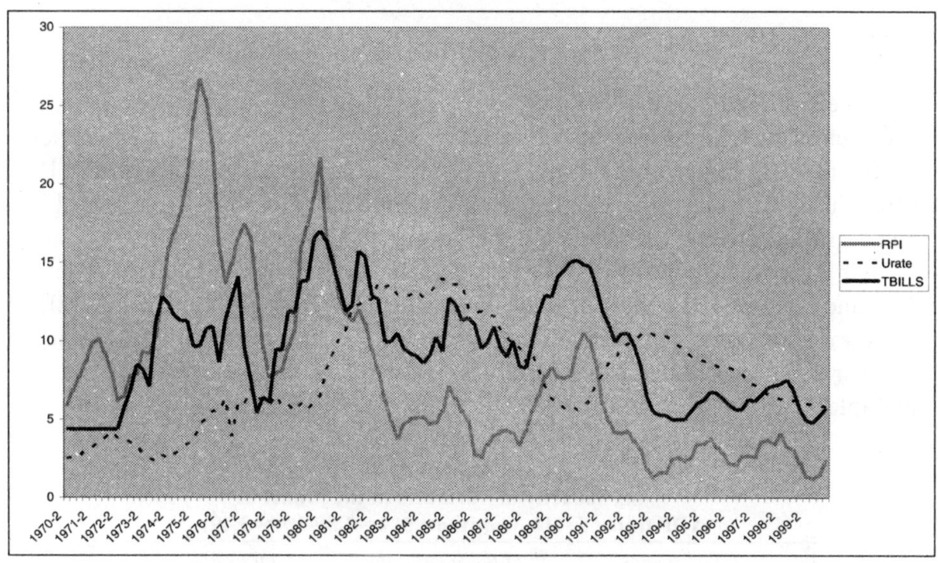

Figure 3
Real interest rates in major industrial economies

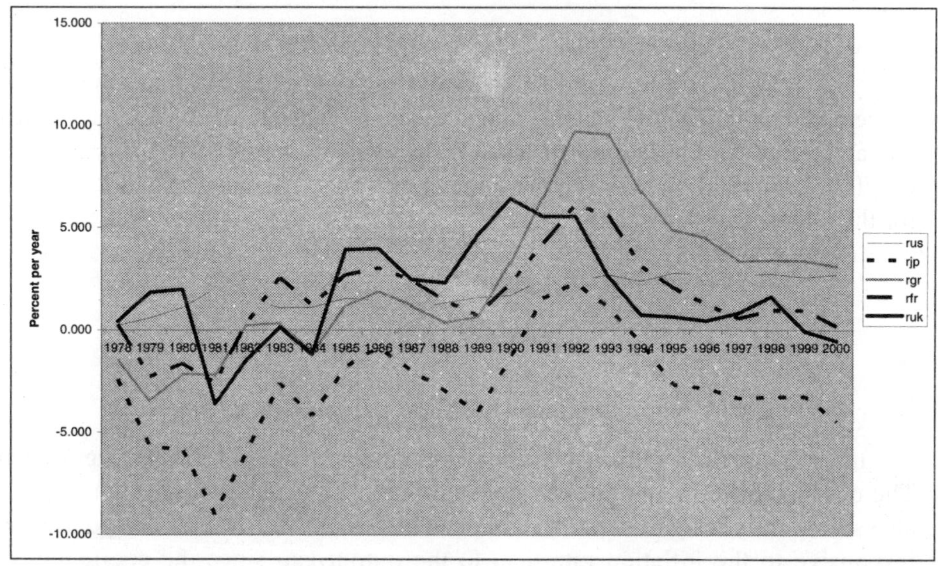

errors are distributed normally, identically and independently. These assumptions imply that those errors are homoscedastic and have no autocorrelation and there is no multi-collinearity among the explanatory variables.

$$y_t - y_t^* = d\left(i_{t-1} - i_{t-1}^*\right) + \varepsilon_{1,t} \tag{11}$$

$$\pi_t = \pi_t^* + c\left(y_{t-1} - y_{t-1}^*\right) + \varepsilon_{2,t} \tag{12}$$

$$i_t = i_t^* + a\left(y_t - y_t^*\right) + b\left(\pi_t - \pi_t^*\right) + \varepsilon_{3,t} \tag{13}$$

Even if relations may be perfect there is still chance of regressions being spurious as the relation may be between nonstationary variables. We follow Dickey-Fuller (1976) Engle and Granger (1987) and Johansen and Juselius (1990) procedures to determine existence or absence of unit roots of a variable or cointegration among variable sin the model.

Unit root test suggests that the interest rate variable is integrated of order one, *I(1)*, and becomes stationary after differencing once. Both output gap and inflation gaps are stationary. The critical and estimated values of coefficients of the unit root for equation of these three variables (from the PC-Give outputs) are as shown in Table 1, along with significant lag lengths.

Table 1
Stationarity of Variables in the Model
ADF tests (T=116, Constant; 5%=-2.89 1%=-3.49)

	Interest rate	*1st Difference of the interest rate*	*Output gap*	*Inflation gap*
Coefficient	-2.723	-6.463**	-6.160**	-7.428**
Lags	2	2	3	1

Next it is shown how the Engle and Granger (1987) or Johansen (1988) procedure can be used to obtain a non-spurious regression between the interest rate and output and inflation gaps even if the interest rate series is non-stationary.

The basic relation between the interest rate and inflation gap and output gap for the UK is as given below.

$$i_t = 9.446 - 0.183\left(y_t - y_t^*\right) + 0.370\left(\pi_t - \pi_t^*\right)$$

t (32.2) (-1.1) (2.84)
(SE) (0.29) (0.13) (0.181)
Normality test: Chi^2(2) = 11.279 [0.0036]**

Interest rate rises with an increase in inflation and the coefficient is significant. The coefficient in the output gap does not have expected positive sign and it is also statistically insignificant. Above result also suggests that interest rate is more responsive to the inflation rate than to the output gap since the coefficient on output is not significant. These test results are comparable to that of Berument and Jelashi (2002), Silvapulle and Hewarathna (2002).

In addition the normality test in line with the Engel and Granger (EG) method of cointegration test suggests that residuals from the above regression of the interest rate on output gap and inflation gap are non-stationary and hence this is a spurious regression.

What about estimating the interest rule in terms of the reduced autoregressive second order difference equation equivalent to that given in equation (5)? This gives reasonable results as:

$$i_t = 1.630 + 0.582 i_{t-1} + 0.244 i_{t-2}$$

t-ratios (2.71) (6.42) (6.69)
r-square = 0.62 Durbin-Watson = 2.0104

All coefficients of the reduced form equation of interest for the UK have expected signs. It is however, difficult to retrieve the structural parameters of the original model from the estimates of the reduced form equation.

Alternative is to use a recursive estimation method where the output gap is estimated as a function of the lagged interest rate and then the inflation gap estimated on the lagged output gap and finally the interest rate rule equation estimated with the predicted values of the output gap and inflation gaps. The output gap is influenced by the interest rate, and the inflation gap is determined by the output gap and then that is determined by the interest rate. The recursive simultaneous equation estimation from UK time series that removes the simultaneity bias looks as following:

Interest rate: i	=	4.969(y-y*) -5.182 (p-p*)
		(7.74) (-7.27)
Output gap: y-y*	=	0.08i + 0.504 (p-p*)
		(7.75) (5.21)
Inflation: p-p*	=	-0.071i + 0.421 (y-y*)
		(-7.27) (5.21)
System R-Square	=	0.8637

The result of the simultaneous equation model has better overall fit even that of the results from the autoregressive model given above. Now the model explains about 86 percent of variation in the interest rate.

The above model can be estimated following Johansen and Juselius (1990) procedure for a cointegrated VAR model. The validity of this approach is based on the rank of the cointegration matrix of the structural coefficients that is crucial for determining the number of cointegration vectors in the model. Consider a VAR model for above three variables.

$$Y_t = A_1 Y_{t-1} + \varepsilon_t$$

where Y_t is vector of interest rate, output gap and inflation gap and ε_t is the vector of normally and identically distributed random error terms. By subtracting Y_{t-1} from both sides

$$\Delta Y_t = (A_1 - I) Y_{t-1} + \varepsilon_t$$

$$\Delta Y_t = \Pi Y_{t-1} + \varepsilon_t \text{ where } \Pi = (A_1 - I)$$

Here Π is the matrix of parameters showing the total long run relationship among variables. By using the cointegration procedure this matrix can further be decomposed into adjustment coefficients (α) and cointegrating vectors (β) as $\Pi = \alpha\beta'$. The matrix β denotes the long run steady state relationship among variables and α is the dynamic process of adjustment towards that equilibrium. The estimation on interest rate, output gap and inflation gap for the UK for 1972:2 to 1999:4 obtained using the PcGive (Doornik and Hendry (2001)) yields following results.

$$\Pi = \begin{bmatrix} -0.03654 & -0.12011 & 0.18569 \\ 0.02982 & -0.24185 & -0.08453 \\ -0.09433 & -0.07224 & -0.53655 \end{bmatrix}$$

$$\alpha = \begin{bmatrix} 0.01810 & 0.09100 & 0.01089 \\ 0.01667 & -0.00346 & -0.00208 \\ -0.00793 & -0.20723 & 0.00692 \end{bmatrix}$$

$$\beta = \begin{bmatrix} 1.0000 & 0.19498 & -6.6460 \\ -13.850 & 1.0000 & 3.6355 \\ -4.3680 & 2.7897 & 1.0000 \end{bmatrix}$$

The number of co-integrating vectors in the Johansen procedure is determined by $\lambda_{trace(r)} = -T\sum_{i=r+1}^{n} \ln\left(1-\hat{\lambda}_i\right)$ and $\lambda_{\max(r,r+1)} = -T\ln\left(1-\hat{\lambda}_{r+1}\right)$ statistics, where λ_i denotes the eigenvalues of the characteristic matrix $\Pi = (A_1 - I)$ and r is an indicator for a reduced rank in (k-r) for k number of explanatory variables. The calculated values of these statistics are compared with the theoretical critical values from Johansen and Juselius (1990) to ascertain the number of cointegrating ranks as following.

These cointegration results are comparable to those found in other applied works such as Cheung and Westerman (2002), *Yamada (2002),* Brooks and Skinner (2000),Camarero, Ordonez and Tamarit (2002) and Silvapulle and Hewarathna (2002), Valente (2003), Mills and Wood (2002).

The order of the rank of Π suggests the number of cointegrating vectors in β. Above $\lambda_{trace(r)}$ and $\lambda_{\max(r,r+1)}$ tests suggest that at least there are two cointegrating vectors in the above model. The long run relation among these variables is shown by a very good fit of the predicted and actual series of above three variables.

Table 2
Cointeg-ation Test Results

rank: H_0	*Trace test [Prob]*	*Max test [Prob]*	*Tracetest (T-nm)*	*Max test (T-nm)*
r = 0	56.86 [0.000]**	34.38 [0.000]**	55.43 [0.000]**	33.52 [0.000]**
r d" 1	22.48 [0.003]**	12.68 [0.087]	21.91 [0.004]**	12.36 [0.097]
r d" 2	9.80 [0.002]**	9.80 [0.002]**	9.55 [0.002]**	9.55 [0.002]**

The fit of the predicted and the actual interest rate is almost perfect as shown in the figures 4.

Figure 4
Prediction from A VAR Model: Actual, Fitted and Cointegrating Vectors.

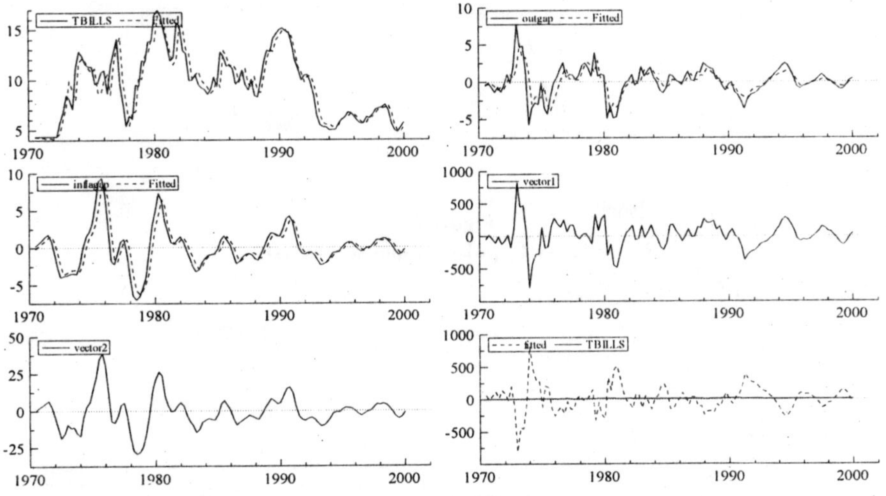

The model estimated above can be used to analyse the impacts of shocks to each of the above equations in terms of incremental and cumulative impulse responses as shown in Figures 5 and Figure 6.

A unique shock to the interest rate by one standard unit reduces the output gap immediately with a lagged response in the rates of inflation; a similar shock to the output equation reduces the interest rate immediately and has lagged response in the rate of inflation rate as shown by graphs in the second row; an unit shock to inflation reduces the interest rate immediately and has lagged response in output gap as shown by graphs in row 3 in Figures 5 and 6. Though the model converges to the steady state over periods, each of these shocks has its own patterns of impacts. The cumulative shocks corresponding to each of three unit shocks on treasury bills rate, output and inflation gaps in Figure 5 are shown by cumulative response graphs in respective positions in Figure 6. Dynamic forecasts along with their confidence bands are shown in Figure 7.

Figure 5
Impulse Response Analysis

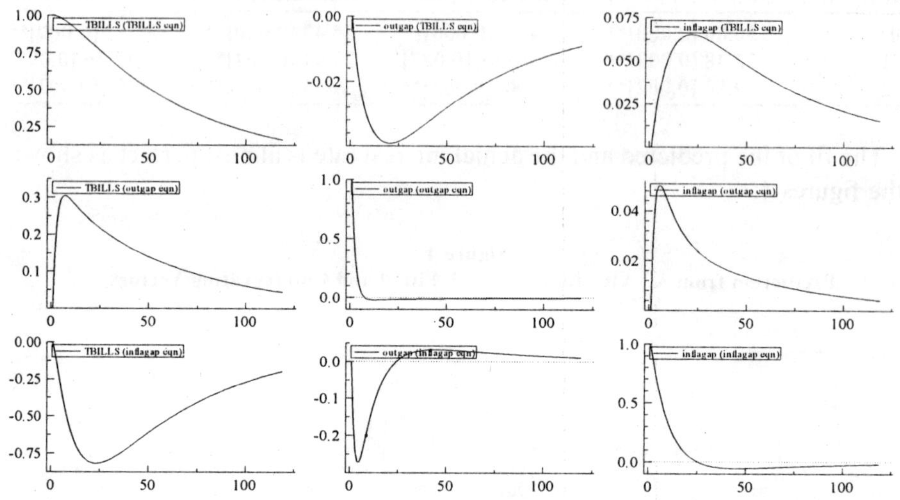

Figure 6
Cumulative Impulse Response Analysis

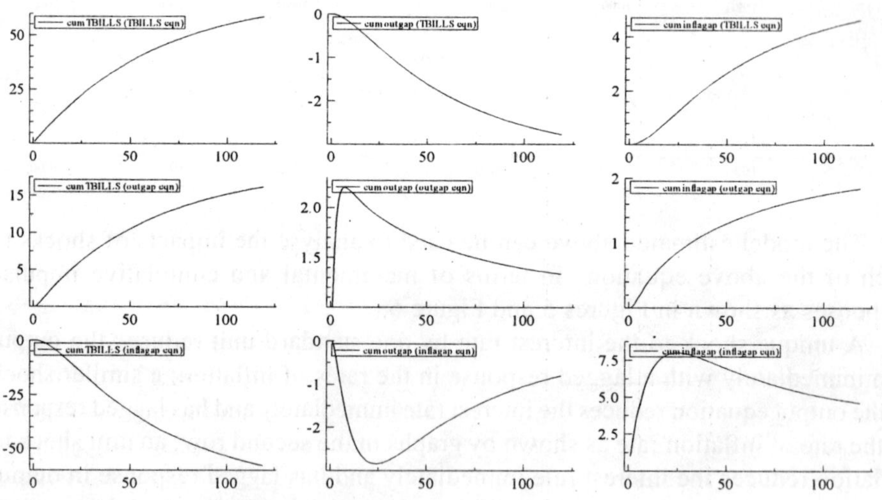

Studying the time profiles of these shocks it becomes obvious that it may take from 4 to 24 quarters for economy to realise the impact of a shock to the interest rate. The above shocks can further be divided in real shocks to the output and the nominal sector shocks in terms of the interest rate. More detailed estimates for various sub-periods between 1973-2000 can be found in Nelson (2000) or in Castelnouvo (2003).

Figure 7
Dynamic Forecasts of Interest Rate, Output-gap and Inflation Gap

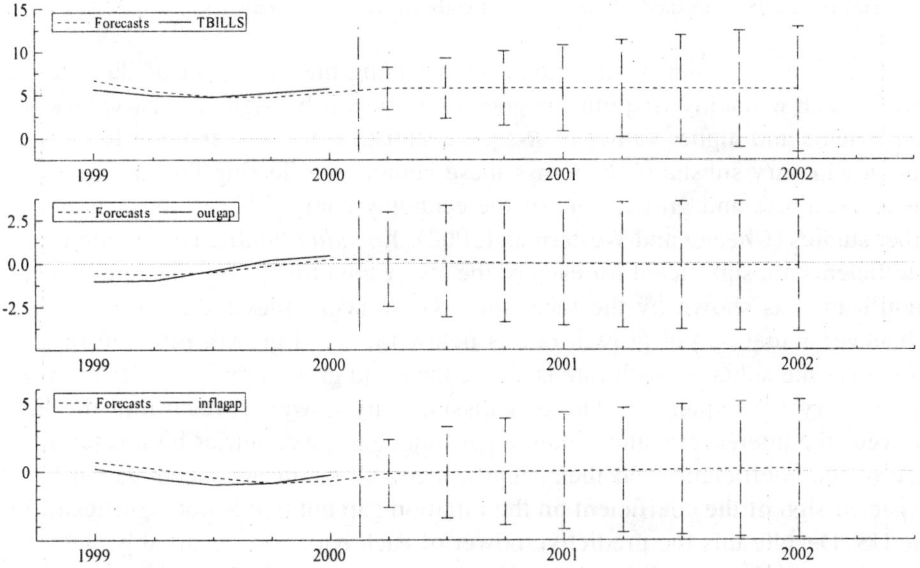

The estimation of the interest rule model for one economy can be extended to a group of economies taken together. An attempt is made here to test it for five major industrial economies France, Germany, Japan, UK and the USA using the annual data set on growth rates of output, inflation and interest rates obtained from the World Bank (2002). Three steps are involved in applying this interest determination model to five major industrial economies. First step involves estimation of the current output gap as a function of the actual interest rates in the previous period relative to a trend interest rate, and the estimation of current inflation gap as a function of output gap in the previous period. These predicted series of output and inflation gaps are used to estimate model generated interest rate for each period in the second step. A comparison is made between the series of the actual interest rates to those predicted by the model in the third stage. Then the quality of predictions of the model are judged using test statistics and studying whether model based prediction can track actual interest rates well and decompose the sources of changes in the interest rate into the real or supply side factors as represented by the output gap and the demand side factors as represented by the inflation gaps.

Table 3
Test of Interest Determination Rule for Five Major Economies

	Output gap	*Inflation gap*	*Constant*	R^2
France	-6.641 (-14.778)	0.670 (1.341)	5.900 (1.341)	0.766
Germany	-10.732 (-15.187)	4.335 (4.953)	5.339 (11.898)	0.752
Japan	-6.775 (-6.554)	-1.794 (-7.061)	-1.312 (-3.487)	0.641
UK	-2.941 (-5.885)	1.006 (2.848)	7.416 (10.203)	0.574
USA	-1.794 (-7.061)	0.360 (0.408)	5.337 (18.955)	0.696

Estimates from a 3SLS method, values in the parenthesis represent *t*-statistics.

Explanatory power of this model in analysing the behaviour of the interest rate in each economy is quite remarkable as shown by significant t-values for coefficients and higher values of *R*-square statistics. Sizes of the coefficients of output gap vary substantially across these countries reflecting the link between the interest rate and growth rate of the economy comparable to those found in other studies (Cheung and Westerman (2002), *Yamada (2002))*. These output gap coefficients are significant for each of the above countries at one percent level of significance as shown by the t-statistics. These economies reduce interest rate whenever actual output growth rate is below the trend growth rate and raise it whenever the actual growth rate is above the trend growth rate in order to avoid inflationary consequences. There is dissimilarity however, regarding the link between the interest rate and inflation gap among these countries both is terms of size of the coefficients and their significance. All countries except Japan have expected sign of the coefficient on the inflation gap but that is not significant for the US. Despite this the predictive power of each equation remarkably suggests for existence of interest rate rule among these economies during the study period.

When we study the interdependence in the interest rate determination among G5 major economies treating them as one by pooling cross section and time series data for entire 1978-2000 period, it generates following result.

$$i_t = 6.25 - 0.29\left(y_t - y_t^*\right) + 0.115\left(\pi_t - \pi_t^*\right)$$

t-ratios (0.80) (-3.30) (1.33)

$$R^2 = 0.43 \quad F = 5.5; N=100$$

From economic point of view this result is not very sensible. In theory the interest rate should rise when output is above its trend but here estimated coefficient has a negative sign showing a reverse result. The coefficient on inflation gap has expected positive sign but it is not significant at 5 percent level of significance. These results do not support the hypothesis of interest rate determination rule at aggregate level by G5 countries for this period though it is supposed to be so in the literature (Asimakopoulos, Goddard and Siriopoulos (2000), Lee (2002), Den Butter and Jenson (2004), Ghazali and Ramlee (2003), Buch (2004)). Each of G5 countries were acting independently in determining its own interest rate.

Analyes on how the interest is determined and how it affects other economies requires more detailed specification of demand, production, portfolio allocation and trade structure of the monetary economy in line with Tobin (1969), Altig, Carlstrom and Lansing (1995), Corsetti and Pesenti (2001) and Vickers (1998). Such modelling is subject for further study but beyond the scope of this paper.

CONCLUSION

Analytical solution for interest rate rules in a three equation model is found using a second order-difference equation technique in terms of model parameters. Those parameters were estimated using the quarterly time series data on treasury bills rate, growth rate of output and inflation rates for UK, the annual time series during the last three decades for Germany, France, Japan, UK and the US. The evidence suggests existence of an interest rule. This empirical model is then applied for impulse response analysis and forecasting.

ACKNOWLEDGEMENTS

Author appreciates comments and suggestions received from editor of this Applied Financial Economics Journal and participants of the Ecomod Conference 2006 in Hong Kong. Earlier version of this paper was published as Bhattarai(2003), a Research Memorandum from the Centre for Economic Policy of the Hull University Business School. Correspondence address: Business School University of Hull, Cottingham Road, HU6 7RX, UK. e-mail: *K.R.Bhattarai@hull.ac.uk. Phone 44-1482-463207.*

REFERENCES

Alesina A, L.H. Summers (1993), Central Bank Independence and Macroeconomic Performance: Some Comparative Evidence *Journal of Money, Credit and Banking*, 25: 2: 151-162, May.

Altig D.E., C.T. Carlstrom and K.L. Lansing (1995), *Computable General Equilibrium Models and Monetary Policy Advice*, Journal of Money Credit and Banking, 27: 4:1472-1493: Nov.

Asimakopoulos I., J. Goddard and C. Siriopoulos (2000), Interdependence between the US and major European equity markets: evidence from spectral analysis. *Applied Financial Economics*, Feb, Vol. 10 Issue 1, p41-47.

Bacchetta P. and F. Ballabriga (2000), The impact of monetary policy and banks' balance sheets: some international evidence. *Applied Financial Economics*, Feb2000, Vol. 10 Issue 1, p15-26.

Ball L. and D. Romer (1990), Real Rigidities and the Non-Neutrality of Money, *Review of Economic Studies*, 57:183-203.

Barro R.J. and D.B. Gordon (1983), Rules, Discretion and Reputation in a Model of Monetary Policy, *Journal of Monetary Economics*, 12: 101-121, North-Holland.

Barro R.J. and D.B. Gordon (1983), A Positive Theory of Monetary Policy in a Natural Rate Model, *Journal of Political Economy*, vol. 91:4: 589-610.

Benigno, P. (2002), A Simple Approach to International Monetary Policy Coordination, *Journal of International Economics*, 57:1: 177-96, June.

Bernanke B.S. and F.S. Mishkin (1997), Inflation Targeting: A New Framework for Monetary Policy, *Journal of Economic Perspectives*, vol. II:2:97-116, Spring.

Berument H. and M.M. Jelashi (2002), Fisher hypothesis a multi-country analysis, *Applied Economics*, 34, 1645-1655.

Bhattarai K. R. (2003), Interest Determination Rule four UK and Other Four Major Industrial Economies, *Research Memorandum*, no. 42 Business School, University of Hull.

Brooks C. and F. Skinner (2000), What will be the risk-free rate and benchmark yield curve following European monetary union? *Applied Financial Economics*, Feb, Vol. 10 Issue 1, p59-69.

Buch, C.M. (2004), Cross-border banking and transmission mechanisms in Europe: evidence from German data. *Applied Financial Economics*, Nov, Vol. 14 Issue 16, p1137-1149.

Camarero M., J. Ordonez and C.R. Tamarit (2002), Monetary transmission in Spain: a structural cointegrated VAR approach, *Applied Economics*, 34: 2201-2212

Castelnouvo E. (2003), Taylor rules, omitted variables, and the interest rate smoothing in the US, *Economic Letters*, 81, 55-59.

Cheung Y.W. and F. Westerman (2002), Output dynamics in G7 countries: stochastic trends and cyclical movements, *Applied Economics*, 34, 2239-2247.

Corsetti, G and P. Pesenti; (2001), Welfare and Macroeconomic Interdependence, *Quarterly Journal of Economics*, May, Vol. 116, iss. 2, pp. 421-45.

Den Butter F.A.G. and P.W. Jansen (2004), An empirical analysis of the German long-term interest rate, Applied Financial Economics, 14, 731–741

Dickey D.A. and W.A. Fuller (1979), Distribution of the Estimator for Autoregressive Time Series with a Unit Root, Journal of the American Statistical Association, 74: 427-431, June.

Dornbush, R. and S. Fisher (1993), Moderate Inflation, World Bank Economic Review, 7:1:1-44.

Doornik J.A and D.F. Hendry (2001), Econometric Modelling Using PCGive Volumes I, II and II, Timberlake Consultant Ltd, London.

Driffil J. (1988), Macroeconomic Policy Games with Incomplete Information: A Survey, *European Economic Review*, 32 (2-3) 513-41.

Ellis C. and S. Price (2003), The impact of price competitiveness on UK producer price behaviour, Working paper No. 178, Bank of England.

Engle R.E. and C.W.J. Granger (1987), Co-integration and Error Correction: Representation, Estimation and Testing. *Econometrica,* Vol. 55, No. 2, pp. 251-276.

Ferris, J.S. and J.A. Galbraith (2003), Indirect Convertibility as a Money rule for Inflation targeting *Applied Financial Economics*, Oct, Vol. 13 Issue 10, p753, 9p;

Fisher, S. (1977), Long-Term Contracts, Rational Expectations, and the Optimal Money Supply Rule, *Journal of Political Economy*, 85:1:191-205, February.

Friedman, M. (1968), The Role of Monetary Policy, *American Economic Review*, LVIII 58:1:1-17, March.

Gali J and Gertler M. (1999), Inflation dynamics: a structural econometric analysis, *Journal of Monetary Economics*, 44(3) 195-222.

Gerlack-Kristen P. (2005), Too little too late, interest rate setting and the cost of consensus, *Economics Letters* 88, 376-381.

Ghazali, N.A. and S. Ramlee (2003), A long memory test of the long-run Fisher effect in the G7 countries. *Applied Financial Economics*, Oct, Vol. 13 Issue 10, p763, 7p;

Goodhart C. (1989), The Conduct of Monetary Policy, *Economic Journal*, 99: 396: 293-346, June.

Hanson J. A. (1980), The Short Run Relation Between Growth and Inflation in Latin America: A Quasi-Rational or Consistent Expectations Approach, *The American Economic Review*, 70:5: 972-989, December.

Hicks, J.R. (1937), Mr. Keynes and the "Classics": A Suggested Interpretations, *Econometrica*, 5:1:147-159.

HM Treasury (2002), "UK Model of Central Bank Independence: An Assessment" in *Reforming Britain's Economic and Financial Policy*, Palgrave pp. 85-109.

Holly S. and M. Weale Eds. (2000), *Econometric Modelling: Techniques and Applications*, pp.69-93, the Cambridge University Press, Great Britain.

Johansen S. (1988), Statistical Analysis of Cointegration Vectors, *Journal of Economic Dynamics and Control* 12 231-254, North Holland.

Johansen J. and Juselius K. (1990), Maximum Likelihood Estimation and Inference on Co-integration - with Application to Demand for Money, Oxford Bulletin of Economics and Statistics, 52, 169-210.

Keynes J.M. (1936), *The General Theory of Employment, Interest and Money*, MacMillan and Cambridge University Press, United Kingdom.

Kydland, F.E. and E.C. Prescott (1977), Rules Rather than Discretion: The Inconsistency of Optimal Plans, *Journal of Political Economy* 85: 3: 473-491.

Laidler D. and M. Parkin (1975), Inflation: A Survey, *The Economic Journal*, 85: 340: 741-809 December.

Lee J. E. (2002), Real interest rate in regional economic blocks, *Applied Economics*, 34:859-864

Lockwood, B.M. Miller, L. Zhang (1998), Designing Monetary Policy When Unemployment Persists *Economica*, August, 65: 259:pp. 327-45.

Mankiw N.G. (1987), The Optimal Collection of Seigniorage, *Journal of Monetary Economics*, 20, 327-341, North Holland.

Mills T.C. and G.E Wood (2002), Wages and prices in the UK, *Applied Economics*, 34:2143-2149

MPC Bank of England (www.bankofengland.co.uk) *The Transmission Mechanism of Monetary Policy*.

Nelson E. (2000), UK monetary policy 1972-97: a guide using Taylor rules, *Bank of England Working Paper No. 120*, London.

Nickell, S. (1990), Inflation and the UK Labour Market *Oxford Review of Economic Policy* 6:4:25-35.

Nordhaus W.D. (1994), Policy Games: Co-ordination and Independence in Monetary and Fiscal Policeis, *Brookings Papers on Economic Activity,0:* 2: 139-216.

Phillips, A.W., (1958), The Relation Between Unemployment and the Rate of Change of Money Wage Rates in the United Kingdom, 1861-1957, *Economica,*, November, 25:283-299.

Phelps E.S. (1968), *Money* Wage Dynamics and Labour Market Equilibrium, *Journal of Political Economy*, 76: 678-711.

Sargent, T.J. (1986), *Rational Expectation and Inflation*, Harper and Row Publishers, New York.

Silvapulle P. and R. Hewarathna (2002), Robust estimation and inflation forecasting *Applied Economics,* 34:2277-2282.

Staikouras, S.K.. (2004), The information content of interest rate futures and time-varying risk premia *Applied Financial Economics*, Jul, Vol. 14 Issue 11, p761-771.

Sugo T. and Y. Teranishi (2005), Optimal Monetary Policy Rule under the non-negativity Constraint on nominal interest rates *Economic Letters* 85: 95-100.

Taylor M.P. (1987), On the long run Solution to Dynamic Econometric Equations under Rational Expectation, *Economic Journal*, 97:385:215-218.

Taylor J. (1993), Discretion Versus Policy Rules in Practice, *Carnegie Rochester Conference Series on Public Policy* 39:0:195-214, Amsterdam.

Tobin, J. (1969), A General Equilibrium Approach to Monetary Theory, *Journal of Money Credit and Banking* 1 February.15-29.

Valente G. (2003), Monetary Policy rules and Regime Shifts, *Applied Financial Economics*, Jul, Vol. 13 Issue 7, p525, 11p.

Vickers J. (1998), Inflation Targeting in Practice: the UK Experience, *Bank of England Quarterly Bulletin*, November, 368-375.

Wetherilt, A.V. (2003), Money Market Operations and short-term Interest Rate Volatility in the United Kingdom *Applied Financial Economics*, Oct, Vol. 13 Issue 10, p701, 19p;

Woodford M. (2001), The Taylor Rule and Optional Monetary Policy, *American Economic Review* 91:2:232-237.

World Bank (2002), *World Development Indicators: a CD-Rom*, Washington DC.

Yamada H. (2002), Real interest rate Equalisation: Some Evidence from three Major World Financial Markets *Applied Economics*, 34:2143-2149

APPENDIX

Summary of Recent Applied Studies on the Determination and Interdependence in the Interest Rates and their Impact among Economies

Authors	*Economic issues*	*Method*	*Summary*	*Journal*
Asimakopoulos, Goddard and Siriopoulos (2000)	US and major European equity markets	spectral analysis	*Lead-lag relation in stock returns in EU and US*	*AE*
Bacchetta and Ballabriga (2000)	The impact of monetary policy and banks' balance sheets: some international evidence.	VAR	*Strong relation between the Interest and output in the US and 13 EU economies*	*AFE*
Brooks and Skinner(2000)	What will be the risk-free rate and benchmark yield curve following European monetary union?	Linear factor model	*UK 3-month yield curve best approximates others in EU*	*AFE*
Berument and Jelashi (2002)	Fisher hypothesis a multi-country analysis	ADF, OLS, ARCH-LM	*Support for Fisher hypothesis for 13 of 26 countries*	*AE*
Mills and Wood (2002)	Wages and prices in the UK	VECM	*Wage growth does not predict inflation*	AE
Silvapulle and Hewarathna (2002)	Robust estimation and inflation forecasting	ECM	*Support Fisher effect on inflation for Australia*	AE
Camarero, Ordonez and Tamarit (2002)	Monetary transmission in Spain	S-CVAR	*Support for endogenous policy reaction of monetary policy*	AE
Cheung and Westerman (2002)	Output dynamics in G7 countries: stochastic trends and cyclical movements	VAR-Co integration	*Existence of common business cycles among G7 countries*	AE
Lee (2002)	Real interest rate in regional economic blocks,	VEC, ARIMA	*Long run relation in real interest rates of APEC, EU and the US*	AE
Castelnouvo (2003)	Taylor rules, omitted variables, and the interest rate smoothing in the US	OLS in first differences	*Test of forward looking Taylor rule in the US*	EL
Yamada (2002)	Real interest rate equalisation: some evidence from three major world financial markets	VAR cointegration	*Departure from long-run real interest rate equalisation is not very large*	AE
Ferris and Galbraith (2003)	Indirect convertibility as a money rule for inflation targeting	Relative price concept	*How indirect converti-bility brings price stability (fixing a basket/ unit of money)*	*AFE*
Valente (2003)	Monetary policy rules and regime shifts	MS-VAR	*Time varying parameter and Markov Switching VAR model for policy rule*	*AFE*
Ghazali and Ramlee (2003)	A long memory test of the long-run Fisher effect in the G7 countries	ARIMA, ARFIMA	*Long run relation between interest rate and inflation in G7 countries.*	*AFE*

Contd....

Authors	*Economic issues*	*Method*	*Summary*	*Journal*
Wetherilt (2003)	Money market operations *and short-term interest rate volelatility in the United Kingdom*	GARCH and VECM	*Reduction in the volatility of market rates along with that in repo rates in uk*	*AFE*
Buch (2004)	Cross-border banking and transmission mechanisms in Europe: evidence from German data.	Credit data analysis	*Activities of commercial banks cause transmission of shocks across countries*	*AFE*
Staikouras (2004)	The information content of interest rate futures and time-varying risk premia	VAR cointegration	*Tests speculative efficiency hypothesis and supports price discovery hypothesis*	*AFE*
Butter and Jenson (2004)	An empirical analysis of German long term interest rate	ARIMA, ECM	*Four theories of interest rate explain German short term rate*	*AFE*
Gerlack-Kristen (2005)	Too little too late, interest rate setting and the cost of consensus	Vote and simulation	*Majority vote better than consensus in setting policy*	EL
Sugo and Teranishi (2005)	Optimal monetary policy rule under the non-negativity constraint on nominal interest rates	Constrained optimisation	*Policy rule optimal even in non-negative constraint on int rate*	EL

AE = Applied Economics,
AFE =Applied Financial Economics,
EL =Economics Letters.

10

Economic Growth: Models and Global Evidence[30]

Keshab Bhattarai

INTRODUCTION

Economic growth is a recent phenomenon in human civilisation. Per capita income in the Western Europe, which was at about the same or even at slightly lower level than that in China and India up to 15th century, had become more than 30 times higher by 2000 (about ten times in terms of PPP). This extraordinary growth in living standards and longevity (Figure A1, A2, A7, A8) in the West was made possible by the use of scientific technology (machines and ideas) in production and use of more sophisticated means of transportation and communications in trade after the industrial revolution that started in late the 16th century (Maddison (1991), Uhling (2002)). In a seminal study Kaldor (1961) has summarised this growth process for the US and the majority of Western countries succinctly in terms of four stylised facts of economic growth. First, labour input has grown more slowly than capital and output. Therefore capital per capita (K/L) and output per capita (Y/L) have increased secularly. Second, the capital output ratio (K/Y) has remained fairly constant, has had no discernible trend and has more or less converged across industrialised economies. Third, the rate of return on capital (profit) and the real interest rate have no trend whereas real wage rates have followed a rising trend as the secular rises in productivity (Y/L) and per capita capital (K/L) have translated into higher real wages. Fourth, the share of income devoted to capital (rK/Y) and to labour (wL/Y) show no trend and remain fairly constant as the capital stock per person tends to grow along with output per person. Romer (1986) and Jones (2002) also illustrate these issues with various numerical examples.

The wide variation in the living standards seen today across countries was caused by differences in the rates of economic growth across countries over time

30. Corresponding Address: *K.R.Bhattarai@hull.ac.uk.* Earlier version of this paper has appeared as a research memorandum from Centre for Economic Policy in the Hull University Business School.

(Figure A1,A2,A3,A4,A9) and it has created imbalance between distributions of population and that of income around the globe. In 2002 seventy eight percent of global population living in developing economies enjoyed only about 21 percent of the global income (Figures A5, A6). Even a small difference in annual growth rates across countries in the past has made a big difference in the level of income over time. If an economy grows at 5 percent per year, it takes 14 years to double its per capita income, while it takes 70 years if it grows by 1 percent per year. Income level can rise 10 times the current level if an economy grows continuously at the rate of 4 percent per year in 58 years, or takes only 23 years if it grows by the rate of 10 percent per year. This means if the poorest country had only 5 percent of the level of income of the richest country, it could still catch up that country in 50 years time if it could maintain the rate of growth of its income at the rate higher than the six percent of that rich country. Such growth rates are not impossible to sustain over a significant time period as is shown by the experiences of the newly emerging economies of Japan and the East Asia. Relative positions in terms of distribution of per capita incomes in the world have changed significantly in the last century for many newly industrialised countries, including China in recent years. The "poor" economies have become "rich" in 50 years time (Figure A2).

Figure A1
Per Capita GDP in OECD Economies (1960-2000)

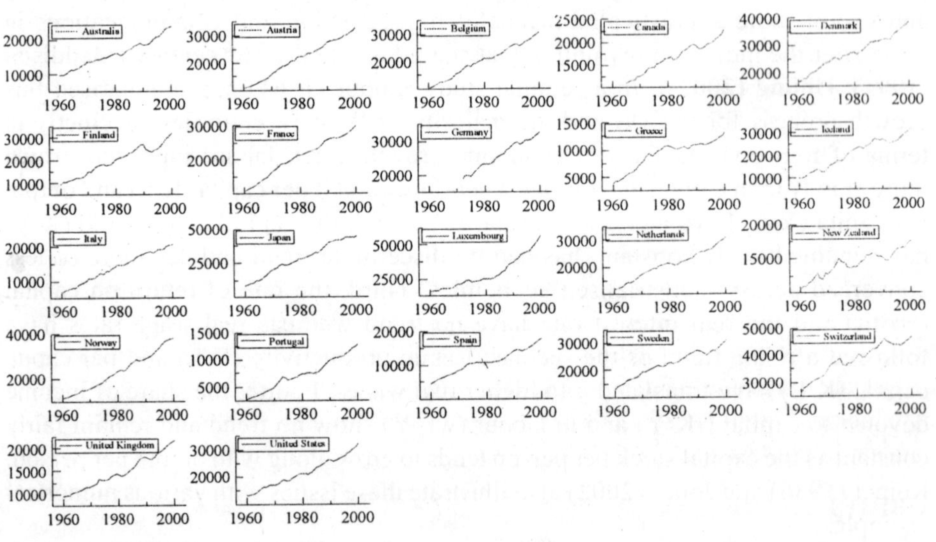

Source: World Bank

Many growth studies have identified accumulation of physical and human capital, as well as improvement in the production technology, and sound economic policies as the most important factors for economic growth (Ramsey (1928), Harrod

(1939), Domar (1947), Solow (1956), Cass (1965), Koopman (1965), Lucas (1988), Romer (1989), Barro (1998) and Barro and Sala-i-Martin (1995), Quah (1997), Rodrik (1999)). International trade has played a big role in the growth process as more open economies have grown faster as small economies have gained proportionately more from the specialisation. Differences in the prospects of economic growth rates between countries have also caused a significant reallocation of both skilled and unskilled workers as they have tended to migrate from poor countries or regions with low wage rates to rich countries or regions with higher wage rates. Growth theories analyse these broad experiences of economic growth across the world.

Figure A2
Per capita Income in Growth Miracle Countries 1960-2000

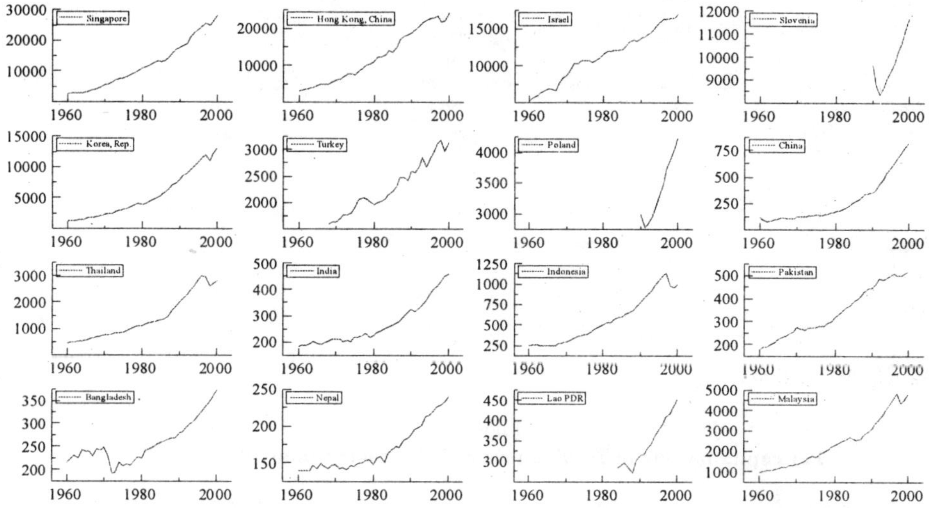

Source: World Bank

The major theories of economic growth are reviewed briefly in section II. Estimates of determinants of economic growth based on panel data for more than 208 countries around the world for years 1960 to 2000 is in section III. Analysis of the convergence or divergence phenomenon is in Section IV followed by conclusions, references, and appendices with more details on the estimates and data set in the last section.

A BRIEF REVIEW OF MODELS OF ECONOMIC GROWTH

Classical economists from Adam Smith to Marshall attributed higher rates of economic growth mainly to the capital accumulation (Roll (1938), Hahn and Matthew (1964), Madison (1991)). New and better equipment raises productivity of workers by improving the technology of production. Higher rates of saving and investment allow more accumulation of capital and generate higher rates of economic growth. They believed in the general equilibrium mechanisms of economic growth and thought that an increase in productivity automatically translates into an increase in the wage rate. They argued that the economy works better if left to itself as supply creates its own demand in the long run (Say's law). They favoured absolute economic freedom and minimum role of the government

Figure A3
Per Capita GDP in Growth Disaster Economies 1960-2000

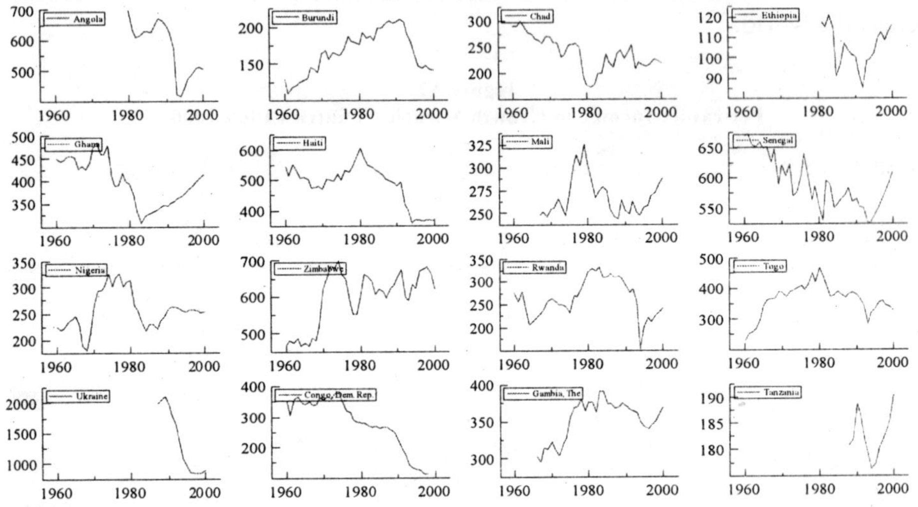

Source: World Bank

Figure A4
Per capita income in Trouble-prone Mid-income Countries 1960-2000

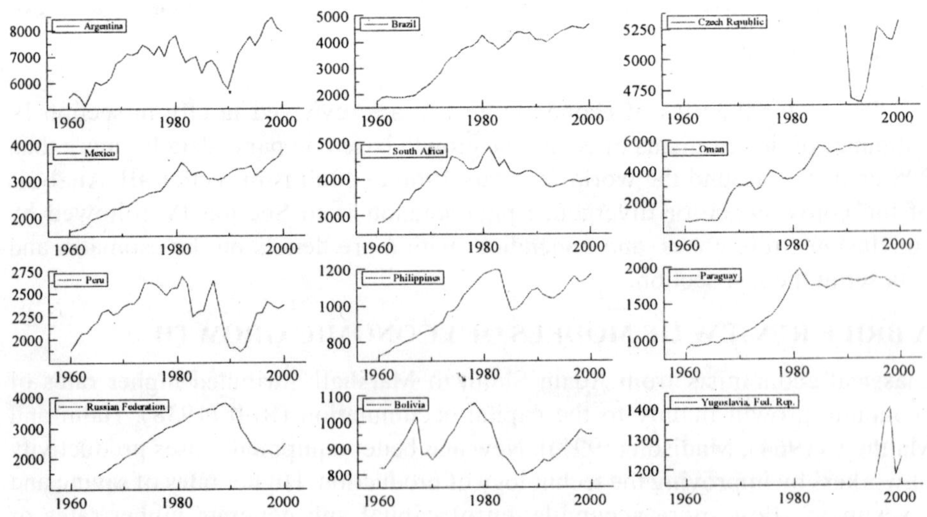

Source: World Bank

in economic activities. These liberal economic ideas were behind the great success of industrial revolution in Great Britain and many other Western economies. The classical ideas have got more accurate analytical framework in works of economists in the subsequent generation. Ramsey's (1928) mathematical theory of saving showed the optimal saving rate for an individual (or a benevolent social planner) who likes to maximise utility over its life time. The dynamic programming approach by Bellman (1957), Solows' neoclassical model of economics growth, the optimal growth framework of Cass (1965) Koopman (1966) added more complete dynamics in the macroeconomics that was focusing more on short run business cycle issues such as fluctuations in employment and output and determination of interest rate and money supply under Keynes (1936) rather than on the long run issue of economic growth. Harrod (1939) and Domar (1946, 1947) following Keynesian model assumed a constant rate of saving and capital output ratio in deriving a simple formula for economic growth. In their model the rate of growth of output related to the rate of saving and capital output ratio as $g = \frac{s}{k}$, where g is the growth rate of output, s is the saving rate and k is the capital output ratio. Under Harrod-Domar models a country with k equal to 4 but wanting to grow at the rate of 5 percent per year, has to save and invest 20 percent of its national income. Such simple calculations were used to formulate national economic plans in many countries after World War II. The lack of substitutability between capital and labour, depending on relative prices of capital and labour, made the Harrod-Domar model less applicable for market economies as it meant a permanent unemployment or growth restrained by the capacity constraint if the warranted rate of growth were different from the actual growth rates. Solow (1956) avoided this shortcoming by incorporating explicit substitutability between capital and labour, illustrating this using either a Cobb-Douglas or a CES production functions. He adopted a constant saving rate (as in the standard Keynesian model) rather than a variable optimal saving rate as in Ramsey (1928). Cass (1965), Koopman (1965) and Uzawa (1968) derived optimal economic growth models in which saving and investment rates also became endogenous to the lifetime utility maximisation behaviour of households and firms (Hahn (1964)).

Growth models have become more prominent in recent years as the most of the economies have realised limitations of demand management policies and focused on reform of goods and factor markets to reform the supply side of their economies. Theoretical models are supported by more in depth empirical growth studies (Maddison (1991), Mankiw et. al. (1992), Barrow and Sala-i-Martin (1995), Temple (1999)). Institutional and policy regimes are considered important determinants of growth in recent years (Barro (1995), Rodrik (1999), Quah(1997), Levin et.al. (1997), Temple (1999)). The basic version of the neo-classical growth model has been extended in many directions for analysis of international trade (Bhagwati (1969), Krugman (1990), Grossman and Helpman (1991)), education and human capital (Dennison (1962), Jorgenson and Fraumeni (1992), technological advancement and assimilation (Parente and Prescott (1991)), fertility and population growth (Tamura (1991), Miles (1999)), economic policies and institutional factors (Turnovskey (1993), Cooley (1995)). Some studies have integrated analysis of long run growth and the analysis of short-run fluctuations (Blackburn (1999), Blake and Weale (2003)).

Figure A5
Per capita income Latin and Central American and Caribbean countries 1960-2000

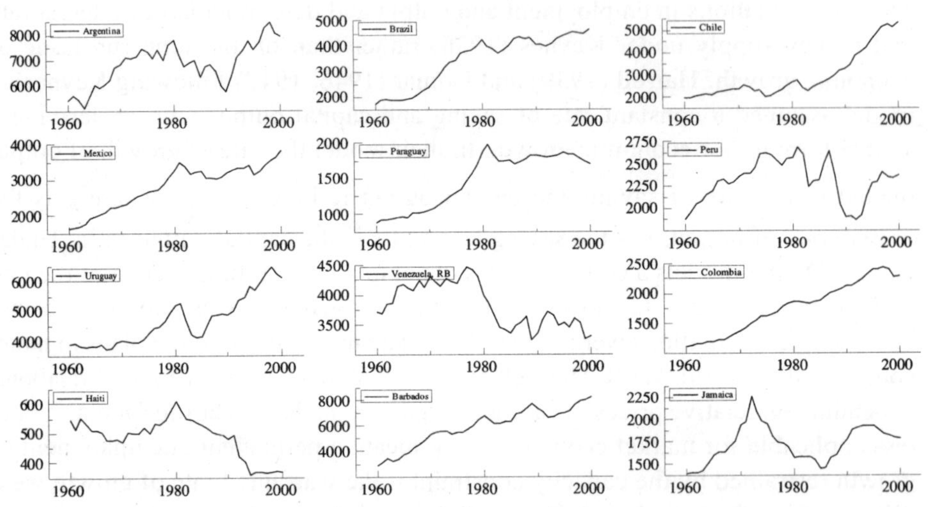

Figure A6
Location of Population across the Globe, 2000 (Out of Six billion)

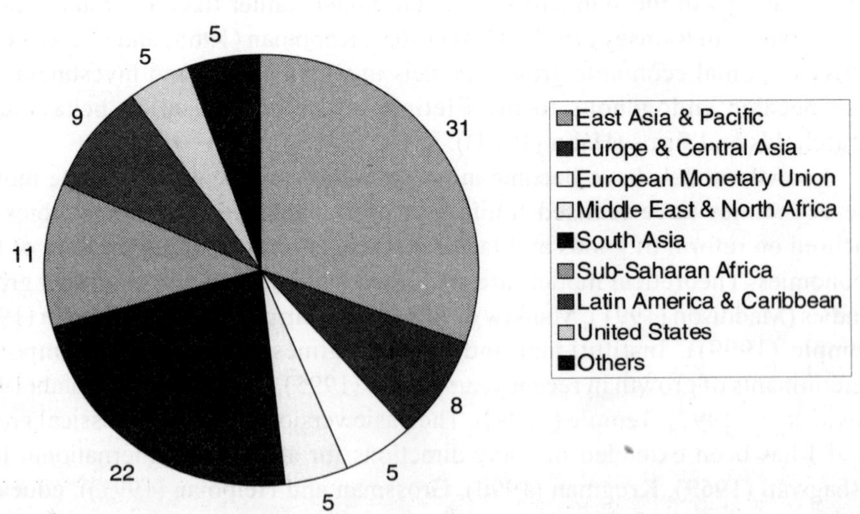

Figure A7
Distribution of Global Income

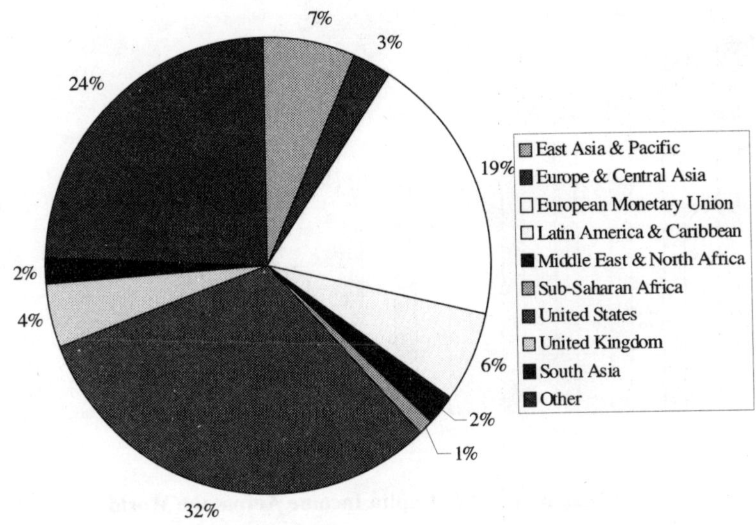

Figure A8
Age Profile of Population in High Income Economies

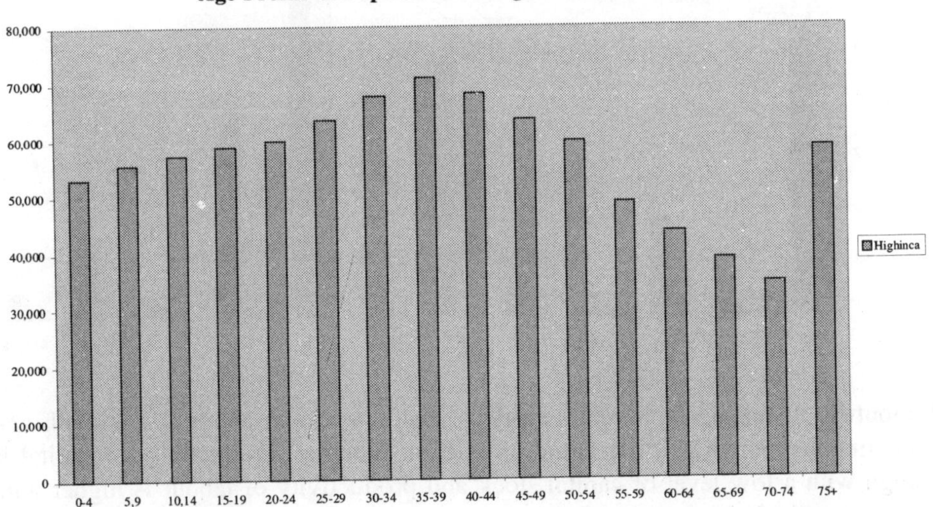

Solow's neoclassical growth model includes maximisation of profit by producers, who pay remuneration to factors equal to their marginal products; maximisation of utility by consumers, who save fixed fraction of their income for future use; model closure by equality of amount of savings to investment; substitution between capital and labour depending on the wage rental ratios. conomic policies can make one input cheaper or expensive relative to another

Figure A9
Age Profile of Population in High Income Economies

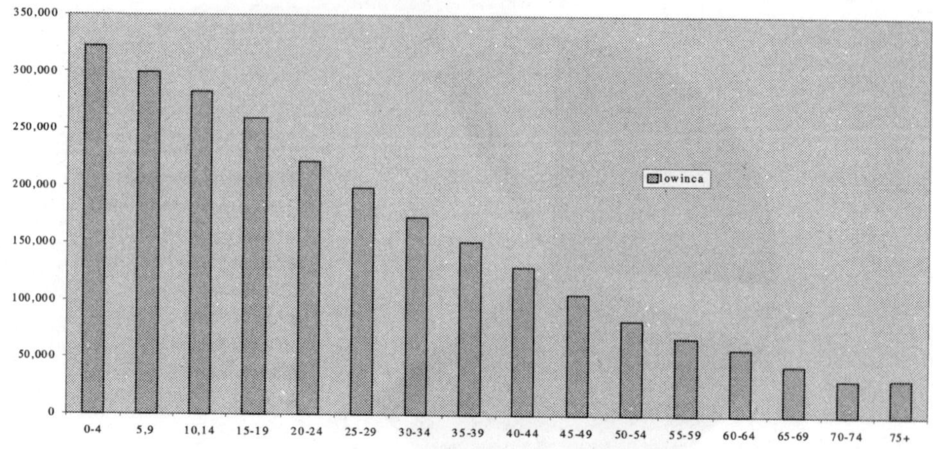

Diaparity in Per Capita Income Across the World

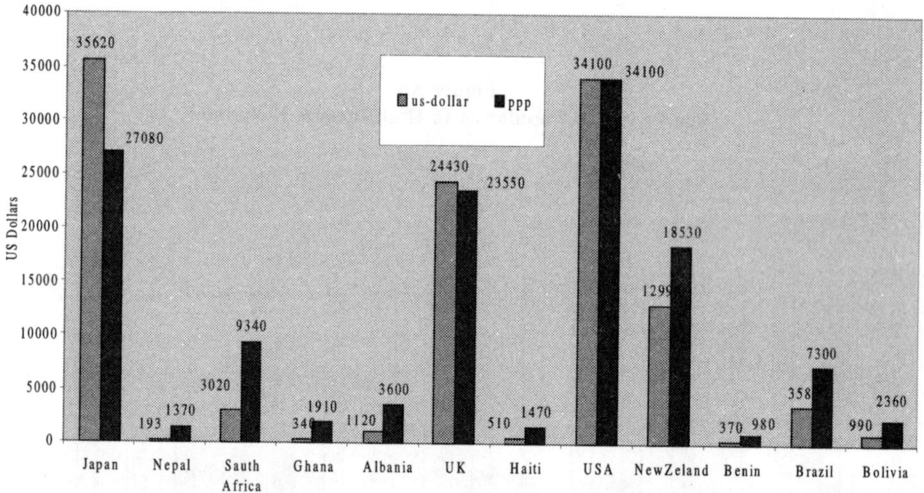

input by distorting their relative prices. Solow's model assumes a smooth and continuous and twice differential production function. Productivity of capital is high with a low level of capital stock and productivity of labour is higher with lower level of labour inputs (Inada conditions). Productivity of capital is higher in labour abundant developing economies than in capital abundant developed economies. Public policy that increases the rate of saving can only influence the level of output but not the rate of growth of output, which can increase only from the exogenous rate of technological progress.

A simple version of the Solow model is often illustrated by using a Cobb-Douglas production function, $Y = AK^{\alpha} L^{\beta}$, where Y is the level of output A the

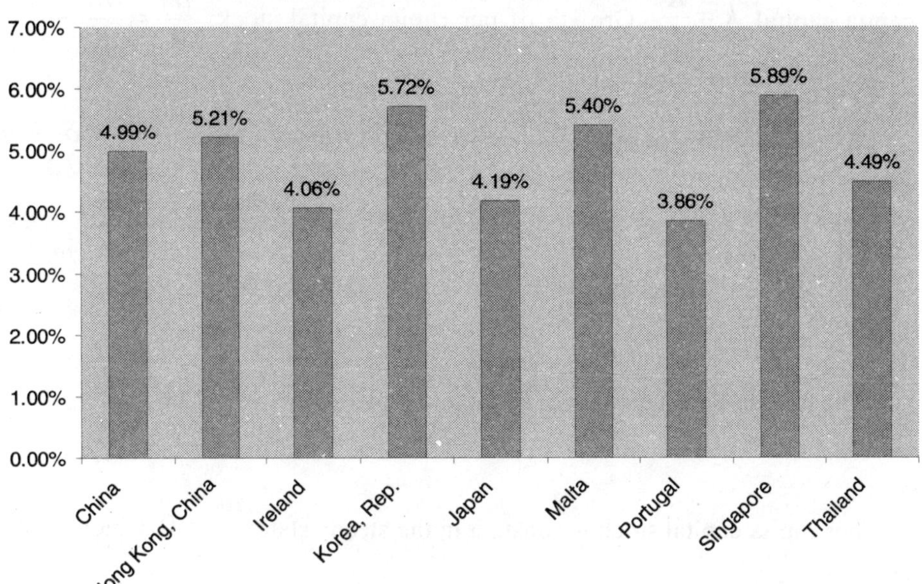

level of technology, L the amount of labour input, K the stock of capital, a the share of capital in output and b the share of labour in output. Shares a and b are positive, below 1; *i.e.* $0 < a < 1$, $0 < b < 1$ and sum to 1, $a < b = 1$ (constant return to scale). By the Euler exhaustion theorem the payment to labour and capital based on their marginal productivity equals the output; $\frac{rK}{Y} + \frac{wL}{Y} = 1$;

$$\alpha = \frac{rK}{Y} = \frac{\alpha AK^{\alpha-1}L^{\beta}.K}{Y} \text{ or } \beta = \frac{wL}{Y} = \frac{\beta AK^{\alpha}L^{\beta-1}L}{Y}.$$

Savings is a fixed fraction of income $S = sY = sAK^{\alpha}L^{\beta}$ and equals gross investment in the steady state, $S = I = (\delta + n + a)K$ in the steady state, where δ is the rate of depreciation, n is the growth rate of population, and a is the rate of technical progress. The change in the capital stock equals the net investment, $dK = I = sY - \delta K = sAK^{\alpha}L^{\beta} - \delta K$. Such net investment causes an accumulation of capital, $K_t = K_{t-1}(1-\delta) + I_t$. The output per effective worker is derived given this capital stock and labour input,

$$y = \frac{Y}{AL} = \frac{AK^{\alpha}L^{\beta}}{AL} = \left(\frac{K}{L}\right)^{\alpha}$$ or simply as $y = k^{\alpha}$ where $y = \frac{Y}{AL}$ and per

capita capital $k=\frac{K}{L}$. Growth of per capita capital stock: $\frac{dk}{k}=\frac{dK}{K}-\frac{dL}{L}=$

$\frac{1}{K}\left[sY-\delta K\right]-n$ and $\frac{dk}{k}=\left[s\frac{Y}{K}-\delta\right]-n$; $\frac{dk}{k}=\left[s\frac{Ay}{k}-\delta\right]-n$;

$\frac{dk}{k}=\left[sAk^{\alpha-1}-\delta\right]-n$.

The fundamental equation of economic growth is: $\frac{dk}{k}=\left[sAk^{\alpha-1}-\delta\right]-n$.

The per capita capital stock is constant in the steady state $\frac{dk}{k}=0$ which implies

$sAk^{\alpha-1}=\delta+n$ and $k^{ss}=\left(\frac{sA}{\delta+n}\right)^{\frac{1}{1-\alpha}}$ Similarly output in the steady state

is $y^{ss}=\left(k^{ss}\right)^{\alpha}=\left(\frac{sA}{\delta+n}\right)^{\frac{\alpha}{1-\alpha}}$ or $y_t=A_t\left(k^{ss}\right)^{\alpha}=A_t\left(\frac{sA}{\delta+n}\right)^{\frac{\alpha}{1-\alpha}}$.

These steady state results imply that countries with higher rate of saving and higher level of technical progress have a higher steady state level of output per capita than countries with lower saving rates and lower level of technical progress. In contrast countries with higher rate of population growth and higher rate of depreciation of capital stock have lower level of per capita output in the steady state. Countries with higher capital share α have higher output in the steady state but countries which differ in the initial capital stock eventually reach the same output level in the steady state. The above results also imply that the growth of per capita income is zero in the steady state unless it is driven by the technical progress.

Thus different economies may have different steady states and may take a long or a short time to reach the steady state depending upon behavioural and technical parameters in the model. In an intensive production $y=k^{\beta}$ with a depreciation rate of 3 percent, saving rates of 20 percent, initial capital stock of 1, zero rate of population growth, and β of 0.75, it takes about 2000 periods for per capital output (y) and per capita capital stock (k) to reach the steady state. Many of the above factors that influence a steady state also may change over time modifying the steady state itself.

Even this simple growth model needs information on the values of parameters such as δ , n , a and s that define the steady state and derive the growth path of the economy. The saving rate is taken as a policy variable that can be influenced by economic policy and recommends a rate of saving that maximises consumption. This is obtained at a point where the marginal product of capital (or slope of the production function) equals the slope of the required investment line. In a golden rule the rate of saving must equal the productivity of capital, $s = \alpha$. More formally this problem is stated as Max $c = y - i$ subject to $i = (\delta + n)k$ or simply maximising $c = y - (\delta + n)k$ with respect to the per capita capital. For a production function $y = k^{\alpha}$, using the first order condition for maximisation $\frac{\partial c}{dk} = \alpha k^{\alpha-1} - (\delta + n) = 0$, the per capita capital stock that maximises per capita consumption $MPK = (\delta + n)$ implies $k = \left(\frac{\alpha}{\delta + n}\right)^{\frac{1}{\alpha-1}}$ ($k = \left(\frac{\alpha}{\delta + n + a}\right)^{\frac{1}{\alpha-1}}$ with the technical progress). If $\alpha = 0.5$ and the level of technology *A*=0.5 and output is given by $Y = 0.5\sqrt{K}\sqrt{L}$ assuming no growth in the labour input, *n* = *0*; a depreciation rate (δ) of 5% then the golden rule rate of saving that maximises consumption is 50 percent.

Technology is the driving force of the growth process in the Solow model in the steady state. Countries with higher rates of saving have higher levels of income in the steady state but a higher growth rate is only possible via a higher rate of technical progress. In a balanced steady state growth path, output per capita and capital per capita grow at a constant rate of population growth rate $y = \frac{Y}{L}$; $\frac{dy}{y} = \frac{dY}{Y} - \frac{dL}{L} = 0 \; g_k - n = 0 \quad g_k = n$; or $k = \frac{K}{L} \quad \frac{dk}{k} = \frac{dK}{K} - \frac{dL}{L} = 0$, $g_k - n = 0$, so $g_k = n$ and $g_y = g_k = n$. Substituting these factors in growth accounting equation

$$\frac{\Delta y}{y} = g_y = a + \alpha g_k + (1-\alpha)n \Rightarrow g - n = \frac{a}{(1-\alpha)}.$$

If the per capita output and the per capita capital stock only grow at the rate of population growth rate then the higher saving rate does not affect the growth rate. Countries with higher rates of saving are able to achieve higher levels of output in the steady state but they cannot have a higher rate of economic growth unless they have a higher rate of technical progress. At the balanced growth path the output grows at the rate of growth of population and there is no increase in the per capita income. Thus only the rate of technological advancement can explain variation in the growth rate of capita output across countries. Technology is exogenous and determined outside the model. For instance if α = 0.3 and g_k = 3% n=1% and g_y=2%, then the technology will progress at the rate of 0.4 percent; $a = g_y - \alpha g_k - (1-\alpha)n$ = 2% -0.3 (3%) - 0.7(1%) = 0.4%.

When there is no technological advancement, growth rate of per capita output $\left(\frac{Y}{L}\right)$ and the per capita capital stock $\left(\frac{K}{L}\right)$ equals growth rate of the labour force (population) then $g_y = g_k = n$. If there is a labour augmenting technology $Y = K^{\alpha}\left(AL\right)^{1-\alpha}$ then a standard way is to analyse per capita output per effective worker $\left(\frac{Y}{AL}\right)$ per capita capital stock per effective worker $\left(\frac{K}{AL}\right)$. Now the growth rate of output and capital stock equals growth rate of technology plus the growth rate of the labour force $g_y = g_k = a + n$. $\frac{Y}{AL} = \left(\frac{K}{AL}\right)^{\alpha}$ or in terms of per effective workers $y = (k)^{\alpha}$

$$\dot{k} = s\left(\frac{Y}{AL}\right) - (\delta + a + n)\frac{K}{AL} = 0 \ ; \ \dot{k} = s(y) - (\delta + a + n)k = 0 .$$

Then the steady state investment requirement per worker is $I = (\delta + a + n)k$. Market clearing implies equality between saving and investment $s(y) = (\delta + a + n)k$ or $sk^{\alpha} = (\delta + a + n)k$. The capital stock per effective worker in the steady state $k_{ss} = \left[\frac{s}{(\delta + a + n)}\right]^{\frac{1}{1-\alpha}}$ and output per effective worker in the steady state is $y_{ss} = \left[\frac{s}{\left(\delta + a + g_L\right)}\right]^{\frac{\alpha}{1-\alpha}}$. Given a constant saving ratio the consumption per effective worker in the steady state is:

$$c_{ss} = (1-s)\left[\frac{s}{(\delta + a + n)}\right]^{\frac{\alpha}{1-\alpha}}.$$

We need to multiply by the index of technology A_t to get the actual per head figures for capital stock, output and consumption, such as

$y_{ss} = A\left[\frac{s}{(\delta + a + n)}\right]^{\frac{\alpha}{1-\alpha}}$. Thus besides differences in s, δ, a and the difference in steady state output also causes a variation in the per capita output in the steady state. Such index of technological growth $A_t = A_0 e^{at}$, can explain divergence in growth rates across various countries based on the difference in A_t.

Role of Human Capital

Human capital (*H*) refers to the average level of skills of individual workers who use physical capital such as buildings, machines and computers to produce goods and services. More skilled workers, who generally have more years of schooling and on the job experience (learning by doing), are more productive. Human capital combined with physical capital may generate a constant marginal product of physical capital as physical and human capital become complementary to each other. When the marginal product of capital is constant and not subject to the law of diminishing returns (as in the neoclassical Solow model), then each marginal unit of capital adds more to the output. Economies with a larger stock of human and physical capital can grow faster than economies with smaller stocks of both of these capitals (for instance average rate of economic growth in the UK and the US economy during 1990 remained impressively between 3% and 4%). Such a complementarity between physical and human capital is illustrated in the literature by assuming that human capital is proportional to the physical capital or $H = \psi K$ together with a restriction of $\gamma + \alpha = 1$. The Solow growth model extended with human capital (*H*) $Y = AK^{\alpha} L^{\beta} H^{\gamma} = A(\psi)^{\gamma} K^{\alpha+\gamma} L^{\beta}$ then implies $Y = A(\psi)^{\gamma} KL^{\beta}$. Now the marginal product of capital is $MPK = \frac{\partial Y}{\partial K} = A(\psi)^{\gamma} L^{\beta}$. If one follows this setup, human and physical capital become complementary to each other. The marginal product of human capital is $MPH = \gamma AK^{\alpha} L^{\beta} H^{\gamma-1} = \gamma Y / H$ and the marginal product of physical capital is $MPK = \alpha AK^{\alpha-1} L^{\beta} H^{\gamma} = \alpha Y / K$. More input of human capital and labour input prevent the marginal product of the physical capital from diminishing. A higher saving rate generates higher capital stock, which is associated with a higher level of technology and workforce and a higher rate of economic growth. This is just like an AK production technology where growth is limitless and output is unbounded. In that case even a small difference in the rate of saving makes a huge difference in level of income over a relatively short period. The importance of human capital in economic growth is obvious from analysis of growth process in more advanced and newly emerging economies. This can be proved by taking a production function that includes human capital $Y = AK^{\alpha} L^{\beta} H^{\gamma}$ with the constant return to scale assumptions, $\alpha + \beta + \gamma = 1$. The sources of growth now also includes rate of growth of skills and expertise of workers $\frac{\Delta y}{y} = g_y = g_a + \alpha g_k + \beta n + \gamma g_h$. Consider the fact that per capita output and capital stock remains constant in the steady state. With this growth accounting equation and set of parameters it can be proved that the higher rate of saving not only influences the level of per capital income but also its rate of growth rate as following:

$$g_y = a + \alpha g_k + \left(1 - \alpha - \gamma\right) n + \gamma g_h$$

$$g_y - n = a + \alpha\left(g_k - n\right) + \gamma\left(g_h - n\right)$$

$$\left(g_y - n\right) - \gamma\left(g_h - n\right) = a + \alpha\left(g_k - n\right)$$

Here the left hand term $\left(g_y - n\right) - \gamma\left(g_h - n\right)$ is the rate of growth of per capita income adjusted for growth in per capita human capital. It equals the growth rate of technology a plus the growth rate of capital stock per person $\alpha\left(g_k - n\right)$ weighted by the share of capital in output. This is higher when the rate of saving is higher and brings a higher rate of economic growth.

Many economists are not happy with the exogenous nature of technological advancement in the Solow model which is the major source of growth in the steady state. Taking on the learning by doing literature (Schultz (1961), Arrrow (1962) and Becker (1964)), Lucas (1988) and Romer (1989), have made technology endogenous by introducing knowledge or human capital in the production function along with the physical capital. Lucas models human capital accumulation to be a direct outcome of time spent on studying and learning rather than at work. If people spend more time in studying, they learn more and become more skilled. This raises per capita human capital available in the economy, which complements with physical capital and raises the skill and the productivity of workers at work. Such a rise in productivity is the major source of economic growth. For instance, a very simple form of Lucas (1988) production function may be written as $Y = K^{\alpha}\left(\theta hL\right)^{1-\alpha}$ where h is human capital per worker; q is the fraction of time spent on working, L the labour supply –(assume this as given). To take a simple illustration if K=100, L=100 h=3 q=0.8, α =0.3; $Y = 100^{0.3}\left(0.8*3*100\right)^{0.7}$ = 185 but without human capital $Y = K^{\alpha}L^{1-\alpha}$ = 100.

Romer (1989) introduces a role for accumulated knowledge in the production process which results from work of researchers in universities or research laboratories. The stock of knowledge that exists in the form of designs, formulas or models is a non-rival good with positive externality as it can be borrowed from the library. He assumes separate production functions for research, intermediate and the final goods sector while illustrating the endogenous process of technical progress and its impact in economic growth. Workers in the research sector produce new ideas that they sell to an intermediate sector, which apply them in production of final goods. Productivity of workers in the final goods sectors rises when they get better tools to work with. Economic growth is ultimately the result of human resources employed in the research sector such as universities and research laboratories. The production function is similar to the labour augmenting technology in the Solow model, $Y = K^{\alpha}\left(AL_Y\right)^{\beta}$. Now technology A is the result of efforts of researchers working in the knowledge sector. Total labour resource (L) can either be used in the knowledge sector L_A or in the production of final goods sector $L_y : L = L_y + L_A$. As presented in Jones (1995) a change in the stock of knowledge depends upon the number of people employed in the knowledge sector L_A, average productivity in the research sector $\bar{\delta}$ and the stock of existing knowledge A as $\bar{\delta} = \delta A^{\phi} L_A^{\lambda}$ and $a = \frac{dA}{A} = \frac{\delta L_A^{\lambda}}{A^{1-\phi}}$. By log differentiating this equation one finds that the growth rate of technology is determined by the rate of population growth in the steady state, $a = \frac{\delta n}{1-\phi}$. Higher rate of growth of population is beneficial rather than harmful for economic growth because the economy can afford to put more people in research. This type of endogenous growth model shows increasing return to scale relative to all inputs used in production. Since there is imperfect competition in the intermediate goods sector it is possible that inventors can extract profits by selling patent rights to producers of intermediate goods. Protecting research in terms of patent rights or subsidies to researchers becomes optimal as research drives up productivity by increasing the stock of knowledge in the whole economy.

Many growth models, as taught in the graduate schools, use dynamic optimisation tool to analyse the capital accumulation process and to identify a set of parameters that are critical to the balanced growth path (Ramsay (1928), Cass (1965), Koopman (1965), Dorfman (1969), Lucas (1988), Romer (1989), (Parente (1994), Perroni (1995)). Such model involves maximising the utility of the infinitely lived household $\int_0^\infty e^{-\rho t}\frac{C_t^{1-\sigma}}{1-\sigma}dt$ subject to the technology constraint $Y_t = A_t K_t^\alpha N_t^{1-\alpha}$ and capital accumulation process $\dot{K}_t = Y_t - N_t C_t - \delta K_t$. When simplified, assuming $A_t = 1$, $N_t = 1$, the optimisation problem is often formulated in the form of a current value Hamiltonian as

$$H(c, K, \theta) = \frac{C_t^{1-\sigma}}{1-\sigma} + \theta\left[K_t^\alpha - C_t - \delta K_{t-1}\right]$$

where C is consumption, a control variable; K is the capital stock, a state variable, θ is the shadow price of the capital stock in terms of the utility, a co-state variable. Market clearing, implicit in the budget constraint, implies that output is either consumed or invested. The optimal path of capital accumulation is found using four first order conditions:

$$\frac{\partial H}{\partial C_t} = 0 \rightarrow C_t^{-\sigma} = \theta_t \tag{1}$$

$$\dot{\theta}_t = \rho\theta_t - \frac{\partial H_t}{\partial K_t} \rightarrow \dot{\theta}_t = \rho\theta_t - \theta_t\left[\alpha K_t^{\alpha-1} - \delta\right] \tag{2}$$

$$\dot{K}_t = K_t^\alpha - C_t - \delta K_t \tag{3}$$

and the transversality condition $\lim_{t\rightarrow\infty} e^{-\rho t}\theta_t K_t = 0$ (4)

The first equation denotes the shadow price of capital in terms of the marginal utility of consumption. The second shows how the shadow price is sensitive to subjective discount factor and accumulation constraint. The final terminal condition implies no need for capital accumulation at the end of the planning horizon. Capital stock, consumption and the shadow price of capital remain constant in the balanced growth path; $\frac{\dot{C}}{C} = g_c$; $\frac{\dot{K}}{K} = g_K$ and $\frac{\dot{\theta}_t}{\theta_t} = g_\theta$. Proof of this follows from (2)

$$\frac{\dot{\theta}_t}{\theta_t} = \rho - \left[\alpha K^{\alpha-1} - \delta\right] \rightarrow \alpha K^{\alpha-1} = \rho - \frac{\dot{\theta}_t}{\theta_t} + \delta \quad (5)$$

This is the most important equation for deriving the equilibrium in this model. It simply states that the marginal productivity of capital should equal the cost of capital, where the shadow price measures the opportunity cost of capital. By assumption the RHS in (5) is constant. This implies that the LHS also should be a constant, therefore, $\frac{\dot{K}}{K} = 0$. Then from the production function, if the capital stock is not growing then the output is also not growing; and so $\frac{\dot{Y}}{Y} = 0$. From the budget constraint when output and capital stocks are not growing the consumption is also not growing; thus $\frac{\dot{C}}{C} = 0$. The shadow price also is not changing in the steady state as is obvious by the log differentiation of (1) $\frac{\dot{\theta}_t}{\theta_t} = -\sigma\frac{\dot{C}_t}{C_t} \rightarrow \frac{\dot{\theta}_t}{\theta_t} = 0$.

The values of capital stock and output in the steady state can be solved from (5): $K_t^{\alpha-1} = \frac{\rho+\delta}{\alpha} \rightarrow K^* = \left(\frac{\rho+\delta}{\alpha}\right)^{\frac{1}{\alpha-1}}$ and $Y^* = \left(\frac{\alpha}{\rho+\delta}\right)^{\frac{\alpha}{1-\alpha}}$.

Though the capital stock does not grow the economy needs positive saving to maintain the capital stock intact: $C^* = K^{*\alpha} - \delta K^*$

$$\text{The saving rate } \frac{\delta\ K^*}{Y^*} = \delta\left(K^*\right)^{1-\alpha} = \delta\left[\left(\frac{\alpha}{\rho+\delta}\right)^{\frac{1}{1-\alpha}}\right]^{1-\alpha} = \delta\left[\left(\frac{\alpha}{\rho+\delta}\right)\right] \quad (6)$$

Thus the saving rate is determined in terms of parameters of preferences and technology rather than being assumed as in the Solow model. The higher discount rate for future consumption implies lower saving rate and more productive capital implies higher saving rate. Higher discount rate of capital reduces the steady state capital but raises the level of saving in the steady state.

The transitional dynamics show a process where by the economy converges towards the steady state once it is disturbed from that path. From the second first order condition derived above, $\dot{\theta}_t = \theta_t\left(\rho - \alpha K_t^{\alpha-1} + \delta\right) \rightarrow$ for $\dot{\theta}_t = 0$, since

$\theta_t > 0$ $K^* = \left(\dfrac{\alpha}{\rho+\delta}\right)^{\frac{1}{1-\alpha}}$ can be used in the (θ_t, K_t)space for the transition dynamics of the shadow price θ_t relative to the steady state capital stock as shown in Figure 1.

Figure 1
Transition dynamics for shadow price of capital stock

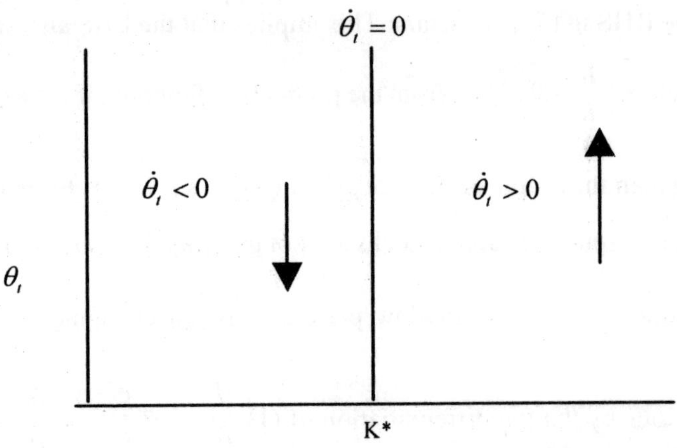

Capital stock can be increased above the steady state only by raising the shadow price of capital above its steady state value or if the shadow price is lowered it will reduce the capital stock. Similarly the transition dynamics of the K_t in the (θ_t, K_t) space relative to the steady state of the shadow price θ_t can be found using FOC (1);

$$C_t^{-\sigma} = \theta_t \rightarrow C_t = \theta_t^{-\frac{1}{\sigma}};\ \dot{K}_t = K_t^{\alpha} - N_t C_t - \delta K_t$$

$$\rightarrow \dot{K}_t = K_t^{\alpha} - \delta K_t - \theta_t^{-\frac{1}{\sigma}} \rightarrow K_t^{\alpha} - \delta K_t = \theta_t^{-\frac{1}{\sigma}} \tag{7}$$

For sufficiently large value of K there is no θ for which (7) will be satisfied. The largest such value of K can be found by setting the right hand side of (7) to zero.

$$K_t^{\alpha} = \delta K_t \rightarrow \bar{K} = \delta^{\frac{1}{\alpha-1}} = \left(\frac{1}{\delta}\right)^{\frac{1}{1-\alpha}} \tag{8}$$

$\bar{K} > K^*$ since $\alpha < 1$ and the $\rho > 1$.

Figure 2
Transition dynamics for capital stock

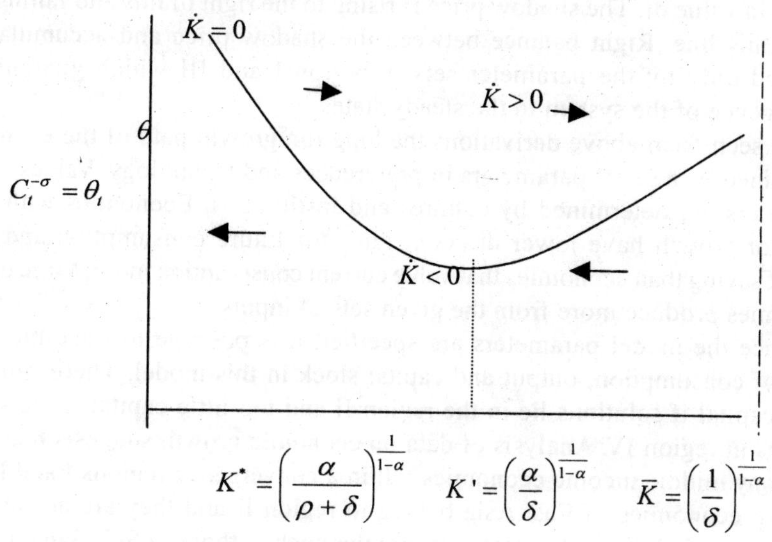

Figure 3
Saddle path for Steady State Solutions

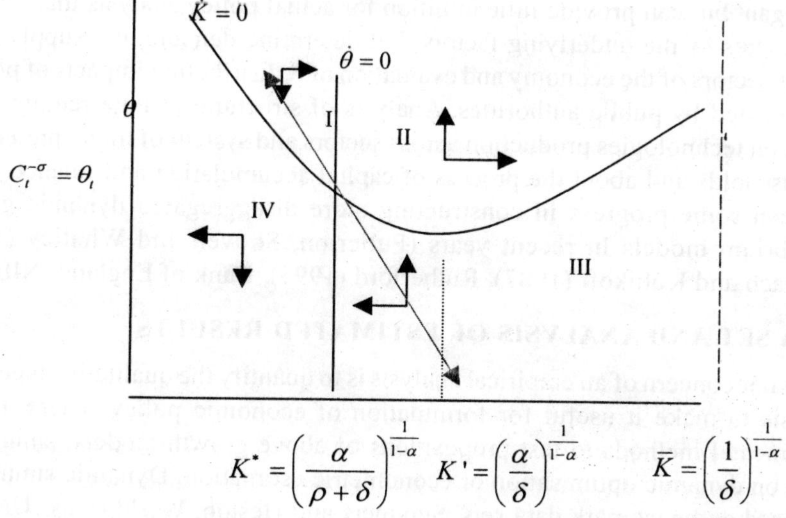

The saddle points for this model consists of points in (θ_t, K_t) space where the economy will converge to its steady state as shown by lines with arrows in region I and II in Figure 3. The $\dot{K}=0$ path shows set of values of θ, for which there will be no change in the stock of capital. Capital stock is rising above this line and falling below this line. Similarly shows capital stock where there is no change in value of. The shadow price is rising to the right of this and falling to the left of this line. Right balance between the shadow price and accumulation is obtained only by the parameter sets in region I and III which guarantee the convergence of the system to the steady state.

As seen from above derivations the long run growth path of the economy is determined by a set of parameters in preferences and technology. Values of these parameters are determined by cultures and institutions. Economies with a hard drive for growth have lower discount rates for future consumption and higher rates of saving than economies that value current consumption more. More efficient economies produce more from the given sets of inputs.

Once the model parameters are specified it is possible to trace the growth paths of consumption, output and capital stock in this model. There can be too much capital if solutions lie in the region II and too little capital if the solution remains in region IV. Analysis of data on economic growth suggests that OECD and many middle income economies fall in a convergence regions I and III. Fast growing economies of East Asia belong to region II and they are accumulating too much capital. Growth disaster economies such as those of Sub-Saharan Africa have not saved enough and caught in poverty trap in region IV of the above figure.

The real economic growth process is much more complicated than explained by the above models. Growth involves structural transformation in production, trade and consumption. Conclusions received from simple single sector models are elegant but can provide little intuition for actual policy analysis that involves assessments of the underlying factors that determine demand and supply in the various sectors of the economy and evaluation of redistribution impacts of policies implemented by public authorities. Analysis of structural change requires more details on technologies production across sectors and system of trade, preferences of households and about the process of capital accumulation and finance. There has been some progress in constructing more disaggregated dynamic general equilibrium models in recent years (Fullerton, Shoven and Whalley (1983), Auerbach and Kotlikoff (1987), Rutherford (1995), Bank of England, NIESR).

DATA SET AND ANALYSIS OF ESTIMATED RESULTS

The major concern of an empirical analysis is to quantify the qualitative theoretical analysis to make it useful for formulation of economic policy. There are two fundamental methods to test propositions of above growth models; simulations based on dynamic optimisation or econometric estimation. Dynamic simulations are based on benchmark data sets. Summers and Heston, World Bank, UNDP or OECD or various national or international surveys provide information for growing number of empirical studies of economic growth. Madison (1991) Mankiw, Romer and Weale (1992), Barrow and Sala-i-Martin (1995), Temple (1999), McMohan and Squire (2003) provide empirical evidence on factors influencing the rates of economic growth across countries. Despite this there is no consensus about the factors affecting the economic growth and very little is known about the causes of economic growth across nations (Temple (1999)). Many issues such as the measurement of variables, specification of functional forms, methods of analysis and approaches for their implementation at the practical level are far from settled making how much the analysis of economic growth assists in bringing better policies still a questionable matter of great theoretical and empirical interest.

We use the World Bank database on macroeconomic variables for 208 countries for a period of 40 years from 1960 to 2000 for empirical investigation of the various propositions illustrated earlier. It is instructive to assess the factors that promote or cause a growth miracle and to contrast them with factors that cause growth disasters. What sorts of economic policies have been used for a ten fold increase in per capita income in Singapore and Korea during that period? Why have the economies of South Asia, Middle East and Latin and Central America not been able to replicate the growth experience of those newly industrialised economies (NIEs)? What sort of policies might have been responsible for reduction in per capita income in Niger, Zambia and Chad and many other developing economies? Why the average growth rates in all G7 countries which were very respectable till 1970, have slowed down after that? How have the economies of the Great Britain and the US been able to sustain a respectable rate of growth in recent years? Why were there set backs in the growth rates in Japan, Germany and France in the 1990s? Why are significant variations seen in growth rates across these countries? Are saving rates, population growth rates, investment rates and trade ratios significant factors in explaining these variations as claimed by the growth models studied earlier? We would like to test these propositions using empirical estimates based on the evidence contained in the above panel data set.

Both theoretical and empirical studies of economic growth have been benefited greatly from the development in computation technology in recent years. The dynamic general equilibrium models use optimising and market clearing conditions to study price based allocations of resources while deriving simulated growth paths of an economy. Econometric models are often used to ascertain the values of important behavioural parameters based on cross section surveys or time series or panel information.

A static panel data growth model relates growth rates, $y_{i,t}$ to K-dimensional vectors of explanatory variables $x_{i,t}$ as in the following equation.

$$y_{i,t} = \alpha_i + x_{i,t}\beta_{i,t} + \lambda_t + e_{i,t}$$

where observations are indexed for $i = 1, \ldots\ldots, N$ countries and for $t = 1, \ldots\ldots, T$ years. Here $x_{i,t}$ includes explanatory variables such as saving, investment, tax, trade ratios or the population growth rate, $\beta_{i,t}$ is the set of unknown parameters, α_i

represent individual specific factors affecting the growth rate, and λ_t denote the time specific effects that influence growth rates.

Doornik and Hendry (2001, chap. 7-10) provide more details on how to estimate coefficients $\beta_{i,t}$ using fixed effect, random effect and the GMM methods referring to models developed by Baltagi (1995) and Arellano and Bond (1991). First it is helpful to stack all observations on growth and explanatory variables with individual and time specific effects as:

$$\begin{bmatrix} y_{i,1} \\ y_{i,2} \\ \cdot \\ \cdot \\ y_{i,T} \end{bmatrix} = \begin{bmatrix} x_{i,1}\beta \\ x_{i,2}\beta \\ \cdot \\ \cdot \\ x_{i,T}\beta \end{bmatrix} + \begin{bmatrix} \alpha_i \\ \alpha_i \\ \cdot \\ \cdot \\ \alpha_i \end{bmatrix} + \begin{bmatrix} \lambda_1 \\ \lambda_2 \\ \cdot \\ \cdot \\ \lambda_T \end{bmatrix} + \begin{bmatrix} e_{1i} \\ e_{2i} \\ \cdot \\ \cdot \\ e_{mi} \end{bmatrix}.$$

One part of the panel data model involves estimating determinant of growth for each country with assessment of time specific effect.

$$y_i = x_i\beta + \lambda_t + \iota_i\alpha_i + e_i$$

Simplifying using a dummy variable D_i to capture country specific and time specific factors that influence economic growth, this model becomes $y_i = x_i\beta + D_i\delta + e_i$ for $i = 1, ..., N$.

$$y = W\beta + e \text{ where } W = [X, D]$$

The coefficient β can be estimated using the Ordinary Least Square (OLS), Least Square Dummy Variable (LSDV), with within estimation method using deviations of variables using time mean, between estimation using means of each individual, or by feasible GLS estimation or using the maximum likelihood estimation method. The general form taken by the estimator of β is $\hat{\beta} = (W'W)^{-1} W'y$.

A dynamic panel data model includes the lagged terms of individual and explanatory variables.

$$y_{i,t} = \sum_{s=1}^{p} a_k y_{i,t-s} + \beta'(L)x_{i,t} + \lambda_t + \alpha_i + e_{i,t}$$

or in short

$$y_i = W_i\delta + \iota_i a_i + e_i$$

The GMM estimator with instrument Z_i (levels, first differences, orthogonal deviations, deviations from individual means, combination of first differences and levels) as given in the PcGive manual by Doornik and Hendry (2001)) is

$$\hat{\delta} = \left[\left(\sum_i W_i^{*} Z_i\right) A_N \left(\sum_i Z_i' W_i\right)\right]^{-1} \left(\sum_i W_i^{*} Z_i\right) A_N \left(\sum_i Z_i' y_i^{*}\right), \text{ with}$$

$$A_N = \left(\frac{1}{N}\sum_i Z_i' H_i Z_i\right)^{-1}$$, where H_i is the individual specific weighting matrix.

The per capita income of various countries are regressed on income in 1960, investment and saving ratios, real interest rate, price index and share of government spending to total GDP to determine the rate of economic growth among three groups of countries. First set of countries had higher rate of economic growth from 1960s onwards. They comprise of China, Hong Kong, Ireland, Korea, Japan, Malta, Portugal, Singapore and Thailand where the governments and markets have worked together to generate growth miracles. The second set includes OECD countries which had steady rate of growth till 1970s but experienced slow-down since then despite having good models to guide economic policies. Then we compare those cases with low income countries, economies of South Asia and Africa and Latina and Central America where growth rates remained lower or even negative.

Table 1

Determinants of Economic Growth in Newly Emerging Growth Miracle Economies

2-step estimation using dynamic panel data model

	Coefficient	*Std.Error*	*t-value*	*t-prob*
Gdpprcap(-1)	0.12036	0.01812	6.64000	0.00000
GDP60	-0.00159	0.00043	-3.73000	0.00000
China	0.00288	0.00137	2.11000	0.03700
Hkong	-0.00171	0.00077	-2.21000	0.02800
Ireland	0.00110	0.00128	0.86300	0.38900
Korea	0.00335	0.00074	4.53000	0.00000
Malta	-0.00197	0.00068	-2.90000	0.00400
Portugal	-0.00061	0.00096	-0.63700	0.52500
Singapore	0.00113	0.00027	4.21000	0.00000
Sy	0.15583	0.04257	3.66000	0.00000
Iy	0.18329	0.02995	6.12000	0.00000
Infl	-0.00510	0.00487	-1.05000	0.29700
Rint	-0.02795	0.06357	-0.44000	0.66100
Xmy	-0.00461	0.00097	-4.74000	0.00000
Japan	-0.00056	0.00086	-0.65300	0.51500
sigma 4.914753	sigma^2 24.1548			
RSS 3526.6004	TSS 2240.0576			
No. of observations 161	No. of parameters 15			

Definition of Variables:

Gdpprcap(-1) : per capita GDP in the previous period

Sy: ratio of saving to GD

GDP60 : per capita GDP in 1960
Iy: ratio of investment to GDP
GDP
Infl: rate of inflation
Govy: ratio of government expenditure of GDP

Rint: real interest rate
Xmy: ratio of trade to
Popg: growth rate of population
Txy: ratio of tax revenue to GDP

Table 2
Determinants of Growth across OECD Countries

	Coefficient	*Std.Error*	*t-value*	*t-prob*
Grpercap(-1)	0.180988	0.05395	3.35	0.00
Sy	0.216942	0.03	7.23	0.00
Iy	-0.00045	0.05464	-0.00824	0.99
Xmy	0.0648251	0.01251	5.18	0.00
Popg	-1.88968	0.4329	-4.37	0.00
Govy	-0.203699	0.0558	-3.65	0.00
Txy	-0.132421	0.0445	-2.98	0.00
Australia	0.972477	0.4075	2.39	0.02
Austria	-1.6312	0.3127	-5.22	0.00
Belgium	-1.8475	0.3254	-5.68	0.00
Canada	-0.463298	0.1385	-3.34	0.00
Denmark	-0.170403	0.04258	-4	0.00
Finland	-0.209737	0.05947	-3.53	0.00
France	0.077469	0.07293	1.06	0.29
Germany	-0.362554	0.04693	-7.73	0.00
Greece	-0.585984	0.06581	-8.9	0.00
Iceland	-0.207666	0.05016	-4.14	0.00
Ireland	-0.411256	0.0768	-5.35	0.00
Italy	-0.0800266	0.0598	-1.34	0.18
Japan	-0.398036	0.06241	-6.38	0.00
Luxembourg	-0.718133	0.1419	-5.06	0.00
Netherlands	-0.221358	0.04843	-4.57	0.00
New Zealand	-0.127106	0.04085	-3.11	0.00
Norway	-0.153097	0.03551	-4.31	0.00
Portugal	-0.216048	0.04225	-5.11	0.00
Spain	-0.114415	0.0264	-4.33	0.00
Switzerland	-0.330109	0.04088	-8.07	0.00
United Kingdom	-0.0111015	0.01851	-0.6	0.55
Constant	6.88023	0.9513	7.23	0.00

Sigma 1.645049; sigma^2 2.71; R^2 = 0.453642; N =390; K 29
Wald (joint): Chi^2(28) = 580.8 [0.000] **
Wald (dummy): Chi^2(1) = 52.31 [0.000] **
AR(1) test: N(0,1) = 3.091 [0.002] **
AR(2) test: N(0,1) = -0.1074 [0.915]

Estimated coefficients, presented in Tables 1 to 7, show that both country specific as well as economic policy variables are important determinants of economic growth. Since 1980 China has experienced the fastest rate of economic growth compared to base country, Thailand. Therefore country specific dummies show lower rates of economic growth in other countries than in China. Income in 1960 is often used to measure the convergence process among these economies. There is a tendency for convergence as higher the level of income in 1960 lower is the rate of economic growth. This result is as expected from the literature. Government spending provides for basic economic infrastructure and it contributes positively towards economic growth. Real interest reflects the cost of capital. Higher real interest is deterrent for economic growth. Higher investment ratio seems to translate to the higher rate of economic growth in these economies. Population growth rate that includes human capital seems important in some countries but not in others.

Table 3
Determinants of Economic Growth in Low Income Countries

	Coefficient	*Std.Error*	*t-value*	*t-prob*
Grpercap(-1)	0.0951008	0.09615	0.989	0.323
Sy	0.073885	0.04722	1.56	0.118
Iy	0.247226	0.1031	2.4	0.017
Xmy	-0.0658137	0.03476	-1.89	0.059
Popg	1.17661	0.4705	2.5	0.013
Infl	-0.00073277	0.0004421	-1.66	0.098
Angola	-2.76705	1.236	-2.24	0.026
Bangladesh	1.6875	0.4195	4.02	0
Benin	0.561721	0.2161	2.6	0.01
Bhutan	0.227747	0.2286	0.996	0.32
Burkina Faso	0.415442	0.1467	2.83	0.005
Burundi	0.15287	0.1287	1.19	0.235
Cameroon	-0.0834596	0.03813	-2.19	0.029
C.African Rep	0.0984396	0.0802	1.23	0.22
Chad	0.406156	0.09907	4.1	0
Comoros	0.0188527	0.09626	0.196	0.845
Congo DmRep.	-0.183401	0.09519	-1.93	0.054
Congo, Rep.	-0.27655	0.11	-2.52	0.012
Cote d'Ivoire	-0.121986	0.05249	-2.32	0.02
Gambia, The	-0.0232108	0.112	-0.207	0.836
Georgia	-0.278447	0.1277	-2.18	0.03
Ghana	0.0900762	0.02431	3.7	0
Guinea-Bissau	0.0738056	0.04113	1.79	0.073
Haiti	0.00512102	0.04598	0.111	0.911
India	0.166295	0.05587	2.98	0.003
Indonesia	0.0842508	0.04013	2.1	0.036
Kenya	0.00188728	0.009427	0.2	0.841
Lesotho	0.138295	0.2026	0.683	0.495
Liberia	-0.182273	0.04636	-3.93	0
Madagascar	0.00146256	0.02168	0.0675	0.946
Malawi	0.051332	0.01687	3.04	0.002
Mali	0.019588	0.02498	0.784	0.433
Mauritania	-0.00072537	0.0426	-0.017	0.986
Moldova	-0.279732	0.05528	-5.06	0
Mongolia	-0.0543321	0.05361	-1.01	0.311
Mozambique	0.101926	0.03887	2.62	0.009
Myanmar	0.0823928	0.03707	2.22	0.027

Contd....

	Coefficient	*Std.Error*	*t-value*	*t-prob*
Nepal	0.0996678	0.01871	5.33	0
Nicaragua	-0.00160759	0.04125	-0.039	0.969
Niger	-0.0176828	0.01763	-1	0.316
Nigeria	-0.0388945	0.01076	-3.62	0
Pakistan	0.0816024	0.01581	5.16	0
Rwanda	0.044232	0.02258	1.96	0.051
Senegal	0.0355324	0.01501	2.37	0.018
Sierra Leone	0.00621669	0.01385	0.449	0.654
Somalia	0.0506883	0.03606	1.41	0.16
Sudan	0.0345439	0.01678	2.06	0.04
Togo	-0.0346172	0.01978	-1.75	0.081
Zambia	-0.024615	0.01354	-1.82	0.07
iy(-1)	-0.152039	0.1063	-1.43	0.153
xmy(-1)	0.0767962	0.0329	2.33	0.02
Constant	-4.08335	2.033	-2.01	0.045
Sigma	5.574104	Sigma^2		31.07063
R^2	0.3144841			
RSS	22339.78428	TSS	3	2588.278128
No. of observations	772	no. of	parameters	53
Wald (joint):	Chi^2(52)	88.72	[0.001] **	
Wald (dummy):	Chi^2(1)	4.034	[0.045] *	
AR(1) test:	N(0,1)	0.7739	[0.439]	
AR(2) test:	N(0,1)	0.3822	[0.702]	

Table 4
Determinants of Growth in South Asia

	Coefficient	*Std.Error*	*t-value*	*t-prob*
Growth(-1)	-0.178123	0.03834	-4.6	5 0.000
Iy	-0.287643	0.1722	-1.6	7 0.100
iy(-1)	0.318337	0.1562	2	4 0.046
Popg	1.89254	0.3437	5.5	1 0.000
popg(-1)	-2.88679	0.4742	-6	9 0.000
xmy(-1)	0.0338384	0.02611	1.3	0 0.200
Rint	0.0435592	0.06249	0.69	7 0.488
Exr	-0.334894	0.2691	-1.2	4 0.218
Exr(-1)	0.345305	0.2863	1.2	1 0.232
Infl(-1)	0.0511216	0.02765	1.8	5 0.069
Govy	-3.86213	7.276	-0.53	1 0.597
Baglad	1.29559	0.8749	1.4	8 0.144
Bhutan	1.23991	0.4283	2.9	0 0.005
India	0.939746	0.3638	2.5	8 0.012
Nepal	0.374721	0.2242	1.6	7 0.100
Constant	3.81139	2.459	1.5	5 0.126
Sigma	2.548947	Sigma^2		6.497133
R^2	0.2456187			
RSS	415.8165132	TSS		551.2020456
Sample Size	83	no. of	parameters	19
Wald (joint):	Chi^2(18)	187.4	[0.000]	**
Wald (dummy):	Chi^2(1)	2.402	[0.121]	
AR(1) test:	N(0,1)	-0.5809	[0.561]	
AR(2) test:	N(0,1)	-1.504	[0.133]	

Table 5
Determinants of growth in Growth-disaster Countries.

	Coefficient	*Std.Error*	*t-value*	*t-prob*
Sy	0.0536652	0.0578	0.929	0.357
Iy	0.387516	0.03472	11.2	0
Popg	1.58804	0.6546	2.43	0.018
Xmy	-0.0645406	0.04199	-1.54	0.13
Infl	-0.000239639	5.52E-05	-4.34	0
Govy	-0.254936	0.05758	-4.43	0
Rint	-0.0128252	0.001408	-9.11	0
Rexch	-0.00829239	0.0006404	-12.9	0
Central African Rep.	-0.567217	1.896	-0.299	0.766
Ghana	0.764814	0.909	0.841	0.404
Nicaragua	-0.267793	0.1168	-2.29	0.025
Sierra Leone	-0.0683136	0.128	-0.534	0.596
Venezuela, RB	-0.294535	0.1456	-2.02	0.048
Constant	-0.894037	2.785	-0.321	0.749
Sigma	4.263287	Sigma^2	18.17	562
R^2	0.3457624			
RSS	1072.361362	TSS	1639.1007	168
No. of observations	79	No. of	Parameters	20
Wald (joint):	Chi^2(19)	180.1	[0.000]	
Wald (dummy):	Chi^2(1)	0.103	[0.748]	
AR(1) test:	N(0,1)	-0.9735	[0.330]	
AR(2) test:	N(0,1)	-1.269	[0.204]	

Table 6
Determinants of Growth in Middle East Countries

	Coefficient	*Std.Error*	*t-value*	*t-prob*
Growth(-1)	0.143673	0.05634	2.55	0.011
Sy	0.310784	0.09445	3.29	0.001
Sy(-1)	-0.36685	0.09985	-3.67	0
Iy	-0.0175073	0.1067	-0.164	0.87
iy(-1)	0.0181627	0.1094	0.166	0.868
Popg	-0.546176	0.3191	-1.71	0.088
popg(-1)	0.521887	0.248	2.1	0.036
Xmy	-0.0329952	0.04531	-0.728	0.467
xmy(-1)	0.0423624	0.04503	0.941	0.348
Infl	-0.0261122	0.01488	-1.75	0.08
infl(-1)	0.0168734	0.01233	1.37	0.172
year(-1)	-0.0202631	0.06147	-0.33	0.742
Constant	43.5594	123.1	0.354	0.724
	Sigma 5.31; sigma^2 28.18; N 282; K =13			
R^2 0.1967839	RSS 7582.5	TSS 9440.1		

No single factor can be isolated that matters for economic growth across all types of countries. Openness and country specific factors are found prominent in emerging economies. These countries also show a tendency for convergence in level of income. Saving and investment ratios have expected signs but were not statistically significant even at 10 percent level of significance. The estimates for

Table 7
Determinants of growth in Latin and Central American Countries
Panel GMM (one Step) Estimation with Individual Effects

	Coefficient	*Std.Error*	*t-value*	*t-prob*
iy	0.1306	0.0522	2.5000	0.0130
xmy	0.0302	0.0209	1.4500	0.1490
infl	-0.0009	0.0002	-4.0000	0.0000
cadef	0.0475	0.0306	1.5500	0.1220
Constant	-4.4425	3.6730	-1.2100	0.2270
Antigua and Barbuda	2.3244	3.0800	0.7550	0.4510
Argentina	0.3609	1.0630	0.3390	0.7340
Bahamas, The	-0.0664	1.2470	-0.0533	0.9580
Barbados	0.9192	1.0350	0.8880	0.3750
Belize	1.4098	2.5280	0.5580	0.5770
Bolivia	2.5282	3.0420	0.8310	0.4060
Brazil	3.9497	2.2790	1.7300	0.0840
Chile	2.1572	2.7650	0.7800	0.4360
Colombia	0.6180	1.8630	0.3320	0.7400
Costa Rica	2.1726	2.1460	1.0100	0.3120
Dominican Republic	0.1568	2.3280	0.0674	0.9460
Ecuador	0.8159	2.3880	0.3420	0.7330
El Salvador	1.1222	1.0850	1.0300	0.3010
Grenada	1.5311	2.6970	0.5680	0.5700
Guatemala	-2.7476	0.4757	-5.7800	0.0000
Guyana	-0.3287	2.7390	-0.1200	0.9050
Haiti	-0.9212	1.9150	-0.4810	0.6310
Honduras	-1.3697	1.3050	-1.0500	0.2940
Jamaica	1.5202	2.5750	0.5900	0.5550
Mexico	-0.1066	2.1300	-0.0500	0.9600
Nicaragua	0.2862	1.8670	0.1530	0.8780
Panama	-0.3209	2.1480	-0.1490	0.8810
Paraguay	1.0235	2.7600	0.3710	0.7110
Peru	1.0299	0.7821	1.3200	0.1880
Puerto Rico	0.9467	0.6354	1.4900	0.1370
St. Kitts and Nevis	0.8115	0.6603	1.2300	0.2200
St. Lucia	0.1886	2.1710	0.0869	0.9310
St. Vincent and the Grenadines	-0.3299	1.7820	-0.1850	0.8530
Suriname	2.5300	2.6500	0.9550	0.3400
Trinidad and Tobago	-0.8258	2.4170	-0.3420	0.7330
Sigma	4.494	Observations	617	
Sigma^2	20.19	Parameters	35	
R^2	0.194			
Wald (Joint)	Chi^2(4)	31.11	[0.000]	**

OECD economies were very consistent with the economic theory. Macro economic variables such as saving rates and the openness of the economy were very significant. Size of the government sector as measured in tax GDP ratio and government spending GDP ratios were found to deter economic growth rates. Country specific factors seem to be more important determinants of economic growth among these OECD economies. Among low income economies saving and investment ratios and population growth rates were found significant determinants of economic growth and higher rate of inflation was deterring economic growth. Country specific factors were dominant factors influencing economic growth among these economies when the US growth rates are taken as a base of comparison. Countries with higher saving and investment ratios are found to have grown faster than with lower ones. Investment ratios, population growth rates and country specific factors were important determinants of growth in South Asian economies. Many other variables such as openness of economy, exchange rate, ratio of government spending were not very significant. Openness, rate of inflation, ratio of government spending to GDP, real interest rate and real exchange rate variables were dragging growth down in growth disaster economies. The saving ratio was not significant but the population growth rates and investment ratios were found to have significant and positive relation with economic growth. Saving rate and previous growth were important determinants of economic growth in the Middle East countries.

Openness had positive and significant impacts but the uncertainty due to inflation has affected growth negatively in Latin American economies as shown in Table 7. Coefficients on investment ratios and current account deficit had expected positive sign but were not significant. There seems to be persistency in economic growth in among these economies. Country specific factors are important in some economies of Latin and Central America but not so in others.

Growth Policies

A sound policy at the national as well as the international level is necessary to speed up such convergence process. Correct policies at the national level improve efficiency in the allocation of resources by promoting the most productive sectors with enhanced saving and investment activities. Transparent and clear tax and trade policies are important in building up credibility of the government activities. Transfer of technology and resources according to the marginal contribution in growth at the international level would also speed up the convergence process. This requires a deep understanding of the process and confidence in each others' actions among the people and policy makers involved in promoting global economies.

A higher growth rate requires the combinations of factors such as a higher saving rate, a lower population growth rate, a low rate of depreciation of capital, development of right technology, free mobility of factors of production across sectors and regions of an economy based upon the marginal productivity of capital and free and liberal international trade. A sound and effective economic policy at home and at the international level can improve growth rates and convergence process in the global economy for a number of reasons (Aghevli (1977), Dollar (1969), Levin and Zervos (1998), Bruno and Easterly (1998)).

At first, correct policies can encourage private saving by means of lower propensity to consume or increase in retained profits of private corporations. Public saving may rise with prudent fiscal policy with reasonable tax rates and lower government spending. In an open economy a higher rate of saving does not necessary translate into a higher investment rate unless accompanied by a correct exchange rate policy. If the real rate of return on the capital asset is negative or much lower than abroad investors would be reluctant to invest in productive assets as it becomes riskier for investors to commit themselves in the long term investment projects. It can cause outflow of capital. In contrast investment tax credit might increase the inflow of foreign capital to complement domestic saving. Secondly, development of human capital is as important as an effort to increase the national saving rate. Highly skilled people produce more and may bring higher rate of technological progress. A more educated work force is able to think about problems more creatively and solve them according to need of the situation. Skilled people also enhance research and development activities useful for final production. Larger size of population can contribute towards growth only when each individual in it is properly trained and skilled. Thirdly many developing economies are caught in poverty traps because of strong barriers to adoption of more appropriate set of technologies in the form of licensing and regulation requirements. Another reason is the distortion of economic incentives among production sectors by different tax and tariff rates. Such distortions affect efficiency in allocation of resources. Heavily taxed sectors get repressed even though they are economically more viable and sectors which get favourable tax treatment may invest more than is economically justifiable. Such distortions may occur across all categories of capital assets. Correct incentives are required to create a "level playing field" for different kinds of capital assets (plant, machinery, building, vehicles) by removing distortions across assets and sectors. An undistorted system assures efficiency in the allocation of resources and is conducive to a higher rate of economic growth. Fifth, economic growth rates are often low in economies, with weak institutions. Investors hesitate to invest unless they are clear about the definition of property rights, legal provision for enforcement of contracts and transparency of tax and trade policies. These are very important in raising the confidence of investors. Sixth, macroeconomic stability – investors hesitate to commit themselves in uncertain policy environment where fiscal and monetary policies are not credible. Sixth, higher economic growth rates also need to be associated with a carefully designed redistribution policy where redistribution occurs more from the creation of productive employment and real wage rates. This would help to prevent social conflict and tensions from stopping or slowing down the growth process. Seventh, a "pay as you go" social security system in many advanced economies puts a greater burden among working people and retards their propensity to save. A fully funded social security system (privatisation of social security system) is beneficial to promote national saving in the economy (Figure A7,A8). Higher proportion of population at lower age cohort in many developing economies, means greater proportion of working age population, that can contribute toward the pension making funding it less serious problem in comparison to that in more advanced economies.

Low income economies are caught in the poverty trap not only because of low productivity of physical capital but also due to inadequate amount of human capital. Lower human capital implies lower marginal product of the physical capital. When it is less than the cost of capital then firms do not invest and it causes a reduction in the stock of capital. In case of sub-Saharan Africa bad policies such as persistent budgetary deficits, overvalued currencies and low investment and saving ratios because of low level of income, lower standard of education, high drop out ratios in the primary and secondary level and high illiteracy, lack of physical infrastructure such as roads and communication networks and facilities drag growth rate down. Ethnic and linguistic diversity and ethnic tribal conflicts, hot tropical climate, lack of appropriate technology for these climates, diseases such as malaria and AIDS and high transportation costs (landlocked-ness for some countries) and lack of transparent and democratic policies are sources of additional problems. Higher rate of foreign aid is less likely to promote growth rates as aids are fungible and donor interest do not match with those of recipients and they are less likely to succeed unless local people are involved in formulating the projects.

CONCLUSION

The neoclassical and endogenous growth models have been reviewed along with empirical analysis of economic growth across highly performing economies, OECD countries, low income economies, economies of South Asia, Africa and the Middle East and Latin America taking each of them separately. Empirical support has been found based on the growth panel data set constructed from the World Bank database for year 1960s to 2000 for 207 countries around the globe. This analysis suggests that the economic growth process is very complex.

It has been shown how the microeconomic factors, such as efficiency in the allocation of resources based on the choices of households and firms, matter for growth and that the greater confidence about the economy raises the rate of saving and investment. It also has been shown that macroeconomic stability with balanced trade and balanced government budget provides an economic framework where private sector can make its rational decision. A positive real interest rate, right exchange rate, open and liberal trade, close cooperation between the private and the public sectors are very essential.

Empirical analysis based on macroeconomic factors ratios of investment, saving, tax and public spending, inflation rates are illustrative but realistic policy requires consideration of country or group specific factors which underpin the growth process in these economies. No single remedy applies to all countries at the same time, each country has some of its own factors, characterised by its own institutions and culture, that have important influences on its rate of saving, capital stock, per capital output and the rate of economic growth, which needs a careful attention.

REFERENCES

Aghevli B.B. (1977), Inflationary Finance and Growth, *Journal of Political Economy*, 85:6: 1295-1307.

Aghion P. and P. Howitt (1998), *Endogenous Growth Theory*, MIT Press, Cambridge MA.

Alesina A. and D. Rodrik (1994), "Distributive Politics and Economic Growth", *Quarterly Journal of Economics*, 109:2:465-90.

Arellano M. and Bond S.R. (1991), Some tests of specification for panel data: Monte Carlo evidence and application to employment equations, *Review of Economic Studies*, 58:2:277-297.

Arrow K.J. (1962), Economic Implications of Learning by Doing, *Review of Economic Studies*, 29:155-73.

Auerbach Alan J. and L. J. Kotlikoff (1987), Dynamic Fiscal Policy. Cambridge University Press.

Baltagi, B.H. (1995), *Econometric Analysis of Panel Data*, John Willey and Sons.

Bank of England (2004), The New Bank of England Quarterly Model, Quarterly Bulletin, 44:2:188- 193, Summer. Economic models of bank of Englánd *www.bangkofengland.co.uk/modcoupdate.htm..*

Barro R.J. (1991), Economic Growth in Cross Section of Countries, Quarterly Journal of Economics, May, 407-433.

Barro R. and X. Sala-i-Martin (1992), Public Finance in Models of Economic Growth, *Review of Economic Studies*, 56:4:645-61.

Barro R.J. and Sala-I-Martin (1995), *Economic Growth*, McGraw Hill.

Becker G.S. (1975), Human Capital, Columbia University, New York.

Bhagwati J. (1969), Optimal Policies and Immiserising Growth, American Economic Review, Cooly Thomas F. (1995), *Frontiers of Business Cycle Research*, Princeton.

Blackburn K. (1999), Can stabilisation policy reduce long-run growth? *Economic Journal* 109:452:67-77.

Blake A.P. and M. Weale (2001), UK Economy, National Institute Economics Review, 175:8-28, January.

Bellman R. (1957), *Dynamic Programming*, Princeton University Press.

Bruno M. and W. Easterly (1998), "Inflation Crises and Long-run Growth" *Journal of Monetary Economics*, 4: 3-26.

Cass, D. (1965), Optimum Growth in Aggregative Model of Capital Accumulation, *Review of Economic Studies*, 32:233-240.

Denison E.F. (1962), The sources of economic growth in the United States, Committee for Economic Development, New York.

Deverajan S., W.R. Easterly and H. Pack (2003), Low Investment is not the Constraint on African Development, *Economic Development and Cultural Change*, 52:3:547-571, April.

Dorfman R. (1969), An Economic Interpretation of Optimal Control Theory, *American Economic Review*, 59: 817-831.

Dollar, D. (1992), "Outward-Oriented Developing Economies Really Do Grow More Rapidly: Evidence from 95 LDCs, 1976-1985" *Economic Development and Cultural Change*, 40:3:523-544.

Domar E. (1947), Capital Expansion, Rate of Growth and Employment" *Econometrica,* 14:2:137-147.

Domar E. (1947), Expansion and Employment, *American Economic Review*, 37:1:35-55.

Doornik J.A. and Hendry D.F. (2001), *Econometric Modelling Using PcGive* Vol. I-III. Timberlake Consultants, London.

Easterly W. and R. Levine (2001), "It's not factor accumulation: Stylized facts and Growth Models" *World Bank Economic Review*, 2001.

Fisher S. (1993), "The Role of Macroeconomic Factors in Growth" *Journal of Monetary Economics,* 32:485-511.

Fullerton, D.J. Shoven and J. Whalley (1983), "Dynamic General Equilibrium Impacts of Replacing the US Income tax with a Progressive Consumption Tax," *Journal of Public Economics* 38: 265-96.

Grossman G. and H. Helpman (1991), Quality Ladders in the Theory of Growth, *Review of Economic Studies*,18:43-61.

Grossman G. and E. Helpman (1991), *Innovation and Growth in the Global Economy*, Cambridge Mass. MIT Press.

Hall R. and C. Jones (1999), "Why do Some Countries Produce so Much More output than others?" *Quarterly Journal of Economics*, February, 104:1:83-116.

Hahn F. (1984), Equilibrium and Macroeconomics, Oxford, Basil Blackwell.

Hahn F.H. and R.C.O. Matthews (1964). The Theory of Economic Growth: A Survey, *Economic Journal*, 296:74:779-902.

Harrod R. (1939), "An Essay in Dynamic Theory", *Economic Journal*, 49:193:14-33.

Jones C.I. (1995), R & D-Based Models of Economic Growth, *Journal of Political Economy*, 103:4:759-784

Holly S. and M. Weale Eds. (2000), Econometric Modelling: Techniques and Applications, pp.69-93, the Cambridge University Press.

Jogenson D.W. and B. Fraumeni (1992), Investment in Education and US Economic Growth, Scandenevian Journal of Economics 94:51-70, September.

Kaldor N. (1961), "Capital Accumulation and Economic Growth" in F.A. Lutz and D.C. Hague ed. The Theory of Capital, New York, St. Martin.

Keynes J.M. (1936), The General Theory of Employment, Interest and Money, MacMillan and Cambridge University Press.

Koopmans, T.C. (1965), On the concept of Optimal Growth. *The Econometric Approach to Development Planning*, Chicago, Rand McNally.

Krugman P.R. and A.J. Venables (1995), "Globalisation and Inequality of Nations" *Quarterly Journal of Economics,* November 857-80.

Levine, R. and S. Zervos (1998), "Stock Markets, Banks and Economic Growth" *American Economic Review*, 88:537-58.

Lin Justin Yifu (2003), Development Strategy, Viability and Economic Convergence, *Economic Development and Cultural Change*, 51:2:277-308, January.

Lucas, R.E. (2002), *Lectures on Economic Growth,* Harvard University Press.

Lucas R.E. (1988), "On the Mechanics of Economic Development", *Journal of Monetary Economics*, 22:1: 3-42.

McMahon G. and L. Squire (2003), *Explaining Growth: A Global Research Project*, Palgrave Macmillan Great Britain.

Maddison A. (1991), *Dynamic of Capital Accumulation and Economic Growth*, Oxford.

Mankiw N.G., D. Romer and D.N. Weil (1992), "Contribution to the Empirics of Economic Growth" *Quarterly Journal of Economics*, 107:407-437, May.

Miller M.H. and Zhang L. (1998), Macroeconomic Policy Options for Managing Capital Flows EDI-NSF China Workshop Vol. "Managing Capital Flows and Financial Risks".

Miles D. and A. Scott (2002), *Understanding the Wealth of Nations*, John Wiley and Sons.

NIESR (Various Issues) UK and World Economies Forecast, *National Institute of Economic Review*, *http://www.niesr.ac.uk*.

Nelson R.R. and H. Pack (1999), The Asian Miracle and Modern Growth Theory, *Economic Journal*, 109:416-436, July.

Parente S.L. (1994), Technology Adoption, Learning-by-Doing, and Economic Growth, *Journal of Economic Theory*, 63:346-369.

Parente S.L. and Prescott E.C. (1993), Changes in the Wealth of Nations, Federal Reserve Bank of Minneapolis, *Quarterly Review*, 17: 3-16, Spring.

Perroni, C. (1995), "Assessing the Dynamic Efficiency Gains of Tax Reform When Human Capital is Endogenous," *International Economic Review* 36:907-925.

Quah D. (1997), "Increasingly Weightless Economies", *Bank of England Quarterly Bulletin*, 37:1: 49-56.

Ramsey, F.P. (1928), "A Mathematical Theory of Saving," *Economic Journal* 38:543-559.

Rodrik D. (1999) "Where did all the growth go? External Shocks, Social conflict, and Growth Collapse" *Journal of Economic Growth*, 4: 4:385-412.

Roll E. (1938), History of Economic Thought, Oxford.

Romer, Paul (1989), Endogenous Technological Change, *Journal of Political Economy*, 98:5: Pt. 2: S71-S102.

Restuccia D. (2004), Barriers to Capital Accumulation and Aggregate Total Factor Productivity, *International Economic Review*, 45:1:225-38.

Rutherford, T.F. (1995), "Extension of GAMS for Complementary Problems Arising in Applied Economic Analysis," *Journal of Economic Dynamics and Control* 19:1299-1324.

Schultz T.W. (1961), Investment in Human Capital, American Economic Review, 51:1-17.

Solow, R.M.(1956), A Contribution to the Theory of Economic Growth, *Quarterly Journal of Economics*, 70:1:65-95.

Tamura R. (1991), Income Convergence in an Endogenous Growth Model, Journal of Political Economy, 99:522-540, June.

Temple J. (1999), The New Growth Evidence, *Journal of Economic Literature*, 37:112-156, March.

Turnovsky S.J. (1993), Macroeconomic Policies, Growth, and Welfare in a Stochastic Economy, *International Economic Review*, 34:4: 953-981.

Uhling H. (1999), A Toolkit for Analysing non-linear Dynamic Stochastic Models Easily, in Marimon and A, Scott ed. Computational Methods for the Study of Dynamic Economics pp. 30-61, Oxford University Press.

Uzawa, H. (1962), "On a Two-Sector Model of Economic Growth," *Review of Economic Studies* 29, 40-47.

11

Is There any Evidence on Unemployment-Inflation Trade-off in OECD Countries in Recent Years?[31]

Keshab Bhattarai

INTRODUCTION

About 36 million people were unemployed across OECD economies in 2005. Economic, social and psychological costs of such a high rates of unemployment, that now averages around 7 percent, are enormous. Economic policies that have aimed to reduce such unemployment rate have become more successful in countries which have deeply appreciated the fundamentals of the labour market than economies that are stuck with rigid labour markets (see graphs in the appendix). Whether or not the unemployment rates can be stabilised towards their natural rates by managing the aggregate demands through fiscal or monetary policies with or without some increase in the price levels is an issue widely investigated in the macroeconomic literature (Keynes (1936), Phillips (1958), Phelps (1968), Friedman (1968), Lucas and Rapping (1969), Lucas (1976) Brunner et. al. (1976), Layard and Nickell (1986, 1990) and Blanchflower and Oswald (1994), Cross (1988), Hoon (2001)). Other models emphasise on wage bargaining outcome between employers and firms (McDonald and Solow (1981), Dixon (1988), Lockwood and Manning (1989), Lockwood, Miller and Zhang (1998), Nickell (1990, 1998)),Caballero and Hammour (1994) and Pissarides (2000)).

Theoretically unemployment cannot exist in the classical general equilibrium system unless the labour market is distorted by rules such as the minimum wage rate. The world is not entirely classical, however. Recessions have been frequent and common. Keynes's suggestion for treating the labour supply as infinitely elastic and adding demand to create employment may have worked well until the late

31. The paper was presented at the 61st International Atlantic Conference Berlin, Germany 15-19 March 2006 and author acknowledges comments and suggestions made by conference participants at that time.

1960s when the majority of the OECD economies had spare productive capacity but all of them went through inflationary spirals when they were close to their potentials for production and faced continued rise in the oil prices in 1970s. Contractionary measures taken to reduce inflation raised the rates of unemployment and these have not been able to come down in many of the OECD economies, mainly due to downward rigidity of nominal wages and prices. After the rational expectations revolution, the issue whether any demand management policy can reduce the employment rate below its natural rate has remained a very controversial one. Raising demand for products through expansionary monetary or fiscal policy to create extra jobs may bring new jobs up to a certain point but can be a futile exercise after an economy crosses that threshold and is likely to initiate a wage price spiral and associated uncertainties if pursued further. Lowering the natural rate of unemployment requires reforms in the structure of the labour market, welfare, transfer and benefit system and unemployment insurance schemes. It is asking for more flexibility in the labour market and removal of some of these distortions often considered as supply side policies.

This paper aims to investigate whether there exists any trade-off between unemployment and inflation as proclaimed by Phillips (1957) and many other subsequent studies among the OECD economies over years. Almost all of these economies have universally adopted inflation targeting regimes and subsequently have opted to limit the role of demand management in regulating economic activities in recent years. Looking at the quarterly data series on unemployment and inflation rates since 1988, it aims also to find out how much evidence can be found on the validity of assertions in line with Phillips' curve among these economies in recent years.

When workers have higher reservation wage rates, the cost conscious employers cannot hire them at that expensive rate. Many workers are likely to remain unemployed. When firms put higher mark-up (over the wage rate) on the prices of goods and services they sell, the workers are bound to raise their mark-up on wage rates that worker apply on the prices of commodities to maintain their real wage rates. Such behaviour creates imperfections in the labour market that can set a process of wage price spiral and disequilibrium in the labour market that manifests itself in higher unemployment rates.

Demand for labour is derived from the demand for output. When an economy is growing fast there will be plenty of demand for labour relative to its supply with a lower rate of unemployment relative to when economy grows slowly. In contrast there are periods when many workers are ready to work but do not find jobs. There are structural reasons for excess supply of labour like this, the main one being the rigidity in the nominal wage rates despite falling prices. On the other side the Keynesian remedy of creating additional demand by expansionary fiscal or monetary policy can push the aggregate demand beyond the productive capacity of the economy and causes inflation to rise. How far the demand management policy is effective in creating jobs and lowering the rate of unemployment is given by the slope of the Phillips curve, which depends on many factors that characterise the economy such as the tax-benefit system, technological progress and efficiency of the job market in matching employees and employers.

In the price-sticky Keynesian models optimal response to an increase in cyclical unemployment, as occurred in 1970s and 1980s and even now in many of the European OECD economies, would be an increase in the level of aggregate demand assuming a perfectly elastic supply curve for output. Following Phillips (1958) it is argued that additional demand not only raises the level of output and employment but also raises the level of prices as employers have to pay higher wage rates to induce more workers to supply their labour. The natural rate and rational expectation hypotheses go even further subsequent to the arguments developed by Phelps (1968) or Friedman (1968) and others about the wage price dynamics in industrial economies. When unions and workers can correctly expect real wage rates about future events in the labour market they adjust their labour supply accordingly leaving the natural rate of unemployment unchanged. This renders monetary policy ineffective to achieve real objectives in the long run. After the rational expectations revolution, the majority of economists tend to believe that only unanticipated policy shocks could have real impacts in the economy (Lucas and Rapping (1969), Lucas (1976)). Consequently inflation targeting has become the major objective of the central banks in the most of the OECD economies and these initiatives have paid off as the price levels have become much more stable in recent years. The persistence of high and varying rates of unemployment among these countries is, however, still an unresolved puzzle.

This paper focuses on the empirical side of this debate. Section II will assess the issue of trade-off using scattered plots of unemployment rates against inflation. Then a series of regressions of levels or first differences of the unemployment rates on inflation will be used to assess whether there is any evidence for the Phillips curve hypotheses in the OECD economies in section III. An examination of the issue of persistence of unemployment using an autoregression model or impulse response analyses from a VAR model for each country will be done in section IV. Finally section V will focus on panel data evidence for all OECD economies and is followed by conclusions, references and appendices.

EXAMINATION OF UNEMPLOYMENT RATE AND INFLATION RELATIONSHIP USING CROSS PLOTS AND COUNTRY SPECIFIC REGRESSIONS

It is hard to see any definite pattern of the relationship between the unemployment rate and inflation in many OECD economies during the periods used in this study. On the quarterly basis the unemployment rate goes up to 25 percent for some countries like Spain and inflation rates up to four percent for Australia. Most observations for other countries lie between these two as shown in details in Figure 1 that plots inflation rate on Y-axis and unemployment rate on X axis for each OECD country from 1988:1-2002:1.

Figure 1
Inflation Rate against Unemployment rate in OECD Economies(1988:1-2001:1)-1

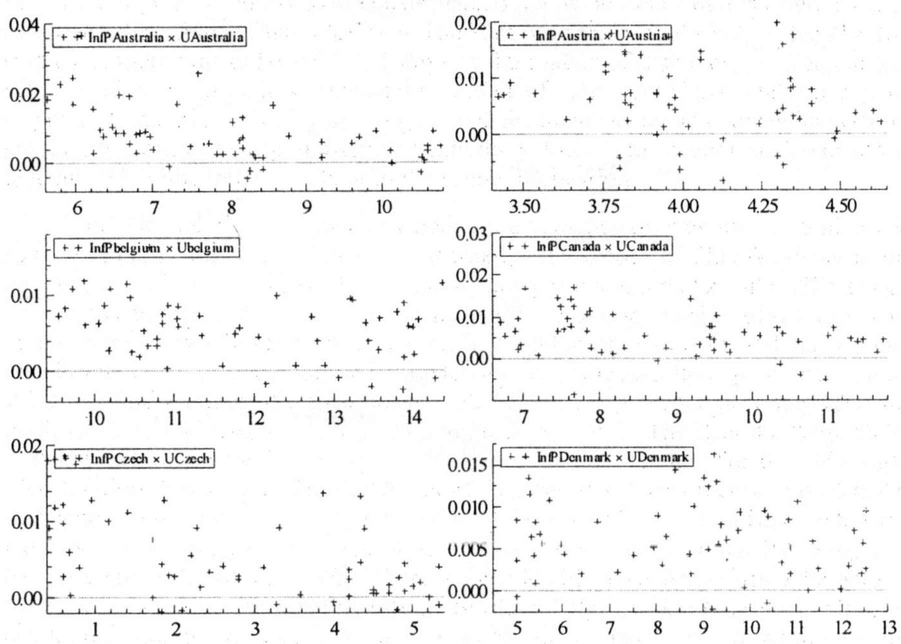

Inflation Rate against Unemployment rate in OECD Economies (1988:1-2001:1)-2

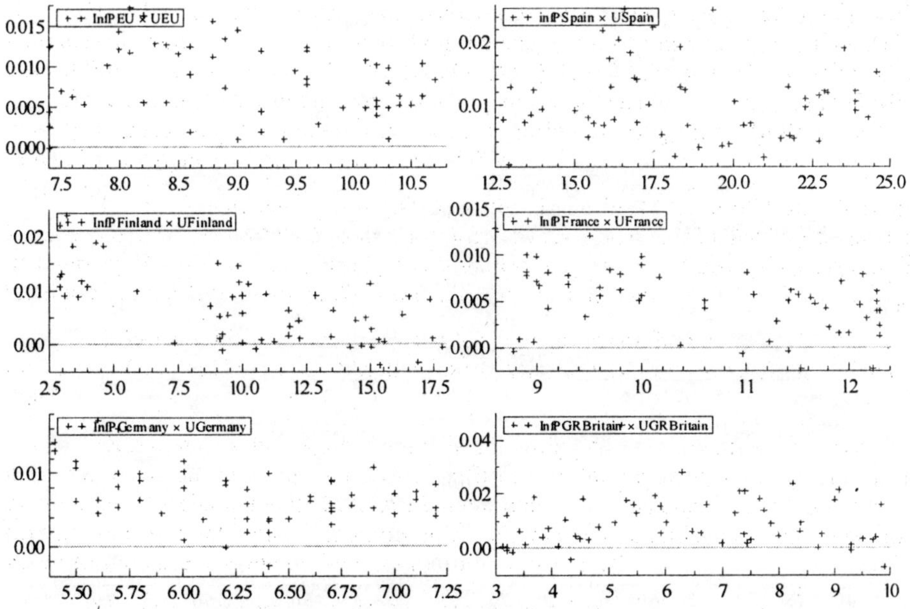

Inflation Rate against Unemployment rate in OECD Economies (1988:1-2001:1) -3

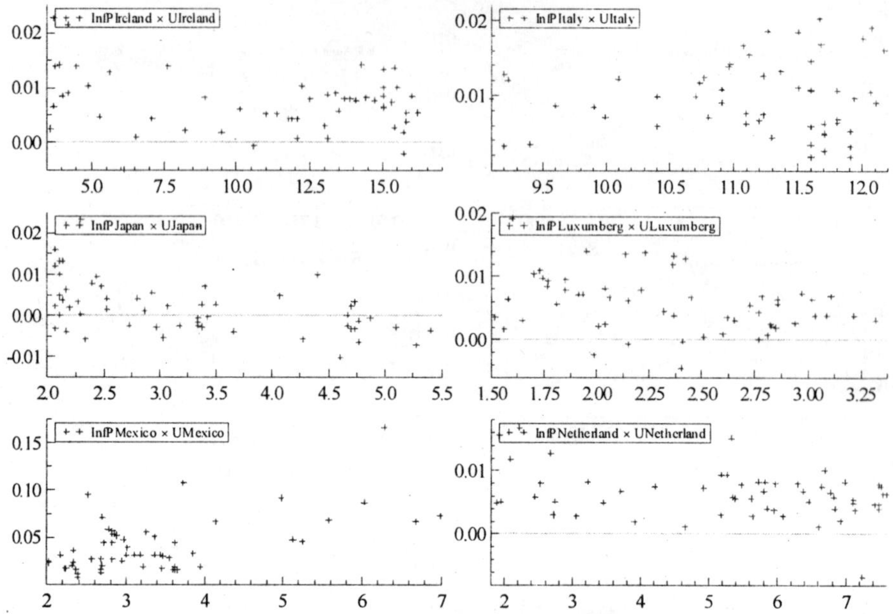

Inflation Rate against Unemployment Rate in OECD Economies (1988:1-2001:1) -3

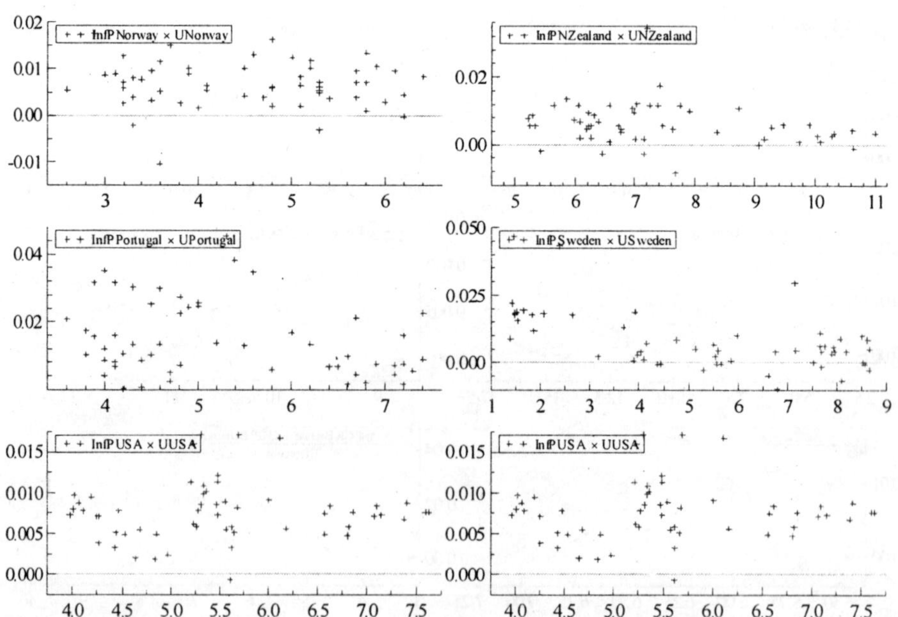

The unemployment rate is highly non-stationary variable but the inflation rate is more stationary. The Unit root test suggests that inflation rates in each country is a stationary I(0) variable but the unemployment rate in each is non-stationary and becomes stationary either by first differencing or in most instances by second differencing in levels or logs as presented in Table 1.

Table 1
Unit Root test for Inflation and Unemployment rate

Country	*Price level*	*Inflation rate*	*Unemployemnt rate*	*Log of unemployment rate*
Australia	I (1), 0	I (0), 0	I (2), 1	I (2), 1
Austria	I (1), 1	I (0), 1	I (1), 3	I (2), 2
Belgium	I (1), 1	I (0), 1	I (2), 3	I (2),1
Canada	I (1), 1	I (0), !	I (1), 0	I (2),3
Czech	I (0), 3	I (0), 1	I (2), 1	I (2),1
Denmark	I (1), 3	I (0), 3	I (2), 2	I (2),2
EU	I (1), 3	I (0), 0	I (1), 0	I (2),2
Spain	I (1), 1	I (0), 0	I (2), 1	I (2),1
Finland	I (1), 1	I (0), 1	I (1), 1	I (2),1
France	I (0), 0	I (0), 1	I (2), 1	I (2),1
Germany	I (0), 3	I (0), 0	I (2), 3	I (2),3
GRBritain	I (0), 2	I (0), 2	I (2), 3	I (2),3
Ireland	I (1), 1	I (0), 2	I (2), 3	I (2),0
Italy	I (1), 1	I (0), 1	I (1), 3	I (2),1
Japan	I (0), 1	I (0), 0	I (2), 1	I (2),2
Luxumberg	I (1), 1	I (0), 1	I (1), 0	I (2),3
Mexico	I (1), 1	I (0), 1	I (1), 3	I (2),3
Netherland	I (1), 2	I (0), 2	I (1), 3	I (2),1
Norway	I (1), 2	I (0), 0	I (1), 0	I (2),2
NZealand	I (1), 1	I (0), 0	I (1), 3	I (2),1
Portugal	I (0), 2	I (0), 1	I (0), 0	I (2),2
Sweden	I (1), 0	I (0), 1	I (1), 0	I (2),1
USA	I (1), 3	I (0), 0	I (2), 1	I (2),1

Many macro economists still believe that an economy may be below or above the natural rate of unemployment in the short run but it will move toward the natural rate of unemployment in the long run. As Friedman (1968) argued the natural rate of output and employment is "ground out" by the equilibrium in goods, labour and money markets. Frictional unemployment, non-accelerating inflation rate of unemployment (NAIRU), or structural unemployment is widely discussed in the literature as an essential process and outcome of the dynamic adjustment mechanism in an economy. Time series models explain the unemployment rate series in terms of trends, cycles, seasonal and random factors and emphasise in the persistency of the unemployment rate because of rigidities in the labour market using sophisticated stochastic processes. Some authors focus on mismatch between creation of new jobs and destruction of old jobs due to new innovations in the production process (Caballero and Hammour (1994), Pissarides (2000)). Others have applied the stochastic Markov switching processes to explain the change in the natural rate of unemployment over time (Bianchi and Zoega (1998)). The rational expectation school shows limitations of the demand management policies in controlling inflation by introducing expectations of prices in wage negotiations by unions and workers. For them stability and growth need to rely more on supply side policies including the reforms in the labour market. Using sophisticated economic models, the real business cycle school, like classical school, ruled out the existence of such involuntary unemployment rate. For them fluctuations in employment rates were considered to be features of inter-temporal optimisation process of individuals and technical shocks (Kydland and Prescott (1982)). There are even suggestions to scrap the notion of the Phillips curve entirely (Summers (1988)) from macroeconomic models.

Table 2
Apparent relation in country regression of unemployment rate on inflation (N=56)

Country	*Inflation Coefficient*	*T-Value*	*R-Square*	*F-Value*	*DW-Statistics*
Australia	-97.640	-4.39	0.261	19.26	0.41
Austria	-6.688	-1.08	.0.021	1.186	0.20
Belgium	-115.899	-2.35	0.094	5.54	0.27
Canada	-57.750	-1.74	0.05	3.04	0.13
Czech	-161.485	-4.74	0.297	22.86	0.335
Denmark	-64.910	-0.842	0.0129	0.709	0.044
EU	-44.170	-1.38	0.034	10907	0.059
Spain	-21.708	-0.22	0.001	0.074	0.034
Finland	-462.83	-0.46	0.438	4.74	0.787
France	-158.690	-3.49	0.184	12.18	0.351
Germany	-56.672	-3.18	0.158	10.1	0.228
GRBritain	8.979	0.288	0.0015	0.0827	0.07
Ireland	-231.64	-1.92	0.064	3.682	0.125
Italy	15.908	0.674	0.008	0.454	0.202
Japan	-70.362	-3.75	0.206	14.05	0.644
Luxumberg	-35.770	-2.54	0.1068	6.458	0.325
Mexico	22.973	5.11	0.326	26.12	0.438
Netherland	-152.643	-2.44	0.0966	5.98	0.214
Norway	-10.284	-0.350	0.0023	0.122	0.316
NZealand	-58.906	-1.66	0.0484	2.745	0.117
Portugal	-28.761	-1.94	0.0661	3.751	0.206
Sweden	-129.605	-4.89	0.307	23.88	0.522
USA	19.840	0.508	0.0047	0.258	0.052

Despite controversies in the literature, the varying rates of unemployment across countries over time is one of the major economic issues and draws overwhelming concerns of public and policy-makers around the world. The rates of unemployment and inflation like the rates growth of the output are the mostly watched macroeconomic indicators by the public who are involved in negotiating contracts and the policy-makers who are responsible for managing the public funds. Interest rate decisions of the Bank of England or the European Central bank or the Federal Reserve or the central banks in the OECD economies focus on achieving a target rate of inflation by stabilising the unemployment rates by minimising the gap between the aggregate demand and aggregate supply (King (2004)). Studies made by Nickell (1998), Phelps and Zoega (1998), Madsen (1998), Cross (1988) significantly highlight on empirical relationship between those two variables for the OECD economies in the recent years and tried to tackle the question of whether a trade-off exists between unemployment and inflation, and the degree of such trade-off using the real world evidence.

COUNTRY SPECIFIC REGRESSIONS OF UNEMPLOYMENT RATES ON INFLATION

There is an apparent trade-off between inflation and unemployment when one regresses unemployment rate to the inflation rate as shown in Table 2 but this relation is spurious one as evidenced by the lower values of Durbin-Watson Statistics relative to R-square from the regressions. The source of spuriousness is the non-stationarity of the unemployment rates. When some of the non-stationarity is removed, the relation between unemployment and inflation completely disappears as shown by the estimated coefficients presented in Table 3.

Table 3
Regression of the first Difference of Unemployment rate on Inflation: Lack of Evidence for Phillips Curve

Country	Inflation Coefficient	T-Value	R-Square	F-Value	DW-stastistics
Australia	-7.398	-1.40	0.035	1.95	0.51
Austria	-2.165	0.805	0.012	0.648	1.15
Belgium	10.672	1.33	0.033	1.78	0.507
Canada	18.598	2.56	0.108	6.569	1.39
Czech	13.503	2.30	0.089	5.309	0.284
Denmark	6.372	0.669	0.008	0.44	0.736
EU	3.701	0.662	0.008	0.44	0.570
Spain	19.001	1.37	0.034	1.882	0.73
Finland	2.155	0.159	0.0005	0.0256	0.221
France	4.247	0.461	0.004	0.212	0.404
Germany	-2.723	-0.558	0.006	0.311	0.885
GRBritain	-3.865	-0.847	0.013	0.717	0.243
Ireland	3.655	0.414	0.003	0.173	0.352
Italy	1.589	0.157	0.001	0.024	2.08
Japan	-3.990	-1.85	0.059	3.416	1.43
Luxumberg	3.635	1.00	0.0182	1.002	0.80
Mexico	3.028	1.86	0.0601	3.454	0.975
Netherland	4.830	0.602	0.006	0.362	0.706
Norway	11.997	0.472	0.009	0.524	2.83
NZealand	2.266	0.237	0.001	0.056	1.34
Portugal	-2.214	-0.404	0.003	0.163	2.11
Sweden	8.005	1.56	0.04	2.447	0.83
USA	4.303	0.516	0.003	0.266	0.86

Above results can highlight some points on why there is a long-standing debate in macroeconomics on whether there exists any trade-off between unemployment and inflation. Resutls are somewhat close to the claims of the Keynesian and new

Keynesian economists who assume a very elastic aggregate supply curve and rigidity in prices and wages in the short run, an expansionary monetary or fiscal policy by raising aggregate demand can have a significant role in reducing unemployment rate. Such an effect occurs because prices and wages adjust at slower rates than the output or employment after an expansionary programme (Keynes (1936), Hicks (1937) Phillips (1958), Phelps and Taylor (1977) Mankiw (1985), Dixon (1988), Ball and Romer (1990), Blanchard. and Summers (1986), Nickell (1986, 1998), Ball (1999)) than the arguments of classical and new classical economists who believe in perfect flexibility of wages and prices in which the result of an expansionary policy is only to raise the price level because money is neutral and there is a proportionate relationship between money and prices, economy is always in full equilibrium because of perfectly flexible prices and wages rates (Yellen (1984) Manning (1995), Layard and Nickell (1990), Nickell and Quintini (2003)).

ANALYSING PERSISTENCY OF UNEMPLOYMENT RATES USING AUTOREGRESSIVE AND VAR MODELS

The autoregressive models show persistence of unemployment rate among the OECD economies (Table 4). When the trends are removed from the unemployment rates by taking its first difference and regressing on inflation almost all coefficients become statistically insignificant except for Canada and Czech Republic. Even for them the positive signs of coefficients are contrary to the Phillips hypotheses. The autocorrelation problem has slightly reduced but there is no statistical basis to claim the truth of Phillips curve hypothesis based on these estimates. These estimates strongly suggest a lack of the Phillips curve phenomenon among OECD economies in recent years.

The inflation targeting policies adopted by most of the OECD countries have reduced variation in inflation in recent years. There are still wide variations in unemployment rates. Enough statistical evidence exists for the persistence hypothesis, either in line with the theory of frictional unemployment, insider-outsider hypothesis, efficiency wage theory, job mismatch or lottery theory of unemployment or structural theory of so called hysteresis and Eurscelosis hypothesis. The estimates from the autoregressive model of order one are enough to prove this persistence in unemployment rates among these countries as presented in Table 4. This however highlights very little in explaining the current unemployment rate as its depends only on its past values.

Further there is an issue of non-stationarity of unemployment rate series. The nature of persistency of the unemployment rate is very strong. It occurs even when unemployment rates are made stationary by second differencing on their logs as shown in Table 5. The second difference (the change of the change in the log of the unemployment rate) is stationary and its period t value is significantly explained by its value in period t-1, an evidence for real persistence phenomenon. This literally means that countries that tend to have higher rates of unemployment rate end up having higher rates of unemployment [which seems like a tautological statement]. Practically it takes a long time to reduce the rate of unemployment once it has been built up like this as reforming labour markets seems to be very difficult in the short run.

Table 4
Random Walk Nature of Unemployment rate: AR(1) Model Estimates

Country	*Coefficients to its own lag*	*T-Value*	*R-Square*	*F-Value*	*DW-Stastistics*
Australia	0.989	34.7	0.96	1203	0.54
Austria	0.901	15.8	0.82	2485	1.15
Belgium	0.990	45.9	0.975	2103	0.468
Canada	0.975	31.9	0.949	1019	1.15
Czech	0.976	48.3	0.977	2333	0.193
Denmark	1.0139	59.6	0.985	3542	0.708
EU	1.006	42.0	0.970	1765	0.563
Spain	1.09	40.7	0.988	1656	0.706
Finland	0.977	51.8	0.980	2680	0.22
France	0.996	39.4	0.967	1549	0.386
Germany	0.968	28.5	0.937	8098	0.888
GRBritain	1.001	49.4	0.978	2444	0.214
Ireland	1.007	95.7	0.990	9154	0.353
Italy	0.947	15.6	0.819	2442	1.99
Japan	10.3	71.5	0.989	5111	1.36
Luxumberg	0.971	29.2	0.941	8555	0.749
Mexico	0.956	23.0	0.908	530.9	0.927
Netherland	1.008	58.9	0.985	3464	0.694
Norway	0.819	11.6	0.714	1349	2.54
NZealand	0.957	27.3	0.932	747.8	1.31
Portugal	0.940	19.3	0.876	374.3	2.04
Sweden	0.973	44.8	0.974	2005	0.779
USA	0.977	33.8	0.955	1142	0.854

When existing theories are unable to explain unemployment rates or inflation rates, it is common for a researcher to turn to the time series models for predicting the likely effects of supply or demand shocks in unemployment rate and inflation, tracing out the marginal and cumulative impacts of shocks over years as evidenced from the impulse response diagrams for each country in Sims' (1981) spirit of "let the data speak for themselves". Even here the data generating processes are very different among countries even unit shocks generate significantly different cumulative shocks (see Appendix 2) from second order VAR of unemployment rate and inflation.

Wage bargaining models of Blanchard (1986) and Nickell (1986,1988), McDonald and Solow (1981) have been applied to explain persistency of unemployment rates in EU economies with rigid labour markets in terms of Euroclerosis (hardening of tissues). In such models the unemployment rate is determined by the bargaining power of workers and firms over the wage rate and the level of employment. The real employment is determined by the interaction of labour demand curve and the union preferences. The union of workers actively engages to secure a higher wage rate and employment for their members and creates more unemployment for non-union workers. Union member increase probability of retaining job by raising the turnover cost, i.e. cost of hiring and firing and training, to employers while they care less about the prospects of the non-union workers.

Table 5
Second difference and persistence in the rate of change of change in unemployment rate

Country	*Inflation Coefficient*	*T-Value*	*R-Square*	*F-Value*	*DW-stastistics*
Australia	-0.353	-2.97	0.14	8.82	1.67
Austria	-0.288	-2.19	0.08	4.78	2.09
Belgium	-0.289	-2.16	0.08	4.65	1.99
Canada	-0.390	-3.06	0.15	9.37	2.02
Czech	-0.028	-0.22	0.001	0.078	1.8
Denmark	-0.409	-3.24	0.17	10.48	2.05
EU	-0.469	-3.79	0.21	14.35	2.08
Spain	-0.125	-0.887	0.05	0.786	2.11
Finland	0.356	2.56	0.111	6.55	1.91
France	0.082	0.599	0.007	0.359	1.82
Germany	-0.459	-3.38	0.180	11.39	1.88
GRBritain	0.166	1.21	0.027	1.457	1.99
Ireland	-0.376	-2.80	0.131	7.857	1.69
Italy	-0.132	-0.931	0.016	0.867	1.97
Japan	-0.535	-4.425	0.310	22.49	2.08
Luxumberg	-0.058	-0.425	0.003	0.181	2.01
Mexico	-0.387	-3.00	0.148	9.006	2.22
Netherland	-0.515	-3.82	0.222	14.6	2.1
Norway	-0.678	-6.43	0.442	4.32	2.2
NZealand	-0.647	-6.34	0.436	40.23	1.91
Portugal	-0.529	-4.55	0.289	20.71	2.3
Sweden	-0.292	-2.20	0.085	4.842	1.95
USA	-0.459	-3.11	0.157	9.685	1.99

The New Keynesian analysis introduces market imperfection to suggest why the aggregate supply is upward-sloping but not as horizontal as suggested by Keynes (Blanchard and Kiyotaki (1987), Manning (1995), Rankin (1992)). Imperfections ultimately results in mark-up behaviour of firms and workers. Most of these market imperfection models treat labour as the only variable input as the plants and machineries cannot be varied in the short run. The simplest form of the market imperfection model contains monopolistic mark up of product prices by firms and similar mark on wage rates by the unions.

When setting the prices (*P*) of commodities firms mark up (θ) over the cost of labour (*W*). Real wage rate conscious workers mark up (γ) over the price. Thus price and wage rates and mark ups and imperfections is often discussed in terms of equations (1)-(6).

$$P_t = (1+\theta)W_t \tag{1}$$

The firms can charge higher mark up if the actual aggregate demand is higher than the trend and lower if the actual unemployment is higher than the natural rate of unemployment. Unions (or workers) care for real wages. They also charge a mark-up over the expected price while negotiating the wage rate from the employer.

$$W_t = (1+\gamma)P_t^e \tag{2}$$

Combining (1) and (2) generates the process of a wage price spiral:

$$P_t = (1+\theta)(1+\gamma)P_t^e \tag{3}$$

Dividing both sides of (3) by P_{t-1} and defining $(1+\pi_t) = \frac{P_t}{P_{t-1}}$, the equation (3) can be written as $(1+\pi_t) = (1+\theta)(1+\gamma)(1+\pi_t^e)$. Using the law of small numbers, this can be approximated by $\pi_t = \pi_t^e + \theta + \gamma$. Both type of mark-ups, and, are normally higher in boom periods and lower during the recession (Burda and Wyplosz (2002 p. 287):

$$\theta + \gamma = a(y_t - \bar{y}) = -b(u_t - \bar{u}) \tag{4}$$

where the term $\theta + \gamma$ are the sum of the mark ups charged by the unions and firms, y is the actual output and $\bar{y}$ is the trend output, thus the term $(y_t - \bar{y})$ reflects the deviation of output from the trend, $(u_t - \bar{u})$ reflects how the actual unemployment rate differs from the natural rate of unemployment. The parameters α and b are positive.

The equation (3) includes only the labour cost. All sorts of non-labour costs in the economy such as an increase in oil prices, increase in the prices of raw materials, increase in the interest rate or the cost of capital are taken by the aggregate supply shock. Then the aggregate supply function or the Phillips curve becomes:

$$\pi_t = \bar{\pi} + \begin{Bmatrix} a(y-\bar{y}) \\ or \\ -b(u-\bar{u}) \end{Bmatrix} + s \tag{4}$$

The short run dynamics of trade-off between inflation and unemployment are given by the expectation augmented Phillips' curve. In case of an adaptive expectation

$$\pi_t - \pi_{t-1} = -b(u_t - u_n) \tag{5}$$

where π_t is inflation rate; u_t is actual unemployment rate; u_n natural rate of unemployment. In terms of unemployment the relation between unemployment and inflation can be written as

$$u_t = u_n - \alpha\left(\pi_t - \pi^e\right) \tag{6}$$

Policy makers may reduce unemployment rate below its natural rate in the short run at the cost of higher inflation rate but the economy moves back to the natural rate of unemployment once workers are able to make more realistic expectation of rise in the price level in their wage contract. For instance suppose the economy is at point a in the beginning and government wants to reduce unemployment rate below the natural rate, u_n, by using expansionary policy which creates extra demand for labour and reduces the unemployment rate. Overtime, however, workers learn that prices have increased. Their expectation of inflation rises. Phillips curve shifts out and becomes vertical without any real impacts in the output and employment.

A PANEL DATA MODEL OF UNEMPLOYMENT-INFLATION TRADE-OFF AMONG OECD COUNTRIES

Blanchflower and Oswald (1994), Nickell (1998), Phelps and Zoega (1998) and Madsen (1998) are the most recent studies about the unemployment-inflation trade-off among OECD economies. Madsen (1998) tests general equilibrium models of Phelps (1994) Layard and Nickell (1986) and Sarantis (1993) for 22 OECD economies in terms of structural demand and supply side variables. These include direct and indirect taxes and benefit ratios, government spending, world interest rate and exchange rate mark-ups, import and export prices, proportion of population of age 20 to 24. Their database is constructed collecting information from the OECD, the IMF, the World Bank and the other international agencies. Cross (1988) includes about 21 studies looking at hystereris hypothesis of unemployment in European economies. Blanchflower and Oswald (1994) estimate wage curve for Britain and US, Canada, Korea and Australia. Study here is less ambitious than these studies and focuses on two types of estimates. The first set of estimates are country specific, where it is investigated whether unemployment inflation trade-off exists for 24 economies taking only one individual country at a time. The second set of estimation is based on the panel data regression which is a more appropriate econometric technique to process information on unemployment rate and inflation across countries over time. It allows us to decompose country specific and time specific factors that influence the rate of unemployment as provided by the expectation augmented Phillips curve in (6). In a standard balanced panel data model the major emphasis lies in splitting total variation within a group and between the groups over time (Hendry (1993), Maddala (2001: chapter 15)). Using subscript i, t to variable to refer to individual and time periods respectively this model can be written as:

$$u_{i,t} = \beta_0 + \beta_1 \pi_{i,t} + e_{i,t} \tag{7}$$

where $u_{i,t}$ is the unemployment rate in country i, $\pi_{i,t}$ is the inflation rate in country i, β_0 and β_1 are the unknown parameters that show relationship between unemployment rate and inflation that need to be estimated using the data series on $u_{i,t}$ and $\pi_{i,t}$. Under the Phillips curve phenomenon we expect β_0 to be positive and β_1 to be negative. The final term $e_{i,t}$ is assumed to be normally, independently and identically distributed random error term with a zero mean but with different variances from one country to another, $e_{i,t} \sim N\left(0, \sigma_i^2\right)$.

The total variation in the unemployment rate can be decomposed into individual and country specific effects as:

$$\beta_{1,OLS} = \frac{\sum_i \sum_t \left(\pi_{i,t} - \bar{\pi}\right)\left(u_{i,t} - \bar{u}\right)}{\sum_i \sum_t \left(\pi_{i,t} - \bar{\pi}\right)^2} = \frac{t_{xy}}{t_{xx}} \tag{8}$$

$$t_{xy} = \sum_i \sum_t \left(\pi_{i,t} - \bar{\pi}\right)\left(u_{i,t} - \bar{u}\right) = \sum_i \sum_t \left(\pi_{i,t} - \bar{\pi}_i + \bar{\pi}_i - \bar{\pi}\right)\left(u_{i,t} - \bar{u}_i + \bar{u}_i - \bar{u}\right)$$

$$= \sum_i \sum_t \left(\left(\pi_{i,t} - \bar{\pi}_i\right)\left(u_{i,t} - \bar{u}_i\right)\right) + T\sum_i \left(\bar{\pi}_i - \bar{\pi}\right)\left(\bar{u}_i - \bar{u}\right) = W_{xy} + b_{xy} \tag{9}$$

Between group effect

$$\hat{\beta}_b = \frac{\sum_t \left(\pi_{i,t} - \bar{\pi}\right)\left(u_{i,t} - \bar{u}\right)}{\sum_t \left(\pi_{i,t} - \bar{\pi}\right)^2} = \frac{b_{xy}}{b_{xx}} \tag{10}$$

Within group effect

$$\hat{\beta}_W = \frac{\sum_i \left(\pi_{i,t} - \bar{\pi}_t\right)\left(u_{i,t} - \bar{u}_t\right)}{\sum_i \left(\pi_{i,t} - \bar{\pi}_t\right)^2} = \frac{W_{xy}}{W_{xx}} \tag{11}$$

$$t_{xx}\beta_{OLS} = t_{xy} = W_{xy} + b_{xy} = \hat{\beta}_W \frac{W_{xx}}{W_{xx} + b_{xx}} + \hat{\beta}_W \frac{b_{xx}}{W_{xx} + b_{xx}} \tag{12}$$

Not all variation in unemployment can be expected to be explained by the rate of inflation even when the Phillips curve hypothesis holds. Other country specific factors are important to be considered, are often analysed, introducing a dummy variable. It is the simplest method of isolating individual or time specific effect in such a regression model. All observations, spanning over i and T dimensions, are stacked together for aggregate relationship but a dummy variable is introduced to pick individual specific or time specific effects.

$$u_{i,t} = \alpha_{1,1} D_{1,i} + \alpha_{1,2} D_{2,i} + .. + \alpha_{1,m} D_{m,i} + \alpha_{1,i} \pi_{i,t} + e_{i,t} \tag{13}$$

Where $D_{1,i} = \left[\begin{array}{l} 1 = if \ \ country \ \ i = 1 \\ 0 \ \ otherwise \end{array} \right.$

The individual effects are picked up by the dummy variable $D_{m,i}$. If there are i-groups, there will be i dummy variables to represent specific effects of each of these groups. The coefficients of each of these dummy variables represent the group specific effect relative to a comparison group. After the static panel, we test a simple dynamic panel which includes a lagged dependent variable term to capture dynamics.

$$u_{i,t} = \beta_0 + \beta_1 \pi_{i,t} + \gamma_1 u_{i,t-1} + e_{i,t} \tag{14}$$

The OX-GiveWin-PcGive software (Doornik and Hendry (2003)), was used to estimate the coefficients. It has user friendly menu and batch file options for computing static or dynamic panel data models using OLS, LSDV, GLS, Maximum Likelihood and GMM estimators. Since errors have different variance across individual countries the model is corrected for heteroscedasticity and autocorrelation.

DATA SET AND ANALYSIS OF RESULTS

The data set for this study is obtained from the macro economic time series database located at the Manchester Information and Associated Services, MIMAS *(www.mimas.ac.uk)*. This dataset was for 23 OECD countries (including the EU aggregates) form 1988:1 to 2002:1 before EU expansion to 25 countries. As shown in Charts in the appendix the data shows a significant variation across OECD countries for both inflation and unemployment rates. Then cross section and time series data are pooled by stacking observations of one country over another and introducing a dummy variable to identify observations for a particular economy. The results of estimation obtained using PCGive are presented in Tables 6 and Table 7.

A number of points can be observed from the results from the static panel data model presented in Table 6. First there is a negative and significant relationship between the unemployment rate and inflation in the pooled data set. This supports the hypothesis underlying a standard Phillips curve which contrasts findings for individual countries. Secondly, the country specific factors are important in explaining variation in the unemployment rates. These factors can be analysed in terms of four theories of unemployment as done in the next section. These help to explain why the EU economies have higher rates of unemployment compared to the US economy. The model can explain only about 77 percent of the variation when regressed on levels and only about 8 percent when in the first difference of unemployment series.

Estimates of a dynamic panel data model, presented in Table 7, explain variation in unemployment and inflation across OECD economies better than the static panel data model presented in Table 6. The overall explanatory power of the model improves even when we introduce just one lag for the dependent variable in estimation. First, the model explains about 71 percent of the total variation in unemployment rate. Secondly, it shows how unemployment is a persistent process. There is, however, some concern about autoregressive model in the literature as these models can explain everything at every time (Phelps and Zeoga (1988) and Nickell (1988)).

Table 6

Results from a Static Panel Data Model (OLS Estimation)

	Determinants of unemployment rate in the OECD economies				*Determinant of the first difference of unemployment in the OECD economies*			
	Coefficient	*Std.Error*	*t-value*	*t-prob*	*Coefficient*	*Std.Error*	*t-value*	*t-prob*
Inflation	-0.006	0.006	-0.917	0.359	-0.029	0.015	-2.000	0.045
Constant	7.982	0.005	1639.000	0.000	0.010	0.011	0.928	0.354
Australia	-3.946	0.006	-708.000	0.000	-0.060	0.013	-4.740	0.000
Austria	3.880	0.005	834.000	0.000	0.113	0.011	10.600	0.000
Belgium	0.905	0.005	184.000	0.000	-0.065	0.011	-5.740	0.000
Canada	-5.193	0.006	-912.000	0.000	-0.111	0.013	-8.500	0.000
Czech	0.741	0.004	207.000	0.000	0.043	0.008	5.250	0.000
Denmark	1.172	0.005	231.000	0.000	0.032	0.012	2.770	0.006
EU	10.663	0.004	2451.000	0.000	0.088	0.010	8.840	0.000
Spain	2.327	0.006	407.000	0.000	-0.082	0.013	-6.270	0.000
Finland	2.596	0.005	504.000	0.000	-0.013	0.012	-1.090	0.276
France	-1.666	0.004	-374.000	0.000	-0.055	0.010	-5.360	0.000
Germany	-1.575	0.004	-354.000	0.000	-0.066	0.010	-6.470	0.000
GRBritain	3.184	0.004	743.000	0.000	0.011	0.010	1.130	0.257
Ireland	3.160	0.005	593.000	0.000	0.074	0.012	6.040	0.000
Italy	-4.738	0.007	-685.000	0.000	-0.087	0.016	-5.500	0.000
Japan	-5.640	0.003	-1614.000	0.000	-0.059	0.008	-7.360	0.000
Luxemburg	-4.573	0.012	-376.000	0.000	0.077	0.028	2.770	0.006
Mexico	-2.628	0.021	-125.000	0.000	-0.095	0.048	-1.970	0.049
Netherland	-3.476	0.005	-669.000	0.000	0.023	0.012	1.980	0.048
Norway	-0.637	0.005	-119.000	0.000	0.009	0.012	0.742	0.458
NZealand	-2.711	0.004	-708.000	0.000	-0.027	0.009	-3.100	0.002
Portugal	-2.732	0.007	-415.000	0.000	-0.020	0.015	-1.340	0.182
Sweden	-2.468	0.004	-677.000	0.000	0.024	0.008	2.870	0.004
USA					Base country			
R^2	0.775042					R^2	0.072053	
RSS	5283.359					RSS	843.3724	
TSS	23485.94					TSS	908.8584	
no. of observations		1310						
no. of parameters		24						
Number of individuals		23						

Higher unemployment in the previous period causes the unemployment rate to be higher even during this period. Thirdly, the country specific effects noticed in the static panel model appear even strongly in the dynamic panel model and it shows that the time specific effect to be less important than country specific effects. On the basis of the above empirical observations variation in the unemployment rates cannot be explained unless one takes account of the country specific factors.

Table 7
Unemployment rate and Inflation: Results from the Dynamic Panel Estimation from the OECD economies (GMM estimations)

	Coefficient	*Standard Error*	*t-value*	*t-prob*
Unemp(-1)	0.3947	0.1049	3.7600	0.0000
Time(-1)	0.0334	0.0032	10.3000	0.0000
Australia	-0.1658	0.0112	-14.7000	0.0000
Austria	0.1740	0.0156	11.1000	0.0000
Belgium	0.1706	0.0171	9.9600	0.0000
Canada	0.0262	0.0045	5.7800	0.0000
Che	0.2357	0.0221	10.7000	0.0000
Denmark	0.0839	0.0143	5.8900	0.0000
EU	-0.1230	0.0079	-15.6000	0.0000
Spain	-0.1886	0.0178	-10.6000	0.0000
Finland	0.0036	0.0106	0.3380	0.7350
France	0.0451	0.0117	3.8600	0.0000
Germany	0.0368	0.0063	5.8300	0.0000
Great Britain	-0.0716	0.0132	-5.4100	0.0000
Ireland	0.0443	0.0254	1.7400	0.0820
Italy	-0.2162	0.0156	-13.9000	0.0000
Japan	0.5464	0.0612	8.9300	0.0000
Luxemburg	0.1478	0.0150	9.8400	0.0000
Mexico	1.2529	0.2865	4.3700	0.0000
Netherlands	0.3800	0.0370	10.3000	0.0000
Norway	-0.0797	0.0051	-15.5000	0.0000
New Zealand	-0.1538	0.0144	-10.6000	0.0000
Portugal	-0.1331	0.0538	-2.4700	0.0130
Sweden	-0.2738	0.0216	-12.7000	0.0000
USA	Base Country			
CPI	1.0005	0.1682	5.9500	0.0000
Constant	1.7581	0.2570	6.8400	0.0000
Sigma	1.266	Singma^2	1.603	
R^2	0.7075527			
RSS	4638.684	TSS	15861.609	
no. of observations	2921 no.	No.of parameters	28	

The above estimates show that Phillips curve phenomenon does not exists for any country when only the Phillips curve is examined only for one individual country and explains only a tiny part of unemployment rate in pooled regression model. The evidence also shows that the unemployment rate is persistent and the country specific factors have dominating influence in it. The natural rate of unemployment is higher in the EU countries than in the United States for country or continent specific reasons[1].

CONCLUSION

Rates of unemployment vary significantly among the OECD economies though the rates of inflation have stabilised at lower rates as a result of inflation targeting policies adopted in recent years. The Phillips curve phenomenon is empirically not significant for an individual OECD economy. The aggregate demand factors, as shown in the aggregate Phillips curve was found to show some trade-off in inflation and unemployment rates in the estimates of a regression model with the quarterly panel data for all OECD economies in 1988:1 to 2002:1. The regression results, however, can explain only a very small part of the variation in the unemployment rates. More country specific supply side and technological factors need to be taken into account to explain persistency of higher rates of unemployment rates in many OECD economies. The classical, frictional unemployment, insider-outsider or the efficiency wage theory of unemployment and creative destruction theories are more relevant in explaining country specific differences in unemployment rates. Countries with more liberal markets such as the US and UK have significantly lower unemployment rates than countries with more rigid labour markets such as Germany, France, Italy or Spain. Many factors may cause such variations. Effective labour market policies require the increased flow of information between employers and employees, transparency in employment rule and regulations, reform in the transfer and benefit system and credibility in economic policy. Training and education programme geared toward innovations and productivity, matching of job between employers and employees, reduction in the cost of job or employee search by means of job data banks can bring efficiency in the labour market and reduce the rate of unemployment.

REFERENCES

Aghevli B.B. (1977), Inflationary Finance and Growth, *Journal of Political Economy,* vol. 85, no.6 pp. 1295-1307.

Bailey M.J. (1956), The Welfare Cost of Inflationary Finance, *Journal of Political Economy,* vol. LXIV No. 2, April, pp. 93-110.

Ball L. (1999), Aggregate Demand and Long-Run Unemployment, *Brookings Paper on Economic Activity,* 2.

Ball L. and D. Romer (1990), Real Rigidities and the Non-Neutrality of Money, *Review of Economic Studies,* 1990 57 183-203.

Ball L., Mankiw G. and D. Romer (1988), "The New Keynesian Economics and Outpput-Inflation Trade-off", *Brookings Papers in Economic Activity,* 1:1-65.

Barro R.J. (1995), Inflation and Economic Growth, *Bank of England Quarterly Bulletin,* vol. 35, no. 2,May, pp. 166-175.

Bean C (1994), European Unemployment: A Survey, *Journal of Economic Perspective,* 32:573-619.

Bianchi and Zoega (1998), Unemployment Persistence: Does the Size of the Shock Matter, *Journal of Applied Econometrics,* 13:283-304 (1998).

Blanchflower D.G. and A. Oswald (1994), Estimating A Wage Curve for Britain, 1973-90. *Economic Journal*, September, 1025-1043. Also Wage Curve, MIT Press.

Blanchard O.J. and L.H. Summers (1986), Hysterisis and the European Unemployment Problem in S.Fischer ed. *Macroeconomic Annual*, NBER.

Blanchard O.J. and Katz L (1997), The Natural Rate of Unemployment, *Journal of Economic Perspective*, 11:51:72.

Blanchard O.J. and Kiyotaki (1987), Monopolistic competition and the effects of aggregate demand, American Economic Review, 77: September, pp 647-66.

Brunner K, A.H. Meltzer and G McGuire (1976), *The Phillips Curve and Labour Markets*, North Holland.

Burda M and C. Wyplosz (B & W hereafter), Macroeconomics: A European Text 3nd edition, Oxford University Press, 2002.

Caballero R.J. and M.L. Hammour (1994), The Cleansing Effect of Recession, *American Economic Review*, 84:1350-68.

Cross R. (1988), *Unemployment, Hysteresis and the Natural Rate Hypothesis*, Basil Blackwell.

Davidson P. (1988), Post Keynesian Employment Analysis and the Macroeconomics of OECD Unemployment, *Economic Journal*, May 817-831.

Dixon Huw (1988), A Simple Model of Imperfect Competition with Walrassian Features in R.Cross ed. *Unemployment, Hysteresis and the Natural Rate Hypothesis*, Basil Blackwell.

Dixon Huw (1988), Controversy: the macroeconomics of unemployment in the OECD, the Economic Journal, 108:779-781, May.

Doornik J.A. and D.F. Hendry (2003), PC-Give Volume I-III, GiveWin Timberlake Consultants Limited, London.

Friedman, M. (1968), The Role of Monetary Policy, *American Economic Review* Vol. LVIII, March No.1.

Fisher, S. (1977), Long-Term Contracts, Rational Expectations, and the Optimal Money Supply Rule, *Journal of Political Economy*, Vol.85, No.1.

Goodhart C. (1989), The Conduct of Monetary Policy, *Economic Journal*, 99, June, pp. 293-346.

Grubb D. (1986), Topics in OECD Phillips Curve, *Economic Journal* 96:55-79.

Hicks, J.R. (1937), Mr. Keynes and the "Classics"; A Suggested Interpretations, *Econometrica* 5:147-159.

Hendry D.F. (1995), *Dynamic Econometrics*, Oxford.

Holly S. and M. Weale (Eds.), *Econometric Modelling: Techniques and Applications*, pp.69-93, the Cambridge University Press, 2000.

Hoon T.H. (2001), Adjustment of wages and Equilibrium Unemployment in a Ricardian global economy, *Journal of International Economics* 54 (2001) 193-209.

Hutchinson M.M. and C.E. Walsh (1998), The Output-Inflation Trade-off and Central Bank Reform: Evidence from New Zealand, *Economic Journal* 108:703-725.

Julius DeAnne (1998), Inflation and growth in a service economy, *Bank of England Quarterly Bulletin*, November, pp. 338-346.

King M. (2004), The Institutions of Monetary Policy, *American Economic Review*, Papers and Proceedings, pp. 94:2:1-13, May.

Kydland, F.E. and Prescott, E.C. (1977), Time to Build and Aggregate Fluctuations. *Econometrica*, 50:pp.1345-1370.

Layard R. and S. Nickell (1986), Unemployment in Britain, *Economica*, 53: S121-69.

Layard R. and S. Nickell (1990), Is Unemployment Lower if Unions Bargain Over Employment?, *Quarterly Journal of Economics*, 3, 773-87.

Layard R.S. Nickell and R. Jackman (1991), *Unemployment*, Oxford University Press.

Lewis Arthur (1954), Economic Development with Unlimited Supply of Labour, *The Manchester School of Economics and Social Studies*, XXII No.2 May.

Lindebeck A. and Snower D.J. (1988), *The Insider-Outsider Theory of Employment and Unemployment*, Cambridge University Press.

Lockwood B. and A. Manning (1989), Dynamic Wage-Employment Bargaining with Employment Adjustment Costs, *Economic Journal* December 1145-1158.

Lockwood B.M. Miller and L Zhang (1998), Designing Monetary Policy when Unemployment Persists, *Economica* (1998) 65 327-45.

Lucas R.E. and L.A. Rapping (1969), Real Wages, Employment and Inflation, *Journal of Political Economy*, vol. 77, issue 5, 721-754.

Maddala, G.S. (2001), *Introduction to Econometrics*, 2nd edition, Wiley

Madsen J.B. (1998), General Equilibrium Macroeconomic Models of Unemployment: Can They Explain the Unemployment Path in OECD? *Economic Journal* 108 May 850-867.

Mankiw G.N. (1985), Small Menu Costs and large Business Cycles: A macroeconomic Model of Monopoly, *Quarterly Journal of Economics*, pp.529-537.

Manning, A. (1995), Development in Labour Market Theory and their Implications for Macroeconomic Policy, *Scottish Journal of Political Economy*, Vol.42, No.3, August.

McDonald I.M and R.M. Solow (1981), Wage Bargaining and Employment, *American Economic Review* Vol.71 No.5, 896:908.

Monetary Policy Committee Bank of England (1999), The Transmission Mechanism of Monetary Policy, *www.bankofengland.co.uk*.

Nickell S. (1998), Unemployment: Questions and Some Answers, *Economic Journal*, 108, 803-816.

Nickell S. and G. Quintini (2003), Nominal Wage Rigidity and the Rate of Inflation, *Economic Journal* 113:490:762-781.

Nickel S. (1990). Unemployment Survey, *Economic Journal*, June, pp 391-439.

Nickell, S. (1990), "Inflation and the UK Labor Market," *Oxford Review of Economic Policy*;6(4) Winter.

OECD (1994), *The OECD Jobs Study: Evidence and Explanations*, Paris, OECD.

Phelps E.S. (1994), *Structural Slumps*, Harvard University Press.

Phelps, Edmund S. (1968), Money-Wage Dynamics and Labor-market Equilibrium, *Journal of Political Economy*, Vol.76, pp. 678-710.

Phelps E.S. and G. Zoega (1998), Natural Rate Theory and OECD Unemployment, *Economic Journal*, 108, 782-801.

Phelps E.S. and J.B. Taylor (1977), Stabilisation Powers of Monetary Policy under Rational Expectations, *Journal of Political Economy*, Vol.85 No. 1, pp. 163-190.

Phillips, A.W., (1958), The Relation Between Unemployment and the Rate of Change of Money Wage Rates in the United Kingdom, 1861-1957, *Economica*, pp.283-299.

Pissarides C.A. (2000), *Equilibrium Unemployment Theory*, MIT Press.

Rankin Neil (1992), Imperfect Competition, Expectations and the Multiple effects of Monetary Growth, *the Economic Journal* 102: 743-753.

Taylor J.B. (1972), Staggered Wage Setting in a Macro Model, *American Economic Review*, 62, pages 1-18.

Sarantis N. (1993), Distribution, Aggregate Demand and Unemployment in the OECD countries, *Economic Journal*, vol. 103 : 459-67.

Sims Christopher A. (1981), Macroeconomics and Reality, Econometrica, 48:1 January, pp. 1-48.

Summers (1988), Should Keynesian Economics Dispense with the Phillips Curve ? in R. Cross ed. *Unemployment, Hysteresis and the Natural Rate Hypothesis*, Basil Blackwell.

Roed K. and T. Zhang (2003), Does Unemployment Compensation Affect Unemployment Duration? *Economic Journal* 113:484:190-206.

Yellen J. L (1984), Efficiency wage models of unemployment, *American Economic Review*, Papers and Proceedings vol.74 No.2, May, pp. 199-205.

NOTES

1. Macroeconomists have proposed many theories to explain why such a natural rate of unemployment exists and varies from one country to another (Mankiw (1988), Dixon (1988), Cross (1988), Phelps and Zeoga (1998), Nickell (1990, 1998), Blanchflower and Oswald (1994), Caballero and Hammour (1994), Manning (1995), Pissarides (2000), Hutchinsion and Walsh (1998)). In the classical model, unemployment is caused by institutional factors such as the minimum wage laws or rule regarding work hours, retirement, tax, benefits and transfers, terms of employment, payment for sickness and family tax credits. There is significant variation across countries in the tax and benefit system and in the flexibility of the labour market (Nickell (1998)). Workers and firms face different constraints in their choices of discrete or continuous work hours and the marginal benefits. Countries with a generous benefit system may generate significant amount of unemployment because such benefit raises the reservation wage of those workers and keeps them away from the labour market.

   The second theory explains unemployment in terms of the frictions in the labour market when firms are in process of to adapting to the new technology. Very elegant models about the creation of new jobs and destruction of old jobs are constructed under creative destruction and job search and mismatch hypotheses (Caballero and Hammour (1994), Pissarides (2000)). Phelps and Zoega (1998) take into account ten different factors for fall in the demand for labour or for the rising trend of the natural rate of unemployment. Namely, external trade shocks, increase in the global real interest rate, increase in the public spending as a share of GDP, slow-down in economic growth, increase in the share of social spending in the GDP, upgrading of educational requirement for jobs. Others point to adjustment problem in the wake of rapid technical progress, increase in energy and oil prices, slow down in productivity, upward pressure in the wage curve either because of expansion in the benefit system or rise in hiring and firing costs, mix of direct and indirect taxes. The natural rate of unemployment hypothesis maintains that above barriers in the efficient functioning of the labour market may cause a rise or fall in employment rate across countries and over time.

Job search and matching processes matter. First, imperfect flow of information means more time for employers with vacant position to find suitable employees and difficulty for applicants to find potential employers. Secondly, it takes time for every new entrant into the job market to get settled in a job. Third, some of the current employees quit their jobs in anticipation of finding a new and better job and are counted as unemployed until they find another job. These frictional features of the labour market are often explained in terms of a model that consists job finding rate (f) of currently unemployed (U) and job separation rates (s) of currently employed (E), both of these rates are influenced by the structure of the labour market. As discussed in Mankiw (1985) a change in the level of unemployment, ΔU, is the difference between job separation and job finding rates $\Delta U = sE - fU$. In a flexible labour market there is a balance between people who quit or are laid off a job and workers who get a new employment. $\Delta U = 0$; $sE = fU$ or $s(L-U) = fU$; $\frac{U}{L} = \frac{s}{s+f}$. Unemployment rate is high in countries with higher separation rates, s and lower for higher job finding rates, f. Government and institutions across OECD economies vary in the effectiveness of intervention for influencing s and f by taking measures such as improving the flow of information between potential employees and employers, providing training for long term unemployed to make them employable. The job matching process by means of creating databases with CVs of potential applicants and vacancies announced by various employers differ. The unemployed have better chances of finding jobs or less need to quit jobs in some countries than in others. Such frictions in the labour market and adjustment process significantly vary across countries. Nickell and Layard (1998) enumerate seven factors that raise frictions or reduce the flexibility of dynamic adjustment between demand and supply of labour. These include the tax wedge (employer social security contribution, consumption taxes), union membership, labour union coverage, the replacement ratio, benefit duration, home owner occupation rate (home ownership prevents mobility (Blanchflower and Oswald (1994)) and co-ordination between employers and employees in wage bargaining and labour market policies. The unemployment rate varies across EU economies since these frictional and labour market rigidity factors differ significantly among them.

The third theory attributes the existence of unemployment to the monopoly powers of the unions and mark-up power of firms. Wage rate and employment levels are settled by bargaining between firms and workers (McDonald and Solow (1981), Lockwood, Miller and Zhang (1998), Lockwood and Manning (1989)) or insider outsider behaviour of unions and their interaction with firms (Lindebeck and Snower (1988), Blanchard and Summers (1986)). Economies vary in mark up prices by firms and mark up of wage rate by unions. Both of these behaviours cause imperfections in the labour market. Institutional factors such as minimum wage, generous unemployment insurance, tax wage, union membership, home ownership, co-ordination between employers and employees cause market imperfection which raise the rigidity in the labour market and imply higher natural rates of unemployment.

The union firm behaviours and the wage negotiation process differ significantly across OECD economies to cause variation in the unemployment rates as observed in Table 1 to 7. Wage bargaining models popularised by Blanchard (1986) and Nickell (1986,1988). McDonald and Solow (1981) that are behind the Eurosclerosis (Hardening of tissues) view of labour market rigidities, had shown how the unemployment rate is determined by the bargaining of workers and firms over the wage rate and the level of employment. Real employment is determined by the interaction of labour demand curve and the union preference. The union of workers actively engages to secure a higher wage rate and employment for their members and incidently create more unemployment for non-union workers. Union member increase probability of retaining job by raising the turnover cost, i.e. cost of hiring and firing and training, to employers while they care less about the prospects of the non-union workers. The fourth theory relates unemployment rate to the efficiency wage. Many firms in the OECD economies pay efficiency wage to their employees. These wage rates are kept slightly higher than the market wage rate in order to reduce the turnover costs or to prevent them from shirking, or to monitor their activities. Employees work more effectively since a higher efficiency wage keeps their morale high. It makes them an impression that the current employers as an ideal one in the entire job market. It also drives away bad applicants and makes less efficient workers less likely to be hired and solves the adverse selection problem. It makes costly to find another job that pays equal amount in case they are caught for shirking. Thus makes them to stick with the current employer. In efficiency wage model by Yellen (1984) the output is a function of employment and effort, $Y = F\left(e(w)N\right)$ where N is the number of employees and ε is effort per worker and w is the real wage rate. Marginal product of labour is equal to real wage rate w^*, $e(w^*)F'\left(e(w^*)N^*\right) = w^*$. Firms do not reduce real wages below w^* because it would reduce productivity of all workers. The efficiency wage, however, creates real wage rigidity, creates the dual labour market and discrimination among observationally distinct groups. This model can explain wide ranging variation of wage rates as well as the unemployment rates across OECD economies.

Unemployment Rates in OECD Economies: 1988:1-2002:1

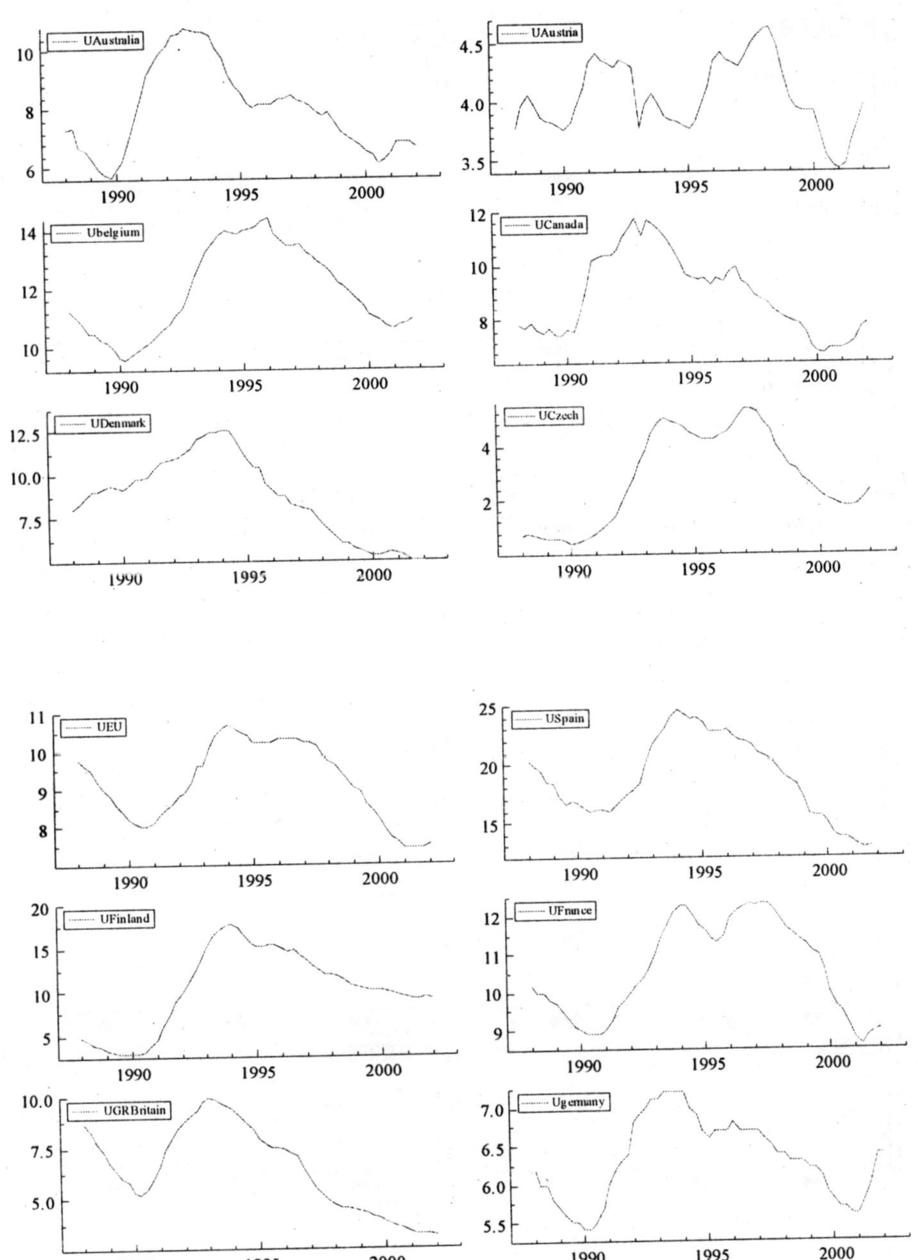

Unemployment Rates in OECD Economies: 1988:1-2002:1

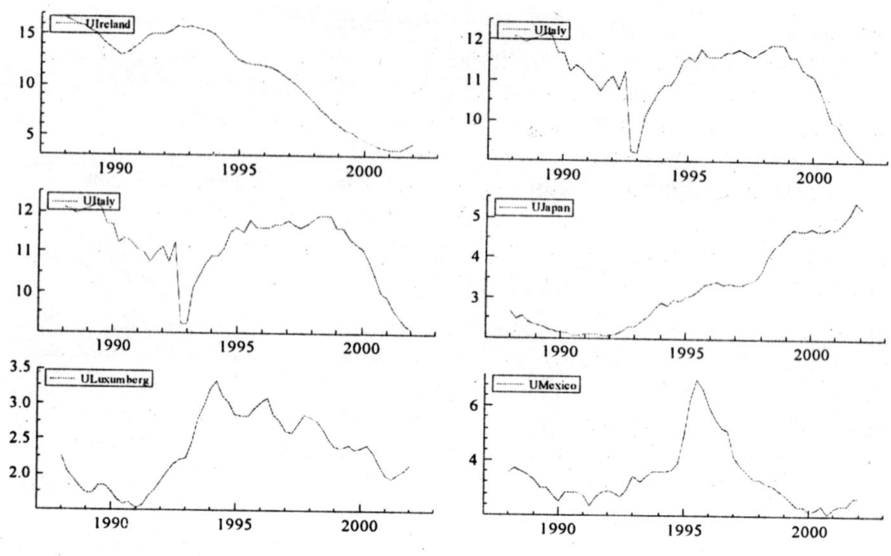

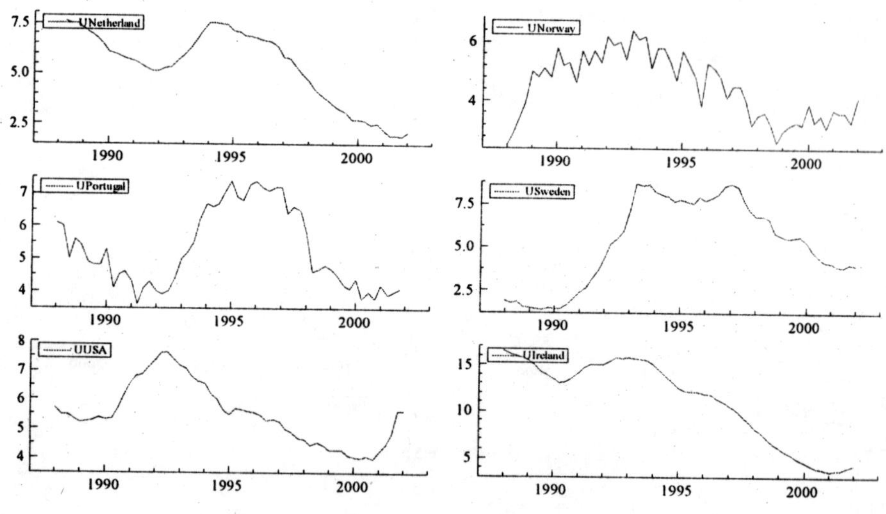

Quarterly Inflation in OECD Economies: 1988:1-2002:1

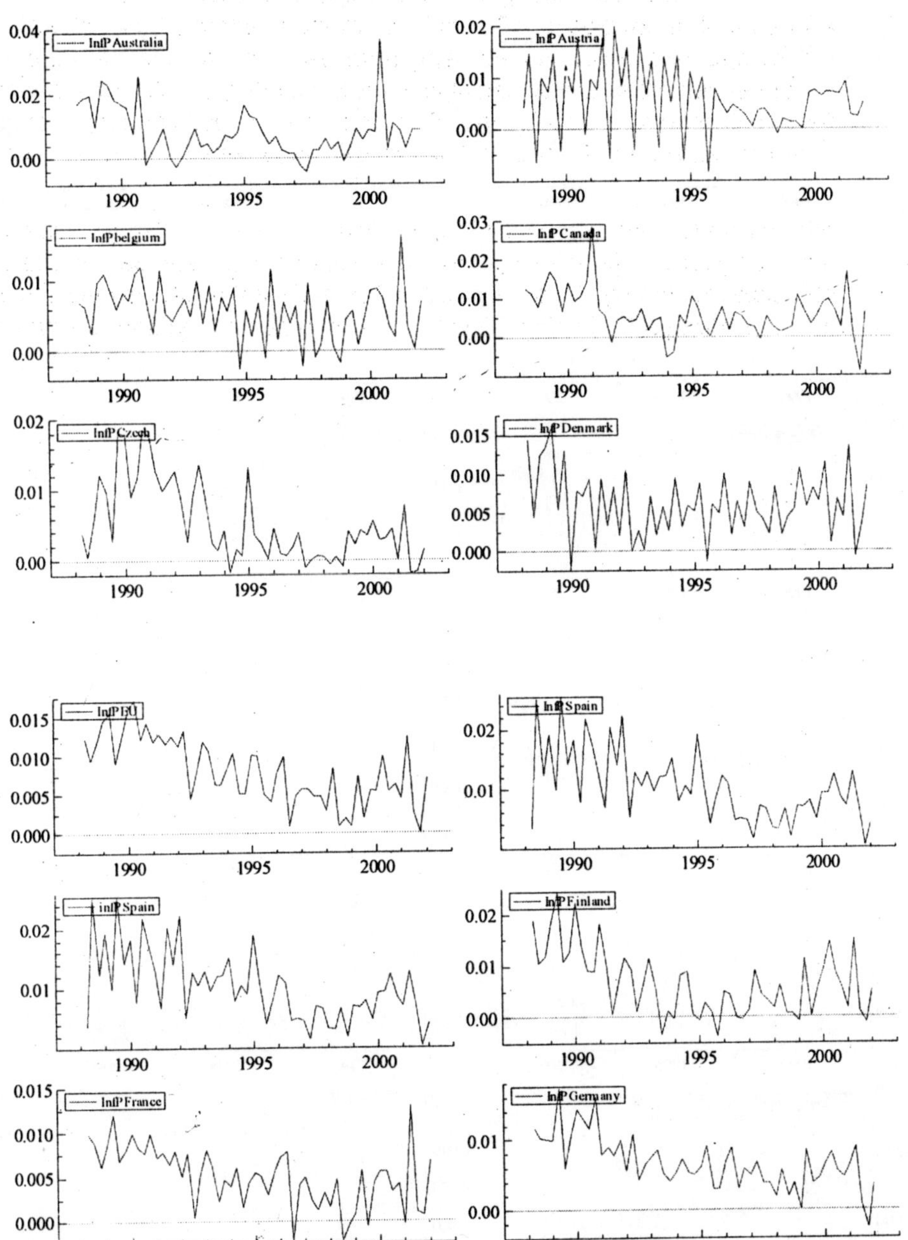

Quarterly Inflation in OECD Economies: 1988:1-2002:1

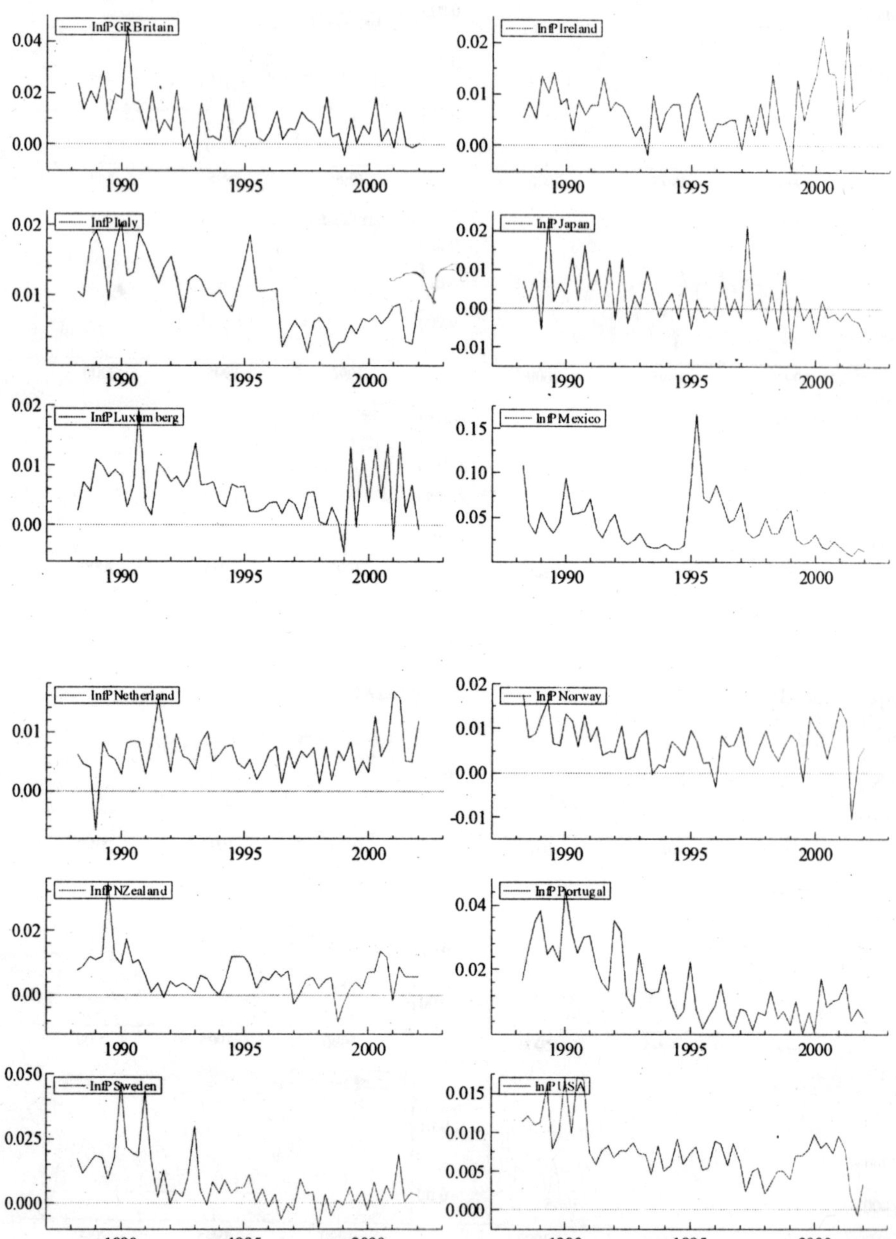

Appendix 2
Impulse Response Analyses in VAR model for OECD Countries
Australia

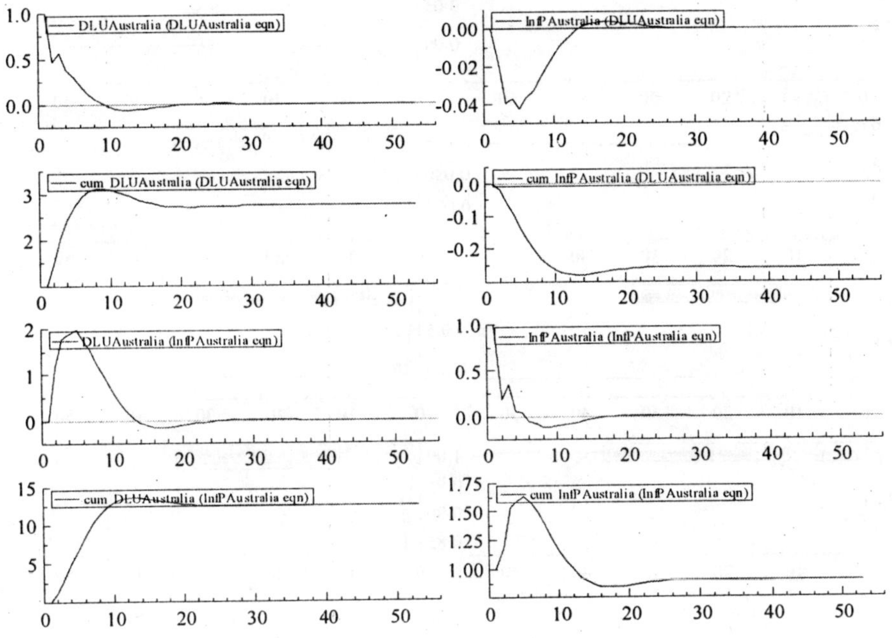

Austria

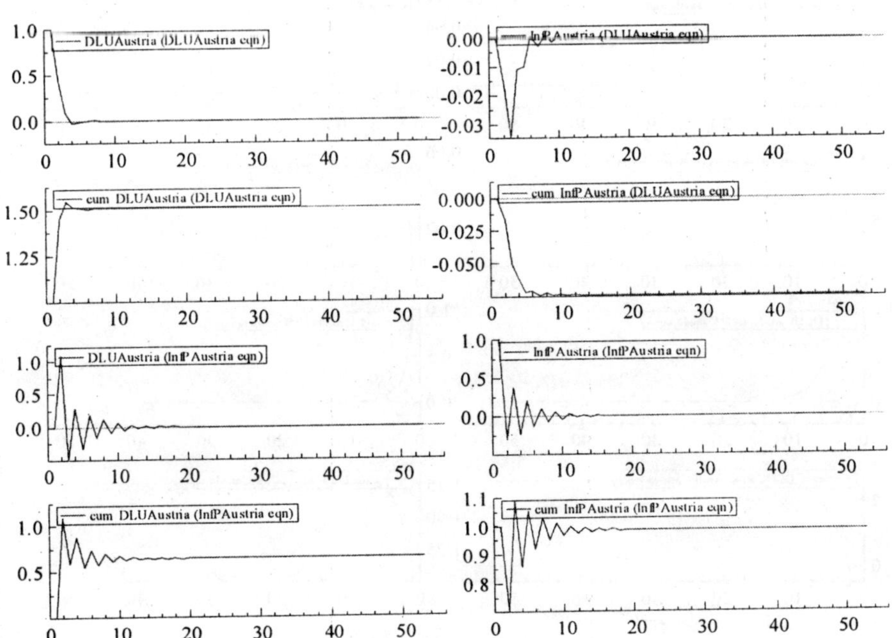

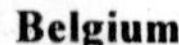
Belgium

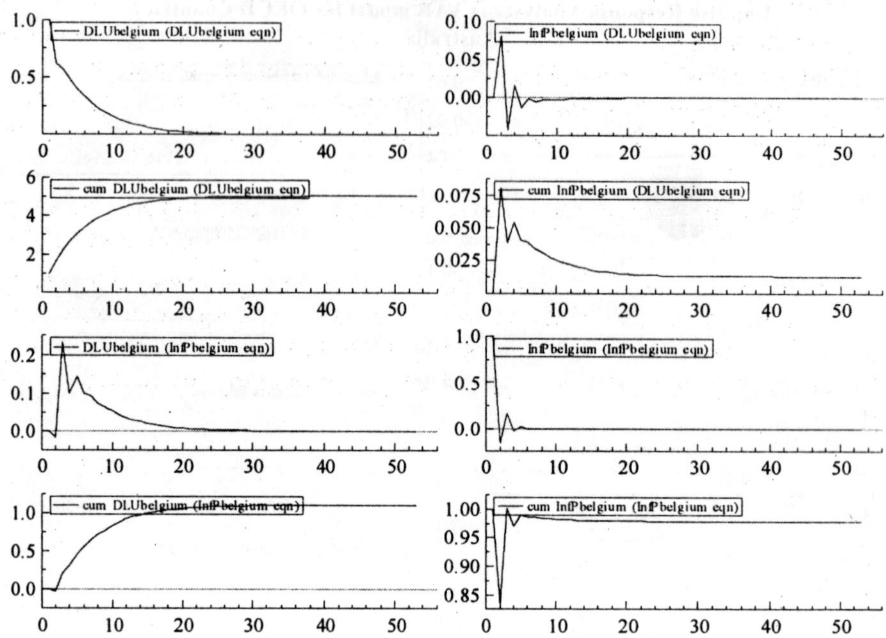
DLUbelgium (DLUbelgium eqn)
lnfPbelgium (DLUbelgium eqn)
cum DLUbelgium (DLUbelgium eqn)
cum InfPbelgium (DLUbelgium eqn)
DLUbelgium (lnfPbelgium eqn)
lnfPbelgium (InfPbelgium eqn)
cum DLUbelgium (InfPbelgium eqn)
cum InfPbelgium (lnfPbelgium eqn)

Canada

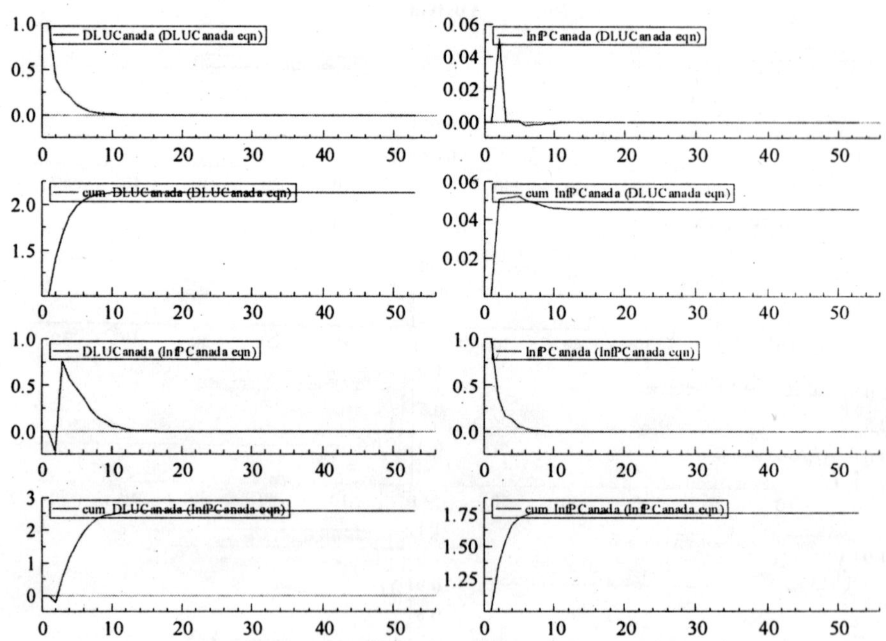
DLUCanada (DLUCanada eqn)
InfPCanada (DLUCanada eqn)
cum DLUCanada (DLUCanada eqn)
cum InfPCanada (DLUCanada eqn)
DLUCanada (lnfPCanada eqn)
lnfPCanada (InfPCanada eqn)
cum DLUCanada (InfPCanada eqn)
cum InfPCanada (lnfPCanada eqn)

Czech Republic

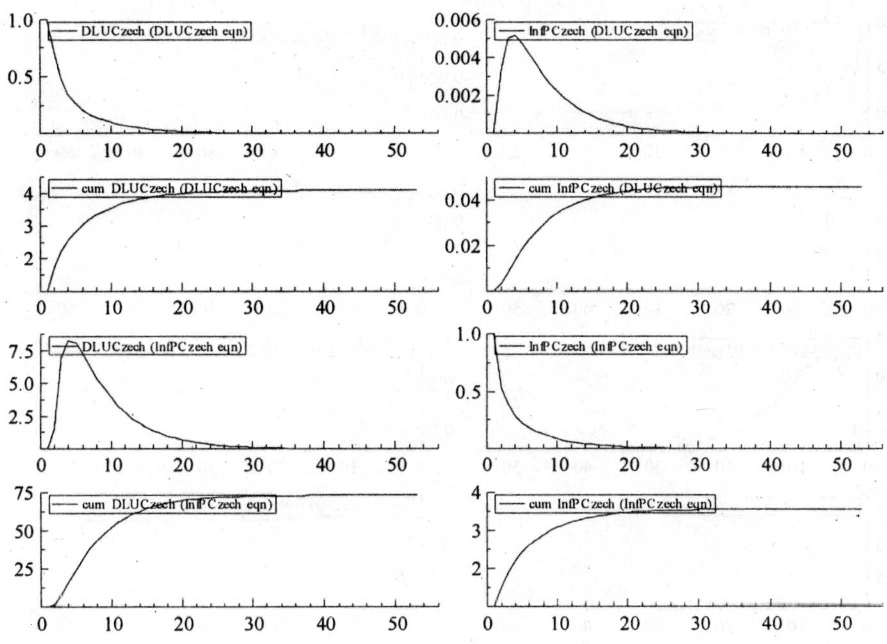

Denmark

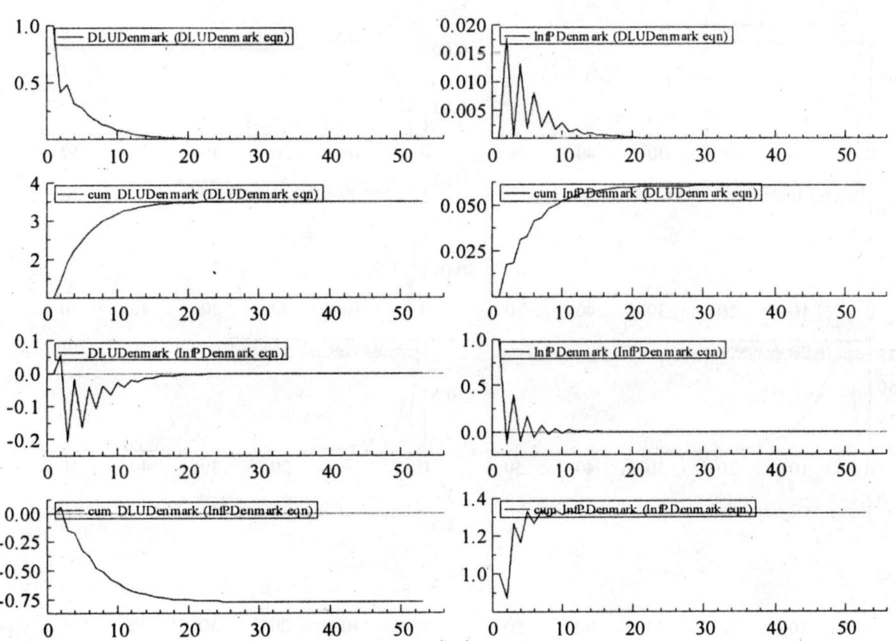

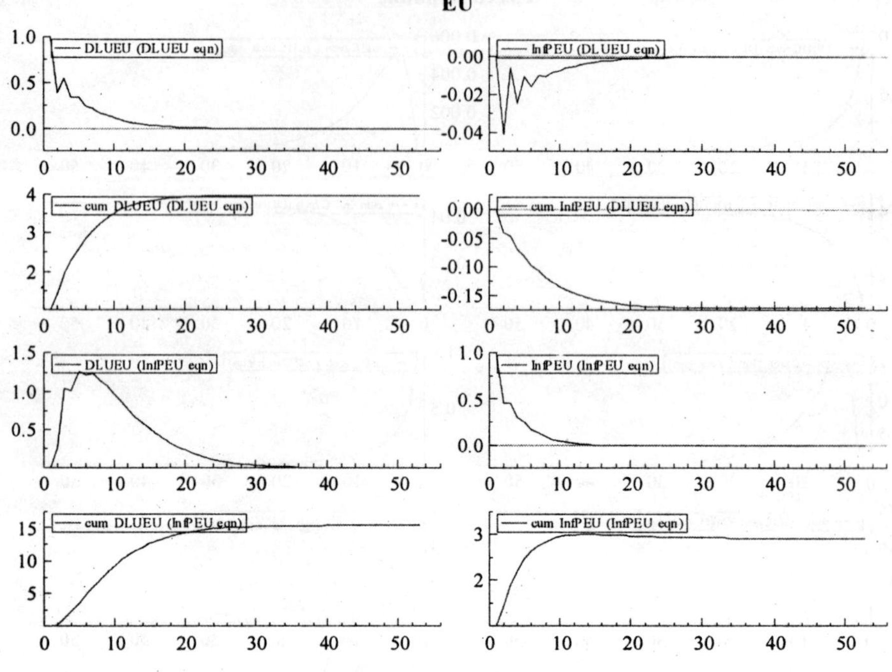
EU
DLUEU (DLUEU eqn)
InfPEU (DLUEU eqn)
cum DLUEU (DLUEU eqn)
cum InfPEU (DLUEU eqn)
DLUEU (InfPEU eqn)
InfPEU (InfPEU eqn)
cum DLUEU (InfPEU eqn)
cum InfPEU (InfPEU eqn)

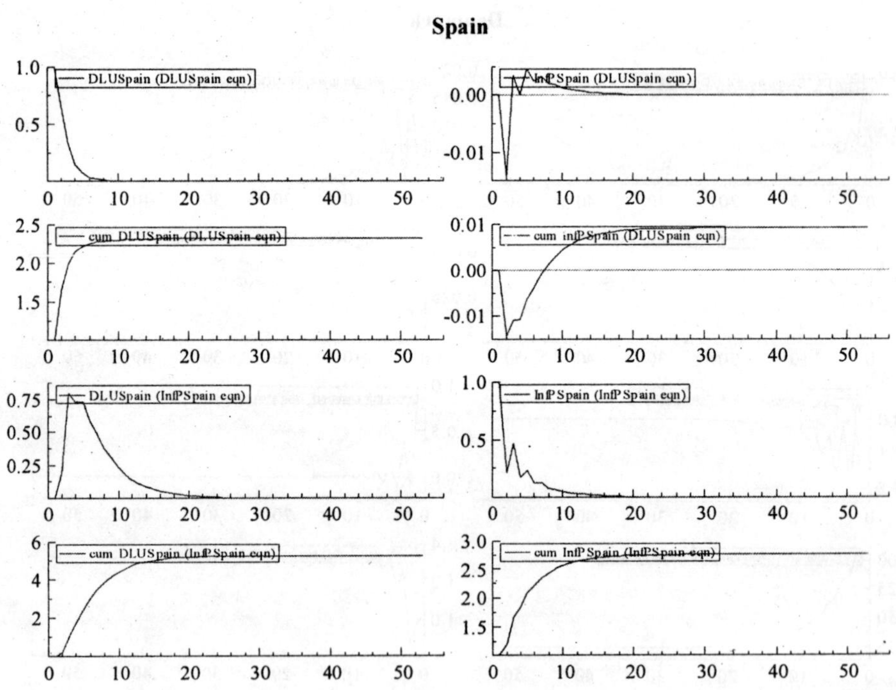
Spain
DLUSpain (DLUSpain eqn)
InfPSpain (DLUSpain eqn)
cum DLUSpain (DLUSpain eqn)
cum InfPSpain (DLUSpain eqn)
DLUSpain (InfPSpain eqn)
InfPSpain (InfPSpain eqn)
cum DLUSpain (InfPSpain eqn)
cum InfPSpain (InfPSpain eqn)

Finland

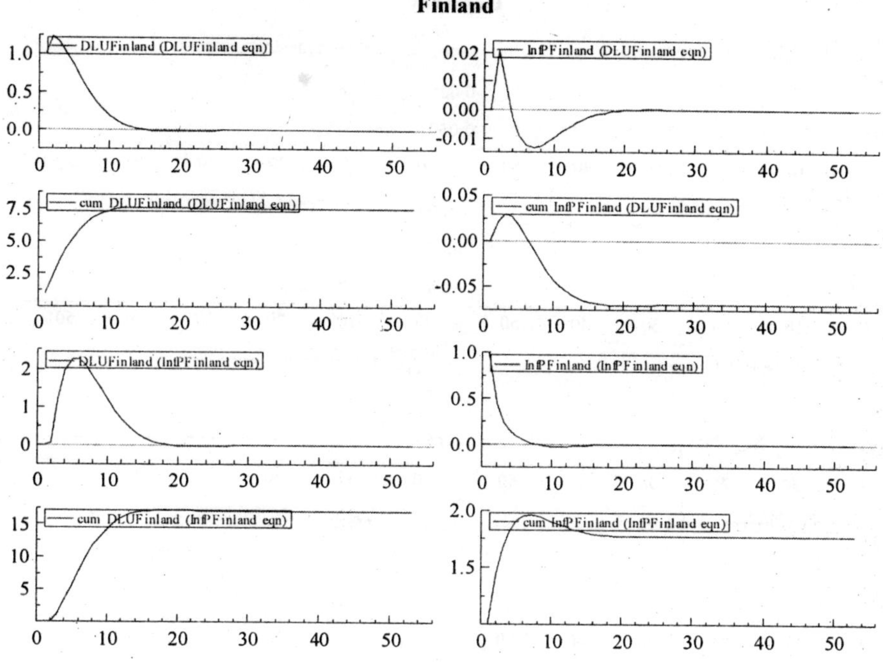

France

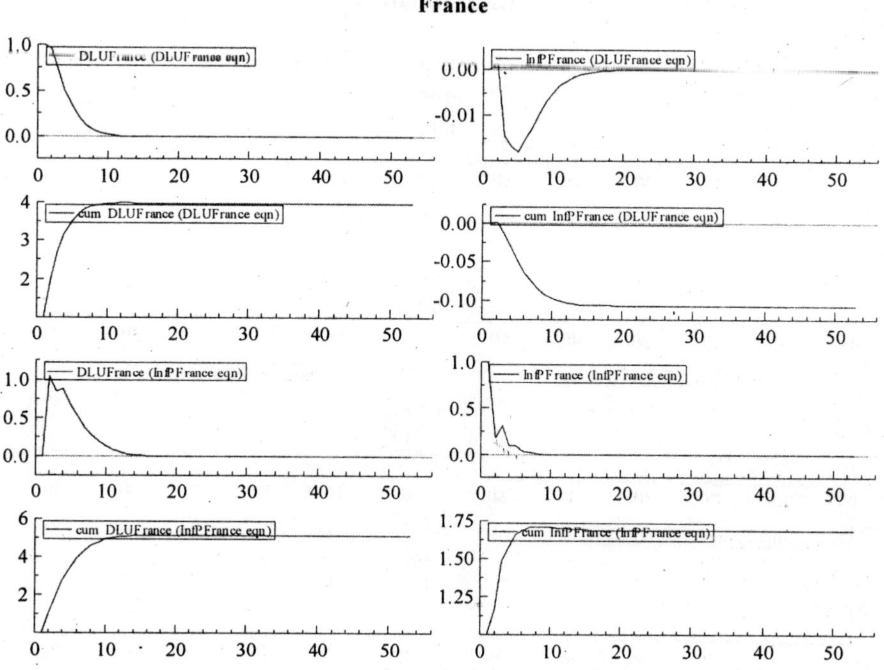

Germany

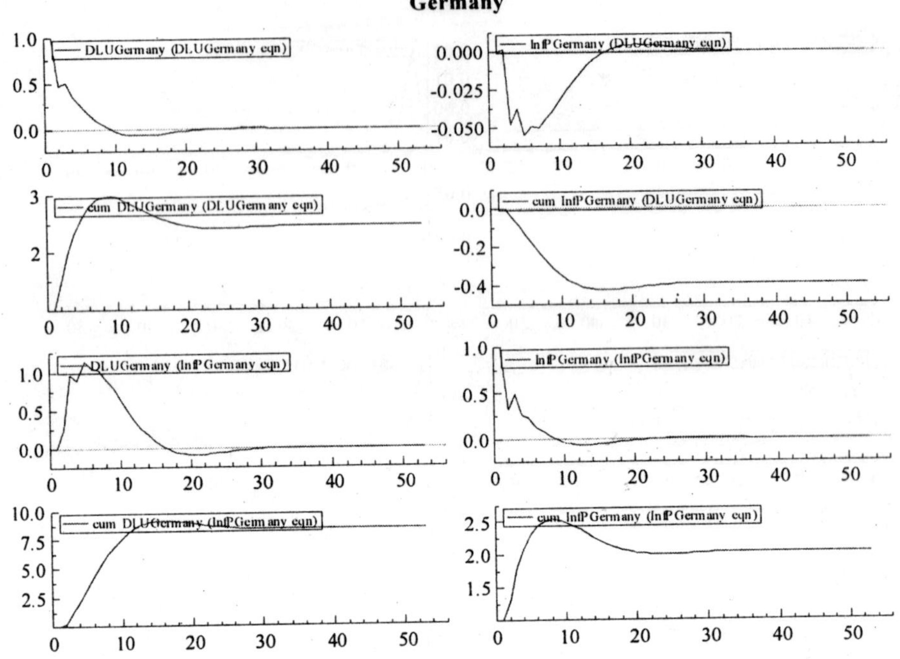

Great Britain

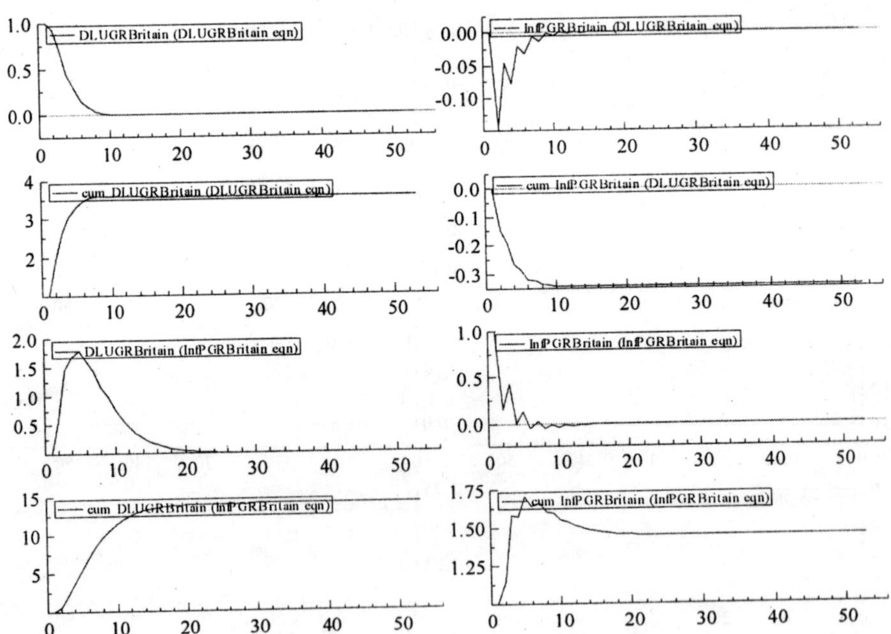

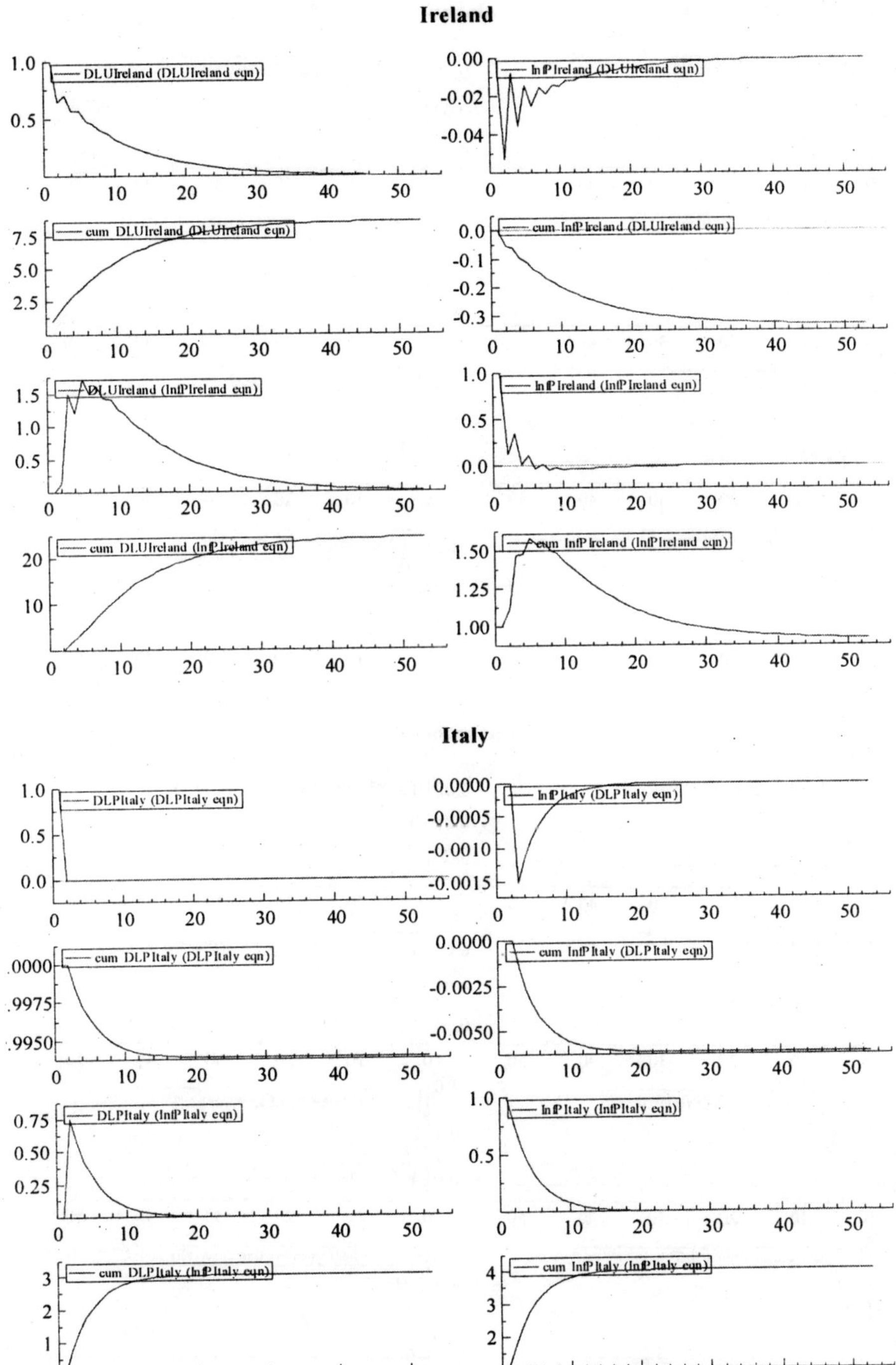
Ireland
DLUIreland (DLUIreland eqn)
InfPIreland (DLUIreland eqn)
cum DLUIreland (DLUIreland eqn)
cum InfPIreland (DLUIreland eqn)
DLUIreland (InfPIreland eqn)
InfPIreland (InfPIreland eqn)
cum DLUIreland (InfPIreland eqn)
cum InfPIreland (InfPIreland eqn)
Italy
DLPItaly (DLPItaly eqn)
InfPItaly (DLPItaly eqn)
cum DLPItaly (DLPItaly eqn)
cum InfPItaly (DLPItaly eqn)
DLPItaly (InfPItaly eqn)
InfPItaly (InfPItaly eqn)
cum DLPItaly (InfPItaly eqn)
cum InfPItaly (InfPItaly eqn)

Japan

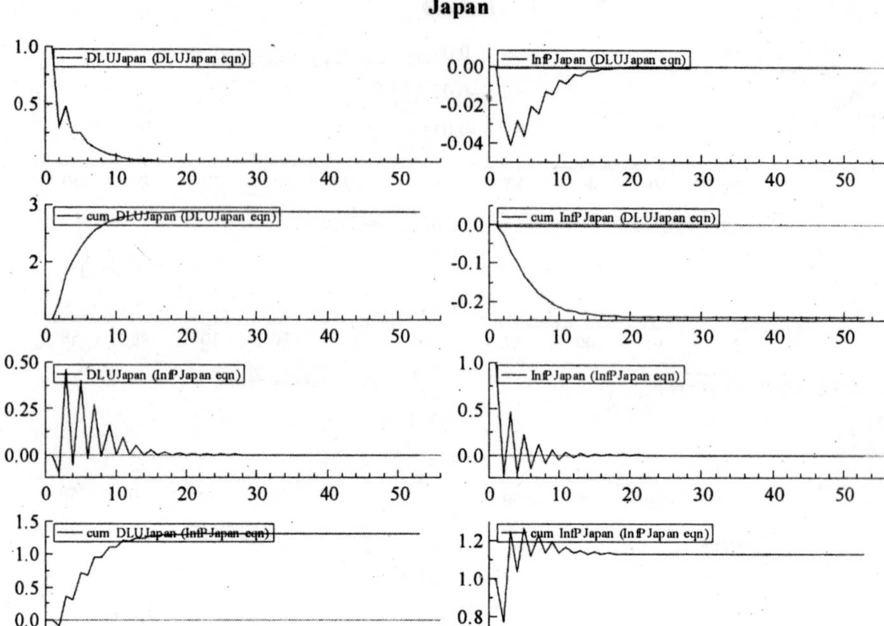

Luxumberg

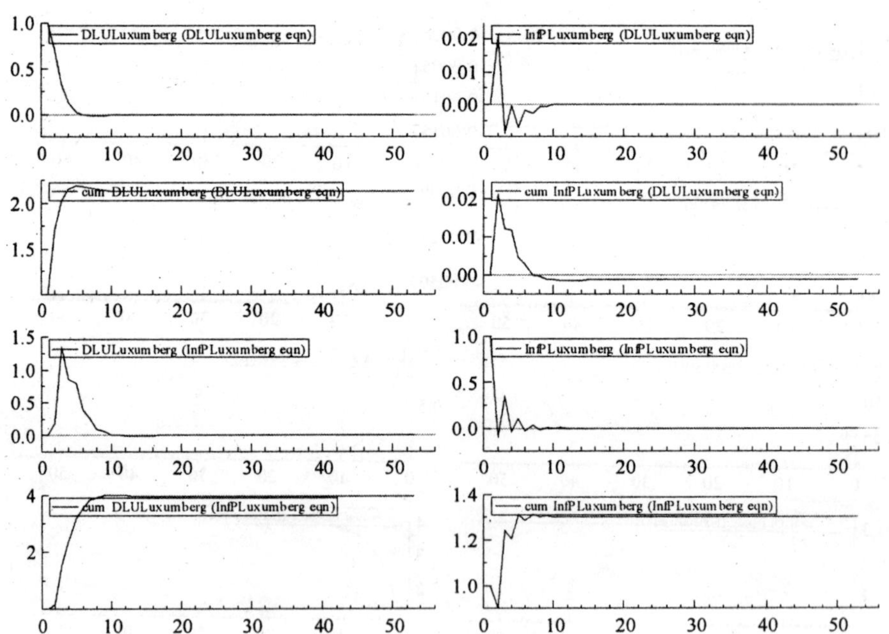

Mexico

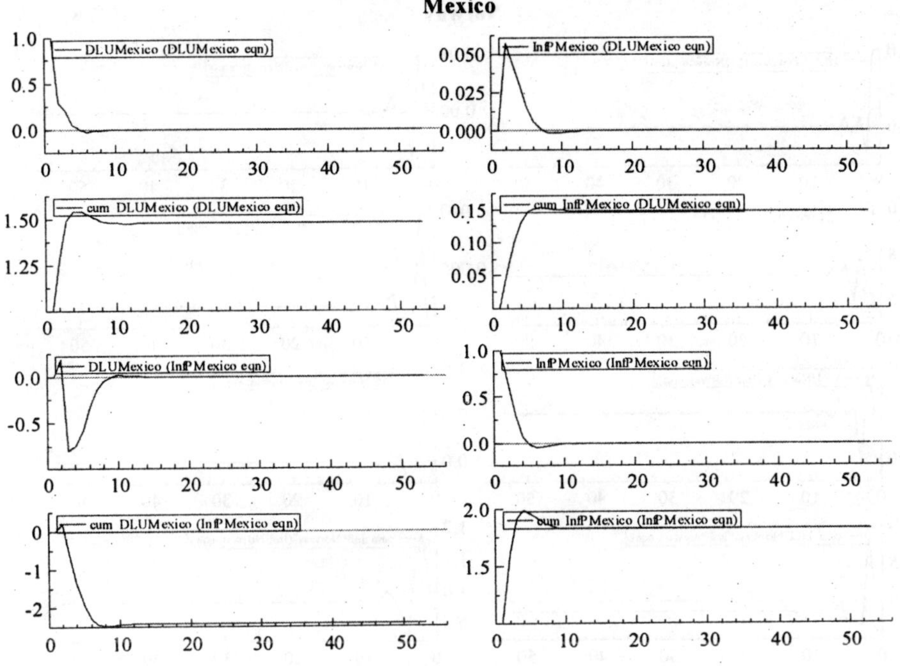

Netherlands

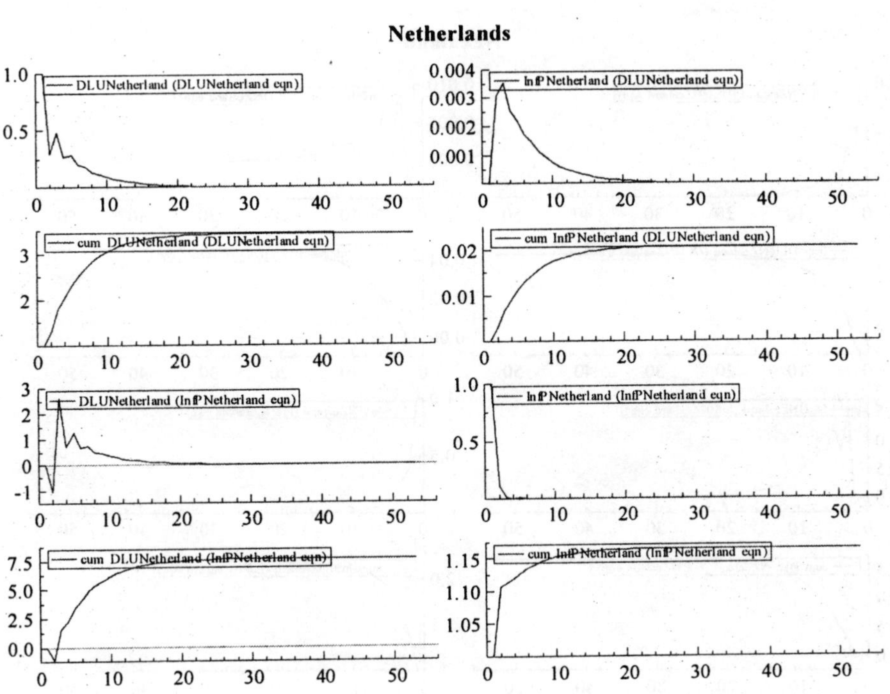

Norway

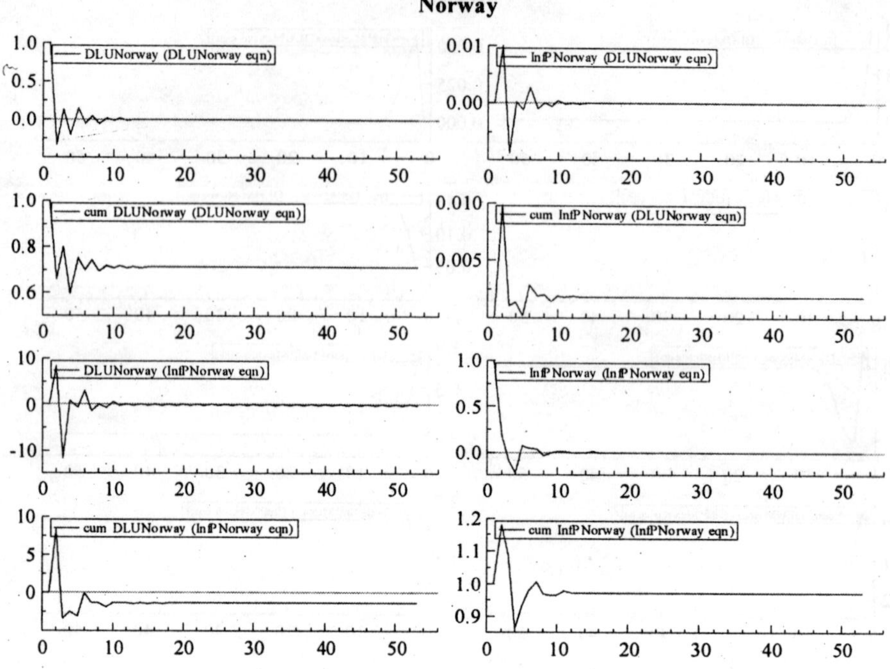

NZealand

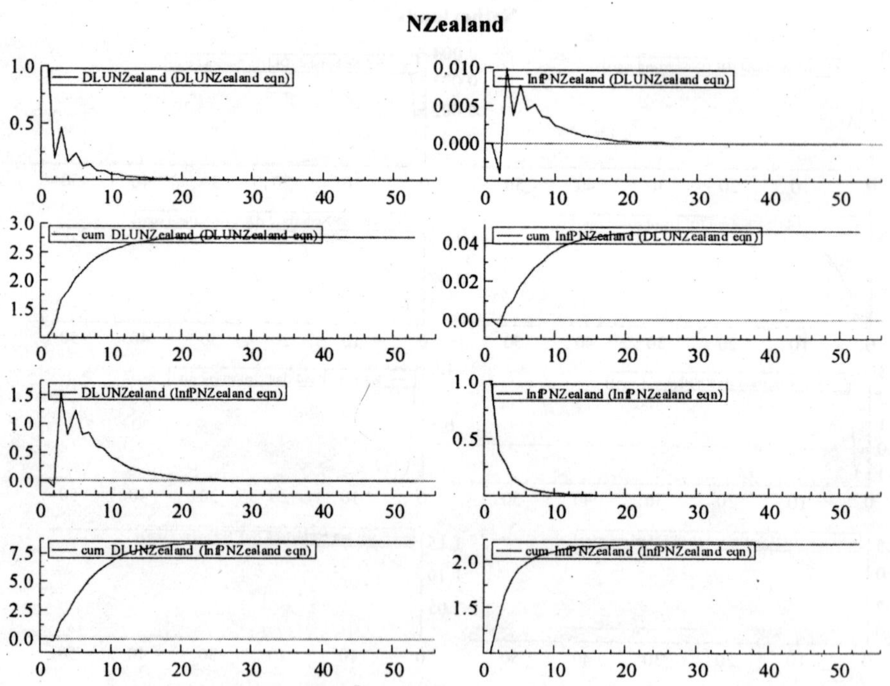

Portugal

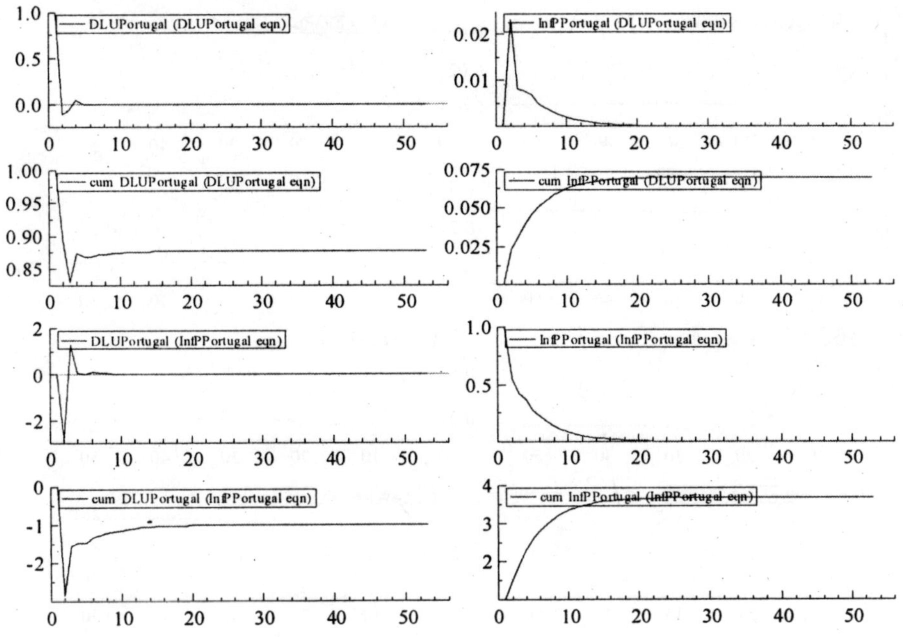
DLUPortugal (DLUPortugal eqn)
InfPPortugal (DLUPortugal eqn)
cum DLUPortugal (DLUPortugal eqn)
cum InfPPortugal (DLUPortugal eqn)
DLUPortugal (InfPPortugal eqn)
InfPPortugal (InfPPortugal eqn)
cum DLUPortugal (InfPPortugal eqn)
cum InfPPortugal (InfPPortugal eqn)

Sweden

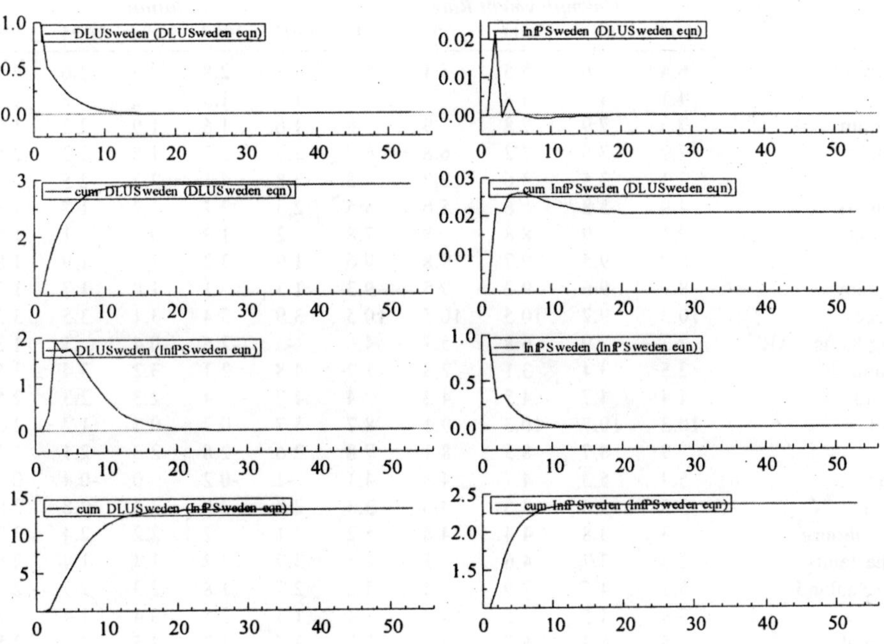
DLUSweden (DLUSweden eqn)
InfPSweden (DLUSweden eqn)
cum DLUSweden (DLUSweden eqn)
cum InfPSweden (DLUSweden eqn)
DLUSweden (InfPSweden eqn)
InfPSweden (InfPSweden eqn)
cum DLUSweden (InfPSweden eqn)
cum InfPSweden (InfPSweden eqn)

USA

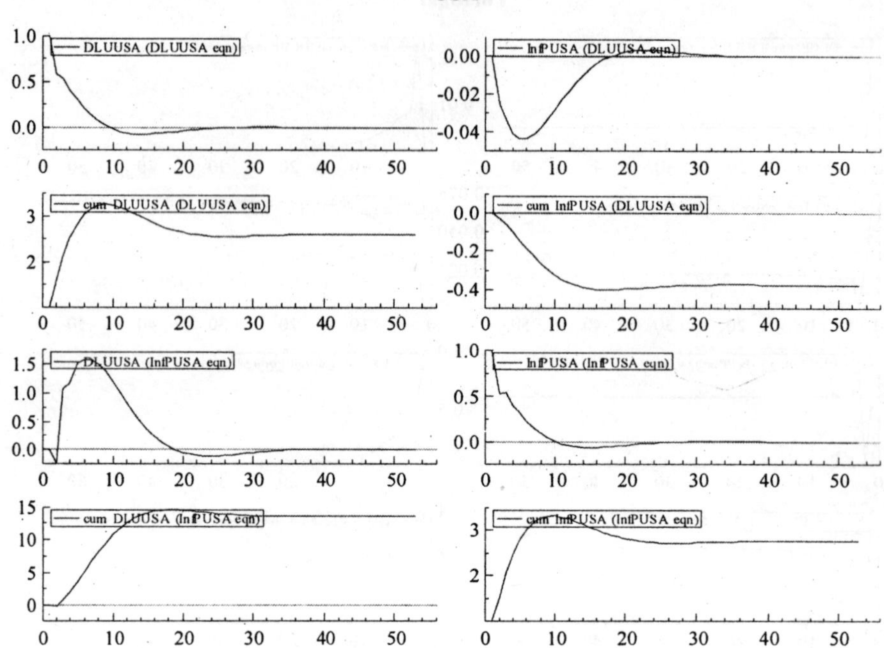

Unemployment rate and Inflation in Advanced Economies in Recent Years, 2002-2006

	Unemployment Rate					*Inflation*				
Country	*2002*	*2003*	*2004*	*2005*	*2006*	*2002*	*2003*	*2004*	*2005*	*2006*
Australia	6.4	6	5.5	5.1	5.1	3	2.8	2.3	2.6	2.7
Austria	4.1	4.3	4.8	5	4.7	1.7	1.3	2	2	1.8
Belgium	7.3	7.9	7.8	7.9	8	1.6	1.5	1.9	2.3	1.9
Canada	7.7	7.6	7.2	6.8	6.7	2.3	2.7	1.8	2.2	2.5
Cyprus	3.1	3.5	3.6	3.2	3	2.8	4.1	2.3	2.5	2.5
Denmark	4.9	5.8	6	5.6	5.5	2.3	2.1	1.2	1.7	1.8
Finland	9.1	9	8.8	8	7.8	2	1.3	0.1	1	1.5
France	8.9	9.5	9.7	9.8	9.6	1.9	2.2	2.3	1.9	1.8
Germany	8.7	9.6	9.2	9.5	9.3	1.3	1	1.8	1.7	1.7
Greece	10.3	9.7	10.5	10.5	10.5	3.9	3.4	3.1	3.5	3.3
Hong Kong SAR	7.3	7.9	6.8	5.7	4.6	-3	-2.6	-0.4	1	1.3
Iceland	2.5	3.4	3.1	2.3	1.7	4.8	2.1	3.2	3.4	3.5
Ireland	4.4	4.7	4.5	4.2	4	4.7	4	2.3	2.3	2.5
Israel	10.3	10.7	10.3	9.1	8.7	5.7	0.7	-0.4	1.2	2.3
Italy	9	8.7	8.5	8.1	7.8	2.6	2.8	2.3	2.1	2
Japan	5.4	5.3	4.7	4.3	4.1	-1	-0.2	0	-0.4	-0.1
Korea	3.3	3.6	3.5	3.6	3.3	2.8	3.5	3.6	2.8	2.9
Luxembourg	3	3.8	4.4	4.8	5.2	2.1	2	2.2	2.4	2.7
Netherlands	2.8	3.7	4.6	5	4.5	3.9	2.2	1.4	1.4	-2.6
New Zealand	5.2	4.7	3.9	4	4.2	2.7	1.8	2.3	2.7	2.7
Norway	3.9	4.5	4.5	4.2	4	1.3	2.5	0.4	1.4	2.1
Portugal	5	6.3	6.7	7.4	7.7	3.7	3.3	2.5	2.3	2.5

Contd....

Country	*Unemployment Rate* 2002	2003	2004	2005	2006	*Inflation* 2002	2003	2004	2005	2006
Singapore	4.4	4.7	4	3.6	3.4	-0.4	0.5	1.7	0.7	1.7
Spain	11.5	11.5	11	9.1	8	3.6	3.1	3.1	3.2	3
Sweden	4	4.9	5.5	5.2	4.9	2	2.3	1.1	0.8	1.8
Switzerland	2.3	3.4	3.5	3.7	3.7	0.6	0.6	0.8	1.3	1.4
Taiwan Province of China	5.2	5	4.4	4.3	4.2	-0.2	-0.3	1.6	2	1.8
United Kingdom	5.2	5	4.8	4.7	4.8	1.3	1.4	1.3	2	1.9
United States	5.8	6	5.5	5.2	5.2	1.6	2.3	2.7	3.1	2.8

International Monetary Fund, World Economic Outlook Database, September 2005

12

Determinants of Wages and Labour Supply in the UK

Keshab Bhattarai & Tomasz Wisniewski[33]

INTRODUCTION

The issue of wage and earnings inequality in the British labour market has been a subject of great controversy. Over the last decades a substantial increase in the cross section variance has been observed and documented (See Gosling *et al.* (1996), Dickens (2000)). There is a common consensus among labour economists that schooling, age, gender, job market experience, professional and vocational background are meaningful factors that can explain part of the existing wage differentials across individuals. However, there is much disagreement on the relative importance of each of these variables for earnings (Rosen (1972), Mincer (1974), Spence and Stiglitz (1975), Heckman (1985), Shultz TP (1998)). In this article, we supplement the aggregate evidence with cross-sectional estimates of an earnings function that fits the UK data well. Moreover, we attempt to provide a full description of workers' response to wage changes and model their labour supply decisions in general. In this respect our study makes a major step forward, as it not only demonstrates the impact of economic factors on participation, but also shows how personal beliefs and political alliance are related to willingness to work. The individual's decision making process is not solely based on a set of economic information, but also on their personal perception of the world and the local environment. For this reason, the psychological profile of an individual can be considered as an extremely relevant factor influencing the decision on whether to enter or remain outside the labour force. Our findings seem to confirm this common sense logic.

33. We appreciate the Social Science Faculty of the Hull University for the research grant #500R054. We are also grateful to the University of Essex for providing us an access to the BHPS data set in the Essex data archive through MIMAS. We also acknowledge R. J. Green, W. Polasek and G. Pelloni and participants of summer econometrics conference under the Centre for Economic Policy at Hull for comments and suggestions. All errors and omissions are of our own. Correspondence regarding this paper should be directed to K.R.Bhattarai@econ.hull.ac.uk.

Furthermore, we estimate the unbiased elasticity of labour supply with respect to the wages that has meaningful microeconomic and macroeconomic underpinnings. An elastic labour supply curve is a core element of a business cycle (Christiano and Eichenbaum (1992), thus the value of considered elasticity is of major significance for devising policy rules aiming to maximise welfare and to stabilise the economy. Numerous studies of the UK labour market vary tremendously in estimated labour supply elasticities (for literature reviews see Elliot (1990) and Killingsworth (1983)). The most of these studies focus on the supply side of the labour market. Full analysis of the labour market requires a general equilibrium approach (Bhattarai and Whalley (1999)).

Big gender differences have been documented. Unlike the female population, men's behaviour is consistent with being on the downward sloping part of the backward-bending labour supply curve. But, so far there is no agreement on the sign of the aggregate labour supply elasticity for men and women. Consequently, we reject the group-estimation approach, so frequently seen in the literature. This allows us to focus clearly on the aggregates.

A number of studies have been made already to analyse theoretical issues related to wage determination and labour supply (Mroz (1987), Angrist (1991), Heckman (1979), Dougherty and Jimnenz (1991)). The literature looking upon empirical aspects is also relatively extensive (for the UK Blundell *et al.* (1992), Miles (1997), Dex(1995), and for the U.S. Kimmel and Kniesner (1998), Nakamura and Nakamura (1981)). Our main contribution to the debate is to provide bias-free estimates with a sample big enough to produce reliable results. Moreover, we incorporate a unique set of regressor not present in other studies, but relevant from the statistical point of view. The primary purpose of this article was to introduce a richer structural model that will improve on previous cross-sectional studies. We use wave 8 of the British Household Panel Survey (over 10 thousand individuals) in order to estimate the wages, participation behaviour and labour supply elasticities. SPSS and Limdep packages are applied for computational purposes.

First, we present the theoretical model of wage determination, methods of resolving self-selection and specification biases and probabilistic models of participation and employment. In section three we proceed onto description of the data set used for this study. Empirical findings on the determinants of wages, participation and labour supply are presented and briefly interpreted in the next section. The study is completed by the conclusions derived from the research in section five.

METHODOLOGY

The Wage Equation

We model logarithmic hourly earnings as determined by both the economic and non-economic individual characteristics. Although various functional specifications of the dependent variable have been tried in the literature, the logarithmic form proved to be the most successful one, both in terms of satisfying the assumption of heteroscedasticity assumption and maximising the explanatory power of the regression (Dougherty and Jimenz, 1991). Due to the fact that the wage level is unobserved for individuals whose market pay is lower than their reservation wage (i.e. for individuals supplying zero hours of labour), the regression is based primarily on a censored sample. We will assume that variation that in the individual's offered logarithmic wages are explained by the following equation:

$$\log w_i = \beta_0 + \beta_1 S_i + \beta_2 Age_i + \beta_3 Age_i^2 + \beta_4 VC_i + \beta_5 Sex_i + \beta_6 E2L_i +$$
$$\beta_7 RGSC_i + \beta_7 Region_i + \varepsilon_i^w = X_i^w\beta + \varepsilon_i^w \qquad [1]$$

where S_i denotes years of schooling, Age proxies labour market experience, VC_i is a dichotomous variable taking positive value if considered individual experienced vocational training, Sex_i is a gender dummy (1 for Male), $E2L_i$ takes a value of 1 if respondent's first language is not English, 0 otherwise, $RGSC_i$ is a vector of 7 dummies representing RG social class on the most recent job, $Region_i$ is a vector of 19 regional dichotomous variables and ε_i^w denotes the disturbance term.

Controlling for self-selection

Self selection bias persists due to the fact that the actual (ex-post) wages for non-workers are unobserved, thus equal to zero (Hausman (1978), Heckman (1978), Heckman and Sadlacek (1985) and Lee (1982)). Nonetheless, had a non-worker been employed, he would have got some pay. In other words, the observed distribution of wage offers is truncated by reservation (shadow) wages. For this reason, any analysis of participation determinants requires a prediction of ex-ante pay for individuals remaining outside paid employment. In order to do so, we utilise a computationally unsophisticated technique (based on Heckman (1979)) that enables the Probit regression estimates to remain free of sample selection bias.

We assumed above that the observed wages are determined in the following way:

$$\log(w_i) = X_i^w\beta + \varepsilon_i^w$$

where X_i^w refers to characteristic relevant to the labour market and b is a column vector of coefficients. Suppose that one wants to estimate a probabilistic model of participation but data on log(w) is missing for certain observations. Furthermore, suppose that one can define an indicator I_i^{empl}, where $I_i^{empl} > 0$ when the individual *i* is in paid employment and $I_i^{empl} < 0$ otherwise (Note, that $I_i^{empl} = X_i^{empl}a + e_i^{empl}$ and X_i^{empl} includes X_i^w and some other relevant variables). Since the wages are observed only when $I_i^{empl} > 0$, the wage equation will be of general form:

$$E(\ln(w_i) | X_i^w, I_i^{empl} > 0) = X_i^w\beta + E(\varepsilon_i^w \hat{o}\, X_i^w, I_i^{empl} > 0)$$
$$= X_i^w\beta + E(\varepsilon_i^w \hat{o}\, e_i^{empl} > - X_i^{empl}\alpha)$$

By estimating

$$\Pr(I_i^{empl} > 0) = \frac{1}{\sqrt{2\pi}} \int_{-\infty}^{X_i^{empl}\alpha} e^{\frac{-t^2}{2}} dt$$

and assuming that $X_i(\varepsilon_i^{w}, \varepsilon_i^{empl})$ is a bivariate normal density one can estimate the last term on the right-hand side of the general wage equation:

$$E(\varepsilon_i^{w} | \varepsilon_i^{empl} > - X_i^{empl}\alpha) = (\delta^{w,empl} / \delta^{empl})\lambda_i$$

and the sample selection correction term (the inverse of Mill's ratio) can be computed as:

$$\lambda_i = \phi(X_i^{empl}\alpha/\delta^{empl})/\Phi(X_i^{empl}\alpha/\delta^{empl})$$

where ϕ and Φ are, respectively, the density and distribution function for a standard normal variable. Thus, the actual model of the wage will now become:

$$\log(w_i) = X_i^{w}\beta + (\delta^{w,empl}/\delta^{empl})\lambda_i + \nu_i$$

Resolving Simultaneity Bias

The wage rate exogeneity assumption usually induces upward sloping bias in estimated wage elasticities (Mroz(1987)), as there are some important unobserved individual effects which are correlated with explanatory variables in the individual labour supply equation. Consequently, the wage appearing as an endogenous explanatory variable in this equation may become stochastic. The lack of control over possible model mispecification leads to the violation of the orthogonality and sphericality assumptions in the regression framework, which results in asymptotically inconsistent estimates (Hausman 1978). To resolve the simultaneity bias we instrument the selectivity bias corrected wage based on the variable set X^{w}. Note, that the used instrument is of exceptionally high quality ($R^2 = 0.92$) and the inconsistencies present in IV regression with weak instruments are unlikely to occur (See Staingler, Stock (1997)).

The Probabilistic Models of Participation

The analysis of labour force states comprises two dichotomous dependent variable models. First, the probability of participating conditional on ability to work[1] is estimated by means of a probabilistic model. To motivate the Probit model, we assume that any given person compares utility if participating, with utility if outside the labour force. Let I_i^{PA} be an indicator of labour force status, so that $I_i^{PA} > 0$ if an individual is either employed or unemployed and I_i^{PA} £ 0 if he remains out of the labour force. Consequently, the probability of participating, given one is able to work can be described as

$$\Pr(P_i | A_i) = \Pr(I_i^{PA} = X_i^{PA}\gamma + e_i^{PA} > 0) = \Pr(e_i^{PA} > -X_i^{PA}\gamma) = F^{PA}(-X_i^{PA}\gamma)$$

where X_i^{PA} is a vector of variables determining participation, such as logarithmic wage, regional unemployment rate, marital status, non-labour income, etc., and F^{PA} is the normal probability density function.

Then, we turn to probability of employment conditional upon participation

$$Pr(E_i \mid P_i) = Pr(I_i^{EP} > 0) = Pr(e_i^{EP} > -X_i^{EP}\phi) = F^{EP}(-X_i^{EP}\Phi)$$

In this particular model $X_i^{EP} = X_i^{PA}$. Having estimated $\log(w_i)$, F^{PA} and F^{EP}, the probability of an individual being employed, given he is able to work can be computed

$$Pr(E_i \mid A_i) = Pr(P_i \mid A_i)^* \, Pr(E_i \mid P_i) = F^{PA}(-X_i^{PA}\gamma)^* \, F^{EP}(-X_i^{EP}\varphi)$$

since all the values on the right-hand side of the above relationship are known.

The model of hours of work supplied weekly

Finally, we focus on a labour-supply model of functional form similar to those frequently found in the literature. Nonetheless, it is quite unique, as it incorporates variables not present in previous studies.

$$\log h_i = \delta_1 + \delta_2\log(w_i) + \delta_3\log(HH_i) + \delta_4 NLI_i + \delta_5 MS_i + \delta_6 Sex_i + \delta_7 Party_i + \delta_7 OTQ_i + \varepsilon_i^h = Z_i^h\delta \qquad [2]$$

where $\log h_i$ is the ith individual's logarithmic hours of work supplied per week, including overtime, w_i is a measure of self-selection corrected instrumented wage, HH_i is the number of hours spend on housework weekly, NLI_i is non-labour income per month in thousands of pounds, MS_i stands for marital status(1 if married), Sex_i is a gender dummy (1 for male), $Party_i$ is a vector of binomial variables describing individual's political preferences, OTQ_i is a vector of continuous variables representing quantified responses to opinion type questions (scale 1-10) and ε_i^h is a stochastic disturbance.

DATA SET AND SAMPLE CHARACTERISTICS

The data set used for our study is from the British Household Panel Survey (BHPS) downloaded from the Essex data archive. It is a nationally representative sample across Great Britain, consisting of around 5,500 households. The panel started in 1991 and the first wave of interviews included 13,840 individuals. The same individuals were contacted, as far as possible, for the subsequent waves of the survey. We use the eighth wave of the survey (1997). We extract the data from the HINDRESP file, which comprises of detailed information on opinions and socio-economic values of 10,300 respondents. The BHPS is an extremely rich source of data that provides almost every piece of information relevant to the labour market and also on the individual's labour supply (Taylor et al (1999)). The data set has been extended to include the ONS 1997 data on regional unemployment rates[2].

The variable collection included by the model is quite unique, as it not only embodies the standard variables utilised by other studies, but also the quantified responses to the opinion-type questions (priorities in life, political views). We conclude that these variables have a significant impact on the individual's labour supply and therefore should not be overlooked. There is however one transparent issue related to usage of these variables, namely the lack of normalisation techniques due to their subjective nature. Consequently, one is only interested in the sign and statistical significance, rather than in the nominal value of their coefficients.

This research focuses on wages and labour market supply, thus specific features of these variables are of particular interest. The frequency distribution of the gross wage rates in the sub-sample of individuals in paid employment is plotted on the graph below. Some descriptive statistics related to this distribution are given in Table 1.

The Frequency Distribution of Gross Wage Rates

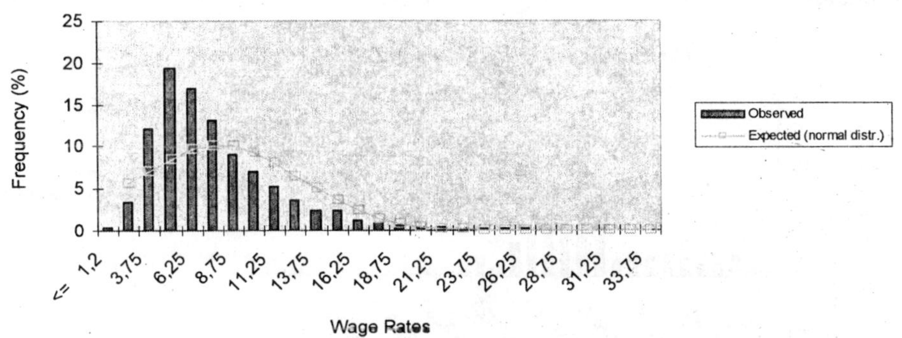

Table 1
Wage Statistics

	Mean	*Median*	*Skewness*	*Kurtosis*
Value	7.254337	6.048609	5.287337	73.23747
S.E.	*(4.890517)*		*(0.034266)*	*(0.068519)*

Source: Own Computations
Note: All values in pounds per hour

The gross wage rate distribution is asymmetric. It is considerably skewed to the right and the median does not coincide with the mean. This result may indicate a smaller number of people have productivity levels above the average. Moreover, the considered distribution is leptokurtic, which is fully consistent with longstanding evidence for Britain (e.g. Lydall (1968)).

The classification of individuals with respect to their current labour force status is demonstrated in Table 2. Given that all survey participants reached the age of 16, there is no strong basis to question the representative character of the sample.

Table 2
Labour force status

Labour force status	*Frequency*	*Percentage of the sample*
Employed	5108	46.8%
Unemployed	372	3.4%
Out of labour force, but able to work	2460	22.6%
Retired, Disabled, Unable to work	2810	25.8%
Total valid cases	10750	98.6%
Missing cases	156	1.4%
Sample size	10906	100%

Source: Own Derivations

As one can clearly see on the following diagram, there are some significant discrepancies if the frequency distribution of hours worked per week, including overtime and the expected values under the normal distribution were to be compared.

The Frequency Distribution of Gross Wage Rates

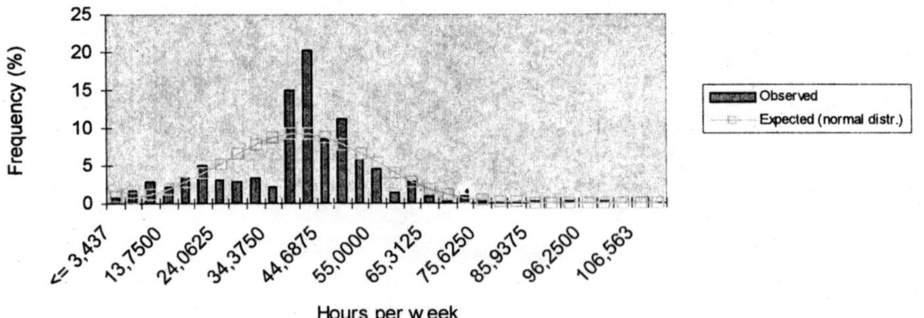

In the sub-sample of employed individuals there is a notable concentration of observations around values of 20 (half-time job) and 40 (full time job). This reflects rigidities and constraints on the labour demand side, which are not explicitly considered in this research due to limitations of the data set. As a result, one can expect the hours of labour supplied model to have relatively low explanatory power. Not surprisingly, we find that a low coefficient of determination is a common feature of all empirical models of hours of labour supplied.

EMPIRICAL RESULTS

We present and discuss empirical results derived from the survey data in this section. The estimated coefficients reflecting the relative importance of various factors in determining wages and labour supply among individuals are given in Tables 3-8.

The Wage Inequalities

We start with regressing the wage equation [1] using the ordinary least squares method on the sub-sample of interviewed workers.

Table 3
The Wage Model Estimates
Dependent Variable - log gross Hourly Earnings *(derived variable)*
Number of observations-5108

Variable	Coefficient	t-stat.	Mean
Intercept	0.042865	0.2773	
Years of schooling *(derived variable)*	0.041662	14.2672	12.136
Age at Date of Interview	0.059554	21.3142	36.662
Age squared	-0.000650	-18.3420	1492.846
Vocational qualifications	0.042175	3.3939	0.389
Sex	0.223546	18.1097	0.500
English 2nd language	-0.222350	-2.7740	0.025
RG Social Class: most recent job			
Professional occupation	0.162362	0.7498	0.073
Managerial and technical	0.073698	0.3422	0.304
Skilled non-manual	-0.210799	-0.9770	0.288
Skilled manual	-0.264472	-1.2254	0.205
Partly skilled occupation	-0.360438	-1.6732	0.177
Unskilled occupation	-0.424298	-1.9709	0.069
Armed forces	0.113362	0.4318	0.020
Region / Metropolitan Area Dummies			
Inner London	0.289657	3.4308	0.048
Outer London	0.252697	3.1381	0.080
R. of South East	0.155620	1.9941	0.219
South West	0.083689	1.0566	0.112
East Anglia	0.046243	0.5614	0.058
East Midlands	0.013843	0.1746	0.110
West Midlands Conurb.	0.061383	0.7387	0.054
R. of West Midlands	0.045400	0.5634	0.078
Greater Manchester	0.151121	1.8403	0.060
Merseyside	0.153563	1.7593	0.039
R. of North West	0.090306	1.1025	0.062
South Yorkshire	0.070065	0.8220	0.044
West Yorkshire	0.050060	0.5990	0.051
R. of Yorks & Humber	0.032916	0.3931	0.050
Tyne & Wear	0.051728	0.6001	0.042
R. of North	0.035033	0.4255	0.059
Wales	0.051493	0.6336	0.068
Scotland	0.106978	1.3404	0.094
Northern Ireland	0.024426	0.2779	0.038

$R^2 = 0.92273928$ Adjusted
$R^2 = 0.92225211$
Note: Mean of dependent variable is 1.8226

Years of schooling are derived from information on the highest completed educational degree or vocational degree by attaching an average number of years to standardised educational levels. This variable proxies human capital acquired through formal education. Because the regression is estimated with log wages the coefficient b_1 has a very useful property. Therefore, in absence of ability bias, it can be interpreted as an estimate of the rate of return to schooling for population j, $\beta_1 = \Delta(\log w_i)/\Delta s_i$ » $\%\Delta w_i/\Delta s_i$. In practice, however, the correlation between schooling and earnings is contaminated by the presence of unobserved ability. Most studies estimating the rate of return to education fail to control for the effects of ability bias, which usually results in overstating the real returns. In recent years some attempts have been made to resolve this problem, by including IQ scores (e.g. Clark and Trash (1987), Card (1994), Blackburn and Neumark (1992)) or results of technical tests (Blackburn and Neumark (1993)) in earnings equations. Nonetheless these variables tend to be highly correlated with the level of schooling, which leads to colinearity problems, with large sampling variances and spurious regressors (for more details see Griliches (1977)). Unfortunately, BHPS does not include any non-academic proxies for ability. The estimated rate of return to schooling includes an upward sloping bias. Nonetheless, the value of 4.166 percent seems to be relatively low compared with commercial interest rates offered by financial institutions in the considered time period. The spot rate on ten year government bonds oscillated in 1997 around 7%. This may be an indication that the general non-vocational training outside the workplace (i.e. schooling) is not as good investment as it is perceived to be. On the other hand, the considered estimate indicates only rate of return to one year of schooling. The cumulative effect is much stronger (Psacharopolous(1985)).

The quadratic specification in terms of age allows us to capture the concavity of age-earning profiles. Murphy and Welch (1990) show that extending this specification, by adding higher-order terms in experience, could reduce the serial autocorrelation of regression residuals and lessen mean squared bias. Nonetheless, the quadratic form is the widely accepted empirical specification, which approximates actual growth of earnings over the career. Moreover it enables us to evaluate almost effortlessly the peaks of age-earnings profiles, as follows:

$$\Delta(\log w_{i,j})/\Delta E_{i,j} = 0$$

$$\Rightarrow \text{(peak of the age earning profile)}_j = -\beta_{2,j} / 2\beta_{3,j}$$

Most of empirical studies based on quadratic functions suggest that average earnings profiles peak around 30 years of labour market experience (e.g. Mincer(1974)). We find that the logarithmic wage rate reaches its maximum at about 45.8 years of age, which is comparable with earlier findings in the literature.

We include vocational qualification variables following Arulampalam and Booth (1998). With NCDS survey data they show that it is only training incidence that matters for the wage growth, and not the number of courses. Inclusion of a specific training variable permits us to isolate the returns to on-the-job investments. Failure to do so can result in overestimation of the returns to initial human capital investments, such as schooling. We find the coefficient of the training binomial variable to be 0.042175. This corresponds to a potential enlargement of the wage rate for individuals completing on-the-job training for the first time by about 4.3077% (=[exp(0.042175)-1]*100).

The size and statistical significance of the sex-related wage gap at first glance seems somewhat controversial. Men earned on average 25 percent more than women. But in fact, the male wage premium is even larger in some other European countries. For instance study by Lauer (2000) estimate the gender wage gap in West Germany to be in order of 36.1%. The inferiority of female wages is often attributed to career interruptions for family reasons. These breaks in career results in loss of on-the-job training and difference in labour market experiences (Gronau (1988), Connolly (1997), Carlson and Wartz (1998), Chinhui and Murphy (1997)). Part of the gap could be also explained by occupational segregation. The female labour force is often seen crowding into lower paid occupations.

As might be expected language fluency has a role to play in describing differences in the log wage rates. Relative to these who are classified as speaking English fluently, there is an approximate 24.9 percent earnings penalty from having inferior language skills. This is an equivalent of the gender gap. Not only are foreigners earning less but, as we will show later, they are less likely to find a job. Our estimate however, seems to be relatively exaggerated compared to other studies (e.g. O'Leary *et al.* (1999)) which could be a consequence of under-representation of the considered group in the sample (only 88 valid cases).

Our results on earning differences across social class are consistent with common sense. Highest wage rate has been observed for professionals and the lowest one for unskilled workers.

We also observe a meaningful variation of wage rates across various regions within the Great Britain. Premiums on wages in Inner London, Outer London and the rest of the South East are 33.6 percent, 28.7 percent and 16.8 percent respectively and are subject to great statistical significance. This may be a strong basis to question the perfectly competitive character of the UK labour market, since individuals with similar labour market characteristics differ in their wage rates across the regions. It is, however, not a direct negation of the microeconomic theory, which says that the wage rate should be equalised with value of the marginal product of labour. Note that the production process in large agglomerations, such as London or Manchester, tends to be more capital intensive and, as a consequence, average productivity per worker may be higher in these regions.

Implications of self-selection Adjustments

The BHPS includes data on expected wages for the sub-sample of unemployed people. Each individual who is actively looking for a job has been questioned on his prediction concerning net wage once employed. This information proves to be very useful in the context of this research, since this allows us to determine if the unemployment spell is a result of excessive wage demands.

Table 4
Do job-seekers have Overoptimistic Wage Expectations?

	Expected net wage rate: jobseeker (derived variable)	*Net wage rate prediction based on the wage model*	*Gross wage rate prediction based on the wage model*
Average	5.124557	3.642086	5.193973
Standard Deviation	3.74482	1.256836	1.792373

Number of Observations: 694

Unemployed seem to overestimate the market value of their labour supply by about 28.9%. Although the gap is rather sizeable, it is not statistically significant. Furthermore, it can be inferred from the data presented in Table 4, in the absence of tax and national insurance deductions, an average job-seeker would be willing to undertake any job at going market wage. This empirical result vividly highlights the beneficial implications of personal income tax cuts for the labour market.

It is apparent that the minimum expected wage rate could be a good proxy for the individual's reservation wage. Modelling such a proxy, or for instance investigating the relationship between excess wage demands and non-labour income should provide some insights onto the trends in unemployment rates. This is quite a profound macroeconomic issue demanding further study. We do not intend to analyse it any further within this paper. The idea, however, has been clearly identified. Its empirical implementation may follow in the near future.

Another intriguing question that can be investigated at this stage is the size of the gap between wage rates of salaried workers and potential wage rates of non-working individuals. Some descriptive statistics relating to this issue are provided in the table below:

Table 5
Differences in wages Predicted by the model *(in pounds per hour)*

	Not Working	*In Paid Employment*	*Whole Sample*
Average	5.8630	7.2543	6.7580
Standard deviation	3.7365	4.8905	4.4307
Number of cases	2832	5108	7940

Source: Own computations

The difference in gross earnings is as big as £1.39 per hour. The magnitude of this discrepancy can be explained solely on the basis of the presented wage model. Therefore, the gap directly quantifies the inferiority of labour market characteristics of the non-working people.

The Probabilistic models of Participation and Employment

Figures in Tables 6 and 7 show results of the Probit analysis on participation in the labour market and employability of individuals already in the labour force.

From these one can evaluate the effect of each variable on participation and the statistical significance of the considered effects. We first model the probability of participating given that one is able to work, and then turn to the chance of being employed once in the labour force.

Binomial Probit Model (Probability of participating given one is able to work)

Dependent	Variable
Participation	
Log likelihood function	-
4546.511	
Restricted log likelihood	-
4929.650	
Chi-squared	
766.2786	
Degrees of freedom 13	

Table 6
Index function for Probability of Participation

Variable	*Coefficient*	*S.E.*	*t-stat*	*Mean of X*
Constant	0.418731464	0.1901692	2.202	
Log wage prediction	0.116349221	0.04553701	2.555	1.7627939
Regional Unemployment Rate	-0.207060363	1.1195939	-0.185	0.0491741
Number of hours spent on housework weekly	-0.013544027	0.00148667	-9.110	10.276700
Non labour income[3]	-0.330800310	0.04175484	-7.922	0.1250598
Married	-0.220534631	0.03363379	-6.557	0.5536524
English second language	-0.417421848	0.17673205	-2.362	0.0073048
Political Party Supported				
Conservative	0.075383701	0.04406321	1.711	0.2001259
Labour	0.297454132	0.03730073	7.974	0.3853904
Liberal	0.319887760	0.05612258	5.700	0.1055416
Opinion Type Questions				
Importance of: Health	-0.1042378013	0.01629281	-6.398	9.556297
Importance of: Money	0.0216673532	0.00751327	2.884	6.421663
Importance of: Having Children	-0.0028306233	0.00573860	-0.493	7.416625
Importance of: Job	0.1165666351	0.00754271	15.454	7.948363

	Predicted		
Actual	0 (inactive)	1 (active)	Total
0 (inactive	599	1880	2479
1 (active)	255	5206	5461
Total	854	7086	7940

Binomial Probit Model (Probability of Working given Participation)

Dependent Working	Variable
Log likelihood function 1212.949	-
Restricted log likelihood 1310.846	-
Chi-squared 195.7941	
Degrees of freedom 13	

Table 7
Index Function for Probability of Working

Variable	*Coefficient*	*S.E.*	*t-stat*	*Mean of X*
Constant	0.639934446	0.0502601	2.098	
Log wage prediction	0.278144375	0.0856109	3.249	1.7772919
Regional Unemployment Rate	-3.94215054	1.9783359	-1.993	0.0491033
Number of hours spent on housework weekly	-0.01186706	0.0029044	-4.086	9.0640908
Non labour income	-0.56294295	0.1053335	-5.344	0.0987165
Married	0.43437977	0.6317260	6.876	0.5209668
English second language	-0.27864439	0.3193311	-0.873	0.0054935
Political Party Supported				
Conservative	0.459919204	0.09366788	4.910	0.1931881
Labour	0.192511218	0.06391944	3.012	0.4110969
Liberal	0.126366160	0.09646776	1.310	0.1146310
Opinion Type Questions				
Importance of: Health	0.0369572972	0.02471114	1.496	9.5061344
Importance of: Money	-0.0190702752	0.01339131	-1.424	6.5222487
Importance of: Having Children	0.0156779815	0.01000925	1.566	7.3479216
Importance of: Job	0.0115251396	0.01613746	0.714	8.2506867

	Predicted		
Actual	0	1	Total
0	353	1	354
1	1	5106	5107
Total	354	5107	5461

The estimates in Table 6 could be extremely useful to forecast the future size of the labour force out of working age population. They could also be used to evaluate work incentives created by a given fiscal policy. Regression results from the second Probit function provide some microeconomic insights onto determinants of level of unemployment.

Results of these models show that the income effect of wage improvements is outweighed by the positive substitution effect for participation. These findings indicate that a 10% increase in the wage rate should be followed by a 1.16

percentage point growth in the participation. The regressor representing hours spent on housework weekly can, to certain extent, reflect the magnitude of fixed costs of employment. It is a very important factor influencing labour supply decisions, especially in the context of married couples (See Cho and Rogerson (1988), Lauer (2000)). The more hours they spend on household work, the less likely they are to participate in the labour market. Its significance and negative impact is confirmed in the reported estimates.

The effect on the willingness to work of people who vote for the three biggest political parties seems to be much larger compared with the rest of the society. No simple normative story can be told in order to explain this result. The supporters of the Conservative party are less likely to participate than individuals associating themselves with the Labour and Liberal Democrat parties. Moreover they tend to supply less hours of labour. Nonetheless, it is relatively easy for them to find a job once they participate in the labour force.

Interestingly, we find that the psychological profile of an individual has a very big influence over his decision on whether to participate. Note however that once he joined the labour force his personal beliefs and opinions have no impact on probability of finding a job. The chance of being employed once participating depends mainly on the local labour market conditions (the unemployment rate regressor becomes statistically significant in the second Probit model - $Pr(E_i | P_i)$). This unique result is somewhat not surprising and seems to conform with common sense intuition. Consider an individual that gets a higher utility level once employed and at the same time is not participating. He will have nothing to lose if he joins the labour force, but the chance of finding an employer depends mostly on his labour market characteristics. Observable variables, such as education and years of experience send the clearest and the strongest signal to the employer during selection procedure. On the other hand, perceptual and psychological notions can be easily misrepresented at the time of the job interview. It takes time for the companies to learn the true productivity, ability and commitment of the hired agents. It becomes expensive to cancel the work contract by the time they know the employee. For this reason, an under-performing employee faces poor promotion perspectives rather than a dismissal. Consequently, we do not observe a significant relationship between $Pr(E_i | P_i)$ and the continuous opinion-type variables.

Estimating the Labour Supply Elasticity and Hours of Work Equation

Now we turn to analysing the hours of work of participants. The OLS estimates of hours of work equation [2] are presented below. These results indicate hours of working people would like to supply as a function of individual specific variables.

The logarithmic specification that we have used provides direct estimate of the wage elasticity of hours of work. Our estimates indicate that the substitution effect of an increase in the wage rate dominates the income effect. For instance a 1 percent rise in the gross wage generates an 0.174% increase in hours of labour supplied. For employed individuals, one would expect the elasticity to be much greater compared with the sample we have quoted. Therefore, we also undertake the necessary steps to obtain the elasticity estimate for the group of people in-paid employment. Its value appears to be 0.295, which confirms the intuition and theory. Until recently the common opinion among labour economists was that the aggregate labour supply curve was negatively sloped. However, the latest evidence has begun to cast doubts on the slope of the overall labour supply curve (for literature review see Elliott (1990), Killingsworth (1983)). Broadly speaking our findings on the elasticities are comparable with these reported in the nineties.

Table 8
The Hours of Labour Supplied Model
Dependent Variable - log hours Worked per week, Including Overtime

		Unrestricted	*Model*
Variable	Beta	t-value	Mean[u]
Intercept	.672	7.791	
Log Wage	.174	14.706	1.77516
Log hours per week on housework	-.197	-15.328	1.01233
Non-labour income per month[4]	-.178	-16.833	0.13764
Marital status	-.031	-2.747	0.56618
Sex	-.041	-3.077	0.48168
Political Party Supported			
Conservative	-.015	-1.188	0.21269
Labour	.038	3.047	0.39793
Lib Dem/Lib/SDP	.009	.771	0.11812
Opinion Type Questions			
Importance of: Health	-.024	-2.293	9.56769
Importance of: Money	.013	1.186	6.43345
Importance of: Having children	-.049	-4.303	7.42828
Importance of: Having a good job	.137	12.538	7.95995
Mean of dependent var.	3.318277		
No. of observations	7940	Adjusted R^2	0.141

Other economic variables included in the equation [2] seem to have the expected direction of impact. Married women tend to supply fewer hours of labour, despite persistence of a strong upward sloping trend in their participation rates. This has been a very prominent labour market feature in the post-war period (see Goldin (1989), Layard et al. (1980)). Single men, on the other hand, are not very keen on housework, but seem to be very devoted to their paid job.

The magnitude of initial endowment (non-labour income) has an enormously significant influence over the labour supply decision. This follows from basic microeconomic principles. Once again, we infer that personal beliefs and political alliances can be important factors in labour supply decision making process as is the participation decision.

CONCLUSIONS

We have explained a big proportion of the differences in wages and labour supply among British individuals. Not only have we considered a wide range of economic characteristics, but also made an attempt to describe individuals' personal profile by means of a additional regressors relating to motivation toward work and political affiliations. This allowed us to illustrate the labour market response of working individuals in the economy. These variables help describe the labour supply decision making process more accurately at a micro level. The estimates reported in this study are free of biases, since we control for self-selection into the labour force and relax the exogeneity assumption on the wage rate. The conclusions reached in this research are, in general, similar compared with these derived in many studies in the late 1990's.

REFERENCES

Angrist J.D., (1991), "Grouped-data Estimation and Testing Simple Labour Supply Models", *Journal of Econometrics,* Vol. 47, pp.243-266.

Arulampalam W., Booth A.L., (2000), "Learning and Earning: Do Multiple Training Events Pay?" forthcoming, *Economica.*

Bhattarai K., Whalley J., (1999), Role of Labour Demand Elasticities in Tax Incidence Analysis with Heterogeneous Labour, *Empirical Economics* 24(4), November pp. 599-619.

Blackburn McKinley L., Neumark D., (1993), "Omitted-Ability Bias as the Increase in the Rate of Schooling", *Journal of Labour Economics,* Vol. XI, No. 3, 521-544.

Blackburn McKinley L., Neumark D., (1992), "Unobserved Ability, Efficiency Wages, and Interindustry Wage Differentials", *Quarterly Journal of Economics 107*, 1421-36.

Blundell, R.W., Ham J.C. and Meghir C. (1969), Unemployment, Labor Force Participation and Hours of Work, UCL Discussion Paper 86-06, May 1986.

Blundell, R, Duncan A. and Meghir C (1992), "Empirical Labour Supply Models: Lone Mothers in the UK", *Economic Journal*, 102(411), March. pp. 265-78.

Card D., (August 1994), "Schooling, Ability and Earnings Revisited", NEBR Working Paper No.4832.

Carlson L.A., Swartz C., (July 1988), "The Earnings of Women and Ethnic Minorities, 1959-79", *Industrial and Labor Relations Review 41,* 530-546.

Chinhui J., Murphy K.M., (1997), "Wage Inequality and Family Labour Supply", *Journal of Labour Economics,* Vol. 15, No.1, pp.72-97.

Clark A., Trash J., (1987), "How much is a Degree Worth?", *Audit*, 109-115.

Connolly S., (1997), "A Model of Female labour Supply in which Supply is Dependent Upon the Chances of Finding a Job", *Applied Economics* 29, 1379-1386.

Chrisitiano L.J., Eichenbaum M., (1992), "Current Real Business Cycle Theories and Aggregate Labour-Market Fluctuation", *American Economic Review* 82, pp.430-450.

Cho J., Rogerson R., (1988), "Family Labour Supply and Aggregate Fluctuations", *Journal of Monetary Economics,* Vol. 21, pp. 233-245.

Dex, Shirley et.al (1995), Household Labour Supply, Research Series, no. 43, Moorfoot, Sheffield, UK Employment Department.

Dickens R., (2000), "The Evolution of Individual Male Earnings in Great Britan: 1975-95", *The Economic Journal,* 110 (January), pp.27-49.

Dougherty C.R.S., Jimenez E., (1991), "The Specification of Earnings Functions: Tests and Implications", *Economics of Education Review,* Vol. 10, No.2, pp.85-98.

Elliott R.F., (1990), *Labour Economics*: *comparative text*, McGraw Hill London, pp.119-120.

Goldin C., (1989), "Life-Cycle Labour-Force Participation of Married Women: Historical Evidence and Implications", *Journal of Labour Economics,* vol.7, no.1, pp.20-47.

Gosling A., Machin S., Meghir C., (1996), "The Changing Distribution of Male Wages in the UK", Centre for Economic Performance Discussion Paper, no.271.

Green W.H. (1998), LIMDEP Version 7: User Manual, Econometric Software Inc.

Griliches Z., (1977), "Estimating the Returns to Schooling: Some Econometric Problems", *Econometrica,* Vol. 45, No 1, pp.1-22.

Gronau R., (1988), "Sex-related Wage Differentials and Women's Interrupted Labour Careers- the Chicken or the Egg", *Journal of Labour Economics,* Vol. 6, No. 3, pp.277-301.

Hausman J.A., (1978), "Specification Tests in Econometrics", *Econometrica,* Vol. 46, No. 6, pp.1251-1271.

Heckman J.J., (1979), "Sample Selection Bias as a Specification Error", *Econometrica,* Vol. 47, No. 1, pp153-161.

Heckman J.J., and G. Sedlacek (1985), "Heterogeneity, Aggregation and Market Wage Functions: An Empirical Model of Self-selection in the Labour Market", *Journal of Political Economy* 93, 6, pp.1077-1125.

Kennan J., (1989), "Simultaneous Equation Bias in Disaggregated Econometric Models", *Review of Economic Studies,* pp.151-156.

Killingsworth M. (1983), *Labour Supply*, Cambridge University Press.

Kimmel J., Kniesner T.J., (1998), "New evidence on labour supply: Employment Versus Hours Elasticities by sex and Marital Status", *Journal of Monetary Economics* 42, 289-301.

Lauer C., (2000), "Gender Wage Gap in West Germany: How Far Do Gender Differences in Human Capital Matter", Discussion Paper No. 00-07, Centre for European Economic Research (ZEW).

Lauer C., Steiner V., (2000), "Returns to Education in West Germany", Discussion Paper No.00-04, Centre for European Economic Research (ZEW).

Layard R., Barton M., Zabalza A., (1980), "Married Women's Participation and Hours", *Economica,* 47, pp. 51-72.

Lee Lung-Fei, (1982), "Some Approaches to the Correction of Selectivity Bias", *Review of Economic Studies,* XLIX, pp.355-372.

Lydall H.F., (1968), *The Structure of Earnings,* London, Oxford University Press.

Miles D., (1997), "A household level study of determinants of income and consumption", *Economic Journal* 107, pp.1-25.

Mincer J., (1974), *Schooling, Experience and Earnings,* New York: Columbia University Press.

Mroz T.A., (1987), "The Sensitivity of an Empirical Model of Married Women's Hours of Work to Economic and Statistical Assumptions", *Econometrica,* Vol. 55, No. 4, 765-799.

Murphy K.M., Welch F., (1990), "Empirical Age-Earnings Profiles", *Journal of Labour Economics*, Vol. VIII, No.2, 202-229.

Nakamura A, Nakamura M., (1981), "A Comparison of the Labour Force Behaviour of Married Women in the United States and Canada, with Special Attention to the Impact of Income Taxes", *Econometrica,* Vol. 49, No.2, pp.451-489.

O'Leary N.C., Murphy P.D., Drinkwater S.J., Blackaby D.H., (1999), "English Language Fluency and the Ethnic Wage Gap in Britain", Discussion Paper No. 99-09, Department of Economics, University of Wales Swansea.

Psacharopolous G., (1985), "Returns to education: a further international update and implications", *Journal of Human Resources,* Vol. XX, Fall.

Rosen S., (1972), "Learning and Experience in Labour Market", *Journal of Human Resources,* 7, pp. 336-342.

Schultz T.P., (1998), "Inequality in the Distribution of Personal Income in the World: How is it Changing and Why", *Journal of Population Economics* 11, pp. 305-405.

Spence M., Stiglitz J., (1975), "The Theory of Screening, Education, and the Distribution of Income", *American Economic Review* 65, pp.283-300.

Staigler D., Stock J.H., (1997), "Instrumental Variables Regression with Weak Instruments", *Econometrica,* Vol. 65, No. 3, pp.557-586.

Taylor M. F., J. Brice, N. Buck and E.P. Lane (1999), British Household Panel Survey User Manual vol A, Essex Data Archive.

Wisniewski D. (Editor)., (December 1997), "Monthly Digest of Statistics", Office of National Statistics, No. 624.

NOTES

1. An individual is able to work if he belongs to the adult population and is neither retired nor disabled.
2. Ed. Wisniewski D., "Monthly Digest of Statistics", Office of National Statistics, No. 624, Dec. 1997.
3. In thousands of pounds per month
4. In Thousands Pounds

13

Income Dynamics of Individuals in the UK: Evidences from Waves 1-8 of the British Household Panel Survey

Keshab Bhattarai[38]

INTRODUCTION

Income patterns over time are different for different individuals. Some people start at a very low level of earnings and experience a rapid rise in income as they gain more job specific experience. Others may have a steady and stagnant income process over years. Still others may even have to face declining growth in income. What are the factors that lead to higher income growth rates and what are the factors that setback the process of income growth has been an issue of great interest among the labour economists.

The years of schooling and job market experience are the most important factors associated with higher income levels. Given other things constant, generally it is believed that an individual with greater number of schooling years earns more than a person with a few years or no schooling. Similarly a person with greater experience earns higher income. Both schooling and experience are perceived to be the main factors enhancing productivity of an individual.

There are a number of factors that set back the income process. Gender bias has been an area of continuous research in the labour economics. Females earn less than male either because of a structural breaks in their career for family reasons or due to gender discrimination in the labour market. Similarly there are cross regional variation in the income process. In the UK several studies have claimed that the inhabitants of the South earn higher level of income than those in the North.

---

38. Correspondence regarding this paper should be directed to K.R.Bhattarai@econ.hull.ac.uk. Phone: 44-1482-466483; Fax: 44-1482-466216.I appreciate the Social Science Faculty for the research grant #500R054 and the Essex data Archive for providing us access to the BHPS data set and Tomasz Wisniewski for excellent research assistantship and. All errors and omissions are of mine.

We aim to investigate income dynamics among individuals in the UK drawing evidences from eight different waves of the British Household Panel Survey (BHPS). We describe our model in section two. Then we give descriptive statistics on wage earning profiles across waves and individuals in section two. We present our panel data estimation in section three with various labour market scenarios in section four followed by conclusions of the study in section five.

The wage model for the full panel might take the following form:

$$w_{i,t} = \alpha_{i,t} + \beta_{i,t} S_{i,t} + \gamma_{i,t} A_{i,t} + \psi_{i,t} A_{i,t}^2 + \lambda_{i,t} G_i + \delta_{i,t} R_{i,t} + \pi_{i,t} P_{i,t} + \theta_t WV_t \quad (1)$$

where $w_{i,t}$ is the wage rate of individual i in year t; $S_{i,t}$ is years of schooling; $A_{i,t}$ is age of individual i in time t; G_i is the gender of an individual, $R_{i,t}$ is regional location, WV_t is wave t, $P_{i,t}$ is professional background of individual i.

Actual structure of the model we have estimated is much simpler than the above model. This is mainly because of the limited number of time periods in the BHPS data set. With only eight waves separate estimation of time specific effects is not possible.

$$w_{i,t} = \alpha + \beta S_{i,t} + \gamma A_i + \psi A_{i,t}^2 + \lambda G_i + \delta_r R_{i,t} + \pi_p P_{i,t} + \theta_t WV_t \quad (1')$$

DATA

The British Household Panel Survey (BHPS) is a longitudinal data set[1]. It started in 1991 with approximately 5500 households and more than 10,300 individuals drawn from 250 different areas of Great Britain. There have been eight waves of BHPS until so far. It includes variables describing the economic, social and regional background of individuals and their labour market status and earnings over years. The BHPS compares to the PSID data set in the United States, which started much earlier in 1968 with 4800 families and about 31,000 individuals.

Table 1
Descriptive Statistics

	Minimum	*Maximum*	*Mean*	*Std. Deviation*	*Skewness*		*Kurtosis*	
	Statistic	*Statistic*	*Statistic*	*Statistic*	*Statistic*	*Std. Error*	*Statistic*	*Std. Error*
WAGE	.40	64.67	7.3291	3.9415	2.421	.024	14.977	.047
Real wage	.38	64.67	6.8506	3.6330	2.470	.024	16.450	.047
AGE	16.00	72.00	38.8614	10.0534	.133	.024	-.580	.047
Schooling	.00	17.00	12.4292	3.7152	-1.324	.024	1.117	.047
<9	.00	1.00	.1357	.3425	2.127	.024	2.526	.047
>500	.00	1.00	.1887	.3913	1.592	.024	.534	.047
PRO	.00	1.00	5.514E-02	.2283	3.898	.024	13.199	.047
MAN	.00	1.00	.3019	.4591	.863	.024	-1.255	.047
SNM	.00	1.00	.2485	.4322	1.164	.024	-.645	.047
SM	.00	1.00	.1831	.3868	1.639	.024	.686	.047
PSO	.00	1.00	.1267	.3326	2.245	.024	3.042	.047
UO	.00	1.00	4.053E-02	.1972	4.661	.024	19.728	.047
ARMY	.00	1.00	1.925E-02	.1374	7.000	.024	47.003	.047

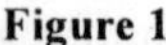

Figure 1

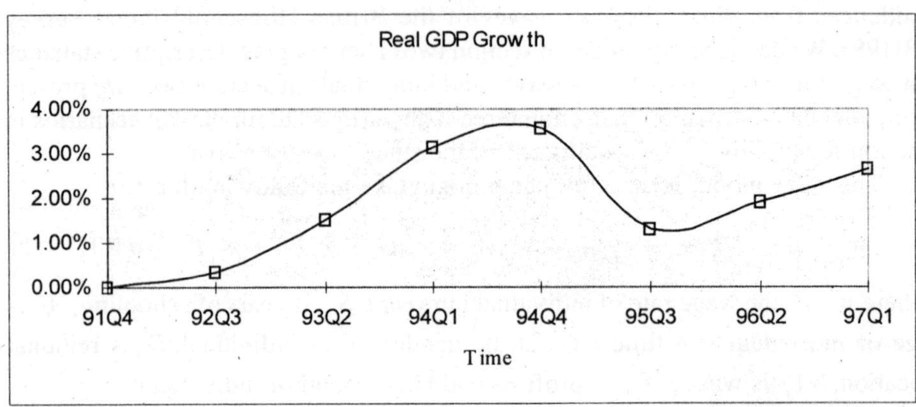

The BHPS provides an unique environment for studying income dynamics. It keeps track of labour market position of individuals that may change substantially as they move along. People get training or further education, may switch jobs and may gain more experience as they rise over the panels. Similarly family characteristics may change as people get married, have children, or get divorced or change their residences. They may retire on pension or migrate to new places.

The BHPS is a balanced panel. We consider 10,808 observations in the whole sample from wave one to eight. Each wave consisted 1351 individuals, which is 12.50 percent of the existing panel. Figures in Table 1 show descriptive statistics of some key variables included in this study. The mean wage of individuals remained 6.85 pounds with their mean age to be 38 years during periods of the panel. Individuals in this panel had 12 years of schooling on average. About 30 percent of working people were in managerial jobs which is significantly higher than the skilled non-manual (25%), skilled manual (18%). About 5.5 percent were professional workers and about 4 percent were unskilled workers.

Table 2

Social Group	*Average real wage rate*
Managers and Professionals	8.697048
Skilled non-manual workers	5.853007
Skilled manual and partly skilled workers	5.634582
Unskilled workers	5.077317

Average real wage rates differed among the social groups. Managers and professional workers on average earned 8.7 gross wage rate per hours while such wage rates was between 5.1 to 5.9 pounds among skilled, non-manual and partly skilled workers. In general we observe a rising trend for the average wages. However, we notice lagged cycles on wages following a business cycle as is evident from Figures 1 and 2. The real GDP growth rates were higher from 1992 to 1994 with a slump in 1995.

ESTIMATION

We use the whole sample to estimate the log real wage function of the individuals included in this survey. The estimated results of wave specific, time trend and simple models as in equation (1) are presented in Table 3.

Table 3
Determinants of log real wages in the BHPS

	Wave specific Model		*Time trend Model*		*Simple Model*	
	Coefficients	*t-stat*	*Coefficients*	*t-stat*	*Coefficients*	*t-stat*
(Constant)	-0.14747	-2.59251	-0.06943	-1.21463	0.077762	1.398395
Schooling	0.02773	24.69335	0.024771	22.89871	0.02236	20.63917
AGE	0.061577	25.59521	0.061922	25.59911	0.064557	26.37733
AGE SQ	-0.00071	-23.6162	-0.00072	-23.7254	-0.00073	-23.9861
REGION	0.108861	13.76351	0.110162	13.85307	0.108349	13.43424
SEX	0.289535	38.1348	0.290434	38.0495	0.291724	37.68031
<9	-0.22086	-20.5803	-0.21948	-20.3914	-0.21897	-20.0628
>500	0.09911	9.982215	0.093538	9.430559	0.094012	9.346495
PRO	0.27677	8.92049	0.22158	7.804683	0.180633	6.313034
MAN	0.242631	8.659276	0.185404	7.434985	0.143636	5.730343
SNM	0.011577	0.409853	-0.04718	-1.85722	-0.09587	-3.7605
SM	-0.07086	-2.49312	-0.13256	-5.14719	-0.18186	-7.0363
PSO	-0.13489	-4.67352	-0.19871	-7.53563	-0.24978	-9.44191
UO	-0.15041	-4.77689	-0.20085	-6.64589	-0.24771	-8.12958
ARMY	-0.0054	-0.15241	-0.01209	-0.33963	-0.01323	-0.36642
W2	0.129078	8.836155	-	-	-	-
W3	0.016599	1.164677	-	-	-	-
W4	0.133982	9.182063	-	-	-	-
W5	0.150253	10.28989	-	-	-	-
W6	0.234902	14.26546	-	-	-	-
W7	0.188706	12.92747	-	-	-	-
W8	0.22254	15.22138	-	-	-	-
TIME	-	-	0.039577	5.361771	-	-
TIME SQ	-	-	-0.00119	-1.50042	-	-
R squared		0.417		0.416		0.399

Most of the coefficients for the wage equation have expected signs and they are statistically significant. We observe rate of return to schooling to be around 2.2 to 2.8 percent. The schooling variable is significant in all of these models. Individuals in this survey realise a six percent gain in wages for one more year of experience in the labour market. However, as indicated by the coefficient of the age square rate of such increase declines as an individual grows older. Similarly our estimates also shows significant bias across gender. Males earn 29 percent more than female even after controlling for schooling, age, region, professional backgrounds. Cross gender inequality is persistent throughout all waves.

Working people in London and South seem to earn 11 percent more wages than people from other part of the country. There are several explanation for this phenomenon in the labour market. The South is generally more capital intensive than the North. Consequently, the marginal productivity of labour is higher in the

South than in the North due to differences in per capita capital stock. Per capital stock seem to be significant even when it is compared between small and large corporations. People working in big firms with over 500 employees gain 10 percent more than by those in medium firms which have employees between 9 to 500. People working in small firms earn 22 less than the people working in the medium firms.

We find wages to differ across working classes. Professionals and managers earn 27 to 14 percent more than normal non-skilled workers. This more reflects returns on human capital of these workers compared to skilled non-manual or skilled manual workers. There are significant variations in wages even across the waves. This reflects wage dynamics across waves.

Table 4
Variation in real wages by the size of the Company

	Big Companies		*Small Business*	
	Coefficients	*t-stat*	*Coefficients*	*t-stat*
(Constant)	0.29994	1.099604	-0.0457	-0.33149
Schooling	0.022003	8.608514	0.024922	7.732276
AGE	0.060397	9.556513	0.05835	9.261173
AGE SQ	-0.00072	-8.85622	-0.00069	-8.9733
REGION	0.129167	7.660593	0.134833	5.584151
SEX	0.255387	15.62679	0.308492	12.72529
PRO	0.120275	0.491738	-0.08024	-1.61605
MAN	0.03926	0.16106	-	-
SNM	-0.20562	-0.84153	-0.21833	-7.06839
SM	-0.22536	-0.92101	-0.38824	-10.9582
PSO	-0.28734	-1.17199	-0.36387	-8.91642
UO	-0.58074	-2.32851	-0.42895	-7.62572
W2	0.125986	3.872638	0.220977	5.109043
W3	0.029339	0.940177	0.100242	2.295374
W4	0.129666	4.149246	0.187425	4.15907
W5	0.130334	4.161889	0.242116	5.341385
W6	0.026827	0.109107	0.09715	2.083886
W7	0.145871	4.711325	0.274512	6.472693
W8	0.201444	6.403804	0.300538	6.962366
R squared		0.401		0.369

Results in Table 3 show significant variation in intercept and coefficients of real log wages across different company sizes. Big companies have larger positive intercept compared to a negative intercept for people working in the small companies. It is noteworthy that the proprietors of small companies get lower wages compared to managers of the big companies.

	Small Companies (<9 employees)	*Big Companies (>500 employees)*
Average real wage rate	5.47783	8.102601

Figure 4

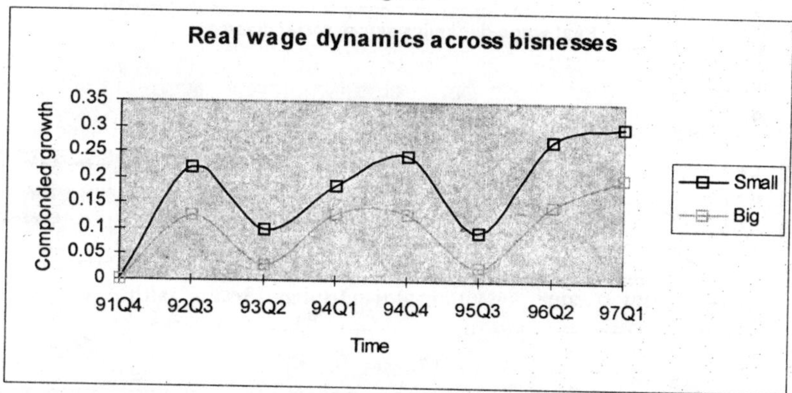

The wages in small companies seem to be growing faster than in the big companies. We suspect this to be occurring due to various policies aimed to promote the small businesses that have been carried out over the years.

VARIATION BY SKILL AND SIZE OF THE EMPLOYER

We use BHPS data set also to estimate log of real wages of four different occupational groups: 1) managers and professionals; 2) skilled non-manual; 3) skilled manual, and 4) partly skilled, and unskilled occupation. Return to schooling and experience are higher for managers and professionals (3.4 percent) than to other three groups. Managers, skilled manual and non-manual workers earn more in bigger than in smaller companies. This cross occupational regression also confirms gender bias in wages.

Table 5
Variation in Wages Across Professional Classes

	Managers and Professionals		*Skilled non-Manual*		*Skilled Manual and Partly Skilled*		*Unskilled Occupation*	
	Coeff.	*t-stat*	*Coeff.*	*t-stat*	*Coeff.*	*t-stat*	*Coeff.*	*t-stat*
(Constant)	-0.24238	-2.30467	-0.279	-3.21818	0.079343	0.997643	0.265824	1.2131
Schooling	0.033991	14.63375	0.025129	9.700202	0.020295	12.37499	0.01783	4.236874
AGE	0.07674	15.00896	0.072049	17.12924	0.045051	11.8383	0.03088	2.958091
AGE SQ	-0.00089	-14.2944	-0.00085	-15.8118	-0.0005	-10.5144	-0.00032	-2.54643
REGION	0.155313	12.07284	0.08104	5.171669	0.074779	5.100802	0.106354	3.106725
SEX	0.205673	16.6282	0.359635	22.84687	0.368248	28.36602	0.275157	8.168141
<9	-0.19619	-9.80429	-0.15601	-7.43583	-0.19338	-10.01	-0.06789	-1.47323
>500	0.081668	5.47145	0.083755	4.03365	0.159345	8.910793	0.016583	0.314742
W2	0.131612	5.324048	0.115727	4.170396	0.107282	4.412229	0.1093	1.578589
W3	0.02364	0.981268	-0.00268	-0.09843	0.028341	1.212702	0.027789	0.42512
W4	0.122919	5.054341	0.117295	4.189873	0.138125	5.634414	0.097687	1.419719
W5	0.135043	5.596049	0.154982	5.445144	0.143342	5.879854	0.127856	1.803636
W6	0.034108	0.930621	0.113121	3.3613	0.350556	13.56767	0.58311	10.77931
W7	0.186893	7.839752	0.181157	6.241838	0.179	7.3533	0.064058	0.869105
W8	0.2438	10.16457	0.195785	6.728269	0.209928	8.637929	0.09961	1.43655
R squared		0.302		0.307		0.331		0.565

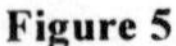

Figure 5

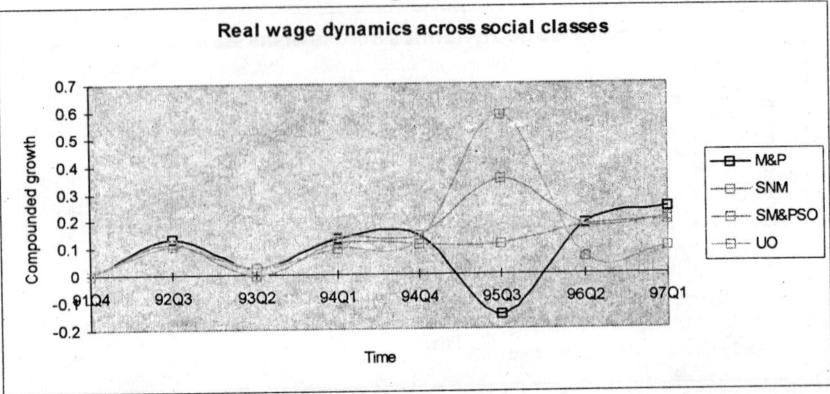

We report the relative wage growth of different classes of working individuals across waves in Figure 5. We notice a large cyclical patterns for unskilled workers peaking around quarter 3 of 1995 while the professionals and managers experienced a decline in their real wages. This signifies underlying structural factors of the British economy. This period is associated with breakdown of several businesses and restructuring of businesses. One the one hand there was redundancy of professional workers, greater number of unskilled workers must have been drawn for sort-term employment in other categories of labour.

Table 6
Regional Variation in log real Wages

	South East	*Rest of the UK*		
	Coefficients	*t-stat*	*Coefficients*	*t-stat*
(Constant)	0.070817	0.628037	-0.18588	-2.83481
Schooling	0.03283	14.53105	0.025668	19.87559
AGE	0.055873	12.01928	0.063831	22.75449
AGE SQ	-0.00064	-11.1071	-0.00074	-20.9837
SEX	0.253966	17.23961	0.300643	33.8597
<9	-0.19384	-9.2052	-0.22896	-18.4183
>500	0.100411	5.300475	0.09737	8.371546
PRO	0.289589	4.955016	0.261049	7.092697
MAN	0.228659	4.190061	0.246252	7.573783
SNM	-0.05313	-0.9588	0.035501	1.08647
SM	-0.12119	-2.14751	-0.05636	-1.71977
PSO	-0.19596	-3.39382	-0.1169	-3.52365
UO	-0.17541	-2.82167	-0.13962	-3.84105
ARMY	-0.03561	-0.51443	0.003636	0.088666
W2	0.127825	4.512517	0.128312	7.55933
W3	-0.01947	-0.70262	0.031207	1.887415
W4	0.10896	3.848974	0.142439	8.401605
W5	0.133526	4.699018	0.155435	9.172799
W6	0.244195	7.584801	0.230597	12.08414
W7	0.163457	5.720786	0.196882	11.64921
W8	0.206867	7.245746	0.227713	13.44049
R squared		0.43		0.401

Figure 6

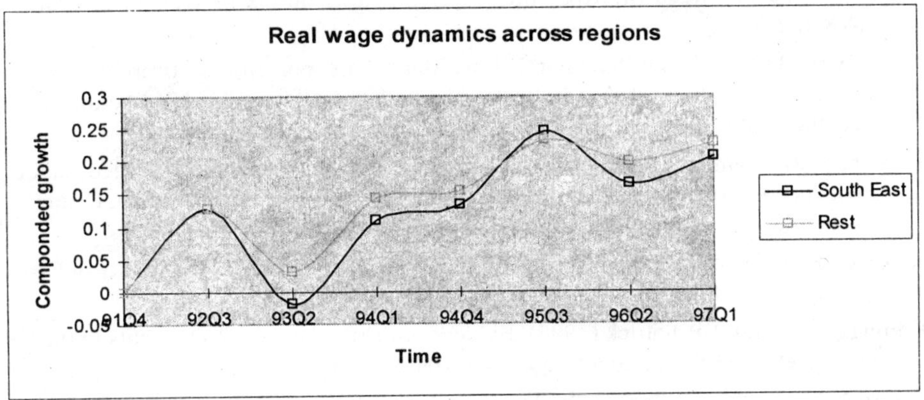

Result on the relative importance of various determinants of wages across regional categories seems to be mixed. While the schooling premium are slightly higher in the South those in the rest of the UK seems to have higher premium in experiences. The company size effect is much stronger in the South than in the North. Across occupational groups managers in the rest of the UK seem to be earning more than those in the South and London.

V. CONCLUSION

We have discussed major determinants of wages in the UK in the period of 1991-1998 using the BHPS data set. We have shown that schooling and experience key determinants of wages. We also show so a significant amount of gender bias among professional and non-professional individuals. While there are clear differences in wage rate across skill classes cross regional variation on the determinants of wages seem to be mixed.

REFERENCES

Arulampalam W., Booth A.L., (1998), "Learning and Earning: Do Multiple Training Events Pay?: D Decade of Evidence from a Cohort of Young British Men", *Journal of Economic Literature,*

Burkhauser R.V. and J.G. Poupore (1997), A Cross Sectional Comparison of Permanent Inequality in the United States and Germany, 10-17.

Chowdhury G., and S. Nickell (1985), "Hourly Earnings in the United States: Another

Look at Unionization, Schooling, Sickness, and Unemployment Using PSID Data", Journal of Labour Economics, vol. 3, no. 1 pp. 38-69.

Dickens Richard (2000), The Evolution of Individual Male Earnings in Great Britain: 1975-95, Economic Journal, 110:27-49.

Elchman Cohn and B.F. Kider (1986), Socioeconomic Background, Schooling, Experience and Monetary Rewards in the United States, Economica 53(212) pp. 497-503.

Fitzgerald J., P. Gottschaldk and R. Moffit ( ), An Analysis of Sample Attrition in Panel Data: The Michigan Study of Income Dynamics, Journal of Human Resources, XXXIII.2.

Green W.H. (1998), LIMDEP Version 7: User Manual, Econometric Software Inc. Haskel Jonathan and R. Jukes (1995) Skilled and Unskilled Employment in UK Manufacturing over the 1980s, International Journal of Manpower 16(2), pp. 36-52.

Haskel Jonathan and Y. Heden (1998), Computers and the Demand for Skilled Labour: Industry and Establishment-level Panel Evidence for the United Kingdom, Center for Economics Policy Research, discussion paper:1907.

Jenkins S.P. (1998), "Modelling Household Income Dynamics" ISER, University of Essex, Colchester CO4 3SQ, UK.

Konings Jozef and P. P. Patrick (1994), Evidence of Efficiency wage payments in the UK firm level panel data, Economic Journal 104(424), pp. 542-55.

Lillard A. Lee and R.J. Willis (1978), Dynamic Aspects of Earning Mobility Econometrica 46:5 pp. 985-1012.

Maddala G.S. (1993), The Econometrics of panel data, Elgar Aldershot UK.

NOTES

1. "The British Household Panel Survey is a multi-purpose study whose unique value resides in the fact that (1) it follows the same representative sample of individuals - the panel - over a period of years; (2) it is household-based, interviewing every adult member of sampled households; (3) it contains sufficient cases for meaningful analysis of certain groups such as the elderly or one parent families; (4) it allows for linkage of data both from other surveys and from local area statistics. The Wave 1 panel consists of some 5,500 households and 10,300 individuals drawn from 250 different areas of Great Britain. Continuing representativeness of the survey is ensured (and loss of panel members minimised) through (a) following panel members wherever they move in the UK; (b) including in the panel the new members of households formed by original panel members; (c) efficient fieldwork practices; (d) training videos for the interviewers; and by (e) regular contact with panel members through special reports and letters." Source: http://www.iser.essex.ac.uk/bhps/index.php#topcent

14

Discreteness and the Welfare Cost of Labour Supply Tax Distortions

Keshab Bhattarai & John Whalley*

INTRODUCTION

The influence that discrete choice in labour supply decisions can have both on the estimation of labour supply elasticities and on the ability of real business cycle models to calibrate to time series on output and employment has been investigated in labour- econometric (Killingsworth 1983) and real business cycle literature (Hansen 1987). However, public finance literature has not analyzed how discreteness can influence estimates of the welfare costs of tax distortions of labour supply.[1] In part, this is because the significance of discrete choice in labour supply for welfare cost estimates is an issue that public finance theorists would not be drawn to, since the issues are quantitative rather than qualitative. But the intuition is that it clearly matters, since in a heterogeneous world, tax induced adjustments will occur discretely for a small number of agents, rather than continuously for all.

Here we use numerical simulation techniques to explore the significance of discrete choice for calculations of the welfare cost of tax distortions of labour supply by constructing observationally equivalent discrete and continuous choice labour supply models.[2] The discrete analogue models we use embody varying forms of agent heterogeneity (over share parameters in preferences, substitution elasticities, endowments), while maintaining equivalence to identical single or multiple agent continuous models through similar model generated aggregate uncompensated labour supply elasticities. Issues arise as to how discrete choice is modelled in the with tax case, and we present two alternative formulations. In

* Bhattarai and Whalley acknowledge financial support from the ESRC under an award for a project on General Equilibrium Modelling of UK Policy Issues. We are grateful to two anonymous referees and to seminar groups at Hull, Warwick and Western Ontario for comments, to Jim Davies, Carlo Perroni and John Shoven for discussions, and to Jim Poterba and Mark Stewart for literature suggestions.

one, households have proportional claims on revenues generated by the tax, and redistribution occurs. In the other, tax revenues are returned to those who pay the tax; no inter-agent redistribution occurs. Each discrete choice analogue asymptotically approaches a comparable continuous case as the grid over which discrete choice occurs becomes everywhere dense. We compare welfare costs of tax distortions across discrete and continuous formulations both where individuals have the extreme choice of working 40 hours a week or remaining out of work, as well as intermediate cases (35 or 15 hours per week). In the continuous models, labour supply responds continuously to wage rate and tax changes as is conventional in the literature.

Results from these exercises are striking. The welfare costs of similar tax distortions are sharply different in discrete and continuous models. For low tax rates, welfare costs are systematically higher in discrete models but for high tax rates the reverse applies. This reflects the feature that distortionary costs are convex in the tax rates in continuous models but closer to the linear in discrete models. These findings are robust whether we use a formulation where redistribution reflecting equal revenue shares occurs across individuals, or where tax revenues are recycled to individuals who pay the taxes. This finding also occurs whether we compare the impacts of taxes under discreteness in labour supply to single representative-agent or heterogeneous-agent continuous household labour supply models. Results are robust across a range of labour supply elasticities and elasticities of substitution in consumption.

As an extension to our basic analysis, we also consider a household optimisation model where there is discrete choice for one household member (the secondary worker) and continuity of choice for the other (the primary worker). Comparisons of welfare costs of tax distortions in two member household cases are similar across discrete and continuous models for single member households. We conclude that discreteness in modelling labour supply behaviour matters not only for labour supply estimation, but also for calculation of the welfare costs of labour supply tax distortions.

DISCRETE AND CONTINUOUS MODELS OF THE WELFARE COST OF LABOUR SUPPLY TAX DISTORTIONS

As we note in our introduction above, the significance of discreteness (and non-linear budget constraints) for the estimation of labour supply elasticities is widely acknowledged in the literature (see Killingsworth 1983 and Hausman 1984). However, issues raised by discreteness in labour supply are little discussed when it comes to calculations of the welfare costs of taxes. The closest to our discussion here that we are able to find is by Blinder and Rosen (1985) who analyze the consequences of discontinuities in welfare and related benefit programs. They do not, however, use the analytic formulations of the welfare costs of taxes that we suggest here, nor offer the observation that discreteness can substantially affect welfare cost estimates.

Continuous Labour Supply Models

The conventional representative single agent continuous model of labour supply behaviour in the presence of a labour income tax is our starting point. This is characterized by the solution to an optimization problem

$$\max \quad U(C, L) \tag{1}$$

$$s.t. \quad PC = w(1 - t)(\bar{L} - L) + R \tag{2}$$

$$t.w.(\bar{L} - L) = R \tag{3}$$

where C is consumption of goods, L is leisure, $\bar{L}$ is the labour endowment, w is the wage rate, P is the price of the consumption good, t is the labour income tax rate, and R is tax revenue.

With revenues recycled in lump sum form, the effect of a labour income tax is to change the slope of the budget constraint, and hence change labour supply behaviour. However, to generate an optimal solution in the presence of taxes when, using the equation representation of the model (equations (1), (2) and (3)) some additional structure is needed. This is because if (1) is maximised subject to (2) and (3), substituting (3) into (2) simply returns the solution (even in the presence of taxes) to the no tax solution. Something else is needed to generate tax distorted optimal outcome.

Adding a tax distorted first order condition

$$\frac{U_c}{U_L} = \frac{P}{w(1 - t)} \tag{4}$$

as an additional constraint to the optimization problem (1), (2), and (3) forces the with tax solution to be different from no tax solution. Alternatively treating R in (2) as parametric, and requiring it to be consistent with its value in (3), rather than directly substituting between the equations, again forces the slope of the with tax budget constraint to be $\frac{P}{w(1 - t)}$, and optimizing behavior in the presence of taxes is different from the no tax equilibrium.

Discrete Choice Labour Supply Models

Discrete choice labour supply models with taxes are more difficult to formulate than for the continuous case above because with discontinuity in the choice set a first order condition similar to (4) no longer holds. We use two alternative discrete versions of a continuous with tax model which differ in their treatment of tax revenues, each of which reverts to the analogous continuous case as the discreteness becomes small. In one, tax revenues are distributed between households in fixed proportions, which can result in significant redistribution between households in the event of a tax change, if individuals respond by switching between discrete labour supply values. In the other, taxes are returned in lump sum form to those who pay taxes (the traditional public finance treatment). As will be seen below, this formulation is not wholly satisfactory as it involves choices among infeasible off budget points and so we treat it as our least preferred version.

In both of our discrete labour supply models, we assume an economy with N heterogeneous individuals with each of them endowed with time each facing a market wage and goods prices, and maximising utility from consumption and leisure subject to their own budget constraint. Under discrete choice, each has the option of either working long hours (eight hours a day or 40 hours a week) or remaining out of work (negligible hours). Whether an individual chooses to work depends upon their preferences over consumption and leisure. These differ across individuals, and so optimisation will yield n_1 individuals out of N as choosing the high labour supply regime, and n_2 $(N- n_1)$ the lower labour supply regime. Each household compares utility across these two regimes and chooses that regime that maximises its utility. Taxes on consumption and labour supply have significant impact on choices for certain individuals. Conventional first order conditions do not guide optimal choices in discrete models. However, numerical analysis can be used to find the best option for each individual in the model.

We use two simple models that take account of the impact of discreteness in labour supply behaviour when analysing the impacts of taxes. In the first, revenues collected from taxes are redistributed among all individuals in fixed proportions. When tax rates rise, some individuals switch between labour supply regimes. As they move from a high labour supply regime to a low labour supply regime revenue falls and lower revenues reduce transfers received by individuals. Thus higher tax rates affect the income of all individuals irrespective of whether they change their labour supply regimes. In the second formulation taxes are returned to individuals who pay them in lump sum from with no inter-individual redistribution of revenue. There is still a distortion of relative prices of consumption and leisure, however, and has impact on choices of labour supply (consumption) and leisure.

The evaluation of high and low labour supply regimes by any household h involves a comparison of utility in the two regimes. In the CES case,

$$UH_h = \left[\alpha_h^{\frac{1}{\sigma_h}} CH_h^{\frac{\sigma_h - 1}{\sigma_h}} + (1-\alpha_h)^{\frac{1}{\sigma_h}} LL_h^{\frac{\sigma_h - 1}{\sigma_h}} \right]^{\frac{\sigma_h}{\sigma_h - 1}} \tag{5}$$

$$UL_h = \left[\alpha_h^{\frac{1}{\sigma_h}} CL_h^{\frac{\sigma_h - 1}{\sigma_h}} + (1-\alpha_h)^{\frac{1}{\sigma_h}} LH_h^{\frac{\sigma_h - 1}{\sigma_h}} \right]^{\frac{\sigma_h}{\sigma_h - 1}} \tag{6}$$

where UH_h is utility in the high labour supply regime, with UH_h and LL_h as its optimal choice of (high level) consumption and (low level) leisure; UL_h is utility in the low labour supply regime with CL_h and LH_h as its (low level) consumption and (high level) leisure. In both equations α_h is the CES share parameter on consumption, and σ_h is the elasticity of substitution between consumption and leisure. The higher the value of the consumption share parameter (α_h), the more likely it is an individual will choose the high labour supply regime, and the higher the value of on average across the whole population the greater the number of people who switch regimes when taxes change. Whether an individual household prefers to remain in a high labour supply (high consumption or low leisure) regime or in a low labour supply (low consumption or high leisure) regime when tax rates change reflects the outcome of the utility comparison. Thus, if

$UH_h > UL_h$ => household chooses the high labour supply regime

$UH_h < UL_h$ => household chooses the low labour supply regime (7)

In the no tax case consumers spend their full income (the value of endowments) on consumption goods and buy back leisure. This implies that in the discrete case each individual considers two budget points, one for the high labour supply regime and one for the low labour supply regime given by:

$$P \cdot CH_h + w \cdot LL_h = w \cdot W_h \tag{8}$$

$$P \cdot CL_h + w \cdot LH_h = w \cdot W_h \tag{9}$$

where P is prices of consumption goods and w is the wage rate and W_h is the total time endowment which, for simplicity, we consider to be 70 hours per week.

Output Y in this model is given by a simple linear constant marginal product technology, which by choice of units we can represent as the labour supplied by individuals who are in the two labour supply regimes, i.e.

$$Y = \sum_{h=1}^{n1} LSH_h + \sum_{h=1}^{n2} LSL_h \tag{10}$$

Economy wide market clearing implies that total consumption for the economy is equal to total output, which by choice of units also equals the total labour supplied by all individuals. Individual consumption depends on regime choice and the economy wide aggregate consumption includes consumption of all individuals, both those who are in higher and lower labour supply regimes. In the no-tax economy consumption of individuals is given by their labour income.

If we assume that both the price of consumption and the wage rate are unity, then consumption is given by:

$$C = \sum_{h=1}^{n1} LSH_h + \sum_{h=1}^{n2} LSL_h \tag{11}$$

The amount of leisure consumed by a given individual is the time endowment less the hours of labour supplied in the high or low labour supply regime.

The imposition of an income tax will modify the budget points and hence the consumption and leisure points in the tax distorted economy are different than those in no tax equilibrium. These can be represented as:

$$UHT_h = \left[\alpha_h^{\frac{1}{\sigma_h}} CHT_h^{\frac{\sigma_h - 1}{\sigma_h}} + (1 - \alpha_h)^{\frac{1}{\sigma_h}} LLT_h^{\frac{\sigma_h - 1}{\sigma_h}} \right]^{\frac{\sigma_h - 1}{\sigma_h}} \tag{12}$$

$$ULT_h = \left[\alpha_h^{\frac{1}{\sigma_h}} CLT_h^{\frac{\sigma_h - 1}{\sigma_h}} + (1 - \alpha_h)^{\frac{1}{\sigma_h}} LHT_h^{\frac{\sigma_h - 1}{\sigma_h}} \right]^{\frac{\sigma_h - 1}{\sigma_h}} \tag{13}$$

where UHT_h and ULT_h are utilities in high and low labour supply regime in the tax distorted economy with CHT_h and LLT_h and CLT_h and LHT_h being the corresponding choices for consumption and leisure. Again the choice of labour supply regimes by an individual depends upon the evaluation of utilities in the presence of taxes, *i.e.*:

$UHT_h > ULT_h$ => high labour supply regime

$UHT_h < ULT_h$ => low labour supply regime. (14)

If t_w is the marginal income tax rate the tax distorted budget points for the high and low labour supply regimes take the form:

$$P \cdot CHT_h + w(1 - t_w) \cdot LLT_h = w(1 - t_w) \cdot W_h + \frac{RV}{N} \tag{15}$$

$$P \cdot CLT_h + w(1 - t_w) \cdot LHT_h = w(1 - t_w) \cdot W_h + \frac{RV}{N} \tag{16}$$

Revenue collections, *RV*, reflect on tax rates on labour income of the n_1 and n_2 individuals in high and low labour supply regimes, *i.e.*:

$$RV = \sum_{h=1}^{n1} t_w \cdot w \cdot LSH_h + \sum_{h=1}^{n2} t_w \cdot w \cdot LSL_h \tag{17}$$

In the discrete choice model an increase in the tax rate affects labour supply only for a limited subset of individuals who switch from their high to low labour supply regime. The majority of individuals still work the same hours as before the imposition of taxes..

Our second formulation of the discrete model for space reasons we only sketch. It retains the same high and low labour supply points as above (40 or 0 in extreme case and 35 and 20 in intermediate case). It also retains the preferences, technology, endowments and the distribution of individuals across share parameters and elasticity of substitution as above. The major difference is that tax revenues are returned back to the same individual who pays the tax with no inter-individual redistribution. Welfare impacts in this model thus reflect a pure tax distortion with no redistribution of revenues as in the first model and in this sense is closer to conventional public finance treatment. However, it involves comparing off budget points and in this sense is less satisfactory.

Change In Labour Supply And The Welfare Costs Of Tax Distortions In Discrete Models

Tax induced changes in labour supply occur in these discrete models, when utility from fewer hours of work in the presence of taxes is higher than utility of working more hours, $UHT_h < ULT_h$. Taxes change behaviour in only a small section of the working population in both discrete model formulations but almost all individuals in the continuous models. We calculate a switching index for each individual as:

$$S_h \begin{matrix} =1 \ \ if \ \ UHT_h < ULT_h \\ =0 \ \ Otherwise \end{matrix} \tag{18}$$

The total number of households who change their behaviour as a result of a tax change is then given as:

$$T = \sum_{h=1}^{N} S^h \tag{19}$$

Changes in total labour supply are obtained by adding up the difference between high and low labour supply hours of individuals who switch, i.e.:

$$\Delta LS_h = \sum_h S_h \left(LSH_h - LSL_h \right) \tag{20}$$

The term in the parenthesis is positive for individuals who switch, and zero for those who remain in the same labour supply regime.

A Comparable Continuous Labour Supply Model

We construct two different continuous labour supply choice models to evaluate welfare costs of tax distortions and which are to compare to cost estimates from comparable discrete models. The first has a representative consumer, whose aggregate labour endowment is the same as the total endowments of all individuals in discrete models. The second has N heterogeneous individuals as in the discrete models. Using these two models enables us to also evaluate the role of agent heterogeneity in discrete/continuous model comparisons. These discrete and continuous models are made comparable to each other by fixing endowments and model parameters so as to generate the same uncompensated aggregate labour supply elasticities across all models.

As in the discrete case, we assume CES preferences for the representative consumer in continuous models, i.e.:

$$U = \left[\delta C^{\frac{\sigma-1}{\sigma}} + (1-\delta) L^{\frac{\sigma-1}{\sigma}} \right]^{\frac{\sigma}{\sigma-1}} \tag{21}$$

These we maximize, subject to the with tax budget constraint

$$PC = w(1-t_w)(\overline{L} - L) + R \tag{22}$$

where revenue collected by the government is $R = t_1 w(\overline{L} - L)$.

The first order condition for utility maximisation is

$$\frac{L}{C} = \left[\frac{(1-\delta)P(1+t)}{\delta \; w(1-t_l)} \right]^{\sigma} \tag{23}$$

We again assume a linear technology with constant marginal product of labour

$$Y = \overline{L} - L \tag{24}$$

The aggregate labour supply is given by

$$LS = \overline{L} - L \tag{25}$$

For the heterogeneous agent model, we use subscripts h for individual variables and sum over h to obtain aggregate variables for the N heterogeneous individuals, and hence

$$U_h = \left[\delta_h C_h^{\frac{\sigma_h-1}{\sigma_h}} + (1-\delta_n) L_h^{\frac{\sigma_h-1}{\sigma_h}} \right]^{\frac{\sigma_h-1}{\sigma_h}} \tag{26}$$

$$R = \sum_h t_1 \; w(\overline{L}_h - L_h) \tag{27}$$

and

$$Y = \sum_h (\overline{L}_h - L_h) \tag{28}$$

where R and Y are the revenue and output functions respectively.

We numerically calculate arc (uncompensated) labour supply elasticities for both discrete and continuous models using a small perturbation in the wage rate around base model values. This gives the model labour supply elasticity (evaluated at the base (or initial) household labour supply values as

$$e = \frac{\Delta LS}{LS}\frac{w}{\Delta w} \tag{29}$$

We achieve aggregate model comparability of the form discussed above using iterative methods. This involves generating similar aggregate (uncompensated) labour supply elasticities in both discrete and continuous models, and equal aggregate labour income in the base (no tax) case. We implement this procedure for numerical examples by first specifying and solving the continuous single agent model, and then manipulating distributions of share and elasticity parameters in preferences in the second version of the continuous model and in two different discrete models until we get identical uncompensated labour supply elasticities across all models.

We use the Hicksian equivalent (EV_h) and compensating variations (CV_h) to measure the welfare costs of tax distortions in money metric utility terms. These welfare estimates reflect variations in utility that occur because of changes in quantities of goods consumed and/or hours of leisure taken by individuals. In the case of a linear homogenous utility functions these equivalent and compensating variations can be measured as:

$$EV_h = \left(\frac{U_h^B - U_h^A}{U_h^A}\right) I_h^n \text{ and } CV_h = \left(\frac{U_h^A - U_h^B}{U_h^B}\right) I_h^O \tag{30}$$

where EV_h and CV_h represent equivalent and compensating variations respectively for household *h*, U_h^A is utility in the counterfactual (A for after tax changes) and U_h^B is the utility before the tax change, I_h^O and I_h^n represent old and new income of individual *h*.

Economy wide welfare costs reflect variations in aggregate money metric utility measures. AEV_h and ACV_h are the summed (economywide) welfare cost measures as a fraction (or percentage) of economy wide income, given by the expressions

$$AEV_h = \frac{\sum_{h=1}^{N} EV_h}{\sum_{h=1}^{N} I_h^O} \text{ and } ACV_h = \frac{\sum_{h=1}^{N} CV_h}{\sum_{h=1}^{N} I_h^n}. \tag{31}$$

These aggregate welfare measures provide the basis for model comparisons of welfare cost estimates for different labour income tax rates.

NUMERICAL IMPLEMENTATION

To analyse the relative performance of discrete and continuous models capturing tax distortions of labour supply we use numerical simulation. The numerical specifications used for both discrete and continuous models are as shown in Table 1. Continuous model 1 has a single representative household, while continuous model 2 and discrete models have *N* individuals. In both continuous models agents choose hours of work in a continuous fashion, while they have limited choices in discrete case. When taxes are collected (not in the base case) tax revenues are redistributed equally among households on a fixed share basis in the discrete model 1, our leading formulation for the discrete case. Discrete models 2 represents a case where revenues are returned to individuals who pay taxes and no redistribution occurs. Individuals differ in preference parameters in continuous 2 and both versions of discrete models. Each individual has endowments equal to 70 hours per week. The single representative consumer in the continuous model 1 has a comparable aggregate labour endowment of 7000.

We use specifications of the above models to compute welfare costs of labour income tax distortions in terms of Hicksian equivalent and compensating variations in money metric utility terms. Two values of work hours, 40 and 1[1] hours per week, are assumed for high and low values of labour supply in both discrete models. In the base case with a linear technology the price of consumption goods and the wage rates are assumed to be unity. Models are made comparable through calibration of uncompensated labour supply elasticities to similar values (reported in Table 1).

Table 2 reports welfare cost estimates for tax distortions set at different rates for both versions of continuous and discrete models with specifications as set out in Table 1. Several interesting results emerge. The first is that for low tax rates, except for the 5% tax case discussed in footnote 3 to the table, welfare cost of estimates for discrete models exceed those of continuous models, while the opposite is true for high tax rates. This is accounted by the observation that, following Harberger intuition, welfare cost estimates are convex in tax rates in the continuous case; while cost estimates are closer to linear in the discrete case. The second is that comparing across continuous models 1 and 2, agent heterogeneity has relatively little impact on welfare cost estimates. This indicates that differences in results between discrete model 1 and continuous model 1 (single agent) reflect discreteness more than agent heterogeneity. Third, comparing across results for discrete model 1 and discrete models 2, welfare costs are higher when taxes have redistributive roles than when they do not as in discrete model 2.

In discrete model 1 when an individual moves from the high to the low labour supply regime in response to a tax, tax collections fall, imposing a loss on all other households because of the per capita distribution of revenues. Even if the individuals who move are close to indifferent in terms of their utility comparisons

Table 1
Specifications Used in Base Case (No Tax) for Simple Numerical Models Exploring the Welfare Cost of Taxes in Comparable Discrete and Continuous Models

	Discrete Model 1[1]	*Discrete Model 2*[2]	*Continuous Model 1*	*Continuous model 2: with agent heterogeniety*
Treatment of tax revenues (when collected)	Redistributed equally per capita	Returned to those who pay the tax	Redistributed equally per capita	Returned to single consumer
Number of households	100	100	1	100
Labour Endowment in Hours per Week	7000 in aggregate, 70 per household	7000 in aggregate, 70 per household	7000	7000 in aggregate, 70 per household
Discrete choice (1 is the numerical approximation used for zero consumption)	High and low discrete leisure consumption values for each household are 40 and 1;	High and low discrete leisure consumption values for each household are 40 and 1;	Not applicable	Not applicable
Share parameter on leisure in utility function, δ	Uniform distribution across households over the range 0.01 to 0.99	Uniform distribution across households over the range 0.01 to 0.99	0.5	Uniform distribution across households over the range 0.1 to 0.91
Net of tax price of consumption goods, P	1.0	1.0	1.0	1
Gross of tax wage, W	1.0	1.0	1.0	1
Point estimate of aggregate uncompensated labour supply elasticity[3] (evaluated at no tax equilibrium)	0.305	0.3	0.302	0.33
Elasticity of substitution in consumption, s (adjusted across models for equivalence)	1.5	0.525	0.67	0.67

1. In this model tax revenues (when collected) are redistributed among households using a fixed proportions distribution scheme.
2. In this model tax revenues (when collected) are returned to those who pay the tax in lump sum form.
3. These are obtained by repeated iteration on model parameters, and hence the values are only approximately equal across the models rather than exactly so.

across states, they would still impose burdens on all other non-movers approximately equal to the taxes they would otherwise have paid if they had remained in the high labour supply state. This fiscal externality occurs because all individuals receive smaller transfers when some individuals pay less to the government while choosing to work only a few hours.

The conclusion thus seems to be that there can be a significant variation in welfare costs of tax distortions between discrete and continuous models. This occurs because taxes induce a large change in labour supply for a small number of individuals in discrete case, whereas it causes a small change for the majority individuals in the continuous case.

Table 2

Hicksian Welfare Cost of Tax Distortions as a Proportion of Base Case Income in the Discrete[1] and Continuous[2] Models Specified in Table 1

Tax rates	*Continuous model 1*		*Discrete model 1*		*Continuous model 2*		*Discrete model 2*[3]	
	EV	CV	EV	CV	EV	CV	EV	CV
0.05	-0.0002	0.0002	-0.0005	0.0005	-0.0002	0.0003	-0.0000	0.0000
0.10	-0.0009	0.0009	-0.0014	0.0014	-0.0007	0.0014	-0.0009	0.0010
0.15	-0.0022	0.0022	-0.0029	0.0029	-0.0016	0.0034	-0.0009	0.0010
0.20	-0.0042	0.0042	-0.0049	0.0050	-0.0031	0.0064	-0.0009	0.0010
0.30	-0.0106	0.0107	-0.0107	0.0109	-0.0098	0.0181	-0.0032	0.0040
0.40	-0.0215	0.022	-0.0189	0.0196	-0.0224	0.0386	-0.0032	0.0040
0.50	-0.0392	0.0408	-0.0298	0.0316	-0.0411	0.0689	-0.0066	0.0092
0.60	-0.0671	0.072	-0.0438	0.0475	-0.0701	0.1174	-0.0110	0.0169
0.70	-0.1122	0.1264	-0.0616	0.0686	-0.111	0.1905	-0.0110	0.0169
0.80	-0.1891	0.2331	-0.0840	0.0961	-0.1752	0.3193	-0.0160	0.0268

1. Both discrete models have 1-40 hours of discrete labour supply choices.
2. The tax revenue is redistributed equally among households in discrete model 1 and given back to households paying the tax in discrete model 2. EVs and CVs reported here are as a proportion of base case aggregate income.
3. In this model the number of individuals affected by tax changes does not alter for some ranges of taxes, explaining the discrete adjustment of welfare cost estimates.

Table 3

Hicksian Welfare Cost of Tax Distortion in less Extreme Forms of Discreteness of Labour Supply Hours: Hicksian EV and CV as a Fraction of Base Case GDP using Discrete Model 1

Income tax rates	*EV*	*CV*	*Number people switching with 35-20 hours*	*Number people switching with 1-40 hours*
0.05	0.0000	0.0000	1	0
0.10	-0.0002	0.0002	2	1
0.15	-0.0006	0.0006	2	1
0.20	-0.0006	0.0006	3	1
0.30	-0.0013	0.0014	5	2
0.40	-0.0033	0.0037	6	2
0.50	-0.0047	0.0052	7	3
0.60	-0.0079	0.0091	9	4
0.70	-0.0118	0.0139	11	4
0.80	-0.0163	0.0197	15	5

Welfare costs estimates of taxes as a fraction of the base case income when individuals have intermediate labour supply choices of 35 and 20 hours labour supply rather than more extreme choices of 40 and 1 are given in Table 3. These results show that welfare costs are even lower when individuals have less extreme discrete choices than when choices are more extreme.

Sensitivity results on welfare cost of taxes for various labour supply elasticities are given in Table 4 for both continuous and discrete models. In these cases the tax change is the same across discrete and continuous cases but the value of the elasticity of labour supply to which calibration takes place changes. In these cases, welfare costs increase in the elasticity with the proportional difference in cost estimates between the discrete and continuous models remaining roughly the same.

The implication of all these results taken as a set is thus to suggest that discreteness is important for assessments of the welfare costs of tax distortions in labour supply.

Table 4
Welfare Costs of 10 percent taxes under Alternative Values of Labour Supply Elasticities to which both Models are Jointly Calibrated

Welfare cost of Income taxes in continuous and discrete labour supply models				
Labour Supply Elasticity	*Continuous 100 Household Model 1*		*Discrete Model 1*	
	EV	*CV*	*EV*	*CV*
0.20	-0.0006	0.0006	-0.0002	0.0002
0.30	-0.0009	0.0009	-0.0007	0.0007
0.50	-0.0016	0.0016	-0.0011	0.0011
0.80	-0.0025	0.0025	-0.0016	0.0017
0.105	-0.0032	0.0032	-0.0014	0.0014
1.550	-0.0038	0.0039	-0.0018	0.0018
2.050	-0.0045	0.0045	-0.0018	0.0018

1. This table gives the sensitivity of welfare costs for 10 percent labour income tax rates reported in Table 2 to various labour supply elasticities.

A TWO LABOUR TYPE ONE HOUSEHOLD DISCRETE CHOICE MODEL

We have deliberately kept the models used in section 3 simple so as to make our main point, namely, that discreteness matters in the measurement of the welfare costs of taxes affecting labour supply. But more elaborate and, hence more realistic, models are needed to underpin any general conclusions as to the role of discreteness in analyzing tax distortions of labour supply.

One particularly relevant issue is that in two person households with both primary and secondary workers, it may be the secondary worker who faces discrete labour supply choices. Secondary workers may he more likely to be involved in choices relating either to a full time job or at home production with zero labour supply. Primary workers may remain in a continuous labour supply regime and can accept overtime or part-time offers according to the need of the work place. In·

such models, the likelihood is that discreteness will have less effect on the welfare costs of taxes, since substitution margins involving continuity of labour supply are present for the household as a whole. A household model with two labour types in which only one is constrained by discrete choice also raises the related issue of whether high labour supply responsiveness by unconstrained primary workers under household utility maximization over goods and both leisure types largely reflects constraints on secondary workers. Discreteness of choice for secondary workers may thus generate data which suggests high labour supply elasticities for primary workers, even though household preferences towards their leisure are no different from those of secondary workers.

We have constructed a two labour type discrete choice household model to examine some of these issues, where we again assume a uniform distribution of households across either preference parameters or substitution elasticities. In this model, each household, h, has a preference function defined over goods and leisure of the two household members (primary and secondary worker, L_1^h and L_2^h).

$$U^h = U^h\left(C^h, L_1^h, L_2^h\right) \tag{32}$$

We again consider two regimes, which now correspond to high and low labour supply (leisure consumption) of the secondary worker. Again, household utility maximisation implies that each household chooses one out of two possible regimes. For analytical convenience, we assume that preferences are additively separable in the discrete and continuous variables. This allows us to determine demands for good, and the type 2 (continuous) leisure by each household, given the values for the discrete labour supply of the secondary worker.

These conditional demand functions for household consumption and leisure of the secondary worker are obtained by maximizing a nested household utility function defined over the continuous variables for each type of leisure and consumption at the first level, and then with discrete leisure and composite consumption-leisure at the household level, given the discrete choice for the secondary worker. The two labour types are assumed to be perfect substitutes in production. Equilibrium is then given by market clearing in the goods market for labour type 2, given the choice of regime for discrete labour type one, and the linear technology. We focus here on results of this model suppressing algebraic details for space reasons.

In the analogue continuous model, the representative household derives utility from a CES function defined over consumption of goods and leisure of household members one and two. Equilibrium in this case is given by household optimising behaviour subject to budget and revenue constraints, and an appropriate tax distorted first order condition for primary labour.

The representative household derives utility from a CES function defined over consumption of goods and leisure of household members one and two, as

$$U = \left[\delta_c C^{\frac{\sigma-1}{\sigma}} + \delta_1 L_1^{\frac{\sigma-1}{\sigma}} + \delta_2 L_2^{\frac{\sigma-1}{\sigma}} \right]^{\frac{\sigma}{\sigma-1}} \tag{33}$$

Income is derived from the two labour endowments and revenue.

$$I = w_1\,(1-t_1)L_1 + w_2\,(1-t_2)L_2 + R \tag{34}$$

Demand functions for goods and leisure are

$$C = \left[\frac{\delta_C}{(1+t)}\right]^{\sigma} \left[\frac{I}{\delta_C^{\sigma}(P(1+t))^{1-\sigma} + \delta_1^{\sigma}(w_1(1-t_1))^{(1-\sigma)} + \delta_2^{\sigma}(w_2(1-t_2))^{1-\sigma}}\right] \tag{35}$$

$$L_1 = \left[\frac{\delta_1}{w_1\,(1+t)}\right]^{\sigma}$$

$$\left[\frac{I}{\delta_C^{\sigma}(P(1+t))^{1-\sigma} + \delta_1^{\sigma}(w_1(1-t_1))^{(1-\sigma)} + \delta_2^{\sigma}(w_2(1-t_2))^{1-\sigma}}\right] \tag{36}$$

and,

$$L_2 = \left[\frac{\delta_2}{w_2\,(1+t)}\right]^{\sigma}$$

$$\left[\frac{I}{\delta_C^{\sigma}(P(1+t))^{1-\sigma} + \delta_1^{\sigma}(w_1(1-t_1))^{(1-\sigma)} + \delta_2^{\sigma}(w_2(1-t_2))^{1-\sigma}}\right] \tag{37}$$

Labour supply of each labour type is

$$LS_1 = \bar{L}_1 - L_1 \tag{38}$$

$$LS_2 = \bar{L}_2 - L_2 \tag{39}$$

Technology is again assumed to be linear,

$$Y = LS_1 + LS_2 \tag{40}$$

where Y is production of the consumption good. Tax revenue consists of sales taxes and income taxes applying to the two types of labour supply.

$$R = t\ PC + t_1\ w_1\ LS_1 + t_2\ w_2\ LS_2 \tag{41}$$

Equilibrium in this case is given by single agent household optimizing behaviour subject to budget and revenue constraints, and the appropriate tax distorted first order conditions.

As with the single labour type model we parameterize comparable discrete and continuous models, where comparability in this case involves the two uncompensated labour supply elasticities for primary and secondary workers rather than, as before, one single elasticity value for aggregate labour supply. We consider the *N* household version of continuous model 4 in which each family member is endowed with 70 hours per week and households differ from each other in preference share parameters and elasticity of substitution between consumption and leisure.

These parameterizations are set out in Table 5. While each household member varies labour supply continuously in models 3 and 4, only the primary worker does so in discrete model 3. The secondary worker chooses a discrete number of hours. We calibrate the discrete model to labour supply elasticities of 0.15 (approximately) for primary workers, and 0.5 (approximately) for the secondary worker to make it comparable with the two versions of the continuous labour supply models. These specifications also allow us to make calculations of welfare costs of tax distortions similar to those reported in Table 4 in the earlier section. Table 6 reports our results.

Table 6
Welfare Costs of Alternative Tax Distortions of to Family Labour Supply Using the Discrete and Continuous Models Specified in Table 5[1]

Tax rates	*Continuous model 3 – Representative Agents*		*Continuous model 4- Heterogeneous agents*		*Discrete model 3 – with primary and secondary workers*	
	EV	*CV*	*EV*	*CV*	*EV*	*CV*
0.05	-0.0003	0.0003	-0.0002	0.0003	-0.00011	0.00011
0.10	-0.0011	0.0011	-0.0010	0.0011	-0.00044	0.00048
0.15	-0.0026	0.0026	-0.0023	0.0026	-0.00105	0.00114
0.20	-0.0049	0.0049	-0.0044	0.0049	-0.00199	0.00215
0.30	-0.0125	0.0126	-0.0111	0.0125	-0.00506	0.00548
0.40	-0.0253	0.0259	-0.0223	0.0256	-0.01032	0.01121
0.50	-0.0457	0.0479	-0.0849	0.0983	-0.01885	0.02059
0.60	-0.0777	0.0843	-0.1176	0.1428	-0.03253	0.03591
0.70	-0.1273	0.1458	-0.1149	0.1410	-0.06825	0.0758
0.80	-0.2484	0.3305	-0.1838	0.2421	-0.11877	0.13331
0.90	-0.3285	0.4893	-0.3034	0.4669	-0.1373	0.13638

1. Discrete models have 0-40 hours of discrete labour supply choices.

Two major points emerge from the results using these household labour supply models. The first is that welfare costs of tax distortions are higher in continuous family labour supply models (continuous 3 and 4) for high tax rates but comparable

Table 5
Specifications Used in Exploring the Welfare Cost of Taxes in Two Member Household Models

Model features	*Continuous Model 3*	*Discrete Model Version 3*	*Continuous heterogeneous model 4*
Number of households	1	100	100
Labour Endowment in potential hours per week.	14000	14000 in aggregate, 140 per household,	14000 in aggregate, 140 per household,
Leisure consumption of primary worker	Continuous variable	Constrained to high and low discrete values for each household ; $L^H = 40$; $L^L = 1$;	Continuous variable
Leisure consumption of secondary worker	Continuous variable	Continuous variable	Discrete variable
Share parameters, d, in the utility function	$d_0 = 0.462 d_1 = 0.345 d_2 = 0.129$	Share parameters of preferences at both levels of nests of utility function are distributed across the 100 households	Share parameters are distributed uniformly across the 100 households
Net of tax price of consumption goods, P	1.0	1.0	1.0
Gross of tax wage, W	1.0	1.0	1.0
Point estimates of aggregate uncompensated labour supply elasticities (evaluated at no tax equilibrium)	0.144[1]0.510[1]	0.146[1]0.517[1]	0.144[1]0.510[1]
Elasticity of substitution in consumption, σ	σ = 0.5	σ = 0.5σ, has a distribution of values. across households	σ = 0.5σ, has a distribution of values across households.

Numerical Difficulties in Calibrating the Discrete two Labour type Model Imply that Elasticities Across the two Models are close but not Identical.

for lower tax rates. The same pattern emerges for discrete model too. This suggests that redistribution impact among households predominates the intra-household labour leisure substitution effect in model 3, in which case some of the effects of taxes on labour income of one family member falls upon that of another family member. Secondly, welfare costs between discrete and continuous models differ by up to factor of five in comparable continuous and discrete family labour supply models, again reflecting the fact that the family as a whole is more capable of absorbing tax shocks in continuous rather than in the discrete models.

CONCLUSION

This paper discusses the influence of discrete labour supply (or leisure) choice in estimates of the welfare costs of taxes on labour supply, issues which appear to be little discussed in the literature. We construct comparable discrete and continuous models of labour supply calibrated to yield similar point estimates of uncompensated elasticities of aggregate labour supply around a base case equilibrium in the presence of taxes. We discuss four different versions of continuous labour supply models in which individuals or families could choose their labour supply continuously and three different versions of discrete models in which their choices are restricted to more extreme and intermediate work hours per week.

Tax distortions in discrete models affect only a subset of individuals or families, who experience large adjustments in their labour supply while the majority still retains their original work hours. This yields only small change for the majority of individuals or families in continuous models. We find that welfare costs of tax distortions differ between continuous labour supply choice models and comparable discrete choice labour supply models. Discreteness matters more than heterogeneity or the redistribution impacts of taxes in these welfare cost calculations. We thus argue that the discreteness perhaps needs to be taken account more than in current literature when evaluating the welfare costs of tax distortions on labour supply, as well as other tax effects.

REFERENCES

Blinder, A.S. and H.S. Rosen, "Notches" *American Economic Review*, vol. 75, No. 4, (September 1985), pp 737-747.

Blundell, R. "Labour Supply and Taxation: A Survey", *Fiscal Studies* vol. 13 No. 3, (August 1992), pp. 15-40.

Blundell R. and T. MaCurdy, "Labor supply: a review of alternative approaches" in *Handbook of Labour Economics*, Part 7, (Elsevier, Norh-Holland: 2000). ISBN: 0-444-50187-8.

Brooke, A., D. Kendrick and A.Meeraus, *GAMS: A Users Guide*, (San Francisco: Scientific Press, 1988).

Cogan, J. F., "Fixed Costs and Labour Supply", *Econometrica*, vol. 49, no.4, (July 1981), pp. 945-963.

Dickens, W.T. and S. Lundberg, "Hours Restrictions and Labour Supply", *International Economic Review*, vol. 34, (February 1993) pp 169-192.

Dex, S., A. Clark and M. Taylor, *Household Labour Supply Employment*, Department Research Series No. 43 (ESRC Centre for Micro-social Change, University of Essex, 1995).

Hansen, G., "Indivisible Labour and the Business Cycle", *Journal of Monetary Economics*, 16, 3, (November 1985) 309-327, North-Holland.

Hausman, J.A., "Labour Supply" in (ed.) J.A. Pechman, *How Taxes Affect Economic Behaviour*, (Washington, D.C: Brookings, 1984)

Khan, S. and K. Lang, "The Effects of Hours Constraints on Labour Supply Estimates", *Review of Economic Statistics*, 73:4 (November 1991) pp. 605-611.

Killingsworth, M., *Labour Supply*, (Cambridge University Press, 1983).

MaCurdy, T., D. Green, H. Paarsch, "Assessing Empirical Approaches for Analyzing Taxes and Labour Supply", *Journal of Human Resources*, Vol. 25, no.3 (Summer 1990) pp. 415-490.

Piggott, J. and Whalley J., "The Tax Unit and Household Production", *Journal of Political Economy*, Vol. 104, No. 2 (April 1996) 398-418.

Preston, I. and Walker I., "Welfare Measurement in Labour Supply Models with Non-linear Budget Constraints", *Institute of Fiscal Studies*, Working Paper no. w92/12, 7 (Ridgmount Street, London WC1E 7AE, 1992).

Rosen, H. S., "Taxes in a Labour Supply Model with Joint Wage-Hours Determination", *Econometrica*, Vol. 44, No. 3 (May 1976) pp. 485-507.

Rosen, H. S., "What is Labour Supply and Do Taxes Affect It?", *American Economic Review*, Vol. 70 no.2 (May 1980) pp.171-176.

Shoven, J.B., and J. Whalley, *Applying General Equilibrium*, (Cambridge University Press: 1992).

Stewart, M.B. and J.K. Swaffield, "Constraints on the Desired Hours of Work of British Men", *Economic Journal*, V. 107, iss. 441, (March, 1997), pp. 520-35

Tummers, M. P. and I. Woittiez, "A Simultaneous Wage and Labour Supply Model with Hours Restrictions", *Journal of Human Resources*, 26(3), (Summer 1991), pp. 393-423.

NOTES

1. There seems to be no discussion of this in existing surveys of taxation and labour supply, including Blundell (1992), and the well known earlier pieces on taxes and labour supply by Rosen (1980), Hausman (1984), and MaCurdy, Green, and Paarsch (1990).
2. See the discussion of the related but different issue of non linear budget constraints and the welfare cost of taxes in Preston and Walker (1992).
3. For numerical reasons we use 1 as the discrete approximation of 0 for low labour supply in our discrete model computations.

15

The Division and Size of Gains from Liberalization in Service Networks

Keshab Bhattarai[43] & John Whalley

INTRODUCTION

We discuss cross border liberalization in flows of network related services, such as telecoms, suggesting that both the division of the gains from liberalization between countries and the size of such gains is likely to differ from the case of trade in goods when tariff barriers are removed at the border. For network related services, no cross border payment is made since senders (callers) pay fully for services (messages). Cross border welfare effects of liberalization still occur since when prices for international calls are lowered both senders and receivers of messages (calls) benefit. Since callers pay the full cost of calls, the addition of a new subscriber to a network confers an externality on existing subscribers who potentially receive calls at no charge. We model such effects as generated by preferences in which individual utility is a function not only of own consumption of network related services (i.e., calls made), but also the consumption of similar services by others within the network (i.e., calls received). We then examine the effects of liberalization across country networks[1], making reference to the sharp reductions in international call rates in recent years which have occurred under deregulation[2].

We first consider a simple two good two-country case involving network-related services and other goods, in which the two countries have different numbers of consumers. We model liberalization as the joining of two previously disjoint country networks into one combined cross country network. When this occurs,

* Earlier versions of this paper were presented at the NBER Summer Institute, Cambridge, the Royal Economic Society meetings and in seminars at Warwick, Copenhagen and Western Ontario. We are grateful to participants in all these sessions for comments. Bhattarai and Whalley acknowledge financial support from the ESRC under an award for a project on General Equilibrium Modeling of UK Policy Issues, and helpful comments from a referee.

consumers in the smaller country receive a larger per capita gain than those in the larger country due to the network externalities since these arise from gaining access to a larger network yielding incoming messages (calls). Country size and the per capita benefit of access to the other country's network tend to offset each other in determining the division of the gains from liberalization, suggesting that the country gains from cross-border network service liberalization can be of similar (absolute) size even where countries differ in size. This is different from the case of trade in goods where the benefits of liberalization accrue disproportionately to the smaller country.

We first examine a case in which the country's gains from liberalization are of equal absolute size in the two countries independently of relative country size (in money metric terms), and then show how it is possible to change preferences and other model parameters in such a way that larger gains accrue to the larger (rather than the smaller) country, or vice versa. In an alternative formulation with two types of network related services (international and domestic), we also show how it is possible to capture price based substitution effects between service categories. This allows us to model network related service trade liberalization as the removal of barriers to international services (which have cross-country network externality effects), rather than simply the joining of two disjoint networks. Using this alternative formulation, we again show that the absolute size of gains can be larger or smaller for the large (or small) country, depending upon the parameter specification used in the model.

We then turn to the relative size of the aggregate gains from liberalization of network related services compared to goods trade liberalization. We characterize inter-country network service interactions as involving service delivery along a joined network, but in ways which, in principle, give each of the two governments in the origin and destination countries the power to tax the same transaction[3]. Phone calls made from, say, the US to India can be regulated or taxed by both governments as messages are either sent or delivered. We evaluate non-cooperative international retaliatory outcomes involving service barrier retaliation in this case, measuring the gains from liberalization by comparing free trade and non-cooperative Nash policy outcomes.

A cross country policy game in a service network reveals three key differences relative to the traditional Nash equilibrium tariff policy game in goods. One is the use of instruments (taxes) by both countries on each bilateral service flow; another is the absence of any restriction that two way service flows be balanced in value terms as the services do not involve any cross country payment (unless taxed by the other government). The third is that inter-country flows along networks can be, and frequently are, unbalanced (more calls from the US to India, than from India to the US). As a result, both governments can have an incentive to charge high taxes in the Nash equilibrium if they can make the first charge on the appropriate bilateral service flow. We find that relative to a non-cooperative Nash outcome, gains from liberalization of network related services are typically larger than gains from liberalization in goods trade in models made comparable in the sense that the service flow parameter values used for trade barriers now apply to similar flows of goods instead of services.

Finally, we apply our framework to the analysis of global telecom liberalization in a model of the EU, the US, Canada, and the Rest of the World, and calibrated to 1999 data. Data on call volumes and pricing are drawn from the World Telecommunications Development Report, and are supplemented by GDP and other data from the World Development Report. Liberalization yields gains similar in proportional size for large and small regions; consistent with the theme of paper of the differences in liberalization between goods and services.

We suggest that our analysis has three main implications. The first is that the benefits of liberalization in network related services, in contrast to goods, are more likely to be approximately equally divided between countries than is true of trade in goods, and this can occur independently of the size of the countries and the number of residents in each. The second is that non-cooperation in network related services trade may involve extremes of retaliation which go beyond even those suggested for goods trade in the optimal tariff literature, and so the gains from liberalization may be larger in network related services than in goods. The third is the large potential size of welfare gains from trans-border liberalization where network externality effects rather than conventional gains from trade apply. The broader implication is the seemingly different nature of cross border liberalization in network related services compared to liberalization in goods.

NETWORK EXTERNALITIES AND THE DIVISION OF GAINS FROM LIBERALIZATION IN A SIMPLE NETWORK SERVICE MODEL

We first consider a world consisting of N countries, each of which has a fixed endowment of resources which, in turn, can be used for producing goods or network related services. Services are consumed via a network, and involve no cross border payment, since services are purchased and consumed by senders of messages along the network[44] Much of service activity, as Melvin (1989) pointed out, is concerned with intermediation through time and/or space. Network related services not only capture activity in telecommunications, but also transportation services where recipients of shipments receive benefits while shipment costs are fully paid by the shipper. They seem not to cover inter-temporal intermediation, such as financial services, which involves intermediaries bringing together agents in order to transact. They directly enter the sender's utility function; but also provide utility to the receiver; hence messages sent by others also appear in the utility function of the receiver. It is this feature which generates network externalities, since service recipients make no payment for incoming messages (calls) even though they receive a welfare benefit. The word externality in such situations denotes a consumption to consumption externality in the sense of Meade; hère the physical interdependence via message flows to recipients is not appropriately priced.

We use a transformation frontier to describe the technology which allows goods and network services in each country to be produced from resource endowments,

$$Y_n = F_n\left(G_n, S_n\right) \text{ (n =1,2)} \tag{1}$$

where Y_n is the fixed resource endowment, G_n is goods production, and S_n is network services production in country n, and Wn, the value of production of goods and network services in country n is given by

$$W_n = P_n^g G_n + P_n^s S_n \tag{2}$$

where P_n^g is the country n price of goods, and P_n^S is the price of network related services in country n. These prices are denominated relative to the country specific resource Y_n (effectively a composite of G_n and S_n) where price is unity. Thus Y_n = W_n. For simplicity, we assume that no direct international trade in either goods or network services occurs. Senders pay for such services in their country of origin, and the prices of the services can differ between the countries. Y_n can also be thought of as the value of the production frontier, where a unit of a composite of G_n and S_n is taken as the numeraire, and has a price of unity. Optimizing behavior on the production side of the model implies

$$\frac{\partial F_N}{\partial G_N} \Big/ \frac{\partial F_n}{\partial S_n} - P_n^G \Big/ P_n^S \tag{3}$$

The transformation frontier (1), along with (2), thus yields an implicit supply function for goods and network services in each country.

We assume that there are T1 households in country 1, and T2 in country 2. Each household in each country derives utility directly from consumption of goods and from sending messages along the network (services). When connected to a service network, households also receive additional utility benefits from the services consumed by others in home and foreign countries, since they are the recipients of messages. We assume such benefits are proportional to the total volume of messages sent along the network; since as the total message volume expands so does the potential number of callers who could be in contact with any particular recipient.

We use a utility function to represent the preferences of each household in which, ST, the total number of calls made along the relevant network, enters multiplicatively with a constant λ[5] which we, for now, take to be common to all individuals,

$$U_n^h = \lambda . ST . U_n^h (G_n^h, S_n^h) \tag{4}$$

where the subscript n refers to countries and the superscript h to households in a country; U is utility, G is consumption of goods, and S is consumption of network related services. *ST* is total consumption of network related services by all the households in the relevant network; the domestic network when networks are disjoint, or the international network when they are linked. In this formulation, the network externality impacts directly on household utility when there is an expansion in the size of the service network to include both home and foreign countries.

We assume, for simplicity, that each household in each country receives a fixed share of the economy wide income

$$I_n^h = \theta_n^h W_n \tag{5}$$

where I_n^h denotes income for household h in country n, and $\sum_h \theta_n^h = 1; \theta_n^h \geq 0$. This income is spent on purchasing goods and network related services. Each household budget constraint implies that

$$I_n^h = P_n^g G_n^h + P_n^S S_n^h \tag{6}$$

Demands for goods and services by each household are obtained from maximization of the utility function (4) subject to the household budget constraint (6).

As no direct trade in network services takes place in this model, in equilibrium the market for goods and services clears in each country; i.e.

$$G_n = \sum_h G_n^h \tag{7}$$

and

$$S_n = \sum_h S_n^h \tag{8}$$

In equilibrium, goods and services prices are thus such that country demands for services match their domestic supply.

We can consider the effects of liberalization involving a joining of the two previously disjoint country service networks using this framework. In this case, the ST term in preferences refers to the combined service consumption across the two countries, rather than the two separate country service consumptions. As only the externality term in preferences changes, when liberalization occurs in this simple case there are no real effects from liberalization; prices and quantities of both goods and services within countries remain the same; only utility changes.

Since any homothetic utility function can be represented as a linear homogenous function with special ordinal properties[6], the welfare implications of liberalization in this case are especially easy to analyze. As noted in Shoven and Whalley (1992), with linear homogenous preferences the Hicksian compensating variation measure of welfare change between equilibria is given by

$$CV^h = \frac{U_N^h - U_0^h}{U_N^h} \cdot I_N^h \tag{9}$$

where U_N^h and U_0^h refer to the old and new utility levels for household h, and I_N^h is the income of household h in the new (post change) equilibrium[7].

Because price and quantities do not change between equilibria, and because the term *ST* is multiplicative in utility from goods and own services, each household's compensating variation in this case can be written as

$$CV^h = \frac{ST^N - ST^0}{ST^N} \cdot I_N^h \qquad (10)$$

where the λ terms cancel, and ST^N and ST^0 denote the aggregate service consumption values relevant for household h in the new and base period (original) equilibria. I_N^h is household h new period equilibrium income.

If preferences are identical across the households in each country, the total welfare impact in the two countries, TCV^1 and TCV^2, can be written as

$$TCV^1 = I_1 \frac{\left(ST^N - ST_1^0\right)}{ST^N} \qquad (11)$$

$$TCV^2 = I_2 \frac{\left(ST^N - ST_2^0\right)}{ST^N} \qquad (12)$$

where ST_1^0 and ST_2^0 refer to the base case aggregate service consumption in countries 1 and 2, I_1 and I_2 are economy wide incomes in country 1 and 2 from (2), and again the λ terms cancel.

The ratio of the welfare gains in the two countries from liberalization is given by

$$\frac{TCV^1}{TCV^2} = \frac{I_1}{I_2} \left(\frac{ST^N - ST_1^0}{ST^N - ST_2^0} \right) \qquad (13)$$

Noting that in this special case $ST^N = ST_1^0 + ST_2^0$, since there is no quantity response under liberalization, (11) implies that

$$\frac{TCV^1}{TCV^2} = 1 \text{ if } \frac{I_1}{I_2} = \frac{ST_1^0}{ST_2^0} \qquad (14)$$

i.e. the two countries will receive a welfare gain under liberalization of equal size if the ratio of national income and service consumption are the same across the countries.

Thus in this simple case it is possible to construct parameterizations in which both countries will receive benefits from network related service liberalization of equal absolute size, even if one country is smaller or larger than the other and has more or less households. The widely accepted propositions concerning the division of gains and country relative size involving liberalization of trade in goods thus seem not to apply to this case in the same way.

THE GAINS FROM LIBERALIZATION IN A TWO SERVICE TYPE MODEL

While illustrating a case where the gains from network related service trade liberalization between countries can be of equal absolute size, the discussion in the previous section nonetheless embodies some important simplifying model features which need further investigation. Liberalization is simply treated as a connection of two separate country networks, and so unchanged relative services to goods prices in each country characterize a liberalization scenario. Also, because the network externality effect is multiplicative in utility, no real effects accompany liberalization; consumption and production of network related services remain unchanged in the new integrated network equilibrium, while household utility changes due to expanded network size.

One can relax these assumptions and extend the framework used above to see if similar results can still be obtained by numerical simulation. Numerical simulation is needed because the model solutions are no longer analytic. To do this, we separately consider two different types of services; one assumed to relate only to domestic and one assumed to relate only to internationally transmitted services (message communications). In this model extension we also give governments the power to tax these two types of services differently when purchased in their own country. A higher tax rate on international rather than on domestic communications can be thought of as reflecting regulation of internationally linked network service transactions. Liberalization in this case involves lowering barriers to international communication, and is reflected in reduced tax rates in all countries on purchases of international network related services. This form of services liberalization, unlike that considered in the previous section, generates relative price effects and, hence, quantity responses.

We use a constant elasticity of transformation (CET) function to describe the transformation of endowments into goods and services, but now one which incorporates two service types S^1 and S^2, one of which is supplied domestically and the other internationally, i.e.

$$Y_n = \left(\eta_n^1 G_n^{\frac{\sigma_n - 1}{\sigma_n}} + \eta_n^2 S_n^{1\,\frac{\sigma_n - 1}{\sigma_n}} + \eta_n^3 S_n^{2\,\frac{\sigma_n - 1}{\sigma_n}} \right)^{\frac{\sigma_n}{\sigma_n - 1}} \tag{15}$$

where Y_n is the fixed resource endowment of country n, G_n is goods production in country n, S_n^1 is production of network service type 1 in country n, and S_n^2 is production of network service type 2 in country n. η_n^1 η_n^2 and η_n^3 are share parameters in production, and σ_n is the country n elasticity of transformation.

The value of production of goods and network services in country n is given by

$$W_n = P_n^g G_n + P_n^{s1} S_n^1 + P_n^{s2} S_n^2 \tag{16}$$

and maximizing the value of production subject to the CET function (15) implies supply functions for country n for the two types of services

$$S_n^1 = G_n \left(\frac{\eta_n^2}{\eta_n^1} \frac{P^g}{P_n^{S_1}} \right)^{\sigma_n} \tag{17}$$

$$S_n^2 = G_n \left(\frac{\eta_n^3}{\eta_n^1} \frac{P^g}{P_n^{S_2}} \right)^{\sigma_n} \tag{18}$$

Each household in each country again derives utility from consumption of goods, but now also from the two types of network services. These households also receive externality benefits from the consumption of network related services by other households along both the home and international networks.

We use Cobb-Douglas preferences for each household of the form[1]

$$U_n^h = G_n^{h^{\alpha_g^h}} \left(S_n^{1,h} \left(\sum_h S_n^{1,h} \right) \right)^{\alpha_1^h} \left(S_n^{2,h} \left(\sum_n \sum_h S_n^{2,h} \right) \right)^{\alpha_2^h} \tag{19}$$

where the *n* subscripts refer to countries, and superscripts *h* refer to households within country *n*. *U* is utility, *G* is consumption of goods, and S^1 and S^2 are consumption of the two service types (domestic and international). As before, household utility increases when country service networks are more fully joined, but these effects now operate differently in the home and international markets.

Each household again receives a fixed share of country income

$$I_n^h = \theta_n^h W_n \tag{20}$$

and this income is spent on purchasing goods and services. Household budget constraints now imply that

$$I_n^h = P_n^g G_n^h + P_n^{S_1} S_n^{1,h} + P_n^{S_2} S_n^{2,h} \tag{21}$$

and demands for goods and services by each household are derived from maximization of Cobb-Douglas household utility functions subject to the household budget constraints (19).

These give goods demands as:

$$G_n^h = \frac{\alpha_{g,n}^h . I_n^h}{P_n^g} \tag{22}$$

and demands for the two types of services as

$$S_n^{1,h} = \frac{\alpha_{1,n}^h . I_n^h}{P_n^{s1}} \tag{23}$$

$$S_n^{2,h} = \frac{\alpha_{2,n}^h . I_n^h}{P_n^{s2}} \tag{24}$$

Markets for goods and network services again clear at country level in equilibrium, i.e.

$$G_n = \sum_h G_n^h \tag{25}$$

$$S_n^1 = \sum_h S_n^{1,h} \tag{26}$$

$$S_n^2 = \sum_h S_n^{2,h} \tag{27}$$

Taxes charged by national governments on S^2 purchased at home can be incorporated into this framework, and distort the relative prices of both network services and goods and also among services, reducing purchases of externality generating international services.

Table 1 reports parameterizations used in a numerical example showing the impacts of network related services liberalization in this two services type model. To capture differences in country size, we assume country 2 has double the resources of country 1 at 1000 rather than 500. We consider 2 households in country 1 and 5 in country 2, with identical preferences within countries. We consider liberalization to be the creation of a link between two disjoint networks.

Results in Table 1 show that, while, the absolute value of the gains from liberalization in network related services differ across the two countries the proportional effects are similar. It is also possible with further changes in specification beyond these used to report results in Table 1 to construct a case where the gains to the two countries go mainly to the small country (as with trade in goods), as in the second specification, or vice versa all in the third specification.

Table 1

Model specifications of the two Services Type Model Yielding Country Gains from Liberalization of Similar Relative size Across Countries and Larger or Smaller Gains for the Larger Country

	Specification yielding gains to both small and large countries	*Specification yielding larger gains to a small country and a loss to the larger country*	*Specification yielding the majority of the gains to the larger country and loss to the smaller country*
Production			
Resources	Country 1 Y_1 =500 Country 2 Y_2 = 1000	Country 1 Y_1 =500 Country 2 Y_2 = 1000	Country 1 Y_1 =500 Country 2 Y_2 = 1000
Transformation Frontier Shares and Elasticities (G, S^1, S^2)	$\eta_1 = 0.4$; $\eta_2 = 0.2$; $\eta_3 = 0.4$;	$\eta_1 = 0.5$; $\eta_2 = 0.25$; $\eta_3 = 0.25$; $\sigma = -0.75$	$\eta_1 = 0.5$; $\eta_2 = 0.25$; $\eta_3 = 0.25$; $\sigma = -0.75$
Demand			
(3 households in country 1 and 5 in country 2, with identical preferences within countries) Demand side shares (G, S^1, S^2)	Country 1 $\alpha_g = 0.4$; $\alpha_1 = 0.4$; $\alpha_2 = 0.4$; Country 2 $\alpha_g = 0.4$; $\alpha_1 = 0.4$; $\alpha_2 = 0.2$;	Country 1 $\alpha_g = 0.2$; $\alpha_1 = 0.2$; $\alpha_2 = 0.6$; Country 2 $\alpha_g = 0.3$; $\alpha_1 = 0.4$; $\alpha_2 = 0.3$;	Country 1 $\alpha_g = 0.2$; $\alpha_1 = 0.2$; $\alpha_2 = 0.6$; Country 2 $\alpha_g = 0.3$; $\alpha_1 = 0.4$; $\alpha_2 = 0.3$;
Taxes			
Pre liberalization (country tax rates on S^2)	$t_1^1 = 3.01$; $t_1^2 = 0.67$;	$t_1^1 = 0.49$; $= 47.1$;	$t_1^1 = 76.5$; $= 0.57$;
Post liberalization (country tax rates on S^2)	$t_2^1 = -0.83$; $t_2^2 = -0.49$;	$t_2^1 = -0.448$; $= 0.97$;	$t_2^1 = -0.57 = -0.44$;
Money Metric Welfare Gains from Liberalization (Hicksian EV as percentage of national income)	$EV_1 = 0.605$ $EV_2 = 1.006$	$EV_1 = 4.42$ $EV_2 = -0.93$	$EV_1 = -0.24$ $EV_2 = 1.79$

Thus, in this more realistic but slightly more complex world the theme is the same as above; namely that with network externalities and cross country service liberalization, there is no presumption (as with goods) that the benefits of liberalization will accrue disproportionately to the small country. Per capita effects and country size seemingly once again operate in opposite directions.

THE SIZE OF THE GAINS FROM LIBERALIZATION IN SERVICE NETWORKS

Having argued that the country division of gains from international liberalization in network related services will typically differ from that for trade in goods, we finally proceed to a discussion of the size of the gains from such liberalization.

We analyze the size of the gains from liberalization in a cross country policy game by comparing Nash equilibria and free trade outcomes. The network related service policy game differs from a conventional tariff game in which both countries apply tariffs to their own imports. In this game, both countries have the ability to tax service flows between countries; the origin country through regulation of the service flow as it leaves its own border, and the destination country through regulation of flows from its own border onward within the country of the eventual recipient of the network related service[1]. Thus, in the two country case four tax rates t_i^j (the tax rates charged by country j on services originating in country i) are involved in the game.

To provide a point of comparison to tariff games in goods trade, we can compute Nash equilibria in a two country tariff game in which *S*, instead of being a network related service, is treated as a conventional commodity, much like *G* and international trade takes place in *G* and *S*. In this calculation, all share and elasticity parameters are as in the two service type model calculations reported on in Table 1, and in a Nash equilibrium tariff rates on imports are determined by commodity and by the country of source. In this case, levels of only two instruments (tariffs on imports by each country) are endogenously determined, rather than four instruments as in the network service case.

We use the two service type model set out in section III above, with the further difference that tax rates charged by the two countries on network related services are endogenously determined in a Nash equilibrium rather than set exogenously. In the process, we determine the two country two tax rate reaction functions.

Table 2 reports results from these calculations, and compares Nash equilibrium outcomes to those under no intervention (free trade in the goods trade model). Because of the network externality accruing to own country residents, origin countries have an incentive to subsidize own consumption of internationally traded services, but destination countries have an incentive to apply a significant tax due to revenues transferred from abroad under the tax. Results in Table 2 suggest that the welfare gains as a % of national income, from moving to no intervention (the analogue of free trade) are larger in the two service type model than in the trade model.

Table 2
Differences in the Welfare Gains from Liberalization in a Service Networks Model and a Tradeable Goods Model Relative to a Nash Equilibrium

	Services Related Network (2 Service Type)	*Model Trade in Goods Model*
Production	Country 1 Y1 =500	Country 1 Y1 =500
Resources Endowment	$\eta 1 = 0.5$; $\eta 2 = 0.25$; $\eta 3 = 0.25$;	$\eta 1 = 0.5$; $\eta 2 = 0.25$; $\eta 3 = 0.25$;
Transformation Elasticities	Country 2 Y2 = 1000	Country 2 Y2 = 1000
Transformation Shares (G, S^1, S^2)	$\eta 1 = 0.5$; $\eta 2 = 0.25$; $\eta 3 = 0.25$;	$\eta 1 = 0.5$; $\eta 2 = 0.25$; $\eta 3 = 0.25$;
Demand	Country 1 $\alpha g = 0.4$;	Country 1 $\alpha g = 0.4$;
Demand side shares (G, S^1, S^2)	$\alpha 1 = 0.4$; $\alpha 2 = 0.2$;	$\alpha 1 = 0.4$; $\alpha 2 = 0.2$;
	Country 2 $\alpha g = 0.4$;	Country 2 $\alpha g = 0.2$;
	$\alpha 1 = 0.4$; $\alpha 2 = 0.2$;	$\alpha_1 = 0.2$; $\alpha_2 = 0.6$;
Nash Equilibrium Tariff Rates	$t_1^1 = 240\%$; $t_1^2 = 107\%$;	$t_1^1 = 235\%$; $t_1^2 = 1008\%$;
(tariff rates on goods and tax	$t_2^2 = 210\%$; $t_2^2 = 99\%$;	$t_2^2 = 183\%$; $t_2^2 = 28\%$;
rates on services)		
Money metric welfare from	EV1 = 3.56%	EV1 = -0.03%
unilateral liberalisation	EV2 = -3.81%	EV2 = -0.07%
(Hicksian EV or CV as a % of		
national income)		

EMPIRICAL ANALYSIS OF GLOBAL TELECOMS LIBERALIZATION

Finally we use the two service type model set out above to analyze the implications of global liberalization in telecoms using an empirically based version of the modelling approach set out above. For these purposes, we consider a global four region telephone service network model consisting of Canada, Europe, USA and the Rest of the World (ROW). We use this to compute the global welfare gains from telecom liberalization using the network related service model presented above. We also analyze the role played by the relative sizes of domestic and global networks in determining the division of gains, using data on the volume of cross-border telephone calls, and the relative size of caller and recipient regions. The size of the domestic network in Canada, for instance, is smaller than that of the USA, even though both countries have inter connected domestic and international networks. European countries have a well developed domestic network, while networks elsewhere in the world are, on average, not as developed as in the three other regional blocs in the model.

To parameterize the model, we specify estimates of preference and technology parameters for each of the regions in the model. In the absence of literature estimates on the relevant elasticities, we have used a value of unity for the transformation elasticities in each region, which we then vary in subsequent sensitivity analysis. The ë parameters in preferences determine the strength of the network externality effects and are important; we have assumed them to be 0.1 in all countries. Using these values, we calibrate share parameters of preference functions and production frontiers using 1999 data on call volumes, implied call prices, and GDP published in the World Telecommunication Development Report (WTDR) (ITU, 1999) and the World Development Report (WDR) (World Bank (2001)).

The 1999 WTDR gives detailed information on the use of telephone networks by country and region, reporting volumes of both international and domestic calls, and revenues generated by the telephone sector in each country, again broken down by domestic and international calls. It also reports total and per capita GDP, as well as other information such as the telephone density and major telephone operating companies in 202 countries and autonomous territories.

We construct base case data on prices and quantities for our model by dividing WTDR revenues by volumes, using the assumption that calls within each group for each country are the same. We use country specific information for Canada and the USA, and use summary statistics for Europe and derive data on the Rest of the World as a residual from world totals minus Canada, USA and Europe. In order to produce a benchmark equilibrium data set for use in calibration, we use merchandise trade data published in the World Development Report, 2001.

Table 3 (and accompanying notes) set out how we have manipulated basic data to obtain a model admissible benchmark equilibrium data set for model calibration.[2] We use this for counterfactual equilibrium analysis in which we reduce the differential pricing in all regions between international and domestic calls by one half, and then perform sensitivity tests in order to assess the robustness of model results to alternative values of elasticity parameters in production.

Calibrating our two service model to the data in table 3 yields the calibrated model parameters reported in table 4. The share parameters in the demand functions are computed using income and price information applied to Cobb-Douglas demand functions, with the sum of share parameters constrained to equal one. Share parameters in the production possibility frontier are computed using information on the value of goods and two types of services produced, and the elasticities of transformation by region. Both sets of share parameters are dominated in their first component by GNP which is large relative to the service categories.

Table 3

Base year (1999) Data used for Calibration of Empirically Based Telecom Services Model

	GDP[1]	*VS1*[2]	*VS2*[2]	*PS1*[3]	*PS2*[4]	*S*[15]	*S*[26]	*M*[7]	*E*[7]	*GE*[7]
Canada	618	12	5	0.09	1.18	132	4	205	214	-9
Europe	9613	180	42	0.07	1.23	2566	34	31	249	-218
USA	8083	170	76	0.09	3.35	1889	23	945	683	262
ROW	11014	159	79	0.03	3.49	5312	23	5415	5359	56

Source: World Telecommunication Union Development Report 1999, ITU, Geneva.

1. GDP, gross domestic product (in billions of US $s) is from table 1 of WTDR.
2. VS1 value of service type 1, VS2 value of service type 2, are derived from table 14 of WTDR and the split between two is based on information in table 4 of WTDR 1994.
3. PS1 are prices of domestic calls reported in table 7 of WTDR, 1999.
4. PS2 are prices of foreign calls obtained by dividing VS2 by S2.
5. S^2 number of international calls, reported in table 12, A-59, WTDR 1999, in million minutes.
6. S^1 is number of domestic calls obtained by dividing VS1 by PS1.
7: M and E are values of merchandise imports and exports obtained from the World

Development Report in millions (World Bank, 2001), Table 20, pp. 268-69. GE is balance of merchandise trade, M-E. Notice that there is a surplus of 91 billions in merchandise trade at the global level.

Table 4
Calibrated Share Parameters in the Empirically Based Telecom Model

	Canada	*Europe*	*USA*	*ROW*
á$_g$	0.619	0.547	0.426	0.196
á$_1$	0.200	0.246	0.437	0.626
á$_2$	0.043	0.030	0.101	0.159
ç$_2$	0.005	0.005	0.006	0.004
ç$_3$	0.002	0.0007	0.002	0.001

Note: α's refer to consumption, *n*'s refer to production shares.
Subscripts 1, 2 and 3 denote non-telecom GDP, domestic phone calls, and international phone calls respectively.

Table 5 reports regional welfare benefits from liberalization in international network related services using this model specification, where the price differential in all regions between domestic and international phone rates is halved. Results show gains for all regions but in proportional terms these are comparable across the smallest and largest region, confirming the conjecture we offered earlier regarding the country division of the gains from liberalization in services and the difference relative to goods liberalization.

Table 5
Regional Welfare Gains from Global Liberalization of Telecoms Services (Hicksian EV as Percentage of GDP (Based on 1999 data))

Canada	*Europe*	*USA*	*ROW*
0.0408	0.0539	0.0549	-0.3398

Table 6
Sensitivity Analysis of Regional Welfare Results for International Telecom Service Liberalization (Welfare effects of Hicksian EV as percentage of GDP)

Countries	*Base Case*	*Doubling*[1] *Transformation Elasticities in all Regions*	*Tripling*[2] *Transformation Elasticities in all Regions*
Canada	0.0408	0.0450	0.0453
Europe	0.0539	-0.0001	-0.0005
USA	0.0549	0.0061	0.0058
ROW	-0.3398	0.00004	-0.0001

We have also performed some limited sensitivity analysis using this model to explore ranges of welfare estimates by region as we vary production side transformation elasticities (the model demand side is Cobb-Douglas). Results are reported in Table 6; money metric welfare effects by region are affected as one might expect.

CONCLUSION

This paper explores international liberalization of network related services, such as telecoms. We argue that in the presence of network externalities, larger per capita benefits accrue to residents of smaller countries when expanding international networks, and this can roughly offset differences in numbers of residents (country size). Hence unlike for trade in goods, gains from liberalization can be of approximately equal absolute size across small and large countries.

We first show this for a simple case and explore this numerically for more complex structures, including for an empirical model implementation to global telcoms liberalization for the US, Europe, Canada and the rest of the world. This theme that the division of gains does not relate to country size in the same way as for the case of liberalization of goods trade prevails across all model calculations. We also show larger gains from liberalization relative to a Nash equilibrium in a network related service model than in a comparable goods model.

REFERENCES

Bousquet, A. and M. Ivaldi (1997), *Information Economics and Policy* v.9, iss.3, pp. 219-39.

Binmore, K. (1999), "Applying Game Theory of Automated Negotiation", *Netnomics*, 1999, Vol.1, iss.1 pp.1-9.

Cairncross, F. (1997), *The Death of Distance :How the Communications Revolution will Change Our Lives*. Orion Business, London.

Chacko, M. and W. Mitchell (1998), Growth Incentives to Invest in a Network Externality Environment, December, Vol. iss. 4, pp.731-44.

Choi, J.P. (1994), "Network Externality, Compatibility, Choice, and Planned Obsolescence", *Journal of Industrial Economics*, Vol. XLII ,June , 167-182.

Economides, N. (1996), "Network Externatilities, Complementarities, and Invitations to Enter", *European Journal of Political Economy*, vol. 12, pp.211-233.

Economides, N. (1996), "Economics of Networks", *International Journal of Industrial Organization,* vol. 14, pp. 673-699.

Garropne, P. (1996), "Network Subscription and Services Usage in European Telecommunications Industries", Information Economics and Policy 8, 25-50.

GAMS Development Corporation (1996), GAMS: The Solver Manuals, Washington D.C.

Harris, R.G. (1995), "Trade and Communication Costs", *Canadian Journal of Economics, Special Issue* November.

International Telecommunication Union (1999), *World Telecommunication Development Report*, Geneva.

Katz, M.L. and C. Shapiro (1986), "Technology Adoption in the Presence of Network Externalities", *Journal of Political Economy*, Vol. 94, No.4, pp. 822-841.

Katz, M.L and C. Shapiro (1985), "Network Externalities, Competition and Compatibility", *America Economic Review*, Vol. 75. no. 3, pp. 424-440.

Kikuchi, T. and T. Ichikawa (2002), "Congestible Communication Networks and International Trade," *Canadian Journal of Economics*, 35, May, pp. 331-340.

Laffont, J.J. and J. Tirole (2000), *Competition in Telecommunications*, The MIT Press, Cambridge Massachussettes.

Liebowitz, S.J. and S.E. Margolis (1994), "Network Externality: An Uncommon Tragedy", *Journal of Economic Perspective*, vol. 8, No.2, Spring, pp. 133-150.

Melvin, J.R. (1989), "Trade in Producer Services: A Heckscher-Ohlin Approach", *Journal of Political Economy*, 97(5) pp. 1180-96.

Roros, O. and H. Bjorn (2001), "Competition and Compatibility among Internet Service Providers", *Information Economics and Policy*, December 2001, V.13, iss. 4 pp. 411-25.

World Bank (2001), World Devélopment Report, Oxford University Press, Washington D.C.

NOTES

1. Katz and Shapiro (1985, 1986) analyze network externalities in an industrial organization structure, and stress the incentives to capture markets in the design of the network. Later contributions include Economides (1996), Liebowitz and Margolis (1994), and Choi (1994), Garrone (1996), Binmore (1999), Bousquet and Ivaldi (1997). Harris (1995) discusses application to trade, but in a different framework from that used here. Kikuchi and Ichikawa (2002) evaluate the influence of congestion in network services on comparative advantage in services trade for larger and smaller countries.
2. See the discussion of this in Cairncross's (1997) book "The Death of Distance".
3. In practice, various sharing agreements between origin and destination countries operate. See ITU (1994) pp. 27-29 for a discussion for how these apply.
4. Much of service activity, as Melvin (1989) pointed out, is concerned with intermediation through time and/or space. Network related services not only capture activity in telecommunications, but also transportation services where recipients of shipments receive benefits while shipment costs are fully paid by the shipper. They seem not to cover inter-temporal intermediation, such as financial services, which involves intermediaries bringing together agents in order to transact.
5. The value of λ determines the strength of the network externality effect. Having ST enter multiplicatively in this way also indicates that it is the potential number of other households in the network that might contact an individual household, rather than the expected number of calls actually received, that yields the external effect. A treatment based on the expected number of calls can also be accommodated within this framework.
6. We are grateful to the referee for correcting our drafting on this part.
7. Alternatively Hicksian equivalent variation measures can be used, which in this case are $EV^h = \frac{U_N^h - U_0^h}{U_0^h} I_0^h$.
8. The λ term from the previous section does not appear here. The externality summation term multiplies the separate S1 and S2 terms rather than all utility.

9. A non-cooperative outcome can thus be thought to correspond to a breakdown of present inter-country telecom revenue sharing arrangement discussed in ITU (1999).
10. Several features of this data set are important for our experiments and results. One is that prices for international calls are sharply above prices for domestic calls (this situation has changed since 1999). Another is that domestic calls are higher in North America than in Europe and ROW, reflecting the higher share of intra continental (e.g. LA/NY) calls to local calls in this region.
11. Base case values are -0.75.
12. Base case values are -0.75.

16

Welfare Gains to UK from a Global Free Trade[56]

Keshab Bhattarai

BACKGROUND

The global trade model presented in this paper explicitly models the UK economy, which is linked to other economies through trade and investment. The UK is part of the wider world economy, where key regions and countries (such as the UK, the EU, USA, Japan, China, Canada-Australia and New Zealand, Africa and other Rest of the World economies) are modelled as separate but linked economies with substantial detail in the representation of production and consumption. Considering a little over 55 percent of the UK's international trade occurs within the EU (see Table 3 below), it is important to illustrate a model which explains the trading relations between the UK and the EU and then between the EU and other trading blocks in the global economy. Here the UK economy is modelled alongside other ten different regions in the global economy.

The GTAP4 data (Hertel (1997)) allows us to build a global model reating the UK as a separate region trading with the EU, the USA, other trading blocks and the rest of the world. This global model enables policy makers to examine the specific impacts of international trade policies pursued at the European level, at a level of various other trading blocks, and at a global level. It also allows for trade policy evaluation on a bilateral as well as on a multilateral basis.

The sectoral structure of the global model presented here is the same as for the open economy model presented in a parallel paper (Bhattarai (2000)). The only difference between these two models is that the global model consists of interdependent economies grouped in one of eleven trading blocks, namely, UK, Europe, USA, Canada-Australia and New Zealand, Japan, China, Asia, Central Europe, Former Soviet Union, oil exporting countries, and the rest of the world, whereas only the UK economy was considered in the small open economy model. Each of the trading regions in the global model has 15 production sectors, a

* Earlier version of this chapter has been published in European Research Studies, Vol. IVv(3-4), 2001.

representative household and a government, which collects taxes from factor incomes and domestically supplied or imported consumption goods and imports and redistributes this revenue through transfers. Goods are differentiated by location of production, i.e. the same good produced in the UK is different from that produced in the USA.

As discussed for the small open economy model, a representative household in each trading region maximises utility subject to a budget constraint, and producers maximise profit subject to technology constraints even in the global model. Households buy both domestic and foreign goods and producers produce for both domestic and foreign markets. Both the utility of households and production by firms are described by standard constant elasticity of substitution (CES) functions; they are concave, monotonic, homothetic and continuous. Equilibrium conditions in each region and at a global level imply that markets for goods and capital clear, competitive firms earn zero economic profit, the income and expenditure of a representative household are equal and trade is balanced. Labour market clears at the regional level in the model. The multi-regional equilibrium model is closed by allowing quantities, prices and income to adjust at global as well as regional level until all excess demand functions are zero and equilibrium conditions are satisfied. We use these market clearing conditions for simplicity and also following the tradition set in Arrow-Debreu general equilibrium models (1954).

The capital inflow or outflow, if any, is allowed to clear any imbalance in international trade. Capital will flow into and out of regions until real returns are equalised across among all regions and sectors. The governments in each region are allowed to carry out their own fiscal and trade policies in order to enhance bilateral and multi-lateral trades. This model explicitly specifies interdependency in global markets, and is an appropriate framework for the evaluation of the effects of various trade and investment promoting measures being pursued by members of the trading community grouped in various trading blocks (See Hartel (1997), Perroni and Whalley (1996), Whalley and Hamilton (1996), Will and Winters (1996) for more discussion on global trade).

THE STRUCTURE OF THE GLOBAL TRADE MODEL

Each region in the global model is endowed with primary factors of production, land, capital, skilled and unskilled labour and natural resources. These non-labour primary factors are either used in producing goods in the same region where these factors are located, or are permitted to move to other regions in response to factor price changes. Labour is mobile across sectors only at the regional level. Production in sector i in region r uses intermediate inputs, and labour and capital from its own region as well as from all other regions.

$$Y_{i,r} = \min\left(\frac{INT_{j,i,r}}{a_{i,j,r}}, \left(K_{i,r}^{\beta_r} L_{i,r}^{1-\beta_r} \right) \right) \tag{1}$$

Here $Y_{i,r}$ is output of the sector *i* good in region *r*, $K_{i,r}$ is capital services originating in region *r* but used to produce the good *i* in region *r*, $L_{i,r}$ are labour services originating in region *r* but used to produce the sector *i* good in region *r*, $INT_{j,i,r}$ is an intermediate input originating in sector *j* of region *r* but used to produce the sector *i* good in region *r*, $a_{j,i,r}$ is a coefficient that gives the amount of the sector *j* intermediate input of region *r* used to produce the sector *i* good in region *r*, and b_r is the share of capital income in sectoral output in region *r*. Land and natural resources are additional inputs in case of agriculture sector.

The output of good a particular region *i*, $Y_{i,r}$, is either supplied to the home region or exported to other regions. This is represented by a constant elasticity of transformation (CET) function:

$$Y_{i,r} = \left(\delta_{i,r} YD_{i,r}^{\eta_{i,r}} + (1-\delta_{i,r}) X_{i,r}^{\eta_{i,r}}\right)^{\frac{1}{\eta_{i,r}}} \qquad (2)$$

where $YD_{i,r}$ is domestic sales of output of good *i* in region *r*, $X_{i,r}$ is exports of good *i* from a region *r*, $d_{i,r}$ is the share of domestic sales of gross output, $Y_{i,r}$, and $h_{i,r}$ is the elasticity of transformation between domestic sales and exports.

Total domestic supplies comes from domestic sales plus imports. Thus absorption of region, *r* is given by a CES aggregation of imports and domestic supplies

$$A_{i,r} = \left(\mu_{i,r} YD_{i,r}^{\sigma_{i,r}} + (1-\mu_{i,r}) M_{i,r}^{\sigma_{i,r}}\right)^{\frac{1}{\sigma_{i,r}}} \qquad (3)$$

Here $A_{i,r}$, is Armington aggregation of domestic and imported goods, $s_{i,r}$ is the elasticity of substitution between imported and domestic products, $m_{i,r}$ is the share of domestic production in the Armington product and $M_{i,r}$ is imports of good *i* to region *r*. The value of imports of goods into regions *r* are equal to value of exports of other region to that region plus transportation costs from the origin to the destination.

Transportation services are proportional to trade:

$$T_{i,r,s} = \tau_{i,r,s} M_{i,r,s} \qquad (4)$$

Here $T_{i,r,s}$ transportation services, $\tau_{i,r,s}$ is transport cost per unit of traded goods $M_{i,r,s}$ amount of good i traded from region r to s.

These international transport services are produced using transport goods supplied by each region.

For simplicity, we represent the utility function in each region by a CES or Cobb-Douglas aggregation of final consumption goods supplied by each region. The total domestic demand is divided between household and government consumption. Household consumption is a Cobb-Douglas aggregation of sector *i* commodities over all *r* regions.

$$U_r = \prod_{i,r} C_{i,r}^{\gamma} \tag{5}$$

Households receive factor income from all regions and transfers from their own government. The income of the representative household in each region is

$$I_r = \sum_i w_r L_{i,r} + \sum_r r_r K_{i,r} + RV_r \tag{7}$$

where I_r is income, w_r is wage rate and r_r is the interest rate and RV_r is the transfer received by a representative household in region r.

Government consumption demand reflects a Cobb-Douglas aggregate of all sector i commodities over all r regions.

$$G_r = \prod_{i,r} GD_{i,r}^{\gamma} \tag{8}$$

$GD_{i,r}^{g}$ is the government consumption of good i in region r. The government in each region collects taxes from factors income, intermediate inputs, imports and domestic sales.

$$G_r = \tau_k r_r \overline{K}_r + \tau_w w_r \overline{L}_r + \tau_{i,r} P_{i,r} Y_{i,r} + \tau_{N,r} P_{i,r} INT_{j,i,r} \tag{9}$$

Here G_r is total government revenue, $i_{k,r}$ is tax rate on capital income, $i_{w,rr}$ is tax rate on labour income, $i_{w,r}$ is tax rate in wage income, $i_{i,r}$ is tax rate on intermediate income, $i_{N,r}$ is tax rate on intermediate input.

A competitive equilibrium in this global economy is such that, given the prices of commodities and factors, demands for good and supply of goods are equal at the regional as well as the global level; factor market clears for each region and at the world level; consumers of each region maximise their utility subject to their income constraints; and the government budget and trade are balanced for each region.

In this global model a competitive equilibrium is given by prices of consumption goods, $P_{i,r}$; the prices of capital; a wage rate for labour, w_r levels of gross output, $Y_{i,r}$; capital use, $K_{i,r}$; sectoral use of labour, $L_{i,r}$; and income I_r such that, given these prices and quantities

(i) households in each region maximise utility subject to their budget constraints;

(ii) firms in each region maximise profits subject to technology constraints;

(iii) labour market clears at the regional level;

(iv) the markets for goods and services and capital clear in each region and at the global level;

(v) the government budget constraint is satisfied for each region, and

(vi) the trade-balance condition is satisfied at the regional and global level.

More specifically, the market clearing condition for the goods market is given by

$$Y_{i,r} = \sum_{r} C_{i,r} + \sum_{rr,j} a_{i,j,r} INT_{i,j,r} \tag{10}$$

The global capital market clearing condition implies

$$\sum_{r} \bar{K}_{r} = \sum_{i,r} K_{r,ri} \tag{11}$$

and labour market clears at the regional level:

$$LS_{r} = \sum_{i} LS_{i,r} \tag{12}$$

When there are *r.n* different markets in the economy, relative prices that clear *rn*-1 markets also clear the *rn*th market as well (Walras (1954)).

Model parameters are calibrated using information on international trade flows and production and consumption flows in each region reported in the GTAP4 data base for 1995 compiled by the Global Trade Analysis Project (GTAP) of the Purdue University in Indiana in the USA. This data base contains data on 50 sector input-output tables and national account series for 45 different regions in the global economy. We follow the GTAPinGAMS approach used by Rutherford (1998, GAMS/MPSGE (1997)) in formulating the model equations. MPSGE (Mathematical Programme for System of General Equilibrium Models) is a programming language with interface to the GAMS (General Algebraic Modelling System) software[1].

DATA SOURCES AND CALIBRATION PROCEDURE IN THE GLOBAL TRADE MODEL

The global trade model presented above requires data on output, imports, exports, consumption and government demand, employment of labour and capital, intermediate inputs, and base year prices for each sector and region included in the model. It also needs tax and tariff rates for each product. We use GTAP4.

The GTAP4 data has been prepared by the Center for Global Trade Analysis, Purdue University (McDougall (1998), Hertel (1997)) for implementing a global trade model from the UK's perspective. This data base consists of 50 GTAP sectors and 45 GTAP regions. We use the GTAP aggregation software of Rutherford (1998)[1] that maps data from the GLOBAL.HAR file of the GTAP4 data base to a GAMS readable data file, GTAP4001.gms. We also take basic features of Rutherford's (1998) regional model structure for implementing the global model.

Table 1
Regional Concordance of Global Trade Model with GTAP Regions

Model Regions	*GTAP Regions*
UK	United Kingdom, Channel Islands, Isle of Man
Europe (EUR)	Germany, Denmark, Sweden, Finland *Rest of EU* (Austria, Belgium, France, French Guiana, Gibraltar, Greece, Gaudeloupe, Holy See, Ireland, Italy, Luxembourg, Martinique, Monaco, Netherlands, Portugal, Reunion, Saint Pierre and Miquelon, San Marino, Spain) *European Free Trade Area* (Iceland, Leichtenstein, Norway, Svalbard and Jan Mayen Is, Switzerland)
Central and Eastern Europe (CEA)	Bulgaria, Czech Republic, Hungary, Poland, Romania, Slovakia, Slovenia
USA	American Samoa, Gaum, Northern Mariana Islands, Puerto Rico, United States Vergin Islands, United States of America
Japan (JPN)	Japan
ACN	Canada, Australia, New Zealand
China	China, Hong Kong, Taiwan
Asia	Malaysia, Singapore, Thailand, Philippines, Vietnam, Korea, India, Sri Lanka, *Rest of Asia* (Bangladesh, Bhutan, Maldives, Nepal, Pakistan)
Former Soviet Union	Armenia, Azerbaijan, Belarus, Estonia, Georgia, Kazakhstan, Kyrgyzstan, Latvia, Lithuania, Moldova, Russian Federation, Tajikistan, Turkmenistan, Ukraine, Uzbekistan
Major Oil Producers (MOP)	Mexico, Indonesia, *Rest of the Middle East* (Bahrain, Iran, Iraq, Isreal, Jordan, Kuwait, Lebanon, Oman, Qatar, Saudi Arabia, Syria, United Arab Emirates, Yemen, Yemen Democratic) *Rest of North Africa* (Algeria, Egypt, Libya, Tunisia)
Rest of the World	Morocco, Western Sahara, Turkey, Venezuela, Columbia, Argentina, Brazil, Chile, Uruguay *Rest of Andean Pact* (Bolivia, Ecuador, Peru) *Central America and Caribbean* (Anguila, Antigua and Barbuda, Aruba, Bahamas, Barbados, Belize, British Virgin Islands, Cayman Islands, Costa Rica, Cuba, Dominica, Dominican Republic, El Salvador, Grenada, Guatemala, Haiti, Honduras, Jamaica, Montserrat, Netherlands Antilles, Nicaragua, Panama, Saint Christopher and Nevis, Saint Lucia, Saint Vincent and the Grenadines, Trinidad and Tobago, Turks and Caicos Isl.) *Rest of the South America* (Guyana, Paraguay, Surinam) *South Africa Customs Union* (Botswana, Lesotho, Namibia, South Africa, Swaziland) *Rest of South Africa* (Angola, Malawi, Mauritius, Mozambique, Tanzania, Zambia, Zimbabwe) *Rest of sub-Saharan Africa* (Benin, Burkina Faso, Burundi, Cameroon, Cape Verde, Central African Republic, Chad, Comoros, Congo, Cote d'Ivoire, Djibouti, Equatorial Guinea, Eritrea, Ethiopia, Gabon, Gambia, Ghana, Guinea, Guinea-Bissau, Kenya, Liberia,

Contd.....

Model Regions	*GTAP Regions*
	Madagascar, Mali, Mauritania, Mayotte, Niger, Nigeria, Rwanda, Sao Tome and Principe, Senegal, Seychelles, Sierra Leone, Somalia, Sudan, Togo, Uganda, Zaire) *Rest of the World* (Afghanistan, Albania, Andorra, Bermuda, Bosnia and Herzegovina, British Indian Ocean Territories, Brunei, Cambodia, Christmas Island, Cocos (Keeling) Islands, Cook Islands, Croatia, Cyprus, Falkland Islands, Faroe Islands, Fiji, French Polynesia, Greenland, Johnston Island Kiribati, Laos, Macao, Macedonia- former Yugoslav Republic, Malta, Marshall Islands, Federation State of Micronesia, Mongolia, Myanmar, Nauru, New Caledonia, Niue, North Korea, Pacific Islands, Palau, Papua New Guinea, Pitcairn Islands, Saint Helena, Solomon Islands, Tokelau, Tonga, Tuvalu, Vanuatu, Wake Island, Wallis and Futura Isl., Western Samoa, Yugoslavia)

We have aggregated the 45 GTAP regions into eleven model regions to represent the global market. These regions are UK, Europe, USA, Canada-Australia and New Zealand, Japan, China, Asia, Central Europe, Former Soviet Union, Major Oil Producers, and the Rest of the World. Countries included in each region are listed in Table 1. This regional classification is made according to the degree of UK's trade linkage in the global economy. Europe region, which consists of continental Europe, Scandinavian economies and other economies in the European Free Trade Area, is the major trading partner of the UK. We treat the UK as a separate region to make this model to represent the UK perspective in the global trade issues. GTAP4 data set provides us the benchmark data set required for the calibration of the regional model.

We aggregate 50 GTAP sectors into fifteen global model sectors in Table 2 consistent with the classification in the small open economy model of the UK. These sectors are agriculture, extraction, other mining, food and drink, other manufacturing, chemical, metal, engineering, utilities, construction, trade and transportation, private services, public services and housing. These sectors closely relate to the classification desired by the Inland Revenue (Bhattarai (1999b)).

GTAP draws on various national and international data sources in creating the global trade database. It takes macroeconomic data on GDP and GDP components and population data from the Bank Economics and Social Database (BESD) of the International Economics Department of the World Bank. A large number of the input output tables were inherited from the Australian Industry Commission's SALTER project (McDougall (1998)). Input output tables for 12 European countries relies on the Central Statistical Offices of those countries, and Eurostat data base which contains input-output tables harmonised in accordance with the European System of Integrated National Accounts (ESA). The UK data in GTAP is drawn from the input-output table 1995 and business and agricultural statistics published by the Central Statistics Office in London.

Table 2
Concordance of sectors in the Global Trade Model with GTAP sectors

Model Sectors	*Commodities*
Agriculture	Paddy, wheat, grains, non-grain crops, wool, other livestock, fisheries, forestry
Extraction	Coal, Oil, Gas
Other mining	Other minerals, non-metallic mineral products,
Food and drink	Processed rice, meat products, milk products, other food products, beverage and tobacco,
Other Manufacturing	textiles, wearing apparel, leather etc., lumber, pulp, paper, etc..
Chemical	chemicals, rubbers, and plastic
Metal	primary ferrous metals
Engineering	fabricated metal products, machinery and equipment
Utilities	Electricity, gas and water
Construction	Construction
Trade and Transportation	Whole sale and retail trade, hotel and restaurants, railways highways subways transport, freight transport, inland and ocean transport, air transport, storage and warehousing, communication
Private services	Monetary and financial services, real estates, accounting, data processing, engineering and technical services, advertising, radio and TV broadcasting, amusement, repairs domestic services, photographic, personal services, business services
Public services	Public administration, health ,education, veterinary, welfare and religious organisations, social and related community services, International and extra-territorial bodies
Housing	Dwellings

Bilateral trade flows are based on the United Nation's COMTRADE database. GTAP's information on tariffs was drawn from UNCTAD's Trade Control Measures Database (TCMD) as well as from the WTO Integrated Database (IDB). TCMD is the most comprehensive database covering tariffs that is currently available. It covers all OECD member countries as well as a number of non-OECD countries. At the global level there are still many countries/ regions which do not have input-output tables or other data sources. GTAP applies the proper regional average technique to fill data gaps in the absence of original data sources[2].

Flows of trade from one region to other regions reflect the comparative advantage enjoyed by an exporting region over importing regions and the production and consumption structure among trading regions. We present the structure of total volume of trade from one region to another in percentage terms in Table 3. Figures in this table show the volume of trade, in percentage terms, originating from a region on each row to other regions listed in columns. About 55 percent of the UK's trade occurs with the European countries, followed by another 14 percent with the United States, and remaining 30 percent spread among other regions. The intra-regional trade is very important in the European region where 58 percent of trade takes place among the member countries themselves. Also note that European region is the most integrated with other regions as reflected its dominance of trade link with other region in the global economy. Asian and the United States follow Europe in the degree of trade integration.

Table 3

Bilateral Trade Composition for 1995 (in percentage terms)

(From a region in the column to various regions in the row)

	USA	*JPN*	*EUR*	*UK*	*ACN*	*CHN*	*FSU*	*CEA*	*ASI*	*MOP*	*ROW*
USA	0.0	27.1	7.4	13.9	55.7	22.7	8.0	4.2	19.5	28.9	19.3
JPN	11.8	0.0	2.6	3.1	12.4	15.3	9.4	4.9	15.2	16.5	7.8
EUR	22.6	14.1	58.0	55.0	7.2	16.8	40.6	53.2	14.0	20.5	30.6
UK	5.6	3.3	8.1	0.0	2.4	2.9	3.2	3.3	3.6	2.3	4.9
CAN	19.2	4.7	1.5	3.6	3.5	3.9	0.9	0.8	3.2	2.3	2.0
CHN	7.0	16.9	2.6	2.8	4.9	16.7	6.9	3.4	12.6	3.6	3.7
FSU	1.0	0.5	1.8	1.4	0.3	0.7	4.3	5.2	1.2	0.4	1.5
CEA	0.7	0.4	3.2	1.8	0.2	0.7	9.1	11.5	0.7	0.6	1.3
ASI	11.6	23.4	4.1	6.2	7.1	11.8	7.7	2.7	18.2	13.8	6.3
MOP	11.2	5.3	4.8	5.9	3.0	3.6	2.7	3.8	5.9	4.2	4.8
ROW	9.3	4.3	5.8	6.3	3.2	5.0	7.2	7.0	5.9	6.7	17.8
Total%	100	100	100	100	100	100	100	100	100	100	100

Source: GTAP Data Base Version 4, 1998; see Table 1 for Countries Included in above Regions.

Volume of the global trade in value terms are given in Table 4 below, which shows that the value of global trade stood around 5.6 trillion us dollars in 1995. This implies the openness of the global economy of around 22 percent in that year. Row sum in this table shows imports and column sum represents exports. In this benchmark data USA, UK, CEA, Asia and ROW regions had deficit in trade accounts whereas Japan, Europe, ACN, China, FSU and MOP regions had surpluses in the trade account. Intra-regional trade in Europe alone had more than 2 trillion US dollars.

Also note that the North-North trade volume is significantly larger than South-South or South-North trade. Rich countries in the North trade more among themselves than with developing countries in the South. The reason for the small share of South-South trade compared to North-South trade lies in predominance of imports of machinery and high-tech manufactured products by developing countries from the rich industrialised countries in the North. The South regions supplies the North only with cheap primary products. For instance, the USA, Japan and European regions were the major trading partners for the Asia and ROW regions. Asia exported more to Europe, USA and the ACN regions than to the ROW or to Asia itself.

Table 4
Volume of Bilateral trade for 1995 (in billion of US $s)
(Imports across the column and exports down the column)

	USA	*JPN*	*EUR*	*UK*	*ACN*	*CHN*	*FSU*	*CEA*	*ASI*	*MOP*	*ROW*	*Global*
USA		131	159	38	154	94	7	4	96	93	64	842
JPN	83		56	9	34	64	8	5	75	53	26	413
EUR	159	68	1244	152	20	69	36	57	69	66	101	2041
UK	39	16	174		7	12	3	4	17	7	16	295
ACN	134	23	33	10	10	16	1	1	16	7	7	257
CHN	49	82	56	8	14	69	6	4	62	12	12	373
FSU	7	3	39	4	1	3	4	6	6	1	5	78
CEA	5	2	69	5	1	3	8	12	3	2	4	114
ASI	82	113	87	17	20	49	7	3	89	45	21	533
MOP	78	26	103	16	8	15	2	4	29	14	16	312
ROW	65	21	125	17	9	21	6	7	29	22	59	381
Global	701	484	2145	276	277	414	89	107	491	322	331	5638

Source: GTAP data base version 4, 1998; see Table 1 for countries included in above regions.

The North-North and South-North trade pattern observed above in aggregate trade flows is also apparent at the sectoral level. We present sectoral trade flows in the appendix A1. For instance, 71 percent of total exports of European agricultural products are sold within the European region, while intra-regional trade for agricultural products is 19 percent in the Asia region. About 54 percent of CEA's agricultural products are exported to Europe compared to 15 percent intra-regional flows.

The composition of regional exports and imports are presented in Table 5 and Table 6. The row sum in Table 5 and 6 show the percentage of sectoral imports and exports in the global economy. Most global trade occurs in the engineering sector which comprised about 34 percent of global trade followed by other manufacturing, chemical and transport sectors. This global trade trend applied also to the UK economy. The columns for individual regions in table 5 and 6 represent sectoral share of imports and exports in each regions respectively. These regional aggregations on trade flows by goods and regions are obtained by aggregating the bilateral flows of GTAP countries. More details on their derivation and various consistency conditions checked for reconciling bilateral trade flows are presented in detail in McDougall (Chapter 3 and 16).

Subsidies and tariff rates are the most important means of protecting domestic industries against foreign competition. The GTAP reports trade-weighted average tariff rates from tariff lines of 6000 to 10,000 commodities. GTAP concordance procedure converts non-tariff distortions into tariff equivalent distortions for the effective tariff rates for year 1995 for the agriculture, energy, manufacturing and transport sectors as presented in Tables A2 and A3 in the appendix. Similarly producer subsidy equivalent (PSE) calculations are made to arrive at effective export taxes/ subsidies for all eight model sectors in Table A3.

Table 5
Sectoral Composition of Imports by Regions for 1995
(gross of tariff in billions of US $s)

	USA	*JPN*	*EUR*	*UK*	*ACN*	*CHN*	*FSU*	*CEA*	*ASI*	*MOP*	*ROW*	*Global%*
AGR	2.1	9.5	4.1	3.4	2.1	4.3	4.1	3.6	4.2	5.0	4.0	4.2
EXT	7.0	11.6	4.7	3.1	3.1	2.3	1.9	7.1	7.4	2.4	6.7	5.5
OMI	2.1	3.3	2.8	2.6	1.9	2.3	1.7	3.0	2.8	3.5	2.1	2.6
FDR	2.7	9.7	6.1	6.4	3.4	3.7	15.6	5.4	4.1	6.8	6.9	5.6
OMA	16.6	13.9	14.6	15.0	12.6	17.5	14.6	16.8	8.9	13.1	13.5	14.3
CHM	7.0	5.7	12.0	10.3	10.3	11.7	7.9	13.2	10.1	10.2	12.6	10.3
MTL	5.4	4.6	7.5	5.9	5.6	7.7	3.2	7.2	8.0	7.6	5.8	6.7
ENG	42.8	17.7	30.3	35.6	44.2	38.2	25.3	30.8	41.5	34.8	33.7	34.2
UTI	0.1	0.0	0.2	0.2	0.0	0.1	0.2	0.1	0.0	0.0	0.1	0.1
CON	0.0	0.0	0.3	0.0	0.0	0.8	0.8	1.5	0.0	1.5	0.8	0.4
TRN	6.5	18.2	7.8	10.5	10.4	5.6	12.0	8.6	5.7	9.2	9.8	8.6
PRS	5.9	5.7	6.8	2.5	5.6	3.5	11.5	2.7	4.5	3.7	2.3	5.3
PUB	1.8	0.1	2.7	4.3	0.8	2.2	1.1	0.1	2.7	2.2	1.7	2.1
Global (%)	100	100	100	100	100	100	100	100	100	100	100	100
Total Value	904.2	474.3	2167	316.1	275.9	438.1	85.05	126.3	627.2	347.7	448	6210

Source: GTAP data base version 4, 1998; see Table 1 for countries included in above regions.

Table 6
Sectoral composition of exports by regions for 1995
(gross of export taxes in billions of US $s)

	USA	*JPN*	*EUR*	*UK*	*ACN*	*CHN*	*FSU*	*CEA*	*ASI*	*MOP*	*ROW*	*Global%*
AGR	5.1	0.1	2.5	1.3	6.5	1.4	6.1	2.9	3.0	3.3	12.2	3.4
EXT	1.2	0.4	2.1	4.5	8.8	0.9	19.2	3.3	2.8	39.0	12.2	5.3
OMI	1.2	1.2	2.4	2.8	3.6	1.7	2.8	3.0	2.3	3.4	6.5	2.5
FDR	3.8	0.4	6.6	5.1	6.8	2.5	3.8	4.7	5.9	2.1	9.9	5.2
OMA	8.1	6.1	12.5	8.5	14.7	31.8	6.8	19.5	17.8	11.1	13.9	13.2
CHM	9.6	7.5	12.6	12.1	6.8	7.2	11.0	9.3	6.3	6.5	6.1	9.7
MTL	3.6	5.8	7.1	5.8	7.8	6.0	25.4	13.2	3.6	3.7	8.9	6.5
ENG	39.7	63.7	32.9	33.7	28.7	30.1	3.8	19.2	37.2	16.3	7.4	33.2
UTI	0.0	0.0	0.3	0.0	0.3	0.1	0.3	0.3	0.0	0.0	0.0	0.1
CON	0.0	0.0	0.6	0.0	0.0	0.2	0.4	4.9	0.3	0.0	0.0	0.4
TRN	14.0	11.4	11.2	15.7	10.9	14.3	13.1	15.9	15.8	10.6	16.1	12.8
PRS	10.4	3.4	6.9	6.1	3.2	2.7	5.3	2.7	3.0	1.4	3.1	5.5
PUB	3.3	0.1	2.3	4.3	1.8	0.9	1.9	1.2	2.1	2.4	3.7	2.3
Global(%)	100	100	100	100	100	100	100	100	100	100	100	100
Total Value	736	503	2224	291	287	422	93	112	518	334	349	5867

Source: GTAP data base version 4, 1998; see Table 1 for countries included in above regions.

Figures in the rows in appendix A2 show tariff rates applied to commodities imported by one region from other regions. Agriculture is the most heavily protected sector among all sectors, followed by manufacturing. For instance, agricultural products from the USA were subject to a 165 percent tariff rate in Japan, 59 percent in Asia, and 34 percent in China. Food and drink sector also is subject to heavy import duties among regions.

From the export taxes (and subsidies) presented in A3, we again see that agriculture receives the highest rate of export subsidy or is subject to the highest export tax rates among these various sectors. Export subsidies on agricultural products from Europe range from 1 percent for exports to the UK to 37 percent for exports to major oil producers. Export subsidy rates were relatively lower in the UK.

WELFARE IMPACTS OF TARIFF REFORMS IN THE GLOBAL TRADE MODEL

We use our global trade model to compute welfare gains to various trading blocks from global free trade for a selected values of substitution elasticity among factors of production (σ), elasticity of substitution between domestic supplies and imports in consumption (σ^m) and transformation elasticity for domestic supplies and exports (σ^d). The results are displayed in Table 7.

The elimination of tariffs increases global trade. Almost all trading communities/regions in the model experience welfare gains from liberalisation. Altogether these gains add up to around 323 billion dollars for 1995. Gains from free trade at the global level is about 1.3 percent of the global GDP. This gain varies significantly from one region to another. Japan gains most by global free trade, which was equivalent to 91 billions dollars (1.93 percent of the Japanese GDP). Europe gains 67 billion but only 0.95 percent of European GDP. UK gains 11 billion dollars. As a percent of GDP China gains the most, about 3.8 percent of GDP. This is not surprising considering the export-led growth process that is undergoing in the Chinese economy over last two decades. Major oil producing countries lose form global trade liberalisation. These welfare figures are very similar to those found in the literature (Whalley (1985), Harrison-Rutherford-Tarr (1997), Ghosh and Whalley (1997)).

Table 7
Hicksian EV by region from global trade liberalization
(Benchmark 1995, for $\sigma = 0.75$; $\sigma^d = 4$; and $\sigma^m = 6$)

Trading blocks or model regions	*Welfare gains from free trade as a percent of GDP*	*Welfare gains in billion of 1995 US dollars*
USA	0.825	54
Japan (JPN)	1.932	91
Europe (EUR)	0.949	67
UK	1.054	11
Australia-Canada and New Zealand (CAN)	3.035	27
China (CHN)	3.723	34
Former Soviet Union (FSU)	0.149	1
Central and East Asia (CEA)	2.143	6
Asia (ASI)	1.849	20
OPEC Countries (MOP)	-0.346	-3
Rest of the World (ROW)	0.886	17
Global gain	1.300	323

See Table 1 for countries included in above regions.

We conduct a sensitivity analysis around key elasticity parameters in the production and utility functions to check the robustness of the results presented above. We make a ten step grid of three key substitution elasticities: substitution elasticity among factors of production (σ), elasticity of substitution between domestic supplies and imports in consumption (σ^m) and transformation elasticity for domestic supplies and exports (σ^d). Welfare gains as a percentage of base year GDP from global free trade are presented in Table 8, which shows welfare improving with increase in the elasticity in all regions except in Former Soviet Union (FSU) Region and major oil producers (MOP) region. Every regions may experience gains from global trade in case of higher values of elasticities.

Table 8
Sensitivity of Welfare to Production and Substitution Elasticities in the Global Model (Welfare gain % of GDP from moving to the global free trade in 1995)

	Substitution Elasticities in Production, Imports and Exports									
Scenario	*S1*	*S2*	*S3*	*S4*	*S5*	*S6*	*S7*	*S8*	*S9*	*S10*
σ	0.75	1.00	1.25	1.50	1.75	2.00	2.25	2.50	2.75	3.00
σ^d	2.25	2.50	2.75	3.00	3.25	3.50	3.75	4.00	4.25	4.50
σ^m	3.25	3.50	3.75	4.00	4.25	4.50	4.75	5.00	5.25	5.50

	Welfare gains % of GDP from moving to the global free trade in 1995 (by region and by the range of values for the elasticity of substituion)									
Scenario	*S1*	*S2*	*S3*	*S4*	*S5*	*S6*	*S7*	*S8*	*S9*	*S10*
USA	0.693	0.715	0.737	0.759	0.781	0.801	0.82	0.838	0.855	0.871
JPN	1.049	1.179	1.317	1.464	1.618	1.779	1.944	2.112	2.282	2.451
EUR	0.824	0.854	0.883	0.911	0.939	0.967	0.996	1.026	1.059	1.093
UK	0.623	0.679	0.737	0.796	0.858	0.921	0.987	1.054	1.124	1.195
CAN	1.437	1.54	1.647	1.761	1.887	2.031	2.195	2.388	2.616	2.894
CHN	1.598	1.786	1.978	2.176	2.382	2.598	2.826	3.069	3.329	3.611
FSU	-0.595	-0.548	-0.498	-0.445	-0.388	-0.328	-0.263	-0.191	-0.111	-0.021
CEA	1.177	1.208	1.247	1.295	1.351	1.421	1.506	1.614	1.748	1.917
ASI	0.164	0.344	0.526	0.712	0.9	1.093	1.291	1.494	1.704	1.92
MOP	-1.331	-1.209	-1.09	-0.973	-0.853	-0.729	-0.599	-0.463	-0.322	-0.175
ROW	-0.088	-0.008	0.075	0.161	0.251	0.344	0.442	0.544	0.652	0.765

See Table 1 for countries included in above regions.

Welfare gains from the liberalisation of the global trade as reported above are based on the comparative static analysis. It can only describe steady state situation, it requires a fully specified dynamic global trade model to track transitional dynamics of policy reform which we have left as an exercise for the next phase of research. It is more encouraging that some work has been already started to this direction (Diao and Somwaru (2002)).

CONCLUSION

This paper reports on a 11 region 15 sector global trade model including the UK as a separate region. The UK is modelled as part of the wider world economy, where key regions and countries (such as the UK, the EU, USA, Japan, China,

Canada-Australia and New Zealand, Africa and other Rest of the World economies) are treated as separate but linked economies with substantial detail in the representation of production and consumption. A representative household in each trading region maximises utility subject to a budget constraint, and producers maximise profit subject to technology constraints even in the global model. Households buy both domestic and foreign goods and producers produce for both domestic and foreign markets. Equilibrium conditions in each region and at the global level imply that markets for goods, labour and capital clear, competitive firms earn zero economic profit, the income and expenditure of a representative household are equal, trade is balanced and all government revenue is transferred to a household. Model parameters are calibrated using information on international trade flows and production and consumption flows in each region reported in the GTAP4 data base for 1995.

This model shows that an elimination of tariffs increases the volume of trade at the global level. Almost all trading communities/regions in our model experience gains from liberalization. Gains from free trade at the global level are 1.3 percent of the global GDP, roughly about 325 billion dollars in 1995. In absolute Japan gains most followed by Europe and the USA. UK gains about 11 billion dollars (6.8 billion pounds) from the multilateral trade liberalisation compared to 3 billion dollar gains from a unilateral liberalisation. The gain occurring to the China is much larger as a share of GDP than any other region included in the model. OPEC economies loose from global scale liberalization. This is mainly due to the removal of subsidies on their imports from developed countries and a significant amount of distortions prevalent in the domestic markets of these economies.

We carry out sensitivity analysis around major model parameters in the production and consumption functions of the model. The results show that the welfare gains reported are sensitive to values of substitution elasticities. It is possible to show much larger gains with higher values of production and trade elasticities. In general, model results show significant welfare gains to the UK economy from the removal of tariffs on international trade.

REFERENCES

Arrow, J.K. and G. Debreu (1954), "Existence of an Equilibrium for a Competitive Economy" *Econometrica* 22, 265-90.

Bhagwati, J.N. and T.N. Srinivasan (1992), Lectures on International Trade, MIT Press.

Bhattarai, K. (2000), Efficiency and Factor Reallocation Effects and Marginal Excess Burden of Taxes in the UK Economy, Hull Economics Research Paper No. 7.

Bhattarai, K. and J. Whalley (1998) "The Division and Size of Gains from Liberalizaiton of Service Networks" NBER Working Paper No. 6712, August.

Bhattarai, K., M. Ghosh and J. Whalley (1999), "On Some Properties of Widely Used Trade Closure", Economics Letters, Vol.62, No.1, pp. 13-21.

Bhattarai, K., M.Ghosh and J. Whalley (1998), "More on Trade Closure", in G. Ranis and K. Raut ed. Trade, Growth and Development: Essays in Honor of Professor T.N. Srinivasan, Yale University.

Brook, A, D. Kendrick, A. Meeraus (1992), GAMS: Users's Guide, release 2.25, The Scientific Press, San Fransisco, CA.

Gerard, D. (1954), The Theory of Value, Yale University Press, New Haven.

Diao X. and Somwaru A. (2000), "An Inquiry on General Equilibrium Effects of MERCOSUR – An Intertemporal World Model", Journal of Policy Modelling 22(5):557-588.

Dirkse, S.P. and M.C. Ferris (1995), "CCPLIB: A collection of nonlinear mixed complementarity problems" *Optimization Methods and Software*. 5:319-345.

Dervis, Kamal, De Melo Jaime, and Robinson, Sherman, 1985: General Equilibrium Models for Development Policy, CUP, New York.

Ghosh, M. and J. Whalley (1997), "The Value of MFN Treatment", *manuscript*, University of Western Ontario.

Goulder, L.H., and L.H. Summers (1989), "Tax Policy, Asset Prices, and Growth: A General Equilibrium Analysis", *Journal of Public Economics*, 38:265-296, North Holland.

Harrison, G.W., T.F. Rutherford and D.G. Tarr (1997), "Quantifying the Uruaguy Round", *Economic Journal* vol. 107 no. 444, September, pp.1405-1430,

Hertel, T. (1997), Global Trade Analysis: Modeling and Applications Cambridge University Press.

Mansur, A. and J. Whalley (1984), "Numerical Specification of Applied General Equilibrium Models: Estimation, Calibration and Data", in Scarf Herbert E and Shoven John B. (1984) Applied General Equilibrium Analysis, CUP.

Will, M. and L.A.Winters (1996), The Uruguay Round and the developing countries, Cambridge University Press.

McDougall, R.A. (1998), Global Trade Assistance and Protection: The GTAP Data Base 4, Global Trade Analysis Project, Purdue University.

Office for National Statistics (ONS (1995)), Input Output:Tables for the United Kingdom, HMSO, London.

———(1992), United Kingdom National Accounts: Sources and Methods.

———(1996), United Kingdom National Accounts: the Blue Book.

Office for National Statistics (ONS (1995)), Family Spending: A report on the 1994-95 Expenditure Survey.

Perroni, C. and J. Whalley (1996), "How evere is Global Retaliation Risk under Increasing Regionalism" , *AER Papers and Proceedings*, vol.86. no. 2, May.

Piggott J. and J.Whalley (1985), UK Tax Polcy and Applied General Equilibrium Analysis, Cambridge University Press.

Rutherford, T.F. (1997), The GAMS/ MPSGE and GAMS/MILES user notes, GAMS Development Corporation, Washington D.C.

Rutherford, T.F. (1997), "GTAPinGAMS:The Dataset and Static Models", Mimio, University of Colorado, Boulder (http://nash.Colorado.edu/tomruth/gtapingams/html/gtapgams.html).

Rutherford, T.F. and D. Tarr (1998), "Regional Trading Arrangements for Chile: Do The Results Differ with a Dynamic Model?", a paper presented at the Dynamic CGE Conference in Denmark.

St-Hilaire, F. and J. Whalley (1983), A Microconsistent Equilibrium data set for Canada for use in Tax Policy Analysis, *Review Income and Wealth*, 29, 175-204.

Shoven, J.B. and J. Whalley (1992), Applying General Equilibrium, CUP, 1992.

Shoven, J.B. and J. Whalley (1984), "Applied General-Equilibrium Models of Taxation and International Trade: An Introduction and Survey", *Journal of Economic Literature*, Vol. XXII, Sept,1984, pp.1007-1051.

Taylor, L. (Ed.) (1990), Socially Relevant Policy Analysis: Structuralist Computable General Equilibrium Models for the Developing World, MIT Press, Cambridge 1990.

Walras, L. Elements of Pure Economics, Allen and Unwin, London, 1954.

Whalley, J. and C. Hamilton (1996), The Trading System: After the Uruguay Round, Institute for International Economics, Washington D.C.

Whalley, J. (1985), Trade Liberalization Among Major World Trading Areas, MIT Press, Cambridge.

Whalley J. and B. Yeung (1983), "External Sector `Closing' Rules in Applied General Equilibrium Models" *Journal of International Economics*, 15, pp. 1- 16.

NOTES

1. The program used is presented in appendix II can be made available upon request for people with access to the GTAP4 data set.
2. See the detailed description of GTAP aggregation in http://nash.colorado.edu/tomruth/gtapingams.html/gtapgams.html.
3. See Whalley and Yeung (1983), Whalley (1985) more discussion on microconsistent data set required for regional trade models.

APPENDIX A

Trade Distortions by Import Tariff and Export Taxes: Illustration in Case of Agriculture Sector

GTAP Import Tariff Rates by Sector for the year 1995 (in %)

	Agriculture										
	USA	*JPN*	*EUR*	*UK*	*ACN*	*CHN*	*FSU*	*CEA*	*ASI*	*MOP*	*ROW*
USA		165	13	17		34	-3	6	59	4	3
JPN	1		6	20	4	4	8	6	13	7	10
EUR	5	27	3		1	1	5	10	46	9	15
UK	1	27	2			-2	-1	10	6	11	27
ACN	1	116	5	5	3	2	2	4	27	4	8
CHN	3	11	5	4	1	3	8	2	24	10	19
FSU	2	1	18	13		17	6	8	13	7	23
CEA	32	6	29	2	1	11	2	-3	30	6	11
ASI	3	9	10	15	2	8		4	21	11	10
MOP	1	6	11	11	1	10	3	6	22	13	20
ROW	8	20	8	22	2	7	1	8	31	14	8

Source: GTAP data base version 4, 1998 see; see Table 1 for countries included in above regions. Tariff rates for other sectors are available upon request.

Appendix 2

GTAP Export Tax Rates on Net Basis by Sectors for 1995 (in %)

	Agriculture										
	USA	*JPN*	*EUR*	*UK*	*ACN*	*CHN*	*FSU*	*CEA*	*ASI*	*MOP*	*ROW*
USA		1	1	1	1		-1				
JPN	-7		-3	-9	-6	-13	-38	-35	-15	-29	-37
EUR	-9	-8	-1	-1	-6	-15	-7	-8	-14	-25	-19
UK	-21	-37			-9	-18	-9	-9	-14	-29	-17
ACN	-1	-1	-2	-2	-2	-1	-2	-1	-3	-1	-3
CHN	7	6	11	11	11	6	11	10	-9	-21	9
FSU	1	5	2	1		1	2	2	1	1	1
CEA	-2	-7	-3	-4	-1	-9	11	5	-5	9	8
ASI	3	4	3	2	5	3	1	4	4	2	4
MOP	3	2	2	1		1	1	3	3		3
ROW	3	4	6	5	3	3	2	8	4	2	7

Source: GTAP data base version 4, 1998; see Table 1 for countries included in above regions. Export tax rates for other sectors are available upon request.

Table A1
Sectoral Composition of Exports 1995
(Total volume in million of US $s)

Agriculture

	USA	*JPN*	*EUR*	*UK*	*ACN*	*CHN*	*FSU*	*CEA*	*ASI*	*MOP*	*ROW*	*Total*	*Total Vol.*
USA	0.00	0.23	0.14	0.02	0.07	0.14	0.01	0.00	0.16	0.14	0.09	1.00	37670
JPN	0.08	0.00	0.06	0.02	0.06	0.49	0.00	0.01	0.17	0.03	0.07	1.00	680
EUR	0.02	0.02	0.71	0.07	0.00	0.02	0.02	0.03	0.01	0.04	0.05	1.00	56582
UK	0.02	0.04	0.65	0.00	0.02	0.03	0.01	0.01	0.04	0.10	0.07	1.00	3849
ACN	0.17	0.16	0.13	0.02	0.03	0.15	0.00	0.00	0.15	0.12	0.06	1.00	18616
CHN	0.05	0.31	0.12	0.01	0.02	0.16	0.02	0.00	0.18	0.09	0.05	1.00	6104
FSU	0.00	0.11	0.44	0.01	0.00	0.07	0.05	0.10	0.11	0.02	0.10	1.00	5690
CEA	0.01	0.02	0.54	0.02	0.00	0.00	0.08	0.15	0.01	0.07	0.10	1.00	3206
ASI	0.11	0.20	0.15	0.03	0.02	0.14	0.03	0.02	0.19	0.07	0.05	1.00	15498
MOP	0.37	0.06	0.22	0.03	0.02	0.03	0.01	0.01	0.09	0.10	0.05	1.00	11170
ROW	0.14	0.06	0.40	0.06	0.02	0.04	0.01	0.02	0.07	0.06	0.12	1.00	42390
Total	16486	21603	77418	8746	5199	15124	3163	3939	18318	15840	15619		201455

Source: GTAP4 data set 1995

Extraction

	USA	*JPN*	*EUR*	*UK*	*ACN*	*CHN*	*FSU*	*CEA*	*ASI*	*MOP*	*ROW*	*Total*	*Total Vol.*
USA	0.00	0.10	0.22	0.03	0.14	0.04	0.00	0.02	0.09	0.16	0.21	1.00	8617
JPN	0.10	0.00	0.03	0.00	0.01	0.31	0.01	0.00	0.49	0.02	0.02	1.00	2080
EUR	0.05	0.00	0.64	0.15	0.03	0.00	0.01	0.02	0.01	0.02	0.05	1.00	46802
UK	0.20	0.00	0.67	0.00	0.02	0.00	0.00	0.02	0.01	0.00	0.06	1.00	13038
ACN	0.58	0.21	0.04	0.01	0.01	0.03	0.00	0.00	0.07	0.01	0.03	1.00	25192
CHN	0.09	0.37	0.09	0.01	0.00	0.07	0.00	0.00	0.24	0.04	0.09	1.00	3947
FSU	0.01	0.01	0.58	0.01	0.00	0.01	0.03	0.27	0.01	0.00	0.06	1.00	17785
CEA	0.02	0.00	0.49	0.02	0.00	0.00	0.10	0.26	0.01	0.02	0.07	1.00	3706
ASI	0.01	0.29	0.01	0.00	0.04	0.14	0.00	0.00	0.42	0.06	0.02	1.00	14419.06
MOP	0.14	0.27	0.24	0.01	0.02	0.03	0.00	0.01	0.20	0.02	0.07	1.00	130105.7
ROW	0.45	0.05	0.18	0.01	0.03	0.02	0.00	0.01	0.06	0.01	0.18	1.00	42546
Total	57340	49457	93745	9180	7511	8686	1504	8259	40370	7217	24969	3E+05	201455

Source: GTAP4 data set 1995.

Other Mining

	USA	*JPN*	*EUR*	*UK*	*ACN*	*CHN*	*FSU*	*CEA*	*ASI*	*MOP*	*ROW*	*Total*	*Total Vol.*
USA	0.00	0.12	0.24	0.05	0.26	0.08	0.01	0.00	0.09	0.08	0.07	1.00	8832
JPN	0.18	0.00	0.11	0.02	0.03	0.24	0.00	0.00	0.36	0.03	0.02	1.00	5776
EUR	0.09	0.03	0.52	0.07	0.01	0.03	0.01	0.03	0.08	0.10	0.04	1.00	53356
UK	0.08	0.02	0.59	0.00	0.02	0.03	0.00	0.01	0.14	0.08	0.03	1.00	8241
ACN	0.20	0.24	0.23	0.06	0.01	0.08	0.00	0.00	0.11	0.03	0.03	1.00	10318
CHN	0.20	0.19	0.14	0.02	0.04	0.13	0.01	0.01	0.15	0.05	0.06	1.00	7301
FSU	0.06	0.02	0.42	0.02	0.01	0.02	0.04	0.25	0.03	0.09	0.02	1.00	2566
CEA	0.05	0.01	0.58	0.03	0.01	0.01	0.04	0.14	0.01	0.05	0.07	1.00	3330
ASI	0.18	0.24	0.19	0.01	0.02	0.13	0.00	0.00	0.15	0.05	0.03	1.00	11922
MOP	0.28	0.19	0.18	0.03	0.02	0.06	0.01	0.00	0.13	0.07	0.04	1.00	11502
ROW	0.09	0.13	0.42	0.09	0.02	0.04	0.01	0.02	0.05	0.04	0.10	1.00	22588
Total	17547	14576	55263	7730	4746	8899	1231	3224	15139	9931	7446		145732

Source: GTAP4 data set 1995.

	Food and Drink												
	USA	*JPN*	*EUR*	*UK*	*ACN*	*CHN*	*FSU*	*CEA*	*ASI*	*MOP*	*ROW*	*Total*	*Total Vol.*
USA	0.00	0.30	0.10	0.02	0.13	0.07	0.05	0.00	0.07	0.14	0.12	1.00	27898
JPN	0.16	0.00	0.04	0.01	0.04	0.35	0.00	0.00	0.31	0.05	0.04	1.00	1930.19
EUR	0.04	0.03	0.60	0.08	0.01	0.01	0.05	0.03	0.02	0.07	0.06	1.00	147794
UK	0.06	0.03	0.59	0.00	0.02	0.03	0.02	0.01	0.06	0.07	0.12	1.00	14879
ACN	0.30	0.22	0.06	0.05	0.06	0.07	0.01	0.00	0.13	0.05	0.05	1.00	19631
CHN	0.08	0.48	0.05	0.01	0.02	0.15	0.03	0.00	0.14	0.02	0.04	1.00	10695
FSU	0.06	0.38	0.20	0.02	0.02	0.05	0.13	0.05	0.07	0.01	0.02	1.00	3549
CEA	0.03	0.01	0.42	0.02	0.01	0.00	0.22	0.15	0.02	0.03	0.09	1.00	5333
ASI	0.10	0.20	0.10	0.02	0.03	0.13	0.01	0.00	0.19	0.13	0.09	1.00	30355
MOP	0.23	0.16	0.24	0.02	0.02	0.05	0.02	0.01	0.08	0.12	0.06	1.00	7050
ROW	0.10	0.08	0.30	0.06	0.02	0.06	0.04	0.02	0.05	0.08	0.20	1.00	34554
Total	22204	34098	1E+05	17152	8635	14371	12426	6019	18569	23847	26304		303668.2

Source: GTAP4 data set 1995.

	Other Manufacturing Sector												
	USA	*JPN*	*EUR*	*UK*	*ACN*	*CHN*	*FSU*	*CEA*	*ASI*	*MOP*	*ROW*	*Total*	*Total Vol.*
USA	0.00	0.13	0.16	0.05	0.21	0.06	0.00	0.00	0.09	0.14	0.15	1.00	59243
JPN	0.22	0.00	0.14	0.03	0.03	0.29	0.00	0.00	0.21	0.05	0.02	1.00	30482
EUR	0.05	0.03	0.63	0.09	0.01	0.02	0.02	0.05	0.02	0.04	0.04	1.00	278152
UK	0.11	0.03	0.62	0.00	0.04	0.03	0.01	0.02	0.04	0.04	0.07	1.00	24679
ACN	0.62	0.11	0.08	0.02	0.04	0.04	0.00	0.00	0.04	0.02	0.03	1.00	42310
CHN	0.25	0.18	0.16	0.03	0.04	0.16	0.01	0.01	0.08	0.03	0.05	1.00	133871
FSU	0.06	0.03	0.50	0.07	0.00	0.02	0.08	0.05	0.05	0.06	0.08	1.00	6344
CEA	0.03	0.00	0.74	0.03	0.01	0.00	0.05	0.08	0.01	0.02	0.04	1.00	21932
ASI	0.22	0.11	0.17	0.05	0.03	0.14	0.01	0.01	0.12	0.08	0.06	1.00	92032
MOP	0.35	0.09	0.24	0.05	0.03	0.06	0.00	0.00	0.08	0.06	0.04	1.00	36931
ROW	0.28	0.03	0.35	0.06	0.02	0.03	0.02	0.02	0.03	0.03	0.13	1.00	48598
Total	1E+05	59764	3E+05	43488	30274	59045	10738	18725	45532	38391	46609		774574

Source: GTAP4 data set 1995.

	Chemical Sector												
	USA	*JPN*	*EUR*	*UK*	*ACN*	*CHN*	*FSU*	*CEA*	*ASI*	*MOP*	*ROW*	*Total*	*Total Vol.*
USA	0.00	0.09	0.21	0.04	0.20	0.10	0.00	0.00	0.10	0.11	0.14	1.00	70893
JPN	0.18	0.00	0.14	0.02	0.03	0.25	0.00	0.00	0.27	0.06	0.03	1.00	37462
EUR	0.06	0.03	0.62	0.08	0.02	0.02	0.01	0.04	0.03	0.04	0.06	1.00	280501
UK	0.11	0.03	0.63	0.00	0.04	0.02	0.01	0.02	0.04	0.05	0.06	1.00	35266
ACN	0.64	0.04	0.05	0.01	0.07	0.05	0.00	0.00	0.07	0.03	0.03	1.00	19606
CHN	0.16	0.10	0.14	0.03	0.04	0.26	0.00	0.00	0.17	0.05	0.05	1.00	30401
FSU	0.10	0.02	0.38	0.04	0.01	0.17	0.05	0.06	0.08	0.02	0.09	1.00	10213
CEA	0.04	0.01	0.45	0.03	0.01	0.02	0.08	0.23	0.03	0.02	0.09	1.00	10513
ASI	0.10	0.08	0.10	0.03	0.03	0.23	0.01	0.00	0.25	0.08	0.08	1.00	32443
MOP	0.18	0.06	0.22	0.02	0.02	0.07	0.01	0.01	0.24	0.08	0.11	1.00	21757
ROW	0.19	0.02	0.21	0.02	0.02	0.02	0.01	0.01	0.05	0.05	0.39	1.00	21112
Total	56697	24545	2E+05	30220	25834	42833	6051	14644	49475	30985	47151		570167

Source: GTAP4 data set 1995.

	Metal												
	USA	*JPN*	*EUR*	*UK*	*ACN*	*CHN*	*FSU*	*CEA*	*ASI*	*MOP*	*ROW*	*Total*	*Total Vol.*
USA	0.00	0.09	0.12	0.06	0.29	0.08	0.00	0.00	0.12	0.16	0.09	1.00	26483
JPN	0.15	0.00	0.05	0.02	0.03	0.29	0.00	0.00	0.35	0.07	0.03	1.00	29215
EUR	0.05	0.01	0.67	0.07	0.01	0.02	0.01	0.03	0.03	0.04	0.05	1.00	158195
UK	0.08	0.02	0.66	0.00	0.03	0.04	0.01	0.01	0.06	0.05	0.05	1.00	16802
ACN	0.56	0.09	0.06	0.02	0.03	0.07	0.00	0.00	0.11	0.03	0.02	1.00	22474
CHN	0.18	0.15	0.13	0.02	0.04	0.18	0.00	0.00	0.20	0.05	0.04	1.00	25225
FSU	0.14	0.09	0.37	0.03	0.01	0.09	0.01	0.02	0.14	0.04	0.06	1.00	23550
CEA	0.02	0.01	0.57	0.04	0.00	0.03	0.02	0.15	0.05	0.05	0.06	1.00	14837
ASI	0.11	0.18	0.06	0.02	0.03	0.18	0.00	0.00	0.27	0.08	0.05	1.00	18487
MOP	0.30	0.10	0.15	0.02	0.01	0.05	0.00	0.00	0.17	0.13	0.06	1.00	12234
ROW	0.17	0.13	0.21	0.03	0.02	0.08	0.00	0.00	0.13	0.07	0.17	1.00	30947
Total	45241	20764	2E+05	17718	14352	29223	2399	8191	41929	22797	22058		378449

Source: GTAP4 data set 1995.

	Engineering												
	USA	*JPN*	*EUR*	*UK*	*ACN*	*CHN*	*FSU*	*CEA*	*ASI*	*MOP*	*ROW*	*Total*	*Total Vol.*
USA	0.00	0.10	0.19	0.06	0.23	0.07	0.01	0.00	0.14	0.12	0.09	1.00	292467
JPN	0.31	0.00	0.14	0.03	0.04	0.14	0.00	0.00	0.22	0.05	0.05	1.00	320151
EUR	0.08	0.02	0.54	0.09	0.02	0.04	0.02	0.04	0.05	0.05	0.07	1.00	731215
UK	0.12	0.03	0.58	0.00	0.03	0.03	0.01	0.02	0.06	0.05	0.06	1.00	97994
ACN	0.81	0.01	0.04	0.02	0.02	0.02	0.00	0.00	0.03	0.02	0.03	1.00	82369
CHN	0.27	0.10	0.19	0.03	0.04	0.15	0.00	0.01	0.14	0.03	0.05	1.00	127017
FSU	0.03	0.00	0.26	0.03	0.01	0.13	0.21	0.09	0.08	0.02	0.13	1.00	3522
CEA	0.03	0.00	0.62	0.04	0.01	0.01	0.06	0.12	0.02	0.03	0.06	1.00	21630
ASI	0.27	0.09	0.13	0.04	0.03	0.11	0.01	0.01	0.22	0.04	0.05	1.00	192815
MOP	0.72	0.01	0.07	0.03	0.04	0.02	0.00	0.00	0.05	0.02	0.04	1.00	54433
ROW	0.15	0.00	0.25	0.04	0.02	0.02	0.02	0.01	0.06	0.05	0.39	1.00	25889
Total	4E+05	80334	6E+05	1E+05	1E+05	1E+05	19562	34858	2E+05	1E+05	1E+05		1949502

Source: GTAP4 data set 1995.

	Private Services												
	USA	*JPN*	*EUR*	*UK*	*ACN*	*CHN*	*FSU*	*CEA*	*ASI*	*MOP*	*ROW*	*Total*	*Total Vol.*
USA	0.00	0.11	0.48	0.04	0.12	0.04	0.02	0.01	0.09	0.05	0.03	1.00	76427
JPN	0.25	0.00	0.14	0.01	0.06	0.15	0.03	0.01	0.29	0.04	0.03	1.00	17042
EUR	0.20	0.03	0.56	0.02	0.02	0.03	0.03	0.01	0.05	0.03	0.02	1.00	152688
UK	0.37	0.04	0.28	0.00	0.04	0.04	0.05	0.02	0.09	0.05	0.03	1.00	17843
ACN	0.35	0.27	0.11	0.01	0.03	0.04	0.02	0.01	0.10	0.03	0.02	1.00	9108
CHN	0.16	0.18	0.27	0.02	0.03	0.08	0.04	0.01	0.13	0.04	0.04	1.00	11510
FSU	0.15	0.17	0.36	0.02	0.02	0.08	0.03	0.01	0.07	0.03	0.05	1.00	4870
CEA	0.15	0.16	0.35	0.02	0.02	0.08	0.03	0.01	0.08	0.03	0.06	1.00	2984
ASI	0.13	0.23	0.23	0.01	0.03	0.11	0.04	0.02	0.10	0.05	0.05	1.00	15611
MOP	0.26	0.15	0.29	0.02	0.02	0.06	0.03	0.01	0.07	0.03	0.07	1.00	4747
ROW	0.13	0.15	0.35	0.02	0.02	0.06	0.03	0.01	0.08	0.04	0.11	1.00	10740
Total	52955	25457	1E+05	7509	15405	14747	9434	3365	27376	12639	9875		323570

Source: GTAP4 data set 1995.

Public Services

	USA	*JPN*	*EUR*	*UK*	*ACN*	*CHN*	*FSU*	*CEA*	*ASI*	*MOP*	*ROW*	*Total*	*Total Vol.*
USA	0.00	0.00	0.45	0.19	0.04	0.10	0.00	0.00	0.13	0.04	0.03	1.00	24653
JPN	0.14	0.00	0.14	0.02	0.02	0.30	0.01	0.00	0.29	0.05	0.03	1.00	499.1201
EUR	0.13	0.00	0.54	0.10	0.01	0.04	0.01	0.00	0.09	0.05	0.04	1.00	50655
UK	0.29	0.00	0.35	0.00	0.02	0.04	0.01	0.00	0.14	0.09	0.06	1.00	12568
ACN	0.19	0.02	0.14	0.06	0.02	0.16	0.01	0.00	0.29	0.06	0.04	1.00	5193
CHN	0.14	0.01	0.31	0.07	0.02	0.10	0.01	0.00	0.20	0.07	0.07	1.00	3963
FSU	0.12	0.01	0.36	0.10	0.01	0.08	0.01	0.00	0.12	0.06	0.12	1.00	1749
CEA	0.12	0.01	0.36	0.10	0.01	0.08	0.01	0.00	0.13	0.07	0.12	1.00	1319
ASI	0.11	0.01	0.29	0.09	0.02	0.14	0.01	0.00	0.16	0.09	0.08	1.00	10649
MOP	0.13	0.01	0.38	0.11	0.01	0.08	0.01	0.00	0.12	0.06	0.11	1.00	8058
ROW	0.11	0.01	0.38	0.10	0.01	0.07	0.01	0.00	0.13	0.07	0.11	1.00	12934
Total	16125	590	57172	13605	2192	9652	962	82.12	16545	7726	7589		132240.1

Source: GTAP4 data set 1995.

Utilities

	USA	*EUR*	*UK*	*CHN*	*FSU*	*CEA*	*ROW*	*Total*	*Total Vol.*
EUR	0.00	0.86	0.11	0.00	0.00	0.01	0.02	1.00	5901
ACN	1.00	0.00	0.00	0.00	0.00	0.00	0.00	1.00	856
CHN	0.00	0.00	0.00	0.98	0.00	0.00	0.02	1.00	623
FSU	0.00	0.42	0.00	0.01	0.46	0.11	0.00	1.00	274
CEA	0.00	0.58	0.00	0.00	0.00	0.12	0.30	1.00	297
MOP	0.90	0.00	0.00	0.00	0.00	0.00	0.10	1.00	86
ROW	0.00	0.04	0.00	0.00	0.00	0.14	0.81	1.00	113
Total	933	5353	668	612	127	156	301		8150

Source: GTAP4 data set 1995.

Construction

	EUR	*ACN*	*CHN*	*FSU*	*CEA*	*ASI*	*MOP*	*ROW*	*Total*	*Total Vol.*
EUR	0.42	0.00	0.06	0.03	0.09	0.01	0.24	0.15	1.00	13958
ACN		0.50					0.33	0.17	1.00	6
CHN	0.09	0.00	0.03	0.06	0.15	0.02	0.40	0.26	1.00	761
FSU	0.21	0.00	0.32	0.03	0.07	0.01	0.20	0.15	1.00	402
CEA	0.22	0.00	0.33	0.03	0.07	0.01	0.20	0.14	1.00	5521
ASI	0.13	0.00	0.35	0.03	0.08	0.01	0.24	0.15	1.00	1429
ROW	0.17		0.30	0.03	0.07	0.03	0.21	0.18	1.00	126
Total	7464	60	3301	696	1880	215	5199	3388		22203

Source: GTAP4 data set 1995.

Table A2

GTAP Import Tariff Rates by Sector for the year 1995 (in %)

Agriculture

	USA	*JPN*	*EUR*	*UK*	*ACN*	*CHN*	*FSU*	*CEA*	*ASI*	*MOP*	*ROW*
USA		165									
13	17		34	-3	6	59	4	3			
JPN	1		6	20	4	4	8	6	13	7	10
EUR	5	27	3		1	1	5	10	46	9	15
UK	1	27	2			-2	-1	10	6	11	27
ACN	1	116	5	5	3	2	2	4	27	4	8
CHN	3	11	5	4	1	3	8	2	24	10	19
FSU	2	1	18	13		17	6	8	13	7	23
CEA	32	6	29	2	1	11	2	-3	30	6	11
ASI	3	9	10	15	2	8		4	21	11	10
MOP	1	6	11	11	1	10	3	6	22	13	20
ROW	8	20	8	22	2	7	1	8	31	14	8

Extraction

	USA	*JPN*	*EUR*	*UK*	*ACN*	*CHN*	*FSU*	*CEA*	*ASI*	*MOP*	*ROW*
USA						6	8	1	6	2	8
JPN			1	1		5	5	4	8	8	2
EUR	2	3			8	7	5	6	28	12	18
UK	1	1			9	7	9	6	24	11	11
ACN						3			5	4	10
CHN	1	2	1		2	1	5	2	5	5	20
FSU	2				9	5	5	1	3	6	6
CEA	1		1		1	8	5	4		4	13
ASI	2	1	1	1		4	5	1	9	4	25
MOP	1	1			3	4	5	2	6	6	10
ROW	1	1		1	4	3	6	2	3	6	12

Other Mining

	USA	*JPN*	*EUR*	*UK*	*ACN*	*CHN*	*FSU*	*CEA*	*ASI*	*MOP*	*ROW*
USA			1	1		9	10	9	10	3	10
JPN	6		4	5	7	9	16	12	9	10	15
EUR	5	1			6	10	16	8	6	13	15
UK	4	3			8	5	18	8	4	12	14
ACN						1	31	3	4	7	7
CHN	6	1	4	5	6	12	11	3	17	13	20
FSU				1		3	13		11	16	7
CEA	8	1	4	4	3	1	18	6	14	20	22
ASI	1		1	2	5	3	22	8	12	10	34
MOP					2	3	43	2	6	11	10
ROW	1				1	3	9	2	5	10	8

Source: GTAP data base version 4, 1998.

Table A2
GTAP Import Tariff Rates by Sector for the year 1995 (in %)

Food and Drink

	USA	*JPN*	*EUR*	*UK*	*ACN*	*CHN*	*FSU*	*CEA*	*ASI*	*MOP*	*ROW*
USA		27	30	14	6	12	12	15	33	12	25
JPN	9		23	36	4	21	14	27	30	17	49
EUR	17	42	3	1	11	21	12	19	42	16	26
UK	9	42	1		7	32	18	31	41	45	30
ACN	7	62	64	81	3	18	4	22	46	14	23
CHN	4	33	21	20	5	12	14	14	34	16	98
FSU	3	21	22	17	2	24	10	16	17	11	31
CEA	15	45	31	29	17	13	16	22	70	20	42
ASI	4	16	17	13	2	9	9	6	39	15	45
MOP	2	10	8	14	3	7	9	15	35	21	42
ROW	13	17	25	54	4	15	9	16	35	10	11

Other Manufacturing

	USA	*JPN*	*EUR*	*UK*	*ACN*	*CHN*	*FSU*	*CEA*	*ASI*	*MOP*	*ROW*
USA		3	4	4	1	10	15	8	12	3	17
JPN	3		5	5	9	30	13	14	12	12	32
EUR	6	8			12	13	13	9	14	15	27
UK	3	6			7	8	17	10	17	14	28
ACN		1	2	2	1	8	16	8	10	7	13
CHN	8	5	8	8	12	31	18	9	19	18	27
FSU	8	4	5	3	14	14	14	8	20	14	12
CEA	8	3	5	6	16	26	17	7	32	14	45
ASI	9	3	7	7	14	24	18	5	20	14	29
MOP	3	1	7	7	11	13	18	10	13	16	22
ROW	9	2	7	7	13	13	18	8	11	14	15

Chemical

	USA	*JPN*	*EUR*	*UK*	*ACN*	*CHN*	*FSU*	*CEA*	*ASI*	*MOP*	*ROW*
USA		2	4	4	1	8	10	10	14	2	9
JPN	3		5	5	8	11	8	8	13	10	13
EUR	3	2			6	8	9	8	19	10	11
UK	3	2			6	8	11	7	21	8	12
ACN		1	3	3	1	8	13	11	12	10	16
CHN	9	3	6	6	13	23	16	8	17	11	15
FSU		2	5	5	4	6	10	11	26	12	8
CEA	1	1	3	3	5	7	11	7	17	12	17
ASI	5	1	4	4	9	12	13	10	22	11	15
MOP	3	2	3	3	7	9	13	10	29	10	9
ROW	1		4	4	2	8	13	8	35	10	9

Source: GTAP data base version 4, 1998.

Metal

	USA	*JPN*	*EUR*	*UK*	*ACN*	*CHN*	*FSU*	*CEA*	*ASI*	*MOP*	*ROW*
USA		1	3	3		9	23	7	10	3	10
JPN	4		4	4	7	11	18	6	13	11	14
EUR	4	1			8	10	12	6	22	14	12
UK	3	1			8	6	15	6	21	13	14
ACN			2	2	1	5	19	6	11	8	16
CHN	4	1	4	4	9	16	14	8	10	11	18
FSU	2		2	2	3	9	13	6	11	10	6
CEA	3	1	3	3	5	8	15	5	13	13	15
ASI	3	2	4	4	8	11	17	7	18	11	23
MOP		1	3	3	3	7	15	8	16	13	11
ROW	1		3	3	3	5	16	6	13	11	9

Engineering

	USA	*JPN*	*EUR*	*UK*	*ACN*	*CHN*	*FSU*	*CEA*	*ASI*	*MOP*	*ROW*
USA		1	3	3	1	9	11	11	9	4	12
JPN	3		5	5	8	15	13	13	12	12	18
EUR	3				7	20	8	8	15	13	14
UK	3	1			7	7	11	7	19	13	12
ACN		1	3	4	2	8	7	12	11	9	15
CHN	3		5	5	6	15	9	11	9	11	14
FSU	1		5	6	6	15	9	12	37	15	10
CEA			4	4	6	27	10	8	30	14	23
ASI	1		4	4	5	8	17	13	9	13	16
MOP			4	3	1	4	7	13	11	15	15
ROW			4	4	6	42	13	11	8	16	14

Utility

	CHN	*FSU*	*ROW*
EUR			1
CHN			1
FSU	1	4	
CEA			1

Construction

	ROW
EUR	1
ACN	1
CHN	1
FSU	1
CEA	1
ASI	1
ROW	1

Source: GTAP data base version 4, 1998.

Transport

	JPN	*FSU*
USA	3	2
JPN		2
EUR	3	2
UK	3	2
ACN	3	2
CHN	3	2
FSU	3	2
CEA	3	2
ASI	3	2
MOP	3	2
ROW	3	2

Private Services

	JPN	*CHN*	*FSU*	*ROW*
USA	3	1	2	
JPN		1	2	1
EUR	3	3	2	1
UK	3	3	2	1
ACN	3	2	2	1
CHN	3	1	2	1
FSU	3	1	2	
CEA	3	1	2	
ASI	3	1	2	1
MOP	3	1	2	
ROW	3	1	2	

Public services

	JPN	*ROW*
USA	2	2
JPN		2
EUR	2	2
UK	2	2
ACN	2	2
CHN	2	1
FSU	2	1
CEA	2	1
ASI	2	2
MOP	2	1
ROW	2	1

Source: GTAP data base version 4, 1998.

Table A3
GTAP Export Tax Rates on Net Basis by Sectors for 1995 (in %)

Agriculture

	USA	*JPN*	*EUR*	*UK*	*ACN*	*CHN*	*FSU*	*CEA*	*ASI*	*MOP*	*ROW*
USA		1	1	1	1		-1				
JPN	-7		-3	-9	-6	-13	-38	-35	-15	-29	-37
EUR	-9	-8	-1	-1	-6	-15	-7	-8	-14	-25	-19
UK	-21	-37			-9	-18	-9	-9	-14	-29	-17
ACN	-1	-1	-2	-2	-2	-1	-2	-1	-3	-1	-3
CHN	7	6	11	11	11	6	11	10	-9	-21	9
FSU	1	5	2	1		1	2	2	1	1	1
CEA	-2	-7	-3	-4	-1	-9	11	5	-5	9	8
ASI	3	4	3	2	5	3	1	4	4	2	4
MOP	3	2	2	1		1	1	3	3		3
ROW	3	4	6	5	3	3	2	8	4	2	7

Extraction

	USA	*JPN*	*EUR*	*UK*	*ACN*	*CHN*	*FSU*	*CEA*	*ASI*	*MOP*	*ROW*
USA		8	8	9	1	8	7	9	7	2	7
EUR		1				1	1	1	1	1	1
ACN		1	1	1		2		1	3	2	3
CHN	28	32	-3	-4	3		7	-3	12	27	14
FSU	4	1	3	3	2	6	3	2	2	1	2
ASI	3	7	1	1	4	2		1	5	2	2
MOP			1	1				1			
ROW	8	2	8	6	4	8	3	4	6	7	2

Other Mining

	USA	*JPN*	*EUR*	*UK*	*ACN*	*CHN*	*FSU*	*CEA*	*ASI*	*MOP*	*ROW*
USA		4	4	4		3	4	2	3	1	2
EUR	1	1			1	1	1	1	1	1	1
CHN	-14	-14	-12	-12	-15	-9	-10	-6	-13	-17	-17
ASI	1	1	1	1	2	1	1		3	1	2
MOP	1	1	2	2	1	2	2	3	1		1
ROW	1			-4	1	-1	-2	-1	1	1	1

Food and Drinking

	USA	*JPN*	*EUR*	*UK*	*ACN*	*CHN*	*FSU*	*CEA*	*ASI*	*MOP*	*ROW*
USA		3	1	3	-1		-3	1		-3	-1
JPN	-2		-7	-7	-4	-3	-19	-32	-9	-40	-2
EUR	-11	-12	-2	-1	-13	-12	-19	-14	-26	-37	-26
UK	-3	-11			-2	-12	-4	-9	-5	-19	-16
ACN	-1	-2	-4	-2	-1	-3	-2	-3	-7	-11	-4
CHN	-3	1	4	-3	-3	1	30	13	-1	-10	-3
FSU	6	3	3	4	3	3	8	1	3	1	2
CEA	-10	-7	-12	-4	-4	-8	-5	-7	-16	-13	-10
ASI	-4	-5	-5	-4	-4	-16	-4	-18	-5	-15	-17
MOP	1	1	1				1	-1			1
ROW	2	1	4	-1	4	4	6	7	5	3	3

Source: GTAP data base version 4, 1998.

Other Manufacturing

	USA	JPN	EUR	UK	ACN	CHN	FSU	CEA	ASI	MOP	ROW
USA		1	1	1		1	1	1	1		1
EUR	1	1			1	1			1	1	1
CHN	10		9	9	8	-1	-3	1	1	2	2
FSU		1		1						1	
ASI	7	3	4	4	5	2	1	1	4	1	1
MOP			-1	-2				-1		-1	-1
ROW	1		1		1	-2					

Chemical

	USA	JPN	EUR	UK	ACN	CHN	FSU	CEA	ASI	MOP	ROW
USA		2	2	2		2	2	2	2		2
EUR										1	1
CHN	-8	-8	-9	-9	-8	-2	-12	-9	-6	-7	-8
ASI	4	2	3	3	2	1	1	1	2	1	1
MOP			1	1			1			1	
ROW	1	5	2	2	1	2	1	2	3	2	2

Metal

	USA	JPN	EUR	UK	ACN	CHN	FSU	CEA	ASI	MOP	ROW
USA		1	1	1		1	1	1	1		1
EUR										1	1
CHN	-4	-5	-6	-5	-4	-3	-9	-6	-4	-5	-7
ASI	1	1	2	2	2	1		2	3	2	1
MOP			1							1	
ROW								1	-1		

Engineering

	USA	JPN	EUR	UK	ACN	CHN	FSU	CEA	ASI	MOP	ROW
USA		1	1	1		1	1	1	1		1
EUR										1	1
ACN		1	1						1	1	1
CHN	-2	-3	-3	-2	-3	-1	-6	-2	-2	-3	-3
ASI	3	3	2	4	3	2		2	4	2	1
MOP						1				1	
ROW	2	2	1	1	2	1					

Utilities

	EUR	CHN	FSU	CEA	ROW
EUR					1
CHN		-9			-11
FSU	-1	-1	-1	-1	
CEA	-1			-1	-1
MOP					4

Construction

	EUR	ACN	CHN	FSU	CEA	ASI	MOP	ROW
EUR		1	1	1	1	1	1	1
ACN	475		475	475	475	475	475	475
FSU	1	1	1	1	1	1	1	1
ROW	1	1	1	1	1	1	1	1

Source: GTAP data base version 4, 1998.

	Transportation										
	USA	*JPN*	*EUR*	*UK*	*ACN*	*CHN*	*FSU*	*CEA*	*ASI*	*MOP*	*ROW*
USA		12	12	12	2	12	12	12	12	7	12
EUR	1	1			1	1	1	1	1	1	1
ASI	1	2	3	2	1	1	2	2	2	2	3
MOP	1	3	3	3	2	4	2	2	3	2	3
ROW	2	1	1	1	1	1	1	1	1	1	1

	Private Services										
	USA	*JPN*	*EUR*	*UK*	*ACN*	*CHN*	*FSU*	*CEA*	*ASI*	*MOP*	*ROW*
USA		8	8	8	1	8	8	8	8	3	8
EUR	1	1			1	1	1	1	1	1	1
FSU	2	2	2	2	2	2	2	2	2	2	2
ASI	1		1	1	1	1		1	1	1	2
ROW	1	2	1	1	1	1	1	1	1	1	1

	Public Services										
	USA	*JPN*	*EUR*	*UK*	*ACN*	*CHN*	*FSU*	*CEA*	*ASI*	*MOP*	*ROW*
ASI			1	1			1	1	1	1	1
MOP	8	8	8	8	8	8	7	6	8	8	8
ROW	1	1	1	1	1	1	1	1	1	1	1

Source: GTAP data base version 4, 1998.

APPENDIX B

$TITLE UK Dataset for the global trade model of the UK economy

```
SET I Sectors/
        agr     Agriculture
        ext     Extraction
        omi     Other mining
        fdr     Food and drink
        oma     Other manufacturing
        chm     Chemical
        MTL     Metals-related industry(IRONSTL & NONFERR)
        eng     Engineering
        uti     Utility
        con     Construction
        trn     Transport distribution and communication
        prs     Private services
        pub     Public service
        hsn     Housing
        CGD     Savings good /;

SET R Aggregated Regions /
        USA     United States
        JPN     Japan
        EUR     Europe
        UK      United Kingdom
        ACN     Australia Canada and New Zealand
        CHN     China
        FSU     Former Soviet Union
        CEA     Central European Associates
        ASI     Other Asia
        MPC     Mexico plus OPEC
        ROW     Other countries /;

SET F Factors of production
    /   LND     Land,
        SKL     Skilled labor,
        LAB     Unskilled labor,
        CAP     Capital,
        RES     Natural resources /
```

$TITLE UK Dataset Mapping from GTAP version 4 to 10 regions and 10 goods

```
$SETGLOBAL source gtap4001

set mapi Mapping for sectors and goods /
      PDR.agr     Paddy rice,
      WHT.agr     Wheat,
      GRO.agr     Grains (other than rice and wheat),
      V_F.agr     Vegetable fruit nuts
      OSD.agr     Oil seeds
      C_B.agr     Sugar cane and beet
      PFB.agr     Plant-based fibers
```

```
OCR.agr    Crops n.e.c.
CTL.agr    Bovine cattle - sheep and goats - horse
OAP.agr    Animal products n.e.c.
RMK.agr    Raw milk
WOL.agr    Wool,
FRS.agr    Forestry,
FSH.agr    Fishing,
COL.ext    Coal,
OIL.ext    Oil,
GAS.ext    Natural Gas,
OMN.omi    Other Minerals,
CMT.fdr    Bovine cattle meat products
OMT.fdr    Meat products n.e.c.
VOL.fdr    Vegetable oils
MIL.fdr    Dairy products
PCR.fdr    Processed rice,
SGR.fdr    Sugar
OFD.fdr    Other food products
B_T.fdr    Beverages and tobacco,
TEX.oma    Textiles,
WAP.oma    Wearing apparel,
LEA.oma    Leather goods,
LUM.oma    Lumber and wood,
PPP.oma    Pulp and paper,
P_C.ext    Petroleum and coal products,
CRP.chm    Chemicals rubber and plastics,
NMM.omi    Non-metallic mineral products,
I_S.mtl    Primary ferrous metals,
NFM.mtl    Non-ferrous metals,
FMP.mtl    Fabricated metal products,
MVH.eng    Motor vehicles
OTN.eng    Other transport equipment
ELE.eng    Electronic equipment
OME.eng    Machinery and equipment,
OMF.oma    Other manufacturing products,
ELY.uti    Electricity
GDT.uti    Gas manufacturing and distribution,
WTR.uti    Water
CNS.con    Construction,
T_T.trn    Trade and transport,
OSP.prs    Other services (private),
OSG.pub    Other services (public),
DWE.hsn    Dwellings,
CGD.cgd    Savings good/;
```

```
SET MAPR mapping GTAP regions /
    AUS.ACN    Australia
    NZL.ACN    New Zealand
    JPN.JPN    Japan
    KOR.ASI    Republic of Korea
    IDN.MPC    Indonesia
```

```
MYS.ASI    Malaysia
PHL.ASI    Philippines
SGP.ASI    Singapore
THA.ASI    Thailand
VNM.ASI    Vietnam
CHN.CHN    China
HKG.CHN    Hong Kong
TWN.CHN    Taiwan
IND.ASI    India
LKA.ASI    Sri Lanka
RAS.ASI    Rest of South Asia
CAN.ACN    Canada
USA.USA    United States of America
MEX.MPC    Mexico
CAM.ROW    Central America and Caribbean
VEN.ROW    Venezuela
COL.ROW    Columbia
RAP.ROW    Rest of Andean Pact
ARG.ROW    Argentina
BRA.ROW    Brazil
CHL.ROW    Chile
URY.ROW    Uruguay
RSM.ROW    Rest of South America
GBR.UK     United Kingdom
DEU.EUR    Germany
DNK.EUR    Denmark
SWE.EUR    Sweden
FIN.EUR    Finland
REU.EUR    Rest of EU,
EFT.EUR    European Free Trade Area
CEA.CEA    Central European Associates
FSU.FSU    Former Soviet Union
TUR.ROW    Turkey
RME.MPC    Rest of Middle East
MAR.ROW    Morocco
RNF.MPC    Rest of North Africa
SAF.ROW    South Africa
RSA.ROW    Rest of South Africa
RSS.ROW    Rest of Sub-Saharan Africa
ROW.ROW    Rest of World /;
```

$TITLE UKGTAPinGAMS — Global Economy Model from UK Perspective

```
*    Note:
*    This is the model implemented in MPSGE.
*    This implementation accomodates both constant-elasticity of
*    transformation between production for domestic and export
*    markets (eta < +INF), and perfect substitution between
*    those markets (eta=+INF).
*    Variables, equations and GAMS keywords are in UPPER case.
*    Sets and parameters are in lower case.
*    Read the dataset using the standard routine:
```

```
$SETGLOBAL dataset uk
$IF EXIST dataset $INCLUDE dataset
$INCLUDE ..\inclib\mrtdata

SCALAR
        eta      Elasticity of transformation - domestic vs. exports    / +inf /,
        esubdm   Elasticity of substitution - domestic vs. imports      / 4 /,
        esubmm   Elasticity of substitution - imports                   / 8 /
        sigmap   Elasticity of substitution - imports                   /0.75/;

    display vim;

$ONTEXT

$MODEL:uk

$SECTORS:
    C(r)                     ! Private consumption
    G(r)                     ! Public provision
    Y(i,r)$vom(i,r)          ! Output
    M(i,r)$vim(i,r)          ! Import aggregation
    A(d,i,r)$va(d,i,r)       ! Armington aggregation of domestic and imports
    YT                       ! Transport

$COMMODITIES:
    PC(r)                                ! Private demand
    PG(r)                                ! Public provision
    PY(i,r)$(vom(i,r) and (1/eta=0))     ! Output price
    PD(i,r)$(vdm(i,r) and 1/ETA)         ! Domestic price
    PX(i,r)$(vxm(i,r) and 1/ETA)         ! Export price
    PM(i,r)$vim(i,r)                     ! Import price
    PA(d,i,r)$va(d,i,r)                  ! Armington composite price
    PF(f,r)$evoa(f,r)                    ! Factor price
    PT                                   ! Transport services

$CONSUMERS:
    RA(r) ! Representative agent

    *   Production:

$PROD:Y(i,r)$(vom(i,r)>0 and 1/eta>0) S:0 T:eta va:sigmap
    O:PD(i,r)       Q:vdm(i,r) A:RA(r) T:ty(i,r)
    O:PX(i,r)       Q:vxm(i,r) A:RA(r) T:ty(i,r)
    I:PA("i",j,r)   Q:vafm(J,i,r) A:RA(r) T:ti(j,i,r)
    I:PF(f,r)       Q:vfm(f,i,r) P:pf0(f,i,r) A:RA(r) T:tf(f,i,r) va:

$PROD:Y(i,r)$(vom(i,r)>0 and 1/eta=0) S:0 va:sigmap
    O:PY(i,r)       Q:vom(i,r) A:RA(r) T:ty(i,r)
    I:PA("i",j,r)   Q:vafm(J,i,r) A:RA(r) T:ti(j,i,r)
    I:PF(f,r)       Q:vfm(f,i,r) P:pf0(f,i,r) A:RA(r) T:tf(f,i,r) va:
```

```
$REPORT:
      V:FD(f,i,r) I:PF(f,r) PROD:Y(i,r)
      V:YD(i,r)$(1/eta>0) O:PD(i,r) PROD:Y(i,r)
      V:YX(i,r)$(1/eta>0) O:PX(i,r) PROD:Y(i,r)

      *    Armington aggregation over domestic versus imports:

$PROD:A(d,i,r)$va(d,i,r) S:esubdm
      O:PA(d,i,r)               Q:va(d,i,r)
      I:PD(i,r)$(1/eta>0)       Q:vd(d,i,r)
      I:PY(i,r)$(1/eta=0)       Q:vd(d,i,r)
      I:PM(i,r)                 Q:vm(d,i,r)

      *    Armington aggregation across imports from different countries:

$PROD:M(i,r)$(vim(i,r)>0 and 1/eta>0) S:esubmm s.TL:0
      O:PM(i,r) Q:vim(i,r)
      I:PX(i,s) Q:vxmd(i,s,r) P:pmx0(i,s,r)
      +    A:RA(S) T:TX(i,s,r) A:RA(r) T:(tm(i,s,r)*(1+tx(i,s,r))) s.TL:
      I:PT#(s) Q:vtwr(i,s,r) P:pmt0(i,s,r) s.TL:
      +    A:RA(r) T:tm(i,s,r)

$PROD:M(i,r)$(vim(i,r)>0 and 1/eta=0) S:esubmm s.TL:0
      O:PM(i,r) Q:vim(i,r)
      I:PY(i,s) Q:vxmd(i,s,r) P:pmx0(i,s,r)
      +    A:RA(S) T:TX(i,s,r) A:RA(r) T:(tm(i,s,r)*(1+tx(i,s,r))) s.TL:
      I:PT#(s) Q:vtwr(i,s,r) P:pmt0(i,s,r)          s.TL:
      +    A:RA(r) T:tm(i,s,r)

      *    Demand for public output:

$PROD:G(r) S:1
      O:PG(r) Q:vg(r)
      I:PA("g",i,r) Q:vgm(i,r) P:pg0(i,r) A:RA(r) T:tg(i,r)

      *    Private Consumption:

$PROD:C(r) S:1
      O:PC(r) Q:vp(r)
      I:PA("c",i,r) Q:vpm(i,r) P:pc0(i,r) A:RA(r) T:tp(i,r)

      *    Inter-national transport services (Cobb-Douglas):

$PROD:YT S:1
      O:PT                      Q:vt
      I:PX(i,r)$(1/eta>0)       Q:vst(i,r)
      I:PY(i,r)$(1/eta=0)       Q:vst(i,r)

      *    Final demand over consumption, savings and government
      *    Services (Cobb-Douglas):
```

```
$DEMAND:RA(r)
    E:PF(f,r)                 Q:evoa(f,r)
    E:PC(num)                 Q:vb(r)
    E:PD(cgd,r)$(1/eta>0)     Q:-vi(r)
    E:PY(cgd,r)$(1/eta=0)     Q:-vi(r)
    E:PG(r)                   Q:-vg(r)
    D:PC(r)                   Q:vp(r)

$OFFTEXT
    $SYSINCLUDE mpsgeset uk

    *   Check the benchmark:

    uk.ITERLIM = 0;
    $INCLUDE uk.GEN
    SOLVE uk USING MCP;

    *   Fix a numeraire to permit comparison with MCP:

    RA.FX(num) = RA.L(num);

    *   Do a cleanup calculation:

    uk.ITERLIM = 8000;
    $INCLUDE uk.GEN
    SOLVE uk USING MCP;
```

$TITLE Test calculation with the MGEUK model (and MCP solver)

```
$INCLUDE mrtuk

    alias (r,rr), (s,ss);
    PARAMETER
    TMRATE import tariff rate
    TXRATE export tax rate
    imports value of import of good i, from region s to region r
    exports value of exports of good i, from region s to region r
    impsum
    trdcomp
    trdsum
    glblgain
    ;

    TMRATE(I,S,R) = ROUND(100 * TM(I,S,R));
    OPTION TMRATE:0:1:1; DISPLAY TMRATE;

    TXRATE(I,S,R) = ROUND(100 * TX(I,S,R));
    OPTION TXRATE:0:1:1; DISPLAY TXRATE;
```

```
imports(i,r,s) = 10000*vxmd(i,r,s);
impsum(s,r) = sum(i, vxmd(i,r,s));
trdcomp(s,r) = impsum(s,r)/sum(ss,impsum(ss,r));
trdsum(r) = sum(s,trdcomp(s,r));
option imports:0:1:1;

display imports, impsum, vxm,vim, txrate, tmrate;

display imports, vxm,vim, trdcomp,txrate, tmrate,trdsum,impsum, imports;

esubdm =4;
esubmm =6;

ty(i,r) = 0;
ti(j,i,r) = 0;
tf(f,i,r) = 0;
tx(i,s,r) = 0;
tm(i,s,r) = 0;
tg(i,r) = 0;
tp(i,r) = 0;

$INCLUDE uk.GEN
SOLVE uk USING MCP;

parameter     prices     Equilibrium consumer prices;

prices(r,"mge") = pc.l(r);

Parameter welfare(r), wdoller;

welfare(r) = 100*(C.l(r) -1);

display welfare;
wdoller(r,"wefare") =welfare(r);
wdoller(r,"gains") = (welfare(r)*sum((f,i),10*(vfm(f,i,r))))/100;
glblgain = 100*sum(r,wdoller(r,"gains"))/sum(rr, sum((f,i),10*(vfm(f,i,rr))));

display wdoller, sigmap, esubdm, esubmm, glblgain;
$exit
parameter ep,epp,welfarr,sigg,sigm,sigd;

sigmap = 0.75;

set steps /s1*s10/;
ep(steps) = 0.25;
epp(steps) =0.25;

esubdm =2;
esubmm =3;
```

```
loop(steps,
ep(steps+1) = ep(steps);
epp(steps+1) = epp(steps);

sigmap = sigmap +ep(steps);
esubdm = esubdm +epp(steps);
esubmm = esubmm +epp(steps);

$INCLUDE uk.GEN
SOLVE uk USING MCP;
welfare(r) = 100*(C.l(r) -1);

welfarr(r,steps) =welfare(r);
sigg(steps) = sigmap;
sigm(steps) = esubmm;
sigd(steps) = esubdm;

);

display imports, vxm,vim, trdcomp,txrate, tmrate,trdsum,impsum, imports;
display welfare, welfarr, sigg, sigm,sigd;
```

17

The Redistributive Effects of Transfer Programe in the UK

Keshab Bhattarai[60] & John Whalley

INTRODUCTION

Most empirical work which seeks to assess the redistributive effects of transfers paid to lower income households (AFDC in the US, income and housing benefit in the UK) assumes that recipient households are made better off by the full amount of net cash transfers received (net of any tax back), with wage and other behavioural responses largely ignored.[1] Considerable energy is devoted in some of this literature to calculating and modelling complex tax back schemes which accompany these transfers; with implicit tax rates varying by household and income characteristics, discontinuities and spikes appearing in tax rate profiles, and other complex institutional features being captured. But as an extensive older review of the then available work on transfer programmes by Danziger, Haveman and Plotrick (1981) says "the redistributive effect of transfers is generally measured by comparing pre-transfer and post transfer income distributions. This comparison assumes that transfers elicit no behavioral response that would cause income without transfers to deviate from observed pre-transfer income"[2]. Subsequent and more recent work in this area, such as Dickert, Houser and Scholz (1994), Moffitt (1991), and Hoynes (1993) have focused on partial equilibrium labour supply impacts of transfer programmes, but with no attention to impacts on other endogenous variables including welfare and wage rates.

The point of departure in this paper is the observation, seemingly not in the literature[3], that with voluntary participation in transfer programmes (with tax back

* Bhattarai and Whalley acknowledge financial support from the ESRC under an award for a project on General Equilibrium Modeling of UK Policy Issues. We are grateful to James Davies, Carlo Perroni, Norman Ireland, and a seminar group at Warwick and Western Ontario for comments, and to Andrew Oswald, Mark Stewart and Philip Trostel for literature suggestions. Correspondence: K.R.Bhattarai@hull.ac.uk or JWhalley@uwo.ca

or withdrawal provisions), the utility, or real income, value of transfers to participants is typically less than the cash transfers received. If, for now, impacts on wage rates are ignored, individuals (or households) compare utility across two regimes; one with benefits and tax back arrangements, and the other with no benefits and no tax back, choosing the higher utility regime. A money metric utility comparison between the regimes (the real income difference) bears no direct relation to the net of tax back cash transfer actually received. Indeed, in an extreme case where an individual (or household) is indifferent between participating and not participating, if they were recorded as a benefit programme participant, the real income gain to them from participation in the transfer programme would be zero, despite the disbursement of public funds to the recipient. We therefore argue that, in general, and ignoring wage rate effects, the real income received by transfer recipients is smaller than the cash transfers actually made, since to the recipient the reference point for valuing them should be the reservation utility in the no benefit - no tax back regime.

Given tax back rates, individuals (or households) will also not participate in transfer programmes until some threshold level of transfers is reached, raising utility under participation above that in the no participation regime. Tax back conditions in benefit programmes thus impose a form of real income entry fee on participation, which must be deducted in evaluating the redistributive effects of transfer programmes. Conditional on participation transfers shift recipients¢ budget constraints parallel. In the homothetic case, after the entry fee has been paid, marginal increases in transfers (for fixed tax back rates) provide recipients corresponding marginal increases in real income in the fixed wage case. Hence, we also argue that the average value of transfers (gain per £ of transfers received) will typically differ from the marginal value (the extra benefit per additional £ of transfers) to recipient households.

We further argue that an additional effect, also seemingly missing from existing literature, needs to enter analyses of the redistribution effects of transfers, namely that when the poor participate in a conditional transfer scheme, the associated withdrawal of low wage labour from the market place drives up the wage of low wage(skill) workers relative to high wage(skill) workers. Thus, with heterogeneous labour by income (skill) range, the withdrawal of low wage labour due to high tax back conditional transfers to the poor raises their wage rate. This set aside effect thus potentially raises the welfare of the poor, and actual redistribution to the poor through transfers may be under estimated for the reasons we give above[4].

We use conditional choice general equilibrium models to assess the importance of these two effects. These models embody both endogenous participation decisions in transfer schemes by households, and heterogeneous labour in production (by income range or skill type). In such models, program participation by low income households is endogenously determined in equilibrium along with the wage distribution, since wage rates change as transfer programmes characteristics (benefit levels, tax-back rates) change.

In these models, the budget sets for households are also non-convex, presenting special computational problems not tackled, as far as we are aware, in existing general equilibrium tax computation literature. Commodity demands by households, including leisure, are no longer analytic, even for conventional CES or Cobb Douglas utility functions. This means that household demands have to be evaluated numerically using optimization techniques within a larger equilibrium structure, including the production side modelling of the economy. In essence, in such models, solution procedures use optimization embedded within wider consistent optimization, since consumer demands are non-analytic.

We first present numerical examples which illustrate the potential significance of the two features we highlight above as missing in existing literature. We then apply our techniques to an assessment of the redistributive effects of UK transfer programmes using 2000/01 data. Relative to previous literature on assessments of benefit programs, our model results show that the welfare (or utility) value of transfers received differs markedly from their cash value; in our central case specification being lower by a factor of around two. Model results also show that incorporating heterogeneous labour in production adds an important and neglected channel for distributional effects from conditional transfer programmes to operate through the induced withdrawal of lower income labour from the market, since this increases the wage rates of low wage labour. The strength of this effect depends crucially on the elasticity of substitution in production, which we relate to literature estimates. This can reduce the tax cost of marginal real income transfers to the poor, since induced wage rate changes reinforce the redistribution effect. These two features emerge under most model parameterizations, including those calibrated to the skill specific labour demand elasticity estimates reported in Hammermesh (1988). These are used in model calibration for cross elasticities of substitution among labour types in production.

The conclusion we thus offer is that assessing the redistributive effects of conditional transfers is neither as straight forward as it appears at first sights, nor is the real income value of such transfers seemingly so large as is implicitly assumed in the literature. Regime choice significantly affects such measures, and their general equilibrium effects through programme induced low wage labour withdrawal need to be taken into account. These effects seem to be absent in available literature in the area, and are important because they can change perceptions as to the redistributive effects of transfers. We offer our conditional choice general equilibrium model as a way forward, and investigate these effects using UK data.

A CONDITIONAL CHOICE GENERAL EQUILIBRIUM MODEL FOR ANALYZING THE REDISTRIBUTIVE EFFECTS OF TRANSFERS

Background

As we note in our introduction above, when analyzing the redistributive effects of transfers the conventional treatment in the literature is to assume that recipients of transfers are made better off by the cash value of the transfers they receive. The welfare effects of programme conditionality through tax back and other arrangements are ignored, as are the impacts of transfers on high and low skill wage differentials through induced low wage labour withdrawal from the market.

These two effects are seemingly ignored in existing literature, but there are related ideas that have been discussed and it is perhaps worth clarifying further our point of departure. In essence we argue that transfers should be valued to recipients using their reservation utility in the no transfer regime as the reference point. This differs from the value of cash actually received. Some prior literature (Brown (1970), Haverman and Garfinkel (1980), Betson and Van der Gaag (1985), Betson and Greenberg (1986) and Greenberg (1997)) has attempted to make adjustments to measured redistributive impacts of transfers for the value of leisure to transfers recipients, but this is a different notion from that we advance here. Also, wage rate endogeneity in the presence of changes in transfer programme may seem an obvious point, but existing literature lacks any treatment of these effects, in part due to the problems of analytically formulating and solving market clearing equilibrium models with endogenously determined wage distributions.

It is also worth emphasizing that, for simplicity, we treat participation in transfer programmes as being based solely on welfare considerations. In so doing we ignore transactions costs, sigma effects from participation, informational inadequacies, and intertemporal considerations that motivate analyses of non participation in Strauss (1977), Fry and Stark (1987), Moffit (1983), Blundell, Fry and Walker (1988), and Blank and Ruggles (1996).

In our formulation the effects of programme conditionality on both participation decisions and the valuation of the benefits of transfers reflect a regime choice problem. If p and w denote the consumption good price and the wage rate, and if household utility evaluated at given benefit and tax-back levels is U_B, and with no benefits and no tax back is U_{NB}, then if

$$U_B\,(p,w) > U_{NB}\,(p,w) \tag{1}$$

the household participates in the benefit programme. However, the value of the transfers to the household is a money metric measure of the difference $(U_B - U_{NB})$, not the level of cash benefits actually received. The real income gain from a marginal increase in benefits (where the benefit level B increases to $B¢$) will, however, be more closely related to the benefit change. In the homothetic case, money metric measure of the real income gain fully reflects the marginal gain from transfer increases of $(B'-B)$, assuming the household participates in the programme at a benefit level B.

These valuation features of conditional transfer programmes are illustrated in Figures 1 and 2. Figure 1 displays the budget set in the presence of conditional transfers. The household decides its consumption/leisure choice given a fixed wage, w, but is also offered participation in a transfer programme which pays a fixed benefit B, while taxes apply to any additional labour income at some (typically high) tax back rate, t_B. The budget set for the household in the presence of these features is no longer convex, being given by the intersection of the no transfer budget and the with transfer budget constraint.

Figure 1
Non-Convex Budget Set in the Presence of Conditional Transfers

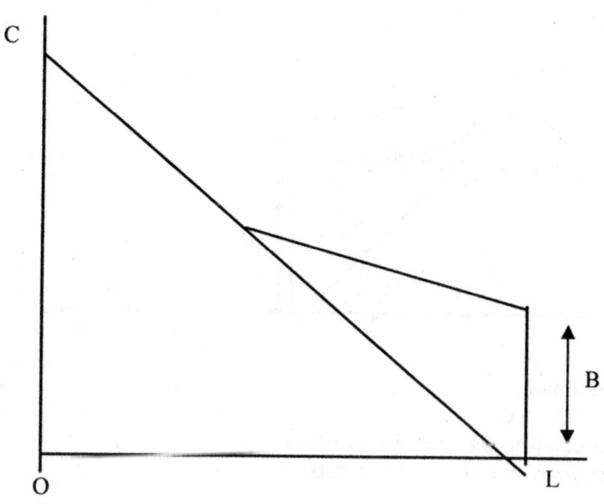

C = Consumption
L = Leisure
B = Transfer

Figure 2
Participation Choice and the Value of Conditional Transfers

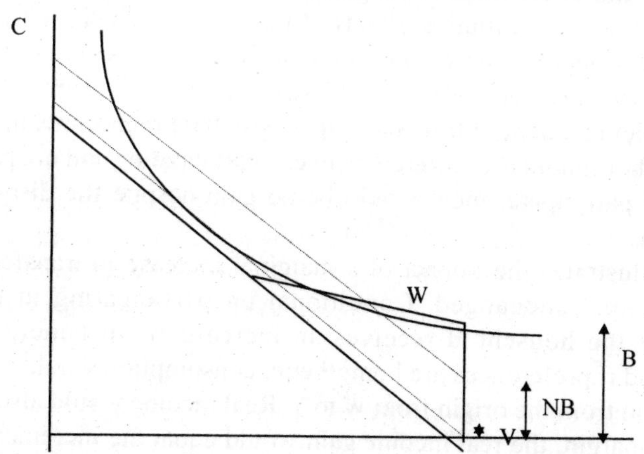

W = Consumption / Leisure point under programme participation
B = Benefit paid
NB = Net benefit paid (after tax back)
V = Money metric measure of the value of net transfers received

Figure 3
The Impact of a Marginal Increase in Transfers

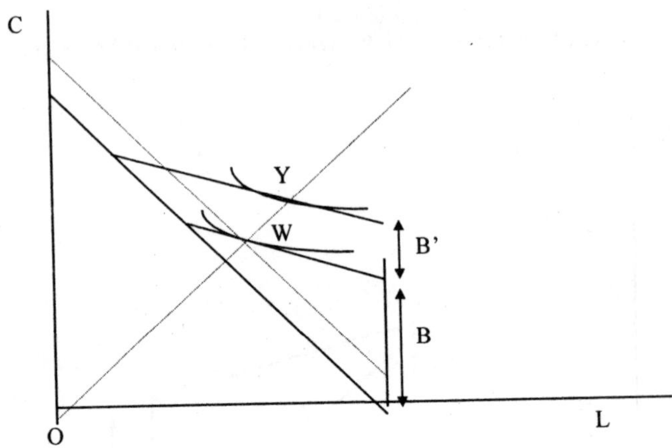

B = Original transfer
B′ = Increase in transfers
W = Original equilibrium point for transfer recipients
Y = Equilibrium with additional transfers, B′

Figure 2 displays the valuation of transfers. The household participates in the transfer programme, receiving B but faces a tax back rate on additional labour income to yield a net benefit of NB; consuming at point W. The utility value of programme participation is, however, smaller than NB because the point of comparison is utility in the no benefit - no tax back regime. In money metric terms, participating in the transfer programme yields a gain of V rather than NB. Thus, studies of the redistributive effects of transfers which show households as gaining from transfers by the amount of cash received (receiving NB on a net basis) overestimate their redistributive effects, since, in utility terms, the household receives a smaller real benefit from participating in the programme. In the extreme case where the household is indifferent between participating and not participating, but chooses to participate, there would be no gain despite the disbursement of funds involved.

Figure 3 illustrates the impact of a marginal increase in transfers when the wage rate remains unchanged. Conditional on participating in the transfer programme, if the household receives an increase B′ in benefits under the programme, and if preferences are homothetic, consumption would move along a radial expansion from the origin from W to Y. Real income would also increase by B′, and at the margin, the real income gain would equal the incremental transfer. Thus, the marginal and average value of transfers to recipients differ. Conditional upon participating in a transfer programme, the real value of additional transfers equals their cash representation, but the average value of all transfers received will be below their cash value, because of the tax back features of these programmes.

The effect of conditional transfers on the wage distribution noted above is also ignored in existing literature, both because of the widely used partial equilibrium assumption that wage rates for transfer recipients remain unaffected by the introduction of transfer programmes and the lack of availability of market clearing equilibrium models with heterogeneous labour in which the wage distribution is endogenously determined. But because of the high tax back rates in transfer programmes, as participation occurs low wage labour withdraws from the market place bidding up their own wage rate, amplifying whatever redistributive effect of transfers occurs in a traditional partial equilibrium model.

In the conditional choice general equilibrium model we use here to value the redistributive impacts of transfers, in contrast to available literature wage, rates across the heterogenous labour types are endogenously determined. We assume that production in the economy involves a single output and heterogeneous labour inputs, profit maximizing behaviour yields labour demand functions by skill type, and as a result, wage rates by skill type are endogenously determined rather than given[5]. In this framework, conditional transfers result in the withdrawal of low skilled labour from the market relative to a no transfer programme regime, and the supply function of low skilled labour shifts. Conditional transfer programmes can thus have the further redistributive effect of raising the wage rate of low skilled labour through conditionality induced labour withdrawal from the market place. This effect can also play an important role in determining the distributional impact of transfer programmes, and is analyzed here alongside the first effect we note above.

A Conditional Choice General Equilibrium Model

We use a general equilibrium model with both transfer participation choice by households and endogenous wage determination by skill type. We numerically solve the model both where transfers and associated tax back arrangements are present and where they are absent. This allows for a comparison of the redistributive effects of transfer programmes based both on conventional analyses and on the modelling approach set out above which captures the two effects missing from previous literature. We later present analyses of model generated estimates of average and marginal redistributive effects of transfers using UK data.

Essentially, we develop a conditional choice general equilibrium model as an extension to the standard general equilibrium tax model set out in Shoven and Whalley (1973, 1992). The main departure from the traditional model is that with non-convex budget sets, household demand functions, including those derived from conventional functional forms such as CES or Cobb-Douglas are no longer analytic. Demands thus need to be solved numerically, and embedded within a larger equilibrium problem, rather than derived algebraically as is usually done. We use GAMS optimization code for this purpose, with numerical (rather than analytical) solutions of household optimization sub models generating demands and communicating with a master economy wide equilibrium formulation, which includes production. The production modelling explicitly incorporates heterogeneity among labour inputs, with skill levels assumed to be collinear with income ranges.

The implications of non-linear budget constraints for the estimation of labour supply elasticities have been extensively discussed in the literature (see Hausman (1981), and Heckman (1978)), but less attention has been given to the impacts of non-convex budget sets on the welfare and redistributive impacts of transfer programmes. These pose the special problems of potentially multiple solutions to household optimization problems, discontinuities in responses to wage rates and transfer programme characteristics as households change regimes, and local rather than global optima being found by numerical optimisation packages used in any simulation analysis.

Using the two household (high and low wage) case for illustrative purposes, we consider a model with a single commodity (consumption good) and two labour (leisure) types. Distorting income taxes collected from the high wage household finance transfers to the low wage household. In the presence of a household income tax at rate t_1, a transfer programme with eligible benefits B, and a tax back rate of t_2 (significantly higher than t_1), demand functions for the consumption good are obtained by solving an optimization problem for each household (ie. for each of the high and low wage types). These optimization problems can be written as

$$\text{Max } U_i(C_i, L_i^e) \quad \text{i} = \text{(H,L)} \tag{2}$$

subject to

$$P_c C_i = \max\begin{bmatrix} \left\{ w_i(1-t_1)(\overline{L_i} - L_i^e) + R_i \right\}, \\ \left\{ w_i(1-t_2)(\overline{L_i} - L_i^e) + B_i + R_i \right\} \end{bmatrix} \tag{3}$$

where C_i and L_i^e are consumption of goods and leisure by household i, P_c is the price of the consumption good, $\overline{L_i}$ is the household labour endowment[6], and w_i is the wage rate applying to the labour type i, which in turn is specific to the i th household type. R_i defines that portion of aggregate tax revenues (net of transfers) that are redistributed to household I, and household (non-transfer) income I_i is given by the maximal portion of the budget constraint (3). In the determination of household demands the R_i are taken as parametric; but in equilibrium, when summed across households, these must equal the revenues actually collected by the government. These household utility maximization problems mirror those represented diagramatically in Figure 2, with choice between the two regimes entering for each household.

We represent production in the model though a production function defined over the consumption goods and the two types of labour inputs.

$$C = F(L_H, L_L) \tag{4}$$

where C defines aggregate consumption, and L_H and L_L are labour inputs supplied by high and low wage households.

Explicit labour income taxes, or tax back rates accompanying the transfer programme, and affect the price of leisure in terms of consumption goods on the expenditure side of the budget constraint (3) for each household. In equilibrium, aggregate the production must equal the sum of consumption demands across households, and labour markets must clear, i.e.

$$C = C_H + C_L \tag{5}$$

$$\overline{L}_H = L_H^e + L_H \tag{6}$$

$$\overline{L}_L = L_L^e + L_L \tag{7}$$

The goods price and wage rates are thus endogenously determined such that in equilibrium the goods and labor markets clear (equations (5), (6) and (7)), and the solutions to the (non-analytic) optimization problems, (2), for each household, yields solutions L_L^*, L_H^* which correspond to optimizing factor input use in production. Wage rates are thus endogeneously determined to clear labour markets; and the model is homogeneous of degree zero in wage rates and prices, so that either the consumption good price or one of the wage rates can be taken as the numeraire.

Set up in this way, tax rates (income and tax back rates) can be exogenous in the model as in the original Shoven-Whalley formulation, and with the revenues (net of expenditures on transfer programmes) dispersed to households endogenously determined. Alternatively, R can be set exogenously, and the income tax rates endogenously determined (with the tax back rates exogenous) to meet a given net of transfer revenue requirement. An R=0 case is where income taxes raised from non transfer participants exactly finance transfers dispersed.

In equilibrium, government budget balance must hold. This can be written in this case as

$$\sum_{i=H,L} B_i N_i + \sum_{i=H,L} R_i = \sum_{i=H,L} (1 - N_i) t_1 w_i L_i + \sum_{i=H,L} N_i t_2 w_i L_i \tag{8}$$

where N_i is an index for household i, which takes the value 1 if household i participates in the conditional transfer programme and 0 otherwise. The first right hand side term reflects income taxes at a rate t_1 on household income. The second term denotes revenues from tax backs at a rate t_2 applied to transfer program participant households, this is not collected from non benefit programme participants.

In this equilibrium structure, household budget sets are non convex and optimizing behaviour cannot be represented by a series of first order conditions from utility maximization. Household optimization problems therefore have to be solved numerically to yield household demands, and separate numerical evaluation of household optimization problem is needed but this must take place at the economywide prices associated with the equilibrium. Equilibrium models of this form with heterogeneous labour inputs and a single output in production have not been widely used in the numerical equilibrium tax literature, where it remains common to work with homogenoous labour in production.

We use the GAMS (Generalised Algebraic Modelling System (Brooke, Kendrick, and Meeraus (1988))) optimization software for this purpose, since this is now widely used by equilibrium modelers, and is thought to be the most suitable optimization code available. The regime choice formulations we adopt are surprisingly difficult to solve numerically, and we use the PATH solver developed by Dirkse and Ferris (1995) to solve the models which follow, since more conventional GAMS solvers (Conopt, Minos) fail. Because of the non-convexities in the household budget sets, at any computed equilibrium we also check optimizing outcomes for each household in both regimes, in order to confirm that a global rather than a local solution to each sub optimization problem has been found.

Once in place this numerical structure can be used in counterfactual equilibrium mode as set out in Shoven and Whalley (1973), first with calibration of the model structure to a base case equilibrium, followed by counterfactual equilibrium computation under a change in model specification (such as the level at which benefits are paid). Calibration also provide a test of the model's ability to replicate the base case equilibrium. These procedures enable equilibria with and without benefits to be compared, and calculations made of the redistributive effects of transfers.

A Simple Numerical Example

In Table 1 we provide a small dimensional example which we have used to evaluate the redistributive effects of conditional transfers in an artificial economy using the model set out above. The parameter values and functional forms we use are illustrative rather than realistic, but nonetheless serve to both show how the model can be applied and underline the central themes of the paper. We use CES preference and production functions, with specified share and elasticity parameters, and a high tax back rate of 80 percent.

The section (a) Table 1 sets out the specification used in the example using data in section (b) of the table. There are 2 labour types, each with CES preferences defined over consumption and leisure. Elasticities in preferences are 1.5 for each household. On the production side, we specify share parameters for each labour type as well as a single elasticity of substitution, which is equal to 1.55. Being greater than one, this elasticity implies that the wage of the low wage labour fall sharply as transfers are eliminated. The income tax rate for high wage household is 0.4, and there is 80 percent tax back rate in low income household.

Tables 2 and 3 report model generated equilibria both in the presence and the absence of transfers. Prices, goods consumption, leisure consumption, taxes and benefits, and welfare are all displayed. Table 3 indicates that if transfers are abolished, the high wage household gains because taxes are no longer paid to finance transfers, and the low wage group loses. However, losses in real income for the low wage are only 25.4 percent of the cash transfers which terminate with the elimination of the transfer programme, despite a fall in the relative wage of the low skilled. The evaluation of programme impact implied by these model results thus differs sharply from that from a more conventional calculation which simply measures cash benefits paid and nets out taxes collected through tax back arrangements, with the net payment taken as the benefit to the transfer recipient.

Table 1
A Simple Numerical Example Illustrating the Evaluation of the Redistributive Effects of Transfer Programmes Using Conditional Choice General Equilibrium Models.

(a)

1. No. of Labour Types:	2 (High and Low Wage)
2. Preferences:	CES with shares 0.86, 0.14 on consumption/leisure for low wagewith shares 0.54, 0.46 on consumption/leisure for high wagewith substitution elasticities 1.5 for low wage, 1.5 for high wage
3. Production:	CES production function with share parameters of 0.24, and 0.76 low and high wage labour. The substitution elasticity in production is set at -1.55. The unit term in the CES function (which controls the position of production function) is set at 1.3. Labour endowments equal 40 and 60 for low and high income households.
4. Tax Rates:	Income tax rates 0.4 for high wage and 0.0 for low wageBenefit tax back rate 0.8 for both households.
5. Benefit Levels:	11 for the low wage worker who participates in the transfer programme (in the with benefit case).
6. Revenue distribution	Low and high wage households receives 2.3 and 7.4 of the net revenues (tax revenues less transfers paid) as a lump sum redistribution

(b)
Above Parameters are Derived from the following set of Baseline data with low and high Income Households

	Low Income Household	*High Income Household*
Gross income	10	20
Benefit	11	0
Transfer	2.3	7.4
Income Tax	0	8
VAT	1.3	3.4
Tax Back	8	0
Gross Consumption	14	16
Leisure	30	40
Labour Endowment	40	60

Table 2
Model Equilibria With and Without Conditional Transfer Programmes for the Numerical Example Specified in Table 1

1. Equilibrium in the Presence of Transfer Programme

A. Prices:	consumption good	1.00	B. Regime Choice	high wage does not Participate in transfer programme.low wage participates in transfers programme	
	high wage	1.00			
	low wage	1.00			
B. Consumption:	consumption by high wage	15.8	D. Taxes/Transfer:	Total Tax Revenues Collected	20.6
	leisure of high wage	40.0		Transfers Paid	11.0
	consumption by low wage	14.0		Net Tax Revenue Redistributed	9.6
	leisure of low wage	30.0			
C. Welfare:	utility high wage	51.0			
	utility low wage	27.7			

2. Equilibrium in the Absence of Transfer Programme

A. Prices:	consumption good	1.00	B. Consumption:	consumption by high wage	48.9
	high wage	1.6		leisure of high wage	28.4
	low wage	0.50		consumption by low wage	17.2
				leisure of low wage	8.9
C. Welfare:	utility high wage	76.3	D. Taxes/Transfer:	Total Tax Revenues Collected	12.0
	utility low wage	24.4		Transfer Paid	0.0
				Net Tax Revenue Redistributed	12.0

Table 3
Comparing Model Based and Conventional Evaluations of the Redistributive Effects of Transfer Programmes Using the Example from Table 1

1. Model Evaluation of the Effects of Eliminating Transfers Programme

	High Wage Household	*Low Wage Household*
Hicksian EV	49.6%	-11.9%
Hicksian CV	-33.3%	13.6%
Wage Rate Changes under programme elimination	High/Low Wage Rate Ratio Before Benefit Elimination	1.00
	High/Low Wage Rate Ratio After Benefit Elimination	3.09

2. Conventional Evaluation of Redistributive Impact of Transfers

Gross Cash Benefits received under programme by low wage household	13.3
Taxes paid by low wage household through tax back	8.0
Net benefit received by low wage household	5.30

3. Ratio of money metric welfare loss to low wage from transfer elimination to loss in net cash benefit	25.4%

AN ASSESSMENT OF THE REDISTRIBUTIVE EFFECTS OF GOVERNMENT TRANSFERS IN THE UK

We have also used the framework set out above to investigate the implications of our conditional choice general equilibrium model for more empirically based assessments of the redistributive impacts of tax financed government transfer programmes. We base our analyses on data produced annually by the UK Statistical Office (Office of National Statistics, ONS), and published in Economic Trends. In this, taxes paid and benefits received from both direct transfers and other selected government expenditures are allocated to deciles of the household population. We use the data for 2000/01 (Economic Trends, April 2001) as the starting point for an analysis of the redistributive effects of transfers using the conditional choice general equilibrium framework we set out above.

We take this data, after some elaboration and adjustment for mutual consistency, as representative of a base case economy wide equilibrium. We calibrate a ten household version of our conditional choice general equilibrium model to this data, with the ten households reflecting the UK household decile groups reported in the ONS data. We use data only on non-retirees to avoid including redistribution through public pensions in our analyses; since for these there is no endogenoulsy determined participation decision. We perform similar counter factual analyses to those reported for the numerical example above, including removal of and incremental increases in cash transfers. In so doing, we incorporate literature estimates on benefit tax back rates, and labour supply (leisure demand) and labour demand (inter labor substitution in production) elasticities.

BASE CASE DATA

The main source for our base case data is Economic Trends (April 2001) which reports components of income for non retired households grouped by income decile[7], and benefits received and taxes paid for each household decile for the UK tax year 2000/01. We use this data to construct a model admissible data set for an analysis of the redistributive effects of transfers in the UK incorporating endogenous participation decisions. Original income in this data is taken as the value of non-leisure production in the model admissible data set; non-contributory benefits give net benefits paid to households in the base year; benefits in kind plus contributory scheme benefits are summed to yield non conditional benefit related transfers which are treated in the model as paid to households in lump sum form. We separate direct taxes, which can be avoided by not working (i.e. consuming leisure), from indirect taxes which must still be paid on transfer financed consumption, even if the household does not work. These are grouped after adjustment for micro consistency, under broad headings, with the constituent elements for each, displayed in Table 4.

To yield a model admissible data set for calibration purposes, a series of further adjustments are made to the base case data ;

(i) **Government Budget Valance:** Government budget balance does not hold in the base 2000/01 data available from UK government sources, while this is a property of equilibrium in the model. In part, this is because not all government expenditures (such as defence) are induced in the Economic Trends data. To achieve budget balance, we proportionally scale all taxes across all deciles in the unadjusted base case data so that this is the case. This is one of several scaling adjustments that can be used to satisfy this requirement of model admissibility.

(ii) **Netting out Benefits and Income Taxes:** In our model representation, households receiving benefits (net of tax back) cannot pay personal income taxes in addition to paying the tax back on benefits. But in the unadjusted data for 2000/01, coexisting income tax payments and transfer receipts occur because each decile consists of an aggregation across different households within the cell. We net out these receipts and payments for each cell, so that each household decile is either a net payer of income taxes, or a net recipient of benefits. After this netting out, 3 out of 10 household groups receive net benefits in the data used in the model; while 7 out of 10 household groups are net payers of income taxes.

(iii) **Setting Model Tax Tates:** We calculate both income and indirect tax rates by decile using unadjusted raw data, assuming that average and marginal tax rates for any household within a decile grouping are the same for all households within the group. We set model tax back rates on additional labour income for the transfer recipients at 80 %. This is lower than the combined 75% withdrawal rate on income support and 20% rate on housing benefit that typically apply in the UK. In reality, and as Dilnot and Duncan (1992) document, tax back rates vary significantly across households, depending upon household characteristics and on how both programmes and income sources interact. We abstract from these complications here by setting a single and common tax back rate in the model across all household deciles receiving transfers.

(iv) **Adding Leisure Consumption:** To incorporate leisure consumption into the base case data used in the model, we use UK time use survey data reported in Dex (1996). This data does not directly provide time use data by income range, and we supplement this with further information on hours of work by decile. The way these data are used is reported on in Table 4, and the associated footnotes (footnote 14, in particular).

(v) **Elasticities:** The two key elasticity parameters in the model are CES substitution elasticities in consumption and production. We calibrate values of these elasticities so as to be broadly consistent with implied literature values of labour supply (and hence leisure demand) elasticities used in household CES preferences, and labour demand elasticities implied by the elasticity specification in the CES production function. We use Killingsworth (1983) as our main source of labour supply

Table 4[1]

Base Case 2000/01 UK data for Household Deciles on Household Incomes, Taxes, and Transfers in £ /Year Per Household

Household deciles	Original income[2]	Noncon-tributory Benefits[3]	Direct Cash Benefits[4]	Direct Tax[5]	Indirect Tax[6]	In-Kind[7] Transfers	Earnings per week[8]	Working weeks[9]	Value of Leisure[10]	Total Income[11]	Consumption[12]
Poorest H1	2149	4525	469	930	2139	4647	160	13	14491	16640	8721
H2	4724	4866	782	1194	2183	4007	210	23	17085	21809	11002
H3	9141	3510	963	1880	2759	3765	223	41	14076	23217	12740
H4	13296	2745	746	2815	3213	3561	243	55	11934	25230	14320
H5	17353	2027	704	2831	3572	3266	272	64	10895	28248	16947
H6	21416	1653	603	4745	3957	3276	306	70	10455	31871	18246
H7	24609	1348	522	5531	4266	2755	355	69	12293	36902	19437
H8	28038	1037	447	6576	4362	2304	403	70	13895	41933	20888
H9	33743	788	386	8175	4537	2189	473	84	8190	41933	24394
Richest H10	56065	778	301	15082	5551	1826	543	91	6871	56420	31831

Source: Based on Table 9 (Appendix 1) of Economic Trends, 2000/01, p. 63, and authors' own calculations. Further explanatory notes are given over.

Notes for Table 4

1. This table is derived from Table 9 (Appendix 1) of Economic Trends, April 2001, p. 63.
2. Original income includes wages and salaries, imputed income from benefits in kind, self-employment income, occupational pensions, annuities, investment and other income.
3. Non-contributory benefits include income support, child benefit, housing benefit, invalid care allowances, attendance allowance, war pension and war widows pensions, disability living allowance, industrial injury disablement benefit, student maintenance awards, government training schemes, family credit and other non-contributory benefits.
4. Direct cash benefit consists of contributory retirement pension, unemployment benefit, invalidity pension and allowance, sickness and industrial injury benefit, widow's benefits, and statutory maternity pay/allowance.
5. Direct taxes include employees' national insurance (NI) contributions.
6. Indirect taxes includes taxes on final goods and services, VAT, duty on tobacco, beer and cider, wines and spirits, hydrocarbon oils, vehicle excise duty, TV licences, stamp duty on house purchase, customs duties, betting taxes, insurance premium tax, fossil fuel levy, air passenger tax, Camelot national lottery fund. It also includes intermediate taxes such as commercial and industrial rates, employer's NI contributions, duty on hydrocarbon oils, vehicle excise and other duties.
7. Benefits in kind consists of education, national health service, housing subsidy, rail travel subsidy, bus travel subsidy, school meals and welfare milk.
8. Earnings per week for top and bottom deciles, and first and third quartiles are taken from the New Earnings Survey 2000. These are interpolated for other deciles.
9. Working weeks are derived by dividing the original income by the weekly earnings.
10. The value of leisure is obtained by multiplying non-working weeks by the weekly earnings rate. The number of non-working weeks is the difference between the working weeks and 104 weeks, which represents the total labour endowment per household with two working members.
11. Original income plus the value of leisure gives the total income of the economy.
12. Consumption for a household is derived by adding cash, in kind and non-contributory benefits to original income and subtracting the direct and indirect taxes paid by the household.

elasticities, and Hamermesh (1988) for labour demand elasticities. We use a substitution elasticity in preferences of 1.5 for all household groups which implies a point estimate of the aggregate labour supply elasticity in the neighbourhood of the base case equilibrium of 0.23 (within in the range suggested by the studies reviewed by Killingsworth). We use a substitution elasticity in production of 1.5 as our central case which yields a point estimate of the demand elasticities for individual labour categories of between -1.05 and -1.5, in the range of skill specific labour demand elasticities suggested by Hamermesh. The wage rate effects in the model are sensitive to the setting of this elasticity, and a value close to unity yields almost no wage rate effects, enabling us to use a model specification with an elasticity in production of unity to abstract from wage rate effects. We thus use two base cases, one with wage rate effects present (elasticity of 1.5) and one with them absent (elasticity close to one).

Model Experiments and Results

To use the model described above to evaluate the redistributive effects of transfers, we perform counterfactual analyses with the model. We first calibrate the model to the base case 2000/01 data. We then compute equilibria in which we remove both benefits and tax back arrangements, and make further small adjustments necessitated by the government budget balance condition in the model.

The government budget constraint in the model can be written as

$$\sum_i B_i + \sum_i Tr_i = VAT + IT + TB \tag{9}$$

where B_i and Tr_i are benefit payments and other transfers received by household i and VAT, IT, and TB represent the collections of indirect taxes, income tax, and from tax back arrangements; and.

If we eliminate benefits paid to each household (B_i) and all tax back arrangements (TB), then if we wish to maintain other transfers to households (Tr_i) at their base levels, some further change is needed in the model to satisfy the budget balance condition (9). Just as in tax incidence analysis where the incidence effects of a tax cannot be discussed independently of the replacement regime (such as no replacement tax, an equal yield sales (or income, or other) tax), in discussing the redistributive effects of transfers what happens to the rest of government activity must be carefully specified and can affect conclusions.

When the B_i and associated TB are eliminated, we keep other (non-benefit) transfers to each individual household (Tr_i) constant in real terms. This means that benefit recipient households suffer the full real income loss from termination of benefits. To achieve government budget balance in the new equilibium we proportionally scale all income tax rates for non participants so that this condition holds in the counterfactual equilibrium. The only direct effect of government policy changes on recipient households from the experiment is their loss of benefits.

Using both the model and the constructed microconsistent data set, we have performed similar experiments to those undertaken for the simple numerical example reported on earlier. Here, however, we produce two cases; one using a production side substitution elasticity for which the wage rate changes across deciles are small, and one for a higher literature based elasticity for which the wage rate effects are substantial.

The results, reported in Table 5, confirm the themes suggested by both the line of argument of the paper and our numerical example, namely that valuing the redistributive effects of transfers in terms of their cash value to recipients is misleading. In case 1 where the choice of substitution elasticity in production (1.05) produces a large wage rate effect, for the bottom three deciles of UK households, the losses in real income when all benefits are eliminated fall well short of the direct losses from benefit elimination. Only 17% of the value of net cash transfers withdrawn is lost in real income terms for the lowest group. The second group loses only 15% of net cash benefits and the third group loses 21%. These ratios fall or rise by decile depending upon the rate of substitution across various categories of labour in production. As argued earlier, with an implicit entry fee being paid by participants in transfer programmes via the comparison to reservation utility, the smaller the benefits as a proportion of income the smaller their average real income value.

Table 5
The Redistributive Effects of Transfers in the Ten Decile Conditional Choice General Equilibrium Model Calibrated to 2000/01 UK Data

	Case 1 Production elasticity set close to one[1]: small wage rate effects		*Case 2* Production elasticity at 1.5: larger wage rate effects	
Deciles receiving benefits in wage	Ratio of real income loss from transfer elimination to cash benefits forgone	% change in wage rate of group	Ratio of real income loss from transfer elimination to cash benefits forgone	% change in wage rate of group
Bottom decile	0.17	-54.4	0.168	-54.7
Next to Bottom decile	0.15	-53.9	0.148	-54.3
Third decile	0.21	-45.8	0.211	-47.3

1. We use a value of 1.05 since computational problems arise as this elasticity assymptotically approaches one.

In the second case in Table 5, we use literature based values of the production side substitution elasticity of 1.5 in our calculations of the redistributive impact of conditional transfers. In these cases, the additional low wage labour entering the market substantially depresses wage rates as benefits are eliminated. As shown in Table 6 wage rates fall by 54.4% for the lowest decile, and by 53.9% and 45.8% for the other two deciles. These wage rate changes inflict big losses on each decile as benefits are eliminated, and the ratios of real income change to benefit loss rise.

Table 6
Impact of Elimination of Benefit on Wage Rates and Shares of Labour income by Decile

	New Wage	*Base Wage*	*New Share*	*Old Share*
h1	0.147	1.026	0.004	0.008
h2	0.153	0.996	0.006	0.011
h3	0.22	0.92	0.013	0.019
h4	0.299	0.751	0.025	0.031
h5	0.384	0.656	0.044	0.045
h6	0.425	0.588	0.066	0.062
h7	0.445	0.569	0.091	0.082
h8	0.45	0.551	0.117	0.103
h9	0.436	0.505	0.15	0.129
h10	1	1	0.692	0.702

These later results clearly indicate parameter sensitivity to our results, but also stress the role that induced wage rate changes can play when evaluating the effects of benefits schemes. By keeping labour off the market, for higher substitution elasticities in production these schemes can potentially significantly drive up the wage rates of the poor. Case 2 indicates that this can also be a significant channel for redistributive impact for conditional transfer schemes.

Taken as set, therefore, the results in Table 5 and Table 6 reinforce the earlier observations that the appropriate reference point for the valuation of the benefit of transfers to recipients is their reservation utility in the no transfer receipt regime, that valuing transfers in terms of cash received overstates their value to recipients, and that induced wage effects can play a key role in evaluating how transfer programmes actually redistribute.

In Table 7, we report on more extensive parametric sensitivity of our results on the redistributive impact of conditional transfers focusing on results for the lowest decile. We consider different combinations of demand and production side elasticities in the model. We report the ratio of the real income to benefit loss and the percentage wage rate change for the lowest model decile. Varying production side elasticities large (50%) changes in wage rate effects occur, and changes of sign occur as the substitution elasticity moves above or below one. Correspondingly, ratio values remain around 0.168, and seems to be more robust to the values of substitution elasticities in use. These results thus show substantial parametric sensitivity, but it is concentrated on variation in production side rather than demand side parameters. In turn, variations in the ratio of real income loss to benefit loss have corresponding variation in wage rate changes. Varying demand side elasticities, while fixing production side elasticities, has little impact on either ratio or wage rate effects.

These results in Table 7 indicate that substitution elasticities between skill categories on the production side are critical parameters for the evaluation of the actual redistribution acheived by benefit programmes, because of their key role in determining the wage rate effects involved. Depending upon whether these elasticities are above or below one, wage rate effects can be positive or negative, and large wage rate effects can occur even for relatively modest departures from unity. Literature estimates suggest an elasticity value close to 1.5, implying significant negative wage rate effects from the elimination of transfers, or conversely significant wage rate induced redistribution in favour of low wage households due to transfers. Further empirical research on the appropriate range for this critical parameter is clearly needed to make more definitive statements as to the redistribution actually involved.

Table 7
Elasticity Sensitivity of the Redistributive Impact of Transfers

Elesticity Specification		*Ratio of real income loss to poorest decile to their cash benefit loss under benefit elimination*			*% change in wage rate of the lowest group*
Demand side (σ_p)	*Production side (σ_p)*	*10th*	*9th*	*8th*	
1.6	1.50	0.168	0.15	0.21	-85
2.05	1.50	0.168	0.15	0.21	-75
2.50	1.50	0.168	0.15	0.21	-66
2.95	1.50	0.168	0.15	0.21	-59
3.40	1.50	0.168	0.15	0.21	-53
1.6	1.05	0.168	0.15	0.21	17
3.40	1.05	0.168	0.15	0.21	6

Finally, in Table 8, we report the redistributive impacts of a two percent marginal increase in benefit levels. Following the earlier discussion, these have almost equi-proportional effects on real income. In these cases, there is also little sensitivity to elasticity values since wage rate effects are small. This is because the income effects on leisure consumption from marginal changes in transfers are themselves small.

Table 8
Valuing Marginal Increases in Transfers

	Ratio of incremental real income gain to transfer increase for the poorest decile	*% wage change under incremental benefit increase for the poorest decile*
Central case specification (1.05)	1.0	0.91
High σ_p case (2.0)	1.0	2.88

CONCLUSION

This paper builds on the observation that when evaluating the redistributive effects of transfers it is the real income equivalent of transfers to recipients that is relevant, and this is typically less than their cash value. This contrasts with current literature which usually assumes that transfer recipients are better off by the amount of cash they receive. Because of conditionality in transfer programmes, households face a choice between receiving transfers with an accompanying tax back scheme on additional labour income, and non participation with no tax back. The reference point which should be used when evaluating the redistributive effects of transfers is thus the utility level in the no transfer regime. For a household indifferent between participating and not participating in such programmes, the value of such transfers is zero, even if participation by them involves receipt of cash. Typically, attaching a tax back scheme to a transfer mechanism will lower the real value of transfers to the recipient.

We report numerical examples and an empirical implementation of a conditional choice general equilibrium model based on 2000/02 UK data. Results from both of these clearly show that the conventional belief that, through transfer programmes, transfer recipients are made better off by the full cash transfer received does not hold. For this UK data, our central case conditional choice general equilibrium model suggests that real gains to transfer recipients in the bottom decile of households may be no more than 87% of cash transfers received. We also show that general equilibrium wage effects from changes in transfer programmes can come into play in potentially a major way, reflecting induced low wage labour withdrawal attributable to tax back schemes. These effects further modify the redistribution attributable to transfers. Both of the effects we emphasize in the paper appear to be neglected in current literature on the evaluation of the redistributive effects of transfer programmes.

REFERENCES

Atkinson A.B. (1996), Public Economics in Action: The Lindahl Lectures Oxford University Press.

Balestrino A. (1999), The Desirability of In-Kind Transfers in the Presence of Distortionary Taxes, Journal of Economic Surveys, September 1999, V. 13, iss. 4, pp.333-54.

Benabou, R. (2002), Tax and Education Policy in a Heterogeneous-Agent Economy: What Levels of Redistribution Maximize Growth and Efficiency?, *Econometrica*, March, V. 70. Iss. 2, pp. 481-517.

Betson D.M and D. Greenberg (1986), "Labor Supply and Tax Rates: Comment", *American Economic Review*, Vol. 76 No. 3, June pp.551-556.

Blank R.M. and P. Ruggles (1996), "When Do Women Use Aid to Families with Dependent Children and Food Stamps? The Dynamics of Eligibility Vesrus Participation" *Journal of Human Resources* XXXI.1 pp.57-89.

Blundell R.V. Fry and I. Walker (1988), "Modelling the Take-Up of Means-Tested Benefits: the Case of Housing Benefits in the United Kingdom" *Economic Journal*, Conference Vol. pp. 58-74.

Browning E.K. (1973), "Alternative Program for Income Redistribution: NIT and the NWT", *American Economic Review*, Vol. 63 No. 1, March, pp. 38-39.

Browning E.K. and J.M. Browning (1987), Public Finance and the Price Systems, 3rd edition, Macmillan, New York.

Browning E.K. and W.R. Johnson (1984), "The Tradeoff between Equality and Efficiency" *Journal of Political Economy*, April 1984, 92, 175-203.

Danziger S., R. Haveman and R.Plotrick (1981), "How Income Transfers Affect Work, Savings and the Income Distribution" *Journal of Economic Literature*, Vol. XIX, No. 3, September, pp.975-1028.

Dickert S., S. Houser and J.K. Scholz (1994), "The Earned Income Tax Credit and Transfer Programs: A Study of Labour Market and Program Participation" in (ed.) J. Poterba *Tax Policy and the Economy*, Vol. 9, 1995, MIT Press for NBER.

Dilnot A. and Duncan Alan (1992), "Lone Mothers, Family Credit and Paid Work", *Fiscal Studies* 13(1), 1-21.

Dirkse S.P. and M.C. Ferris (1995), "CCPLIB: A collection of nonlinear mixed Complementarity Problems" *Optimization Methods and Software*. 5:319-345.

Economic Trends (1996), Office of National Statistics, London.

Fry V. and F. Stark (1987), "The Take-Up of Supplementary Benefit: Gaps in the 'Safety Net'?" *Fiscal Studies* 8 4 pp.

Garfinkel I. and R.H. Haveman (1977), Earnings Capacity, Poverty, and Inequality Academic Press, London.

Greenberg D.H. (1997), "The Leisure Bias in Cost-benefit Analyses of Employment and Training Programs" *Journal of Human Resources* XXXI.2 pp.413-439.

Hamermesh D.S. (1993), Labor Demand, Princeton University Press, New Jersey.

Hausman A.J. (1984), "Labour Supply" in (ed.) J.A. Pechman, How Taxes Affect Economic Behaviour, Brookings, Washington D.C.

Heckman J. (1974), "Shadow Prices, Market Wages, and Labour Supply" *Econometrica* Vol. 42, no. 4, pp. 679-694.

Hoynes H.W. (1993), "Welfare Transfers in two-parent Families: Labour Supply and Welfare Participation under AFDC-UP" NBER Working Paper No. 4407, July.

Killingsworth M. (1983), Labour Supply, Cambridge University Press.

Masters S. and I. Garfinkel (1977), Estimating the Labour Supply Effects of Income-Maintenance Alternatives Academic Press, London.

Moffit R. (1992), "Incentive Effects of the US Welfare System: A Review" *Journal of Economic Literature*, March, pp. 1-61.

Office of the National Statistics (2001), Economic Trends, April, London.

Office of the National Statistics (2000), New Earnings Survey, H.M.S.O. London.

Shoven J.B. and J. Whalley (1992), Applying General Equilibrium, Cambridge University Press.

Shoven J.B. and J. Whalley (1973), "General Equilibrium with Taxes: A Computational Procedure and an Existence Proof " *Review of Economic Studies*, 40, 475-90.

Strauss J. (1977), "Information and Participation in Public Transfer Program" *Journal of Public Economics*, 8(3) December, pp.385-96.

Yelowitz A.S. (1995), "The Medicaid Notch, Labor Supply, and Welfare Participation: Evidence from Eligibility Expansions" *Quarterly Journal of Economics*, Vol.110, No. 4, pp.909-939.

NOTES

1. These transfers are large (Danziger, et al (1981) some years ago put them at 10 percent of GDP for the US), and they play a key role in assessments of the overall redistributive impact of government tax and transfer activity. Browning and Johnson (1984), while admittedly using a broad notion of transfers, suggested that the bottom 25 percent of households in the US receive 65 percent of their income in transfers.
2. Thus, in Chapter 6 of Atkinson (1994) where tax benefit models are discussed, detailed presentation of implicit marginal tax rates implied by complex and overlapping UK schemes appears, but wage rates are treated as exogenous. The same is true of the discussion in Dilnot and Duncan (1992). Yelowitz's (1995) recent paper also discusses the complex interacting effects of welfare programmes in the US displaying their effects on the non-convex budget sets that we also emphasize here, but without any welfare analysis of gains and losses and behavioural response under alternative schemes.
3. The closest discussion we are able to find is that by Browning (1973) of the welfare costs of the negative income tax, and the related discussion in Browning and Browning (1987). Browning diagramatically sets out the regime choice problem we discuss here, but does not focus on the real value of transfers and offers no numerical or explicit general equilibrium analysis.
4. When combined with existing estimates of the marginal welfare costs of taxes (Browning (1978), Stuart (1984), Ballard, Shoven and Whalley (1985)) which suggests high marginal dead-weight losses of taxes, and much lower average costs; a picture for the social cost of distortionary tax financed redistribution in OECD countries also emerges from our analysis. This suggests that the average social cost per dollar of tax financed redistribution should be upward revised above existing dead-weight losse stimates from taxes due to the added distortionary cost from conditionality in transfer schemes; but the marginal social cost per dollar of tax financed redistribution should be downward revised due to the labour withdrawal low wage rate effect.
5. In the UK model presented later, we are able to remove wage rate effects across the various labour types by using substitution elasticities in production close to one (constant factor shares). This allows us to isolate the conditionality effects on transfer valuation from wage effects.
6. $(\overline{L_i} - L_i^e)$ is labour supply for household i.
7. The income concept used in the published data is equivalized disposable income.

18

Welfare and Distributional Impacts of Financial Liberzation in an open Economy: Lessons from a Multi-sectoral Dynamic Model for Nepal

Keshab Bhattarai [68]

INTRODUCTION

Nepal is going through series of conflicts and tensions over last 20 years mainly caused by lower rate of economic growth and lack of clear policy of redistribution and alleviating the massive degree of poverty both in rural and urban areas. This paper focuses on how the process of economic development can be augmented by liberalizing financial markets that has been a central theme in policy debate world-wide[1]. Nepalese policy makers also chose this route in 1992 by adhering to a policy that emphasized deregulation of financial institutions, privatization of public enterprises and liberalization of trade for the efficient allocation of resources to promote long-run growth[2]. Though the reform measures[3] have removed many of existing distortionary elements,[4] debate on the potential efficiency and redistribution effects of further reforms continues.

The major argument advanced in this paper is that financial sector reforms in Nepal have released extra resources for investment by improving efficiency in resource allocation, and increased the volume of savings available for productive investment as spending was cut on unproductive assets such as land, jewelry and precious metals. It also argues that the Nepalese reform process has redistributed income from urban to rural households. Financial liberalization has increased the

68 [1] I acknowledge important guidance from Bruce Bolnick, Thomas F. Rutherford and John Whalley in the process of the research. I am thankful to John Adams, Jonathan Haughton and Stephen Parente and seminar groups in Northeastern University Boston, Universities of Warwick and Hull in the UK for comments. Earlier version of this paper was presented at the "Using Dynamic CGE model for Policy Analysis conference June 14-16, 1998" held in Denmark and has appeared as a working paper from Centre for Economic Policy of the University of Hull. Contact address: University of Hull HU6 7RX, Hull UK K.R.Bhattarai@hull.ac.uk phone: 44-1482-463207; fax: 44-1482-463484.

demand for rural labor to complement added capital stocks in rural-labor intensive sectors. Greater increases in wage rates for rural labor than for urban labor are reflected in an increase in the welfare level of rural households. The impact of liberalization is greater when economy is allowed to borrow in international markets than when all imports need to be paid by exports at the same period. It has a greater impact if the productivity of rural land grows faster than the population.

The welfare and distributional impacts of financial reforms discussed above results from changes in the volume of saving and investment. However, economic theory yields ambiguous predictions about such changes. Whether the volume of saving increases with financial liberalization or not, depends upon whether the income effect from a change in the rate of interest dominates the accompanying substitution effect, namely saving will increase only if the substitution effect is stronger than the income effect. Also, financial sector reform is often accompanied by an increase in the real interest rate. Standard theory states that when the cost of investment funds increases, the amount of investment is likely to fall. The net effect of the reforms on investment then depends upon whether the reallocation of capital after the liberalization can compensate for the effect of an increase in the cost of funds after liberalization. Thus not only the size but also the direction of the changes in saving and investment owing to financial liberalization is an empirical issue. Specifically by removing distortions, does financial liberalization promote capital accumulation and output? Is there an overall gain in welfare after the liberalization? If welfare improves, by how much does it improve? Is the gain in welfare from reform distributed equally among consumers located in rural and urban areas? Do urban consumers with a better access to the financial institutions benefit more from liberalization than rural consumers, as is commonly perceived? These are central questions we want to investigate in this paper.

We consider the economy-wide long-run consequences of financial sector liberalization using a forward-looking multi-sectoral computable general equilibrium (CGE) model of the Nepalese economy[5] with financial intermediation. This model is an appropriate tool to study welfare and redistribution consequences of financial sector reform to households and producers in a developing economy. Though numbers of financial institutions, the cost of funds, the volume of savings and investment, assets and liabilities and freedom of financial institutions on the allocation of credits are important measures to ascertain the degree of competition in the financial system, these measure alone are not sufficient to evaluate wide ranging welfare and redistributive effects of reform. General equilibrium analysis is required to correctly quantify the benefits of reform and its distribution among households. It provides meaningful guidelines to policy makers in choosing the most dominating policy option in which gainers can compensate most to the losers.

The forward looking CGE modeling framework presented here builds on standard applied general equilibrium[6] analyses that have been in use for policy analyses in more disaggregated institutional and sectoral structures since mid 1970s. (Shoven and Whalley (1973, 1984, 1992), Robinson (1991), Mercenier and Srinivasan (1995)). Advancement in mixed complementarity modeling algorithm and software (Rutherford (1995), and Dirske and Ferris (1995)) have made numerical analysis of a fairly decentralized forward-looking models much easier in recent years than it used to be in the past. Though a number of CGE models with forward-looking behavior by economic agents exist in the literature,[7] none of the previous studies apply a forward-looking modeling framework to study the multi-sectoral impact of financial sector liberalization. The point of departure in the model presented here lies on explicit incorporation of an investment cost index in a multi-sectoral forward-looking behavioral framework to study the impacts of financial sector reforms over time. With more detailed modeling of investment saving behavior the policy prescription generated by this model may be more consistent in explaining the development process of the Nepalese economy.

THE FORWARD LOOKING COMPUTABLE GENERAL EQUILIBRIUM MODEL OF NEPAL

We consider urban and rural households who allocate their life time income to maximize utility by choosing an optimal path of consumption and saving. These households provide factor services to producers of goods and services, who sell products both in domestic and foreign markets. The capital stock, determined overtime by the volume of savings and investment, complements labor input. In central case, we assume that labor force grows exogenously. Output expands along with increase in labor and capital inputs, its level is consistent with the demand of consumers, investors, the government and foreign sectors.

Consumers' Intertemporal Problem

In the model representative households located in urban and rural areas of the economy allocate lifetime income to maximize utility over an infinite horizon; i.e.

$$\text{Max} \sum_{t=0}^{\infty} \beta^t U(C_t^h) \tag{1}$$

where β is the the discount factor, and it depends on the rate of time preference; C_t^h is composite consumption; U is a time separable utility function. We choose a constant relative risk aversion (CRRA) CES utility function to represent U in (1).[8]

$$U(C_t^h) = \frac{\left(C_t^h\right)^{1-\sigma} - 1}{1-\sigma} \tag{2}$$

here $1/s$ measures the elasticity of substitution between the present and future consumption. The smaller is s the more slowly marginal utility falls as consumption rises, so households are more willing to allow changes in consumption over time. Thus smaller s implies higher elasticity of substitution between current and future consumption or the higher degree of consumption smoothing and substitution over time.

Each type of households faces an inter-temporal budget constraint which implies that its the present value of consumption cannot exceed its present value of life time income (wealth).

$$\sum_{t=0}^{\infty} R_t^{-1} P_t C_t^h = WH^h \tag{3}$$

where, $R_t^{-1} = \prod_{s=0}^{t-1} \frac{1}{1+r_s}$ is a discount factor to convert future expenses in the present value terms; r_s represents the real interest on financial assets; P_t is vectors of relative prices, and C_t is composite consumption goods, which is composed of sectoral consumption goods, $C_t = \prod_{i=1}^{n} C_{i,t}^{\alpha_i^h}$ where α_i^h gives the share of spending on good i by household h. WH_h is the life time wealth of household h and is defined as:

$$WH^h = \frac{J_0^h}{1+r_0^c} + \frac{J_1^h}{(1+r_0^c)(1+r_1^c)} + ... + \frac{J_2^h}{\Pi_s^t (1+r_s^c)} + ... = \sum_{t=0}^{\infty} R_t^{-1} J_t^h \tag{4}$$

where J_t^h is disposable household income in period t. It includes labor and capital income plus transfers.

We combine equation (1) to (4) to form Lagrangian of consumers' the inter-temporal allocation problem in (5).

$$\Im^h = \sum_{t=0}^{\infty} (\frac{1}{1+\rho})^t (\frac{C_t^{h^{1-\sigma}} - 1}{1-\sigma}) + \lambda.[\sum_{t=0}^{\infty} R_t^{-1} P_t C_t^h - WH_t^h] \tag{5}$$

Here, λ is the shadow price of income in terms of present value of utility, and b in (1) is replaced by $\frac{1}{1+\rho}$, where ρ is the rate of time preference.

We derive consumption function by taking first order condition on (5):

$$\frac{C_{t+1}}{C_t} = \left(\left(\frac{1+r_t}{1+\rho} \right) \frac{P_t}{P_{t+1}} \right)^{\frac{1}{\sigma}} \tag{6}$$

or using a steady state assumption on the growth rate

$$C_{t+1} = \left(\left(\frac{1+r_t}{1+\rho} \right) \frac{P_t}{P_{t+1}} \right)^{\frac{1}{\sigma}} C_0 (1+g)^{t-1} \tag{6'}$$

Thus the consumption level at time t, in the steady state, is a function of growth rate, the rate of interest and intertemporal prices of commodities.

Consistency of the intertemporal budget constraint implies that:

$$\sum_t R_t^{-1}[C_0 + \Omega_1 C_0 + \Omega_2 C_0 + ...] = WH^h \tag{7}$$

where $\Omega_t = [\beta^t R_t^{-1} \frac{P_t}{P_0}]^{\frac{1}{\sigma}}$

Economy wide savings is total of household savings, S_t^h, which in turn is the portion of income not consumed :

$$S_t = \sum_h S_t^h = \sum_h J_t^h - \sum_h C_t^h \tag{8}$$

The consumption saving decisions are two sides of the same coin. Once we know the level consumption we also know the level of savings. Saving like consumption is influenced by the rate of interest prevailing in the economy and the time preference of individuals. The efficiency in the financial system can contribute to rise in the level of saving, depending upon the value of *s*, by influencing the decision between the current and future consumption and reducing the wedge between the cost of capital to investors and gains received by the savers.

Savings of households are intermediated through the financial institutions to investors, who use those savings to purchase investment goods from different sectors. Like consumers investors in each of n production sectors solve an intertemporal profit maximization problem. They combine goods produced in a set of n sectors to deliver an unit of investment in sector j. Therefore, the unit cost of investment in sector j is a weighted average of the prices of components of sector n goods used for investment purpose. One unit of investment at period t produces once unit of capital stock in period t+1:

$$\Pi_{j,t}^I = P_{j,t+1}^k - \sum_i P_{i,t} a_{i,j}^I \leq 0 \tag{9}$$

Here $\Pi_{j,t}^I$ is profit from one unit of investment at period t, $P_{j,t+1}^k$ is the price of capital in period *t+1*, and $a_{i,j}^I$ is the investment coefficient matrix. One unit of capital at the start of period 1 generates a rate of return ($r_{j,t}^k$) today and delivers 1-d unit at the start of the subsequent period. The arbitrage condition in capital accumulation implies that:

$$\Pi_{j,t}^k = (1-\delta)P_{j,t+1}^k + r_{j,t}^k - P_{j,t}^k \leq 0 \tag{10}$$

Entering capital (K_0) stock is transferred into initial capital stock for the various sectors, $K_{i,0}$, according to a fixed coefficient transformation process. Once the initial capital is allocated among different sectors, $K_{i,t}$, the law of motion of capital in a sector is explained by the following equation.

$$K_{j,t+1} = I_{j,t} + (1-\delta_K)K_{j,t} \tag{11}$$

where,

$$I_{i,t} = \sum_j a^I_{i,j,t} I_{j,t} \tag{12}$$

Net investment demand, $I_{i,t}$, in each sector is the sum of investment by origin. The relationship given by $a^I_{i,j,t}$ is called capital coefficient matrix of the economy.

We assume that in the terminal period the investment in each sector grows at the rate of the population so that economy can continue along the steady state growth path even after the terminal period as given by the following equation.

$$I_{j,t} = (g + \delta_{K,j})K_{j,t} \tag{13}$$

g = growth rate of the economy, which equals the growth rate of the labor force in terms of efficiency units, and δ_K = rate of depreciation.

Holding aggregate stock of capital fixed to the savings of households in the beginning of each period, the objective of firms in jth sector of the economy is to maximize the present value of profit subject to the constraints of production technology. Zero profit for sector j written in dual form in terms of composite prices of commodities and inputs is the following form (See appendix for details):

$$\begin{aligned}\Pi^y_{j,t} &= [(\theta^x_j PX^{1+\eta}_{j,t} + (1-\theta^x_j)PD^{1+\eta}_{j,t})]^{\frac{1}{1+\eta}} \\ &-\theta^v_j PV^v_j - (1-\theta^v_j)\sum_j a_{i,j}P_{i,t} \le 0\end{aligned} \tag{14}$$

The exact meaning of the symbols of the above profit function are following:

$\Pi^y_{j,t}$ unit profit of activity in sector j

$PX_{j,t}$ price of exports

$PD_{j,t}$ price of domestic sales

PV^v_j price of value added per unit of output in activity j

$P_{i,t}$ price of final goods used as intermediate goods

θ^x_j share parameter for exports in total production

θ^v_j share of costs paid to labor and capital

$a_{i,j}$ input output coefficients.

The equation (14) is an unit profit function. The profit of operating these firms are given by the differences between the revenue from sales and the cost of supply. The unit revenue function is constant elasticity transformation (CET) composite of unit price of domestic sales and unit price of exports. The unit costs are divided between value-added, i.e. payments to labor and capital, and the unit intermediate input costs.

In this model, the gross output in each sector is given by a nested production function between the value added and the intermediate inputs.

$$Y_{j,t} = \min(V_{j,t}, a_{i,j}Y_{j,t}) \tag{15}$$

Where Yj,t is the output of sector j in period t, Vj,t is the value added part and $a_{i,j}$ is the intermediate inputs per unit of gross output produced in sector j.

We use Shephard's lemma to derive the demand for labor and capital from (14). The demand for labor is:

$$L_{j,t} = Y_{j,t} \frac{\partial \Pi^V_{j,t}}{\partial PV_{j,t}} \frac{\partial PV_{j,t}}{\partial PL_{j,t}} \tag{16}$$

where $L_{j,t}$ is a composite of rural (unskilled) and urban (skilled) labor. Equilibrium in the labor market requires that demand for labor be equal to supply of labor:

$$\sum_j L_{j,t} \frac{\partial \Pi^L}{\partial PL^{LC}_t} \leq \overline{L}_t \tag{17}$$

$\overline{L}_t$ in the above equations is a composite of urban and rural labor. The ratio of urban to rural labor employed by firms mainly depends upon the ratio of urban to rural wage rates.

The demand for capital in sector j, again by Shephard's lemma is given by:

$$K_{j,t} = Y_{j,t} \frac{\partial \Pi^V_{j,t}}{\partial PV_{j,t}} \frac{\partial PV_{j,t}}{\partial PK_{j,t}} \tag{18}$$

where $Y_{j,t}$ is activity level; $PK_{j,t}$ is price of capital $PV_{j,t}$ is price of value added. In equilibrium the demand for capital is equal to its supply:

$$\sum_j K_{j,t} = \overline{K}_t \tag{19}$$

$\overline{K}_t$ is the aggregate capital stock in the economy, which grows according to the low of motion of capital stock as given by equation 13. $\sum_j K_{j,t}$ is the total demand for capital by various sectors of the economy.

When an economy is repressed, the arbitrage condition implied by (9) $P^k_{j,t+1} = \sum_j P_{i,t} a^I_{i,j}$ does not exactly hold. There is additional distortionary cost $\tau_{j,t}$ on top of the cost of materials required for per unit investment. The overall cost of investment is rather given by:

$$P^k_{j,t+1} = \left(1+\tau_{j,t}\right)\sum_i P_{i,t} a^I_{i,j} \tag{9'}$$

where,

$\tau_{j,t}$ = per unit wedge between the return to saving and the cost of investment.

$P^k_{j,t+1}$ = present value price of sector j capital at the beginning of next period

$P_{i,t}$ = present value price of sector i commodity at period t

In repressionary situation certain portion of saving dissipates in the process of financial intermediation. Therefore the total investment in the economy less than the total savings i.e. the amount of savings net of intermediation costs. Moreover, additional resources may be available by liquidating the real unproductive assets (ΔRA)of the households and firms.

$$c(S_t - \Delta RA_t) = I_t \tag{20}$$

Here c is the proportion of saving available for investment purpose, or, 1-c being the cost of financial intermediation. In this model cost of financial intermediation is represented by the distortionary cost of repression.

Calibration to a Steady State

In the steady state all sectors of the economy grow at the same rate, *g*. The bench mark rate of return is calibrated assuming the non-distorted economy being in the steady state in the base year. Calibration of dynamic component follows the relationship between the current and future prices of capital and investment goods. Specifically, investment produces one unit of capital stock in period 2 (P^k_2) from one unit of output in the period one, P^I_1 . The present value of one unit of capital in period 2 is equal to $(1-r)P^k_1$.

$$P^I_1 = 1 = P^k_2 = (1-r)P^k_1 \Rightarrow P^k_1 = \frac{1}{1-r}P^k_2 \tag{21}$$

Here 1-r is the discount rate between two periods, and is approximation to 1/(1+r). $\frac{P^k_{t+1}}{P^k_t} = (1-r)$

One unit of capital at the beginning of period one earns a rate of return today, r_1^k and delivers 1-d unit of capital for the start of the next period.

$$P_1^k = r_1^k + (1-\delta)(1-r)P_2^k \tag{22}$$

This relationship applies to all other periods included in the model. Using base year prices equal to 1 to P_2^k and P_1^k by using relationship between P_2^k and P_1^k we get:

$$\frac{1}{1-r} = r_1^k + (1-\delta) \tag{23}$$

which gives the cost of capital to be equal to the rate interest plus the rate of depreciation: $r_1^k = \frac{r}{1-r} + \delta$.

The base-year social accounting matrix (SAM) contains information on capital income V_1 and it is related to rate of return and capital stock, $V_1 = r_1^k K_1$. Now substituting for r_1^k between the steady state interest rate r and the parameters of the model:

$$K_1 = \frac{V_1}{\frac{r}{1-r} + \delta} \tag{24}$$

Then substituting this value of K_1 in I_1 function the relationship between the investment and capital earning component of value added may be expressed as:

$$\frac{I_1}{V_1} = \frac{\delta + g}{\frac{r}{1-r} + \delta} \tag{25}$$

If the ratio of investment and capital earning ($\frac{I_1}{V_1} = 1$) is equal to one then

$g = \frac{r}{1-r}$ or $r = \frac{g}{1+g}$.

When $\frac{I_1}{V_1} \neq 1$, then the key parameter to calibrate is the rate of depreciation, which can be calculated using the relationship between the interest rate, growth rate, depreciation and earning of capital as following :

$$\delta_j = g\frac{V_j}{I_j - V_j} - \frac{r}{1-r}\frac{I_j}{I_j - V_j} \quad (26)$$

In a repressionary regime the cost of capital is distorted by a repressionary component of intermediation, t_j. This can be expressed as:

$$r_1^k = \frac{\bar{r}_j^k}{1-\tau_j} \quad (27)$$

here r_1^k is actual cost of capital, $\bar{r}_j^k$ is rate of interest in steady state, and τ_j is distortionary element in the financial market. The price of capital becomes

$$P_1^k = r_1^k(1-\tau_i) + (1-\delta)(1-r)P_2^k \quad (28)$$

or the cost of capital $r_1^k = \frac{1}{1-\tau_j}\left[\frac{r}{1-r} + \delta\right]$ (29)

Now adjusting (26) to take account of distortions in the capital market :

$$\frac{I_1}{V_1} = \frac{\delta + g}{\frac{r}{1-r} + \delta}(1-\tau_j) \quad (30)$$

or

$$\tau_j = 1 - \frac{\bar{r}_j^k}{\delta + g}\frac{I_j}{V_j}$$

Thus the spread between the true cost of capital $\bar{r}_j^k$ and the actual cost of capital r_1^k depends upon the ratio of investment to capital and ratio of natural rate of interest to depreciation plus the growth rate of the economy.

Government Budget and BOP Closures

In the core part of the model the government's budget is balanced in every period, and, therefore government is not involved in intertemporal savings. This essentially implies all government expenditure is basically the government consumption.

The sources of revenue for the government are taxes on value added[9], tariffs on imports, sales taxes, income taxes and capital taxes. Lump sum income taxes are collected from total household income, and such income taxes are assumed to grow at the rate of population growth rate. In addition there are other sources of government revenue such as export taxes, taxes on tourism, revenue generated from import-licensing and refund of excise taxes from India.

Government transfers its revenues to households and firms in the form of consumption and production subsidies, and it also serves domestic and foreign debt. In the core part of the model we assume all sorts of government non-transfer spending to public consumption.

This is an open economy model. We follow standard Armington specification of international trade in this model. For each tradable sectors constant elasticity of transformation (CET) function defines relation between exports and domestic supply, and constant elasticity of substitution (CES) function explains relation between domestic supply and imports in forming a composite good that goes to the utility function of the households. We use two level nests in trade to take account of different natures of trade relations between India and rest of the world (ROW). More detailed discussion of trade specification is available elsewhere (see Bhattarai (1997) and also the appendix of this paper).

We consider two rules of BOP closure. In the first case no foreign borrowing is allowed; imports need to be paid by exports[10]. In the second case intertemporal borrowing and lending is permitted. It is presented in the form of CAPFLOW scenario in the next section.

The elasticities of substitution between domestic and imported products in consumption and the elasticity of transformation between domestic sales and foreign sales are taken based on sensitivity analyses.

Finally, the market clearing condition for goods market is given by:

$$A_{j,t} = C_{j,t} + \sum_{j=1}^{12} a_{i,j} Y_{j,t} + G_{j,t} + \sum_{j} a_{i,j}^{I} I_{j,t} + DST_{j,t} + TD_{j,t} \tag{31}$$

here $A_{j,t}$ is total supply in the economy in a sector j should be equal to sum of various components of demand as given on the right hand side, i.e. the consumption of households: $C_{j,t} = \sum_{h} C_{j,h,t}$, intermediate demands: $\sum_{j} a_{i,j} Y_{j,t}$, government demand: $G_{j,t}$, investment demand: $I_{j,t} = \sum_{j} a_{i,j} I_{j,,t}$, inventory demand: $DST_{j,t} = DSTR_{j,t} \cdot Y_{j,t}$, and demand by tourists: TD_{t}^{s}; for simplicity we assume that demand by tourists grows at the rate of growth of the economy.

Definition of a Competitive Equilibrium

A competitive equilibrium is a set of sequences of prices of composite commodities, $P_{i,t}$; prices of domestic goods sold in domestic markets, $PD_{i,t}$; prices of exported commodities, $PX_{i,t}$; prices of capital goods, $P^k_{j,t}$; prices of terminal capital , $PTK_{j,t}$; wage rates for each categories of labor, $w_{h,t}$; prices of government services, PG_t ; prices of provisions for tourism, PT_t ; value of transfers to the households, PR_t ; prices of consumption, PU_t ; welfare index, PW_t ; rental rate of capital for each sector, r_1^k : R+→R, and sequences of gross output, $Y_{i,t}$; total supply of commodities, $A_{i,t}$; sectoral capital stock, $K_{i,t}$; sectoral investment, $I_{i,t}$; exports, $X_{i,t}$; government services, GOV_t ; level of household utility from consumption, U_t ; and total welfare, W such that given these prices and commodities

(i) households solve intertemporal utility maximization problems subject to life time income constraints,

(ii) investors solve intertemporal profit maximization problem subject to arbitrage conditions in capital markets

(iii) producers solve their profit maximization problem subject to technology and resource constraints

(iv) markets for goods and services, labour, capital clear

(v) government account constraints are satisfied,

(vi) balance of payments condition is fulfilled

(vii) financial markets are in equilibrium

In this equilibrium, consumers have perfect foresight, capital accumulation is consistent with households optimization, income and expenditure balance over the life period. An agent is doing the best he can in light of actions taken by others and actions taken together are technically feasible. This ensures the compatibility of plans of individuals or correspondence between consumers' preferences and firms' technology.

There are mainly two limitations of this model. First, analytical solution of this model is very complex and unrewarding. We rely on numerical methods that generate a set of relative prices consistent with the equilibrium. Absolute prices do not matter in general equilibrium models, it generates the same equilibrium even if all prices are multiplied by a constant. For analyses of model results we basically compare ratios of prices in terms of a numeraire in benchmark and counterfactual scenarios, not the absolute differences in prices.

Second, the model presented here does not contain any adjustment costs or penalties. The role of dynamics in such a model is not to show the pattern of adjustment, but to track the prices of commodities with a multiperiod character, e.g. the capital stock. The model is suitable to study the impact of a certain policy that changes the steady state of the model and thus the growth and welfare of the households over a model horizon.

In spite of these limitations the model is capable of generating results that are interesting from a point of view of a policy maker. We use a welfare index as the criterion for making the best policy choice from the various options available to a policy maker.

Measure of Welfare

General equilibrium solutions are used to compute equivalent or compensating variations in consumer welfare from given changes in policy regimes. In this model the overall welfare is given by sum of utility over periods measured in terms of prices of composite consumption.

$$UW^h = \sum_t^{\infty} PU_t^h U_t^h \tag{32}$$

Here UW^h is a measure of welfare to household h for the period of model horizon, PU_t^h is the price of composite consumption in period t, and U_t^h is the utility to a household from consumption of goods and services in the economy.

We use welfare measures in order to quantify the impacts of various policy measures. A policy experiment that has greater value of UW^h is more desirable than the one with lower one.

We can also use this model to study the behavior of output, employment, capital accumulation and overall and sectoral prices for a fairly decentralized open economy. This advancement in numerical analysis of an economy is made possible by the development of MPSGE/GAMS software and algorithms to solve the mixed-complementary problem with nested functions, computation of a standard model with a more elaborate specification is not a problem (See Rutherford, (1995)). The task was made even easier by base year micro-consistent data readily available from the ADB model (See Maxwell Stamp's report to ADB 1992). The dataset and the GAMS/MPSGE program used for computation of the model are provided in Appendices I and II. Author appreciates guidance from Professor Rutherford in developing this program as a part of the research for doctoral degree from the Northeastern University in Boston.

ANALYSIS OF MODEL RESULTS

Analyses of model results show that financial liberalization improves efficiency on allocation of resources by eliminating the distortionary costs of capital in the various sectors of the economy. Enhancement in efficiency allows expansion in capital stock, employment and total output over period. Overall welfare of consumers increases. Welfare gains of rural households are higher than the welfare gains of urban households. This indicates a significant effect of liberalization on the redistribution of income. The degree of liberalization matters. The impact of complete liberalization is greater than the impact of a partial or a sector specific piecemeal liberalization for both efficiency and redistribution.

Financial liberalization here means the removal of distortions in the user cost of capital across sectors. The percentage distortions from a steady state rate of return across sectors, represented by t_j in the model, are given by in table 1. In repression, agricultural and manufacturing sectors pay up to a 60 percent higher rate than in an undistorted steady state, while modern sectors such as public services, electricity, transport sectors received subsidies ranging from 4.7 percent to 112 percent in their capital use. Thus rental rates are not necessarily tied down to the rate of returns or productivity of capital and an artificial rule of allocation makes the rates of return vary from one sector to another.

Table 1
Capital Market Distortions In The Base Year
(As % of Steady State User Cost of Capital - Tau (τ_j))

Food-crop	*Cash-crop*	*Food-proc*	*Text-iles*	*Chemi-cal*	*Capi tal*	*-Trans port*	*Elec-tric*	*Cons-truct*	*Tour-ism*	*Ser-vices*	*Public*
0.591	0.591	0.591	0.578	0.536	0.424	-0.047	-0.157	-0.336	0.161	0.011	-1.118

In the liberalized regime rates of return to capital equalize across various sectors, this is the key to the efficiency and distribution effects we have discussed in this paper. We consider economy-wide and sector specific piecemeal liberalization. Economy-wide liberalization is further classified into a partial and a complete liberalization depending upon the amount of reduction in the distortion. In the case of economy-wide liberalization the distortionary cost of financial intermediation (t_j), the spread between the lending and borrowing rates, is changed across all sectors at the same rate. In the partial economy-wide liberalization t_j is reduced by a fifty percent in each sector, and it is set equal to zero in a complete liberalization. In the case of piecemeal liberalization, the distortionary cost of financial intermediation is reduced only for one or a few selected sectors. For instance, would a cut in the subsidy on the user cost of capital to the public sector increases the volume of investment in other sectors? Or does a reduction in the premium on cost of capital in food sector or a cash crop sector matter? We search for answers to these questions solving the model for a 30 years' horizon.

The impact of financial liberalization policy varies according to conditions and structure of the entire economy upon which these policies are undertaken. We capture these conditions selecting five different scenarios (1) the baseline is calibrated assuming a steady state equilibrium in the base-year; (2) complete market scenario (CAPFLOW) represents a steady state growth rate across all sectors, unrestricted borrowing and lending permitted to close the balance of payment (BOP) gap along with exogenous interest rate; (3) the incomplete market scenario (BOPCON) assumes a common steady state growth rate across all sectors and a period by period BOP constraint; (4) in black-hole scenario (BKLHOLE) we study a special feature of repression in the Nepalese economy by allowing leakage of savings to accumulation of unproductive assets such as jewelry, purchases of precious metals, hoarding of urban land or foreign exchange when households anticipate a negative rate of return on their financial assets. This raises the real cost of financial intermediation. This scenario takes period by period BOP constraint and steady state growth path. (5) non-steady state scenario (NONSS) covers cases where supply of some factors grow at different rate than the steady state growth rate assumed in the model. Here, we assume that the urban labor grows twice faster than the steady state growth rate and land productivity grows at 1/3 of the steady state growth rate. In addition as in CAPFLOW scenario we allow free flows of capital with exogenous interest rates.

The overall gains in welfare from financial sector liberalization under these various scenarios are presented in Table 2. The overall welfare effects in CAPFLOW and NONSS model are comparable to findings of many other studies in the tax reforms and trade liberalization literature (Shoven and Whalley (1984) Robinson (1989) and Deverajan et. al (1996)).

Table 2
Welfare Indices Under Different Scenarios

	Capital Flow Scenario (CAPFLOW)			Non steady State Scenario (NONSS)			Black Hole Scenario (BLKHOLE)		
	Rural	*Urban*	*Overall*	*Rural*	*Urban*	*Overall*	*Rural*	*Urban*	*Overall*
Partial	1.103	0.747	1.0674	1.045	0.822	1.0227	0.905	0.920	0.9065
Complete	1.166	0.441	1.0935	1.166	0.947	1.1441	0.855	0.880	0.8575

The greatest welfare gain is up to 14.4 percent more than the baseline welfare in NONSS scenario under complete liberalization, compared with 9.3 percent gain in CAPFLOW scenarios. These results indicate the importance of growth conditions in the labor market and the growth in productivity of agricultural land in analyzing the impacts of financial liberalization. They also highlight the importance of international capital flows. However, if savings leak in unproductive assets high cost of intermediation reduces overall welfare as shown in the Blackhole scenario. The rural households loose more than urban households because of high cost of financial intermediation. Welfare gains under partial liberalization are smaller than in the case of complete liberalization but still sizable. Overall welfare under partial liberalization is up 6 percent in CAPFLOW scenario compared to 2 percent in NONSS scenario. If accumulation in unproductive assets persists reduction in welfare is less with a partial than in a complete liberalization.

The redistribution impacts of liberalization are noticeable. Model solutions generally show that the process of financial liberalization is in favor of rural households in comparison to the urban households. This result might seem counter-intuitive as one would expect urban households to benefit more from the financial liberalization than the rural households. In repression, firms in urban areas have more access to financial institutions compared to those in rural areas and credit rates are kept artificially low by means of interest rate subsidies for one or another reason, i.e. promoting small scale enterprises, enhancing self-sufficiency or increasing exports. After liberalization various channels of capital and labor markets are also open to rural households making them relatively better off than the urban households.

The financial liberalization eliminates cheap credit facilities for privileged firms located in urban areas, forcing all firms to compete for capital on the basis of productivity. Firms operating with a heavy subsidy under repression, i.e. the public sector, can attract less capital and tend to substitute labor to capital after liberalization. Firms employing unskilled labor intensively, such as textiles, food-crops and cash-crop sectors expand their investment and production in response to increased access to funds in liberalized regime. They demand more unskilled labor than skilled labor to complement the additional capital. Given the fact that the endowment of unskilled labor is larger than the endowment of skilled labor in the Nepalese economy an easy access to credit markets for labor intensive firms has positive consequences in the market for rural labor. An increase in the demand for labor raises their wage rates. The higher relative wages of unskilled labor benefit rural households which by our assumption supply only unskilled type of labor.

Liberalization of the formal financial sector also has a widespread effect on informal credit markets in the rural sector. Nepal's rural credit market is dominated by the informal sector. In repression, access of rural firms or households to financial institutions is limited and the local money lenders exercise their market power charging a very high rate of interest. This creates additional distortions in rural sectors as reflected in the high cost of fund to rural sectors such as food crop and cash crop sectors. After liberalization more savings and loans flow through formal channels. Therefore local money lenders have to provide attractive lending and borrowing rates if they want to sustain their business. This implies liberalization opens competition even in the rural areas where the formal financial institutions are not accessible. Cheap credit facilities increase rural investment and the productivity of the rural labor.

Enhancement in welfare and a significant redistribution of income in favor of rural households occurs through improvement in allocation of capital resources and expansion in output. In the liberalized regime capital is allocated according to its marginal productivity. Investors look at the rate of return while allocating investment across sectors. It means that more productive sectors receive more capital. Reallocation of capital continues until the rate of return across the sectors is equal and all of these returns are equal to the cost of capital net of depreciation. Model results presented in Table 3 show the impact of financial liberalization on capital stock.

The capital stock grows faster in complete liberalization than in partial liberalization. For instance, the index of capital stock in the textile sector in 1918 is 2.88 in the case of partial liberalization, and 4.72 in case of complete liberalization. Thus the impact of complete liberalization in this sector is 61 percent higher than that in the partial liberalization. Similarly, the capital stock index in the public service sector in complete liberalization is 73 percent of partial liberalization. The impact in other sectors varies between these two extremes and depends upon the level of investment following liberalization. The Figure 1 below shows investment indices in textiles. food crops, cash-crop sector significantly compared to the baseline and while the level of investment recovers back to the baseline after five or six years.

Table 3
Impacts of Financial Liberalization on Capital Stock Under CAPFLOW Scenario

	Food-crop	*Cash-crop*	*Food-proc*	*Text-iles*	*Chemi-cal*	*Capi-tal*	*Trans-port*	*Elec-tric*	*Cons-truct*	*Tour-ism*	*Ser-vices*	*Public*
Complete	2.37	3.02	2.11	4.72	1.73	1.12	1.07	1.06	1.07	1.02	0.81	0.62
Partial	1.73	2.02	1.61	2.88	1.42	1.08	1.06	1.06	1.05	1.02	0.91	0.84
Base	1.00	1.00	1.00	1.00	1.00	1.00	1.00	1.00	1.00	1.00	1.00	1.00
Base year Cap. Stock	80031	32746	14427	11267	10056	7077	21590	2673	20144	3892	26821	17058

The capital stock shrinks in public services and service sectors implying substitution of labor for capital in these sectors following the removal of interest rate subsidies after the liberalization. The stronger capital re-allocation effect under a complete liberalization compared to a partial liberalization implies that conventional practice of creating special rules for the promotion of selected sectors is not effective in the long run. The best rule for a greater accumulation of capital is to remove these special rules and let the capital market operate according to demand and supply forces of the liberalized market economy.

From the model results it is safe to conclude that the substitution effect dominates the income effect of the increase in the rate of interest on savings and the capital reallocation effect dominates the increase in the cost of capital on the investment side. The magnitude of saving effects depend upon the intertemporal elasticity of substitution (s), as mentioned earlier a small s implies higher degree of consumption smoothing and more pronounced saving effect due to liberalization. Thus both supply and demand in the capital market respond positively to liberalization policies. The overall effect of liberalization increases both savings and investment which ultimately leads to a higher rate of capital accumulation and growth after liberalization.

An increase in overall welfare is possible through increase in output and redistribution effects that results from the changes in composition of sectoral output compared to the base year. Model results presented in Table 4 show that output increases in all sectors after liberalization. But the output expansion in primary rural-labor intensive sectors, such as textiles, food-crops, cash-crops and chemical (mining and querying) sectors, are greater than in secondary sectors, i.e. transportation, electricity, tourism and construction. For instance, output index of textile sector in 2018 was 4.4 in partial liberalization compared to 5.7 in complete liberalization as given in Figure 2.

Output increases even in the public and services sectors in spite of some reductions in capital stocks in these sectors compared to baseline model. This suggests that in response to the elimination of subsidies on interest rates, these sectors substitute labor for capital in the liberalized regime. From sensitivity analyses, substitution of labor for capital is higher for larger values of elasticity of substitution between capital and labor.

Table 4

Output Impacts Of Liberalization Under Capflow Scenario

	Food-crop	*Cash-crop*	*Food-proc*	*Text-iles*	*Chemi-cal*	*Capi-tal*	*-Trans port*	*Elec-tric*	*Cons-truct*	*Tour-ism*	*Ser-vices*	*Public*
Complete	1.856	2.533	1.976	5.738	2.273	1.685	1.633	1.788	1.947	1.591	1.375	1.796
Partial	1.826	2.226	1.904	4.026	2.083	1.723	1.7	1.801	1.817	1.664	1.561	1.772
Base	1.00	1.00	1.00	1.00	1.00	1.00	1.00	1.00	1.00	1.00	1.00	1.00

Expansion in output is even greater than that of capital stock for every sector. None of the production sectors are experiencing any reduction in the level of output compared to baseline model. This reflects the fact that producers maximize profits by substituting capital and labor until the wage rental ratios are equal to marginal productivity ratios of capital and labor. Even if the capital stock de-accumulates in public and service sectors because of factor substitution, the production index is still greater than one. A careful comparison of the capital accumulation path and output path indicates this underlying process of substitutions between capital and labor by producers intending to maximize intertemporal profits. An increase in the capital stock complements urban and rural labor in the production of goods and services in the economy. However, the increase in the capital stock is a neither a necessary nor a sufficient conditions for an increase in output. The level of output can expand even by an increase in the employment of labor for a given stock of capital. Changes in wage rental ratios imply changes in capital labor ratios in order to fulfill the requirements for profit maximization. Thus, increases in the capital stock leads to an increase in output but the output can increase even by an increase in the labor for a given stock of capital. Firms operating the expanding sectors tend to increase employment of both labor and capital to raise production sufficient enough to meet the increased demand for goods and services in the economy.

Expansion in output is supported by increases in final and intermediate demands. Growth in demand for consumption good from a sector may take the forms of increased consumption of households increased level of investment, higher intermediate demand and increased volume of exports. Even the government demand increases after an increase in revenues due to expansion in income.

By reducing the cost of capital the financial liberalization lowers commodity prices supplied by domestic producers. A large proportion of demand met by imports before liberalization, particularly in the expanding sectors such as food crops, cash crops and textiles, are met by internal production after liberalization.

The output indices are very intuitive in considering the growth strategy for the Nepalese economy. If distortions are removed the economy starts growing through expansion of primary sectors, agriculture and its related sectors. Producers in these sectors respond to reduced cost of production by increasing output. The production of textiles expands to meet internal and international demands. The expansion rate of ancillary sectors, i.e. transport, electricity, construction and services is lower than the growth rates of the primary sectors. Given the structure of the model, financial sector liberalization policy actually turns out to be equivalent to an agriculture-led growth strategy for the Nepalese economy.

So far we have only reported welfare impacts of economy wide complete and partial liberalization. Table 5 presents the overall welfare gains by sector specific piecemeal liberalization. The highest welfare gain of 3.8 percent occurs through the piecemeal liberalization of textile sector, followed by 2.4 percent from the agriculture sector. These gains are positive except in case of construction and tourism sectors which do not have strong linkages with the rest of the economy (Bhattarai (1997)). As explained above financial liberalization releases extra resources in unskilled labor intensive sectors by increasing their productivity and wage rate more than for urban labor.

Table 5
Welfare Indices under sector specific liberalization

	Distortion as a % of cost of capital in the model	*Welfare Indices in Piecemeal Liberalization under CAPFLOW*		
			baseyear	
	TAU (t)	*Rural*	*Urban*	*Overall*
Food-Crop	0.591	1.063	0.669	1.0236
Cash-crop	0.591	1.035	0.874	1.0189
Food-Proc.	0.591	1.015	0.919	1.0054
Textiles	0.578	1.051	0.917	1.0376
Chemical	0.536	1.015	0.917	1.0052
Capital	0.424	1.006	0.948	1.0002
Construct	-0.336	0.994	1.029	0.9975
Tourism	0.161	1.001	0.988	0.9997

Financial liberalization is more effective when intertemporal borrowing and lending are permitted in the model. The rental cost of capital is higher in solutions of BOPCON scenario where several instruments of the financial system become inapplicable because of limited financial markets. If the economy cannot participate internationally, markets are not free, so the liberalization has little reallocation effect. In face of a period by period BOP constraint, thus the effect of liberalization on welfare is minimal.

From analysis of welfare figures both in complete, partial and piecemeal liberalization considered so far we can conclude that in general financial liberalization leads to an overall increase in welfare, and the welfare gain of rural households is larger than that of urban households.

Wage Rate Impacts of Liberalization

Wage earnings are key components of income in the intertemporal budget constraints of households. A rise in wage rates increases income, consumption and utilities and hence overall welfare across the model horizon. Redistribution takes place over the period if wage rates of rural households increases faster than wage rates of the urban households or vice-versa. As can be seen from table 6, the increase in wage rates of rural labor in comparison to the urban labor is the major source of income redistribution due to financial liberalization. We present the complete path of indices of gains in wage rates of rural labor relative to urban labor under partial and full liberalization in table 6. Wage gains of rural labor are greater in non steady state scenario where the urban labor force grows twice than the rural labor force and agricultural productivity growth is one third of the growth rate of the rural labor force. An increase in urban labor supply causes a slower growth rate of urban wages in comparison to rural wage rates.

Table 6
Ratio of Rural/Urban Wage Increases Under Different Model

Assumptions Scenario	*Capital Flow Scenario (CAPFLOW)*		*Non Steady State Scenario (NONSS)*		*Black Hole (BLKHOLE)*	
	Partial	*Complete*	*Partial*	*Complete*	*Partial*	*Complete*
1990	1.028	1.049	0.995	1.024	1.029	1.049
1995	1.010	1.016	1.036	1.043	1.010	1.016
2000	1.003	1.010	1.081	1.083	1.003	1.010
2005	1.004	1.009	1.125	1.132	1.002	1.009
2010	1.003	1.010	1.176	1.179	1.003	1.010
2015	1.003	1.009	1.213	1.219	1.003	1.009

There are various explanations for relatively larger wage gains by rural labor. Reforms in the financial sector provide an easy access to credit to rural labor intensive firms in urban areas. These firms increase the demand for rural labor to complement addition in capital stock acquired from cheap credits. The competition in credit markets reduces interest rates in the informal markets in rural areas. Rural firms are able to purchase more capital stock which make rural labor more productive. Households also convert their savings from unproductive assets to formal channels in order to earn interest. This re-conversion of capital takes places in rural sectors favoring rural households more than urban households.

Lower rates of credit lead to more investment and greater demand for labor. Gradually segmentation of the labor market characteristic in a repressed economy fades away as an integrated labor market in which rural labor is paid according to its productivity emerges.

In all scenarios the wage rate increase is higher for rural labor relative to the wage rates of urban labor. Greater demand for rural labor drives up the rural wage rate after liberalization. Significantly higher rural wage rate in NONSS model is indicative of cuts in urban wages due to a higher growth rate of the urban labor force.

Model results in table 6 show that increase in wage rates depends upon the degree of liberalization. Wage rate effects are higher in case of complete liberalization than in the case of partial liberalization.

CONCLUSIONS

The major conclusions from the model analyses are the following:

1. By equalizing rates of return across sectors, financial liberalization insures efficiency in the allocation of resources. Efficiency in resource allocation increases the capital usage in sectors that were more repressed before liberalization. It causes a reduction, or slower growth, of capital use in sectors that used to be subsidized before repression. Output expands with an increase in the capital stock.
2. The benefits of liberalization accrue more to the rural households than to the urban households. Following liberalization rural labor intensive sectors invest more with increased access to financial institutions. More labor is required to complement additional capital. Demand for unskilled labor increases faster than the demand for skilled labor. This means an increase in the wage rate of rural labor is greater than the increase in the wage rate of the urban labor. Consequently welfare gains of rural households are larger in comparison to the welfare gains of urban households. In this sense, liberalization redistributes income from urban to rural households. The redistribution of welfare occurs by increasing the wages of unskilled labor relative to skilled labor.
3. Numerical solutions of the model imply that the substitution effect of the increase in the rate of interest dominates the income effect on the savings side and the efficiency in capital reallocation effect dominates the increased cost of capital effect on the investment side. The overall effect is on increase in both savings and investment after the liberalization leading to a higher level of capital stock and output in each sector and higher level of welfare to both urban and rural households.
4. Conflicts and tension seen in Nepal over last twenty years can be solved by adopting a policy that promotes growth which redistributes income to poor households and thus gradually alleviates the mass poverty. Dynamic multi-household multi-sectoral general equilibrium as discussed in this paper may help to put all parts of economy together while making the policy analyses and to assess the effective monitoring the impacts of those policies in the life time welfare of households located in urban and rural areas.

REFERENCES

Abel Andrew B. and O.J. Blanchard (1983), "An Intertemporal Model of Saving and Investment", *Econometrica* Vol. 51, No. 3, May.

Adelman Irma and S. Robinson (1978), Income Distribution Policy in Developing Countries: A Case of South Korea, Standford University Press, Stanford, California.

Auerbach Alan J. and L.J. Kotlikoff (1987), Dynamic Fiscal Policy. Cambridge University Press.

Ballard Charles L. (1983), Evaluation of the Consumption Tax with Dynamic General Equilibrium Models, Ph.D. Dissertation, Stanford University.

Ballard Charles L., D. Fullerton, J.B. Shoven and J.Whalley (1985). A General Equilibrium Model for Tax Policy Evaluation, University of Chicago Press, Chicago.

Barro, Robert J. abd X. Sala-I-Martin (1995), Economic Growth, McGraw Hill, London.

Bhattarai Keshab R. (1997), Financial Deepening and Economic Development in Nepal:A Forward Looking CGE Model with Financial Intermediation, Ph.D. dissertation Northeastern University, Boston, Massachussetts.

Buehrer Timothy S. and F.di Mauro (1993), "A Computable General Equilibrium Model of Nepal", Manuscript.

Devarajan, Shantayanan, and J.D. Lewis (1990), "Policy Lessons from Trade Focused Two-Sector Models", *Journal of Policy Modeling* 12(4):625-657.

Dirkse and Ferris (1994), "A Pathsearch Damped Newton Method for Computing General Equilibria" Computer Science Department, University of Wisconsin, Wisconsin Madison.

Dixit Praveen M. (1995), Economic Reform in Nepal: A Cursory Assessment, Country Report No. 17, IRIS, 2105 Morrill Hall, College Park, MD 20742.

Elbers Chris (1992), Spatial Disaggregation in General Equilibrium Models: With an Application to the Nepalese Economy, Free University Press, Amsterdam.

Feltenstein, Andrew (1986), "An Intertemporal General Equilibrium Analysis of Financial Crowding Out", *Journal of Public Economics*, 31:1: 79-104.

Go Delfin S. (1993), "External Shocks, Adjustment Policies and Investment in a Developing Economy: Illustrations from a forward-looking CGE model of the Philippines" , *Journal of Development Economics* 44 229-261

King Robert G. and R. Levine (1993), "Finance and Growth: Schumpeter Might Be Right", *Quarterly Journal of Economics*, Aug., pp.717-737.

Leeper Eric M. and C.A. Sims, (1994), "Towards a Modern Macroeconomic Model Usable for Policy Analysis" in NBER *Macroeconomics Annual*, pp.81-139.

Lucas Robert (1988), "On the Mechanics of Economic Development", *Journal of Monetary Economics*, 22(1988) 3-42 North-Holland.

Mansur Ahsan and J. Whalley (1986), "Numerical Specification of Applied General Equilibrium Models: Estimation, Calibration and Data" in Scarf Herbert E and Shoven John B. Applied General Equilibrium Analysis, Cambridge University Press.

Maxwell Stamp (1992), "Assessing Development Options: A Computable General Equilibruim Framework For Nepal", A Report to the Asian Development Bank Manila.

McKinnon Ronald I. (1993), The order of Economic Liberalization: Financial Control in the Transition to a Market Economy, John Hopkins UP, Baltimore.

Mercenier Jean and T.N. Srinivasan ed. (1994), Applied General Equilibrium and Economic Development: Present Achievement and Future Trends, University of Michigan Press, Ann Arbor.

Mercenier Jean and P. Michel (1994), "Discrete-Time Finite Horizon Approximation of Infinite Horizon Optimization Problems with Steady-State Invariance" *Econometrica*, vol. 62, No. 3, May, 635-656.

Ministry of Finance (1994), Economy Survey, Kathmandu Nepal.

Nepal Rastra Bank (1988), Multi-Purpose Household Budget Survey: A Study on Income Distribution, Employment and Consumption Patterns in Nepal, Kathmandu, Nepal.

Pagano Marco (1993), "Financial Markets and Growth: An Overview", *European Economic Review*, 37(2-3,April) 613-622.

Rebelo Sergio, (1991), "Long-run Policy Analysis and Long-run Growth" *Journal of Political Economy*, Vol. 99, No.

Robinson Sherman (1991), "Macroeconomics, Financial Variables, and Computable General Equilibrium Models", *World Development*, vol. 19, no.11, pp.1509-1523, Pergamon Press plc.

Romer David (1996), Advanced Macro Economics, McGraw Hill.

Romer Paul M. (1986), "Capital Accumulation in the Theory of Long-Run Growth", in Barro Ed. Business Cycle Theory, Harvard University Press.

Rutherford Thomas F. (1995),"Extension of GAMS for Complementary Problems Arising in Applied Economic Analysis", Journal of Economic Dynamics and Control, 19, 1299-1324.

Scarf Herbert E and J.B. Shoven (1986), Applied General Equilibrium Analysis, CUP.

Shoven John B. and J. Whalley (1992), Applying General Equilibrium, CUP.

Shoven John B. and J. Whalley (1984), "Applied General-Equilibrium Models of Taxation and International Trade: An Introduction and Survey", *Journal of Economic Literature*, Vol. XXII, Sept, pp.1007-1051.

Taylor Lance ed. (1990), Socially Relevant Policy Analysis: Structuralist Computable General Equilibrium Models for the Developing World, MIT Press, Cambridge.

Whalley John (1985), Trade Liberalization Among Major World Trading Areas, MIT Press, Cambridge.

NOTES

1. (McKinnon 1(973), Taylor (1983), King and Levine (1993), Pagano (1993),.
2. The economic liberalization project started during 1992 represents a breakthrough towards consistent economic policy-making in Nepal. This was a reform package that included various reforms: on fiscal management, on external trade, on the financial system, on tax system, on industrial policy, privatization of public enterprises, and on institutional and legal frameworks. All these reforms were basically intended to increase the role of market forces in determining the allocation of resources in the economy. Therefore, the reform of the financial system and development of the capital market for more efficient mobilization of domestic resources received a high priority in the package.

3. The reform program was under the initiative of the Eighth Plan (1992-97) prepared by the National Planning Commission and Extended Structural Adjustment Facility of International Monetary Fund (IMF 1992, Dixit 1995a, MOF 1995).
4. Before the 1992 reforms, the Nepalese financial sector was characterized by ceilings on interest rates, credit controls, high reserve requirement, tight regulations on entry and exit of financial institutions, controls on foreign exchange, uncontrolled budgetary deficits and underdeveloped capital markets. The financial repression from all these features resulted in higher transaction costs for borrowers, and often negative rates of interest for savers. High subsidies on credits to selected sectors coexisted with higher interest rates for other sectors.
5. There exist a multi-regional multi-sectoral model of Nepalese economy (Elbers (1988)), foreign aid and economic development model (Bhattarai (1990)) and a trade model (Buehrer-Philippo (1993) works on Asian Development Bank's model and Maxwell Stamp's work on a general equilibrium model for Nepal) None of these study effects of financial liberalization and none of them take a forward-looking approach.
6. While the development of growth literature in the mainstream macroeconomics during the last decade has been encouraging application of these models in policy analysis has not been fully successful owing to the limited institutional structures and scant sectoral details in these models (Leeper and Sims (1994)).
7. Ramsey (1929), Koopmans (1957), Uzawa (1962,1964),Cass (1965), Ballard-Fullerton-Shoven-Whalley (1985), Charles Ballard (1983) Aurbach and Kotlikoff(1987), Goulder and Summers (1989) Fullerton and Rogers (1993) Go (1994)..
8. When $\sigma = 1$, $U(C_t) = \log C_t$.
9. From the fiscal year 1996/97 the government is adopting a value-added tax (VAT) system to replace sales and excise taxes imposed on consumers and producers. Given the self-enforcing mechanism of VAT against other indirect taxes are believed to reduce leakage of tax-revenues, though its implementation seem challenging if one considers illiteracy of 67 percent of population in the country. In ideal conditions revenue generated from VAT and taxes on the final product would be the same.
10. In the model number of sectors trading with India and rest of the world are seven and eight respectively.

APPENDIX
Nests in Production Technology and Trade

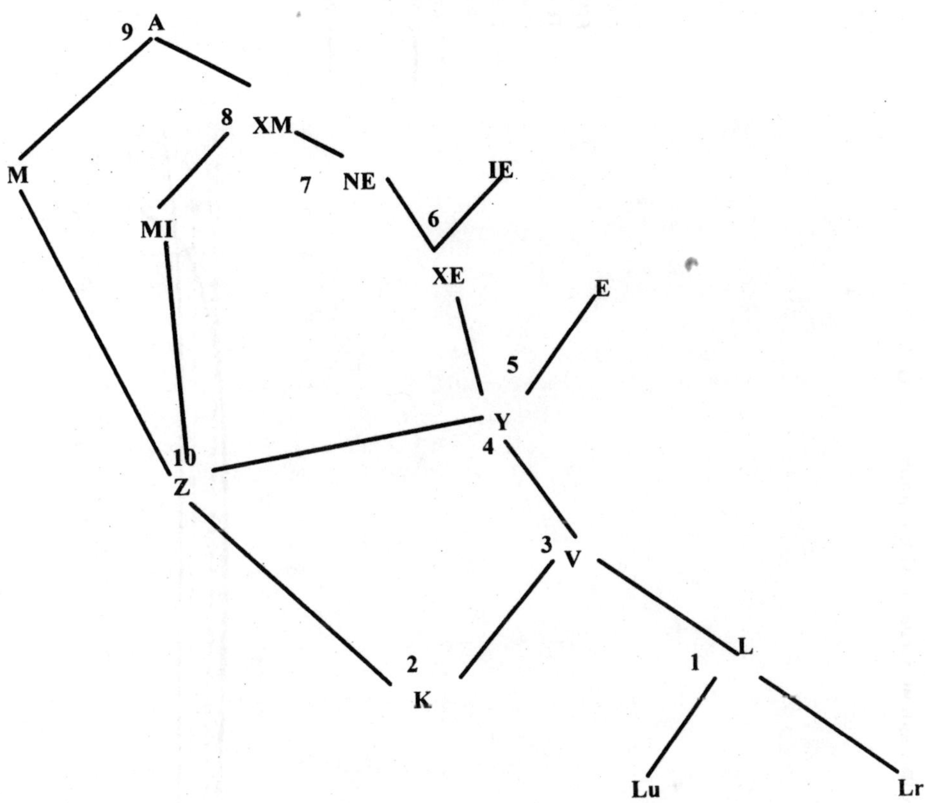

This diagram gives a graphical representation of the nested structure of production, trade and sales in the model Economy. The sectoral subscripts are suppressed here for simplicity. The meanings of nodes, noted 1 to 10, are as following: (1) CES composite labor from skilled and unskilled labor (L);

(2) capital accumulation and capital allocation functions (K), (3) value added function (V); (4) Leontief function between value added and intermediate inputs (Y), (5) Constant elasticity of transformation (CET) export function between the Nepalese markets and the other economies (E,Y,XE) (6) Constant elasticity of transformation export (CET) function between domestic sales and exports to India (IE, XE, NE) (7) Constant elasticity of substitution (CES) function between domestically supplied goods and imports from India (MI, XM, NE) (8) Constant elasticity of substitution (CES) between the Nepal-India market and the other economies (M, A, XM); (9) Total absorption in the economy (A); (10) Intermediate inputs (Z).

Figure 1
Investment Index in Capflow Scenario with Complete Liberalization

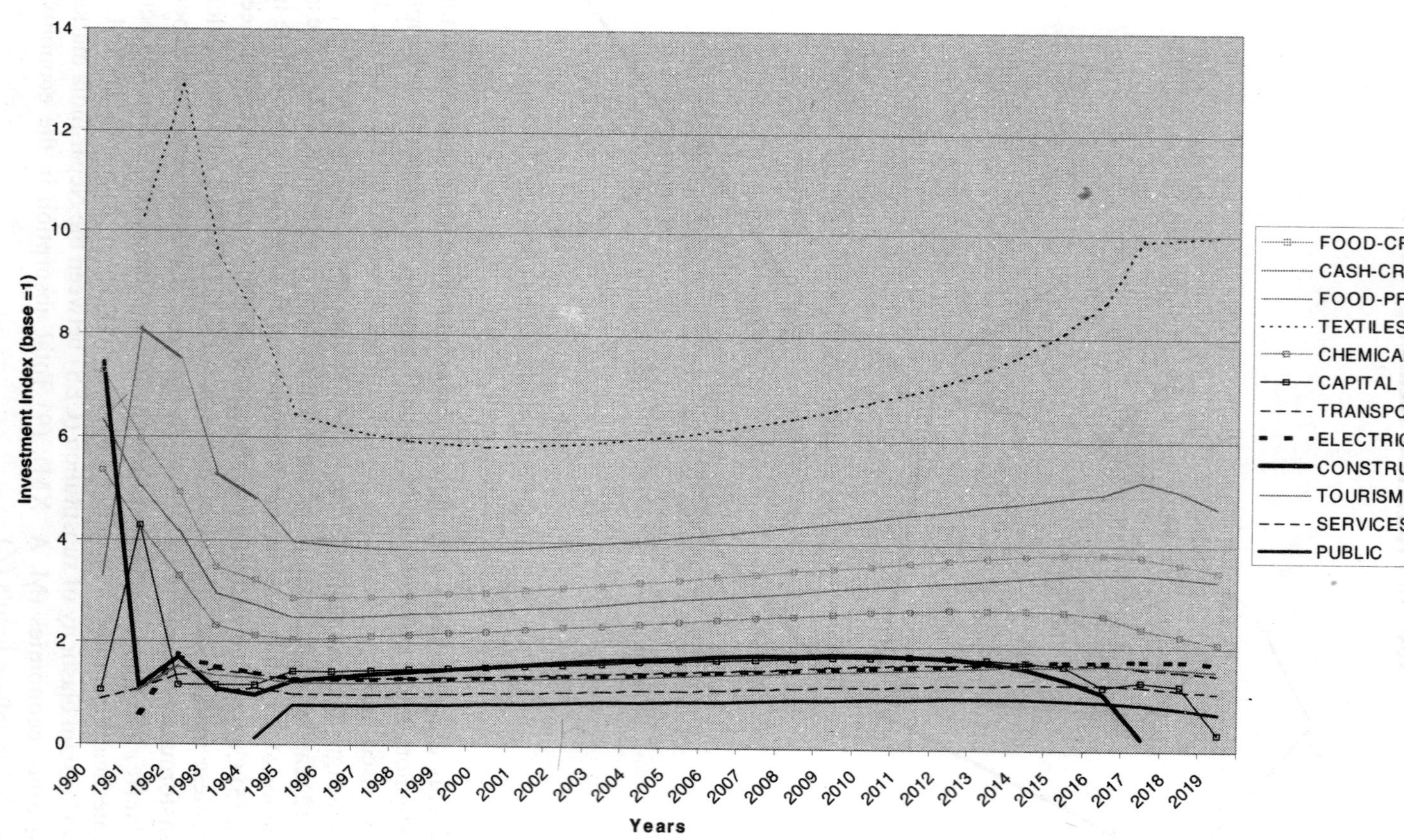

Figure 2
Path of Output Caplow Scenario with Complete Liberalization

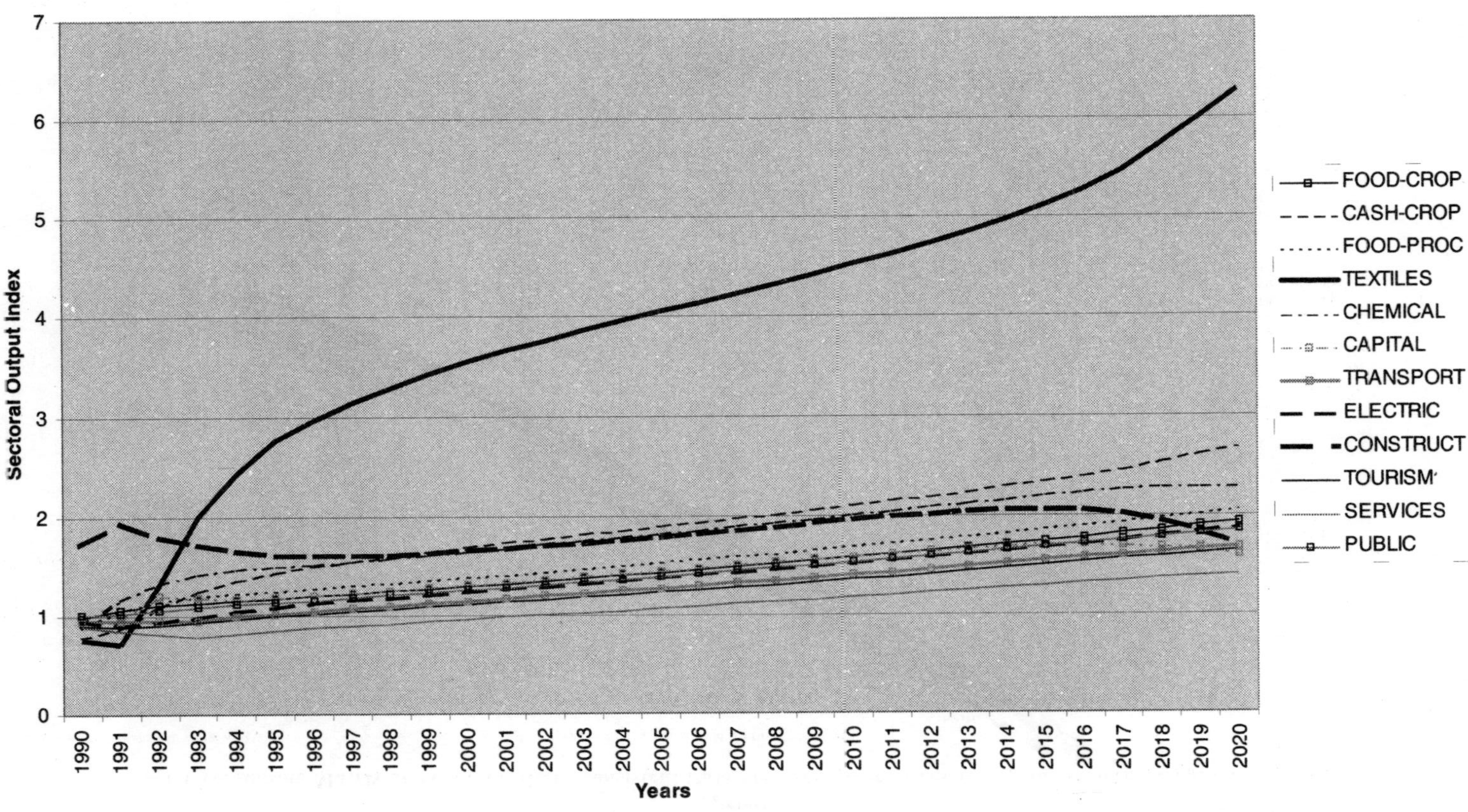

Appendix 1

Social Accounting Matrix of Nepal for Micro-consistent Data Set Used for the Benchmark and Reference Path of the Model

Appendix IV: Nepal SAM 1990/91

		Activities				Activities				Activities				
		Food-Crop	Cash-Crop	Agro-Process	Textiles	Chemicals	Capital Goods	Transport	Electricity/W	Construction	Hotels and R	Other Service	Public Services	Food-Crop
	Food-Crop													52524.732
A	Cash-Crop													
C	Agro-Processing													
T	Textiles													
I	Chemicals													
V	Capital Goods													
I	Transport													
T	Electricity/W/G													
I	Construction													
E	Hotels and Rest													
S	Other Services													
	Public Services													
	Food-Crop	5319.847	1011.540	3762.978	0.000	0.000	0.000	0.000	0.000	0.000	1170.105	6.384	0.000	
C	Cash-Crop	5648.229	314.546	347.228	4013.569	2691.578	1738.541	1.194	0.000	264.234	0.000	294.285	0.000	
O	Agro-Process	0.000	4.879	2.833	1.986	60.261	6.696	35.898	0.263	0.000	48.868	27.940	783.223	
M	Textiles	0.000	2.195	0.683	107.094	,11.928	6.708	51.078	0.390	0.000	0.057	112.593	130.203	
M	Chemicals	24.254	12.992	6.127	29.677	172.329	45.050	159.896	9.603	2380.971	56.580	652.633	297.229	
O	Capital Goods	21.930	3.406	1.341	8.933	10.325	343.970	158.506	11.684	2352.431	0.000	3056.319	515.039	
D	Transport	550.367	143.483	26.304	133.132	100.105	85.416	2505.014	9.550	236.548	267.801	4617.214	2044.980	
I	Electricity/W	0.360	3.103	4.972	50.936	68.010	25.623	156.672	8.919	0.572	103.705	171.044	26.561	
T	Construction	0.000	0.000	0.000	0.000	0.000	0.000	0.000	0.000	0.000	0.000	0.000	0.000	
I	Hotels and R	0.000	0.425	0.156	0.562	1.419	1.440	241.359	0.254	0.523	30.976	115.438	83.410	
E	Other Service	598.829	99.996	6.934	98.362	98.081	50.306	4224.293	175.279	740.709	160.301	6711.432	925.660	
S	Public Service	0.000	0.000	3.135	143.826	54.927	454.141	0.000	0.000	230.276	0.000	0.000	0.000	
	Lab-Rural	10170.876	4400.109	419.027	406.733	639.521	94.589	2387.523	0.152	4815.254	84.991	974.731	5105.196	
Factors	Lab-Urban	699.382	104.336	153.535	683.136	170.218	164.555	270.712	283.535	737.678	347.908	1794.524	1459.128	
	Capital	30124.091	10344.205	3754.409	2050.871	1846.226	1004.180	2087.765	584.312	1663.069	839.100	7628.745	1.677	
	Urban													
Households	Rural													
	Toursists													
	Government	196.153	177.020	415.791	495.265	282.318	347.535	57.181	-14.681	6.825	3.306	657.587	0.000	0.000
Capital Acco	Phys. Cap.													
	Stocks													
External	India													906.736
	Row													112.047
Total		53354.318	16622.235	8905.453	8224.082	6207.246	4368.750	12337.091	1069.260	13429.090	3113.698	26820.869	11372.306	53543.515

source: ADB SAM for Savings and Economic Survey Tables 6.6, 7.3, 7.1, 7.5, 8.10 and 8.11

Table 6.6: Foreign exchange reserve of banks; Table 7.1: Currency holding

Table 7.3: Total deposit; Table 8.10: Foreign Debt; Table 8.11: Internal Borrowing of Govt

Table 7.5 For assets of other financial institutions.

Social Accounting Matrix of Nepal for Micro-consistent Data Set Used for the Benchmark and Reference Path of the Model

	Commodities				Commodities			Appendix IV: Nepal SAM 1990-91	Factors				Households		
Capital Good	Transport	Electricity/W	Construction	Hotels and R	Other Service	Public Services		Lab-Rural	Lab-Urban	Capital		Urban	Rural	Toursists	Government
															-8.657
															-6.253
															-3.253
															-58.870
															-0.354
4262.163															-1.112
	12337.092														
		1066.160													
			13429.089												
				3113.699											
					25057.631										
						11372.305									
												2902.316	38787.425		
												413.141	3036.367		
												1110.546	9081.676		
												437.612	4754.927	232.874	
												662.899	5701.840		
												544.646	5652.421	236.502	
												268.546	1209.435	139.197	
												43.064	416.192		
												0.000	0.000		
												137.115	658.408	1842.212	
												4052.828	8078.595	847.715	
															10486.000
									6337.347	7952.422					
								29498.703		48485.356					
2528.444									531.300	663.200		312.731	1664.969	289.100	
										4827.671		2295.024	1070.105		11977.342
2432.801		13.574			1016.896										
8506.668					895.911							1965.800			1086.500
17730.076	12337.092	1079.734	13429.089	3113.699	26970.438	11372.305		29498.703	6868.647	61928.649		15146.268	80112.360	3587.600	23471.343

APPENDIX 2

GAMS/MPSGE Program to Compute the Dynamic General Equilibrium Model of Nepal

```
$TITLE An Intertemporal CGE Model for Nepal — ref case w/ capital flows

    SET     MDL Alternative models /CAPFLOW, BOPCON, NONSS, BLKHOLE/;
    SET     TP /1990*2025/, TFIRST(TP) /1990/, TLAST(TP), HORIZON(TP);
    SET     SC Two of the scenarios /PARTIAL, COMPLETE/;

    SCALAR  CAPFLOW Switch for free capital flows            /1/,
            BLKHOLE Switch for rent-seeking losses           /1/,
            NONSS Switch for non-steadystate growth path     /0/,
            DEBUG Switch for benchmark replication           /0/;

$INCLUDE scenario

    *   Set switches for alternative model structures:

    IF (STRUCT("CAPFLOW"),
         BLKHOLE = 0;
         NONSS = 0;
         CAPFLOW = 1;
    );
    IF (STRUCT("BOPCON"),
         BLKHOLE = 0;
         NONSS = 0;
         CAPFLOW = 0;
    );
    IF (STRUCT("BLKHOLE"),
     BLKHOLE = 1;
         NONSS = 0;
         CAPFLOW = 1;
    );
    IF (STRUCT("NONSS"),
         BLKHOLE = 0;
         NONSS = 1;
         CAPFLOW = 1;
    );

    SCALAR BOPCON Switch for period by period capital flow constraints;
    BOPCON = 1 - CAPFLOW;

    $INCLUDE nepaldat.gms

    *   Initialize as though we are solving the entire horizon
    *   in one shot:

    SCALAR      G          POTENTIAL GROWTH RATE /0.02/
         NR     NET INTEREST RATE          /0.05/
         DEPR   DEPRECIATION RATE          /0.07/
         GOVFX  Government foreign exchange balance
         GOVEXP Government net income;
```

```
SET URBAN(HH) /URBAN/;

PARAMETER QREF(TP)          STEADY STATE QUANTITY INDEX
          PREF(TP)          PRESENT VALUE PRICE
          QLAND(TP)         GROWTH RATE OF ARABLE LAND
          QLABOR(LC,TP)     GROWTH RATE OF LABOR
          YEAR(TP)          YEAR ASSOCIATED WITH PERIOD TP
          INCBAL(*)         CHECK OF INCOME BALANCE
          I0(J)             BASE YEAR INVESTMENT BY SECTOR
          LAND(I)           LAND INPUTS
          VKCHK(I,*)        CAPITAL VALUE CROSS-CHECKS
          TAU(I)            CALIBRATED SPREAD IN CAPITAL RENTS,
          RK0(*)            BASE YEAR USER COST OF CAPITAL
          K0(I)             BASE YEAR CAPITAL STOCK
          FXCHK             CROSS CHECK OF FOREIGN EXCHANGE

          W0(HH)            REFERENCE CONSUMPTION LEVEL
          THETA(HH)         HOUSEHOLD SHARE OF GOVERNMENT
                            INCOME&EXPENSE
          KSHR(HH)          HOUSEHOLD SHARE OF INITIAL CAPITAL
          LSHR(HH)          HOUSEHOLD SHARE OF LAND
          EXOGFX(TP,HH)     EXOGENOUS FOREIGN INCOME
          INCADJ(HH)        INTER-HOUSEHOLD TRANSFERS
          BOPDEF            BASE YEAR FOREIGN EXCHANGE DEFICIT

          ESUBT(HH)         INTERTEMPORAL ELASTICITY OF SUBSTITUTION
                            / RURAL 0.25, URBAN 0.5 /;
*     Set up the time horizon:

YEAR(TP) = 1990 + (ORD(TP)-1);
LOOP(TARGET, HORIZON(TP) = YES$(YEAR(TP) LE YEAR(TARGET)) );
TLAST(TP) = YES$(ORD(TP) EQ CARD(HORIZON));

*     Check income balances in the base year data:

INCBAL(HH) = SUM(I,D0(I,HH)) + SAVING(HH) -
    ( ENDOW("L",HH)
    + ENDOW("K",HH)
    + SUM(R,ER(R)*(REMIT(R,HH)-FTRN(HH,R)))
    - ER("ROW")*LOANS(HH)
    - TAXREV(HH) );

INCBAL("GOVT") = SUM(I,D0(I,"GOVT")) + SAVING("GOVT") - (
          SUM((I,R), X0(I,R) * TX(I,R))
        + SUM((I,R), M0(I,R) * TM(I,R))
        + SUM(I, D0(I,"TOURIST") * TTR)
        + SUM(J, Y0(J)*TI(J))
        + SUM(HH, TAXREV(HH))
        + SUM(LC,INCTAX(LC))
        + TAXREV("CORP")
        + FSAV
        + ER("ROW")*(LOANS("AID")-LOANS("GOVT"))
        + ER("INDIA")*LOANS("REFUND")
        - SUM(I,D0(I,"STOCK")) );
```

```
DISPLAY INCBAL;

*   Move non-capital inputs from the investment demand to the stock
*   change vector:

SET IK(I)     Capital formation goods /CAPITAL, CONSTRUCT/;

D0(I,"STOCK") = D0(I,"STOCK") + SUM(J,IMA(I,J))$(NOT IK(I));
IMA(I,J)$(NOT IK(I)) = 0;
I0(J) = SUM(I, IMA(I,J));

*   Extract land rents from capital income in the agricultural
*   sectors:

SET IAGR(I) Agricultural goods /FOOD-CROP,CASH-CROP,FOOD-PROC/;
LAND(IAGR) = VK0(IAGR) - I0(IAGR) / 0.3;
VK0(IAGR) = VK0(IAGR) - LAND(IAGR);
DISPLAY LAND;

*   Report statistics on the rates of return to capital and land, etc:

VKCHK(I,"KVS") = (PROFIT(I)+SUPPLY(I,"DEP")) /
                 (LAND(I) + PROFIT(I)+SUPPLY(I,"DEP") + SUM(LC,WAG(I,LC)));
VKCHK(I,"LAND") = LAND(I) /
                 (LAND(I) + PROFIT(I)+SUPPLY(I,"DEP") + SUM(LC,WAG(I,LC)));
VKCHK(I,"PROFITSHR") = PROFIT(I)/VK0(I);
VKCHK(I,"IKRATIO") = I0(I) / VK0(I);

*   Calibrate the spread from the base year investment, growth,
*   depreciation, interest rate and capital rents:

TAU(I) = 1 - (DEPR + NR/(1-NR))*I0(I)/((DEPR+G)*VK0(I));
RK0("RISKLESS") = NR/(1-NR) + DEPR;
RK0(I) = ( NR/(1-NR) + DEPR ) / (1-TAU(I));
K0(I) = VK0(I) / RK0(I);

DISPLAY RK0;

*   Reporting capital-output ratio:

VKCHK(I,"KYRATIO") = K0(I) / Y0(I);
VKCHK(I,"TAU") = TAU(I);
DISPLAY VKCHK;

*   Steady state growth path quantity and price indices:

QREF(TP) = (1+G)**(ORD(TP)-1);
PREF(TP) = (1-NR)**(ORD(TP)-1);
QLAND(TP) = QREF(TP);
QLABOR(LC,TP) = QREF(TP);

DISPLAY QREF,PREF;

*   Calibrated foreign exchange flows (the whole economy):
```

```
BOPDEF =
    FSAV
    + SUM(R, TY(R))
    + ER("ROW")              * LOANS("GOVT")
    + ER("ROW")              * LOANS("AID")
    + ER("INDIA")            * LOANS("REFUND")
    + ER("ROW")              * SUM(HH, LOANS(HH))
    + SUM((HH,R), ER(R) * REMIT(R,HH))
    - SUM((HH,R), ER(R) * FTRN(HH,R));

FXCHK = BOPDEF - SUM((I,R), M0(I,R)-X0(I,R));
DISPLAY FXCHK;

$ONTEXT

$MODEL:NEPAL

$SECTORS:
    W(HH)                               ! Welfare index
    Y(I,TP)$HORIZON(TP)                 ! PRODUCTION
    K(I,TP)$HORIZON(TP)                 ! CAPITAL
    INV(I,TP)$HORIZON(TP)               ! INVESTMENT
    X(I,TP)$(VX0(I)$HORIZON(TP))        ! EXPORT
    A(I,TP)$HORIZON(TP)                 ! ARMINGTON AGGREGATION
    GOV(TP)$HORIZON(TP)                 ! GOVERNMENT OUTPUT
    U(HH,TP)$HORIZON(TP)                ! UTILITY INDEX
    T(TP)$HORIZON(TP)                   ! PROVISION OF TOURISM

$COMMODITIES:
    P(I,TP)$HORIZON(TP)                 ! SUPPLY PRICE
    PD(I,TP)$HORIZON(TP)                ! DOMESTIC OUTPUT PRICE
    PX(I,TP)$(VX0(I)$HORIZON(TP))       ! EXPORT PRICE AGGREGATE
    RK(I,TP)$HORIZON(TP)                ! CAPITAL RENTAL RATE
    PK(I,TP)$HORIZON(TP)                ! CAPITAL PRICE
    PL(LC,TP)$HORIZON(TP)               ! WAGE RATE
    PLAND(TP)$HORIZON(TP)               ! RENTAL RATE ON LAND
    PG(TP)$HORIZON(TP)                  ! GOVERNMENT OUTPUT
    PT(TP)$HORIZON(TP)                  ! TOURSIST PRICE
    PR(TP)$HORIZON(TP)                  ! PRICE INDEX FOR GOVERNMENT
                                        TRANSFER
    PU(HH,TP)$HORIZON(TP)               ! CONSUMPTION PRICE
    PW(HH)                              ! Welfare price index
    PTK(I)                              ! TERMINAL INVESMENT PREMIUM
    PVPFX$CAPFLOW                       ! PRESENT VALUE EXCHANGE RATE
    PFX(TP)$(BOPCON$HORIZON(TP))        ! PRESENT VALUE EXCHANGE RATE

$CONSUMERS:
    TOURIST(TP)$HORIZON(TP)             ! TOURISM DEMAND
    GOVT(TP)$HORIZON(TP)                ! GOVERNMENT
    RA(HH)                              ! REPRESENTATIVE AGENT
    FININT(TP)$(BLKHOLE$HORIZON(TP)) ! FINANCIAL INTERMEDIATION COST

$AUXILIARY:
    TK(I)                               ! TERMINAL CAPITAL DEMAND
```

```
$PROD:Y(I,TP)$HORIZON(TP) s:0 t:ETRNDX(I) VA:1 L(VA):3
     O:PD(I,TP)          Q:(Y0(I)-VX0(I)) A:GOVT(TP) T:TI(I)
     O:PX(I,TP)          Q:VX0(I)  A:GOVT(TP) T:TI(I)
     I:P(J,TP)           Q:IOF(J,I)
     I:PL(LC,TP)         Q:WAG(I,LC)        L:
     I:PLAND(TP)         Q:LAND(I)          VA:
     I:RK(I,TP)          Q:K0(I) P:RK0(I)   VA:

$PROD:K(I,TP)$HORIZON(TP+1) s:0
     O:RK(I,TP)          Q:K0(I)
+              A:RA("URBAN")$(NOT BLKHOLE) A:FININT(TP)$BLKHOLE T:TAU(I)
     O:PK(I,TP+1)        Q:(K0(I)*(1-DEPR))
     I:PK(I,TP)          Q:K0(I)

$PROD:K(I,TP)$TLAST(TP) s:0
     O:RK(I,TP)          Q:K0(I)
+              A:RA("URBAN")$(NOT BLKHOLE) A:FININT(TP)$BLKHOLE T:TAU(I)
     O:PTK(I)            Q:(K0(I)*(1-DEPR))
     I:PK(I,TP)          Q:K0(I)

$PROD:INV(I,TP)$HORIZON(TP+1) s:0
     O:PK(I,TP+1)        Q:I0(I)
     I:P(J,TP)           Q:IMA(J,I)

$PROD:INV(I,TP)$TLAST(TP) s:0
     O:PTK(I)            Q:I0(I)
     I:P(J,TP)           Q:IMA(J,I)

*    EXPORT ACTIVITY — THIS IS A CET COMPOSITE OUTPUT OVER
*    FLOWS TO DIFFERENT TRADING PARTNERS.

$PROD:X(I,TP)$(VX0(I)$HORIZON(TP)) t:ETRNXX(I) O:PVPFX#(R)$CAPFLOW
+    Q:(X0(I,R)*PREF(TP)) P:(PX0(I,R)/PREF(TP)) A:GOVT(TP) T:TX(I,R)
 O:PFX(TP)#(R)$BOPCON Q:X0(I,R) P:PX0(I,R) A:GOVT(TP) T:TX(I,R)
 I:PX(I,TP)     Q:VX0(I)

*    ARMINGTON SUPPLY AGGREGATES DOMESTIC AND IMPORTED GOODS.
*    LIKE EXPORTS, HERE WE HAVE ONE IMPORT COEFFICIENT FOR EACH
*    REGION R.

$PROD:A(I,TP)$HORIZON(TP) s:SIGMADM(I) m:SIGMAMM(I)
 O:P(I,TP)      Q:S0(I)
 I:PD(I,TP)     Q:(Y0(I)-VX0(I))
 I:PVPFX#(R)$CAPFLOW
+    Q:(M0(I,R)*PREF(TP)) P:(PM0(I,R)/PREF(TP)) A:GOVT(TP) T:TM(I,R) m:
 I:PFX(TP)#(R)$BOPCON Q:M0(I,R) P:PM0(I,R) A:GOVT(TP) T:TM(I,R) m:

$PROD:GOV(TP)$HORIZON(TP)
     O:PG(TP)Q:(SUM(I,D0(I,"GOVT")))
     I:P(I,TP)  Q:D0(I,"GOVT")

$PROD:U(HH,TP)$HORIZON(TP) s:1
     O:PU(HH,TP)         Q:(SUM(I,D0(I,HH)))
     I:P(I,TP)  Q:D0(I,HH)
```

```
$PROD:W(HH) s:ESUBT(HH)
     O:PW(HH)            Q:W0(HH)
     I:PU(HH,TP)$HORIZON(TP) Q:(QREF(TP)*SUM(I,D0(I,HH))) P:PREF(TP)

$PROD:T(TP)$HORIZON(TP)
     O:PT(TP)            Q:(SUM(I,D0(I,"TOURIST"))+TAXREV("TOURIST"))
     I:P(I,TP)           Q:D0(I,"TOURIST") A:GOVT(TP) T:TTR

$DEMAND:FININT(TP)$(BLKHOLE$HORIZON(TP))
     D:PFX(TP)$BOPCON
     D:PVPFX$CAPFLOW

$DEMAND:TOURIST(TP)$HORIZON(TP)
     E:PVPFX$CAPFLOW          Q:(PREF(TP)*QREF(TP)*SUM(R, TY(R)))
     E:PFX(TP)$BOPCON         Q:(QREF(TP)*SUM(R, TY(R)))
     D:PT(TP)                 Q:(QREF(TP) * SUM(R, TY(R)))

$DEMAND:GOVT(TP)$HORIZON(TP)
     E:PVPFX$CAPFLOW          Q:(QREF(TP)*PREF(TP)*GOVFX)
     E:PFX(TP)$BOPCON         Q:(QREF(TP)*GOVFX)
     E:P(I,TP)                Q:(-QREF(TP)*D0(I,"STOCK"))
     E:PL(HH,TP)              Q:(QLABOR(HH,TP)*(TAXREV(HH)+INCTAX(HH)))
     D:PR(TP)                 Q:(QREF(TP)*GOVEXP)

$DEMAND:RA(HH)
     E:PFX(TP)$((BLKHOLE*BOPCON)$HORIZON(TP)$URBAN(HH))
  +  Q:(SUM(I,                TAU(I)*K0(I)*RK0(I)*QREF(TP)))
     E:PVPFX$((BLKHOLE*CAPFLOW)$URBAN(HH))
  +  Q:(SUM((I,TP)$HORIZON(TP),TAU(I)*K0(I)*RK0(I)*QREF(TP)*PREF(TP)))
     E:PW("URBAN")            Q:INCADJ(HH)
     E:PVPFX$CAPFLOW          Q : ( S U M ( T P $ H O R I Z O N ( T P ) ,
PREF(TP)*EXOGFX(TP,HH)))
     E:PFX(TP)$BOPCON         Q:EXOGFX(TP,HH)
     E:PR(TP)$HORIZON(TP)     Q:(QREF(TP)*GOVEXP*THETA(HH))
     E:PL(HH,TP)$HORIZON(TP)Q:(QLABOR(HH,TP)*(ENDOW("L",HH)-
TAXREV(HH)))
     E:PLAND(TP)$HORIZON(TP)
Q:(QLAND(TP)*SUM(I,LAND(I))*LSHR(HH))
     E:PK(I,TFIRST)           Q:(K0(I)*KSHR(HH))
     E:PG(TP)$HORIZON(TP)     Q:(-QREF(TP)*SUM(I,D0(I,"GOVT"))*THETA(HH))
     E:PTK(I)                 Q:(-K0(I)*KSHR(HH))         R:TK(I)
     D:PW(HH)                 Q:W0(HH)

$CONSTRAINT:TK(I)
     PTK(I)*I0(I) =E= SUM((J,TLAST), P(J,TLAST)*IMA(J,I));

$OFFTEXT
$SYSINCLUDE mpsgeset NEPAL

P.L(I,TP)              = PREF(TP);
PFX.L(TP)              = PREF(TP);
PD.L(I,TP)             = PREF(TP);
PX.L(I,TP)$VX0(I)      = PREF(TP);
RK.L(I,TP)             = PREF(TP)*RK0(I);
```

```
PK.L(I,TP)              = PREF(TP)/(1-NR);
PL.L(LC,TP)             = PREF(TP);
PLAND.L(TP)             = PREF(TP);
PG.L(TP)                = PREF(TP);
PT.L(TP)                = PREF(TP);
PU.L(HH,TP)             = PREF(TP);
PR.L(TP)                = PREF(TP);

Y.L(I,TP)               = QREF(TP);
K.L(I,TP)               = QREF(TP);
INV.L(I,TP)             = QREF(TP);
X.L(I,TP)$VX0(I)        = QREF(TP);
A.L(I,TP)               = QREF(TP);
GOV.L(TP)               = QREF(TP);
U.L(HH,TP)              = QREF(TP);
T.L(TP)                 = QREF(TP);

*   Allocate 20 megabytes of workspace for the solver:

NEPAL.WORKSPACE = 10;
NEPAL.OPTFILE = 1;

*   Set price distortion levels:

TLAST(TP) = YES$(ORD(TP) EQ CARD(HORIZON));

DISPLAY HORIZON, TLAST, TAU;

PTK.L(I)    = SUM(TLAST, PK.L(I,TLAST)*(1-NR));
TK.L(I) = (1+G)*SUM(TLAST,QREF(TLAST));

W0(HH) = SUM(TP$HORIZON(TP),PREF(TP)*QREF(TP)*SUM(I,D0(I,HH)));

GOVFX =     FSAV + ER("ROW")            * LOANS("GOVT")
            + ER("ROW")                 * LOANS("AID")
            + ER("INDIA")               * LOANS("REFUND");

GOVEXP = GOVFX - SUM((I), D0(I,"STOCK"))
            + SUM(HH, TAXREV(HH)+INCTAX(HH))
            + SUM(I, D0(I,"TOURIST")*TTR)
            + SUM((I,R), M0(I,R)*TM(I,R))
            + SUM((I,R), X0(I,R)*TX(I,R))
            + SUM(I, Y0(I) *TI(I));

EXOGFX(TP,HH) = QREF(TP) * (
                        + ER("ROW") * LOANS(HH)
                        + SUM(R, ER(R) * REMIT(R,HH))
                        - SUM(R, ER(R) * FTRN(HH,R) ) );

THETA(HH) = SAVING(HH) / SUM(H, SAVING(H));

KSHR(HH) = ENDOW("K",HH) / SUM(H, ENDOW("K",H));

LSHR("RURAL") = 1;
```

```
INCADJ(HH) =
     PW.L(HH)*W0(HH)
     + SUM(I, PTK.L(I)*(K0(I)*KSHR(HH))*TK.L(I))
     + SUM(TP$HORIZON(TP), PG.L(TP) *QREF(TP)*SUM(I,D0(I,"GOVT"))
     *THETA(HH))
     - SUM(TP$HORIZON(TP), PREF(TP)*EXOGFX(TP,HH))
     - SUM(TP$HORIZON(TP), QREF(TP) * (
               PR.L(TP)          * GOVEXP*THETA(HH)
               + PL.L(HH,TP)     * (ENDOW("L",HH)-TAXREV(HH))
               + PLAND.L(TP)     * SUM(I,LAND(I))*LSHR(HH) ))
     - SUM((I,TFIRST), PK.L(I,TFIRST)*(K0(I)*KSHR(HH)));

INCADJ("URBAN") = INCADJ("URBAN")
     - SUM((I,TP)$HORIZON(TP), K0(I)*K.L(I,TP)*RK.L(I,TP)*TAU(I));
DISPLAY INCADJ;

*    Work with a non-steady state baseline:
*    Assume that arable land grows at 1/3 the growth rate of other
*    factors, and urban labor grows at twice the underlying growth
*    rate:

IF (NONSS,
     QLAND(TP) = (1+G/3)**(ORD(TP)-1);
     QLABOR("URBAN",TP) = (1+2*G)**(ORD(TP)-1);
);

IF (DEBUG,

 NEPAL.ITERLIM = 0;
$INCLUDE NEPAL.GEN
 SOLVE NEPAL USING MCP;

ELSE

 TAU(I)$SCENARIO(I) = 0;
 TAU(I)$SCENARIO("PARTIAL") = TAU(I) / 2;
 TAU(I)$SCENARIO("COMPLETE") = 0;
$INCLUDE NEPAL.GEN
 SOLVE NEPAL USING MCP;
);
PARAMETER
SOLUTION ACTIVITY LEVELS AND FUTURE VALUE PRICES (% CHANGE FROM
BASELINE);

*    Record all the activity levels from this solution:

SOLUTION("L",TLAST,TP,I,"Y",STRUCT,SCENARIO)$HORIZON(TP)
     = ROUND(100 * (Y.L(I,TP)-QREF(TP))/QREF(TP), 1);
SOLUTION("L",TLAST,TP,I,"K",STRUCT,SCENARIO)$HORIZON(TP)
     = ROUND(100 * (K.L(I,TP)-QREF(TP))/QREF(TP), 1);
SOLUTION("L",TLAST,TP,I,"INV",STRUCT,SCENARIO)$HORIZON(TP)
     = ROUND(100 * (INV.L(I,TP)-QREF(TP))/QREF(TP), 1);
SOLUTION("L",TLAST,TP,I,"X",STRUCT,SCENARIO)$(VX0(I)$HORIZON(TP))
     = ROUND(100 * (X.L(I,TP)-QREF(TP))/QREF(TP), 1);
```

```
SOLUTION("L",TLAST,TP,I,"A",STRUCT,SCENARIO)$HORIZON(TP)
    = ROUND(100 * (X.L(I,TP)-QREF(TP))/QREF(TP), 1);
SOLUTION("L",TLAST,TP,HH,"U",STRUCT,SCENARIO)$HORIZON(TP)
    = ROUND(100 * (U.L(HH,TP)-QREF(TP))/QREF(TP), 1);
SOLUTION("L",TLAST,TP,"x","T",STRUCT,SCENARIO)$HORIZON(TP)
    = ROUND(100 * (T.L(TP)-QREF(TP))/QREF(TP), 1);

PARAMETER PNUM(TP) NUMERAIRE PRICE INDEX (RURAL CONSUMPTION
BASKET);
PNUM(TP) = PU.L("RURAL",TP);

*    Record all the prices from this solution:

SOLUTION("P",TLAST,TP,I,"P",STRUCT,SCENARIO)$HORIZON(TP) =
    ROUND(100 * ( P.L(I,TP) / PNUM(TP) - 1), 1);
SOLUTION("P",TLAST,TP,I,"PD",STRUCT,SCENARIO)$HORIZON(TP) =
    ROUND(100 * ( PD.L(I,TP) / PNUM(TP) - 1), 1);
SOLUTION("P",TLAST,TP,I,"PX",STRUCT,SCENARIO)$(VX0(I)$HORIZON(TP))
    = ROUND(100 * ( PX.L(I,TP) / PNUM(TP) - 1), 1);
SOLUTION("P",TLAST,TP,I,"RK",STRUCT,SCENARIO)$HORIZON(TP) =
    ROUND(100 * ( RK.L(I,TP) / PNUM(TP) - 1), 1);
SOLUTION("P",TLAST,TP,I,"PK",STRUCT,SCENARIO)$HORIZON(TP) =
    ROUND(100 * ( PK.L(I,TP) / PNUM(TP) - 1), 1);
SOLUTION("P",TLAST,TP,LC,"PL",STRUCT,SCENARIO)$HORIZON(TP) =
    ROUND(100 * ( PL.L(LC,TP) / PNUM(TP) - 1), 1);
SOLUTION("P",TLAST,TP,HH,"PU",STRUCT,SCENARIO)$HORIZON(TP) =
    ROUND(100 * ( PU.L(HH,TP) / PNUM(TP) - 1), 1);
SOLUTION("P",TLAST,TP,"x","PLAND",STRUCT,SCENARIO)$HORIZON(TP) =
    ROUND(100 * ( PLAND.L(TP) / PNUM(TP) - 1), 1);
SOLUTION("P",TLAST,TP,"x","PT",STRUCT,SCENARIO)$HORIZON(TP) =
    ROUND(100 * ( PT.L(TP) / PNUM(TP) - 1), 1);
SOLUTION("P",TLAST,TP,"x","PG",STRUCT,SCENARIO)$HORIZON(TP) =
    ROUND(100 * ( PG.L(TP) / PNUM(TP) - 1), 1);
SOLUTION("P",TLAST,TP,"x","PFX",STRUCT,SCENARIO)$(BOPCON$HORIZON(TP))
    = ROUND(100 * ( PFX.L(TP) / PNUM(TP) - 1), 1);

*    Save the activity levels and prices in the solution file so
*    that they may be retrieve to the PC:

PUT KSOL '$offlisting'/;
$BATINCLUDE gams2txt SOLUTION
DISPLAY SOLUTION;
```

APPENDIX 3

```
$STITLE 1990/91 Base Year Data for Nepal (nepaldat.gms)

SET
    F Primary factors /L, K/,

    I Sectors /
            FOOD-CROP Agricultural food crops
            CASH-CROP Agricultural cash crops
            FOOD-PROC Food processing
            TEXTILES Textile goods
            CHEMICAL Chemical and minerals
            CAPITAL Metal products
            TRANSPORT Transport
            ELECTRIC Electricity
            CONSTRUCT Construction
            TOURISM Tourism and distribution
            SERVICES Private services
            PUBLIC Public services /

HH Households and labor categories /RURAL, URBAN /,
R Trading partners /INDIA, ROW/;

ALIAS (I,J), (LC,HH), (H,HH);

PARAMETER

ER(R) Base year exchange rates
            / INDIA 1.68
            ROW 49.78 /

INCTAX(HH) Income tax payments ('91 million Nepal Rs) /
            URBAN 855.1 /

TAXREV(*) Tax revenue ('91 million Nepal Rs) /
            URBAN 312.7
            RURAL 1664.9
            CORP 663.2
            TOURIST 289.1 /

TY0(R) Gross tourist income ('91 million Nepal rs) /
            INDIA 1593.8
            ROW 1993.8 /


LOANS Financial flows associated with various loans /

*     Foreign aid income and loans M. US$
            AID 295.5

*     Govt payments on foreign loans M.US$
            GOVT 31.5
```

```
*     Private payments on foreign loans M.US$
              URBAN 44.6

*     Indian exise tax refund (million Indian Rs)
              REFUND 448.7

*     Loans to government from private sector M.RP
              LOAN 154.3 /

      FTRN(HH,R) Payments by households to foreigners M.US$
              / URBAN.ROW 69.0 /;

TABLE REMIT(R,HH) Ghorka remitances in foreign currency - M. US$ & India Rp
              RURAL URBAN
              ROW 19.3 28.1
              INDIA 939.7 33.8;

TABLE ENDOW(F,HH) Factor income M. N Rp
              RURAL URBAN
              L 29498.7 6338.3
              K 48485.4 7952.4;

TABLE IOF(I,J) Input-output flows ('91 million Nepal Rs)

FOOD-CROP CASH-CROP FOOD-PROC TEXTILES CHEMICAL CAPITAL
FOOD-CROP 5319.847 1011.540 3762.978
CASH-CROP 5648.229 314.546 348.228 4013.569 2691.578 1738.541
FOOD-PROC 4.879 2.833 1.986 60.261 6.696
TEXTILES 2.195 0.683 108.094 11.928 6.708
CHEMICAL 24.254 12.992 6.127 29.677 172.329 45.050
CAPITAL 21.930 3.406 1.341 8.933 10.325 343.970
TRANSPORT 550.367 143.483 26.304 133.132 100.105 85.416
ELECTRIC 0.360 3.103 4.972 50.936 68.010 25.623
TOURISM 0.425 0.156 0.562 1.419 1.440
SERVICES 598.829 99.996 6.934 98.362 98.081 50.306
PUBLIC 3.135 143.826 54.927 454.141

+ TRANSPORT ELECTRIC CONSTRUCT TOURISM SERVICES PUBLIC

FOOD-CROP 1170.105 6.384
CASH-CROP 1.194 264.234 294.285
FOOD-PROC 35.898 0.263 48.868 28.940 783.223
TEXTILES 51.078 0.390 0.057 112.593 130.203
CHEMICAL 159.896 9.603 2380.971 56.580 652.633 298.229
CAPITAL 158.506 11.684 2352.431 3056.319 515.039
TRANSPORT 2505.014 9.550 236.548 268.801 4618.214 2044.980
ELECTRIC 156.672 8.919 0.572 103.705 171.044 26.561
TOURISM 241.359 0.254 0.523 30.976 115.438 83.410
SERVICES 4224.293 175.279 740.709 160.301 6711.432 925.660
PUBLIC 230.276
```

*SOURCE: THESE TABLES ARE FROM NEPAL91.GMS FROM TIMOTHY BUEHRER, HARVARD UNIVERSITY AND

*FILIPPO DI MAURO OF ADB, MANILA.

TABLE IMA(I,J) Capital formation matrix ('91 million Nepal Rs)

FOOD-CROP CASH-CROP FOOD-PROC TEXTILES CHEMICAL CAPITAL
FOOD-CROP 364.405 208.046
CASH-CROP 310.472 85.370 0.308 1.810 4.136
CAPITAL 413.962 76.175 182.655 258.304 219.796 121.884
CONSTRUCT 1549.419 875.346 295.142 376.623 408.506 302.251

+ TRANSPORT ELECTRIC CONSTRUCT TOURISM SERVICES PUBLIC

CAPITAL 1299.240 346.107 1049.805 158.560 144.980 256.837
CONSTRUCT 304.409 150.197 581.400 358.897 5394.889 2833.010

TABLE WAG(I,LC) Wage bill by sector and labor category ('91 million Nepal Rs)
RURAL URBAN
FOOD-CROP 10170.876 699.382
CASH-CROP 4400.109 104.336
FOOD-PROC 419.027 153.535
TEXTILES 406.733 683.136
CHEMICAL 639.521 170.218
CAPITAL 94.589 164.555
TRANSPORT 2388.523 270.712
ELECTRIC 0.152 283.535
CONSTRUCT 4815.254 738.678
TOURISM 84.991 348.908
SERVICES 974.731 1794.524
PUBLIC 5105.196 1459.128

* TABLE UPDATED ACCODRIN TO POPULATION CENSUS, 1991.

TABLE XLE(I,LC) Employment by sector and labor category (1000 persons)

RURAL URBAN
FOOD-CROP 5778.945 150.786
CASH-CROP 826.567 11.635
FOOD-PROC 48.149 9.308
TEXTILES 104.324 22.339
CHEMICAL 48.150 12.100
CAPITAL 48.149 9.308
TRANSPORT 256.797 21.408
ELECTRIC .015 18.616
CONSTRUCT 353.097 49.331
TOURISM 24.075 13.031
SERVICES 320.997 94.009
PUBLIC 216.673 53.520

* The table below is somewhat special in that it contains both SAM data
* and data related to the parameters of the functions of the model. For
* instance the items called sigc and sigcm are parameters for the
* Armington functions used to calculate import demand.

```
TABLE ZZ(*,I) MISCELLANEOUS PARAMETERS AND INITIAL DATA

FOOD-CROP CASH-CROP FOOD-PROC TEXTILES CHEMICAL CAPITAL
M0 112.047 2180.373 1842.668 2069.570 1714.674 8506.668
MI0 906.736 601.761 691.503 804.708 2333.491 2432.801
E0 263.374 242.016 68.038 5246.832 1.029 81.211
IE0 574.869 363.380 246.923 453.168 33.271 26.489
DT0 241.935 234.490 302.076 194.229 1478.884
IDT0 12.305 21.923 26.889 69.318 173.150
QR0 98.784 178.534 80.900 392.782
SALES0 99.291 72.239 66.874 19.104 338.220
SALESI0 16.720 8.415 49.144 33.584 146.408
ETDUTY 2.720 2.500 0.703 54.190 0.011 0.839
EITDUTY 5.937 3.753 2.550 4.680 0.344 0.274
ITN0 0.000 0.0093 0.0619 0.0085 0.050 0.000
XD0 53354.318 16622.235 8905.454 8224.082 6208.245 4368.751
K 80031 32746 14427 11267 10056 7077
DEP 424.000 973.281 163.364 218.539 409.220 119.130
SIGC 0.75 0.75 1.50 1.50 1.50 1.50
SIGCM 1.50 2.50 2.5 2.0 1.50 1.50
SIGT 0.75 0.75 1.50 1.50 1.50 1.50
SIGTE 1.50 2.50 2.5 2.0 1.50 1.50
TAX 196.153 178.020 415.791 495.265 282.318 348.535
EC0
CONSU 2902.316 413.141 1110.546 438.612 662.899 544.646
CONSR 38788.426 3036.366 9081.676 4754.928 5701.839 5652.421
TCONS 232.874 236.502
ID 572.451 402.097 4528.304
DST 10.468 10.468 398.700 231.404 406.521 284.319

+ TRANSPORT ELECTRIC CONSTRUCT TOURISM SERVICES PUBLIC
M0 895.911
MI0 13.574 1016.896
E0 1162.988
IE0 3.100 600.251
XD0 12338.092 1069.260 13429.089 3113.699 26820.871 11372.305
K 21590 2673 20144 3892 26821 17058
DEP 624.639 100.243 659.357 64.901 789.381 281.617
SIGC 0.75 0.75 0.75 0.75 1.50 0.75
SIGCM 0.75 2.50 0.75 0.75 2.50 0.75
SIGT 0.75 0.75 0.75 0.75 1.50 0.75
SIGTE 0.75 2.50 0.75 0.75 2.50 0.75
TAX 58.181 -14.681 6.825 3.306 658.587
CONSU 268.546 43.064 138.115 4052.828
CONSR 1209.435 416.194 658.410 8078.593
TCONS 139.197 1842.212 848.715
GD0 10486.000
ID 13429.089
DST 101.120 ;
* THESE TABLE RELY ON ECONOMCI SURVEY, OF MINISTRY OF FINANCE, AND QUARTERLY BULLETINE OF NRB.

PARAMETER M0(I,R) Value of imports by sector and partner M. N.Rp
     X0(I,R) Value of exports by sector and partner M. N.Rp
```

```
    SUPPLY(I,*) Additional output statistics
    ELAST(I,*) Elasticities of substitution and transformation
    MDUTY(I,R) Import duty collections M.N Rp
    RENT(I,R) Import quota rents M. N Rp
    MTAX(I,R) Import sales tax
    EDUTY(I,R) Export duty collections M.N Rp
    TARIFF(I,R) Tariff rate applied to Nepali exports
    D0(I,*) Components of final demand;

SUPPLY(I,"XD0") = ZZ("XD0",I);
SUPPLY(I,"K") = ZZ("K",I);
SUPPLY(I,"DEP") = ZZ("DEP",I);
SUPPLY(I,"TAX") = ZZ("TAX",I);
ELAST(I,"SIGC" ) = ZZ("SIGC",I);
ELAST(I,"SIGCM") = ZZ("SIGCM",I);
ELAST(I,"SIGT" ) = ZZ("SIGT",I);
ELAST(I,"SIGTE") = ZZ("SIGTE",I);

M0(I,"INDIA") = ZZ("M0",I);
M0(I,"ROW") = ZZ("MI0",I);

X0(I,"INDIA") = ZZ("E0",I);
X0(I,"ROW") = ZZ("IE0",I);

MDUTY(I,"INDIA") = ZZ("DT0",I);
MDUTY(I,"ROW") = ZZ("IDT0",I);

RENT(I,"ROW") = ZZ("QR0",I);

MTAX(I,"ROW") = ZZ("SALES0",I);
MTAX(I,"INDIA") = ZZ("SALESI0",I);

EDUTY(I,"INDIA") = ZZ("ETDUTY",I);
EDUTY(I,"ROW") = ZZ("EITDUTY",I);

TARIFF(I,"INDIA") = ZZ("ITN0",I);

D0(I,"URBAN") = ZZ("CONSU",I);
D0(I,"RURAL") = ZZ("CONSR",I);
D0(I,"GOVT") = ZZ("GD0",I);
D0(I,"TOURIST") = ZZ("TCONS",I);
D0(I,"INVEST") = ZZ("ID",I);
D0(I,"STOCK") = ZZ("DST",I);

* THERE APPEARS TO HAVE BEEN A MISTAKE IN SPECIFICATION OF X0.
* THIS SHOULD BE AT INTERNATIONAL PRICES:

DISPLAY M0,X0,SUPPLY,ELAST,MDUTY,RENT,MTAX,EDUTY,TARIFF,D0;

* Check supply-demand relations:

SET FD /GOVT, TOURIST, INVEST, STOCK/; FD(HH) = YES;

PARAMETER MKT Check of supply-demand balance;
```

```
MKT(I) = SUPPLY(I,"XD0")
      + SUM(R, M0(I,R) + MDUTY(I,R) + MTAX(I,R) + RENT(I,R))
      - SUM(R, X0(I,R)) + SUM(R, EDUTY(I,R))
      - SUM(FD, D0(I,FD))
      - SUM(J, IOF(I,J));

DISPLAY MKT;
MKT(I)$SUPPLY(I,"XD0") = ROUND(100 * MKT(I) / SUPPLY(I,"XD0"));
DISPLAY "Percentage deviation:", MKT;

* Move imbalance into stock:

D0(I,"STOCK") = D0(I,"STOCK") - MKT(I);

PARAMETER LABMKT(LC) Labor payments - receipts balance;
LABMKT(LC) = ENDOW("L",LC) + INCTAX(LC) - SUM(I, WAG(I,LC));
DISPLAY LABMKT, INCTAX;

* ADJUST FACTOR ENDOWMENTS:

ENDOW("L",LC) = SUM(I, WAG(I,LC)) - INCTAX(LC);

* Fix tax payment to the public sector so that capital
* earns a 10% rate of return:

SUPPLY("PUBLIC","TAX") = SUPPLY("PUBLIC","XD0")
                        - SUPPLY("PUBLIC","DEP")
                        - SUM(J, IOF(J,"PUBLIC"))
                        - SUM(LC, WAG("PUBLIC",LC))
                        - 0.1 * SUPPLY("PUBLIC","K");

PARAMETER PROFIT(I) Sectoral profits net depreciation;
PROFIT(I) = SUPPLY(I,"XD0") - SUPPLY(I,"TAX") - SUPPLY(I,"DEP")
            - SUM(J, IOF(J,I)) - SUM(LC, WAG(I,LC));
DISPLAY PROFIT;

PARAMETER ROR(I) Net rate of return;
ROR(I) = NA;
ROR(I)$SUPPLY(I,"K") = PROFIT(I) / SUPPLY(I,"K");
DISPLAY ROR;

PARAMETER CAPMKT Capital earnings;
CAPMKT = SUM(I, PROFIT(I)) - TAXREV("CORP") - SUM(HH, ENDOW("K",HH));
DISPLAY CAPMKT;

* ADJUST CAPITAL ENDOWMENT EARNINGS TO CLEAR THIS MARKET:

ENDOW("K","URBAN") = ENDOW("K","URBAN") + CAPMKT;

PARAMETER SAVING(*) Benchmark savings;
SAVING(HH) = SUM(R, REMIT(R,HH)*ER(R)) + SUM(F, ENDOW(F,HH))
            - SUM(I, D0(I,HH)) - SUM(R,FTRN(HH,R)*ER(R))
            - TAXREV(HH) - ER("ROW")*LOANS(HH);
```

```
DISPLAY SAVING;
SCALAR DEPR0;
DEPR0 = SUM(I, SUPPLY(I,"DEP"));
SAVING("GOVT") = SUM(I, D0(I,"INVEST")) - SUM(HH, SAVING(HH)) - DEPR0;

PARAMETER TINCBAL INCOME BALANCE FOR TOURIST;
TINCBAL = SUM(R, TY0(R)) - TAXREV("TOURIST") - SUM(I, D0(I,"TOURIST"));
DISPLAY TINCBAL;

PARAMETER FSAV IMPLICIT FOREIGN SAVINGS;

FSAV = SUM((I,R), M0(I,R) - X0(I,R))
      - SUM(R, TY0(R))
      - ER("ROW")         * LOANS("GOVT")
      - ER("ROW")         * LOANS("AID")
      - ER("INDIA")       * LOANS("REFUND")
      - ER("ROW")         * SUM(HH,LOANS(HH))
      - SUM((R,HH), ER(R) * REMIT(R,HH))
      + SUM((HH,R), ER(R) * FTRN(HH,R));

DISPLAY FSAV;

PARAMETER
 IOC(I,J) INPUT OUTPUT COEFFICIENT
      Y0(I)             BASE YEAR SECTORAL OUTPUT ..
      VX0(I)            VOLUE OF SECTORAL EXPORTS NET OF TAXES
      X0(I,R)           AMOUNT OF SECTORAL EXPORT TO INDIA AND ROW
      PX0(I,R)          SECTORAL EXPOR PRICES TO INDIA AND ROW
      S0(I)             SUPPLY OF COMPOSITE COMMODITY OF THE SECTOR I
      M0(I,R)           AMOUNT OF SECTORAL IMPORTS FROM INDIA ANR ROW
      PM0(I,R)          IMPORT PRICES FROM INDIA AND ROW
      IDTOT0            TOTAL INVESTEMENT DEMAND IN THE BASE YEAR
      ID0(I)            INVESTMENT BY ORIGIN
      D0(I,*)           COMPONENTS OF FINAL DEMAND
      TI(I)             INDIRECT TAX RATE
      TX(I,R)           INDIRECT TAX ON INTERNATIONAL TRADE
      TM(I,R)           TARIFFS
      VK0(I)            BASE YEAR RETURN TO CAPITAL GROSS DEPRECIATION
      TY(R)             INCOME OF INDIAN AND FOREIGN TOURISTS
      ETRNDX(I)         ELASTICITY OF TRANSFORMATION OF EXPORTS
      ETRNXX(I)
      SIGMADM(I)        ELASTICITY BETWEEN IMPORTS AND DOMESTIC
                        PRODUCTS
      SIGMAMM(I)        ELASTICITY OF SUBSTITUTION
      ALPHAK(I)         CAPITAL'S SHARE OF OUTPUT
      ALPHAL(I,HH)      LABOR'S SHARE IN OUTPUT;
      ETRNDX(I) = 2;
      ETRNXX(I) = 5;
      SIGMADM(I) = 4;
      SIGMAMM(I) = 8;

Y0(I) = SUPPLY(I,"XD0");
IOC(I,J)=(IOF(I,J))/Y0(J);
ALPHAL(I,HH) = WAG(I,HH)/Y0(I);
```

```
ALPHAK(I) = 1-SUM(HH,ALPHAL(I,HH));
VX0(I) = SUM(R, X0(I,R) - EDUTY(I,R));
TX(I,R)$X0(I,R) = EDUTY(I,R) / X0(I,R);
PX0(I,R) = 1 - TX(I,R);
TM(I,R)$M0(I,R) = (MDUTY(I,R) + MTAX(I,R) + RENT(I,R)) / M0(I,R);
PM0(I,R) = 1 + TM(I,R);
S0(I) = SUM(R, PM0(I,R)*M0(I,R)) + Y0(I) - VX0(I);
ID0(I) = D0(I,"INVEST");
IDTOT0 = SUM(I, ID0(I));
VK0(I) = PROFIT(I) + SUPPLY(I,"DEP");
TI(I) = SUPPLY(I,"TAX") / Y0(I);
TY(R) = TY0(R);
MKT(I) = S0(I) - SUM(J, IOF(I,J)) - ID0(I) - D0(I,"TOURIST")
- D0(I,"GOVT") - SUM(HH, D0(I,HH)) - D0(I,"STOCK");
DISPLAY IOC,MKT, ALPHAL, ALPHAK;
SCALAR TTR; TTR = TAXREV("TOURIST") / SUM(I, D0(I,"TOURIST"));
```

19

General Equilibrium Modelling of UK Tax Policy[79]

Keshab Bhattarai & John Whalley

INTRODUCTION

This paper summarises activity thus far in the general equilibrium tax modelling area undertaken at Warwick University as part of a wider project on "General Equilibrium Analysis of UK Policy Issues" supported by the ESRC Macromodelling Consortium. Some of this work has been undertaken jointly with the Research Division of the Inland Revenue, to whom we are indebted for collaborative support on the data front.

We set out the basic approach, summarise a standard general equilibrium tax model for the UK providing some initial results, and indicate some extensions to the approach which have been undertaken in stand alone research papers.

GENERAL EQUILIBRIUM TAX MODELS[1]

Broad Approach

In a traditional general equilibrium model of either the tax or non tax variety, a number of consumers are identified, each with an initial endowment of commodities and preferences. Under optimization, the latter yield household demand functions for each commodity, with market demands given by the sum of the individual consumer's demands. Market demands depend on all prices, are continuous, nonnegative, homogeneous of degree zero (i.e., there is no money illusion), and satisfy Walras's law (i.e., that at any set of prices the total value of consumer expenditures equals consumer incomes). The production side of such models incorporates technology described by either constant-returns-to-scale activities or

79 This paper has been prepared for a volume on *Econometric Modelling: Techniques and Applications* to be edited by Sean Holly and Martin Weale, and draws on an earlier presentation to a conference on Macroeconomic Modelling and Economic Policy organised by the National Institute for Economic and Social Research, January 8/9, 1998. We are grateful to the Research Division of the Inland Revenue for their collaborative support of this work.

nonincreasing returns-to-scale production functions, and has producers maximise profits.

An equilibrium is characterised by a set of relative prices and levels of production by each industry such that market demand equals supply for all commodities (including disposals if any commodity is a free good). Since producers are assumed to maximise profits, this implies that in the constant-returns-to-scale case no one does any better than break even at the equilibrium prices. The zero homogeneity of demand functions and linear homogeneity of profits in prices (i.e., doubling all prices doubles money profits) implies that only relative prices are of any significance in this model; the absolute price level has no impact on the equilibrium outcome.

Taxes typically appear in these models in *ad valorem* form (see Shoven and Whalley (1973); Shoven (1974)), either as producer taxes on inputs or consumer taxes on incomes or expenditures, revenues either being redistributed to consumers or used to finance publicly provided goods and services. The taxes that characterise modern tax systems (personal, corporate, sales, excise, property, social security, resource, and other taxes) are usually represented in model-equivalent *ad valorem* form. The equilibrium behaviour of the model can be investigated as taxes change and, on that basis, policy evaluations made.

A Numerical Example

A numerical example is a good way to illustrate this approach; although, in representing actual economies, much more specificity is required than the general form of the model usually admits. Particular functional forms for production and demand functions need to be chosen and parameter values selected. The tax policy instruments to be analysed need to be incorporated, and the treatment (or model closure) of the various items such as foreign trade, savings, and public goods all need to be settled.

A simple numerical example of a tax-policy-oriented general equilibrium model is presented by Shoven and Whalley (1984). In this example, there are two final goods (manufacturing and nonmanufacturing), two factors of production (capital and labour), and two classes of consumers (a "rich" consumer group that owns all the capital and a "poor" group that owns all the labour). There are no consumer demands for factors (i.e., there is no labour-leisure choice). Each consumer group generates demands by maximising a constant elasticity of substitution (CES) utility function subject to its budget constraint. CES production functions are assumed.

The CES utility functions are

$$U^c = \left[\sum_{i=1}^{2} \left(a_i^c\right)^{1/\sigma_c} \left(X_i^c\right)^{\left(\sigma_c - 1\right)/\sigma_c} \right]^{\sigma_c/(\sigma_c - 1)} \qquad (2.1)$$

where X_1^c is the quantity of good i demanded by the cth consumer, a_1^c are share parameters, and σ_c is the substitution elasticity in consumer c's CES utility function. The consumer's budget constraint is $P_1X_1^c + P_2X_2^c \le P_LW_L^c + P_K^cW_K^c = I^c$, where P_1 and P_2 are the consumer prices for the two goods, W_L^c and W_K^c are consumer *c*'s endowment of labour and capital, and I^c is the income of consumer *c*.

Maximising this utility function subject to the budget constraint yields the commodity demands

$$X_i^c = \frac{a_i^c I^c}{P_i^{\sigma_c}\left(a_i^c P_1^{(1-\sigma_c)} + a_2^c P_2^{(1-\sigma_c)}\right)} \qquad i = 1, 2; c = 1, 2 \qquad (2.2)$$

The production functions are

$$Q_i = \phi_i\left[\delta_i L_i^{(\sigma_i-1)/\sigma_i} + (1-\delta_i)K_i^{(\sigma_i-1)/\sigma_i}\right]^{\sigma_i/(\sigma_i-1)} \qquad i = 1, 2 \qquad (2.3)$$

where Q_i denotes output of the *i*th industry, ϕ_i is a scale or unit parameter, δ_i is a distribution parameter, K_i and L_i are capital and labour factor inputs, and σ_i is the elasticity of factor substitution in industry *i*.

This example has six production function parameters (i.e., ϕ_i, δ_i, and σ_i for i = 1, 2), six utility function parameters (i.e., $a_1^1, a_2^1, a_1^2, a_2^2, \sigma_1$ *and* σ_2, and four exogenous variables (the endowment of labour (W_L) and capital (W_K) for each of the two consumers).

Table 1
Production and Demand Parameters and Endowments used by Shoven and Whalley (1984) for their two-sector General Equilibrium Numerical Example

			ϕ_i	δ_i	σ_i
Production Parameters					
Manufacturing			1.5	0.6	2.0
Nonmanufacturing			2.0	0.7	0.5
Demand Parameters					
Rich Consumers			Poor consumers		
α_1^1	α_2^1	σ^1	α_1^2	α_2^2	σ^2
0.5	0.5	1.5	0.3	0.7	0.75
Endowments			K	L	
Rich households			25	0	
Poor households			0	60	

An equilibrium for the model is given by the four prices P_1, P_2, P_L, and P_K and eight quantities $x_1^1, x_1^2, x_2^1, x_2^2$ *and* $K_1, K_2, L_1,$ *and* L_2, which meet the equilibrium conditions that market demand equals market supply for all inputs and outputs and that zero profits apply in each industry. Once the parameters are specified and the factor endowments are known, a complete general equilibrium model is available. Tax and other policy variables can then be added as desired.

Table 1 presents the values for the parameters and the exogenous variables used by Shoven and Whalley in their example. The equilibrium solution is reported in Table 2 for a case where a 50 percent input tax applies to the use of capital in manufacturing. Only relative prices are relevant in this model and, somewhat arbitrarily, labour is chosen as the numeraire. At the equilibrium prices, total demand for each output equals production, and producer revenues equal costs. Labour and capital endowments are fully employed, and consumer incomes from sale of factors plus transfers equal consumer expenditures. Because of the assumption of constant returns to scale, the per-unit costs in each industry equal producer selling prices, meaning that economic profits are zero. Expenditures by each household exhaust their income. Shoven and Whalley illustrate how this general equilibrium model can be adapted for policy evaluation work by comparing the with-tax equilibrium solution reported in Table 2 to the no-tax equilibrium solution to obtain measures of the welfare costs of such a tax.

Empirical Implementation and Model Structure

The differences between the model actually used to analyse tax policy proposals and the numerical example above lie in their dimensionality (i.e., the number of sectors and consumer types modelled.) their parameter specification procedures and use of data, and their inclusion of more complex policy regimes than a simple tax on one factor in one sector.

Although the appropriate general equilibrium model for any particular policy analysis varies with the issue, most tax models are variants of static, two-factor models, that have long been employed in public finance and international trade. Most involve more than two goods even though factors of production are classified into two broad categories of capital and labour services. In some models these are further disaggregated into subgroups (for instance, labour may be identified as skilled or unskilled). Intermediate transactions are usually incorporated either through fixed or flexible input-output coefficients.

The rationale for proceeding this way is that tax and policy issues are frequently analysed using a general equilibrium theoretical framework, and it is natural to retain the same basic structure in applied work. This is especially the case if the major contribution of the numerical work is to advance from qualitative to quantitative analysis. Also, most data on which the numerical specifications of tax models are based come in a form consistent with the two-sector approach. National accounts data, for instance, identify wages and salaries and operating surplus as major cost components. Input-output data provide intermediate transaction data, with value added broken down in a similar way. This all suggests a model in which capital and labour are identified as the principal factor inputs.

The partition between goods and factors in two-sector models is used in tax models to simplify computation. By using factor prices to generate cost-covering goods prices, consumer demands can be calculated and the derived demands for factors that meet consumer demands evaluated. Thus, even a model with a large number of goods can be solved by working only with the implicit system of excess factor demands.

Table 2
Equilibrium Solution for Shoven and Whalley's Example with a 50% Input tax on Capital in Manufacturing

Equilibrium Prices						
Manufacturing output				1.47		
Nonmanufacturing output				1.01		
Capital				1.13		
Labour				1.00		
Production side: Outputs						
		Quantity	Revenue			
Manufacturing		22.39	32.83			
Nonmanufacturing		57.31	57.64			
Inputs						
	Capital	Capital (incl. tax)	Labour cost	Labour cost	Total cost	Cost per uit output
Manufacturing	4.04	6.83	1.00	26.00	32.83	1.47
Nonmanufacturing	20.96	23.64	34.00	34.00	57.60	1.00
Demand side						
		Manufacturing	Nonmanufacturing	Expenditure		
Rich households		8.94	15.83	29.10		
Poor households		13.40	41.48	61.37		
	Labour income	Capital income	Transfers	Total income		
Rich households	0	28.19	0.91	29.10		
Poor households	60.00	0	1.37	61.37		

There are a range of more specific model design issues that are also encountered with tax models, including the treatment of investment, foreign trade, and government expenditures. Where there are no international capital flows, the level of investment in the model reflects household saving decisions (broadly defined to include corporate retentions). These are based on constant-savings propensities in static models and on explicit intertemporal utility maximisation in dynamic models. Government expenditures usually reflect transfers and real expenditures, with the latter frequently determined from assumed utility-maximising behaviour for the government. In this approach, the government is treated as a separate consumption-side agent that buys public goods and services. In a few cases (such as Piggott and Whalley 1985), tax models have been used with public goods explicitly appearing in household utility functions, although this complicates the basic approach.

As regards the treatment of time, some of the static equilibrium tax models have been sequenced through time to reflect changes in the economy's capital stock due to net saving. Models such as those due to Summers (1981), Auerbach, Kotlikoff, and Skinner (1983), and Fullerton, Shoven, and Whalley (1983) have been used to analyse intertemporal issues in tax policy, such as whether a move from an income tax to a consumption tax (under which saving is less heavily taxed) is desirable. This approach links a series of single-period equilibria through saving decisions that change the capital stock of the economy. Saving, in turn, is based on maximisation of a utility function defined over current and expected future consumption. Myopic expectations (i.e., expected future rates of return on assets are assumed equal to current rates of return) are often used to simplify computation. Saving in the period augments the capital stock in all future periods. The general equilibrium computed for each period has all markets clearing, including that for newly produced capital goods. The economy passes through a sequence of single-period equilibria in which the capital stock grows. Tax changes that encourage higher savings typically cause lowered consumption in initial years and eventually higher consumption due to the larger capital stock.

Functional Forms

When building a tax model to represent an actual economy, in addition to selecting the model structure one also has to choose particular functional forms. Typically the major constraint on the choice of demand and production functions is that they be consistent with the theory and are analytically tractable. This involves choosing functions that satisfy the usual demand- and production-side restrictions assumed in general equilibrium models, such as Walras's law. It also requires that excess-demand responses be easy to evaluate for any price vector considered as a candidate equilibrium solution for the model.

The choice of a specific functional form by any given modeller usually depends on how elasticities are to be used in the model. The general approach is one of selecting a functional form that best allows key parameter values (e.g., income and price elasticities) to be incorporated while retaining tractability. This largely explains why the functional forms used in general equilibrium tax models are so often drawn from the family of "convenient" forms [Cobb-Douglas, CES, linear expenditure system (LES), and translog, generalised Leontief, or other flexible functional forms].

Demands from Cobb-Douglas utility functions are easy to work with but have unitary income and uncompensated own-price elasticities and zero cross-price elasticities; restrictions are typically implausible. If all expenditure shares for CES functions are small, compensated own-price elasticities equal the elasticity of substitution in preferences. It may thus be unacceptable to model all commodities as having essentially the same compensated own-price elasticities. One alternative is to use hierarchical or nested CES functions, although here the issues that arise are the global properties of these more flexible functional forms, such as concavity. Unitary income elasticities implied by Cobb-Douglas or CES functions can be relaxed by using LES functions with a displaced origin, but the origin displacements need to be specified.

On the production side, where only two primary factor enter the model, CES value-added functions are usually assumed. If more than two factors are used, hierarchical CES functions or translog cost functions are again used. Intermediate requirements functions may be modelled as fixed coefficients, or intermediate substitutablity may be introduced.

Choice of Parameter Values

Parameter values for the functions used in tax models are crucial in determining the results of simulations for various tax policies. The procedure most commonly used in these models has come to be labelled "calibration" (Mansur and Whalley (1984)). Under this approach, the economy under consideration is assumed to be in equilibrium in the presence of existing tax policies, that is, at a so-called benchmark equilibrium. Parameters for the model are then calculated such that the model can reproduce the equilibrium data as a model solution.

A feature of this calibration procedure that has both attracted interest and raised concerns is that there is no statistical test of the resulting model specification implied by calibration. The procedure for calibrating parameter values from a constructed equilibrium observation is deterministic. This typically involves the key assumption that the benchmark data represent an equilibrium for the economy under investigation, and required parameter values are then calculated using the model equilibrium conditions. If the equilibrium conditions are not sufficient to identify the model, additional parameter values (typically elasticities) are exogenously specified until the model is identified. These are usually based on a literature search or, less frequently, on separate estimation. In contrast to econometric work that often simplifies the structure of the economic portion of models to allow for substantial richness in statistical specification, the procedure in these models is the opposite. The richness of the economic structure only allows for a crude statistical model that, in the case of calibration to a single year's data, becomes deterministic.

If the widespread use of deterministic calibration in these models is troubling, it is perhaps worthwhile outlining some of the reasons why this calibration approach is so widely used. First, in some of the tax models, several thousand parameters may be involved, and to simultaneously estimate all of the model parameters using time series methods requires either unrealistically large numbers of observations or overly severe identifying restrictions. Partitioning models into submodels (such as a demand and production system) may reduce or overcome this problem, but partitioning does not fully incorporate the equilibrium restrictions that are emphasised in calibration. Also, benchmark data sets are usually constructed in value terms, and their separation into price and quantity observations with consistent units through time as would be required for time series estimation. Finally, the dimensions used in these models make the construction of benchmark equilibrium data sets a nontrivial exercise. Some of the large-scale data sets have required upwards of 18 months work, so that if time series are to be constructed, the required workload may not be sustainable.

Calibration usually involves one year's data. or a single observation represented by an average over a number of years, and it is only in the Cobb-Douglas case that the benchmark data uniquely identify a set of parameter values. In other cases, the required values for the relevant elasticities needed to identify other parameters in the model are usually based on other sources. Typically, heavy reliance is placed on literature surveys of elasticities, and as other modellers have also observed, the literature on elasticity values is sparse (and sometimes contradictory). Also although this procedure might sound straightforward, it can also be difficult because of differences among studies in estimates.

Elasticity values in these models specify the curvature of isoquants and indifference surfaces, with their position given by the benchmark equilibrium data. Because the curvature of CES indifference curves and isoquants cannot be inferred from the benchmark data, extraneous values of substitution elasticities are required. Similarly, for LES demand functions, income elasticities are needed upon which to base the origin coordinates for utility measurement.

In practice, data representing benchmark equilibria for use in calibration are constructed from national accounts and other government data sources. In these data, available information does not satisfy microconsistency conditions (e.g., payments to labour from firms will not equal labour income received by households), and a number of adjustments are needed to ensure that the equilibrium conditions of the models hold. In these, some data are taken as correct and others adjusted to reflect consistency. Tax-related data sets of this type are described in St-Hilaire and Whalley (1983), Piggott and Whalley (1985), and Ballard, Fullerton, Shoven, and Whalley (1985).

Because these benchmark data are usually produced in value terms, in using the data in a general equilibrium model units must be chosen for goods and factors so that separate price and quantity observations are obtained. A commonly used convention, originally adopted by Harberger (1962), is to assume units for both goods and factors such that they have a price of unity in the benchmark equilibrium.

Solving General Equilibrium Models

The early general equilibrium tax models typically used Scarf's algorithm for their solution (see Scarf (1967), Scarf and Hansen (1973)). More recent models rely on optimization software such as GAMS (the Generalised Algebraic Modelling System). In this latter approach, all equilibrium conditions are written as constraints for an optimization problem with an arbitrary (or convenient) objective function. Any solution to the optimization problem which lies in the contstraint set is, by construction, an equilibrium.

A GAMS model in this format essentially is a set of statements in GAMS syntax (Brook, Kendrick and Meeraus (1992)) which declare sets, data, parameters, variables, equations, and and assigns model relationships in a natural way legible to any model user. A specific GAMS formulation, MPSGE, has also become popular for generating a specific set of large scale standard Arrow-Debreu applied general equilibrium models (Rutherford (1997)). This declares the full model equations in symbolic form. After models are generated, either in GAMS or MPSGE format, a one line command instructs solvers to solve the declared models. It is possible to declare a number of models consisting of different equations in the same file, and include statements to solve these models sequentially with loops over time or counterfactual experiments. The class of these models can reflect linear, non-linear, mixed complementarity, integer or discrete programming problems. Optimization solvers (MINOS5 and CONOPT) are the most popular for solving non-linear and linear programming problems in GAMS, while PATH is a more powerful solver to for mixed complementarity problems (Dirkse and Ferris (1995)). At the end of the GAMS program file, a series of reporting statements are included to handle the report. In recent versions of GAMS a user has more control over the output generated from the model; the results of desired variables can be displayed, put in tabular spreadsheet format, or plotted directly at the end of the model execution.

Evaluating Impacts of Policy Changes

Theoretical literature on welfare economics is usually followed in making comparisons between equilibria in order to arrive at policy evaluation based on these tax models. For welfare impacts, Hicksian compensating (CV) and equivalent variations (EV) are commonly used as summary measures of welfare impact by agent. Economywide welfare measures are often computed by aggregating CVs or EVs over consumer groups. Although this is consistent with practice in the cost-benefit literature, the theoretical shortcomings in using the sum of CVs or EVs as an aggregate welfare criterion are well known.

Models also provide a detailed evaluation of who gains, who loses, and by how much as a result of a policy change. No single summary measure need be chosen if the policy analyst is interested only in the detailed impacts of any policy change. In some tax models, new (policy change) equilibria are computed under the restriction that government revenues remain constant. In these models, this usually implies replacing one set of taxes with another, but with new tax rates endogenously determined to preserve revenues. In other models government revenues change, but where this occurs the welfare impact from changes in the amount of public service needs to be factored into any economywide welfare measure.

In addition to welfare impacts, other impacts of tax changes can be investigated, such as income distribution effects using Lorenz curves or Gini coefficients. Alternative income concepts (e.g., gross of tax or net of tax) can also be used in such calculations. Changes in relative prices can be evaluated, as can changes in the use of factors of production across industries or changes in the product composition of consumer demands.

Uniqueness of Equilibrium

One final point to keep in mind is that the applied general equilibrium approach to tax policy may not be particularly instructive if the equilibrium solution in any model is not unique for any particular tax policy. Uniqueness, or lack of it, has been a long-standing interest of general equilibrium theorists (see Kehoe (1980)). There is, however, no theoretical argument that guarantees uniqueness in the tax models currently in use. With some of the models, researchers have conducted *ad hoc* numerical experimentation (approaching equilibria from different directions and at different speeds) but have yet to find a case of nonuniqueness. In the case of the US tax model due to Ballard, Fullerton, Shoven, and Whalley (1985), uniqueness has been numerically demonstrated by Kehoe and Whalley (1985). The current working hypothesis adopted by most tax modellers seems to be that uniqueness can be presumed in the models discussed here until a clear case of nonuniqueness is found.

A UK TAX MODEL

We next discuss a simple version of a UK tax model built under project support. This is a single household model with a variety of tax instruments (sales, income and VAT taxes) similar to that considered earlier by Piggott and Whalley (1985), with a labour-leisure choice component to the model. For this model, we briefly discuss the specification of preferences and technology and then describe the construction of micro-consistent data sets required for model calibration We discuss the methods used for calibration and choice of the elasticity parameters in preferences and production functions. Since the models replicate a base year economy in the presence of taxes, we can solve for a counterfactual equilibrium without taxes in order to evaluate the welfare costs of tax distortions.

The data for this model draws on Input-Output tables for the UK economy (ONS (1995)).[2] We discuss a model for the one household case, with the same sectoral disaggregation as available in the 1990 UK Input-Output table (ONS (1995)). Model parameters are inferred from a fully micro-consistent UK data set for 1990, constructed using these data, and supplemented by literature based estimates of behavioural elasticities. The flexibility of the modelling format allows parameters to be calibrated to later years as and when relevant information becomes available.

Demands

The household maximises a CES utility function defined over commodities and leisure, subject to a budget constraint. This utility function can be written as

$$U_h = \left(\sum_i \alpha_{i,h} C_{i,h}^{\rho_h} + \beta_h L_h^{\rho_h} \right)^{\frac{1}{\rho_h}} \tag{3.1}$$

where U_h is the utility of household h, $C_{i,h}$ is the consumption of good i by household h, L_h is the leisure taken by household h, $\alpha_{i,h}$ is the share of income of household h spent on consumption of good i, β_h is the share of full income spent on leisure, and ρ_h is the elasticity parameter in the utility function, the elasticity of substitution between goods (and leisure) being equal to $\sigma = \dfrac{1}{1-\rho_h}$ (Varian (1992)). In versions of the model in which leisure does not appear $\beta_h = 0$.

Households receive income from capital and labour endowments, and transfers from the government. They pay taxes on household and capital income. The disposable income of a households is given by

$$I_h = r(1-t_k)\bar{K}_h + (1-t_l^h)w\bar{L}_h + TR_h \qquad (3.2)$$

where I_h is the full income of the households, $\bar{K}_h$ is the endowment of capital, $\bar{L}_h$ is the endowment of labour, TR_h are the transfers received by the household h, r is the rental rate of capital, w is the wage rate, t_l^h is tax rate on household h's labour income[3], and t_k is tax rate on capital income.

The demand functions for goods and leisure are obtained by maximising (1) with respect to (2), and take the following form

$$C_{i,h} = \left(\frac{\alpha_{i,h} I_h}{\left(P_i(1+t_i^v)\right)^{\sigma_h} \left(\sum_i \alpha_{i,h} \left(P_i\left(1+t_i^v\right)\right)^{1-\sigma_h} + \beta_h \left(w\left(1-t_l^h\right)\right)^{1-\sigma_h} \right)} \right) \qquad (3.3)$$

where t_i^v is value added tax rate and t_l^h tax rate on labour income.

Consumption of leisure is given by

$$L_h = \left(\frac{\beta_h . I_h}{\left(w\left(1-t_l^h\right)\right)^{\sigma_h} \left(\sum_i \alpha_{i,h} \left(P_i\left(1+t_i^v\right)\right)^{1-\sigma_h} + \beta_h \left(w\left(1-t_l^h\right)\right)^{1-\sigma_h} \right)} \right) \qquad (3.4)$$

In versions of the model model where there is no demand for leisure households have demand functions only for goods. In that case equation (3.4) does not exist, and equation (3.3) is modified with the setting β_h =0.

In the one household case, the labour supply of each household LS_h is given by the difference between the household labour endowment, and the demand for leisure, L_h.

$$LS_h = \overline{L}_h - L_h \tag{3.5}$$

In equilibrium, this labour supply by household must be consistent with the total demand for labour derived from the profit maximisation behaviour of firms as set out in the following section.

Production

Producers use labour and capital in each of N sectors to yield value added according to CES functions.

$$Y_i = \Omega_i((1-\delta_i)(K_i)^{\gamma_i} + \delta_i(LS_i)^{\gamma_i})^{\frac{1}{\gamma_i}} \quad (i = 1..N) \tag{3.6}$$

where Y_i is the value added of sector i, Ω_i is a shift parameter in the production function, K_i and LS_i are the amounts of capital and labour used in sector *i*, δ_i is the share parameter on labour in the CES function, and γ_i is the CES factor substitution parameter.

The gross output of each sector reflects the use of value added, Y_i and intermediate inputs. We assume fixed coefficients both among intermediate inputs, and between value added and intermediate inputs; M_{ij} is the intermediate use of good *i* in the production of good *j* and X_j is the gross output of sector *j*. At any set of prices, producers in each sector maximise profits subject to their technology constraint

$$\max \Pi_i = P_i X_i - wL_i - rK_i - \sum_j P_j M_{ji} \tag{3.7}$$

where Π_i is the profit of sector *i*. In equilibrium, factor demands by sectors are determined where the value marginal product of factors equal factor prices, and there are no positive profits for producers.

Government Budget

The government collects revenue from taxes on capital and labour income and value-added taxes. All the tax revenues collected are transferred to households in lump sum form; i.e.

$$\sum_h TR_h = \sum_i t_k rK_i + \sum_h t_i^v P_i C_{i,h} + \sum_h t_i^h wLS_h \tag{3.8}$$

where t_k is the tax rate on capital income, t_i^v is the *ad valorem* tax rate on final sales, t_l^h is the tax rate on labour income of the household.

These taxes, particularly when they are levied at different rates on different sectors and households, have distortionary impacts on the allocation of resources in the economy. These are captured by the model. Government budget balance is a property of an equilibrium

Model Equilibrium Conditions

In this model a competitive equilibrium is given by prices of consumption goods, P_i; the prices of capital, P^k ; a wage rate for labour, w and levels of gross output, Y_i; capital use, K_i ; and sectoral use of labour, L_i ; such that, given these,

(i) markets for goods and services, labour and capital clear; and

(ii) the government budget constraint is satisfied,

More specifically the market clearing condition for the goods market is given by

$$X_i = C_i + \sum_{j=1}^{N} a_{ij} X_j \tag{3.9}$$

where $C_i = \sum_h C_{ih}$ is household final consumption, and $\sum_j a_{ij} X_j$ the intermediate demand.

The capital market clearing condition implies

$$\sum_h \bar{K}_h = \sum_i K_i \tag{3.10}$$

and labour market clearing implies:

$$\sum_h LS_h = \sum_i LS_i \tag{3.11}$$

Government budget balance is given by (3.9). When there are n different markets in the economy, relative prices that clear n-1 markets also clear the nth market as well.

Data Sources and Calibration

The implementation of the UK model begins with input-output data. 1990 input-output information is published in the ONS publication *Input-Output Tables for the United Kingdom*, and are available for up to 123 sectors. The breakdown of consumption spending and the distribution of income across households is limited in this source. We therefore take an eight-sector version of the input-output table (see Table 3) to represent the inter-sectoral linkages in UK production. The input-output table shows the quantities of labour and capital services which producers purchase (see Table 4). It also shows how commodities supplied by the various sectors are bought either by households for final consumption (see Table 5), or by other sectors as intermediate inputs. The zero profit conditions for producers in the benchmark data are met in the input-output data for the various sectors of the economy. This essentially means that the value of output equals payments to labour and capital services and intermediate inputs.

We make two modifications to this input-output data for use in the model. First, in an initial closed economy formulation of the model we do not explicitly consider import and export functions. We modify the data such that exports and imports balance for the economy as a whole, and there are no foreign transfers in the model[4].

Table 3
Aggregated Input-Output Table of the UK Economy, 1990 (£ millions)

	Agri[1]	*Energy*[2]	*Manuf*[3]	*Constr*[4]	*Distr*[5]	*Transp*[6]	*BusServ*[7]	*OtherServ*[8]
Agri	2,853	0	9,059	3	536	32	0	88
Energy	550	22,203	5,377	598	2,670	2,241	1,824	694
Manuf	3,774	2,896	60,613	14,961	13,372	4,290	8,763	3,410
Constr	186		791	23,022	760	128	1,808	999
Distr	873	1,220	12,171	2,891	4,438	2,700	2,472	742
Transp	266	1,253	7,251	846	12,956	8,091	10,599	1,303
BusServ	1,010	1,648	21,717	9,008	18,348	7,336	49,008	11,278
OtherServ	375	331	3,518	403	1,118	949	3,314	6,059

Source: ONS (1995), Input-Output Tables of the United Kingdom.

Table 4
UK Value added and indirect business taxes 1990 (£ millions)

	Agri[1]	*Energy*[2]	*Manuf*[3]	*Constr*[4]	*Distr*[5]	*Transp*[6]	*BusServ*[7]	*OtherServ*[8]
Labour	2,966	7,918	69,787	16,703	50,599	22,953	52,776	88,656
Capital	5,228	14,255	29,176	16,923	19,175	16,365	23,047	42,359

Source: ONS, Input-Output Tables of the United Kingdom, 1995.

Table 5
UK Final demands 1990 (£ millions)

	Agri[1]	*Energy*[2]	*Manuf*[3]	*Constr*[4]	*Distr*[5]	*Transp*[6]	*BusServ*[7]	*OtherServ*[8]
Total FD	5059	18597	109143	57953	105376	23534	40058	140253
VAT	876	2485	9015	655	14943	2852	3224	8518

Source: ONS, Input-Output Tables of the United Kingdom, 1995.

Notes:
1. Agriculture, Forestry and Fishing (1-3). Numbers in parentheses in this and other notes refer to input-output classifications.
2. Coal, Oil, Gas, Electricity, Water supply (4-9).
3. All Manufacturing (10-90).
4. Construction (91).
5. Wholesale, Retail Services, Hotel and Entertainment (92-95).
6. Railways, Air, Road, Sea, Postal and Telecommunications (96-102).

7. Business Services, Banking, Insurance, Accountancy (103-114).
8. Other Services, Public Administration, Education, Health (115-123)

The second modification relates to the treatment of final demand. We only consider one category of final demands and do not explicitly incorporate investment and government demands into the model. For simplicity, we also do not separate government consumption and investment.

This model is thus a closed economy single household static model, with the government collecting taxes and redistributing income by means of transfers to households. The government collects revenue from taxes on capital income, value-added taxes on commodities and taxes on household income. The value-added tax influences the composition of final demand. The household income tax and accompanying transfers influence the labour supply decisions of the household sector. Differences in tax rates on capital income across sectors distort the allocation of capital resources among various sectors. In a competitive environment, resources are diverted from heavily taxed sectors to less taxed sectors. Production taxes and subsidies paid to producers both apply, having the effect of reducing the selling price below the cost of production.

Parameters and Elasticities

We use literature based estimates of elasticities of substitution between labour and capital in the production functions in calibration, and elasticities of substitution among various commodities (including leisure) that enter the utility function of households in the model is based on literature values reported in Table 6. Data on input-output transactions, value-added, taxes and final demand as presented above are then used to calibrate parameters on the consumption and production sides of this model. Model parameters are chosen in such a way that its solution replicates base year quantities, when base year prices are given to the model with the calibrated parameters. The resulting calibrated parameters are shown in Table 6.

Table 6
Calibrated Share Parameters in Production and Consumption in UK tax Model

Sectors	*Calibrated Share Parameter on Capital Inputs*	*Calibrated Share Parameter on Labour Inputs*	*Calibrated Share Parameters for Household Expendituresby Product*
Agri	0.638	0.362	0.006
Energy	0.643	0.357	0.023
Manuf	0.295	0.705	0.137
Constr	0.503	0.497	0.073
Distr	0.275	0.725	0.132
Transp	0.416	0.584	0.030
BusServ	0.304	0.696	0.050
OtherServ	0.323	0.677	0.176

Table 7
Elasticity Parameters used in the UK Tax Model

Sectors	*Elasticity of Substitution in Production Functions*	*Central Tendency Values of own Price Elasticities of Household Demand Functions*
Agri	0.50	0.468
Energy	0.75	0.659
Manuf	0.45	0.592
Constr	0.50	0.25
Distr	0.80	0.642
Transp	0.80	0.977
BusServ	0.80	0.461
OtherServ	0.50	0.461

Source: Piggott and Whalley (1985)

The Welfare Costs of Taxes

This basic model captures three different tax instruments: taxes on capital income, value-added taxes on sales of final goods and taxes on household labour income. Tax rates on capital income are taken from information in the UK input-output tables. Value added tax rates and tax rates on household labour income are calculated from the data on income and sales taxes contained in *Economic Trends* (ONS, 1995). (See Tables 8 and 9).

Table 8
Production Side Tax Rates in the UK Tax Model

Sectors[1]	*Tax Rate on Capital Income (%)*	*Value-added Tax Rates (%)*
Agri	8.6	23
Energy	23.1	23
Manuf	6.0	23
Constr	1.7	23
Distr	46.5	23
Transp	6.2	23
BusServ	25.2	23
OtherServ	1.7	23

1. See Table 3 for a key to Sectoral Abbreviations

Table 9
Household Tax Rates in the UK Tax Model

Household Labour Income Tax Rate (%)	*Transfers as Fraction of Household Income*
22	0.273

To assess the welfare impacts of alternative UK tax policies, the model computes compensating and equivalent variations based on consumers' money metric welfare associated with various tax changes. It also computes the marginal excess burdens involved when raising additional tax revenues from various sources.

Model results (Table 10) indicate that the removal of all taxes in the UK model yields a gain equal to 1.762 percent of the benchmark income. The largest welfare gain results from the removal of household labour income tax distortions which equal to 1.132 percent of benchmark income. Among the three tax measures, taxes on capital income show the lowest welfare cost, equal to 0.33 percent of income in the benchmark equilibrium.

Table 10
Welfare effects of the removal of tax distortions in the UK model (EV as a % of GDP)

	Removal of VAT	*Removal of Taxes on Capital Income*	*Removal of Taxes on Household Labour Income*	*Removal of all three Taxes*
Hicksian EV for representative household as % of GDP	1.002	0.33	1.132	1.762
	VAT	Capital income	Household labour income	All taxes
MEB £1 of extra revenue when raised by taxes	0.132	-0.028	0.234	0.191

Table 10 also reports the marginal cost of public funds (MEB) for the three categories of taxes in this initial UK model. The marginal excess burden is 23 pence per pound of revenues raised from taxes on household income and 13 pence per pound if extra revenues are raised by means of VAT. However, revenues raised by capital taxes improve the welfare in the economy. This outcome is due to the distortionary nature of capital taxes in the base year, which partly reflects distortions elsewhere in sales and other taxes. In the model data, for instance, capital income from the distribution sector is taxed at 46.5 percent, while capital income from construction and other sectors is subject only to 1.7 per cent tax rate on capital income.

EXTENSIONS OF THE BASIC APPROACH

Disaggregation and Elaboration

This basic UK model has already been expanded on in several ways in the project. We have disaggregated the households sector into ten different categories so that we can analyse incidence effects of taxes. We use data reported in the Family Expenditure Survey and income distribution data published in *Economic Trends*. As data tables in the latter sources are presented for ten deciles ranked by household income, we have expanded the UK model set out above to capture ten household groups. In the model, households are grouped by income decile, each endowed with labour and capital. Households receive income by supplying labour and capital, and receive transfers from the government. Rich households have proportionately larger capital endowments, and are liable for higher rates of taxes than poor households. In turn, poor households receive larger transfers from the government than those received by rich households. The income distribution data in the model includes income on wages and salaries, income from investment, and transfers by decile.

We have also extended the model to include an international trade sector, using two different variants. One is a small open economy model of the UK and the other is a world trade model, including the UK. The latter can be used to analyse multilateral trade policy initiatives, such as the impacts of the Uruguay Round decisions in the WTO.

Discreteness of Labour Supply Choices and Tax Distortions of Labour Supply

Bhattarai and Whalley[5] have also use this modelling approach to investigate the significance of discrete choice for calculations of the welfare cost of tax distortions of labour supply by constructing observationally equivalent discrete and continuous choice UK based labour supply models[6]. The discrete analogue models they use embody varying forms of agent heterogeneity (over share parameters in preferences, substitution elasticities, endowments), while maintaining equivalence to identical single agent continuous models through similar model generated aggregate uncompensated labour supply elasticities. Issues arise as to how discrete choice is modelled in the with tax case, and they present two alternative formulations. In one, tax revenues are returned to those who pay the tax; no interagent redistribution occurs. In the other, households have proportional claims on revenues generated by the tax, and redistribution occurs. The discrete analogue forms both asymptotically approach the continuous case as the grid over which discrete choice occurs becomes everywhere dense.

Results from these exercises are striking. In simple numerical examples using their first discrete formulation (tax revenues recycled to those who pay the tax), the discrete choice model produces sharply lower welfare costs of taxes if model calibration is made to the same uncompensated labour supply elasticities in both discrete and continuous models. Welfare costs of similar *ad valorem* labour supply tax distortions differ between models by factors of around 5, being sharply lower in the discrete formulation. On the other hand, under their second discrete choice formulation, which maintains fixed shares of households in tax revenues, the discrete choice model produces sharply higher welfare cost estimates. This is because households who switch from high to low labour supply inflict a fiscal externality on those remaining in their original state, since revenues fall. For an individual close to indifferent between high and low discrete labour supply states, when switching to the low labour supply state they experience little or no gain, while all other individuals collectively experience a loss represented by the tax revenue foregone. The factors of proportionality in results between discrete and continuous models change as the form of discreteness changes (step size across uniform parameter distributions, numbers of individuals, model parameters used for the population distributions), but not markedly.

They also consider cases where there is discrete choice for one household member (the primary worker) and continuity of choice for the other (the secondary worker); and consider household rather than individual optimization. Differences in results between mixed discrete-continuous choice models are smaller, but other insights also emerge. These include the influence of discreteness of choice for one household member over the labour supply behaviour of the other, with implications for the literature on labour supply elasticities for primary and secondary workers. They investigate differences in model results empirically using UK data and literature based parameter estimates instead of numerical examples. Results indicate slightly smaller but still significant factors of proportionality to those which occur in numerical examples. The conclusion is that discreteness in modelling labour supply behaviour matters, not only for labour supply estimation but also for the calculation of welfare costs of labour supply taxation. The formulation chosen also critically affects whether estimates are raised or lowered.

The Redistributive Effects of Transfers

Bhattarai and Whalley (1997b) also use this modelling approach to investigate the redistributive effects of transfers in the UK. The point of departure in their analysis is the observation, seemingly not in the literature, that with voluntary participation in transfer programmes (with tax back or withdrawal provisions), the utility, or real income, value of transfers to participants is typically less than the cash transfers received. This is because individuals (or households) compare utility across two regimes; one with benefits and tax back arrangements, and the other with no benefits and no tax back, choosing the higher utility regime. A money metric utility comparison between the regimes (the real income difference) bears no direct relation to the net of tax back cash transfers actually received. Indeed, in an extreme case where an individual (or household) is indifferent between participating and not participating, if they were recorded as a benefit programme participant, the real income gain to them from participation in the transfer programme would be zero, despite the disbursement of public funds to the recipient. This analysis argues that, in general, and ignoring wage rate effects, the real income received by transfer recipients is smaller than the cash transfers actually made, since to the recipient the reference point for valuing them should be the reservation utility in the no benefit-no tax back regime.

Given tax back rates, individuals (or households) will also not participate in transfer programmes until some threshold level of transfers is reached, raising utility under participation above that in the no participation regime. Tax back conditions in benefit programmes thus impose a form of real income entry fee on participation, which must be deducted when evaluating the redistributive effects of transfer programmes. Conditional on participation in transfer programmes, transfers shift recipients' budget constraints parallel. In the homothetic case, after the entry fee has been paid, marginal increases in transfers (for fixed tax back rates) provide recipients with corresponding marginal increases in real income in the fixed wage case.

They also argue that an additional effect, also seemingly missing from existing literature, needs to enter analyses of the redistribution effects of transfers, namely that when the poor participate in a conditional transfer scheme, the associated withdrawal of low wage labour from the market place drives up the wage of low wage(skill) workers relative to high wage(skill) workers. Thus, with heterogeneous labour income(skill) range, the withdrawal of low wage labour due to high tax back conditional transfers to the poor raises their wage rate. This set aside effect potentially substantially raises the welfare of the poor. Thus, conventional redistribution to the poor through transfers may be overestimated for the reasons given above, but induced redistribution via changes in the wage distribution can provide significant redistribution.

Bhattari and Whalley use conditional choice general equilibrium models to assess the importance of these two effects. These models embody both endogenous participation decisions in transfer schemes by households, and heterogeneous labour in production (by income range or skill type). In such models, programme participation by low income households is endogenously determined in equilibrium, along with the wage distribution since wage rates change as transfer programmes characteristics (benefit levels, tax-back rates) change. The budget set for households are non-convex, presenting special computation problems not tackled, as far as we are aware, in existing general equilibrium tax computation literature. Commodity demands by households, including leisure, are no longer analytic, even for conventional CES or Cobb-Douglas utility functions. This means that household demands have to be evaluated numerically using optimisation techniques within a larger equilibrium structure, including the production side modelling of the economy. The larger model is itself solved through separate application of numerical optimization methods; in essence optimization embedded within a wider optimization, since consumer demands are non-analytic.

The bottom line conclusion they offer is that assessing the redistributive effects of conditional transfers is neither as straightforward as it at first sight appears, nor is the real income value of such transfers seemingly so large as is implicitly assumed in the literature. Regime choice significantly affects such measures, and their general equilibrium effects through programme-induced low wage labour withdrawal need to be taken into account. These effects seem to be virtually ignored in available literature in the area, and are important because they can radically change perceptions as to the redistributive effects of transfers.

CONCLUDING REMARKS

This paper discusses applied general equilibrium tax modelling, and initial applications to UK policy issues under an ESRC supported research project on General Equilibrium Modelling of UK Policy Issues. Future activity on the project will reflect the objectives outlined in the original project proposal. Further work also remains to be done on model applications to the analysis of other UK policy issues (e.g. effects on the UK of the Uruguay Round of GATT negotiations, possible effects of a carbon tax on UK economic performance, and analysis of UK social security issues) through the development of a other of issue-driven modelling structures. The original project proposal set out a research agenda through the years 1998-99. Furthering the development of general equilibrium and dynamic modelling techniques and providing a better integration with other disciplines, including econometrics, while contributing to the dissemination of general equilibrium modelling techniques and relevant software tools will remain the focus of the remainder of project.

REFERENCES

Auerbach, A.J., L.J. Kotlikoff and J. Skinner (1983), "The Efficiency Gains from Dynamic Tax Reform", *International Economic Review*, 24, 81-100.

Ballard, C., D. Fullerton, J.B. Shoven and J.Whalley (1985), *A General Equilibrium Model for Tax Policy Evaluation*, University of Chicago Press, Chicago, IL.

Bhattarai, K. and J. Whalley (1997a), "Discreteness and the Welfare Cost of Labour Supply Tax Distortions", NBER Working Paper No.6280, November.

Bhattarai, K and J. Whalley (1997b), "The Redistrbutive Effects of Transfers", NBER Working Paper No.6281, November.

Brook, A., D. Kendrick and A. Meeraus (1992), *GAMS: User's Guide*, release 2.25, Scientific Press, San Francisco, CA.

Dirkse, S.P. and M. Ferris, (1995), "The PATH Solver: a Non-monotone Stabilization Scheme for Mixed Complementarity Problems", *Optimization Mehods and Software*, 5, 123-156.

Economic Trends (1995), Office of National Statistics, London.

Fullerton, D., J.B. Shoven and J. Whalley (1983), "Replacing the U.S. Income Tax with a Progressive Consumption Tax. A Sequenced General Equilibrium Approach", *Journal of Public Economics*, 20, 3-23.

Harberger, A.C. (1962), "The Incidence of the Corporation Income Tax", *Journal of Political Economy*, 70, 215-40.

Kehoe, T. (1980), "An Index Theorem for General Equilibrium Models with Production", *Econometrica*, 48, 1211-32

Kehoe, T. and J. Whalley (1985), "Uniqueness of Equilibrium in a Large Scale Numerical General Equilibrium Model", *Journal of Public Economics*, 28, 247-54.

Mansur, A., and J. Whalley (1984), "Numerical Specification of Applied General Equilibrium Models: Estimation, Calibration and Data", in H. Scarf and J.B. Shoven, eds., *Applied General Equilibrium Analysis*, Cambridge University Press, New York.

Piggott, J.R. and J. Whalley (1985), *Economic Effects of U.K. Tax-Subsidy Policies: A General Equilibrium Appraisal,* Cambridge University Press, Cambridge.

Preston, I. and I.Walker (1992), "Welfare Measurement in Labour Supply Models with Non-linear Budget Constraints", Institute of Fiscal Studies, Working Paper No. 292/12. London.

Rutherford, T.F. (1997), *The GAMS/MPSGE and GAMS/MILES User Notes*, GAMS Development Corporation, Washington, DC.

Scarf, H.E. (1967), "On the Computation of Equilibrium Prices", in W.J. Fellner, ed., *Ten Economic Studies in the Tradition of Irving Fisher*, Wiley, New York.

Scarf, H.E. and T. Hansen (1973), *The Computation of Economic Equilibria*, Yale University Press, New Haven, CT.

Shoven, J.B. (1974), "A Proof of the Existence of General Equilibrium with *ad Balorem* Commodity Taxes", *Journal of Economic Theory*, 8, 1-25.

Shoven, J.B. and J. Whalley (1973), "General Equilibrium with Taxes: A Computational Procedure and an Existence Proof", *Review of Economic Studies*, 40, 475-90.

Shoven, J.B. and J. Whalley (1984), "Applied General Equilibrium Models of Taxation and International Trade", *Journal of Economic Literature*, September 1007-51.

St.-Hilaire, F. and J. Whalley (1983), "A Microconsistent Equilibrium Data Set for Canada for Use in Tax Policy Analysis", *Review of Income and Wealth*, June 175-204.

Summers, L.H. (1981), "Capital Taxation and Accumulation in a Life Cycle Growth Model", *American Economic Review*, 71, 533-44

Taylor, L. (ed.), (1990), *Socially Relevant Policy Analysis: Structuralist Computable General Equilibrium Models for the Developing World*, MIT Press, Cambridge, MA.

Varian, H.R. (1992), *Microeconomic Analysis*, 3rd edition, W.W. Norton and Company, New York.

Whalley, J.(1985), *Trade Liberalization Among Major World Trading Areas*, MIT Press, Cambridge, MA.

NOTES

1. The Discussion in this Section Draws on Whalley (1985).
2. We use data for 1990. Data for a later Year was not Available at Construction Stage, but 1995 Data has Since been Released.
3. The effect of tax distortions on the labour leisure choice can be captured through a subsidy to the consumption of leisure at rate t_l^h.
4. Elaboration of this model to more fully include is to follow in the project.
5. See Bhattarai and Whalley (1997a).
6. See the Discussion of the Related but Different Issue of non linear Budget Constraints and the Welfare cost of Taxes in Preston and Walker (1992).

20

The Role of Labour Demand Elasticities in Tax Incidence Analysis with Heterogeneous Labour

Keshab Bhattarai[86] & John Whalley

INTRODUCTION

This paper builds on the observation that existing empirically based incidence analyses drawing either on shifting assumptions[1], or on general equilibrium tax models treat labour as bearing the burden of its own income and payroll taxes[2]. The implicit assumption is that labour is a homogenous input which is perfectly mobile across industries and yields leisure which is consumed by households. A key set of parameters in incidence analyses conducted with these models have been presumed to be the labour supply elasticities which are the subject of some attention in both calibration and sensitivity analysis. Labour demand elasticities do not enter these analyses.

We argue that with homogeneous labour in production, the implicit labour demand function facing each household is highly elastic since, if small relative to the aggregate, each is a price taker in labour markets. The implication is that labour will bear most of the burden of its own labour taxes, independently of labour supply elasticities used. Conventional sensitivity analysis on labour supply elasticities will show little variation in tax incidence profiles. On the other hand, varying labour demand elasticities will allow for the shifting of tax burdens to other groups or households.

We investigate differences in model analyses of tax incidence using comparable nested models in which labour is either homogenous or heterogeneous in production, so that labour demand elasticities also enter. Each model is calibrated to a ten decile household data set containing data on consumption, taxes, and leisure for the UK for 1994. Labour supply elasticity calibration is based on

86. Bhattarai and Whalley acknowledge financial support from the ESRC under an award for a project on General Equilibrium Modelling of UK Policy Issues. We are thankful to Baldev Raj and two referees for comments on earlier versions of this paper.

estimates from Killingsworth (1983), with the labour demand elasticity used in calibration in the heterogeneous labour model drawing on estimates from Hamermesh (1993). Significant differences in incidence profiles are found across the two models. The heterogeneous model shows significant variations in incidence profiles as labour demand elasticities change, while the homogeneous good model shows little sensitivity to labour supply elasticities. The implication drawn is the need to more carefully specify labour demand elasticities in tax incidence analyses.

TAX INCIDENCE MODELS WITH HETEROGENEOUS AND HOMOGENEOUS

Labour Supply

It seems clear that if labour supplied by household groups is heterogeneous with imperfect substitutability in production across skill levels, then both labour demand and labour supply elasticities are needed in tax incidence analyses. If labour is treated as homogeneous across households, then if each household is small and a taker of wage rates, they implicitly face a perfectly elastic labour demand function. In this case, varying the labour supply elasticity will not change the conclusion that labour bears the burden of their own income taxes, even if tax rates differ across households.

If the labour demand elasticity is less than infinite, as labour supply functions shift due to household specific taxes, some of the burden of the tax is shifted elsewhere. The implication is that if heterogeneous labour models are used for tax incidence analysis and model parameters calibrated to both labour demand and labour supply elasticities, tax incidence results can differ[3] (and potentially sharply so) from those generated by the homogenous labour model conventionally used.

We choose the household as the basic unit of tax incidence analysis not only because consumption and labour-leisure choice decisions are made at the household level, but also it is adapted in the data on income and consumption used in the empirical analysis of incidence profiles in the paper.

A heterogeneous Labour Household Tax Model

We consider an economy with households differentiated according to their skill levels, which, for our empirical application, we take to be collinear with income ranges. Each household is endowed with a fixed amount of time, which it can divide between leisure and work. A production function specifies how the various labour types combine to yield a single consumption good. Each of them buys the consumption good using income earned by selling its labour on the market along with transfers received from government, effectively buying back its leisure at its net of tax wage. Households maximize utility by choosing bundles of consumption goods and leisure subject to their budget constraint. Hours of work (labour supply), consumption and leisure are thus obtained by solving each household's optimization problem.

Taxes distort the consumption-leisure choice of households. Tax rates are household specific, and government budget balance holds with transfers the sole expenditure item. In empirical implementation, we use a single tax rate on labour income for each household to represent the composite of income and payroll taxes, and a composite indirect tax rate for each household which reflects sales (VAT) and excise taxes. These latter rates differ by household due to differing consumption patterns in the data.

More specifically, we assume CES preferences for each household as

$$U^h = \left[\alpha^h C^{h\frac{\sigma^h - 1}{\sigma^h}} + (1-\alpha^h) L^{h\frac{\sigma^h - 1}{\sigma^h}} \right]^{\frac{\sigma^h}{\sigma^h - 1}} \tag{1}$$

where U^h is utility, α^h is the share of income spent on the consumption good, (1- α^h) is the share parameter on leisure, C^h and L^h are consumption and leisure respectively of household *h*, and σ^h is the elasticity of substitution between consumption and leisure of household *h*.

The income for household *h* equals the time endowment valued at the net of tax wage plus transfers received from government, i.e.

$$I^h = (1 - t_l^h) w^h \bar{L}^h + RH^h \tag{2}$$

where I^h is the full income of household *h*, w^h is the gross of tax wage rate for household *h*, and t_l^h is the household specific income tax rate. $\bar{L}^h$ is the time endowment of household *h* to be divided between labour supply and leisure, and RH^h are transfers received by household *h*.

Maximization of utility (1), subject to (2), yields demand functions for consumption and leisure for each household as,

$$C^h = \left[\frac{\alpha\alpha^h}{P(1+t_C^h)} \right]^{\sigma^h}$$

$$\left[\frac{I^h}{\alpha\alpha^h (P(1+t_C^h))^{1-\sigma^h} + (1-\alpha^h)(w^h(1-t_I^h))^{1-\sigma^h}} \right] \tag{3}$$

$$L^h = \left[\frac{(1-\alpha^h)}{w^h(1-t_I^h)}\right]^{\sigma^h}$$

$$\left[\frac{I^h}{\alpha^h(P(1+t_C^h))^{1-\sigma^h} + (1-\alpha^h)(w^h(1-t_I^h))^{1-\sigma^h}}\right] \quad (4)$$

where w^h is the gross of tax wage rate for labor of type h (supplied by household h), P is the price of the consumption good, and t_C^h is the consumption (or indirect) tax rate faced by household h. The budget balance condition for households implies that on the expenditure side

$$I^h = P(1+t_c^h)C^h + w^h(1-t_I^h)L^h \quad (5)$$

Each household supplies labour to the market which reflects the difference between its labour endowment and its demand for leisure,

$$LS^h = \overline{L}^h - L^h \quad (6)$$

where LS^h is labour supplied by household h. The economy wide labour supply is the sum of labour supplied across the individual households. In equilibrium, equation (6) is also the labour market clearing condition for labour of type h.

In the model, we assume that the labour each household supplies is differentiated by skill level from the labour supplied by all other households, and we represent this through a CES production technology for the single output Y in which all labour types enter, i.e.

$$Y = \lambda\left(\sum_h \delta^h LS^{h\frac{\sigma_p-1}{\sigma_p}}\right)^{\frac{\sigma_p}{\sigma_p-1}} \quad (7)$$

where LS^h is the input (labour supply) of type h, δ^h is the share parameter in production on each category of labour, λ is a units term and σ_p is the elasticity of substitution among labour types in production.

Producers pay the gross of tax wage rate when hiring labour from each household, and households receive the net of income tax wage. For simplicity, we assume that only one consumption good is produced in this economy, and producers maximize profit, Π, given by

$$\Pi = PY - \sum_h w^h LS^h \tag{8}$$

where the P is price of the consumption good, and is the labour input of type h.

Profit maximization results in the labour demand function for each labour type h as,

$$LD^h = \frac{1}{\lambda}\left(\delta^h + \sum_{hh} \delta^{hh}\left(\frac{\prod\limits_{hh \neq h} w^{hh}}{w^h}\right)^{\sigma_p - 1}\right)^{\frac{\sigma_p}{\sigma_p - 1}} \tag{9}$$

where LD^h is labour demand of type h, and in equilibrium also equals labour supply LS^h.

The government in this economy raises revenues, R, by taxing income and consumption, i.e,

$$R = \sum_h t_I^h w^h LS^h + \sum_h t_c^h PC^h \tag{10}$$

We assume a single period in which all output is consumed (there is no saving). In equilibrium, P and the household wage rates, w^h, are endogeneously determined such that there is market clearing in the consumption good

$$Y = \sum_h C^h \tag{11}$$

and there is market clearing for each labour type,

$$LS^h = LD^h \tag{12}$$

As transfers to households are the only government expenditure item, government budget balance also requires that in equilibrium $R = \sum_h RH^h$. Thus, for each household h, in equilibrium labour supplied of each type equals its use in production, and a profile of skill specific equilibrium wage rates will be determined. For convenience, in this model, we can choose the numeraire of this system to be that the price of the consumption good is equal to 1.

A Homogeneous Labour Tax Model

In contrast to the heterogeneous labour model, when labour is homogeneous in production we need only specify a model with labour as the single input into production. We assume a constant marginal product of labour production function, which is linear in (total) labour [1].

$$Y = \lambda \sum_h LS^h \tag{13}$$

A single wage applies to all households' labour supply because of the homogeneity of labour inputs, and the relationship between the wage rate and the price of the consumption good is given by

$$P = \frac{w}{\lambda} \tag{14}$$

Households still differ in their preferences as in (1), still face household specific income and consumption tax rates, but unlike in the heterogeneous labour model face a common wage rate. Equilibrium in this case is given by market clearing for the single labour type in the model; with, in this case, one single wage rate endogenously determined.

This homogeneous labour model is thus a special case of the model presented above, and nests into the more general heterogeneous labour model.

IMPLEMENTATION OF HOMOGENEOUS AND HETEROGENEOUS LABOUR TAX

Incidence Models

We perform tax incidence analyses using two models above by calibrating[2] each to a base year data set, specifying labour demand and labour supply elasticity values, and performing counterfactual equilibrium analyses. The base case data set we use reflects the UK economy for the UK tax year 1994/95[3]. We use data on incomes, taxes and benefits by household decile compiled by the UK Treasury and reported in the UK government statistical publication Economic Trends (1996). This source reports data for non retired households grouped by income[4] decile, benefits received both in cash and in kind, and direct and indirect taxes paid by each household decile.

Base Case Data

For modelling purposes, we require a base case data set which is fully model admissible. This means that all variables which appear in each model should be identified in the data set, and all of the model equilibrium conditions need to be satisfied. Among these are conditions that the value of consumption across households should equal the value of production (a zero profit condition in production implies that income received from supplying labour equals the value of production). All households should also be represented by data which satisfies household budget balance, and government expenditures equal government receipts (government budget balance).

The basic data we use, while having most of the information we need, is deficient for our purposes in number of respects. Household leisure consumption is not identified. Government budget balance is violated in the data, since all taxes paid by households are identified but only those government expenditures leading directly to direct household benefits (cash transfers, education, and health care appear, but defence, for instance, is missing). In the basic data, government expenditures in aggregate are thus substantially less than tax revenues. Also, individual household budget constraints do not automatically hold.

A series of adjustments and modifications are therefore necessary to the basic data set before it can be used for model calibration. These are set out in more detail in Appendix 1, but can be summarised as follows. We scale the in kind portion of government benefits for each decile such that government expenditures equal taxes collected. Transfers received by each decile in the model are thus the sum of cash and in kind benefits provided by government. We use wage rate data by household and UK time use survey data to construct data on the value of leisure time by household for each decile, valuing time at the net of tax wage. We then make further adjustments to ensure full consistency of the data set to the model, including modifications such that household budget constraints hold in the data.

Table1
Model Admissible Household data set by Deciles of Income for Non-retired Households, UK 1994/95[1]

Households[2]	*(a) Gross of tax labor income*[a]	*(b) Transfers*[a]	*(c) Income and other direct taxes paid*[a,3]	*(d) Indirect taxes paid*[a,4]	*(e) Consump- tiongross of indirect taxes*[a,5]	*(f) Leisure*[a,6]	*(g) Income tax rate*[7]	*(h) Indirect tax rate*[8]
Decile 1 (Poor)	3079	14638	930	2139	16787	14491	0.05	0.13
Decile 2	5918	12880	1194	2183	17604	17085	0.06	0.12
Decile 3	11021	11040	1880	2759	20181	14076	0.09	0.14
Decile 4	16111	9867	2815	3213	23163	11934	0.11	0.14
Decile 5	21184	8559	3831	3572	25912	10895	0.13	0.14
Decile 6	26161	8205	4745	3957	29621	10455	0.14	0.13
Decile 7	30140	6858	5531	4266	31467	12293	0.15	0.14
Decile 8	34614	5645	6576	4362	33683	13895	0.16	0.13
Decile 9	41918	5166	8175	4537	38909	15449	0.17	0.12
Decile 10 (Rich)	71147	4440	15082	5551	60505	6871	0.20	0.09

Notes: All figures in this table noted with superscript **a** are millions of £, for the tax year 1994/95.

The resulting model admissible data set across ten UK households is displayed in Table 1. In this data, gross income is concentrated in the higher deciles, with transfers concentrated in the lower deciles. The household profile of leisure consumption reflects the interaction of hours (falling as we move to the higher income ranges) and wage rates at which leisure is valued (rising by income range). The two tax rate profiles are for average (not marginal) tax rates. For income taxes they rise by income range, but not by as much as might be thought from an examination of tax rate schedules. This is because of income tax allowances, caps on social (national) insurance contributions, untaxed housing capital income, and UK tax shelters (pensions, savings in tax sheltered vehicles), all of which have a major influence on the average tax rate profile. The indirect tax rates fall by income range due to the influence of excise taxes, particularly on petrol, but also on drink, both of which are a considerably larger fraction of expenditures for the poor than the rich.

Using information on elasticities, we calibrate both the homogeneous and heterogeneous labour models to this benchmark equilibrium data set. To do this, we first take the benchmark data set from Table 1 in value terms, and decompose it into separate price and quantity observations. Following Harberger (1962), and Shoven and Whalley (1992) we choose units both for labour by type, and for consumption, as those amounts which sell for £1 in the base case equilibrium. Using this convention all prices and wages are one in the base case, and all quantities are as given by the base case observations in Table 1. The calibrated versions of each model replicate this base case data as a model solution.

Elasticities

The elasticity parameters needed for the models are the ten household specific substitution elasticities in consumption (CES preferences) which are used in both models, and the substitution elasticity in production (in the CES production function) in the heterogeneous labour model. Direct estimates of these elasticities are not available in the literature. Elasticities in consumption over goods and leisure must be inferred from literature estimates of labour supply elasticities. Elasticities of substitution in production between labour types must be inferred from literature estimates of labour demand elasticities for various types of labour.

From the production function (7), we can use the first order conditions for profit maximization and the derived labour demand function (9). The elasticity of labour demand in production is given by $e_{LD}^{h} = \frac{\partial LD^{h}}{\partial w^{h}} \frac{w^{h}}{LD^{h}}$ and differentiating (9) w.r.t. w^{h} gives

$$e_{LD}^{h} = \frac{-\sigma_{p} \sum_{hh \neq h} \delta^{hh} \left(\prod_{h \neq h} w^{hh} \right)^{\sigma_{p}-1}}{w^{h^{\sigma_{p}-1}} \left[\delta^{h} + \sum_{hh} \delta^{hh} \left(\frac{\prod_{h \neq h} w^{hh}}{w^{h}} \right)^{\sigma_{p}-1} \right]} \tag{15}$$

In the base case all gross of tax wage rates are unity, and if, in addition, household labour shares are small, e_{LD}^{h} effectively collapses to $-\sigma p$. We choose the elasticity of substitution between labour types in production which, from (15), we can calibrate numerically to values of labour demand elasticities found in the literature (Hamermesh (1993)), and use other sensitivity cases discussed below to reflect ranges around a central case value. As there are ten household demand elasticities in the model around the base case equilibrium, and only one free parameter, σ^p, in calibration we choose such that elasticities across households (which do not vary that much) are within a desired range.

Labour supply elasticities, in contrast, are found using the leisure demand function (4). Point estimates of labour supply elasticities for each household in the neighbourhood of the benchmark equilibrium can be generated by noting that

$$\frac{\partial LS^h}{\partial w^h}\frac{w^h}{LS^h} = \frac{\partial LS^h}{\partial L^h}\frac{\partial L^h}{\partial w^h}\frac{w^h}{L^h}\frac{L^h}{LS^h} = (-1)\eta_{LE}\frac{L^h}{LS^h} \tag{16}$$

We use the leisure demand function (4) to derive the leisure demand elasticity, η_{LE} which is given by

$$\eta_{LE}^h = -\left(\sigma^h + \frac{(\sigma^h - 1)(1-\alpha^h){w^h}^{1-\sigma^h}}{\alpha^h P^{1-\sigma^h} + (1-\alpha^h){w^h}^{1-\sigma^h}}\right) \tag{17}$$

The point estimate of the labour supply elasticity for each household, given σ^h, is :

$$e_{LS}^h = \left(\sigma^h + \frac{(\sigma_p - 1)(1-\alpha^h){w^h}^{1-\sigma^h}}{\alpha^h P^{1-\sigma^h} + (1-\alpha^h){w^h}^{1-\sigma^h}}\right)\frac{L^h}{LS^h} \tag{18}$$

In the neighbourhood of the base case, where the price of goods and all wage rates are unity, this collapses to

$$e_{LS}^h = \left(\sigma^h + (\sigma_p - 1)(1-\alpha^h){w^h}^{1-\sigma^h}\right)\frac{L^h}{LS^h} \tag{19}$$

and if $\left(1-\alpha^h\right)$ is small[1] $e_{LS}^h \approx \sigma^h \dfrac{L^h}{LS^h}$.

We choose values for labour supply elasticities from literature estimates and using (16) these imply leisure demand elasticities. Using those as point estimates around the benchmark equilibrium, and using (18), elasticities of substitution in preferences are determined for each household decile. The equation (18) yields an implicit function for σ^h, which we solve numerically.

Table 2

Model Production and Consumption side Elasticities, and Literature Justification

A. Range of labour supply elasticities based on those reported in Killingsworth (1983)

Range of values	*Labour supply elasticity assumed for each household*	*Range of elasticities of substitution in consumption implied for household deciles*
High	1.0	0.52-10.5
Mid (central case)	0.3	0.38-3.50
Low	0.15	0.32-1.57

B. Range of labour demand elasticities based on those reported in Hamermesh (1993)

Range	*Range of Labour Demand Elasticities by Decile*	*Elasticity of Substitution used in Production*
High	-1.81 to -2.10	1.93
Mid Range (central case)	-1.05 to -1.24	1.32
Low	-0.58 to -0.67	0.71

Table 2 sets out the elasticity ranges we use for in the two models and the implied substitution elasticities in consumption and production. These are approximately consistent with ranges of parameter estimates reported by Hamermesh (1993) for labour demand, and Killingsworth (1983) for labour supply.

In the model, there are 10 separate labour demand elasticities for each labour type. These elasticities vary, and hence we calibrate the model to point estimates of these elasticities in the neighbourhood of the benchmark equilibrium. In addition, there is only one free model parameter (the elasticity of substitution among labour types in production) so that exact calibration for each household type labour demand elasticity is not feasible. We thus vary the single production side elasticity until the household labour demand elasticities, which are similar across households, are within the desired range.

RESULTS

We have used the heterogeneous and homogeneous labour models described above and calibrated to UK data for the 1995/96 tax year to investigate the behaviour of tax incidence results across models. We do this for different tax experiments, different labour supply elasticity (consumption/leisure substitution) configurations, freezing the labour demand elasticity specification; and for different labour demand elasticity specifications, freezing the labour supply elasticity specification.

The essence of tax policy analysis lies in comparing welfare changes between benchmark and counterfactual equilibria. How much a typical household has gained or lost because of changes in policy in money metric terms, or how much money is required to bring him/her back to their original welfare can be measured at either original or new prices. The Hicksian equivalent variation (*EV*) is a money metric measure of the welfare change between benchmark and counterfactual scenarios using benchmark (old) prices. It is the difference in money metric utility at old prices corresponding to benchmark and counterfactual model solutions; i.e.

$$EV = E(U^N, P^0) - E(U^0, P^0) \tag{20}$$

where superscripts N and O represent new and old values for the variable on which they appear, U is the utility, and E is the expenditure function which depends on prices and utility level.

If utility functions are of the linear homogeneous type, then original and new equilibria can be thought of in terms of a radial expansion of the utility surface. In this case the change in money metric welfare between benchmark and counterfactual solutions of the model is proportional to the change in utility or the percentage change along the radial projection between the two consumption points.

$$EV = \frac{U^N - U^0}{U^0} I^0 \tag{21}$$

where N and O represent new and old values of the variables as before, and I represents the income.

In Table 3 we report tax incidence calculations for a case where we replace the pre existing pattern of labour income tax rates by household by a yield preserving uniform rate income tax across households. We consider cases where we freeze labour supply elasticities first at 0.3, and then at 1.0, and vary the ranges we use for labour demand elasticities in the heterogeneous labour model. We compare model results across the homogeneous labour model and the various specifications of the heterogeneous model for these labour supply elasticities.

Table 3
Comparing Homogeneous and Heterogeneous Labour Models

Specification

- *Experiment:* replacing existing labour income taxes by yield preserving uniform rate
- *Elasticity Specification:* Labour supply elasticity 0.3 and 1.0 in two cases, labour demand elasticities range from -0.58 to -2.1.

Results:

Welfare gains/losses by decile in terms of Hicksian EV as a fraction of base income (with low labour supply elasticity (0.3))

Decile	*Homogeneous Labour Model*	*Heterogeneous Labour Model Labour Demand Elasticities Ranges as Specified in Table 2*		
		Low (-0.58 to -0.67)	*Middle (-1.05 to -1.24)*	*High (-1.8 to-2.1)*
1 poor	-0.0581	-0.0134	-0.0501	-0.0591
2	-0.0485	-0.0173	-0.0434	-0.0493
3	-0.0424	-0.0334	-0.0401	-0.0430
4	-0.0299	-0.0306	-0.0296	-0.0303
5	-0.0143	-0.0211	-0.0153	-0.0146
6	-0.0064	-0.0159	-0.0078	-0.0066
7	0.0044	-0.0059	0.0028	0.0042
8	0.0173	0.0060	0.0155	0.0171
9	0.0272	0.0154	0.0253	0.0270
10 rich	0.0670	0.0562	0.0660	0.0666

Results:

Welfare gains/losses by decile in terms of Hicksian EV as a fraction of base income (with low labour supply elasticity (1.0))

Decile	Homogeneous Labour Model	Heterogeneous Labour Model Labour Demand Elasticities Ranges as Specified in Table 2		
		Low (-0.58 to -0.67)	Middle (-1.05 to -1.24)	High (-1.8 to-2.1)
1 poor	-0.0577	-0.0376	-0.0503	-0.0585
2	-0.0481	-0.0709	-0.0442	-0.0486
3	-0.042	-0.2191	-0.0420	-0.0421
4	-0.0295	-0.2944	-0.0312	-0.0294
5	-0.014	-0.3300	-0.0150	-0.0140
6	-0.0061	-0.1114	-0.0060	-0.0061
7	0.0047	0.3908	0.0066	0.0045
8	0.0176	0.0739	0.0221	0.0172
9	0.0276	0.1476	0.0349	0.0270
10 rich	0.0676	-0.0025	0.0737	0.0670

Results in Table 3 show the redistribution across households in these cases. Richer households gain because their taxes fall, and poorer households lose since the replacement tax is at a uniform rate and their taxes rise. However, there is considerable variation in the redistribution profile across the two elasticity cases for the heterogeneous labour model. Considerably more redistribution occurs in the high elasticity case since wage rate changes in response to the tax replacement are small; low income households bear most of the burden of their higher taxes, and high income households gain by most of their tax saving.

As one moves across labour demand elasticity specifications the redistributive effects from the tax changes become larger, with wage changes less pronounced. Labour demand elasticities have a significant influence on the perceived tax incidence effects from the tax replacement. From various sensitivity analyses, we find that as labour demand elasticities increase, the income tax incidence profile in the heterogeneous labour model approaches that of the homogeneous labour model for any given value of the labour supply elasticity.

In Table 4 we explore how the model comparisons change as we vary labour supply elasticities. We consider the same tax replacement, i.e. replacing the existing profile of income tax rates by a uniform rate income tax across households, but only consider the mid range specification of labour demand elasticities, changing labour supply elasticities in both homogeneous and heterogeneous labour models.

Results in Table 4 show that the incidence profile changes relatively little between heterogeneous and homogeneous labour models as labour supply elasticities increase. The low income households lose about 5-6 percent of the base year income in both heterogeneous and homogeneous labour models irrespective of different values of labour supply elasticities. For middle range values of labour demand elasticities (irrespective to any specific value of labour supply elasticity), income tax incidence profiles of replacing base case labour income taxes by yield preserving labour income tax rates become comparable across two models.

Table 4
Impacts of Varying Labour Supply Elasticities on Incidence Profile Comparisons

Specification

- Experiment: replacing existing labour income taxes by yield preserving uniform rate
- Elasticity specification: Labour supply elasticity 0.3, mid range demand elasticities in the heterogeneous labour model.

Results:

Welfare gains/losses by households, Hicksian EV as a fraction of base income

Decile	*Labour Supply Elasticity (0.15)*		*Labour Supply Elasticity (0.3)*		*Labour Supply Elasticity (1.0)*	
	Homogeneous labour Model	*Heterogeneous labour Model*	*Homogeneous labour Model*	*Heterogeneous labour Model*	*Homogeneous labour Model*	*Heterogeneous labour Model*
1 poor	-0.0582	-0.0500	-0.0581	-0.0501	-0.0577	-0.0585
2	-0.0486	-0.0431	-0.0485	-0.0434	-0.0481	-0.0486
3	-0.0426	-0.0395	-0.0424	-0.0401	-0.0420	-0.0421
4	-0.0300	-0.0290	-0.0299	-0.0296	-0.0295	-0.0294
5	-0.0144	-0.0149	-0.0143	-0.0153	-0.0140	-0.0140
6	-0.0065	-0.0075	-0.0064	-0.0078	-0.0061	-0.0061
7	0.0043	0.0028	0.0044	0.0028	0.0047	0.0045
8	0.0172	0.0150	0.0173	0.0155	0.0176	0.0172
9	0.0270	0.0244	0.0272	0.0253	0.0276	0.0270
10 rich	0.0668	0.0650	0.0670	0.0660	0.0676	0.0670

Table 5
Incidence Comparison for Different Tax Changes for the Heterogeneous Labour and Homogeneous Labour Models

Specification

- Labour Supply Elasticity set at 0.3
- Labour Demand Elasticities set at Mid Range Values in the heterogeneous labour model.

Results:

Welfare gains/losses by households, Hicksian EV as a fraction of base income

Decile	*Labour Income Tax*		*Labour and Sales Tax*		*Only Sales Tax*	
	Homogeneous labour Model	*Heterogeneous labour Model*	*Homogeneous labour Model*	*Heterogeneous labour Model*	*Homogeneous labour Model*	*Heterogeneous labour Model*
1 poor	-0.0581	-0.0501	-0.0551	-0.0489	0.0029	0.0026
2	-0.0485	-0.0434	-0.0478	-0.0434	0.0006	0.0006
3	-0.0424	-0.0401	-0.0324	-0.0307	0.0101	0.0096
4	-0.0299	-0.0296	-0.0167	-0.0166	0.0132	0.0129
5	-0.0143	-0.0153	-0.0008	-0.0014	0.0134	0.0134
6	-0.0064	-0.0078	0.0039	0.0032	0.0100	0.0102
7	0.0044	0.0028	0.0164	0.0155	0.0116	0.0118
8	0.0173	0.0155	0.0235	0.0225	0.0058	0.0061
9	0.0272	0.0253	0.0217	0.0208	-0.0057	-0.0054
10 rich	0.0670	0.0660	0.0314	0.0307	-0.0337	-0.0338

As final sets of results in Table 5 we present incidence results for three different yield preserving tax changes; the first one only involves income taxes, the second one involves income and sales taxes, and the last one involves only sales taxes. We use a 0.3 labour supply elasticity and mid range labour demand elasticities.

In both the income tax case and the combined income and sales tax case we find low income households lose and high income households gain when base case taxes are replaced by yield preserving tax rates, but the pattern of gains is different in the upper tail of the distribution across heterogeneous and homogeneous models.

CONCLUSIONS

In this paper we analyze how labour demand elasticities, long neglected in empirically based tax incidence analysis, affect incidence conclusions. Using a data set for the UK for tax year 1994/95 covering 10 household deciles we use two models to evaluate the incidence effect of various tax changes, specially the replacement of the existing pattern of income tax rates by a uniform rate yield preserving alternative. We consider two models, one with labour heterogeneous in production, i.e. 10 different labour types (one for each decile) in production; and the other with labour homogeneous across households i.e. only one type of labour in production. The substitution elasticity among labour types in production determines labour demand elasticities. Our results suggest that labour demand elasticities do indeed matter for tax incidence conclusions.

REFERENCES

Auerbach Alan J. and L.J. Kotlikoff (1987), *Dynamic Fiscal Policy*, Cambridge University Press.

Ballard Charles L., D. Fullerton, J.B. Shoven and J. Whalley (1985), *A General Equilibrium Model for Tax Policy Evaluation,* University of Chicago Press, Chicago.

Dirkse S.P. and M.C. Ferris (1995), "CCPLIB: A Collection of Nonlinear Mixed Complementarity Problems" *Optimization Methods and Software*. 5:319-345.

Dex S., A.Clark and M.Taylor (1995), *Household Labour Supply Employment*, Department Research Series No. 43 (ESRC Center for Micro-social Change, University of Essex).

Economic Trends (1996), Office of National Statistics, London.

Gillespie W. (1965), "Effect of Public Expenditure in Distribution of Income", in R. Musgrave (ed.) *Essays in Fiscal Federalism,* Brookings, Washington DC, pp. 122-186.

Hamermesh D.S. (1993), *Labour Demand,* Princeton University Press, New Jersey.

Harberger A.C. (1962), "The Incidence of the Corporation Income Tax", *Journal of Political Economy,* 70, 215-40.

Killingsworth M. (1983), *Labour Supply,* Cambridge University Press.

Kydland F.E., and E.C. Prescott "Time to Build and Aggregate Fluctuations." *Econometrica 50,* Nov., 1345-70.

Mansur A. and J. Whalley (1986), Numerical Specification of Applied General Equilibrium Models: Estimation, Calibration and Data, in Scarf Herbert E and Shoven John B. (ed.) *Applied General Equilibrium Analysis,* Cambridge University Press.

Pechman J.A and B.A. Okner (1974), *Who Bears the Burden of Taxes?* Brookings Institute, Washington D.C.

Piggott J. and J. Whalley (1985), *UK Tax Policy and Applied General Equilibrium Analysis,* Cambridge University Press.

Shoven J.B. and J. Whalley (1992), *Applying General Equilibrium,* Cambridge University Press.

Shoven J.B. and J. Whalley (1972), "A General Equilibrium Calculation of the Effects of Differential Taxation of Income from Capital in the U.S. "*Journal of Public Economics* 1, 281-322.

Watson Mark W. (1993), "Measures of Fit for Calibrated Models", *Journal of Political Economy,* Vol. 101, No. 6 pp.1011-1041.

NOTES

1. See Pechman and Okner (1974), and Gillespie (1965) as examples of this approach.
2. See Shoven and Whalley (1972) for a simple 2 sector 2 household Harberger tax model; Piggott and Whalley (1985) for a 100 household model of the UK; Ballard, Fullerton, Shoven and Whalley (1985) for a 15 household model of the US; and Auerbach and Kotlikoff (1987) for a 55 overlapping generations dynamic structure applied to US data.
3. One reason for the relative absence of heterogeneous labour models in empirically based general equilibrium work is the seeming difficulty of solution in the non-nested production function case. We solve it using the new PATH algorithm developed and employed with GAMS by Michael Ferris (see Appendix 2 for details).
4. This is a special case of the production function (7) in the model above, for the case where becomes infinite.
5. Calibration, here, denotes the exact calibration of each model to a model admissible data set which is constructed from unadjusted data from a variety of statistical sources. This is the sense of calibration discussed by Mansur and Whalley (1984) and differs from the calibration procedures used by real business cycles researchers (see Kydland and Prescott (1982)). In this latter work, no readjustments are made to data, and model parameter values chosen by reference to literature sources with a view to seeing how close model solution can be made to actual data. See also Watson (1993).
6. April 5th 1994 to April 4th 1995. This is the year used in recording tax and household income data by the UK tax authorities.
7. The income concept used in the published data is "household equivalized disposable income".
8. See Appendix 1 for more detail.
9. These households are grouped by "original" household income as in Economic Trends (1995). Original income is pre tax/pre transfer income.
10. This Includes all Social Insurance Contributions.
11. This includes VAT and all excises (especially on petrol, tobacco, drink).

12. This is gross of indirect taxes.
13. This is from UK time use survey data; leisure time is valued at the net of tax wage.
14. This includes income tax and social insurance contributions.
15. This includes the VAT plus specific excise taxes.
16. Typically, however, consumption share parameters on leisure are not small.

APPENDIX 1

Data Sources

This appendix presents details on various data sources and adjustments that underlie Table 1. The main data sources are Table 3A (Appendix 1) of Economic Trends, 1995/96, p. 36, New Earnings Survey 1995 and Time Use Survey reported in Dex et al. (1995).

The gross income in column (a) of Table 3A comprises original income and direct taxes (see Table 1 in text). Original income includes wages and salaries, imputed income from benefits in kind, self-employment income, occupational pensions, annuities and other income. Direct taxes include employees' national insurance (NI) contributions. The household average direct tax rate to be income and other taxes divided by gross of tax income plus transfers.

A1
Components of Gross of Tax Labour Income in Table 1 (see Text)
(£ million 1995/1996 UK Tax year)

	H1	*H2*	*H3*	*H4*	*H5*	*H6*	*H7*	*H8*	*H9*	*H10*	*Total*
Original income2	2149	4724	9141	13296	17353	21416	24609	28038	33743	56065	210534
Direct taxes5	930	1194	1880	2815	3831	4745	5531	6576	8175	15082	50759
Total	3079	5918	11021	16111	21184	26161	30140	34614	41918	71147	261293

The UK Economic Trends data distinguishes five different concepts of income: original, income, gross income, disposable income, post tax income and final income. Original income plus cash benefits equal gross income, disposable income is gross income minus direct taxes. Post tax income is disposable income minus indirect taxes. Final income equals post tax income plus in kind benefits.

Table A2
Gross Consumption by Households in Table 1 (see Text)
(£ million 1995/1996 UK Tax year)

Decile	*H1*	*H2*	*H3*	*H4*	*H5*	*H6*	*H7*	*H8*	*H9*	*H10*	*Total*
Gross income	3079	5918	11021	16111	21184	26161	30140	34614	41918	71147	261293
Transfers	14638	12880	11040	9867	8559	8205	6858	5645	5166	4440	86479
Direct taxes	930	1194	1880	2815	3831	4745	5531	6576	8175	15082	50759
Total	16787	17604	20181	23163	25912	29621	31467	33683	38909	60505	297013

The transfers presented in column (b) of Table 1 in the text include direct cash benefits, in kind transfers, and consumption of publicly provided goods services such as national defence. Direct cash benefits consist of retirement pension contributions, unemployment benefit, invalidity pension and allowance, sickness and industrial injury benefit, widow's benefits, and statutory maternity pay/ allowance. Non-contributory benefits include income support, child benefit, housing benefit, invalid care allowances, attendance allowance, disability living allowance, industrial injury disablement benefit, student maintenance awards, government training schemes, family credit and other non-contributory benefits. Benefits in kind consist of education, national health service, housing subsidy, rail travel subsidy, bus travel subsidy, school meals and welfare milk.

The gross consumption of each household, included in column (e) of Table 1 in the text, is derived by adding cash, in kind and non-contributory benefits to original income and subtracting the direct and indirect taxes paid by the household. Consumption thus is gross of indirect taxes that include taxes on final goods and services, VAT, duty on tobacco, beer and cider, wines and spirits, hydrocarbon oils, vehicle excise duty, TV licences, stamp duty on house purchase, customs duties, betting taxes, fossil fuel levy, and Camelot national lottery fund. It also includes intermediate taxes such as commercial and industrial rates, employer's NI contributions, duty on hydrocarbon oils, vehicle excise and other duties.

Table A3

The Value of Leisure Consumption by Households in Table 1 (see text)

	H1	*H2*	*H3*	*H4*	*H5*	*H6*	*H7*	*H8*	*H9*	*H10*	*Total*
Earnings/week/ households (£)	160	210	223	243	272	306	355	403	473	543	319
Working weeks	13	23	41	55	64	70	69	70	71	91	57
Leisure weeks	91	81	63	49	40	34	35	34	33	13	47
Value of leisure by household (£ million)	14491	17085	14076	11934	10895	10455	12293	13895	15449	6871	127444

The value of leisure reported in Table 1 in the text has been obtained by multiplying non-working weeks by the weekly earnings rate. The number of non-working weeks is the difference between the working weeks and 104 weeks. The total working week represents the total labour endowment per household with two working members. Earnings per week for top and bottom deciles, and first and third quartiles are taken from the New Earnings Survey 1995. These are interpolated for other deciles. Working weeks are derived by dividing the original income by the weekly earnings.

APPENDIX 2

Solution Method of the Model

Both homogeneous and heterogeneous labour models discussed in this paper are set up as a mixed complementarity problems and solved in GAMS software using the PATH solver.

Dirkse and Ferris (1995) state the basic idea behind the PATH solver in terms of a "zero finding problem". For any function $F: \Re^n \rightarrow \Re^n$ with lower bound $-\infty \leq l$ and an upper bound $\leq \upsilon \leq +\infty$ the problem *is to* find $z \in \Re^n$ such that

either $z_i = l_i$ and $F_i(z)$ ³ 0

or $z_i = l_i$ and $F_i(z)$ £ 0

or $l_i \leq z_i \leq u_I$ and $Fi(z) = 0$

PATH Constructs a Solution using a Damped Newton Method such as

$$0 = F_{B(x)} = F_{x(B)} + (x - x_B)$$

where x_B is the Euclidean projection of x onto the Box $B := [l, u]$. A vector x solves this non-linear equation only if $z = x_B$ solves the MCP. A more detailed explanation of this algorithm is beyond the scope of this paper, many technical papers on the topic are available in Ferris's homepage : http://www.cs.wisc.edu/~ferris/.

GAMS syntax (Brook, Kendrick and Meeraus (1992)) permits us to generate a non linear mixed complemetarity model by declaring and assigning sets, data, parameters, variables, equations in the model. PATH is invoked by the "OPTION MCP = PATH" statement in the GAMS code and a command line "solve <model name> using MCP" instructs GAMS to solve the model using the PATH solver. We use batch files to compute incidence profiles across various scenarios for different values of elasticities and tax rates for households.

21

On Some Properties of a Trade Closure Widely Used in Numerical Modelling

Keshab Bhattarai[103], Madanmohan Ghosh & John Whalley[1]

INTRODUCTION

In the numerical modelling trade policy literature, it is common to use the so-called Armington assumption of product heterogeneity. The justifications offered for using this treatment are problems in accommodating cross hauling in trade data, difficulties in calibrating models to literature based trade elasticities, and removing problems of specialization in response to model shocks. A procedure widely followed is to use an Armington treatment on both the import and export side, with domestic products (which are both produced and consumed) treated as qualitatively different from products imported from abroad or exported to abroad. For small economies who are takers of prices on world markets, this structure combined with price taking behaviour is commonly used to study the effects of trade liberalization (see, de Melo, Dervis and Robinson (1985), Deverajan and Lewis (1990), Robinson (1991), Harrison, Rutherford and Tarr (1993), and Rutherford (1995) and papers in the volume edited by Mercinier and Srinivasan (1995)).

The Armington treatment when used for small open price taking economies sub divides each domestically produced good into separate exported and domestically consumed goods using a transformation frontier, while on the import side domestic products and foreign imports are modelled as imperfect substitutes in preferences. The prices of domestically produced and consumed goods are thus delinked from world prices which now only apply to consumed imports and produced exports.

---

103. Bhattarai and Whalley acknowledge financial support from the ESRC under an award for a project on General Equilibrium Modelling of UK Policy Issues.
Correspondence:k.bhattarai@warwick.ac.uk; phone: 44-1203-523035; Fax: 44-1203-523032.

To solve this structure for an equilibrium, one has first to specify trade balance as a characteristic of the system. We argue here that this widely used treatment has some unattractive, and even unpleasant, properties. This we term unusual, since in most trade models external sector balance is a property of the equilibrium, deriving from a domestic version of Walras Law, and not an element of the model. We show how peculiar features of behaviour can arise for simple versions of this structure. If, for instance, preferences are Cobb-Douglas, then independently of the specification of production (transformation) elasticities, the model will generate fixed export volumes under any world price change. World price changes have no effect on either domestic production or consumption of the domestically produced good. If preferences are CES and elasticities are less than one, higher world prices for imports generate lower imports but higher exports; a perverse offer curve which assymptotically approaches the import axis and is truncated at an upper bound on exports in the two traded good case.

If we then take the same single country structure, and replicate it and use it in a 2 country model, we can also show cases where a Nash equilibrium of the two country tariff game does not exist, because of the perverse slopes of the offer curves. We can also produce global equilibria across which a country which reduces its tariffs increases its imports but reduces its exports.

We do not argue that the large number of numerical models which currently use this structure necessarily exhibit these features, but we do argue that the potential exists for peculiar properties to be unknowingly built into numerical models if modellers are unaware of these properties. De Melo and Robinson (1989) in an earlier paper exploring this structure concluded that (p. 62) " An external closure with symmetric product differentiation for imports and exports is theoretically well behaved, and gives rise to normally shaped offer curves." Our results suggest that this need not be the case; indeed some of our observations about the properties of this structure are implicit in the analytics that de Melo and Robinson present. Thus, while the two sided Armington product differentiation structure continues to be widely used in applied work, our analysis suggests potential pitfalls.

We present the basic structure of this widely used trade treatment in Section II, and some numerical results showing regular and perverse offer curves resulting from the closure structure. Section III deals with the two country case, which is followed by the conclusion in section IV.

A SIMPLE ONE COUNTRY PRODUCT DIFFERENTIATION TRADE MODEL

We consider a small open 2 good economy which is a price taker for both exports (E) and imports (M) and also uses tariffs on imports. $\overline{P}_M$ and $\overline{P}_E$ designate the fixed world prices at which the small economy trades internationally. It thus faces a perfectly elastic supply function for imports and a perfectly elastic demand for its exports.

We consider a domestically produced and consumed good, D, which enters preferences along with imports. These are given by

$$U = U(D, M) \tag{1}$$

Production represented by a transformation frontier defined over exported goods, E, and, D, i.e.

$$T = T(E, D) \tag{2}$$

A commonly used formulation is for (1) to be CES (constant elasticity of substitution), with (2) CET (constant elasticity of transformation).

From optimizing behaviour on the demand side,

$$\frac{U_D}{U_M} = \frac{P_D}{\overline{P}_M(1+t)} \tag{3}$$

where U_D and U_M are the first derivatives of the utility function with respect to D and M, P_D is the price of the domestic good, and *t* is the tariff rate on imports.

Economy wide income, I, is given by

$$I = P_D D + \overline{P}_E E + R \tag{4}$$

where R is tariff revenue. Given t, $\overline{P}_M$, and $\overline{P}_E$, (4) and (3) determine demands for the domestically produced and consumed commodity, which we denote as D^D, and if E is known, also import demands M. From (2), and prices P_D and $\overline{P}_E$, profit maximizing behaviour gives

$$\frac{T_E}{T_D} = \frac{\overline{P}_E}{P_D} \tag{5}$$

where T_D and T_E are the first derivatives of the transformation frontier with respect to D and E. (5) and (2) in combination give the export supplies *E*, and the supply of the domestically produced and consumed good, which we denote as D^S.

An equilibrium for this system is given by the price of the domestic good, P_D, such that there is market clearing in the domestically produced and consumed good, i.e.,

$$D^D = D^S \tag{6}$$

To both solve for and characterize an equilibrium in this structure, external sector balance needs to be specified

$$\overline{P}_M M - \overline{P}_E E = B \tag{7}$$

where B is the exogenous trade imbalance; B will equal zero if there is zero trade balance. This resolves the simultaneity between income, exports, and hence import demands. This treatment of trade balance is unusual since trade balance is usually a property of an international trade equilibrium, and implied by Walras Law (domestically). In this set up this is not the case, trade balance must be specified as a model feature, rather than emerge as a property of an equilibrium.

Once particular functional forms are adopted with assigned parameters, their comparative static properties can be explored in this structure, and a range of problems can, however, arise. If, for instance, Cobb-Douglas preferences are used, then independently of the specification of the transformation frontier, the implied offer curve for the domestic economy involves constant E[1]. This is a reflection of the constant expenditure shares implied by Cobb-Douglas, since in this case changes in world prices can be accommodated by changes in M, with no further change in E or D. Such properties would not characterize a homogenous good trade model with unitary elasticities in preferences, and would not occur independently of the specification of production.

If we change from Cobb-Douglas to CES preferences, we introduce bowness to the home country offer curve, but there are two alternative regimes depending upon the value of elasticity of substitution in preferences. In one regime offer curves are perversely sloped , and in the other more usual in slope.

In Figure 1 we display numerically simulated offer curves for different values of σ_U (the elasticity of substitution in preferences) for an arbitrarily specified numerical example, and in Table 1 we report the parameterization used and co-ordinates of the curves. Here, the perverse offer curves for the low elasticity specification imply falling E with rising M, opposite to conventionally sloped offer curves in traditional trade models. Approaching the M axis implies infinite amounts of low priced imports for an infinitesimally small amount of high priced exports. Approaching the E axis implies infinite amounts of low priced exports financing an infinitesimally small amount of high priced imports. In reality, E will face an upper bound reflecting the maximal E value in production given finite resources and the production frontier (2).

Table 1

Offer Curves Generated by a Simple Product Differentiation Model for Alternative Substitution Elasticities in Preferences

A. Numerical Specification of Model

Production specification	*T= 100; E share = 0.4; D share = 0.6; Transformation elasticity = 0.8*
Demand specification	D share = 0.7; M share = 0.3; Demand Elasticity (varied as below through the setting of elasticities of substitution in preferences,)
World price ratio	Varied to generate offer curve

B. Model Behaviour

Perverse Cases

$(\frac{P_M}{P_E})$	$\sigma_U = 0.5$		$\sigma_U = 0.75$		$\sigma_U = 1.0$	
	Imports	*Exports*	*Imports*	*Exports*	*Imports*	*Exports*
0.5	127.2	63.6	154.8	77.4	176.0	88.0
1.0	75.8	75.8	82.8	82.8	88.0	88.0
2.0	44.4	88.8	44.2	88.3	44.0	88.0
3.0	32.2	96.5	30.5	91.6	29.3	88.0
4.0	25.4	101.8	23.5	93.8	22.0	88.0

Non-perverse Cases

$(\frac{P_M}{P_E})$	$\sigma_U = 1.5$		$\sigma_U = 2.0$		$\sigma_U = 4.0$	
	Imports	*Exports*	*Imports*	*Exports*	*Imports*	*Exports*
0.5	204.5	102.2	221.7	221.7	249.9	125.0
1.0	95.0	95.0	99.4	99.4	107.6	107.6
2.0	43.8	87.5	43.6	43.6	43.3	86.7
3.0	27.7	83.2	26.7	26.7	24.8	74.4
4.0	20.0	80.2	18.8	18.8	16.5	66.1

Figure 2 displays the own tariff distorted offer curve for the same single country case. In the perverse case, the tariff distorted offer curve shifts to the left, as do the non perverse and perfectly inelastic offer curves.

PRODUCT DIFFERENTIATION IN A MULTI COUNTRY MODEL

It is possible to also use the structure we set out above to represent individual countries in a multi-country model[2]. Under this model formulation, there are preferences and technology (equations (1) and (2)) for each country, and trade balance (7)) is again specified for each country. The difference relative to the single country case is that P_M and P_E are now endogenously determined to clear global markets. In this case, the Armington assumption implies heterogeneity across the domestically produced goods in the two countries, not across the traded goods (i.e. the domestic goods D differ across countries rather than the traded goods M and E).

This structure generates two separate country offer curves; and given the discussion above a range of possibilities present themselves. Where both offer curves are non perverse, an intersection of two conventionally sloped offer curves characterizes equilibrium country behaviour with respect to induced changes in world prices as is conventional (either due to foreign country tariff changes, or

Figure 1
Graphical Representation of Perverse and Non-perverse Offer Curves Generated by the Model set out in Table 1

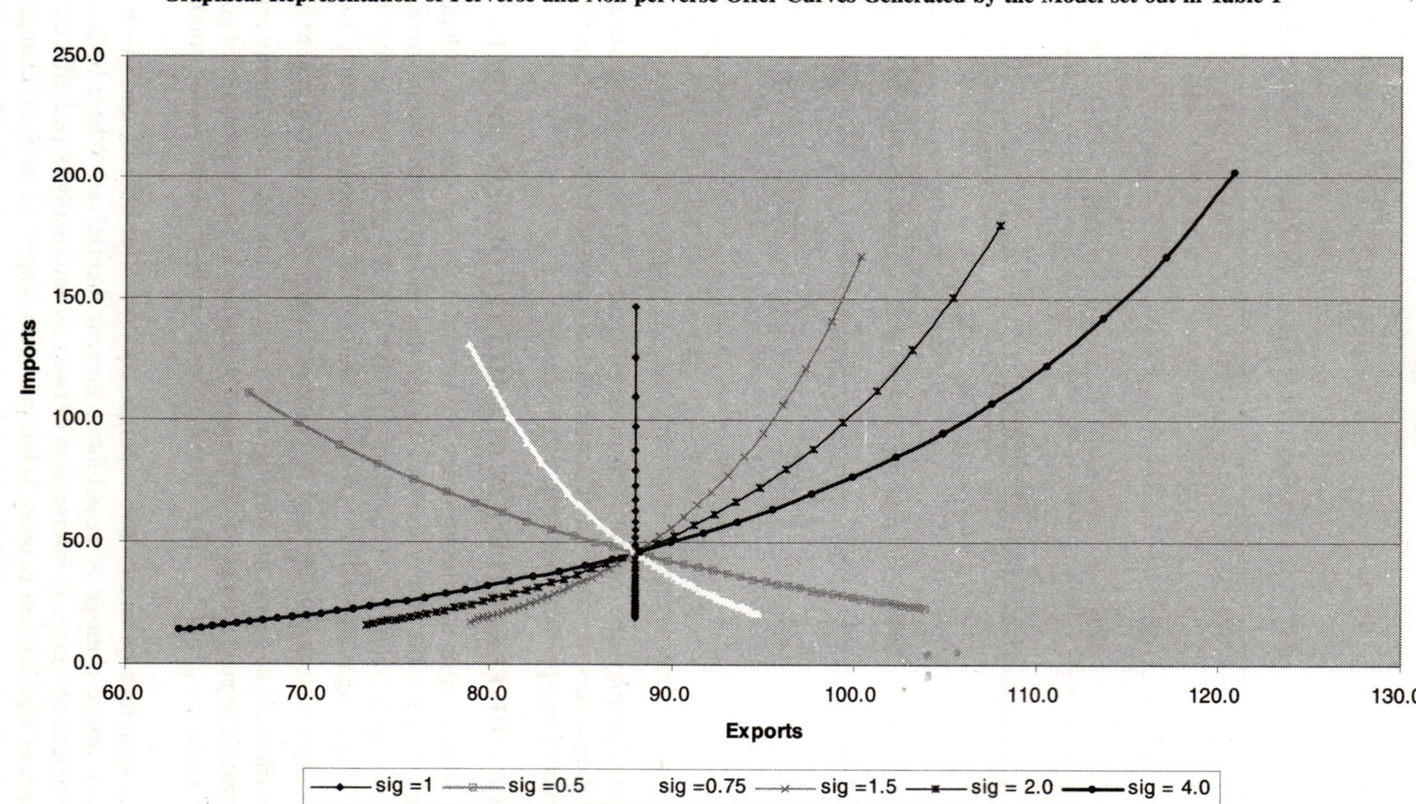

Note:
SIGT refers to a tariff distorted offer curve generated using substitution elasticities as specified.

Figure 2
Tariff Distorted Perverse and Non-perverse Offer Curves

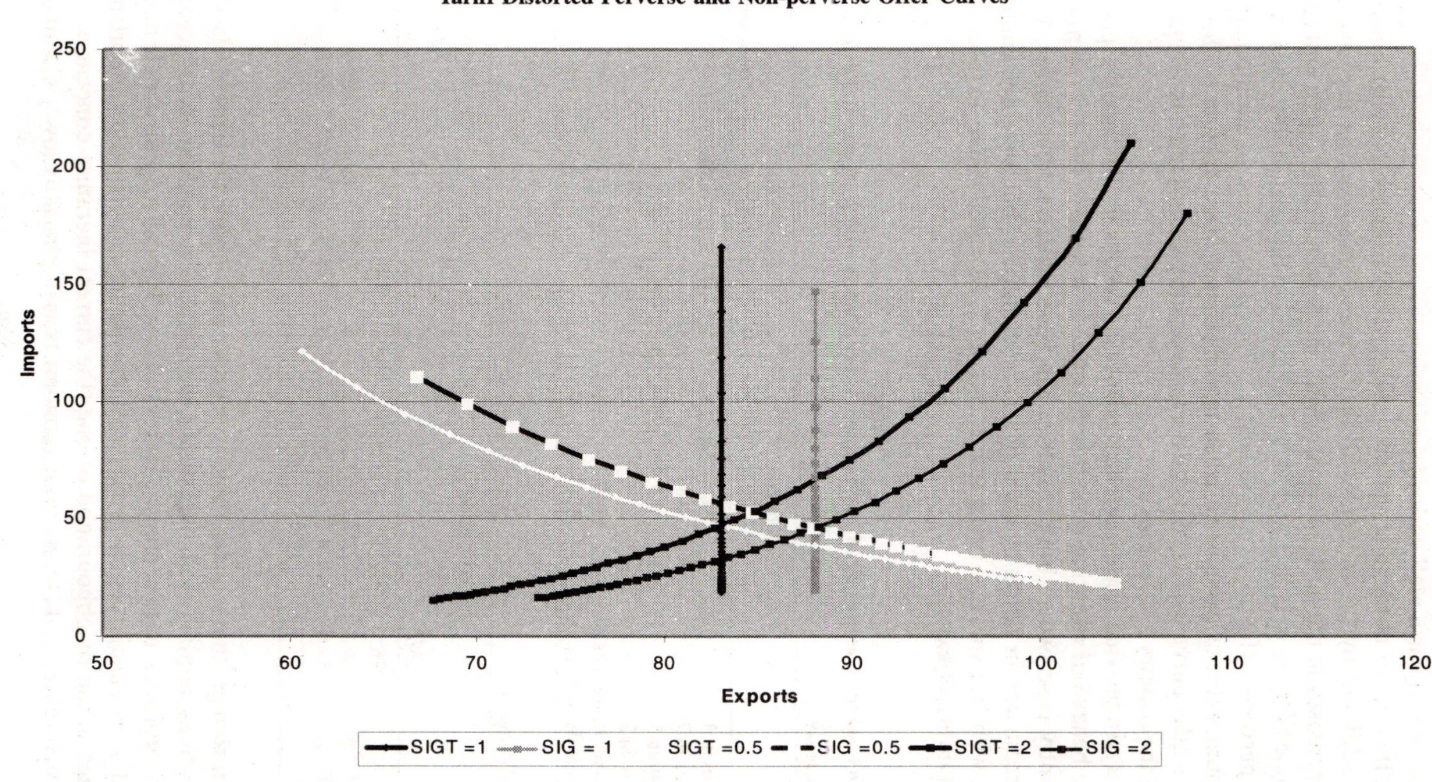

Note:
SIGT refers to a tariff distorted offer curve generated using substitution elasticities as specified.
SIG refers to a non-distorted offer curve generated using substitution elasticities as specified.

technology or demand shifts), and a Nash tariff game (as in Johnson (1954) and Gorman (1957)) has a well defined equilibrium.

But if either or both countries have perverse offer curves, peculiar behaviour can be exhibited by the model. With one perverse and one non perverse offer curve, increases in the tariff of country with the perverse offer curve will reduce the volume of trade in both E and M, but increases in the tariff of the country with the non perverse offer curve will reduce E while M increases. In addition, a Nash equilibrium will not exist since when maximizing welfare subject to the other country's offer curve wishes, the non perverse country wishes to go to an extremal point of the country's offer curve.

We again provide some numerical simulation results to illustrate the possible perverse behaviour resulting from this structure in this case. Table 2 reports on a two country case, where both countries can have perverse offer curves. In this case, a reduction in tariffs by country 1 reduces imports but increases country 1 exports, with the same also being true of country 2. As noted above no meaningful Nash equilibrium exists.

Table 2
Two Country Cases of Product Variation Trade Models with Perverse Behaviour

A. Specification

	Shares		*Elasticities*	
	M	*D*	*Perverse*	*Non-perverse*
Preferences in 1	0.5	0.5	0.5	1.5
Preferences in 2	0.5	0.5	0.5	1.5
Technology in 1	0.5	0.5	-3.5	-1.5
Technology in 2	0.5	0.5	-3.5	-1.5
EconomywideResources in 1	1000			
EconomywideResources in 2	500			

B. Model Behaviour

	Perverse Case				*Non-Perverse Case*			
	Country 1		*Country 2*		*Country 1*		*Country 2*	
	M1	*X1*	*M2*	*X2*	*M1*	*X1*	*M2*	*X2*
No tariff	36.5	125.1	125.1	36.5	53.4	92.9	92.9	53.4
10% tariff	36.8	122.8	122.8	36.8	53.2	89.6	89.6	53.2
20% tariff	37.0	120.7	120.7	37.0	53.0	86.6	86.6	53.0
50% tariff	37.7	115.0	115.0	37.7	52.5	78.9	78.9	52.5

Even though these undesirable properties only apply for certain elasticity configurations, applied modellers would, we presume, not want to introduce them into their structures used to analyze policy options. Typically, applied trade models are used with elasticities in preferences which are calibrated to import price elasticities in the neighbourhood of one (the current literature concensus, even though such values strike many trade economists as implausibly low[3]). Commonly, values in excess of one are used, suggesting that the problems we highlight may be avoided, but their possible presence is a source of unease, as well as raising queries over whether the offer curves, even in these cases, are specified in the way that modellers believe them to be in term of their implied model responses.

CONCLUSION

We discuss a structure widely used in applied trade models involving price taking behaviour for both imports and exports, with Armington product differentiation between domestic and traded goods on both the export and import sides. We note the need to impose trade balance as a condition in order to solve the model, rather than for trade balance to be a property of an international equilibrium via Walras Law (which is more usual). We argue that in simple analogues of this structure, implied offer curves can be perverse with exports falling as imports rise with falling import prices. Similar outcomes are possible in the two country case, and here the Nash equilibria of tariff games may not exist. In the special case where preferences over domestic products and imports have unit elasticity of substitution, changes in world prices merely result in changes in import volumes, which allow exports and consumption and production of domestic goods to be unchanged in the new equilibrium. No propagation of trade disturbances beyond imports occurs in such cases.

We do not claim that al! uses of this structure in large scale trade models inevitably lead to these features; but modellers using this approach should be aware of the somewhat unfortunate properties that can result in some situations, and need to ensure that the foreign trade behaviour of their system is as they intended it to be.

REFERENCES

De Melo, J. and S. Robinson (1989),"Product Differentiation and the Treatment of Foreign Trade in Computable General Equilibrium Models of Small Economies", Journal of International Economics, 27 47-67.

De Melo, J. and D. Roland-Holst (1994), Tariffs and Exports Subsidies when Domestic Markets Are Oligopolistic: Korea, in Mercenier Jean and Srinivasan, T.N. ed. *Applied General Equilibrium and Economic Development: Present Achievement and Future Trends,* University of Michigan Press, Ann Arbor.

Dervis, K., J. de Melo , and S. Robinson (1985), *General Equilibrium Models for Development Policy,* CUP, New York.

Devarajan, S., and J. D. Lewis (1990), Policy Lessons from Trade Focused Two-Sector Models, Journal of Policy Modeling 12(4):625-657.

Gorman W.M. (1958), Tariffs, Retaliation and the Elasticity of Demand for Imports, Review of Economic Studies, June 25(3), pp. 133-62.

Harrison, G.W, T.F. Rutherford (1997), "Burden Sharing, Joint Implementation, and Carbon Coalitions", Working Paper no. 97-11, Department of Economics, University of Colorado at Boulder.

Harrison, Glenn W, T.F. Rutherford and D.G. Tarr (1993), "Trade Reform in the Partially Liberalized Economy of Turkey", the World Bank Economic Review, Vol. 7 No. 2, 191-217.

Johnson H.G. (1953-54), Optimal tariffs and Retaliation, Review of Economic Studies, 21(2), pp.142-43.

Mercenier J. and Srinivasan, T.N. ed. (1994) *Applied General Equilibrium and Economic Development: Present Achievement and Future Trends,* University of Michigan Press, Ann Arbor.

Perroni, C. and J. Whalley (1994), "The New Regionalism: Trade Liberalization or Insurance", NBER working paper No. 4626.

Robinson, S. (1991), Macroeconomics, Financial Variables, and Computable General Equilibrium Models, World Development, Vol. 19, No.11, pp.1509-1523, Pergamon Press plc.

Rutherford, T.F. (1995) Extension of GAMS for Complementary Problems Arising in applied Economic Analysis, Journal of Economic Dynamics and Control,19, 1299-1324.

NOTES

1. In an appendix, de Melo and Robinson (1989) analytically derive the elasticity of the offer curve for this system and note that their formula implies an offer curve elasticity $\frac{\partial E}{\partial M}\frac{M}{E}$ of ∞, yielding the same behavior we note above.
2. Harrison and Rutherford (1997) use a multi country structure of this form to evaluate international burden sharing under global carbon tax initiatives.
3. See the discussion of these elasticities in Perroni and Whalley (1994).

22

More On Trade Closure[107]

Keshab Bhattarai[108], Madanmohan Ghosh & John Whalley[2]

INTRODUCTION

Over his career, T.N. has made contributions in a wide array of areas, and not always only through his written works. In the 1970s T.N. attended meetings and conferences where numerical general equilibrium modellers presented their trade models some of which sought to analyze the effects of trade liberalization on various economies. T.N. picked up on the issue of trade closure, how the specification of the rest of the world and their trade behaviour influences the model outcome. T.N. highlighted the seeming inconsistency of having financial variables (exchange rates) in what were presented as real side models, and other points.

This present paper, as its title suggests, offers more on trade closure beyond the immediate debate that T.N. initiated. It takes as its point of departure the claim by modellers who responded to T.N. that the only exchange rate at issue in their closure treatment is the real exchange rate (the relative price of traded and non traded goods), and that in a formulation with product differentiation on both the demand and supply sides the issues that T.N. identified no longer apply. We argue that a new set of issues arise such as perversely sloped offer curves in small open economy trade models and ill-defined Nash equilibria in case of two country trade models. In small open economy models with Cobb-Douglas preferences trade shocks impacts only on demand side seemingly independently of the production side specifications. In two country models with perverse offer curves each trading country tends to reach extreme point of the partners offer curve and hence Nash equilibrium may not exist. T.N. has long argued that there is no short cut to well defined theoretical structures, and the debate on model closure is a direct reflection

107. This paper was presented in a conference organized in honour of T.N. Srinivasan in April, 1998.

108. Bhattarai and Whalley are grateful to the ESRC for financial support.

of his earlier contributions. Our contribution is merely a further twist on the earlier development that T.N. started.

TRADE CLOSURE

The need for trade closure arises from the development of detailed single economy models for the analysis of trade liberalization, or other trade policy changes. As Figure 1 suggests, substantial modelling effort is typically put into the development of a detailed representation of the economy in question. Some treatment is then needed of the world that the single economy trades with, and in particular its trade behaviour, through the export demand and import supply functions that the country faces in world markets.

The pitfalls with trade closure are well illustrated by the simple homogenous good trade structure discussed in Whalley and Yeung (1984), which in turn is reflective of closure structures actually in use in some of the applied models in the early 1980's. For the two good case, they set out a system of closure as representing the behaviour of the rest of the world through three equations. The first is an export demand function

$$E = E_O \left(\frac{P_E}{e} \right)^{\eta} \qquad -\infty < \eta < 0 \tag{1}$$

where E_o represents base period exports and is the endogenously model determined price of exportable in own country currency. As foreign buyers of exports purchase these at world prices, this is divided by an exchange rate term e to yield the prices paid by buyers, h seemingly defines the price elasticity of the export demand function, and varying the parameter h allows modellers to vary the export demand elasticity that the country in question faces.

Figure 1
Closure in General Equilibrium Trade Models

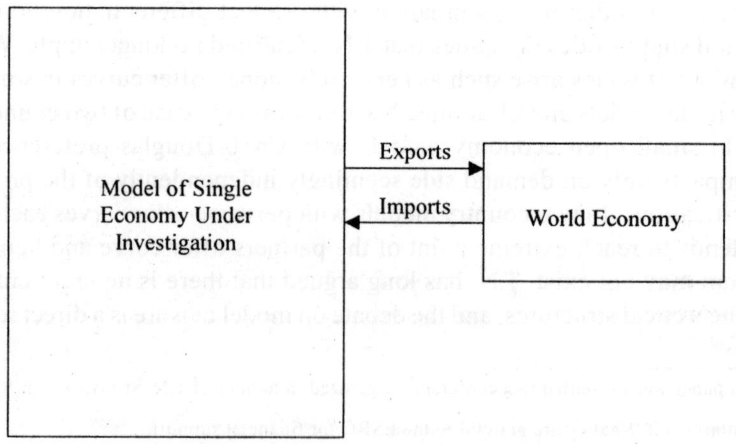

A related equation can be written down for the import supply function for the world to the domestic market, but with a change in sign for the elasticity parameter

$$\text{Imports} \qquad M = M_O \left(\frac{P_M}{e} \right)^{\mu} \qquad \infty > \mu > 0 \tag{2}$$

where M_o is base period imports, P_M is the own country price of importables, (P_M/e) is the world price of imports for world suppliers to the country, and *m* is a further elasticity term, now interpreted as the import supply elasticity.

A trade balance condition (at either world or own country prices) completes the specification

$$P_M M - P_E E \tag{3}$$

As T.N. pointed out, for such structures there cannot be any meaningful exchange rate term in this closure system if the own country model structure to which the closure is appended is (as is typical) a real side barter economy. This follows directly by substituting (1) and (2) into (3) and solving out for *e*. This solution can, in turn, be substituted back into (1) and (2) to give export demand and import supply functions as

$$E = E_O P_E^{-1} \left(\frac{M_O}{E_O} \right)^{-\eta/(\mu-\eta)} P_M^{-(\mu+1)\eta/(\mu-\eta)} P_E^{\mu(\eta+1)/(\mu-\eta)} \tag{4}$$

$$M = M_O P_M^{-1} \left(\frac{M_O}{E_O} \right)^{-\mu/(\mu-\eta)} P_M^{-(\mu+1)\eta/(\mu-\eta)} P_E^{\mu(\eta+1)/(\mu-\eta)} \tag{5}$$

No exchange rate really exists within the structure; its presence is an illusion created by the closure structure. Moreover, as Whalley and Yeung show, *h* and *m* also define the true export demand and import supply elasticities. These come from equations (4) and (5) as

$$\varepsilon_E^{FD} = \frac{\partial E}{\partial P_E} \frac{P_E}{E} = \frac{\eta(1+\mu)}{(\mu-\eta)} \tag{6}$$

$$\varepsilon_M^{FS} = \frac{\partial M}{\partial P_M} \frac{P_M}{M} = \frac{-\mu(1+\eta)}{(\mu-\eta)} \tag{7}$$

and are in fact interconnected in the two good case by the relationship between the two export demand and import supply elasticities and the elasticity of the offer surface. Thus, for this system, modellers may believe that they control two independent elasticity parameters (*h* and *m*), while in reality they only control one parameter ε^{OC} which implies the two jointly determined model elasticities.

$$\varepsilon^{OC} = \frac{\eta}{1+\eta}\frac{1+\mu}{\mu} \tag{8}$$

Modellers, therefore can easily misinterpret their model specification on the elasticity front if they adopt this form of closure treatment.

Another closure issue identified by T.N. involved the claim by some modellers to be separately incorporating price-making behaviour, say, on the export side and price-taking behaviour on the import side through their closure specification. As Figure 2 makes clear, in the simple two good case, only one relative price is involved in trade and the domestic economy has to be either a price taker in both imports and exports (a straight line offer curve), or a price maker in both (bowness in the offer curve). Mixed price-making/price-taking rule in the simple two good case would thus seem to be inconsistent.

Figure 2
World Offer Curves as Closure, and Price-Making Price-Taking Behaviour

A. Price Taking in Both E, M

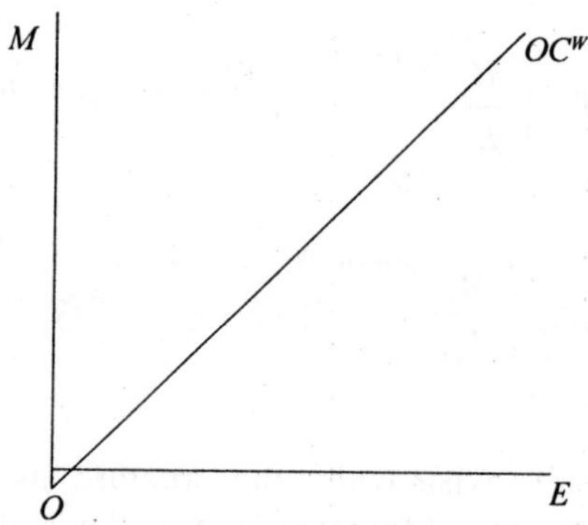

B. Price-Making in Both E, M

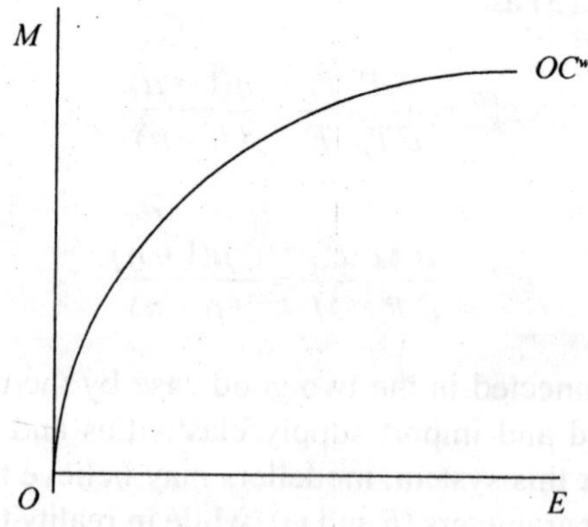

MORE ON TRADE CLOSURE[1]

In more recent numerical modelling trade policy literature, it is common to use the so-called Armington assumption of product heterogeneity; domestic products (which are both produced and consumed) treated as qualitatively different from products imported from abroad or exported to abroad. Such specification is useful in studying cross hauling phenomena in trade data in place of complete specialization characteristic of the Neoclassical trade models. This essentially involves using a constant elasticity of transformation (CET) frontier to separate each domestically produced good into exported and domestically consumed goods and a CES function to show imperfect substitution between domestic products and foreign imports. The price-taking behaviour is commonly used both for imports and exports, prices of domestically produced and consumed goods are delinked from world prices which now only apply to consumed imports and produced exports. Any difference between the value of imports and exports are met by a net foreign transfer in the trade balance equation (see, de Melo, Dervis and Robinson (1985), Devarajan and Lewis (1990), Robinson (1991), Harrison, Rutherford and Tarr (1993), and Rutherford (1995) and papers in the volume edited by Mercinier and Srinivasan (1995)). We argue that this widely used trade closure has some unattractive properties.

A trade balance condition specified as above is unusual to most trade models where external sector balance is a property of the equilibrium, deriving from a domestic version of Walras Law, and not an element of the model. Here, we note some peculiar features of behaviour that arise from simple versions of this structure. If, for instance, preferences are Cobb-Douglas, then independently of the specification of production (transformation) elasticities, the model will generate fixed export volumes under any world price change. World price changes have no effect on either domestic production or consumption of the domestically produced good. If preferences are CES and elasticities are less than one, higher world prices for imports generate lower imports but higher exports; a perverse offer curve which asymptotically approaches the import axis and is truncated at an upper bound on exports in the two traded good case.

Using the similar structure in a 2 country model, we can also show cases where a Nash equilibrium of the two country tariff game does not exist, because of the perverse shape of the offer curves. It could also be shown that global equilibria may be obtained under which a country that reduces its tariffs increases its imports but reduces its exports.

De Melo and Robinson (1989) exploring this structure concluded that (p. 62) "An external closure with symmetric product differentiation for imports and exports is theoretically well behaved, and gives rise to normally shaped offer curves". Our results suggest that this need not be the case; though some of our observations about the properties of this structure might be implicit in the analytics that de Melo and Robinson present.

Model Specification

For illustration first we consider a small open 2 good economy which is a price taker for both exports (E) and imports (M) and also uses tariffs on imports. $\bar{P}_M$ and $\bar{P}_E$ are the fixed world prices at which the small economy trades internationally. Thus the economy faces a perfectly elastic supply function for imports and a perfectly elastic demand for its exports.

A representative consumer gets utility by consuming a domestically produced good, D and an imported good M and hence the utility function is given by

$$U = U(D, M) \tag{9}$$

A commonly used functional form for the utility function in (9) is constant elasticity of substitution (CES).

Total production, T, is allocated between domestic sales and exports by using a transformation frontier given by

$$T = T(E, D) \tag{10}$$

Most often such transformation frontier is explained by a CET (constant elasticity of transformation) function.

From optimizing behaviour on the demand side implies that the ratio of the marginal rate of substitution between D and M in preferences should equal the ratio of prices of domestic goods to imported goods (inclusive of tariffs).

$$\frac{U_D}{U_M} = \frac{P_D}{\bar{P}_M(1+t)} \tag{11}$$

where U_D and U_M are the first derivatives of the utility function with respect to D and M, P_D is the price of the domestic good, and t is the tariff rate on imports.

Economy wide income, I, is given by the sum of the value of domestic sales plus exports and tariff revenue.

$$I = P_D D^D + \bar{P}_E E + R \tag{12}$$

where R is tariff revenue. Given t, $\bar{P}_M$, $\bar{P}_E$ (11) and (12) determine demands for the domestically produced and consumed commodity, which we denote as D^D, and if E is known, import demands M. From (10), and prices P_D and $\bar{P}_E$, profit maximizing behaviour gives

$$\frac{T_D}{T_E} = \frac{P_D}{\bar{P}_E} \tag{13}$$

where T_D and T_E are the first derivatives of the transformation frontier with respect to D and E. Equations (13) and (10) in combination give the export supplies E, and the supply of the domestically produced and consumed good, which we denote as D^S.

To both solve for and characterize an equilibrium in this structure, external sector balance needs to be specified

$$\bar{P}_M M - \bar{P}_E E = B \tag{14}$$

where B is the exogenous trade imbalance; B will equal zero if there is zero trade balance.

This treatment of trade balance is unusual since trade balance is usually not implied by Walras Law (domestically), a property of an international trade equilibrium. In this set up trade balance must be specified as a model feature, rather than it emerges as a property of an equilibrium. This resolves the simultaneity between income, exports, and hence import demands.

An equilibrium for this system is given by the price of the domestic good, P_D, such that there is market clearing in the domestically produced and consumed good, i.e.

$$D^D = D^S \tag{15}$$

We illustrate that a range of problems in comparative static properties of trade structure can arise for particular set of functional forms and parameters, often used in the trade literature. If, for example, Cobb-Douglas preferences in consumption are used, then independently of the specification of the transformation frontier, the implied offer curve for the domestic economy involves constant exports[1]. This reflects the constant expenditure shares implied by Cobb-Douglas, as in this case changes in world prices can be accommodated by changes in M, with no further change in E or D. Such properties would not characterize a homogenous good trade model with unitary elasticities in preferences, and would not occur independently of the specification of production.

Even with CES preferences, which introduces bowness to the home country offer curve, depending upon the value of elasticity of substitution in preferences two alternative regimes may appear, one with perversely sloped offer curves and the other with more usual slope.

We compute coordinates of offer curves for different values of s_U (the elasticity of substitution in preferences), and for given share and shift parameters for an arbitrarily specified numerical example, and display results in Table 1 and Figure 3. Here, the perverse offer curves for the low elasticity specification imply falling E with rising M, opposite to conventionally sloped offer curves in traditional trade models. An offer curve approaching the M axis implies infinite amounts of low priced imports for an infinitesimally small amount of high priced exports. Similarly an offer curve approaching the E axis implies infinite amounts of low priced exports financing an infinitesimally small amount of high priced imports. In reality, E will face an upper bound reflecting the maximal E value in production given finite resources and the production frontier (10).

Table 1
Offer Curves Generated by a Simple Product Differentiation Model for Alternative Substitution Elasticities in Preferences

A. Numerical Specification of Model

Production specification	*T= 100; E share = 0.4; D share = 0.6; Transformation elasticity = 0.8*
Demand specification	D share = 0.7; M share = 0.3; Demand Elasticity (varied as below through the setting of elasticities of substitution in preferences,)
World price ratio	Varied to generate offer curve

B. Model Behaviour

Perverse Cases

	$\sigma_U = 0.5$		$\sigma_U = 0.75$		$\sigma_U = 1.0$	
$(\frac{P_M}{P_E})$	*Imports*	*Exports*	*Imports*	*Exports*	*Imports*	*Exports*
0.5	127.2	63.6	154.8	77.4	176.0	88.0
1.0	75.8	75.8	82.8	82.8	88.0	88.0
2.0	44.4	88.8	44.2	88.3	44.0	88.0
3.0	32.2	96.5	30.5	91.6	29.3	88.0
4.0	25.4	101.8	23.5	93.8	22.0	88.0

Non-perverse Cases

	$\sigma_U = 1.5$		$\sigma_U = 2.0$		$\sigma_U = 4.0$	
$(\frac{P_M}{P_E})$	*Imports*	*Exports*	*Imports*	*Exports*	*Imports*	*Exports*
0.5	204.5	102.2	221.7	221.7	249.9	125.0
1.0	95.0	95.0	99.4	99.4	107.6	107.6
2.0	43.8	87.5	43.6	43.6	43.3	86.7
3.0	27.7	83.2	26.7	26.7	24.8	74.4
4.0	20.0	80.2	18.8	18.8	16.5	66.1

Offer curves with and witout tariffs are drawn in Figure 4 from the computational results in Table 2. In the perverse case, imposition of tariff shifts the offer curve to the left, as do the non perverse and perfectly inelastic offer curves.

We modify the above model to represent a multi-country model[1] by allowing changes in P_M and P_E endogenously to clear global markets. Under this formulation, preferences and technology (equations (9) and (10)) for each country, and trade balance (15)) are again specified for each country. The Armington

Figure 3

Graphical Representation of Perverse and Non-perverse Offer Curves Generated by the Model set out in Table 1

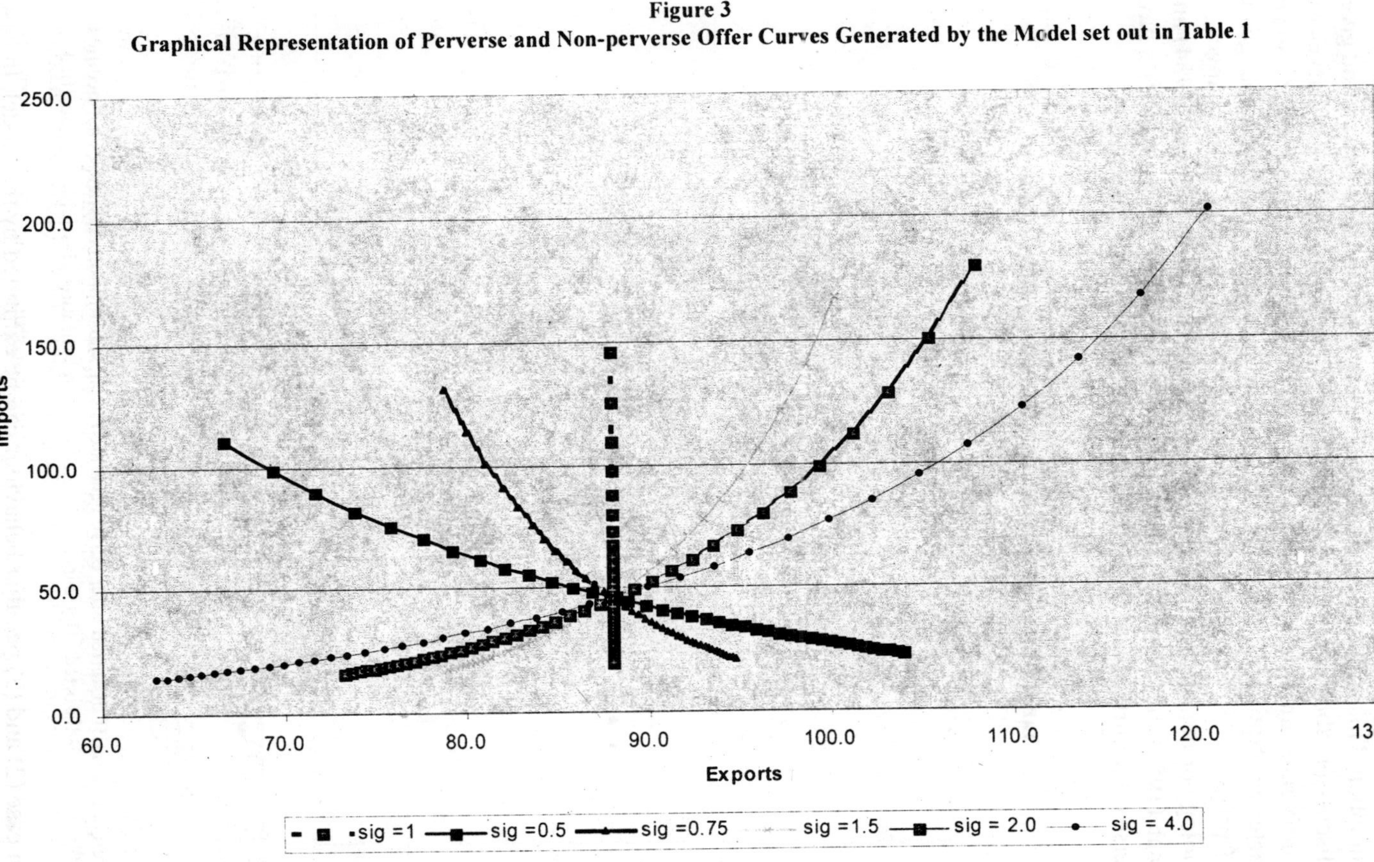

Note:
SIGT refers to a tariff distorted offer curve generated using substitution elasticities as specified.

assumption implies that domestically produced goods for domestic consumption are different from that produced for export sales and that for imported for domestic consumption. This structure generates two separate country offer curves; and given the discussion above three possibilities appear (1) where both offer curves are non perverse, an intersection of two conventionally sloped offer curves characterizes equilibrium country behaviour with respect to induced changes in world prices as is conventional (either due to foreign country tariff changes, or technology or demand shifts), and a Nash tariff game (as in Johnson (1954) and Gorman (1957)) has a well defined equilibrium ; (2) either of two countries have perverse offer curves; and (3) both countries have perverse offer curves.

Figure 4
Tariff Distorted Perverse and Non-perverse Offer Curves

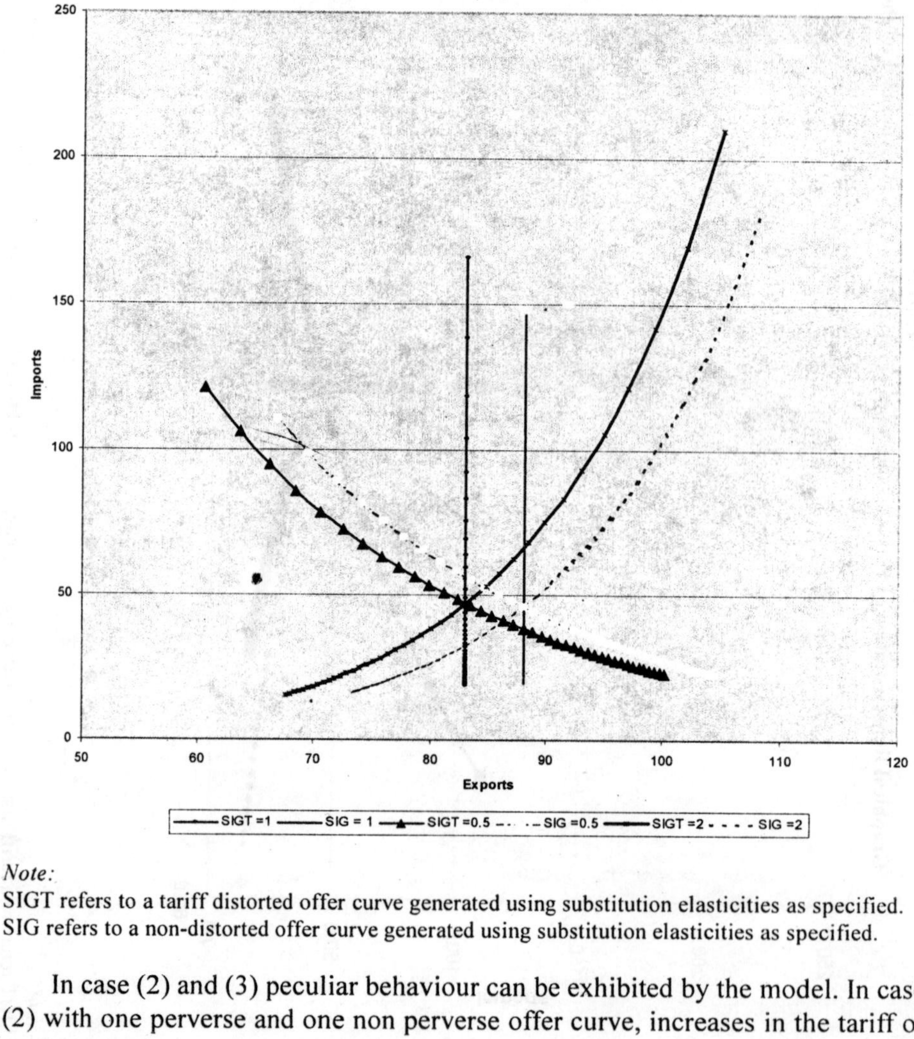

Note:
SIGT refers to a tariff distorted offer curve generated using substitution elasticities as specified.
SIG refers to a non-distorted offer curve generated using substitution elasticities as specified.

In case (2) and (3) peculiar behaviour can be exhibited by the model. In case (2) with one perverse and one non perverse offer curve, increases in the tariff of country with the perverse offer curve will reduce the volume of trade in both *E* and *M*, but increases in the tariff of the country with the non perverse offer curve will reduce *E* while *M* increases. In addition, a Nash equilibrium will not exist since when maximizing welfare subject to the other country's offer curve wishes, the non perverse country wishes to go to an extremal point of the country's offer curve.

We again provide some numerical simulation results to illustrate the possible perverse behaviour resulting from the price taking Armington structure. Table 2 reports on a two country case, where both countries can have perverse offer curves. In this case, a reduction in tariffs by country 1 reduces imports but increases country 1 exports, with the same also being true of country 2. As noted above no meaningful Nash equilibrium exists in case of (2) and (3).

Table 2
Two Country Cases of Product Variation Trade Models with Perverse Behaviour

A. Specification

	Shares *M*	*D*	*Elasticities* *Perverse*	*Non-perverse*
Preferences in 1	0.5	0.5	0.5	1.5
Preferences in 2	0.5	0.5	0.5	1.5
Technology in 1	0.5	0.5	-3.5	-1.5
Technology in 2	0.5	0.5	-3.5	-1.5
Economywideresources in 1	1000			
Economywideresources in 2	500			

B. Model Behaviour

	Perverse case				*Non-Perverse case*			
	Country 1		*Country 2*		*Country 1*		*Country 2*	
	M1	*X1*	*M2*	*X2*	*M1*	*X1*	*M2*	*X2*
No tariff	36.5	125.1	125.1	36.5	53.4	92.9	92.9	53.4
10% tariff	36.8	122.8	122.8	36.8	53.2	89.6	89.6	53.2
20% tariff	37.0	120.7	120.7	37.0	53.0	86.6	86.6	53.0
50% tariff	37.7	115.0	115.0	37.7	52.5	78.9	78.9	52.5

In Armington trade models, commonly values in excess of one are used for elasticities, suggesting that the problems we highlight may be avoided. Undesirable properties noted above appear only when elasticity configurations are 1 or below 1. However, typically applied trade models are used with elasticities in preferences which are calibrated to import price elasticities in the neighbourhood of one (the current literature consensus, even though such values strike many trade economists as implausibly low[2]) possible presence of perverse behavour is a source of unease. Applied trade models need to be specified in the way that modellers believe that the offer curves generated from them be in term of their implied model responses.

CONCLUSION

Closure rules used in applied Armington trade models involve price-taking behaviour for both imports and exports, and product differentiation between domestic and traded goods. In such models, most often a CET function describes transformation between domestic sales and exports and a CES function explains the substitution between imports and domestically produced goods for domestic consumption. A trade balance condition is imposed to solve the model, rather than trade balance being a property of an international equilibrium via Walras Law (which is more usual). When the elasticity of substitution equals one or is less than one implied offer curves can be perverse with exports falling as imports rise with falling import prices. The Nash equilibria of tariff games may not exist in the two country case. When domestic products and imports have unit elasticity of substitution, changes in world prices merely result in changes in import volumes, with no change in exports and consumption and production of domestic goods in the new equilibrium. Trade disturbances do affect nothing but imports.

We do not claim that all Armington trade models generate perverse offer curves; but modellers using trade closure should be aware of the somewhat unfortunate properties that can result in some situations, which they did not intend it to be. This is a point long stressed by T.N., and simply re-emphasized here.

REFERENCES

De Melo, J. and S. Robinson (1989), "Product Differentiation and the Treatment of Foreign Trade in Computable General Equilibrium Models of Small Economies", *Journal of International Economics*, 27 47-67.

De Melo, J. and D. Roland-Holst (1994), Tariffs and Exports Subsidies when Domestic Markets Are Oligopolistic: Korea, in Mercenier Jean and Srinivasan, T.N. ed. *Applied General Equilibrium and Economic Development: Present Achievement and Future Trends*, University of Michigan Press, Ann Arbor.

Dervis, K., J. de Melo, and S. Robinson (1985), *General Equilibrium Models for Development Policy*, CUP, New York.

Devarajan, S., and J.D. Lewis (1990), Policy Lessons from Trade Focussed Two-Sector Models, Journal of Policy Modeling 12(4):625-657.

Gorman, W.M. (1957), Tariffs, Retaliation and the Elasticity of Demand for Imports, *Review of Economic Studies*, June 25(3), pp. 133-62.

Harrison, G.W., and T.F. Rutherford (1997), "Burden Sharing, Joint Implementation, and Carbon Coalitions", Working Paper No. 97-11, Department of Economics, University of Colorado at Boulder.

Harrison, G.W., and T.F. Rutherford and D.G. Tarr (1993), "Trade Reform in the Partially Liberalized Economy of Turkey", *The World Bank Economic Review*, Vol.7 No.2, 191-217.

Johnson, H.G. (1953-54), Optimal tariffs and Retaliation, Review of Economic Studies, 21(2), pp.142-43.

country with the perverse offer curve will reduce the volume of trade in both E and M, but increases in the tariff of the country with the non perverse offer curve will reduce E while M increases. In addition, a Nash equilibrium will not exist since when maximizing welfare subject to the other country's offer curve wishes, the non perverse country wishes to go to an extremal point of the country's offer curve.

We again provide some numerical simulation results to illustrate the possible perverse behaviour resulting from the price taking Armington structure. Table 2 reports on a two country case, where both countries can have perverse offer curves. In this case, a reduction in tariffs by country 1 reduces imports but increases country 1 exports, with the same also being true of country 2. As noted above no meaningful Nash equilibrium exists in case of (2) and (3).

Table 2

Two Country Cases of Product Variation Trade Models with Perverse Behaviour

A. Specification

	Shares		*Elasticities*	
	M	*D*	*Perverse*	*Non-perverse*
Preferences in 1	0.5	0.5	0.5	1.5
Preferences in 2	0.5	0.5	0.5	1.5
Technology in 1	0.5	0.5	-3.5	-1.5
Technology in 2	0.5	0.5	-3.5	-1.5
Economywideresources in 1	1000			
Economywideresources in 2	500			

B. Model Behaviour

	Perverse case				*Non-Perverse case*			
	Country 1		*Country 2*		*Country 1*		*Country 2*	
	M1	*X1*	*M2*	*X2*	*M1*	*X1*	*M2*	*X2*
No tariff	36.5	125.1	125.1	36.5	53.4	92.9	92.9	53.4
10% tariff	36.8	122.8	122.8	36.8	53.2	89.6	89.6	53.2
20% tariff	37.0	120.7	120.7	37.0	53.0	86.6	86.6	53.0
50% tariff	37.7	115.0	115.0	37.7	52.5	78.9	78.9	52.5

In Armington trade models, commonly values in excess of one are used for elasticities, suggesting that the problems we highlight may be avoided. Undesirable properties noted above appear only when elasticity configurations are 1 or below 1. However, typically applied trade models are used with elasticities in preferences which are calibrated to import price elasticities in the neighbourhood of one (the current literature consensus, even though such values strike many trade economists as implausibly low[2]) possible presence of perverse behavour is a source of unease. Applied trade models need to be specified in the way that modellers believe that the offer curves generated from them be in term of their implied model responses.

CONCLUSION

Closure rules used in applied Armington trade models involve price-taking behaviour for both imports and exports, and product differentiation between domestic and traded goods. In such models, most often a CET function describes transformation between domestic sales and exports and a CES function explains the substitution between imports and domestically produced goods for domestic consumption. A trade balance condition is imposed to solve the model, rather than trade balance being a property of an international equilibrium via Walras Law (which is more usual). When the elasticity of substitution equals one or is less than one implied offer curves can be perverse with exports falling as imports rise with falling import prices. The Nash equilibria of tariff games may not exist in the two country case. When domestic products and imports have unit elasticity of substitution, changes in world prices merely result in changes in import volumes, with no change in exports and consumption and production of domestic goods in the new equilibrium. Trade disturbances do affect nothing but imports.

We do not claim that all Armington trade models generate perverse offer curves; but modellers using trade closure should be aware of the somewhat unfortunate properties that can result in some situations, which they did not intend it to be. This is a point long stressed by T.N., and simply re-emphasized here.

REFERENCES

De Melo, J. and S. Robinson (1989), "Product Differentiation and the Treatment of Foreign Trade in Computable General Equilibrium Models of Small Economies", *Journal of International Economics*, 27 47-67.

De Melo, J. and D. Roland-Holst (1994), Tariffs and Exports Subsidies when Domestic Markets Are Oligopolistic: Korea, in Mercenier Jean and Srinivasan, T.N. ed. *Applied General Equilibrium and Economic Development: Present Achievement and Future Trends*, University of Michigan Press, Ann Arbor.

Dervis, K., J. de Melo, and S. Robinson (1985), *General Equilibrium Models for Development Policy*, CUP, New York.

Devarajan, S., and J.D. Lewis (1990), Policy Lessons from Trade Focussed Two-Sector Models, Journal of Policy Modeling 12(4):625-657.

Gorman, W.M. (1957), Tariffs, Retaliation and the Elasticity of Demand for Imports, *Review of Economic Studies*, June 25(3), pp. 133-62.

Harrison, G.W., and T.F. Rutherford (1997), "Burden Sharing, Joint Implementation, and Carbon Coalitions", Working Paper No. 97-11, Department of Economics, University of Colorado at Boulder.

Harrison, G.W., and T.F. Rutherford and D.G. Tarr (1993), "Trade Reform in the Partially Liberalized Economy of Turkey", *The World Bank Economic Review*, Vol.7 No.2, 191-217.

Johnson, H.G. (1953-54), Optimal tariffs and Retaliation, Review of Economic Studies, 21(2), pp.142-43.

Mercenier, J. and T.N. Srinivasan ed. (1994), *Applied General Equilibrium and Economic Development: Present Achievement and Future Trends*, University of Michigan Press, Ann Arbor.

Perroni, C. and J. Whalley (1994), "The New Regionalism: Trade Liberalization or Insurance", NBER Working Paper Mo. 4626.

Robinson, S. (1991). Macroeconomics, Financial Variables, and Computable General Equilibrium Models, World Development, Vol. 19, No.11, pp.1509-1523, Pergamon Press plc.

Rutherford, T.F. (1995), Extension of GAMS for Complementary Problems Arising in applied Economic Analysis, *Journal of Economic Dynamics and Control*,19, 1299-1324.

Whalley, J. and B. Yeung (1984), External Sector Closing Rules in Applied General Equilibrium Models, *Journal of International Economics*, 16, 123-38

NOTES

1. This section heavily relies on our earlier paper "On Some Unusual Properties of Trade Closure Widely Used in Numerical Modelling" forthcoming in Economic Letters.
2. In an appendix, de Melo and Robinson (1989) analytically derive the elasticity of the offer curve for this sytem and note that their formula implies an offer curve elasticity of ∞ implying the same behaviour we note above.
3. Harrison and Rutherford (1997) use a multi country structure of this form to evaluate international burden sharing under global carbon tax initiatives.
4. See the discussion of these elasticities in Perroni and Whalley (1994).